T0214949

PHP 8 Solutions

Dynamic Web Design and Development
Made Easy

Fifth Edition

David Powers

apress®

PHP 8 Solutions: Dynamic Web Design and Development Made Easy

David Powers
London, UK

ISBN-13 (pbk): 978-1-4842-7140-7   ISBN-13 (electronic): 978-1-4842-7141-4
https://doi.org/10.1007/978-1-4842-7141-4

Managing Director, Apress Media LLC: Welmoed Spahr
Acquisitions Editor: Steve Anglin
Development Editor: Matthew Moodie
Coordinating Editor: Mark Powers

Cover designed by eStudioCalamar

Cover image by Hazel Clifton on Unsplash (`www.unsplash.com`)

Distributed to the book trade worldwide by Apress Media, LLC, 1 New York Plaza, New York, NY 10004, U.S.A. Phone 1-800-SPRINGER, fax (201) 348-4505, e-mail `orders-ny@springer-sbm.com`, or visit `www.springeronline.com`. Apress Media, LLC is a California LLC and the sole member (owner) is Springer Science + Business Media Finance Inc (SSBM Finance Inc). SSBM Finance Inc is a **Delaware** corporation.

For information on translations, please e-mail `booktranslations@springernature.com`; for reprint, paperback, or audio rights, please e-mail `bookpermissions@springernature.com`.

Apress titles may be purchased in bulk for academic, corporate, or promotional use. eBook versions and licenses are also available for most titles. For more information, reference our Print and eBook Bulk Sales web page at `http://www.apress.com/bulk-sales`.

Any source code or other supplementary material referenced by the author in this book is available to readers on GitHub via the book's product page, located at `www.apress.com/9781484271407`. For more detailed information, please visit `http://www.apress.com/source-code`.

Printed on acid-free paper

In memory of Toshiko, my friend, companion, and wife of many years.

Table of Contents

About the Author

David Powers is the author of more than 30 highly successful video training courses and books on PHP. He began his professional career as a radio and TV journalist for the BBC, spending a large part of it in Japan reporting on the rise and collapse of the bubble economy. His background of reporting on complex issues in plain, jargon-free language reveals itself in his writing about PHP and web development.

David first became involved with web development in the early 1990s as Editor of BBC Japanese TV. With no marketing budget, he developed a bilingual web site to promote the channel. After leaving the BBC, he went on to develop a bilingual online database for an international consultancy, as well as teaching web development courses at two universities in the United Kingdom. In addition to writing and creating video training courses, he's a trustee of a charity in North London that provides educational facilities for retired people and those no longer in full-time employment.

About the Technical Reviewer

Satej Kumar Sahu works in the role of Senior Enterprise Architect at Honeywell. He is passionate about technology, people, and nature. He believes through technology and conscientious decision-making, each of us has the power to make this world a better place. In his free time, he can be found reading books, playing basketball, and having fun with friends and family.

Acknowledgments

Many people have contributed to this book, each one helping improve it as it has moved over five editions. I'm particularly grateful to Chris Mills, the editor of the first edition, whose idea it was to move away from the cookbook formula of isolated solutions that left the reader with little or no idea about the practical use of a technique. Chris's successors, Ben Renow-Clarke (for the second and third editions) and Mark Powers (for the fourth and fifth editions), have both provided a light touch, nudging me in the right direction and forgiving my late delivery times. By the way, if you think we're keeping it in the family, Mark is no relation in spite of his splendid surname.

A big thank you is due to the technical reviewers of this edition, Matt Wade and Satej Sahu. By the time a book gets to its fifth edition, an author hopes to get something of a free ride, expecting all the problems to have been sorted out in previous editions. Fortunately for you, the reader, they subjected my code and text to detailed analysis, making many helpful suggestions. As a result, the book has been greatly improved. Any errors or inconsistencies that remain are my responsibility alone.

Thanks are also due to everyone involved in the production chain at Apress. A book would never see the light of day without their diligent work behind the scenes.

Finally, I would like to pay tribute to my late wife, Toshiko, who put up with me disappearing for hours on end working on the first three editions of this book. We should have spent more time together. Miss you.

Introduction

PHP 8 is a major update of one of the most widely used languages for developing dynamic web sites. It was released in November 2020. So how could a book released less than 12 months later have managed to get to its fifth edition? Quite simply, this is the fifth iteration of my book *PHP Solutions* that was first published in 2006. When the fourth edition came out in 2019, it was felt important to indicate which version of PHP it covered. So, although the structure of the book remains close to the original, the code has gone through major revision each time.

The fact that *PHP Solutions* has remained so popular owes a great deal to the concept of the book's first editor, Chris Mills. He wanted a book that dealt with practical problems in easily digestible bites; but we agreed that it shouldn't be yet another code "cookbook," a format that was popular at the time. The problem with the cookbook approach is that the reader is presented with a potentially useful block of code but no indication of how it might be used in a real-world situation. *PHP Solutions* aims to provide solutions to practical problems rather than a series of meaningless exercises.

How Easy Is It?

I've always felt concerned about unduly raising readers' expectations with the subtitle of this book, Dynamic Web Design and Development Made Easy. PHP is not difficult, but nor is it like an instant cake mix: just add water and stir. Every web site is different, so it's impossible to grab a script, paste it into a web page, and expect it to work. My aim is to help web designers with little or no knowledge of programming gain the confidence to dive into the code and adjust it to their own requirements.

You don't need any previous experience of PHP or another programming language to be able to use this book; but it does move at a fast pace. After the first few chapters, you start working with relatively advanced features of the language. Don't let that put you off. Regard it as a challenge.

How you use the book will depend on your level of experience. If you're new to PHP and programming, start at the beginning and work your way gradually through the book. It's organized as a logical sequence with each chapter building on knowledge and skills gained in previous ones. When describing the code, I try to explain what it does in plain language. I avoid jargon, but not technical terms (each new term is described briefly when it's first encountered). If you have more experience with PHP, you can probably jump straight into whatever interests you. Even if the code makes sense to you without my explanations, I hope the text throws light onto my thought processes when solving a problem with PHP.

A Word of Caution About PHP Versions

Because hosting companies are often slow to upgrade the version of PHP that they offer, previous editions of this book provided workarounds for older versions of PHP. This time, I don't. In some respects, this is a gamble. As of mid-2021, less than one percent of web servers running PHP were using PHP 8. This means code that works perfectly in a local testing environment is likely to break when it's uploaded to a remote server unless you have upgraded to PHP 8. However, active support for the last version of PHP 7 (7.4) ends in November 2021, shortly after this book's publication.

PHP isn't like that old car you've been running for years and doesn't need changing as long as you give it sufficient love and oil. PHP is constantly being updated, not only to add new features but also to fix bugs and security issues. Even if you're not interested in the new features, you should be interested in security fixes. The Internet can be a wild place with lots of unsavory characters trying to find exploitable holes in web sites. This book contains a lot of advice on security, but it can't protect you from security issues that are uncovered in the PHP core. Making sure that your remote server is kept up to date is an indispensable insurance policy to minimize your risks. And it shouldn't cost you any extra because PHP is free (although hosting companies charge for their services).

If you really need code that's compatible with PHP 7, check out the fourth edition of this book. Better still, make the move to the most up-to-date version of PHP.

What's New in This Edition?

All the code has been extensively reviewed and updated to take advantage of time-saving new features in PHP 8, including named arguments, constructor property promotion, and the match expression. This particularly affects the custom classes in Chapters 9–11. They have been radically rewritten using named arguments to avoid the need for public methods to modify their behavior. There are fewer changes in the second half of the book from Chapter 12 onward because the only significant change PHP 8 makes to interacting with a database is that PDO (PHP Data Objects) now throws an exception by default when it encounters an error. Nevertheless, each chapter has been thoroughly reviewed and revised.

Using the Example Files

All the files necessary for working through this book can be downloaded from the Apress web site via the **Download Source Code** button located at www.apress.com/9781484271407.

Set up a PHP development environment, as described in Chapter 2. Unzip the files and copy the php8sols folder and all its contents into your web server's document root. The code for each chapter is in a folder named after the chapter: ch01, ch02, and so on. Follow the instructions in each PHP solution, and copy the relevant files to the site root or the work folder indicated.

Where a page undergoes several changes during a chapter, I have numbered the different versions like this: index_01.php, index_02.php, and so on. When copying a file that has a number, remove the underscore and number from the filename, so index_01.php becomes index.php. If you are using a program that prompts you to update links when moving files from one folder to another, do not update them. The links in the files are designed to pick up the right images and style sheets when located in the target folder. I have done this so you can use a file comparison utility to check your files against mine.

If you don't have a file comparison utility, I strongly urge you to install one. It will save you hours of head-scratching when trying to spot the difference between your version and mine. A missing semicolon or mistyped variable can be hard to spot in dozens of lines of code. Windows users can download WinMerge for free from http://winmerge.org/. I use the file comparison utility built into my favorite script editor, PhpStorm. BBEdit on a Mac includes a file comparison utility. If you're comfortable using Terminal on a Mac, the diff utility is installed by default.

Layout Conventions

To keep this book as clear and easy to follow as possible, the following text conventions are used throughout:

Important words or concepts are normally highlighted on the first appearance in **bold type**.

Code is presented in `fixed-width font`.

New or changed code is normally presented in **`bold fixed-width font`**.

Pseudocode and variable input are written in *`italic fixed-width font`*.

Menu commands are written in the form Menu ➤ Submenu ➤ Submenu.

Where I want to draw your attention to something, I've highlighted it, like this:

■ **Ahem, don't say I didn't warn you.**

CHAPTER 1

■ ■ ■

What Is PHP 8?

PHP 8, released in late November 2020, is a major update of one of the most popular programming languages. According to Web Technology Surveys (https://w3techs.com/technologies/details/pl-php/all/all), PHP is deployed on more than four in every five web sites that use a server-side language. In spite of its popularity, PHP has a lot of detractors, mainly because of the way the language evolved in the early years. This resulted in the names of related functions and the order of arguments being sometimes inconsistent. And some of its features posed a security risk in inexperienced hands. Concerted efforts to improve the language since 2012 have eliminated most of the problems.

PHP is now a mature, powerful language that's become the most widely used technology for creating dynamic web sites. It's used by major enterprises, including Wikipedia, Mailchimp, and Tumblr, as well as powering the popular WordPress, Drupal, and Joomla content management systems. PHP brings web sites to life in the following ways:

- Sends feedback from your web site directly to your mailbox
- Uploads files through a web page
- Generates thumbnails from larger images
- Reads and writes to files
- Displays and updates information dynamically
- Uses a database to display and store information
- Makes web sites searchable
- And much more...

By reading this book, you'll be able to do all that. Not only is PHP easy to learn; it's platform-neutral, so the same code runs on Windows, macOS, and Linux. All the software you need to develop with PHP is open source and free.

In this chapter, you'll learn about the following:

- How PHP has grown into the most widely used technology for dynamic web sites
- How PHP makes web pages dynamic
- How difficult—or easy—PHP is to learn
- Whether PHP is safe
- What's new in PHP 8
- What software you need to write PHP

© David Powers 2022
D. Powers, *PHP 8 Solutions*, https://doi.org/10.1007/978-1-4842-7141-4_1

How PHP Has Grown

PHP started out in 1995 with rather modest ambitions. It was originally called Personal Home Page Tools (PHP Tools). One of its main goals was to create a guestbook by gathering information from an online form and displaying it on a web page. Within three years, it was decided to drop Personal Home Page from the name, because it sounded like something for hobbyists and didn't do justice to the range of sophisticated features that had since been added. That left the problem of what the initials PHP should stand for. In the end, it was decided to call it PHP Hypertext Preprocessor; but most people simply call it PHP.

PHP has continued to develop over the years, adding new features all the time. One of the language's great attractions is that it remains true to its roots. Although it has support for sophisticated object-oriented programming, you can start using it without diving into complex theory. PHP's original creator, Rasmus Lerdorf, once described it as "a very programmer-friendly scripting language suitable for people with little or no programming experience as well as the seasoned web developer who needs to get things done quickly." You can start writing useful scripts right away, yet be confident in knowing that you're using a technology with the capability to develop industrial-strength applications.

■ **Note**   Much of the code in this book uses features that are new to PHP 8. It is not guaranteed to work on older versions of PHP.

How PHP Makes Pages Dynamic

PHP was originally designed to be embedded in the HTML of a web page, and that's the way it's often still used. For example, to display the current year in a copyright notice, you could put this in your footer:

```
<p>&copy; <?php echo date('Y'); ?> PHP 8 Solutions</p>
```

On a PHP-enabled web server, the code between the <?php and ?> tags is automatically processed and displays the year like this:

© 2021 PHP 8 Solutions

This is only a trivial example, but it illustrates some of the advantages of using PHP:

- The year is automatically updated at the stroke of midnight on New Year's Day.

- The date is calculated by the web server, so it's not affected if the clock in the user's computer is set incorrectly. However, as you'll learn later, PHP follows the server's time zone; but this can be adjusted programmatically.

Although it's convenient to embed PHP code in HTML like this, it's repetitive and can lead to mistakes. It can also make your web pages difficult to maintain, particularly once you start using more complex PHP code. Consequently, it's common practice to store a lot of dynamic code in separate files and then use PHP to build your pages from the different components. The separate files—or *include files*, as they're usually called—can contain only PHP, only HTML, or a mixture of both.

As a simple example, you can put your web site's navigation menu in an include file and use PHP to include it in each page. Whenever you need to change the menu, you edit only the include file, and the changes are automatically reflected in every page that includes the menu. Just imagine how much time that saves on a web site with dozens of pages!

With an ordinary HTML page, the content is fixed by the web developer at design time and uploaded to the web server. When somebody visits the page, the web server simply sends the HTML and other assets, such as images and the style sheet. It's a simple transaction—the request comes from the browser, and the fixed content is sent back by the server. When you build web pages with PHP, much more goes on. Figure 1-1 shows what happens.

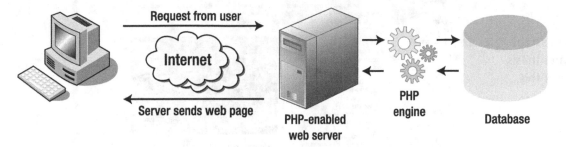

Figure 1-1. *The web server builds each PHP page dynamically in response to a request*

When a PHP-driven web site is visited, it sets in motion the following sequence of events:

1. The browser sends a request to the web server.

2. The web server passes the request to the PHP engine embedded in the server.

3. The PHP engine processes the code in the requested page. In many cases, it might also query a database before building the page.

4. The server sends the completed page back to the browser.

This process usually takes only a fraction of a second, so the visitor to a PHP web site is unlikely to notice any delay. Because each page is built individually, PHP sites can respond to user input, displaying different content when a user logs in or showing the results of a database search.

Creating Pages That Think for Themselves

PHP is a server-side language. The PHP code remains on the web server. After it has been processed, the server sends only the output of the script. Normally, this is HTML, but PHP can also be used to generate other web languages, such as JSON (JavaScript Object Notation) or XML (Extensible Markup Language).

PHP enables you to introduce logic into your web pages that is based on alternatives. Some decisions are made using information that PHP gleans from the server: the date, the time, the day of the week, information in the page's URL, and so on. If it's Wednesday, it will show Wednesday's TV schedules. At other times, decisions are based on user input, which PHP extracts from online forms. If you have registered with a site, it will display personalized information—that sort of thing.

How Hard Is PHP to Use and Learn?

PHP isn't rocket science, but don't expect to become an expert in 5 minutes. Perhaps the biggest shock to newcomers is that PHP is far less tolerant of mistakes than browsers are with HTML. If you omit a closing tag in HTML, most browsers will still render the page. If you omit a closing quote, semicolon, or brace in PHP, you'll get an uncompromising error message like the one shown in Figure 1-2. This affects all programming languages, such as JavaScript and C#, not just PHP.

A missing
parenthesis
turns this...

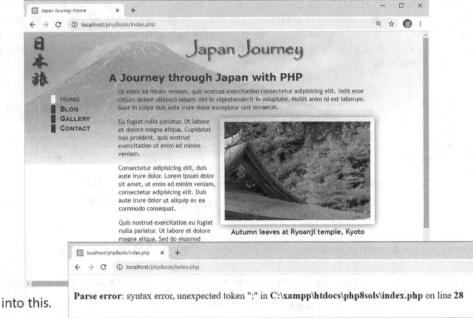

into this.

Figure 1-2. *Server-side languages like PHP are intolerant of most coding errors*

If you use a visual design tool and never look at the underlying code, it's time to rethink your approach. Mixing PHP with poorly structured HTML is likely to lead to problems. PHP uses loops to perform repetitive tasks, such as displaying the results of a database search. A loop repeats the same section of code—usually a mixture of PHP and HTML—until all results have been displayed. If you put the loop in the wrong place or if your HTML is badly structured, your page is likely to collapse like a house of cards.

If you're not already in the habit of doing so, it's a good idea to check your pages using the World Wide Web Consortium's (W3C) Nu HTML Checker (`https://validator.w3.org/nu/`).

■ **Note** The W3C is the international body that develops standards such as HTML and CSS to ensure the long-term growth of the Web. It's led by the inventor of the World Wide Web, Tim Berners-Lee. To learn about the W3C, see `www.w3.org/Consortium/mission`.

Can I Just Copy and Paste the Code?

There's nothing wrong with copying the code in this book. That's what it's there for. I've structured this book as a series of practical projects. I explain what the code is for and why it's there. Even if you don't understand exactly how it all works, this should give you sufficient confidence to know which parts of the code to adapt to your own needs and which parts are best left alone. But to get the most out of this book, you need to start experimenting and then come up with your own solutions.

PHP has thousands of built-in functions that perform all sorts of tasks, such as converting text to uppercase, generating thumbnail images from full-sized ones, or connecting to a database. The real power comes from combining these functions in different ways and adding your own conditional logic.

How Safe Is PHP?

PHP is like the electricity or kitchen knives in your home: handled properly, it's very safe; handled irresponsibly, it can do a lot of damage. One of the inspirations for the first edition of this book was a spate of attacks that exploited a vulnerability in email scripts, turning web sites into spam relays. The solution is quite simple, as you'll learn in Chapter 6, but even many years later, I still see people using the same insecure techniques, exposing their sites to attack.

PHP is not unsafe, nor does everyone need to become a security expert to use it. What is important is to understand the basic principle of PHP safety: *always check user input before processing it*. You'll find that to be a constant theme in this book. Most security risks can be eliminated with very little effort.

The best way to protect yourself is to understand the code you're using.

What's New in PHP 8?

The list of new features and changes in PHP 8 is extensive; but the most important is the adoption of a Just In Time (JIT) compiler. This changes the way PHP code is converted into machine code that the server can understand. As the name implies, JIT is designed to speed up performance. Zeev Surasky, one of the authors of the JIT proposal, has created a short video (https://youtu.be/dWH65pmnsrI) to demonstrate the dramatic improvement JIT is capable of. However, such improvements in speed affect only processor-intensive calculations—at least for the time being. WordPress runs no faster on PHP 8 than on PHP 7, which is where the real speed gains over previous versions were made.

Many of the new features in PHP 8 are designed to make code more concise and efficient. For example, named arguments eliminate the need to repeat the default values of multiple arguments to a function if you want to change only one of them. Constructor property promotion greatly simplifies the declaration of properties in a class definition, typically reducing the number of lines by one third. The new nullsafe operator similarly reduces the amount of code needed to call a method or fetch the property on the result of an expression only if it's not null. Details of these and other new features are covered in Chapters 3 and 4.

An important consideration of migrating existing code to a new version of PHP is whether incompatible changes will break your application. If you have been following recommended best practices, you're unlikely to have problems. However, there are some important changes that you should be aware of, as follows:

- The error control operator (@) will no longer silence fatal errors.

- Non-strict comparisons between numbers and non-numeric strings using two equal signs (==) now convert the number to a string and compare the strings. This means that some comparisons that previously equated to true are now false.

- Methods with the same name as the class are no longer interpreted as constructors. You must use __construct() instead.

- You can no longer define case-insensitive constants.

- match is now a reserved keyword.

- #[is no longer regarded as the start of a comment because this syntax is used for a new feature called attributes. This affects only an opening square bracket after #.

■ **Note** See www.php.net/manual/en/migration80.incompatible.php for a complete list of backward-incompatible changes in PHP 8.

What Software Do I Need to Write PHP?

Strictly speaking, you don't need any special software to write PHP scripts. PHP code is plain text and can be created in any text editor, such as Notepad on Windows or TextEdit on macOS. Having said that, your life will be a lot easier if you use a program that has features designed to speed up the development process. There are many available—both free and on a paid-for basis.

What to Look for When Choosing a PHP Editor

If there's a mistake in your code, your page will probably never make it as far as the browser, and all you'll see is an error message. You should choose a script editor that has the following features:

- **PHP syntax checking**: This used to be found only in expensive, dedicated programs, but it's now a feature in several free programs. Syntax checkers monitor the code as you type and highlight errors, saving a great deal of time and frustration.

- **PHP syntax coloring**: Code is highlighted in different colors according to the role it plays. If your code is in an unexpected color, it's a sure sign you've made a mistake.

- **PHP code hints**: PHP has so many built-in functions that it can be difficult to remember how to use them, even for an experienced user. Many script editors automatically display tooltips with reminders of how a particular piece of code works.

- **Line numbering**: Finding a specific line quickly makes troubleshooting a lot simpler.

- **A "balance braces" feature**: Parentheses (()), square brackets ([]), and curly braces ({}) must always be in matching pairs. It's easy to forget to close a pair. All good script editors help find the matching parenthesis, bracket, or brace.

The program you're already using to build web pages might already have some or all of these features. Even if you don't plan to do a lot of PHP development, you should consider using a dedicated script editor if your web development program doesn't support syntax checking. The following dedicated script editors have all the essential features, such as syntax checking and code hints. It's not an exhaustive list, but rather one based on personal experience:

- **PhpStorm** (`www.jetbrains.com/phpstorm/`): Although this is a dedicated PHP editing program, it has excellent support for HTML, CSS, and JavaScript. It's my favorite program for developing with PHP. It's sold on an annual subscription. If you cancel after a minimum of 12 months, you get a perpetual license for an older version.

- **Visual Studio Code** (`https://code.visualstudio.com/`): An excellent code editor from Microsoft that runs not only on Windows but also on macOS and Linux. It's free and has built-in support for PHP.

- **Sublime Text** (`www.sublimetext.com/`): If you're a Sublime Text fan, there are plug-ins for PHP syntax coloring, syntax checking, and documentation. Free for evaluation, but you should buy the relatively inexpensive license for continued use.

- **Zend Studio** (`www.zend.com/products/zend-studio`): Powerful, dedicated PHP editor created by Zend, the company run by leading contributors to the development of PHP. It runs on Windows, macOS, and Linux. Different pricing applies to personal and commercial use.

- **Eclipse PHP Development Tools (PDT)** (`https://projects.eclipse.org/projects/tools.pdt`): Similar to Zend Studio but with the advantage of being free. It runs on Eclipse, the open source IDE that supports multiple computer languages. If you have used Eclipse for other languages, you should find it relatively easy to use. PDT runs on Windows, macOS, and Linux.

So Let's Get On with It…

This chapter has provided only a brief overview of what PHP can do to add dynamic features to your web sites and what software you need to do so. The first stage in working with PHP is to set up a testing environment. The next chapter covers what you need for both Windows and macOS.

CHAPTER 2

■ ■ ■

Getting Ready to Work with PHP

Now that you've decided to use PHP to enrich your web pages, you need to make sure that you have everything you need to get on with the rest of this book. Although you can test everything on your remote server, it's usually more convenient to test PHP pages on your local computer. Everything you need to install is free. In this chapter, I'll explain the various options for Windows and macOS. The necessary components are normally installed by default on Linux.

This chapter covers

- Checking if your web site supports PHP

- Creating a local testing setup with a ready-made package in Windows and macOS

- Deciding where to store your PHP files

- Checking the PHP configuration on your local and remote servers

Checking Whether Your Web Site Supports PHP

The easiest way to find out whether your web site supports PHP is to ask your hosting company. The other way to find out is to upload a PHP page to your web site and see if it works. Even if you know that your site supports PHP, do the following test to confirm which version is running:

1. Open your script editor, and type the following code into a blank page:

    ```
    <?php echo phpversion();
    ```

2. Save the file as phpversion.php. It's important to make sure that your operating system doesn't add a .txt filename extension after the .php. If you're using TextEdit on a Mac, make sure that it doesn't save the file in Rich Text Format (RTF). If you're at all unsure, use phpversion.php from the ch02 folder in the files accompanying this book.

3. Upload phpversion.php to your web site in the same way you would an HTML page and then type the URL into a browser. Assuming you upload the file to the top level of your site, the URL will be something like www.example.com/phpversion.php.

    If you see a three-part number like 8.0.3 displayed onscreen, you're in business: PHP is enabled. The number tells you which version of PHP is running on your server.

© David Powers 2022
D. Powers, *PHP 8 Solutions*, https://doi.org/10.1007/978-1-4842-7141-4_2

4. If you get a message that says something like "Parse error," it means PHP is supported but that you have made a mistake in typing the code in the file. Use the version in the ch02 folder instead.

5. If you just see the original code, it means PHP is not supported.

■ **Caution** The code in this book uses features that are new to PHP 8. If your web server is running an older version of PHP, many of the techniques described in this book will not work.

Deciding Where to Test Your Pages

Unlike ordinary web pages, you can't just double-click PHP pages in Windows File Explorer or Finder on a Mac and view them in your browser. They need to be **parsed**, or processed, through a web server that supports PHP. If your hosting company supports PHP, you can upload your files to your web site and test them there. However, you need to upload the file every time you make a change. In the early days, you'll find you have to do this often because of a minor mistake in your code. As you become more experienced, you'll still need to upload files frequently because you'll want to experiment with different ideas.

Using a local test environment is the most efficient way to develop with PHP. The rest of this chapter is devoted to showing you how to do this, with instructions for both Windows and macOS.

What You Need for a Local Test Environment

To test PHP pages on your local computer, you need to install the following:

- A web server, which is a piece of software that displays web pages, not a separate computer

- PHP

- A MySQL or MariaDB database and phpMyAdmin, a web-based front end for administering the database

---

■ **Tip** MariaDB (`https://mariadb.org/`) is a community-developed drop-in replacement for MySQL. The code in this book is fully compatible with both MySQL and MariaDB.

All the software you need is free. The only cost to you is the time it takes to download the necessary files, plus, of course, the time to make sure everything is set up correctly. In most cases, you should be up and running in less than an hour, probably considerably less. As long as you have at least 1 GB of free disk space, you should be able to install all the software on your computer—even one with modest specifications.

■ **Tip** If you already have a PHP 8 test environment on your local computer, there's no need to reinstall. Just check the section at the end of this chapter titled "Checking Your PHP Settings."

The simplest way to set up a test environment is to use a package that installs Apache, PHP, MySQL (or MariaDB), and phpMyAdmin in a single operation. On my computers, I use XAMPP for Windows (`www.apachefriends.org/index.html`) and MAMP for macOS (`www.mamp.info/en/`). Other packages are available; it doesn't matter which you choose.

Setting Up on Windows

Make sure that you're logged on as an administrator before proceeding.

Getting Windows to Display Filename Extensions

By default, most Windows computers hide common three- or four-letter filename extensions, such as `.doc` or `.html`, so all you see in dialog boxes and Windows File Explorer is `thisfile` instead of `thisfile.doc` or `thisfile.html`.

Use these instructions to enable the display of filename extensions in Windows 10:

1. Open File Explorer (Windows key + E).

2. Select View to expand the ribbon at the top of the File Explorer window.

3. Select the "File name extensions" check box.

Displaying filename extensions is more secure—you can tell if a virus writer has attached an `.exe` or `.scr` executable file to an innocent-looking document.

Choosing a Web Server

Most PHP installations run on the Apache web server. Both are open source and work well together. However, Windows has its own web server, Internet Information Services (IIS), which also supports PHP. Microsoft has worked closely with the PHP development team to improve the performance of PHP on IIS to roughly the same level as Apache. So which should you choose?

Unless you need IIS for ASP or ASP.NET, I recommend that you install Apache, using XAMPP or one of the other all-in-one packages, as described in the next section. If you need to use IIS, you can install PHP from `https://php.iis.net/`.

Installing an All-in-One Package on Windows

There are two popular packages for Windows that install Apache, PHP, MySQL or MariaDB, phpMyAdmin, and several other tools on your computer in a single operation: XAMPP (`www.apachefriends.org/index.html`) and EasyPHP (`www.easyphp.org`). The installation process normally takes only a few minutes. Once the package has been installed, you might need to change a few settings, as explained later in this chapter.

Versions are liable to change over the lifetime of a printed book, so I won't describe the installation process. Each package has instructions on its web site.

Setting Up on macOS

The Apache web server and PHP are preinstalled on macOS, but they're not enabled by default. Rather than using the preinstalled versions, I recommend that you use MAMP, which installs Apache, PHP, MySQL, phpMyAdmin, and several other tools in a single operation.

To avoid conflicts with the preinstalled versions of Apache and PHP, MAMP locates all the applications in a dedicated folder on your hard disk. This makes it easier to uninstall everything by simply dragging the MAMP folder to the Trash if you decide you no longer want MAMP on your computer.

Installing MAMP

Before you begin, make sure you're logged in to your computer with administrative privileges:

1. Go to www.mamp.info/en/downloads/ and select the link for MAMP & MAMP PRO. This downloads a disk image that contains both the free and paid-for versions of MAMP.

2. When the download completes, launch the disk image. You'll be presented with a license agreement. You must click Agree to continue with mounting the disk image.

3. Follow the onscreen instructions.

4. Verify that MAMP has been installed in your Applications folder.

■ **Note** MAMP automatically installs both the free and paid-for versions in separate folders called MAMP and MAMP PRO. The paid-for version makes it easier to configure PHP and to work with virtual hosts, but the free version is perfectly adequate, especially for beginners. If you want to remove the MAMP PRO folder, don't drag it to the Trash. Open the folder and double-click the MAMP PRO uninstall icon. The paid-for version requires both folders.

Testing and Configuring MAMP

By default, MAMP uses nonstandard ports for Apache and MySQL. Unless you're using multiple installations of Apache and MySQL, change the port settings as described in the following steps:

1. Double-click the MAMP icon in Applications/MAMP. If you're presented with a panel inviting you to learn more about Standard View, this is a feature that's new in the paid-for version only. To prevent the panel from being displayed each time you start MAMP, deselect the check box at the bottom left of the panel. Then click the Close button at the top left to dismiss the panel.

2. In the MAMP control panel, set the PHP version drop-down menu to 8.0.2 or later (see Figure 2-1). If you get a warning that your site might not behave as expected in PHP 8, click OK. You can prevent this warning from appearing again by selecting the check box.

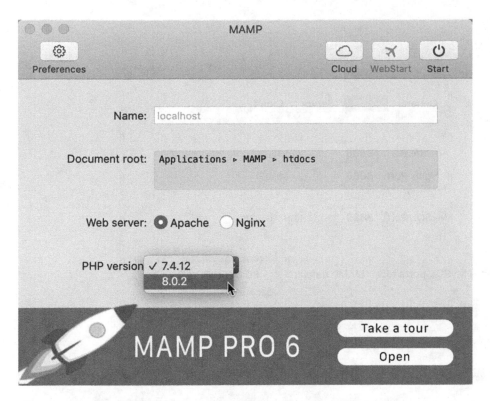

Figure 2-1. *Selecting the PHP version in the MAMP control panel*

3. Click the Start icon at the top right of the MAMP control panel. Your default browser eventually launches and presents you with the MAMP welcome page.

4. If your browser doesn't launch automatically, click the WebStart icon at the top of the MAMP control panel.

5. Check the URL in the browser address bar. It begins with localhost:8888. The :8888 indicates that Apache is listening for requests on the nonstandard port 8888.

6. Minimize the browser and click the Preferences icon at the top left of the MAMP control panel.

7. Select Ports at the top of the panel that opens. It shows that Apache and MySQL are running on ports 8888 and 8889 (see Figure 2-2).

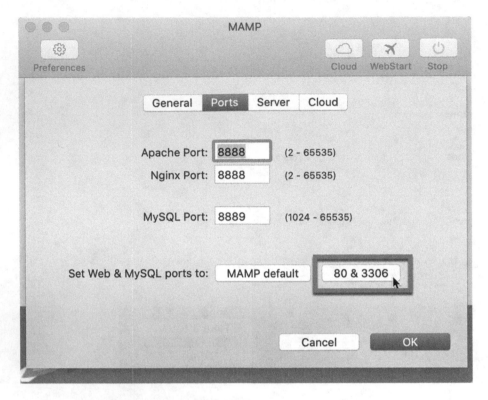

Figure 2-2. *Changing the Apache and MySQL ports*

8. Click the 80 & 3306 button as shown in Figure 2-2 to change the web and MySQL
    ports to the standard values: 80 for Apache and 3306 for MySQL.

9. Click OK and enter your Mac password when prompted to restart the servers.

■ **Tip**   Apache won't restart if any other program is using port 80. If you can't find what's preventing Apache
from using port 80, open the MAMP Preferences panel and click the MAMP default button. Then click OK again.

---

10. When the servers have started up again, click the WebStart button in the MAMP
    control panel to load the welcome page into your browser. This time, the URL
    shouldn't have a colon followed by a number appearing after localhost because
    Apache is now listening on the default port.

Where to Locate Your PHP Files (Windows and Mac)

You need to create your files in a location where the web server can process them. Normally, this means that
the files should be in the server's document root or in a subfolder of the document root. The default location
of the document root for the most common setups is as follows:

- **XAMPP**: C:\xampp\htdocs

- **EasyPHP**: C:\EasyPHP\www

- **IIS**: C:\inetpub\wwwroot

- **MAMP**: /Applications/MAMP/htdocs

To view a PHP page, you need to load it in a browser using a URL. The URL for the web server's document root in your local testing environment is http://localhost/.

■ **Caution** If you need to reset MAMP back to its default ports, you will need to use http://localhost:8888 instead of http://localhost.

If you store the files for this book in a subfolder of the document root called php8sols, the URL is http://localhost/php8sols/ followed by the name of the folder (if any) and file.

■ **Tip** Use http://127.0.0.1/ if you have problems with http://localhost/. 127.0.0.1 is the loopback IP address all computers use to refer to the local machine.

Checking Your PHP Settings

After installing PHP, it's a good idea to check its configuration settings. In addition to the core features, PHP has a large number of optional extensions. The all-in-one packages install all the extensions that you need for this book. However, some of the basic configuration settings might be slightly different. To avoid unexpected problems, adjust your configuration to match the settings recommended in the following pages.

Displaying the Server Configuration with phpinfo()

PHP has a built-in command, phpinfo(), that displays details of how PHP is configured on the server. The amount of detail produced by phpinfo() can feel like massive information overload, but it's invaluable for determining why something works perfectly on your local computer yet not on your live web site. The problem usually lies in the remote server having disabled a feature or not having installed an optional extension.

The all-in-one packages make it easy to run phpinfo():

- **XAMPP**: Click the Apache Admin button in the XAMPP control panel to launch the XAMPP welcome page in a browser. Then click the PHPInfo button at the top of the page.

- **MAMP**: Scroll down to the PHP section of the MAMP welcome page and click the phpinfo link.

Alternatively, create a simple test file and load it in your browser using the following instructions:

1. Make sure that Apache or IIS is running on your local computer.

2. Type the following in a script editor:

```
<?php phpinfo();
```

There should be nothing else in the file.

3.   Save the file as phpinfo.php in the server's document root (see "Where to Locate Your PHP Files (Windows and Mac)" earlier in this chapter).

■ **Caution**   Make sure your editor doesn't add a .txt or .rtf extension after .php.

---

4.   Type http://localhost/phpinfo.php in your browser address bar and press Enter.

5.   You should see a page similar to that in Figure 2-3 displaying the version of PHP followed by extensive details of your PHP configuration.

PHP Version 8.0.3	*php*
System	Windows NT DAVID8 10.0 build 19041 (Windows 10) AMD64
Build Date	Mar 2 2021 23:26:36
Build System	Microsoft Windows Server 2016 Standard [10.0.14393]
Compiler	Visual C++ 2019
Architecture	x64
Configure Command	cscript /nologo /e:jscript configure.js "--enable-snapshot-build" "--enable-debug-pack" "--with-pdo-oci=c:\php-snap-build\dep-aux\oracle\x64\instantclient_19_9\sdk,shared" "--with-oci8-12c=c:\php-snap-build\dep-aux\oracle\x64\instantclient_12_1\sdk,shared" "--with-oci8-19=c:\php-snap-build\dep-aux\oracle\x64\instantclient_19_9\sdk,shared" "--enable-object-out-dir=../obj/" "--enable-com-dotnet=shared" "--without-analyzer" "--with-pgo"
Server API	Apache 2.0 Handler
Virtual Directory Support	enabled
Configuration File (php.ini) Path	*no value*
Loaded Configuration File	C:\xampp\php\php.ini
Scan this dir for additional .ini files	(none)
Additional .ini files parsed	(none)
PHP API	20200930
	20200930

Figure 2-3. Running the phpinfo() command displays full details of your PHP configuration.

6.   Make a note of the value for the Loaded Configuration File item. This tells you where to find php.ini, the text file that you need to edit in order to change most settings in PHP.

7.   Scroll down to the section labeled Core and compare the settings with those recommended in Table 2-1. Make a note of any differences so you can change them as described later in this chapter.

Table 2-1. Recommended PHP configuration settings

Directive	Local value	Remarks
display_errors	On	Essential for debugging mistakes in your scripts. If set to Off, errors result in a completely blank screen, leaving you clueless as to the possible cause.
error_reporting	32767	This sets error reporting to the highest level.
file_uploads	On	Allows you to use PHP to upload files to a web site.
log_errors	Off	With display_errors set to On, you don't need to fill your hard disk with an error log.

8. The rest of the configuration page shows you which PHP extensions are enabled. Although the page seems to go on forever, the extensions are all listed in alphabetical order. To work with this book, make sure the following extensions are enabled:

- **gd**: Enables PHP to generate and modify images and fonts.

■ **Note** If your testing environment is running on Windows and the gd extension is not listed, you can easily turn it on by following the instructions in the next section.

- **mysqli**: Connects to MySQL/MariaDB. (Note the "i," which stands for "improved." Since PHP 7, the older mysql one is no longer supported.)

- **PDO**: Provides software-neutral support for databases (optional).

- **pdo_mysql**: Alternative method of connecting to MySQL/MariaDB (optional).

- **session**: Sessions maintain information associated with a user and are used, among other things, for user authentication.

You should also run phpinfo() on your remote server to check which features are enabled. If the listed extensions aren't supported, some of the code in this book won't work when you upload your files to your web site. If PDO and pdo_mysql aren't listed, you can use mysqli instead.

■ **Caution** The output displayed by phpinfo() reveals a lot of information that could be used by a malicious hacker to attack your web site. Always delete the file from your remote server after checking your configuration.

If any of the settings in your setup are different from these recommendations, you will need to edit the PHP configuration file, php.ini, as described in the next section.

Editing php.ini

The PHP configuration file, php.ini, is a very long file, which tends to unnerve newcomers to programming, but there's nothing to worry about. It's written in plain text, and one reason for its length is that it contains copious comments explaining the various options. That said, it's a good idea to make a backup copy before editing php.ini in case you make a mistake.

How you open `php.ini` depends on your operating system and how you installed PHP:

- If you used an all-in-one package, such as XAMPP, on Windows, double-click `php.ini` in Windows File Explorer. The file opens automatically in Notepad.

- If you installed PHP on IIS, `php.ini` is normally located in a subfolder of Program Files. Although you can open `php.ini` by double-clicking it, you won't be able to save any changes you make. Instead, right-click Notepad and select Run as administrator. Inside Notepad, select File ➤ Open and set the option to display All Files (*.*). Navigate to the folder where `php.ini` is located, select the file, and click Open.

- On macOS, use a plain-text editor to open `php.ini`. If you use TextEdit, make sure it saves the file as plain text, not Rich Text Format.

Lines that begin with a semicolon (`;`) are comments. Except for turning on the gd extension on Windows, the lines you need to edit do not begin with a semicolon.

Use your text editor's Find functionality to locate the directives you need to change to match the recommendations in Table 2-1. Most directives are preceded by one or more examples of how they should be set. Make sure you don't edit one of the commented examples by mistake.

For directives that use `On` or `Off`, just change the value to the recommended one. For example, if you need to turn on the display of error messages, edit this line

```
display_errors = Off
```

by changing it to this:

```
display_errors = On
```

To set the level of error reporting, you need to use PHP constants, which are written in uppercase and are case-sensitive. The directive should look like this:

```
error_reporting = E_ALL
```

If your testing environment is running on Windows and the gd extension isn't listed when you run `phpinfo()`, find the following line in `php.ini`:

```
;extension=gd
```

Remove the semicolon from the beginning of the line.

■ **Note**   On macOS and Linux, PHP normally needs to be compiled with the gd extension enabled, so this simple fix won't work. Check with the site where you downloaded your PHP installation for any options that are available.

After editing `php.ini`, save the file and then restart Apache or IIS so that the changes take effect. If the web server won't start, check the server's error log file. It can be found in the following locations:

- **XAMPP**: In the XAMPP control panel, click the Logs button alongside Apache and then select Apache (error.log).

- **MAMP**: In /Applications/MAMP/logs, double-click apache_error.log to open it in Console.

- **EasyPHP**: Right-click the EasyPHP icon in the system tray and select Log Files ➤ Apache.

- **IIS**: The default location of log files is C:\inetpub\logs.

The most recent entry in the error log should give you an indication of what prevented the server from restarting. Use that information to correct the changes you made to php.ini. If that doesn't work, be thankful you made a backup of php.ini before editing it. Start again with a fresh copy and check your edits carefully.

What's Next?

Now that you've got a working test bed for PHP, you're no doubt raring to go. The last thing I want to do is dampen any enthusiasm, but before using PHP in a live web site, you should have a basic understanding of the rules of the language. So, before jumping into the cool stuff, read the next chapter, which explains how to write PHP scripts. Even if you have extensive experience of PHP, be sure to check the sections that deal with changes in PHP 8.

CHAPTER 3

▄ ▄ ▄

How to Write PHP Scripts

This chapter offers a quick overview of how PHP works and gives you the basic rules. It's aimed primarily at readers who have no previous experience of PHP or coding. Even if you've worked with PHP before, check the main headings to see what this chapter contains and brush up your knowledge on any aspects that you're a bit hazy about.

This chapter covers

- Understanding how PHP is structured

- Embedding PHP in a web page

- Storing data in variables and arrays

- Getting PHP to make decisions

- Looping through repetitive tasks

- Using functions for preset tasks

- Displaying PHP output

- Understanding PHP error messages

PHP: The Big Picture

At first glance, PHP code can look quite intimidating, but once you understand the basics, you'll discover that the structure is remarkably simple. If you have worked with any other computer language, such as JavaScript or jQuery, you'll find they have a lot in common.

Every PHP page *must* have the following:

- The correct filename extension, usually .php

- PHP tags surrounding each block of PHP code (the closing PHP tag is normally omitted if the file contains only PHP code)

A typical PHP page will use some or all of the following elements:

- Variables to act as placeholders for unknown or changing values

- Arrays to hold multiple values

- Conditional statements to make decisions

- Loops to perform repetitive tasks

- Functions or objects to perform preset tasks

Let's take a quick look at each of these in turn, starting with the filename and the opening and closing tags.

21

D. Powers, *PHP 8 Solutions*, https://doi.org/10.1007/978-1-4842-7141-4_3

Telling the Server to Process PHP

PHP is a **server-side language**. The web server—usually Apache—processes your PHP code and sends only the results, usually as HTML, to the browser. Because all the action is on the server, you need to tell it that your pages contain PHP code. This involves two simple steps:

- Give every page a PHP filename extension; the default is .php. Use a different extension only if you are specifically told to do so by your hosting company.

- Identify all PHP code with PHP tags.

The opening tag is <?php and the closing tag is ?>. If you put the tags on the same line as surrounding code, there doesn't need to be a space before the opening tag or after the closing one, but there must be a space after the php in the opening tag like this:

```
<p>This is HTML with embedded PHP<?php //some PHP code ?>.</p>
```

When inserting more than one line of PHP, it's a good idea to put the opening and closing tags on separate lines for the sake of clarity:

```
<?php
// some PHP code
// more PHP code
?>
```

You may come across <? as an alternative short version of the opening tag. However, <? isn't enabled on all servers. Stick with <?php, which is guaranteed to work.

When a file contains only PHP code, it's strongly recommended to omit the closing PHP tag. This avoids potential problems when working with include files (see Chapter 5).

■ **Note**   To save space, most examples in this book omit the PHP tags. You must always use them when writing your own scripts or embedding PHP into a web page.

Embedding PHP in a Web Page

PHP can be used as an **embedded** language. This means that you can insert blocks of PHP code inside ordinary web pages. When somebody visits your site and requests a PHP page, the server sends it to the PHP engine, which reads the page from top to bottom looking for PHP tags. HTML and JavaScript pass through untouched, but whenever the PHP engine encounters a <?php tag, it starts processing your code and continues until it reaches the closing ?> tag (or the end of the script if nothing follows the PHP code). If the PHP produces any output, it's inserted at that point.

■ **Tip**   A page can have multiple PHP code blocks, but they cannot be nested inside each other.

Figure 3-1 shows a block of PHP code embedded in an ordinary web page and what it looks like in a browser and in a page source view after it has been passed through the PHP engine. The code calculates the current year, checks whether it's different from a fixed year (represented by $startYear on line 26 of the code on the left of the figure), and displays the appropriate year range in a copyright statement. As you can see from the page source view at the bottom right of the figure, there's no trace of PHP in what's sent to the browser.

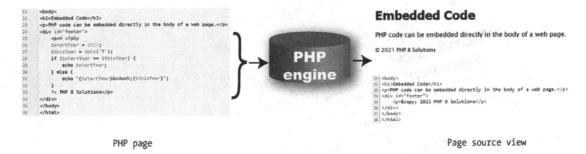

Figure 3-1. The PHP code remains on the server; only the output is sent to the browser

---

■ **Tip**   PHP doesn't always produce direct output for the browser. It may, for instance, check the contents of form input before sending an email message or inserting information into a database. Therefore, some code blocks are placed above or below the main HTML code or in external files. Code that produces direct output, however, goes where you want the output to be displayed.

Storing PHP in an External File

As well as embedding PHP in HTML, it's common practice to store frequently used code in separate files. When a file contains only PHP code, the opening <?php tag is mandatory, but the closing ?> tag is optional. In fact, the recommended practice is to leave out the closing PHP tag. However, you *must* use the closing ?> tag if the external file contains HTML after the PHP code.

Using Variables to Represent Changing Values

The code in Figure 3-1 probably looks like a very long-winded way to display a single year or range of years. But the PHP solution saves you time in the long run. Instead of your needing to update the copyright statement every year, the PHP code does it automatically. You write the code once and forget it. What's more, as you'll see in Chapter 5, if you store the code in an external file, any changes to the external file can be reflected on every page of your site.

    This ability to display the year automatically relies on two key aspects of PHP: **variables** and **functions**. As the name suggests, functions do things; they perform preset tasks, such as getting the current date and converting it into human-readable form. I'll cover functions a little later, so let's work on variables first. The script in Figure 3-1 contains two variables: $startYear and $thisYear.

■ **Tip**   A **variable** is simply a name that you give to something that may change or that you don't know in advance. Variables in PHP always begin with $ (a dollar sign).

23

We use variables all the time in everyday life without thinking about it. When you meet somebody for the first time, you might ask "What's your name?" It doesn't matter whether the person is called Tom, Dick, or Harriet; the word "name" remains constant. Similarly, with your bank account, money goes in and out all the time (mostly out, it seems), but as Figure 3-2 shows, it doesn't matter whether you're scraping the bottom of the barrel or as rich as Croesus. The amount available is always called the balance.

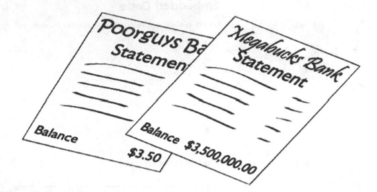

Figure 3-2. *The balance on your bank statement is an everyday example of a variable—the label stays the same, even though the value may change from day to day*

So "name" and "balance" are everyday variables. Just put a dollar sign in front of them, and you have two ready-made PHP variables, like this:

```
$name
$balance
```

Simple.

Naming Variables

You can name a variable just about anything you like, as long as you keep the following rules in mind:

- Variables always begin with a dollar sign ($).

- Valid characters are letters, numbers, and the underscore.

- The first character after the dollar sign must be a letter or the underscore(_).

- No spaces or punctuation marks are allowed, except for the underscore.

- Variable names are case-sensitive: $startYear and $startyear are not the same.

When naming variables, choose something that tells you what it's for. The variables you've seen so far—$startYear, $thisYear, $name, and $balance—are good examples. It's a good idea to capitalize the first letter of the second or subsequent words when combining them (sometimes called **camel case**). Alternatively, you can use an underscore ($start_year, $this_year, etc.).

■ **Tip**   Accented characters commonly used in Western European languages are valid in variables. For example, $prénom and $förnamn are acceptable. In practice, you can also use other alphabets, such as Cyrillic, and nonalphabetic scripts, such as Japanese kanji, in variable names; but at the time of this writing, such use is undocumented, so I recommend sticking to the preceding rules.

Don't try to save time by using really short variables. Using $sy, $ty, $n, and $b instead of the more descriptive ones makes code harder to understand—and that makes it hard to write. More important, it makes errors more difficult to spot. As always, there are exceptions to a rule. By convention, $i, $j, and $k are frequently used to keep count of the number of times a loop has run, and $e and $t are used in error checking. You'll see examples of these later in this chapter.

■ **Caution**   Although you have considerable freedom in the choice of variable names, you can't use $this, because it has a special meaning in PHP object-oriented programming. It's also advisable to avoid any of the keywords listed at www.php.net/manual/en/reserved.php.

Assigning Values to Variables

Variables get their values from a variety of sources, including the following:

- User input through online forms
- A database
- An external source, such as a news feed or XML file
- The result of a calculation
- Direct assignment in the PHP code

Wherever the value comes from, it's normally assigned with an equal sign (=), like this:

```
$variable = value;
```

The variable goes on the left of the equal sign, and the value goes on the right. Because it assigns a value, the equal sign is called the **assignment operator**.

■ **Caution**   Familiarity with the equal sign from childhood makes it difficult to get out of the habit of thinking that it means "is equal to." However, PHP uses two equal signs (==) to signify equality. This is a major cause of beginner mistakes, and it sometimes catches more experienced developers, too. The difference between = and == is covered in more detail later in this chapter.

Ending Commands with a Semicolon

PHP is written as a series of commands or statements. Each statement normally tells the PHP engine to perform an action, and it must always be followed by a semicolon, like this:

```
<?php
do this;
now do something else;
?>
```

As with all rules, there is an exception: you can omit the semicolon after the last statement in a code block. However, *don't do it* except when using the short echo tag as described later in this chapter. Unlike JavaScript, PHP won't assume there should be a semicolon at the end of a line if you leave it out. This has a nice side effect: you can spread long statements over several lines for ease of reading. PHP, like HTML, ignores whitespace in code. Instead, it relies on semicolons to indicate where one command ends and the next one begins.

■ **Tip** A missing semicolon will bring your script to a grinding halt.

Commenting Scripts

PHP treats everything as statements to be executed unless you mark a section of code as a comment. The following three reasons explain why you may want to do this:

- To insert a reminder of what the script does
- To insert a placeholder for code to be added later
- To disable a section of code temporarily

When a script is fresh in your mind, it may seem unnecessary to insert anything that isn't going to be processed. However, if you need to revise the script several months later, you'll find comments much easier to read than trying to follow the code on its own. Comments are also vital when you're working in a team. They help your colleagues understand what the code is intended to do.

During testing, it's often useful to prevent a line of code, or even a whole section, from running. PHP ignores anything marked as a comment, so this is a useful way of turning on and off code.

There are three ways of adding comments: two for single-line comments and one for comments that stretch over several lines.

Single-Line Comments

The most common type of single-line comment begins with two forward slashes, like this:

```
// this is a comment and will be ignored by the PHP engine
```

PHP ignores everything from the double slashes to the end of the line, so you can also place comments alongside code (but only to the right):

```
$startYear = 2018; // this is a valid comment
```

Comments aren't PHP statements, so they don't end with a semicolon. But don't forget the semicolon at the end of a PHP statement that's on the same line as a comment.

An alternative style uses the hash or pound sign (#), like this:

```
# this is another type of comment that will be ignored by the PHP engine
$startYear = 2018; # this also works as a comment
```

This style of commenting often indicates sections of a longer script, like this:

```
##################
## Menu section ##
##################
```

■ **Caution** PHP 8 uses #[as the opening syntax of a new feature called attributes that provide metadata for the declarations of classes, functions, and some other features (see `www.php.net/manual/en/language.attributes.overview.php`). If you use an opening square bracket immediately after # as a comment, PHP 8 will generate a parse error.

Multiline Comments

For a comment to stretch over several lines, use the same style as in Cascading Style Sheets (CSS) and JavaScript. Anything between /* and */ is treated as a comment, like this:

```
/* This is a comment that stretches
   over several lines. It uses the same
   beginning and end markers as in CSS. */
```

Multiline comments are particularly useful when testing or troubleshooting, as they can be used to disable long sections of a script without the need to delete them.

■ **Tip** Good comments and well-chosen variable names make code easier to understand and maintain.

Using Arrays to Store Multiple Values

PHP lets you store multiple values in a special type of variable called an **array**. A simple way of thinking about arrays is that they're like a shopping list. Although each item might be different, you can refer to them collectively by a single name. Figure 3-3 demonstrates this concept: the variable $shoppingList refers collectively to all five items—wine, fish, bread, grapes, and cheese.

Figure 3-3. Arrays are variables that store multiple items, just like a shopping list

Individual items—or **array elements**—are identified by means of a number in square brackets immediately following the variable name. PHP assigns the number automatically, but it's important to note that the numbering always begins at 0. So the first item in the array, wine in our example, is referred to as $shoppingList[0], not $shoppingList[1]. And although there are five items, the last one (cheese) is $shoppingList[4]. The number is referred to as the array **key** or **index**, and this type of array is called an **indexed array**.

■ **Caution**   PHP 8 changes the way that automatic numbering works. If you create an array with the first key as a negative number (as described in Chapter 4), subsequent keys will add 1 to the previous number. Prior to PHP 8, subsequent keys after a negative number always started from zero.

PHP uses another type of array in which the key is a word (or any combination of letters and numbers). For instance, an array containing details of this book might look like this:

```
$book['title'] = 'PHP 8 Solutions: Dynamic Web Design and Development Made Easy';
$book['author'] = 'David Powers';
$book['publisher'] = 'Apress';
```

This type of array is called an **associative array**. Note that the array key is enclosed in quotes (single or double, it doesn't matter).

Arrays are an important and useful part of PHP. You'll use them a lot, starting with Chapter 5, when you'll store details of images in an array to display a random image on a web page. Arrays are also used extensively with databases as you fetch the results of a search in a series of arrays.

■ **Note**   You can learn the various ways of creating arrays in Chapter 4.

PHP's Built-In Superglobal Arrays

PHP has several built-in arrays that are automatically populated with useful information. They are called **superglobal arrays**, and they normally begin with a dollar sign followed by an underscore. The only exception is $GLOBALS, which contains references to all variables in the **global scope** of the script (see "Variable Scope: Functions as Black Boxes" in Chapter 4 for a description of scope).

Two superglobals that you will see frequently are $_POST and $_GET. They contain information passed from forms through the Hypertext Transfer Protocol (HTTP) post and get methods, respectively. The superglobals are all associative arrays, and the keys of $_POST and $_GET are automatically derived from the names of form elements or variables in a query string at the end of a URL.

Let's say you have a text input field called "address" in a form; PHP automatically creates an array element called $_POST['address'] when the form is submitted by the post method or $_GET['address'] if you use the get method. As Figure 3-4 shows, $_POST['address'] contains whatever value a visitor enters in the text field, enabling you to display it onscreen, insert it in a database, send it to your email inbox, or do whatever you want with it.

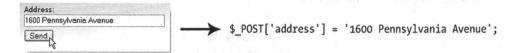

Figure 3-4. *You can retrieve the values of user input through the $_POST array, which is created automatically when a form is submitted using the post method*

You'll work with the $_POST array in Chapter 6 when you send the content of an online feedback form by email to your inbox. Other superglobal arrays that you'll use in this book are $_SERVER, to get information from the web server in Chapters 5, 14, and 15, $_FILES to upload files to your web site in Chapter 8, and $_SESSION, to create a simple login system in Chapters 11 and 19.

■ **Caution**   Don't forget that variable names in PHP are case-sensitive. All superglobal array names are written in uppercase. $_Post or $_Get, for example, won't work.

Understanding When to Use Quotes

If you look closely at the PHP code block in Figure 3-1, you'll notice that the value assigned to the first variable isn't enclosed in quotes. It looks like this:

```
$startYear = 2021;
```

Yet all the examples in "Using Arrays to Store Multiple Values" *did* use quotes, like this:

```
$book['title'] = 'PHP 8 Solutions: Dynamic Web Design and Development Made Easy';
```

The simple rules are as follows:

- **Numbers**: No quotes
- **Text**: Requires quotes

As a general principle, it doesn't matter whether you use single or double quotes around text or a **string**, as text is called in PHP and other computer languages. The situation is a bit more complex, as explained in Chapter 4, because there's a subtle difference in the way single and double quotes are treated by the PHP engine.

■ **Note**   The word "string" is borrowed from computer and mathematical science, where it means a sequence of simple objects—in this case, the characters in text.

Quotes must always be in matching pairs, so you need to be careful about including apostrophes in a single-quoted string or double quotes in a double-quoted string. Examine the following line of code:

```
$book['description'] = 'This is David's latest book on PHP.';
```

At first glance, there seems to be nothing wrong with it. However, the PHP engine sees things differently than the human eye does, as Figure 3-5 demonstrates.

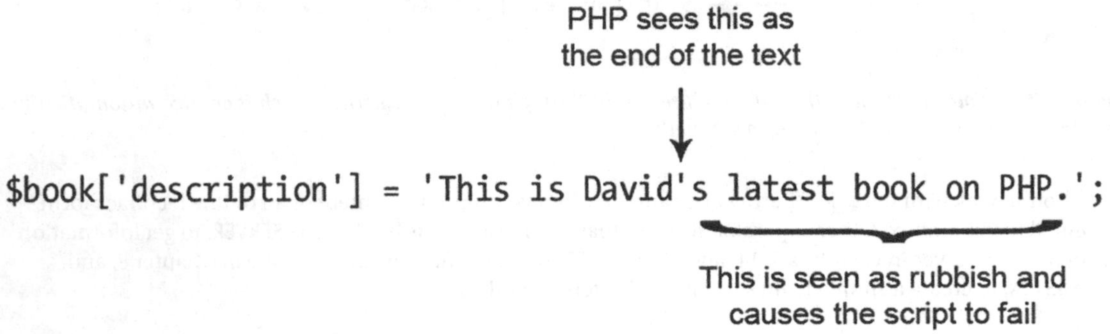

PHP sees this as
the end of the text

↓

```
$book['description'] = 'This is David's latest book on PHP.';
```

This is seen as rubbish and
causes the script to fail

Figure 3-5. An apostrophe inside a single-quoted string confuses the PHP engine

There are two ways around this problem:

- Use double quotes if the text includes any apostrophes.

- Precede apostrophes with a backslash (this is known as **escaping**).

So either of the following is acceptable:

```
$book['description'] = "This is David's latest book on PHP.";
$book['description'] = 'This is David\'s latest book on PHP.';
```

The same applies with double quotes in a double-quoted string (although with the rules reversed). The following code causes a problem:

```
$play = "Shakespeare's "Macbeth"";
```

In this case, the apostrophe is fine, because it doesn't conflict with the double quotes, but the opening quotes in front of *Macbeth* bring the string to a premature end. To solve the problem, either of the following is acceptable:

```
$play = 'Shakespeare\'s "Macbeth"';
$play = "Shakespeare's \"Macbeth\"";
```

In the first example, the entire string has been enclosed in single quotes. This gets around the problem of the double quotes surrounding *Macbeth* but introduces the need to escape the apostrophe in *Shakespeare's*. The apostrophe presents no problem in a double-quoted string, but the double quotes around *Macbeth* both need to be escaped. So, to summarize

- Single quotes and apostrophes are fine inside a double-quoted string.

- Double quotes are fine inside a single-quoted string.

- Anything else must be escaped with a backslash.

■ **Tip**   Use single quotes most of the time and reserve double quotes for situations where they have a special meaning, as described in Chapter 4.

Special Cases: True, False, and Null

Although text should be enclosed in quotes, three keywords—true, false, and null—should never be unless you want to treat them as strings. The first two mean what you expect; null means "nonexistent value."

■ **Note**   True and false are known as **Boolean values**. They're named after nineteenth-century mathematician George Boole whose system of logical operations became the basis of much modern-day computing.

As the next section explains, PHP makes decisions based on whether something equates to true or false. Putting quotes around false has surprising consequences. Consider the following code:

```
$OK = 'false';
```

This does exactly the opposite of what you might expect: it makes $OK true! Why? Because the quotes around false turn it into a string, and PHP treats strings as true. (There's a more detailed explanation in "The Truth According to PHP" in Chapter 4.)

The keywords true, false, and null are *case-insensitive*. The following examples are all valid:

```
$OK = TRUE;
$OK = tRuE;
$OK = true;
```

So, to recap, PHP treats true, false, and null as special cases:

- Don't enclose them in quotes.

- They are case-insensitive.

Making Decisions

Decisions, decisions, decisions... Life is full of decisions. So is PHP. They enable it to change the output according to circumstances. Decision-making in PHP uses **conditional statements**. The most common of these uses if and closely follows the structure of normal language. In real life, you may be faced with the following decision (admittedly not very often in Britain): if the weather's hot, I'll go to the beach.

In PHP pseudocode, the same decision looks like this:

```
if (the weather's hot) {
    I'll go to the beach;
}
```

The condition being tested goes inside parentheses, and the resulting action goes between curly braces. This is the basic decision-making pattern:

```
if (condition is true) {
    // code to be executed if condition is true
}
```

■ **Tip**   Conditional statements are control structures and are not followed by a semicolon. The curly braces keep together one or more individual statements that are intended to be executed as a group.

The code inside the curly braces is executed *only* if the condition is true. If it's false, PHP ignores everything between the braces and moves on to the next section of code. How PHP determines whether a condition is true or false is described in the following section.

Sometimes, the if statement is all you need, but you often want a default action to be invoked if the condition isn't met. To do this, use else, like this:

```
if (condition is true) {
    // code to be executed if condition is true
} else {
    // default code to run if condition is false
}
```

If you want more alternatives, you can add more conditional statements like this:

```
if (condition is true) {
    // code to be executed if condition is true
} else {
    // default code to run if condition is false
}
if (second condition is true) {
    // code to be executed if second condition is true
} else {
    // default code to run if second condition is false
}
```

In this case *both* conditional statements will be run. If you want only one code block to be executed, use elseif like this:

```
if (condition is true) {
    // code to be executed if first condition is true
} elseif (second condition is true) {
    // code to be executed if first condition fails
    // but second condition is true
} else {
    // default code if both conditions are false
}
```

You can use as many elseif clauses in a conditional statement as you like. *Only the first condition that equates to true will be executed; all others will be ignored, even if they're also true.* This means you need to build conditional statements in the order of priority that you want them to be evaluated. It's strictly a first-come, first-served hierarchy.

■ **Note**   Although elseif is normally written as one word, you can use else if as separate words.

Making Comparisons

Conditional statements are interested in only one thing: whether the condition being tested equates to true. If it's not true, it must be false. There's no room for half measures or maybes. Conditions often depend on the comparison of two values. Is this bigger than that? Are they both the same? And so on.

To test for equality, PHP uses two equal signs (==), like this:

```
if ($status == 'administrator') {
    // send to admin page
} else {
    // refuse entry to admin area
}
```

■ **Caution**   Using a single equal sign on the first line ($status = 'administrator') opens the admin area of your web site to everyone. Why? Because this automatically sets the value of $status to administrator; it doesn't compare the two values. It's a common mistake, but one with potentially disastrous consequences. To compare values, you must use two equal signs. A more powerful comparison operator uses three equal signs; it's described in Chapter 4.

Numerical comparisons are performed using the mathematical symbols for less than (<) and greater than (>). Let's say you're checking the size of a file before allowing it to be uploaded to your server. You could set a maximum size of 50 KB like this (1 kilobyte = 1024 bytes):

```
if ($bytes > 51200) {
    // display error message and abandon upload
} else {
    // continue upload
}
```

■ **Note** Chapter 4 describes how to test for multiple conditions simultaneously.

Using Indenting and Whitespace for Clarity

Indenting code helps to keep statements in logical groups, making it easier to understand the flow of the script. PHP ignores any whitespace inside code, so you can adopt any style you like. Just be consistent so that you can spot anything that looks out of place.

Most people find indenting four or five spaces makes for the most readable code. Perhaps the biggest difference in styles lies in the position of curly braces. It's common to put the opening brace on the same line as the preceding code, with the closing brace on a new line after the code block, like this:

```
if ($bytes > 51200) {
    // display error message and abandon upload
} else {
    // continue upload
}
```

However, others prefer this style:

```
if ($bytes > 51200)
{
    // display error message and abandon upload
}
else
{
    // continue upload
}
```

The style isn't important. What matters is that your code is consistent and easy to read.

Using Loops for Repetitive Tasks

Loops are huge timesavers because they perform the same task over and over again, yet involve very little code. They're frequently used with arrays and database results. You can step through each item one at a time looking for matches or performing a specific task. Loops are particularly powerful in combination with conditional statements, allowing you to perform operations selectively on a large amount of data in a single sweep. Loops are best understood by working with them in a real situation. Details of all looping structures, together with examples, are in Chapter 4.

Using Functions for Preset Tasks

Functions do things...lots of things, mind-bogglingly so in PHP. A typical PHP setup gives you access to several thousand built-in functions. You'll only ever need to use a handful, but it's reassuring to know that PHP is a full-featured language.

The functions you'll be using in this book do truly useful things, such as get the height and width of an image, create thumbnails from existing images, query a database, send email, and much, much more. You can identify functions in PHP code because they're always followed by a pair of parentheses. Sometimes, the parentheses are empty, as in the case of phpversion(), which you used in phpversion.php in the previous chapter. Often, though, the parentheses contain variables, numbers, or strings, like this line of code from the script in Figure 3-1:

```
$thisYear = date('Y');
```

This code calculates the current year and stores it in the variable $thisYear. It works by feeding the string 'Y' to the built-in PHP function date(). Placing a value between the parentheses like this is known as **passing an argument** to a function. The function takes the value in the argument and processes it to produce (or **return**) the result. For instance, if you pass the string 'M' as an argument to date() instead of 'Y', it will return the current month as a three-letter abbreviation (e.g., Mar, Apr, May). As the following example shows, you capture the result of a function by assigning it to a suitably named variable:

```
$thisMonth = date('M');
```

■ **Note**   Chapter 16 covers in depth how PHP handles dates and time.

Some functions take more than one argument. When this happens, separate the arguments with commas inside the parentheses, like this:

```
$mailSent = mail($to, $subject, $message);
```

It doesn't take a genius to work out that this sends an email to the address stored in the first argument, with the subject line stored in the second argument and the message stored in the third one. Most functions return a value, so the result is stored in the variable $mailSent (in this case, true or false, depending on success or failure). You'll see how this function works in Chapter 6.

■ **Tip**   You'll often come across the term "parameter" in place of "argument." Technically speaking, parameter refers to a variable used in the function definition, while argument refers to an actual value passed to the function. In practice, both terms tend to be used interchangeably.

As if all the built-in functions weren't enough, PHP lets you build your own custom functions, as described in the next chapter. Even if you don't relish the idea of creating your own functions, throughout this book you'll use some that I have made. You use them the same way as built-in functions.

Displaying PHP Output

There's not much point in all this wizardry going on behind the scenes unless you can display the results on your web page. The two main ways of doing this in PHP are using echo and print. There are some subtle differences between the two, but they are so subtle you can regard echo and print as identical. I prefer echo for the simple reason that it's one fewer letter to type.

You can use echo with variables, numbers, and strings; simply put it in front of whatever you want to display, like this:

```
$name = 'David';
echo $name;   // displays David
echo 5;       // displays 5
echo 'David'; // displays David
```

When using echo or print with a variable, the variable must contain only a single value. You cannot use them to display the contents of an array or of a database result. This is where loops are so useful: you use echo or print inside the loop to display each element individually. You'll see plenty of examples of this in action throughout the rest of the book.

You may see scripts that use parentheses with echo and print, like this:

```
echo('David'); // displays David
```

The parentheses make no difference. Unless you enjoy typing for the sake of it, leave them out.

Using the Short Echo Tag

When you want to display the value of a single variable or expression (and nothing else), you can use the short echo tag, which consists of an opening angle bracket, a question mark, and the equal sign, like this:

```
<p>My name is <?= $name ?>.</p>
```

This produces the same output as this:

```
<p>My name is <?php echo $name ?>.</p>
```

Because it's shorthand for echo, no other code can be in the same PHP block, but it's particularly useful when embedding database results in a web page. It goes without saying that the value of the variable must be set in a previous PHP block before you can use this shortcut.

■ **Tip** Because no other code can be in the same PHP block, it's common practice to omit the semicolon before the closing PHP tag when using the short echo tag.

Joining Strings Together

Although many other computer languages use the plus sign (+) to join text (strings), PHP uses a period, dot, or full stop (.), like this:

```
$firstName = 'David';
$lastName = 'Powers';
echo $firstName.$lastName; // displays DavidPowers
```

As the comment on the final line of code indicates, when two strings are joined like this, PHP leaves no gap between them. Don't be fooled into thinking that adding a space after the period will do the trick. It won't. You can put as much space on either side of the period as you like; the result will always be the same, because PHP ignores whitespace in code. In fact, it's recommended to leave a space on either side of the period for readability.

To display a space in the final output, you must either include a space in one of the strings or insert the space as a separate string, like this:

```
echo $firstName . ' ' . $lastName; // displays David Powers
```

■ **Tip** The period—or **concatenation operator**, to give it its correct name—can be difficult to spot among other code. Make sure the font size in your editor is large enough to see the difference between periods and commas.

Working with Numbers

PHP can do a lot with numbers, from simple addition to complex math. The next chapter contains details of the arithmetic operators you can use with PHP. All you need to remember at this stage is that numbers must not contain any punctuation other than a decimal point. This must be a dot or period. The use of a comma, as is common in many European countries, is not permitted. Similarly, PHP will choke if you use commas or spaces as the thousands separator (although since PHP 7.4.0 you can use an underscore for readability—PHP strips out the underscores when processing the code).

Understanding PHP Error Messages

Error messages are an unfortunate fact of life, so you need to understand what they're trying to tell you. The following illustration shows a typical error message:

Severity of error   What went wrong   Where it went wrong

  ↓   ↓   ↓

Parse error: syntax error, unexpected token "echo" in **C:\xampp\htdocs\php8sols\ch03\error.php** on line **16**

PHP error messages report the line where PHP discovered a problem. Most newcomers—quite naturally—assume that's where to look for their mistake. Wrong...

Most of the time, PHP is telling you that something unexpected has happened. In other words, the mistake lies *before* that point. The preceding error message means that PHP discovered an echo command where there shouldn't have been one.

Instead of worrying what might be wrong with the echo command (probably nothing), start working backward, looking for anything missing, probably a semicolon or closing quote on a previous line.

Sometimes, the message reports the error on the last line of the script. That frequently means you have omitted a closing curly brace somewhere further up the page.

These are the main categories of errors, presented here in descending order of importance:

- **Fatal error**: Any HTML output preceding the error will be displayed, but once the error is encountered—as the name suggests—everything else is killed stone-dead. A fatal error is often caused by referring to a nonexistent file or function.

- **Parse error**: This means there's a mistake in your code syntax, such as mismatched quotes or a missing semicolon or closing brace. It stops the script in its tracks, and it doesn't even allow any HTML output to be displayed.

- **Warning**: A warning indicates a serious problem, such as a missing include file. (Include files are the subject of Chapter 5.) However, the error is usually not serious enough to prevent the rest of the script from being executed.

- **Deprecated**: This warns you about features that are scheduled to be removed from a future version of PHP. If you see this type of error message, you should seriously consider updating your script, as it could suddenly stop working if your server is upgraded.

- **Strict**: This type of error message warns you about using techniques that are not considered good practice.

- **Notice**: This advises you about relatively minor issues, such as the use of a nondeclared variable. Although this type of error won't stop your page from displaying (and you can turn off the display of notices), you should always try to eliminate them. Any error is a threat to your output.

Why Is My Page Blank?

Many beginners are left scratching their heads when they load a PHP page into a browser and see absolutely nothing. There's no error message, just a blank page. This happens when there's a parse error—in other words, a mistake in the code—and the `display_errors` directive in `php.ini` is turned off.

If you followed the advice in the previous chapter, `display_errors` should be enabled in your local testing environment. However, most hosting companies turn off `display_errors`. This is good for security, but it can make it difficult to troubleshoot problems on your remote server. As well as parse errors, a missing include file often causes blank pages.

You can turn on the display of errors for an individual script by adding the following code right at the top of the page:

```
ini_set('display_errors', '1');
```

Put this code on the first line after the opening PHP tag or in a separate PHP block at the top of the page if the PHP is lower down the page. When you upload the page and refresh the browser, you should see any error messages generated by PHP.

If you still see a blank page after adding this line of code, it means there's an error in your syntax. Test the page locally with `display_errors` turned on to find out what's causing the problem.

■ **Caution**   After correcting the error, remove the code that turns on the display of errors. If something else breaks in the script at a later stage, you don't want to expose potential vulnerabilities on your live web site.

PHP Quick Checklist

This chapter contains a lot of information, but hopefully it has given you a broad overview of how PHP works. Here's a reminder of some of the main points:

- Always give PHP pages the correct filename extension, normally `.php`.

- Enclose PHP code between the correct tags: `<?php` and `?>`.

- Avoid the short form of the opening tag: `<?`. Using `<?php` is more reliable.

- Omit the closing PHP tag in files that contain only PHP code.

- PHP variables begin with $ followed by a letter or the underscore character.

- Choose meaningful variable names and remember they're case-sensitive.

- Use comments to remind you what your script does.

- Numbers don't require quotes, but strings (text) do.

- The decimal point is the only punctuation allowed in numbers.

- You can use either single or double quotes around strings, but the outer pair must match.

- Use a backslash to escape quotes of the same type inside a string.

- To store related items together, use an array.

- Use conditional statements, such as `if` and `if . . . else`, for decision-making.

- Loops simplify repetitive tasks.

- Functions perform preset tasks.

- Display PHP output with `echo` or `print`.

- With most error messages, work *backward* from the position indicated.

- Keep smiling—and remember that PHP is *not* difficult.

The next chapter fills in essential details that you can refer to as you progress through this book.

CHAPTER 4

▪ ▪ ▪

PHP: A Quick Reference

Whereas the previous chapter offered a bird's-eye view of PHP for beginners, this chapter goes into detail. Don't try to read it at a single sitting. Dip into it when you need to find out how to do something specific, such as build an array or use a loop to repeat an action. The following sections don't cover every aspect of PHP, but they'll help expand your understanding of the rest of the book.

This chapter covers

- Understanding data types in PHP
- Using arithmetic operators for calculations
- Understanding how PHP treats variables in strings
- Creating indexed and associative arrays
- Understanding what PHP regards as true and false
- Using comparisons to make decisions
- Executing the same code repeatedly inside a loop
- Modularizing code with functions
- Using generators to yield a series of values
- Understanding classes and objects
- Creating new variables dynamically

Using PHP in an Existing Web Site

PHP code is normally processed only in pages that use the .php filename extension. Although you can mix .html and .php pages in the same web site, it's a good idea to use only .php, even if not every page contains dynamic features. This gives you the flexibility to add PHP to pages without breaking existing links or losing search engine rankings.

Data Types in PHP

PHP is what's known as a **weakly typed** language. In practice, this means that, unlike some other computer languages (e.g., Java or C#), PHP doesn't care what type of data you store in a variable.

Most of the time, this is very convenient, although you need to be careful with user input because data from an online form is always transmitted as text. Checking user input carefully is one of the major themes of later chapters.

Even though PHP is weakly typed, it uses the following data types:

- **Integer**: This is a whole number, such as 1, 25, 42, or 2006. Integers must not contain commas as thousands separators. However, since PHP 7.4.0, you can use underscores between digits for better readability, for example, 1_234_567. The PHP engine removes the underscores automatically.

- **Floating-point number**: This is a number that contains a decimal point, such as 9.99, 98.6, or 2.1. PHP does not support the use of the comma as the decimal point, as is common in many European countries. You must use a period. Like integers, floating-point numbers can contain underscores as thousands separators since PHP 7.4.0. (This type is also referred to as **float** or **double**.)

■ **Caution** Integers that begin with a leading zero are treated as octal numbers. So, for example, 08 will generate a parse error because it's not a valid octal number. On the other hand, there is no problem using a leading zero in a floating-point number, for example, 0.8.

- **String**: A string is text of any length. It can be as short as zero characters (an empty string) and has no upper limit on 64-bit builds. In practice, other considerations, such as available memory or passing values through a form, impose restrictions.

- **Boolean**: This type has only two values, `true` and `false`. However, PHP treats other values as implicitly true or false. See "The Truth According to PHP" later in this chapter.

- **Array**: An array is a variable capable of storing multiple values, although it may contain none at all (an empty array). Arrays can hold any data type, including other arrays. An array of arrays is called a **multidimensional array**.

- **Object**: An object is a sophisticated data type capable of storing and manipulating values. See "Understanding PHP Classes and Objects" later in this chapter.

- **Resource**: When PHP connects to an external data source, such as a file or database, it stores a reference to it as a resource.

- **Null**: This is a special data type that indicates that a variable's value is nonexistent.

■ **Note** The PHP online documentation lists two other types that describe the behavior of a structure rather than the type of data. An **iterable** is a structure, such as an array or generator, that can be used in a loop, normally to extract or generate the next value in a series each time the loop runs. A **callable** is a function invoked by another function.

An important side effect of PHP's weak typing is that if you enclose an integer or floating-point number in quotes, PHP automatically converts it from a string to a number, allowing you to perform calculations without the need for any special handling. This can have unexpected consequences. When PHP sees the plus sign (+), it assumes you want to perform addition, and thus it tries to convert strings to integers or floating-point numbers, as in the following example (the code is in data_conversion_01.php in the ch04 folder):

```
$fruit = '2 apples ';
$veg = '2 carrots';
echo $fruit + $veg;  // displays 4
```

PHP sees both $fruit and $veg begin with a number, so it extracts the number and ignores the rest.

■ **Caution** Although the automatic conversion works, PHP 8 generates warning messages about "a non-numeric value." A number on its own in quotes presents no problem.

However, if the string doesn't begin with a number, PHP 8 triggers a fatal TypeError because + cannot be used to combine two strings, as shown in this example (the code is in data_conversion_02.php):

```
$fruit = '2 apples ';
$veg = 'and 2 carrots';
echo $fruit + $veg;  // displays warning about "non-numeric value" followed by fatal error
```

Checking the Data Type of a Variable

When testing scripts, it's often useful to check the data type of a variable. This can help explain why a script produces unexpected results. To check the data type and contents of a variable, simply pass it to the var_dump() function like this:

```
var_dump($variable_to_test);
```

Use data_tests.php in the files for this chapter to see the output generated by var_dump() for different types of data. Just change the name of the variable between the parentheses on the final line.

Explicitly Changing a Variable's Data Type

Most of the time, PHP automatically converts a variable's data type to the one appropriate to the current context. This is known as **type juggling**. However, it's sometimes necessary to change the data type explicitly using a **casting operator**. Table 4-1 lists the most commonly used casting operators in PHP.

Table 4-1. *Commonly used PHP casting operators*

Casting operator	Alternatives	Operation
(array)		Casts to an array
(bool)	(boolean)	Casts to a Boolean
(float)	(double), (real)	Casts to a floating-point number
(int)	(integer)	Casts to an integer
(string)		Casts to a string

To convert the data type of a variable, precede it with the appropriate casting operator like this:

```
$input = 'coffee';
$drinks = (array) $input;
```

This assigns the value of $input as an array to $drinks containing the string 'coffee' as its only element. Casting a string to an array like this can be useful when a function expects an array rather than a string as an argument. In this example, the data type of $input remains a string. To make a cast permanent, reassign the casted value to the original variable like this:

```
$input = (array) $input;
```

Checking Whether a Variable Has Been Defined

One of the most common tests used in conditional statements is to check whether a variable has been defined. Simply pass the variable to the isset() function like this:

```
if (isset($name)) {
    //do something if $name has been defined
} else {
    //do something else, such as give $name a default value
}
```

■ **Tip** See "Setting a Default Value with the Null Coalescing Operator" later in this chapter for a less verbose way of assigning a value to a variable that hasn't yet been defined.

Doing Calculations with PHP

PHP can perform a wide variety of calculations, from simple arithmetic to complex math. This chapter covers only the standard arithmetic operators. See www.php.net/manual/en/book.math.php for details of the mathematical functions and constants supported by PHP.

■ **Note** A **constant** represents a fixed value that cannot be changed. All PHP predefined constants are in uppercase. Unlike variables, they do not begin with a dollar sign. For example, the constant for π (pi) is M_PI. You can find a full list at www.php.net/manual/en/reserved.constants.php.

Arithmetic Operators

The standard arithmetic operators all work the way you would expect, although some of them look slightly different from those you learned at school. For instance, an asterisk (*) is used as the multiplication sign, and a forward slash (/) is used to indicate division. Table 4-2 shows examples of how the standard arithmetic operators work. To demonstrate their effect, $x has been set to 20.

Table 4-2. *Arithmetic operators in PHP*

Operation	Operator	Example	Result
Addition	+	$x + 10	30
Subtraction	-	$x - 10	10
Multiplication	*	$x * 10	200
Division	/	$x / 10	2
Modulo	%	$x % 3	2
Increment (add 1)	++	$x++	21
Decrement (subtract 1)	--	$x--	19
Exponentiation	**	$x**3	8000

The modulo operator converts both numbers to integers by stripping the decimal portion before processing and returns the remainder of a division, as follows:

```
5 % 2.5    // result is 1, not 0 (the decimal fraction is stripped from 2.5)
10 % 2     // result is 0
```

Modulo is useful for working out whether a number is odd or even. $number % 2 always produces 0 or 1. If the result is 0, there is no remainder, so the number is even.

Using the Increment and Decrement Operators

The increment (++) and decrement (--) operators can come either before or after the variable. Their position has an important effect on the calculation.

When the operators come before the variable, 1 is added or subtracted before any further calculation is carried out, as shown in the following example:

```
$x = 5;
$y = 6;
--$x * ++$y // result is 28 (4 * 7)
```

When they come after, the main calculation is carried out first, and then 1 is either added or subtracted, like this:

```
$x = 5;
$y = 6;
$x-- * $y++ // result is 30 (5 * 6), but $x is now 4, and $y is 7
```

Determining the Order of Calculations

Calculations in PHP follow the same rules of precedence as standard arithmetic. Table 4-3 lists arithmetic operators in order of precedence, with the highest precedence at the top.

Table 4-3. *Precedence of arithmetic operators*

Group	Operators	Rule
Parentheses	()	Operations contained within parentheses are evaluated first. If these expressions are nested, the innermost is evaluated foremost.
Exponentiation	**	
Increment/ decrement	++ --	
Multiplication and division	* / %	If an expression contains two or more of these operators, they are evaluated from left to right.
Addition and subtraction	+ -	If an expression contains two or more of these operators, they are evaluated from left to right.

Combining Calculations and Assignment

PHP offers a shorthand way of performing a calculation on a variable and reassigning the result to the variable through **combined assignment operators**. The main ones are listed in Table 4-4.

Table 4-4. *Combined arithmetic-assignment operators used in PHP*

Operator	Example	Equivalent to
+=	$a += $b	$a = $a + $b
-=	$a -= $b	$a = $a - $b
*=	$a *= $b	$a = $a * $b
/=	$a /= $b	$a = $a / $b
%=	$a %= $b	$a = $a % $b
**=	$a **= $b	$a = $a ** $b

Adding to an Existing String

The same convenient shorthand allows you to add new material to the end of an existing string by combining a period and an equal sign, like this:

```
$hamlet = 'To be';
$hamlet .= ' or not to be';
```

Note that you need to create a space at the beginning of the additional text unless you want both strings to run on without a break. This shorthand, known as the **combined concatenation operator**, is extremely useful when combining many strings, such as is required when building the content of an email message or looping through the results of a database search.

■ **Tip** The period in front of the equal sign is easily overlooked when copying code. When you see the same variable repeated at the beginning of a series of statements, it's often a sure sign that you need to use `.=` instead of `=` on its own. However, the variable must already exist before you use the combined concatenation operator. If you try to initialize a variable with `.=`, it will generate a warning about an undefined variable.

All You Ever Wanted to Know About Quotes—and More

Computers always take the first matching quote as marking the end of a string. Since your strings may include apostrophes, the combination of single and double quotes isn't enough. Moreover, PHP gives variables and escape sequences (certain characters preceded by a backslash) special treatment inside double quotes. Over the next few pages, I'll unravel this tangle and make sense of it all for you.

How PHP Treats Variables Inside Strings

Choosing whether to use double quotes or single quotes might just seem like a question of personal preference, but there's an important difference in the way that PHP handles them:

- Anything between single quotes is treated literally as text.

- Double quotes act as a signal to process variables and special characters known as **escape sequences**.

In the following example, $name is assigned a value and then used in a single-quoted string. So $name is treated like normal text (the code is in `quotes_01.php`):

```
$name = 'Dolly';
echo 'Hello, $name';  // Hello, $name
```

If you replace the single quotes on the second line with double ones (see `quotes_02.php`), $name is processed, and its value is displayed onscreen:

```
$name = 'Dolly';
echo "Hello, $name";  // Hello, Dolly
```

■ **Note** In both examples, the string on the first line is in single quotes. What causes the variable to be processed is the fact that it's embedded in a double-quoted string, not how it originally got its value.

Using Escape Sequences Inside Double Quotes

Double quotes have another important effect: they treat escape sequences in a special way. All escape sequences are formed by placing a backslash in front of a character. Table 4-5 lists the main escape sequences supported by PHP.

Table 4-5. *The main PHP escape sequences*

Escape sequence	Character represented in double-quoted string
\"	Double quote
\n	New line
\r	Carriage return
\t	Tab
\\	Backslash
\$	Dollar sign

■ **Caution**   With the exception of \\, the escape sequences listed in Table 4-5 work only in double-quoted strings. In a single-quoted string, they are treated as a literal backslash followed by the second character. A backslash at the end of the string always needs to be escaped. Otherwise, it's interpreted as escaping the following quotation mark.

Embedding Associative Array Elements in a String

There's a nasty "gotcha" with associative array elements in a double-quoted string. The following line of code attempts to embed a couple of elements from an associative array called $book:

```
echo "$book['title'] was written by $book['author'].";
```

It looks OK. The keys of the array elements use single quotes, so there's no mismatch of quotes. Yet, if you load quotes_03.php into a browser, you get this enigmatic error message:

Parse error: syntax error, unexpected string content "", expecting "-" or identifier or variable or number in **C:\xampp\htdocs\php8sols\ch04\quotes_03.php** on line **15**

The solution is to enclose the associative array elements in curly braces like this (see quotes_04.php):

```
echo "{$book['title']} was written by {$book['author']}.";
```

The values are now displayed correctly, as shown in the following screenshot:

PHP 8 Solutions: Dynamic Web Design and Development Made Easy was written by David Powers.

Indexed array elements, such as $shoppingList[2], don't need this special treatment because the array index is a number and is not enclosed in quotes.

Avoiding the Need to Escape Quotes with Heredoc Syntax

Using a backslash to escape one or two quotation marks isn't a great burden, but I frequently see examples of code where backslashes seem to have run riot. The PHP **heredoc syntax** offers a relatively simple method of assigning text to a variable without any special handling of quotes.

■ **Note** The name "heredoc" is derived from here-document, a technique used in Unix and Perl programming to pass large amounts of text to a command.

Assigning a string to a variable using heredoc involves the following steps:

1. Type the assignment operator, followed by <<< and an identifier. The identifier can be any combination of letters, numbers, and the underscore, but it can't begin with a number. The same combination is used later to identify the end of the heredoc.

2. Begin the string on a new line. It can include both single and double quotes. Any variables will be processed in the same way as in a double-quoted string.

3. Place the identifier on a new line after the end of the string. To ensure the heredoc works in all versions of PHP, the identifier *must* be at the beginning of the line; and nothing else should be on the same line except the final semicolon.

■ **Note** The closing identifier can be indented in PHP 8.

It's a lot easier when you see it in practice. The following simple example can be found in heredoc.php in the files for this chapter:

```
$fish = 'whiting';
$book['title'] = 'Alice in Wonderland';
$mockTurtle = <<< Gryphon
"Oh, you sing," said the Gryphon. "I've forgotten the words."
```

So they began solemnly dancing round and round Alice, every now and then treading on her toes when they passed too close, and waving their fore-paws to mark the time, while the Mock Turtle sang this, very slowly and sadly:–

```
"Will you walk a little faster?" said a $fish to a snail.
"There's a porpoise close behind us, and he's treading on my tail."
(from {$book['title']})
Gryphon;
echo $mockTurtle;
```

In this example, Gryphon is the identifier. The string begins on the next line, and *the double quotes are treated as part of the string*. Everything is included until the identifier at the beginning of a new line. However, the identifier repeated in the body of the heredoc is treated as part of the text. As the following screenshot shows, the first instance of Gryphon is treated as part of the string because it's not at the beginning of a new line. Also, the heredoc displays the double quotes and processes the $fish and $book['title'] variables:

"Oh, you sing," said the Gryphon. "I've forgotten the words." So they began solemnly dancing round and round Alice, every now and then treading on her toes when they passed too close, and waving their fore-paws to mark the time, while the Mock Turtle sang this, very slowly and sadly:— "Will you walk a little faster?" said a whiting to a snail. "There's a porpoise close behind us, and he's treading on my tail." (from Alice in Wonderland)

■ **Caution**   Although heredoc syntax avoids the need to escape quotes, the associative array element $book['title'] still needs to be enclosed in braces, as described in the previous section. Alternatively, assign it to a simpler variable before using it in a double-quoted string or heredoc.

To achieve the same effect without using the heredoc syntax, you need to add the double quotes and escape them like this:

```
$mockTurtle = "\"Oh, you sing,\" said the Gryphon. \"I've forgotten the words.\" So they
began solemnly dancing round and round Alice, every now and then treading on her toes
when they passed too close, and waving their fore-paws to mark the time, while the Mock
Turtle sang this, very slowly and sadly:– \"Will you walk a little faster?\" said a $fish
to a snail. \"There's a porpoise close behind us, and he's treading on my tail.\" (from
{$book['title']})";
```

The heredoc syntax is mainly of value when you have a long string and/or lots of quotes. It's also useful if you want to assign an XML document or a lengthy section of HTML to a variable.

Creating Arrays

There are two types of arrays: indexed arrays, which use numbers to identify each element, and associative arrays, which use strings. You can build both types by assigning a value directly to each element. For example, the $book associative array can be defined like this:

```
$book['title'] = 'PHP 8 Solutions: Dynamic Web Design and Development Made Easy';
$book['author'] = 'David Powers';
$book['publisher'] = 'Apress';
```

To build an indexed array the direct way, use numbers instead of strings as the array keys. By default, indexed arrays are numbered from 0, so to build the $shoppingList array depicted in Figure 3-3 in the previous chapter, you would declare it like this:

```
$shoppingList[0] = 'wine';
$shoppingList[1] = 'fish';
$shoppingList[2] = 'bread';
$shoppingList[3] = 'grapes';
$shoppingList[4] = 'cheese';
```

Although both are perfectly valid ways of creating arrays, there are shorter ways of doing it.

Building an Indexed Array

The quick way is to use the shorthand syntax, which is the same as an array literal in JavaScript. You create the array by enclosing a comma-separated list of values between a pair of square brackets, like this:

```
$shoppingList = ['wine', 'fish', 'bread', 'grapes', 'cheese'];
```

■ **Caution**   The comma must go outside the quotes, unlike in American typographic practice. For ease of reading, I have inserted a space following each comma, but it's not necessary to do so.

The alternative is to pass a comma-separated list to array(), like this:

```
$shoppingList = array('wine', 'fish', 'bread', 'grapes', 'cheese');
```

PHP numbers each array element automatically, beginning from 0, so both methods create the same array as if you had numbered them individually.

To add a new element to the end of the array, use a pair of empty square brackets, like this:

```
$shoppingList[] = 'coffee';
```

PHP uses the next number available, so this becomes $shoppingList[5].

■ **Note**   Prior to PHP 8, items added to an indexed array took the next number available only if the last number in the existing array was positive. If the last number was negative, the new addition was set to 0. Now, if the last number is negative, the new index is incremented by one. For example, if the final index is –4, the next one will be –3.

Building an Associative Array

Associative arrays use the => operator (an equal sign followed by a greater than sign) to assign a value to each array key. Using shorthand square bracket syntax, the structure looks like this:

```
$arrayName = ['key1' => 'element1', 'key2' => 'element2'];
```

Using array() achieves the same outcome:

```
$arrayName = array('key1' => 'element1', 'key2' => 'element2');
```

So this is the shorthand way to build the $book array:

```
$book = [
    'title'        => 'PHP 8 Solutions: Dynamic Web Design and Development Made Easy',
    'author'     => 'David Powers',
    'publisher'  => 'Apress'
];
```

It's not essential to put the opening and closing brackets on separate lines nor to align the => operators as I have done, but it makes code easier to read and maintain.

■ **Tip**   Both the shorthand syntax and array() permit a single trailing comma after the last array element. This applies equally to indexed and associative arrays.

Creating an Empty Array

There are two reasons you might want to create an empty array, as follows:

- To create (or **initialize**) an array so that it's ready to have elements added to it inside a loop
- To clear all elements from an existing array

To create an empty array, just use an empty pair of square brackets:

```
$shoppingList = [];
```

Alternatively, use array() with nothing between the parentheses, like this:

```
$shoppingList = array();
```

The $shoppingList array now contains no elements. If you add a new one using $shoppingList[], it will automatically start numbering again at 0.

Multidimensional Arrays

Array elements can store any data type, including other arrays. You could create an array of arrays—in other words, a multidimensional array—with details of several books, like this (using shorthand syntax):

```
$books = [
    [
        'title'     => 'PHP 8 Solutions: Dynamic Web Design and Development Made Easy',
        'author'    => 'David Powers'
    ],
    [
        'title'     => 'PHP 8 Revealed',
        'author'    => 'Gunnard Engebreth'
    ]
];
```

This example shows associative arrays nested inside an indexed array, but multidimensional arrays can nest either type. To refer to a specific element, use the key of both arrays, for example:

```
$books[1]['author']   // value is 'Gunnard Engebreth'
```

Working with multidimensional arrays isn't as difficult as it first looks. The secret is to use a loop to get to the nested array. Then you can work with it in the same way as an ordinary array. This is how you handle the results of a database search, which is normally contained in a multidimensional array.

Using print_r() to Inspect an Array

Pass the array to print_r() like this to inspect its contents during testing (see inspect_array.php):

```
print_r($books);
```

Often, it helps to switch to source view to inspect the details, as browsers ignore indenting in the underlying output:

Array ([0] => Array ([title] => PHP 8 Solutions: Dynamic Web Design and Development Made Easy [author] => David Powers) [1] => Array ([title] => PHP 8 Revealed [author] => Gunnard Engebreth))

```
 9  Array
10  (
11      [0] => Array
12          (
13              [title] => PHP 8 Solutions: Dynamic Web Design and Development Made Easy
14              [author] => David Powers
15          )
16
17      [1] => Array
18          (
19              [title] => PHP 8 Revealed
20              [author] => Gunnard Engebreth
21          )
22
23  )
```

■ **Tip**   Always use `print_r()` to inspect arrays. `echo` and `print` don't work. To display the contents of an array on a web page, use a `foreach` loop, as described later in this chapter.

The Truth According to PHP

Decision-making in PHP conditional statements is based on the mutually exclusive Boolean values of `true` and `false`. If the condition equates to `true`, the code within the conditional block is executed. If `false`, it's ignored. Whether a condition is `true` or `false` is determined in one of these ways:

- A variable set explicitly to one of the Boolean values
- A value PHP interprets implicitly as `true` or `false`
- The comparison of two non-Boolean values

Explicit Boolean Values

If a variable is assigned the value `true` or `false` and is used in a conditional statement, the decision is based on that value. The keywords `true` and `false` are case-insensitive and must not be enclosed in quotes, for example:

```
$ok = false;
if ($ok) {
    // do something
}
```

The code inside the conditional statement won't be executed, because $ok is `false`.

Implicit Boolean ("Truthy" and "Falsy") Values

Using implicit Boolean values provides a convenient shorthand, although it has the disadvantage—at least to beginners—of being less clear. Implicit Boolean values—or "truthy" and "falsy" values, as they're sometimes called—rely on PHP's relatively narrow definition of what it regards as false, namely:

- The case-insensitive keywords false and null
- Zero as an integer (0), a floating-point number (0.0), or a string ('0' or "0")
- An empty string (single or double quotes with no space between them)
- An empty array
- SimpleXML objects created from empty tags

Everything else is true.

■ **Tip** This explains why PHP interprets "false" (in quotes) as true. It's a string, and all strings—except an empty one—are true. Also note that –1 is considered true like any other non-zero number.

Making Decisions by Comparing Two Values

Many true/false decisions are based on a comparison of two values using **comparison operators**. Table 4-6 lists the comparison operators used in PHP.

Table 4-6. *PHP comparison operators used for decision-making*

Symbol	Name	Example	Result
==	Equality	$a == $b	Returns true if $a and $b are equal; otherwise, returns false.
!=	Inequality	$a != $b	Returns true if $a and $b are different; otherwise, returns false.
===	Identical	$a === $b	Determines whether $a and $b are identical. They must not only have the same value but also must be of the same data type (e.g., both integers).
!==	Not identical	$a !== $b	Determines whether $a and $b are not identical (according to the same criteria as the previous operator).
>	Greater than	$a > $b	Returns true if $a is greater than $b.
>=	Greater than or equal to	$a >= $b	Returns true if $a is greater than or equal to $b.
<	Less than	$a < $b	Returns true if $a is less than $b.
<=	Less than or equal to	$a <= $b	Returns true if $a is less than or equal to $b.
<=>	Spaceship	$a <=> $b	Returns an integer less than zero if $a is less than $b, an integer greater than zero if $a is greater than $b, or zero if $a and $b are equal.

As you'll see in Chapter 9, the spaceship operator is useful for custom sorting. It got its name from the author of books on Perl, where the operator originated. He decided it was easier than constantly referring to the "less-than-equal-to-or-greater-than operator."

It's important to remember that a single equal sign only assigns a value. When comparing two values, use the equality operator (==), the identical operator (===), or their negative equivalents (!= and !==).

■ **Caution** PHP 8 changes the way the equality operator (==) compares numbers to strings by converting the number to a string and testing whether they're the same. In previous versions, the comparison was performed the other way round by converting the string to a number. This results in some edge cases now returning `false` where they previously returned `true`. See `www.php.net/manual/en/migration80.incompatible.php` for details.

Testing More Than One Condition

Frequently, comparing two values is not enough. PHP allows you to set a series of conditions using **logical operators** to specify whether all or just some need to be fulfilled.

The most important logical operators in PHP are listed in Table 4-7. The logical Not operator applies to individual conditions rather than to a series.

Table 4-7. *The main logical operators used for decision-making in PHP*

Symbol	Name	Example	Result
&&	And	$a && $b	Equates to true if both $a and $b are true
||	Or	$a || $b	Equates to true if either $a or $b is true; otherwise, false
!	Not	!$a	Equates to true if $a is *not* true

Technically speaking, there is no limit to the number of conditions that can be tested. Each condition is considered in turn from left to right, and as soon as a defining point is reached, no further testing is carried out. When using &&, every condition must be fulfilled, so testing stops as soon as one turns out to be `false`. Similarly, when using ||, only one condition needs to be fulfilled, so testing stops as soon as one turns out to be `true`:

```
$a = 10;
$b = 25;
if ($a > 5 && $b > 20) // returns true
if ($a > 5 || $b > 30) // returns true, $b never tested
```

Always design tests to provide the speediest result. If all conditions must be met, evaluate the one most likely to fail first. If only one condition needs to be met, evaluate the one most likely to succeed first. If a set of conditions needs to be considered as a group, enclose them in parentheses, as follows:

```
if (($a > 5 && $a < 8) || ($b > 20 && $b < 40))
```

■ **Note** PHP also uses AND in place of && and OR in place of ||. However, AND and OR have much lower precedence that can lead to unexpected results. To avoid problems, it's advisable to stick with && and ||.

Using the switch Statement for Decision Chains

The switch statement offers an alternative to if . . . else for decision-making. The basic structure looks like this:

```
switch(variable being tested) {
    case value1:
        statements to be executed
        break;
    case value2:
        statements to be executed
        break;
    default:
        statements to be executed
}
```

The case keyword indicates possible matching values for the variable passed to switch(). Each alternative value must be preceded by case and followed by a colon. When a match is made, every subsequent line of code is executed until the break or return keyword is encountered, at which point the switch statement comes to an end. A simple example follows:

```
switch($myVar) {
    case 1:
        echo '$myVar is 1';
        break;
    case 'apple':
    case 'orange':
        echo '$myVar is a fruit';
        break;
    default:
        echo '$myVar is neither 1 nor a fruit';
}
```

The main points to note about switch are as follows:

- The expression following the case keyword is normally a number or a string. You can't use a complex data type like an array or object.

- To use comparison operators with case, you must repeat the expression being tested. For example, case > 100: won't work, but case $myVar > 100: will. There's a practical example of this situation in "PHP Solution 8-4: Joining an Array with Commas" in Chapter 8.

- Every subsequent case will also be executed, unless you end a case with break or return.

57

- You can group several instances of the case keyword together to apply the same block of code to all of them. So, in the preceding example, if $myVar is "apple" or "orange," the following line will be executed.

- If no match is made, any statements following the default keyword are executed. If no default has been set, the switch statement exits silently and continues with the next block of code.

Using a match Expression for Decision Chains

PHP 8 introduces match expressions that compare a value with multiple alternatives. It's similar to switch but with some important differences. The basic syntax looks like this:

```
$return_value = match($value) {
    single_conditional_expression => return_expression,
    conditional_expression1, conditional_expression2 => return_expression,
} ;
```

The switch example in the preceding section would be rewritten like this:

```
$result = match ($myVar) {
    1 => '$myVar is 1',
    'apple', 'orange' => '$myVar is a fruit',
    default => '$myVar is neither 1 nor a fruit'
};
echo $result;
```

This is not only more concise than switch; there are other significant differences, namely:

- match returns a value. It cannot be used to output a value directly with echo or print.

- There *must* be a semicolon after the closing curly brace.

- match performs strict comparisons with the identity operator (===), whereas switch uses the looser equality operator (==). This means that the value being compared must be of the same type as the conditional expression. In the preceding example, if the value passed to match is the string '1' (in quotes), it won't match the number 1 in the first conditional expression.

- If nothing matches, PHP throws an UnhandledMatchError. You can avoid this by always setting a default at the end.

- There is no need to use break. The match expression stops evaluating the conditional expressions as soon as it finds a match.

You can also use a match expression to test nonidentical conditions by passing true as the argument. The following example compares a value against a range of integers by repeating the value inside each conditional expression:

```
$age = 23;

$result = match (true) {
    $age >= 65 => 'senior',
    $age >= 25 => 'adult',
```

```
    $age >= 18 => 'young adult',
    default => 'child',
}; // $result is 'young adult'
```

■ **Note**   All the examples at www.php.net/manual/en/control-structures.match.php have a trailing comma after the final expression. This is optional in practice.

Using the Ternary Operator

The **ternary operator** (?:) is a shorthand method of representing a conditional statement. Its name came from the fact that it normally uses three operands. The basic syntax looks like this:

```
condition ? value if true : value if false;
```

Here is an example of it in use:

```
$age = 17;
$fareType = $age >= 16 ? 'adult' : 'child';
```

The second line tests the value of $age. If it's greater than or equal to 16, $fareType is set to adult; otherwise, $fareType is set to child. The equivalent code using if . . . else looks like this:

```
if ($age >= 16) {
    $fareType = 'adult';
} else {
    $fareType = 'child';
}
```

You can leave out the value between the question mark and the colon. This has the effect of assigning the value of the condition to the variable if the condition is true. The preceding example could be rewritten like this:

```
$age = 17;
$adult = $age >= 16 ?: false; // $adult is true
```

In this case, the expression before the question mark is a comparison, so it can equate to only true or false. However, if the expression before the question mark is "truthy" (implicitly true), the value itself is returned. For example:

```
$age = 17;
$years = $age ?: 'unknown';  // $years is 17
```

The problem with the preceding example is that if the variable being used as the condition hasn't been defined, it generates an error. A better solution is to use the null coalescing operator as described in the next section.

■ **Caution** Chaining or nesting ternary expressions is not recommended because the code can be difficult to understand and the outcome hard to predict. PHP 8 requires nested ternary expressions to be wrapped in parentheses to indicate the order in which they are to be evaluated. Failure to do so generates a fatal error.

Setting a Default Value with the Null Coalescing Operator

The **null coalescing operator** is a convenient way of assigning a default value to a variable when another variable—such as one containing user input from an online form—hasn't been defined. The operator consists of two question marks (??) and is used like this:

```
$greeting = $_GET['name'] ?? 'guest';
```

This attempts to set the value of $greeting to whatever is stored in $_GET['name']. But if $_GET['name'] hasn't been defined—in other words, it's null—the value after the ?? ('guest') is used instead. The null coalescing operator can be chained like this:

```
$greeting = $_GET['name'] ?? $nonexistent ?? $undefined ?? 'guest';
```

PHP tests each value in turn and assigns the first non-null one to the variable.

■ **Caution** The null coalescing operator rejects only **null** values—in other words, variables that don't exist or have been explicitly set to null. In the preceding examples, $_GET['name'] would be set to an empty string if a form were submitted without entering a value in a field called name. Although PHP treats this as false, it's not null. Consequently, $greeting would be set to an empty string.

Executing Code Repeatedly with a Loop

A **loop** is a section of code that is repeated until a certain condition is met. Loops are often controlled by setting a variable that counts the number of iterations. By incrementing the variable each time, the loop comes to a halt when the variable gets to a preset number. Loops are also controlled by running through each item of an array. When there are no more items to process, the loop stops. Loops frequently contain conditional statements, so although they're very simple in structure, they can be used to create code that processes data in often sophisticated ways.

Loops Using while and do . . . while

The simplest type of loop is called a while loop. Its basic structure looks like this:

```
while (condition is true) {
    do something
}
```

The following code displays every number from 1 through 100 in a browser (you can test it in while.php in the files for this chapter). It begins by setting a variable ($i) to 1 and then uses the variable as a counter to control the loop, as well as displays the current number onscreen:

```
$i = 1;  // set counter
while ($i <= 100) {
    echo "$i<br>";
    $i++; // increase counter by 1
}
```

■ **Tip**   In the previous chapter, I warned against using variables with cryptic names. However, using $i as a counter is a common convention. If $i is already in use, the normal practice is to use $j or $k as counters.

A variation of the while loop uses the keyword do and follows this basic pattern:

```
do {
    code to be executed
} while (condition to be tested);
```

The difference is that the code within the do block is executed at least once, even if the condition is never true. The following code (in dowhile.php) displays the value of $i once, even though it's greater than the maximum being tested in the condition:

```
$i = 1000;
do {
    echo "$i<br>";
    $i++; // increase counter by 1
} while ($i <= 100);
```

The danger is forgetting to set a condition that brings the loop to an end or setting an impossible condition. This is known as an **infinite loop** that freezes your computer or causes the browser to crash.

The Versatile for Loop

The for loop is less prone to generating an infinite loop because all the conditions of the loop are declared on the first line. The for loop uses the following basic pattern:

```
for (initialize loop; condition; code to run after each iteration) {
    code to be executed
}
```

The output of the following code is identical to the previous while loop, displaying every number from 1 to 100 (see forloop.php):

```
for ($i = 1; $i <= 100; $i++) {
    echo "$i<br>";
}
```

The three expressions inside the parentheses control the action of the loop (note that they are separated by semicolons, not commas):

- The first expression is executed before the loop starts. In this case, it sets the initial value of the counter variable $i to 1.

- The second expression sets the condition that determines how long the loop should run. This can be a fixed number, a variable, or an expression that calculates a value.

- The third expression is executed at the end of each iteration of the loop. In this case, it increases $i by 1, but there is nothing stopping you from using bigger increments. For instance, replacing $i++ with $i+=10 in this example would display 1, 11, 21, 31, and so on.

■ **Note**   The first and third expressions inside the parentheses at the start of a for loop can contain multiple statements separated by commas. For example, the loop might use two counters that are incremented or decremented independently.

Looping Through Arrays and Objects with foreach

The final type of loop in PHP is used with arrays, objects, and generators (see "Generators: A Special Type of Function That Keeps on Giving" later in this chapter). It takes two forms, both of which use temporary variables to handle each element. If you only need to do something with the element's value, the foreach loop takes the following form:

```
foreach (variable_name as element) {
    do something with element
}
```

The following example loops through the $shoppingList array and displays the name of each item (the code is in foreach_01.php):

```
$shoppingList = ['wine', 'fish', 'bread', 'grapes', 'cheese'];
foreach ($shoppingList as $item) {
    echo $item.'<br>';
}
```

■ **Caution**   The foreach keyword must *not* have a space between for and each.

Although the preceding example uses an indexed array, you can also use the basic form of the foreach loop with an associative array to access the value of each element.

The alternative form of the foreach loop gives access to both the key and the value of each element. It takes this slightly different form:

```
foreach (variable_name as key => value) {
    do something with key and value
}
```

This next example uses the $book associative array from the "Creating Arrays" section earlier in this chapter and incorporates the key and value of each element into a simple string, as shown in the following screenshot (see foreach_02.php):

```php
foreach ($book as $key => $value) {
    echo "$key: $value<br>";
}
```

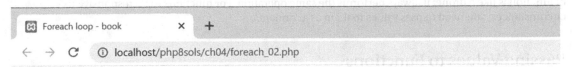

title: PHP 8 Solutions: Dynamic Web Design and Development Made Easy
author: David Powers
publisher: Apress

■ **Note** Apart from arrays, the main use of a foreach loop is with **iterators** and **generators**. You'll see how to use iterators and generators in Chapters 8 and 9.

Breaking Out of a Loop

To bring a loop prematurely to an end when a certain condition is met, insert the break keyword inside a conditional statement. As soon as the script encounters break, it exits the loop.

To skip the code in a loop when a certain condition is met, use the continue keyword. Instead of exiting, it immediately returns to the top of the loop (ignoring the code in the loop body that follows continue) and deals with the next element. For example, the following loop begins with a condition that skips the current element if $photo has no value (the empty() function returns true if a variable doesn't exist or is false):

```php
foreach ($photos as $photo) {
    if (empty($photo)) continue;
    // code to display a photo
}
```

Modularizing Code with Functions

In addition to the large number of built-in functions, PHP lets you create your own. You write the code only once, rather than needing to retype it everywhere you need it. If there's a problem with the code in your function, you can update it in just one place rather than hunting through your entire site.

Building your own functions in PHP is easy. You simply wrap a block of code in a pair of curly braces and use the function keyword to name the new function. The function name is always followed by a pair of parentheses. The following—admittedly trivial—example demonstrates the basic structure of a custom-built function (see `functions_01.php` in the files for this chapter):

```php
function sayHi() {
    echo 'Hi!';
}
```

Simply putting `sayHi();` in a PHP code block results in Hi! being displayed onscreen. This type of function is like a drone: it always performs the same operation. For functions to be responsive to circumstances, you need to pass values to them as arguments.

Passing Values to Functions

Let's say you want to adapt the `sayHi()` function to display someone's name. You do this by inserting a variable between the parentheses in the function declaration (technically, this is known as inserting a parameter in the **function signature**). The same variable is then used inside the function to store whatever value is passed to the function. The revised version in `functions_02.php` looks like this:

```php
function sayHi($name) {
    echo "Hi, $name!";
}
```

You can now use this function inside a page to display the value of any variable or literal string passed to `sayHi()`. For instance, if you have an online form that saves someone's name in a variable called `$visitor` and Mark visits your site, you can give him the sort of personal greeting shown in the following screenshot by putting `sayHi($visitor);` in your page.

Hi, Mark!

A downside of PHP's weak typing is that if Mark is being uncooperative, he might type 5 into the form instead of his name, giving you not quite the type of high five you might have been expecting.

Hi, 5!

■ **Tip** Always check user input before using it in any critical situation. You'll learn how to do this as you progress through this book.

To pass more than one argument to a function, separate the variables (parameters) with commas in the function signature.

Setting Default Values for Arguments

To set a default value for an argument passed to a function, assign a value to the variable in the function signature like this (see `functions_04.php`):

```php
function sayHi($name = 'bashful') {
    echo "Hi, $name!";
}
```

This makes the argument optional, allowing you to invoke the function like this:

```php
sayHi();
```

The following screenshot shows the result:

Hi, bashful!

However, you can still pass the function a different value to use instead of the default.

■ **Tip** Optional arguments must always come at the end of the function signature after required ones. This won't work: `function sayHi($name = 'bashful', $title);`. This will: `function sayHi($title, $name = 'bashful');`.

Variable Scope: Functions as Black Boxes

Functions create a separate environment that is rather like a black box. Normally what goes on inside the function has no impact on the rest of the script, unless it returns a value, as described in the next section. Variables inside a function remain exclusive to the function. This example should illustrate the point (see `functions_05.php`):

```php
function doubleIt($number) {
    $number *= 2;
    echo 'Inside the function, $number is ' . $number . '<br>';   // number is doubled
}
$number = 4;
doubleIt($number);
echo 'Outside the function $number is still ' . $number;   // not doubled
```

The first four lines define a function called doubleIt(), which takes a number, doubles it, and displays it onscreen. The rest of the script assigns the value 4 to $number. Then it passes $number as an argument to doubleIt(). The function processes $number and displays 8. After the function comes to an end, $number is displayed onscreen by echo. This time, it's 4 and not 8, as the following screenshot shows:

Inside the function, $number is 8
Outside the function $number is still 4

This demonstrates that $number in the main script is totally unrelated to the variable with the same name inside the function. This is known as the **scope** of the variable. Even if the value of the variable changes inside a function, variables with the same name outside are not affected unless the value is passed to the function by reference, as described later in this chapter.

■ **Tip** Where possible, avoid using the same variable names in the rest of your script as those inside functions. It makes your code easier to understand and to debug.

PHP superglobal variables (www.php.net/manual/en/language.variables.superglobals.php), such as $_POST and $_GET, are not affected by variable scope. They're always available, which is why they're called superglobal.

Returning Values from Functions

There's more than one way to get a function to change the value of a variable passed to it as an argument, but the most important method is to use the return keyword and to assign the result either to the same variable or to another one. This can be demonstrated by amending the doubleIt() function like this (the code is in functions_06.php):

```php
function doubleIt($number) {
    return $number *= 2;
}
$num = 4;
$doubled = doubleIt($num);
echo '$num is: ' . $num . '<br>';    // remains unchanged
echo '$doubled is: ' . $doubled;     // original number doubled
```

$num is: 4
$doubled is: 8

This time, I have used different names for the variables to avoid confusing them. I have also assigned the result of doubleIt($num) to a new variable. The benefit of doing this is that both the original value and the result of the calculation are now available. You won't always want to keep the original value, but it can be very useful at times.

■ **Tip** Functions don't always need to return a value. The return keyword can be used on its own to halt any further processing.

Generators: A Special Type of Function That Keeps on Giving

When a function encounters return, it immediately terminates and returns a value or nothing. Generators are special functions that create simple iterators for use inside a loop to produce a series of values. Instead of using the return keyword, they use yield. This enables a generator to yield values one at a time, keeping track of the next one in the series until it's called again or runs out of values.

A generator can use an internal loop to generate the values it yields, or it can have a series of yield statements. The simple example in generator.php uses both techniques like this:

```php
function counter($num) {
    $i = 1;
    while ($i < $num) {
        yield $i++;
    }
    yield $i;
    yield $i + 10;
    yield $i + 20;
}
```

The counter() generator takes a single argument, $num. It initializes a counter $i to 1 and then uses a loop that continues running while $i is less than $num. The loop yields $i and increments it by 1. After the loop comes to an end, a series of yield statements yields three further values.

After initializing the generator by assigning it to a variable, you can use it in a foreach loop like this:

```php
$numbers = counter(5);
foreach ($numbers as $number) {
    echo $number . ' ';
}
```

This produces the series of numbers shown in the following screenshot:

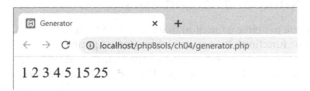

For this trivial example, it would be simpler to create an array of the values and use that directly in a loop. The major advantage of generators is that they use considerably less memory than arrays for a large number of values. Chapter 9 presents a practical example of a generator to process the contents of a file.

Passing by Reference: Changing the Value of an Argument

Although functions don't normally change the value of variables passed to them as arguments, there are occasions when you do want to change the original value rather than capture a return value. To do so, when defining the function, prefix the parameter you want to change with an ampersand, like this:

```php
function doubleIt(&$number) {
    $number *= 2;
}
```

Notice that this version of the doubleIt() function doesn't echo the value of $number, nor does it return the value of the calculation. Because the parameter between the parentheses is prefixed by an ampersand, the original value of a variable passed as an argument to the function will be changed. This is known as **passing by reference**.

The following code (found in functions_07.php) demonstrates the effect:

```php
$num = 4;
echo '$num is: ' . $num . '<br>';
doubleIt($num);
echo '$num is now: ' . $num;
```

```
┌──────────────────────────────────────────────────┐
│ ⊠ Passing by reference      ×   +                 │
├──────────────────────────────────────────────────┤
│ ←  →  C   ① localhost/php8sols/ch04/functions_07.php│
├──────────────────────────────────────────────────┤
│ $num is: 4                                         │
│ $num is now: 8                                     │
```

The ampersand is used only in the function definition, not when the function is invoked.

Generally speaking, it's not a good idea to use functions to change the original values of variables passed to them as arguments because there can be unexpected consequences if the variable is used elsewhere in a script. However, there are situations in which it makes a lot of sense to do this. For example, the built-in array-sorting functions use pass by reference to affect the original array.

■ **Note**   Objects are always passed by reference, even if the function definition doesn't prefix the parameter with an ampersand. This also applies to iterators and generators, which implement built-in PHP classes.

Functions That Accept a Variable Number of Arguments

The rather inelegantly named **splat operator** allows you to define a function that accepts an arbitrary number of arguments (technically known as a **variadic function**). It consists of three dots or periods preceding the last (or only) parameter in the function signature. The splat operator converts the values passed to the function into an array, which can then be used inside the function. The code in functions_08. php contains the following trivial example:

```php
function addEm(...$nums) {
    return array_sum($nums);
}
```

```
$total = addEm(1, 2, 3, 4, 5);
echo '$total is ' . $total;
```

The comma-separated numbers passed to the function are converted to an array and then passed to the built-in array_sum() function that adds up all the values in an array. The following screenshot shows the output:

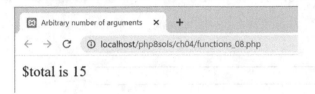

$total is 15

Automatically Unpacking an Array Passed to a Function

The splat operator has the opposite effect when it precedes an array passed as an argument to a function: it unpacks it so that each element is treated as a separate argument. The following example in unpack.php shows how it works:

```
function add ($a, $b) {
    return $a + $b;
}
$nums = [1,2,4,7,9];
echo 'The result is ' . add(...$nums);
```

The add() function expects two separate values and adds them together. $nums is an array of five integers. When the array preceded by the splat operator is passed to the function, the first two elements are automatically extracted and added together, and the result is returned. The excess arguments are silently ignored, producing the result shown in the following screenshot:

The result is 3

■ **Caution** Although excess elements are ignored, the array must contain at least as many values as the function expects.

Optionally Specifying Data Types

As PHP has matured, many developers have sought greater control over the data types accepted and returned by functions. This sparked fierce controversy among the community because PHP's weak data typing has been one of the main reasons for its success—not having to worry about data types makes the language a lot easier for beginners to learn. The compromise was to introduce optional **type declarations**.

To specify that an argument must be of a specific type, precede the parameter in the function signature with one of the types listed in Table 4-8.

Table 4-8. *Type declarations*

Type	Description
Class/interface name	Must be an instance of the given class or interface
self	Must be an instance of the same class
parent	Must be an instance of the current class's parent class
array	Must be an array
callable	Must be a valid callable function
bool	Must be a Boolean value
float	Must be a floating-point number
int	Must be an integer
string	Must be a string
iterable	Must be an array or implement the Traversable interface
object	Must be an object
mixed	Can be any value

■ **Note** The first three type declarations in Table 4–8 are used only with classes, which are described in "Understanding PHP Classes and Objects" later in this chapter. An **interface** specifies which methods a class must implement.

Type declarations for classes, interfaces, arrays, callable functions, and objects enforce the use of the correct data type by throwing an error if a different type is used. However, bool, float, int, and string type declarations behave differently. Instead of throwing an error, they silently convert the argument to the specified data type. The code in functions_09.php adapts the doubleIt() function from "Returning Values from Functions" earlier in this chapter by adding a type declaration like this:

```php
function doubleIt(int $number) {
    return $number *= 2;
}
```

The following screenshot shows what happens when the value passed to the function is 4.9:

$num is: 4.9
$doubled is: 8

The number is converted to an integer before it's processed. It's not even rounded to the closest integer. The decimal fraction is simply stripped off.

■ **Tip**   You can change the behavior of `bool`, `float`, `int`, and `string` type declarations by enabling strict typing in each script. However, the implementation of strict typing can be confusing. My personal recommendation is to use type declarations only for classes, interfaces, and arrays, unless you deliberately want to convert the submitted value to the specified type. You can learn how to enable strict typing in the PHP documentation at `www.php.net/manual/en/functions.arguments.php`.

You can also specify the data type that a function returns. The available types are the same as listed in Table 4-8 with the addition of void. The return type declaration consists of a colon and type between the closing parenthesis and opening curly brace in the function signature. The example in `functions_10.php` adapts the `doubleIt()` function like this:

```
function doubleIt(int $number) : float {
    return $number *= 2;
}
```

I've deliberately chosen this illogical example to demonstrate that setting `float` as the return type silently converts the value returned by the function to a floating-point number. But it doesn't override the type declaration for the parameter. Passing 4.9 as the argument to the function still returns 8; but `var_dump()` reveals that PHP treats it as a floating-point number, as the following screenshot shows:

$num is: 4.9
$doubled is: float(8)

Using `bool`, `int`, and `string` as return type declarations also performs silent data type conversion unless strict typing is enabled. Other return type declarations throw errors if the function returns the wrong data type.

Specifying Multiple Data Types

Previous versions of PHP permitted only one data type to be declared. PHP 8 now permits **union types**, which allow you to combine two or more data types in a declaration. Simply separate the types with a vertical pipe like this:

```
string|array
```

This accepts either a string or an array. Union types can also be used for return type declarations.

If you want to specify that `null` is also acceptable, there are two ways to do so. With a union type, declare `null` as one of the types like this:

```
string|array|null
```

If you are specifying that the value can be of a single type or `null`, precede the type declaration with a question mark like this:

```
?string
```

This is the equivalent of the following union type:

```
string|null
```

You cannot use `null` as a standalone type. It can only be an alternative to the specified type(s).

■ **Note**   The code in this book uses type declarations only in situations where there is a genuine benefit of doing so, for example, to check that the correct data type has been passed to a function.

Using Named Arguments

Normally, all arguments need to be passed to a function in the same order as the parameters in the function signature unless they are optional. However, this can be inconvenient if the function takes several optional arguments and you need to change only one of the options. PHP 8 solves this problem with the introduction of **named arguments**, which allow you to submit values to a function in any order.

A useful example of named arguments is with the built-in function `htmlentities()`, which takes a string and converts all characters that have HTML entity equivalents (such as replacing & with &). The function signature looks like this:

```
htmlentities ( string $string , int $flags = ENT_COMPAT , string|null $encoding = null ,
bool $double_encode = true ) : string
```

The last three arguments have default values, so are optional. The final argument converts everything, including existing HTML entities. So, for example, if your string contains an ampersand that has already been converted to an HTML entity like this

```
Fish &amp; Chips
```

when you pass it to `htmlentities()`, the default is to convert the ampersand again, producing

```
Fish &amp;amp; Chips
```

To prevent this, you need to set the final argument to `false`. In previous versions of PHP, this involved setting all four arguments like this:

```
$output = htmlentities($myText, ENT_COMPAT, null, false);
```

Named arguments are passed by prefixing the value with the parameter name (minus the leading $) followed by a colon, simplifying the code to this:

```
$output = htmlentities($myText, double_encode: false) ;
```

Where to Locate Custom-Built Functions

If your custom-built function is found on the same page it's being used, it doesn't matter where you declare the function; it can be either before or after it's used. It's a good idea, however, to store functions together, either at the top or the bottom of a page. This makes them easier to find and maintain.

Functions used in more than one page are best stored in an external file that is included in each page. Including external files with `include` and `require` is covered in detail in the next chapter. When functions are in external files, you must include the external file *before* calling any of its functions.

Creating Anonymous Functions

Anonymous functions allow the creation of functions that don't have a specified name. They're useful in situations where you need a function that will be used only once, such as a **callback function**.

■ **Tip** A callback function is a function passed into another function as an argument, which is then invoked inside the outer function to complete some kind of routine or action. You'll see practical examples of anonymous callbacks in Chapter 8.

The basic syntax of an anonymous function is the same as a normal function, except that it has no name. If you are passing it as an argument to another function, it looks like this:

```
function ($arguments) {
    // body of function
}
```

As a simple example, this anonymous function doubles a number and returns the result:

```
function ($num) {
    return $num * 2;
}
```

You can also assign an anonymous function to a variable like this:

```
$anon = function ($arguments) {
    // body of function
};
```

■ **Caution**   There must be a semicolon after the closing curly brace because this is a statement assigning the function to a variable.

Assigning the function to a variable is useful when the body of the function contains a lot of code that could make it difficult to read if passed directly as an argument to another function. When passing it as a callback argument, pass the variable on its own. In any other context, invoke the anonymous function by appending a pair of parentheses to the variable and pass it the arguments like this:

```
$anon($arguments);
```

If you want to pass values from the parent scope to an anonymous function, you do so with the use construct like this:

```
function ($arguments) use ($fromParentScope) {
    // body of function
    // do something with $fromParentScope
}
```

Values passed through the use construct can be modified by the anonymous function by preceding the parameter with an & in the same way as described in "Passing by Reference: Changing the Value of an Argument" earlier in this chapter.

Using the Concise Anonymous Syntax of Arrow Functions

If anonymous functions save typing, arrow functions save even more. The syntax looks like this:

```
fn ($arguments) => expression
```

The number-doubling anonymous function from the preceding section can be rewritten as an arrow function like this:

```
fn ($num) => $num * 2
```

The function keyword is shortened to fn. There are no curly braces; and the return keyword is omitted. You can also assign an arrow function to a variable like this:

```
$anon = fn ($num) => $num * 2;
```

Arrow functions can automatically access variables from the parent scope. In the following example, the arrow function adds the value of $y from the parent scope to the argument ($x):

```
$y = 3;
$anon = fn ($x) => $x + $y;
echo $anon(5);  // displays 8
```

However, arrow functions cannot modify values from the parent scope. The following has no effect:

```
$y = 3;
$anon = fn () => $y++;
echo $anon();  // displays 3; the value of $y is not changed
```

To change a value from the parent scope, you need the more verbose syntax of an anonymous function and pass the value by reference to the use construct as described in the preceding section.

Understanding PHP Classes and Objects

Classes are the fundamental building blocks of **object-oriented programming** (OOP), an approach to programming that's designed to make code reusable and easier to maintain. PHP has extensive support for OOP, and new features are frequently implemented in an object-oriented manner.

An **object** is a sophisticated data type that can store and manipulate values. A **class** is the code that defines an object's features and can be regarded as a blueprint for making objects.

Using PHP Built-In Classes

Among PHP's many built-in classes, two of particular interest are the DateTime and DateTimeZone classes, which deal with dates and time zones. To create an object, you use the new keyword with the class name like this:

```
$now = new DateTime();
```

This creates an **instance** of the DateTime class and stores it in a DateTime object called $now that is aware not only of the date and time it was created but also of the time zone used by the web server. Most classes have properties and methods, which are like variables and functions, except that they're related to a particular instance of a class. For example, you can use the DateTime class's methods to change certain values, such as the month, year, or time zone. A DateTime object is also capable of performing date calculations, which are much more complicated using ordinary functions.

You access an object's properties and methods using the -> operator (a hyphen followed by a greater than symbol). To reset the time zone of a DateTime object, pass a DateTimeZone object as an argument to the setTimezone() method like this:

```
$westcoast = new DateTimeZone('America/Los_Angeles');
$now->setTimezone($westcoast);
```

This changes $now to the current date and time in Los Angeles, regardless of where the web server is located, automatically making any adjustments for daylight saving time.

You access an object's properties using the -> operator in the same way:

```
$someObject->propertyName
```

Building Custom Classes

You can define your own classes in PHP in much the same way as defining a function. The difference is that a class normally contains a collection of functions (known as **methods**) and variables (known as **properties**) designed to work together. Each function inside a class should normally focus on a single task. The code should also be generic so it isn't tied to a specific web page. You can also create **subclasses** (also known as **child classes**) to add to or modify the functionality of an existing class.

Defining a PHP class is straightforward. You use the `class` keyword followed by the class name and then put all the code for the class between a pair of curly braces. By convention, class names begin with an uppercase letter, and classes are stored in a separate file with the same name as the class. You cannot use any of the reserved words listed at `www.php.net/manual/en/reserved.php` as the name of a class.

Most classes have a constructor function to initialize any properties when you create a new instance of an object. The basic constructor syntax looks like this:

```
__construct($arguments) {
    // initialization of object
}
```

■ **Caution**   PHP 8 no longer treats a method with the same name as the class as a constructor. You must use `__construct()`. Note that it begins with two underscores, not one.

Accessing Methods and Properties in a Class

PHP classes use the reserved variable `$this` to refer to the current instance of an object. To invoke one of the class's methods inside the class definition, use the arrow operator like this:

```
$this->myMethod();
```

Similarly, you set the value of a property by accessing it using the arrow operator and assigning a value like this:

```
$this->myProperty = 4;
```

Setting the Visibility of Class Methods, Properties, and Constants

The class definition can set the visibility of methods, properties, and constants by prefixing the declaration with one of the following keywords:

- `public`: This makes it visible anywhere, including outside the class definition, allowing you to call a method, access or change the value of a property, or use the value of a constant.

- `protected`: This restricts access to inside the class definition or to a parent or child class.

- `private`: This restricts access to the defining class.

When declaring a property, you must define its visibility, followed optionally by a data type. Declaring the visibility of methods and constants is optional. Methods and constants without any explicit visibility are treated as `public`.

It's common practice to declare properties at the top of a class definition. If you assign the property a default value, it must be an actual value, not the result of an expression derived from another variable. One way of changing the default value is to pass an argument to the constructor and reassign it to the property like this:

```
class MyClass {
    protected int myValue = 42;

    public function __construct(int $value) {
        $this->myValue = $value;
        // other initialization code
    }
}
```

Using Constructor Property Promotion

PHP 8 introduces a shorthand syntax for declaring and setting a value of a property. When a constructor argument includes a visibility modifier, PHP interprets it as both an object property and a constructor argument and assigns the argument value to the property. This avoids the need to declare the property separatately. So the example in the previous section can be simplified like this:

```
class MyClass {
    public function __construct(protected int myValue = 42) {
        // other initialization code
    }
}
```

If nothing else needs initialization, the constructor method can be empty.

Declaring and Using Class Constants

To create a class constant, declare it within the class definition using the `const` keyword, optionally preceded by a visibility declaration. For example, this sets 42 as a constant that can be accessed only in child or parent classes:

```
protected const ULTIMATE_ANSWER = 42;
```

The normal convention is to use all uppercase for the names of constants as a reminder that the value of a constant cannot be changed.

■ **Note** Although the value of a constant cannot be changed inside a class or by an instance of the class, it can be redefined by a child class.

To access the value of a constant within a class or a child class, use the self or parent data type as appropriate followed by the **scope resolution operator** (a pair of colons) like this:

```
self::ULTIMATE_ANSWER
parent::ULTIMATE_ANSWER
```

If the class constant has been made explicitly public or defined without a visibility declaration, you can access its value outside the class definition through an instance of the class using the scope resolution operator. For example, this accesses the value of a class constant on an object called $myObject:

```
$myObject::ULTIMATE_ANSWER
```

Using a Namespace to Avoid Naming Conflicts

Once you start using scripts and classes created by others (including those in this book), there's a danger of multiple classes having the same name. PHP solves this problem by using namespaces to group related classes, functions, and constants.

A common strategy is to store class definitions in a folder structure that describes their functionality and to give the top-level folder a unique name based on a domain or company name. Namespaces can have sublevels, so the folder structure is replicated as sub-namespaces separated by backslashes. The namespace is also declared separately, allowing you to use simple class names.

For example, in Chapter 9 you will build a class called Upload. To avoid naming conflicts, it will be created in a namespace called Php8Solutions\File.

You declare a namespace at the top of a file using the namespace keyword followed by the namespace like this:

```
namespace Php8Solutions\File;
```

___

■ **Caution**   PHP uses a backslash as the namespace separator on all operating systems. Don't be tempted to change it to forward slashes on Linux or macOS.

___

So the fully qualified name of a class called Upload in this namespace is Php8Solutions\File\Upload.

Importing a Namespaced Class

To avoid having to use the fully qualified name every time you refer to a namespaced class, you can import the class at the start of a script with the use keyword like this:

```
use Php8Solutions\File\Upload;
```

___

■ **Caution**   The use keyword must be declared at the top level of a script. It cannot be nested inside a conditional statement.

___

You can then refer to the class as Upload rather than using the fully qualified name. In fact, you can assign an alias to the imported class with the as keyword, like this:

```
use Php8Solutions\File\Upload as FileUploader;
```

The class can then be referred to as FileUploader. Using an alias is mainly useful in large applications where two classes from different frameworks have the same name. Importing a class with the use keyword is simply a declaration that you want to use the class with a shorter name. You still need to include the class definition (including external files is the subject of Chapter 5).

■ **Note**   This chapter covers only the essentials of working with classes and objects in PHP. For more details, consult the documentation at www.php.net/manual/en/language.oop5.php.

Handling Errors and Exceptions

Since PHP 7, most errors are reported by **throwing an exception**—or generating a special type of object that contains details of what caused the error and where it arose. If you've used previous versions of PHP, the only difference you'll probably notice is that the wording of error messages or the type of error is different. However, there's a subtle difference between exceptions thrown as a result of internal errors, such as a parse error or a missing include file, and those thrown by a script.

When PHP throws an exception as the result of an internal error, it immediately brings the script to a halt. If you have turned on the display of error messages, as recommended in a testing environment, PHP displays a message indicating what's happened. Sometimes these messages can be difficult to interpret, so it's often a good idea to **catch the exception**. You do this by wrapping your main script in a block called try and putting the error-handling code in a catch block like this:

```
try {
    // main script goes here
} catch (Throwable $t) {
    echo $t->getMessage();
}
```

■ **Tip**   The Throwable type declaration in the catch block covers both internal errors and exceptions thrown by scripts (user exceptions).

This produces an error message that's usually much easier to understand than the lengthy message generated by some errors.

You can throw custom exceptions with the keyword throw like this:

```
if (error occurs) {
    throw new Exception('Houston, we have a problem.');
}
```

The string inside the parentheses is used as the error message, which can be caught in a catch block.

■ **Caution**   Error messages are vital to help you resolve problems during development. But when you deploy your scripts on a live web site, they can reveal information that could be useful to a malicious attacker. When you go live, replace error messages in `catch` blocks with a neutral message. Alternatively, use the `catch` block to redirect visitors to an error page.

Creating New Variables Dynamically

PHP supports the creation of what's known as a **variable variable**. That's not a typographical error. A variable variable creates a new variable that derives its name from an existing variable. The following example shows how it works (see `variable_variables.php`):

```
$location = 'city';
```

The preceding statement assigns the string "city" to a variable called `$location`. You can use this to create a variable variable by using *two* dollar signs, like this:

```
$$location = 'London';
```

The variable variable takes the value of the original variable as its name. In other words, `$$location` is the same as `$city`:

```
echo $city; // London
```

You'll see a practical example of this technique in the mail-processing script in Chapter 6.

■ **Tip**   To indicate that the double $ is intentional, you can wrap curly braces around the variable being used to create the variable variable like this: `${$location}`. The braces are optional, but make the code easier to read.

Now to the Solutions

The first four chapters have been devoted to theory—important, but not much fun. The rest of the book gets down to practical matters: getting PHP to solve real-world problems. So, without further ado, let's get on with PHP 8 Solutions.

CHAPTER 5

■ ■ ■

Lightening Your Workload with Includes

The ability to include the contents of one file inside another is one of the most powerful features of PHP. It's also one of the easiest to implement. This means code can be incorporated into multiple pages—for example, common elements, such as a header, footer, or navigation menu. PHP merges the content into each page on the server, allowing you to update a menu or other common elements by editing and uploading a single file—a great timesaver.

As you work through this chapter, you'll learn how PHP includes work, where PHP looks for include files, and how to prevent error messages when an include file can't be found. You'll also learn to do some cool tricks with PHP, such as creating a random image generator.

This chapter covers the following topics:

- Understanding the different include commands
- Telling PHP where to find your include files
- Using PHP includes for common page elements
- Protecting sensitive information in include files
- Automating a "you are here" menu link
- Generating a page's title from its filename
- Automatically updating a copyright notice
- Displaying random images complete with captions
- Handling errors with include files
- Changing your web server's `include_path`

Including Code from External Files

The ability to include code from other files is a core part of PHP. All that's necessary is to use one of PHP's include commands and tell the server where to find the file.

D. Powers, *PHP 8 Solutions*, https://doi.org/10.1007/978-1-4842-7141-4_5

Introducing the PHP Include Commands

PHP has four commands that can be used to include code from an external file, namely:

- `include`
- `include_once`
- `require`
- `require_once`

All do basically the same thing, so why have four? The fundamental difference is that `include` attempts to continue processing your script, even if it can't locate the specified file, whereas `require` is used in the sense of mandatory: if the file is missing, the PHP engine stops processing and throws a fatal error. In practical terms, this means you should use `include` if your page would remain usable even without the contents of the external file. Use `require` if the page depends on the external file.

The other two commands, `include_once` and `require_once`, prevent the same file from being included more than once in a page. Attempting to define a function or class more than once in a script triggers a fatal error. So `include_once` or `require_once` ensures that functions and classes are defined only once, even if the script tries to include the external file more than once, as might happen if the commands are in conditional statements.

■ **Tip**   If in doubt, always use `require`, except for files that define functions and classes, when you should use `require_once`. Relying on your script still working even if the external file can't be found can expose you to security risks.

Where PHP Looks for Include Files

To include an external file, use one of the four include commands followed by the file path in quotes (single or double, it doesn't matter). The file path can be either absolute or relative to the current document. For example, any of the following will work (as long as the target file exists):

```
require 'includes/menu.php';
require 'C:/xampp/htdocs/php8sols/includes/menu.php';
require '/Applications/MAMP/htdocs/php8sols/includes/menu.php';
```

■ **Note**   PHP accepts forward slashes in Windows file paths for include commands.

You can optionally use parentheses with the include commands, so the following would also work:

```
require('includes/menu.php');
require('C:/xampp/htdocs/php8sols/includes/menu.php');
require('/Applications/MAMP/htdocs/php8sols/includes/menu.php');
```

When using a relative file path, it's recommended to use ./ to indicate that the path begins in the current folder. Thus, it's more efficient to rewrite the first example like this:

```
require './includes/menu.php'; // path begins in current folder
```

What *doesn't* work is using a file path relative to the site root, like this:

```
require '/includes/menu.php'; // THIS WILL NOT WORK
```

This won't work because PHP include commands interpret a leading forward slash as the root of the hard disk. In other words, PHP treats this as an absolute path, not one relative to the site root. PHP also looks in the include_path as defined in your PHP configuration. I'll return to this subject later in this chapter. Before that, let's put PHP includes to practical use.

PHP Solution 5-1: Moving the Menu and Footer to Include Files

Figure 5-1 shows how four elements of a page benefit from a little PHP magic with include files.

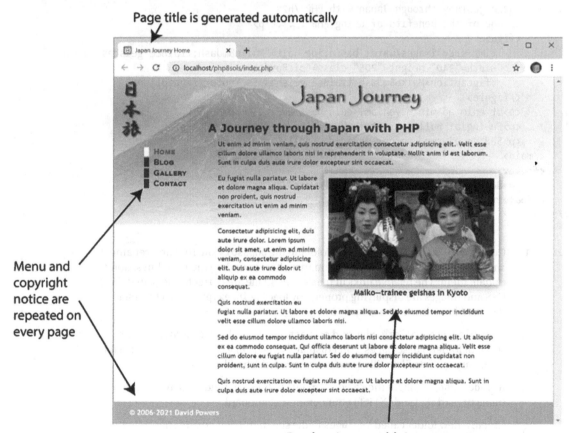

Figure 5-1. Identifying elements of a static web page that could be improved with PHP

The menu and footer appear on every page of the Japan Journey site, so they're prime candidates for include files. Listing 5-1 shows the code for the body of the page with the menu and footer highlighted in bold. (The second link in the navigation menu is deliberately different from Figure 5-1. You'll change it later.)

Listing 5-1. The static version of index.php

```
<header>
    <h1>Japan Journey</h1>
</header>
<div id="wrapper">
    <nav>
        <ul>
            <li><a href="index.php" id="here">Home</a></li>
            <li><a href="blog.php">Journal</a></li>
            <li><a href="gallery.php">Gallery</a></li>
            <li><a href="contact.php">Contact</a></li>
        </ul>
    </nav>
    <main>
        <h2>A journey through Japan with PHP</h2>
        <p>One of the benefits of using PHP . . .</p>
        <figure>
            <img src="images/water_basin.jpg" alt="Maiko&mdash;trainee geishas in Kyoto"
            width="340" height="205" class="picBorder">
            <figcaption>Maiko&mdash;trainee geishas in Kyoto</figcaption>
        </figure>
        <p>Ut enim ad minim veniam, quis nostrud . . .</p>
        <p>Eu fugiat nulla pariatur. Ut labore et dolore . . .</p>
        <p>Sed do eiusmod tempor incididunt ullamco . . .</p>
    </main>
    <footer>
        <p>&copy; 2006&ndash;2021 David Powers</p>
    </footer>
</div>
```

1. Copy index_01.php from the ch05 folder to the php8sols site root and rename it index.php. If you are using a program that offers to update the page links, don't update them. The relative links in the download file are correct. Check that the CSS and images are displaying properly by loading index.php into a browser. It should look the same as Figure 5-1.

2. Copy blog.php, gallery.php, and contact.php from the ch05 folder to your site root folder. These pages won't display correctly in a browser yet because the necessary include files still haven't been created. That'll soon change.

3. In index.php, highlight the <nav> element as shown in bold in Listing 5-1, and then cut (Ctrl+X/Cmd+X) it to your computer clipboard.

4. Create a new folder called includes in the site root. Then create a file called menu.php inside the folder you have just created. Remove any code inserted by your editing program; the file must be completely blank.

5. Paste (Ctrl+V/Cmd+V) the code from your clipboard into menu.php and save the file. The contents of menu.php should look like this:

```
<nav>
    <ul>
        <li><a href="index.php" id="here">Home</a></li>
        <li><a href="blog.php">Journal</a></li>
        <li><a href="gallery.php">Gallery</a></li>
        <li><a href="contact.php">Contact</a></li>
    </ul>
</nav>
```

Don't worry that your new file doesn't have a DOCTYPE declaration or any <html>, <head>, or <body> tags. The other pages that include the contents of this file will supply those elements.

6. Open index.php and insert the following in the space left by the nav unordered list:

```
<?php require './includes/menu.php'; ?>
```

This uses a document-relative path to menu.php. Using ./ at the beginning of the path is more efficient because it explicitly indicates that the path starts in the current folder.

■ **Tip** I'm using the require command because the navigation menu is mission critical. Without it, there would be no way to navigate around the site.

---

7. Save index.php and load the page into a browser. It should look exactly the same as before. Although the menu and the rest of the page are coming from different files, PHP merges them before sending any output to the browser.

■ **Note** Don't forget that PHP code needs to be processed by a web server. If you have stored your files in a subfolder of your server's document root called php8sols, you should access index.php using the URL http://localhost/php8sols/index.php. See "Where to Locate Your PHP Files (Windows and Mac)" in Chapter 2 if you need help finding the server's document root.

---

8. Do the same with the footer. Cut the lines highlighted in bold in Listing 5-1 and paste them into a blank file called footer.php in the includes folder. Then insert the command to include the new file in the gap left by the <footer>:

```
<?php include './includes/footer.php'; ?>
```

This time, I've used include rather than require. The <footer> is an important part of the page, but the site remains usable if the include file can't be found.

■ **Caution**   If an include file is missing, for example, if you accidentally delete it, you should always replace it or remove the include command. Don't rely on the fact that `include` tries to process the rest of the page even if it can't find the external file. Always fix problems as soon as you become aware of them.

---

9. Save all pages and reload `index.php` in your browser. Again, it should look identical to the original page. If you navigate to other pages in the site, the menu and footer should appear on every page. The code in the include files is now serving all pages.

10. To prove that the menu is being drawn from a single file, change the text in the Journal link in `menu.php`, like this:

    ```
    <li><a href="blog.php">Blog</a></li>
    ```

11. Save `menu.php` and reload the site. The change is reflected on all pages. You can check your code against `index_02.php`, `menu_01.php`, and `footer_01.php` in the ch05 folder.

As Figure 5-2 shows, there's a problem. The style that indicates which page you're on doesn't change (it's controlled by the here ID in the `<a>` tag).

Figure 5-2. *The current page indicator still points to the Home page*

That's easily fixed with PHP conditional logic. Before doing so, let's examine how the web server and the PHP engine handle include files.

Choosing the Right Filename Extension for Includes

When the PHP engine encounters an include command, it stops processing PHP at the beginning of the external file and resumes at the end. That's why the include files contain only raw HTML. If you want the external file to use PHP code, the code must be enclosed in PHP tags. Because the external file is processed as part of the PHP file that includes it, an include file can have any filename extension.

Some developers use .inc as the filename extension to make it clear that the file is intended to be included in another file. However, most servers treat .inc files as plain text. This poses a security risk if the file contains sensitive information, such as the username and password to your database. If the file is stored within your web site's root folder, anyone who discovers the name of the file can simply type the URL in a browser address bar, and the browser will obligingly display all your secret details!

On the other hand, any file with a .php extension is automatically sent to the PHP engine for parsing before it's sent to the browser. As long as your secret information is inside a PHP code block and in a file with a .php extension, it won't be exposed. That's why some developers use .inc.php as a double extension for PHP includes. The .inc part reminds you that it's an include file, but servers are only interested in the .php on the end, which ensures that all PHP code is correctly parsed.

For a long time, I followed the convention of using .inc.php for include files. But since I store all my include files in a separate folder called includes, I've decided that the double extension is superfluous. I now use just .php.

Which naming convention you choose is up to you, but using .inc on its own is the least secure.

PHP Solution 5-2: Testing the Security of Includes

This solution demonstrates the difference between using .inc and .php (or .inc.php) as the filename extension for an include file. Use index.php and menu.php from the previous section. Alternatively, use index_02.php and menu_01.php from the ch05 folder. If you use the download files, remove the _02 and _01 from the filenames before using them.

1. Rename menu.php to menu.inc and edit index.php accordingly to include it:

    ```
    <?php require './includes/menu.inc'; ?>
    ```

2. Load index.php into a browser. You should see no difference.

3. Amend the code inside menu.inc to store a password inside a PHP variable, like this:

    ```
    <ul>
        <li><a href="index.php" id="here">Home</a></li>
        <?php $password = 'topSecret'; ?>
        <li><a href="blog.php">Blog</a></li>
        <li><a href="gallery.php">Gallery</a></li>
        <li><a href="contact.php">Contact</a></li>
    </ul>
    ```

4. Reload the page. As Figure 5-3 shows, the password remains hidden in the source code. Although the include file doesn't have a .php filename extension, its contents have been merged with index.php, so the PHP code is processed.

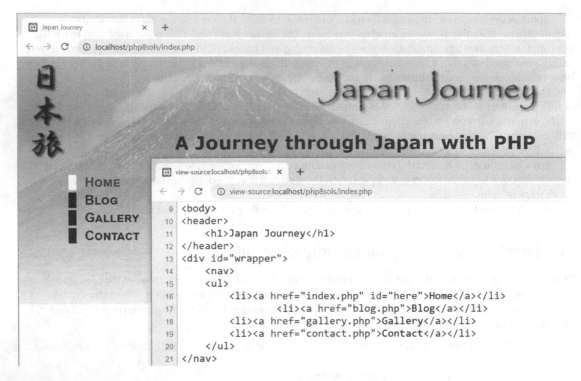

Figure 5-3. There's no output from the PHP code, so only the HTML is sent to the browser

5.   Now load menu.inc directly in the browser. Figure 5-4 shows what happens.

Neither the server nor the browser knows how to deal with an .inc file, so
the entire contents are displayed onscreen: raw HTML, your secret password,
everything.

```
<nav>
    <ul>
        <li><a href="index.php" id="here">Home</a></li>
        <?php $password = 'topSecret'; ?>
        <li><a href="blog.php">Blog</a></li>
        <li><a href="gallery.php">Gallery</a></li>
        <li><a href="contact.php">Contact</a></li>
    </ul>
</nav>
```

Figure 5-4. Loading menu.inc directly in a browser exposes the PHP code

6. Change the name of the include file to menu.inc.php and load it directly into your browser by adding .php to the end of the URL you used in the previous step. This time, you should see an unordered list of links. Inspect the browser's source view. The PHP isn't exposed.

7. Change the name back to menu.php and test the include file by loading it directly in your browser and viewing the source code again.

8. Remove the password PHP code you added to menu.php in step 3 and change the include command inside index.php back to its original setting, like this:

```php
<?php require './includes/menu.php'; ?>
```

PHP Solution 5-3: Automatically Indicating the Current Page

Let's fix the problem with the menu not indicating the current page. The solution involves using PHP to find out the filename of the current page and then using conditional statements to insert an ID in the corresponding <a> tag.

Continue working with the same files. Alternatively, use index_02.php, contact.php, gallery.php, blog.php, menu_01.php, and footer_01.php from the ch05 folder, making sure to remove the _01 and _02 from any filenames.

1. Open menu.php. The code currently looks like this:

```html
<nav>
    <ul>
        <li><a href="index.php" id="here">Home</a></li>
        <li><a href="blog.php">Blog</a></li>
        <li><a href="gallery.php">Gallery</a></li>
        <li><a href="contact.php">Contact</a></li>
    </ul>
</nav>
```

The style that indicates the current page is controlled by the id="here" highlighted on line 3. You need PHP to insert id="here" into the blog.php <a> tag if the current page is blog.php, into the gallery.php <a> tag if the page is gallery.php, and into the contact.php <a> tag if the page is contact.php.

Hopefully, you have got the hint by now—you need an if statement (see "Making Decisions" in Chapter 3) in each <a> tag. Line 3 needs to look like this:

```php
<li><a href="index.php" <?php if ($currentPage == 'index.php') {
    echo 'id="here"'; } ?>>Home</a></li>
```

The other links should be amended in a similar way. But how does $currentPage get its value? You need to find out the filename of the current page.

2. Leave menu.php to one side for the moment and create a new PHP page called get_filename.php. Insert the following code (alternatively, use get_filename. php in the ch05 folder):

```
<? php echo $_SERVER['SCRIPT_FILENAME'];
```

3. Save get_filename.php and view it in a browser. On a Windows system, you should see something like the following screenshot: (The version in the ch05 folder contains the code for this step and the next, together with text indicating which is which.)

C:/xampp/htdocs/php8sols/get_filename.php

On macOS, you should see something like this:

/Applications/MAMP/htdocs/php8sols/get_filename.php

$_SERVER['SCRIPT_FILENAME'] comes from one of PHP's built-in superglobal arrays, and it always gives you the absolute file path for the current page. What you need now is a way of extracting just the filename.

4. Amend the code in the previous step like this:

```
<?php echo basename($_SERVER['SCRIPT_FILENAME']);
```

5. Save get_filename.php and click the Reload button in your browser. You should now see just the filename: get_filename.php.

The built-in PHP function basename() takes a file path as an argument and extracts the filename. So there you have it—a way of finding the filename of the current page.

6. Amend the code in menu.php like this (the changes are highlighted in bold):

```
<?php $currentPage = basename($_SERVER['SCRIPT_FILENAME']); ?>
<nav>
    <ul>
        <li><a href="index.php" <?php if ($currentPage == 'index.php') {
            echo 'id="here"';} ?>>Home</a></li>
        <li><a href="blog.php" <?php if ($currentPage == 'blog.php') {
            echo 'id="here"';} ?>>Blog</a></li>
```

```
            <li><a href="gallery.php" <?php if ($currentPage == 'gallery.php') {
                echo 'id="here"';} ?>>Gallery</a></li>
            <li><a href="contact.php" <?php if ($currentPage == 'contact.php') {
                echo 'id="here"';} ?>>Contact</a></li>
        </ul>
    </nav>
```

■ **Tip** I used double quotes around here, so I wrapped the string 'id="here"' in single quotes. It's easier to read than "id=\"here\"".

---

7. Save menu.php and load index.php into a browser. The menu should look no different from before. Use the menu to navigate to other pages. This time, as shown in Figure 5-5, the border alongside the current page should be white, indicating your location within the site. If you inspect the page's source view in the browser, you'll see that the here ID has been automatically inserted into the correct link.

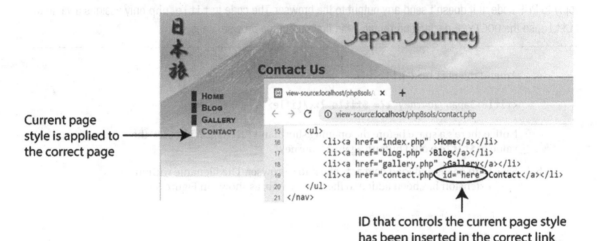

Figure 5-5. Conditional code in the include file produces different output for each page

8. If necessary, compare your code with menu_02.php in the ch05 folder.

PHP Solution 5-4: Automating a Page's Title from Its Filename

This solution uses basename() to extract the filename and then uses PHP string functions to format the name ready for insertion in the <title> tag. It works only with filenames that tell you something about the page's contents, but that's a good practice anyway.

1. Create a new PHP file called title.php and save it in the includes folder.

2. Strip out any code inserted by your script editor and type in the following code:

```
<?php $title = basename($_SERVER['SCRIPT_FILENAME'], '.php');
```

■ **Tip** Don't add a closing PHP tag at the end. It's optional when nothing follows the PHP code in the same file. Omitting the closing tag helps avoid a common error with include files known as "headers already sent." You'll learn more about this error in PHP Solution 5-9.

The basename() function used in PHP Solution 5-3 takes an optional second argument: a string containing the filename extension preceded by a leading period. Adding the second argument strips the extension from the filename. So this code extracts the filename, strips the .php extension, and assigns the result to a variable called $title.

3. Open contact.php and include title.php by typing this above the DOCTYPE:

```
<?php include './includes/title.php'; ?>
```

■ **Note** Normally, nothing should precede the DOCTYPE declaration in a web page. However, this doesn't apply to PHP code, if it doesn't send any output to the browser. The code in title.php only assigns a value to $title, so the DOCTYPE declaration remains the first output the browser sees.

4. Amend the <title> tag like this:

```
<title>Japan Journey <?= $title ?></title>
```

Notice there's a space before the opening shorthand PHP tag. Without it, the value of $title would butt up against "Journey."

5. Save both pages and load contact.php into a browser. The filename without the .php extension has been added to the browser tab, as shown in Figure 5-6.

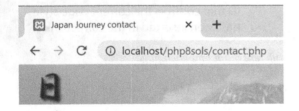

Figure 5-6. *Once you extract the filename, you can generate the page title dynamically*

6. What if you prefer an initial capital letter for the part of the title derived from the filename? PHP has a neat little function called ucfirst(), which does exactly that (uc stands for "uppercase"). Add another line to the code in step 2, like this:

```
<?php
$title = basename($_SERVER['SCRIPT_FILENAME'], '.php');
$title = ucfirst($title);
```

This might look confusing if you're new to programming, so let's examine what's going on here. The first line of code after the PHP tag gets the filename, strips .php off the end, and stores it as $title. The next line passes the value of $title to ucfirst() to capitalize the first letter and stores the result back in $title. So, if the filename is contact.php, $title starts out as contact, but by the end of the following line, it has become Contact.

■ **Tip** You can shorten the code by combining both lines into one, like this:

```
$title = ucfirst(basename($_SERVER['SCRIPT_FILENAME'], '.php'));
```

When you nest functions like this, PHP processes the innermost one first and passes the result to the outer function. It makes your code shorter, but it's not so easy to read.

---

7. A drawback with this technique is that filenames consist of only one word—at least they should. Spaces are not allowed in URLs, which is why some web design software or the browser replaces spaces with %20, which looks ugly and unprofessional in a URL. You can get around this problem by using an underscore.

   Change the filename of contact.php to contact_us.php.

8. Amend the code in title.php like this:

   ```
   <?php
   $title = basename($_SERVER['SCRIPT_FILENAME'], '.php');
   $title = str_replace('_', ' ', $title);
   $title = ucwords($title);
   ```

   The middle line uses a function called str_replace() to look for every underscore and replace it with a space. The function takes three arguments: the character(s) you want to replace, the replacement character(s), and the string you want to change.

■ **Tip** You can also use str_replace() to remove character(s) by using an empty string (a pair of quotes with nothing between them) as the second argument. This replaces the string in the first argument with nothing, effectively removing it.

   Instead of ucfirst(), the final line of code uses the related function ucwords(), which gives each word an initial cap.

9. Save title.php and load the renamed contact_us.php into a browser. Figure 5-7 shows the result.

Figure 5-7. *The underscore has been removed, and both words have been given initial caps*

10. Change the name of the file back to `contact.php` and reload the file into a browser. The script in `title.php` still works. There are no underscores to replace, so `str_replace()` leaves the value of $title untouched, and `ucwords()` converts the first letter to uppercase, even though there's only one word.

11. Repeat steps 3 and 4 with `index.php`, `blog.php`, and `gallery.php`.

12. The home page of the Japan Journey site is called `index.php`. As Figure 5-8 shows, applying the current solution to this page doesn't seem quite right.

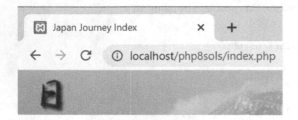

Figure 5-8. *Generating the page title from index.php produces an unsatisfactory result*

There are two solutions: either don't apply this technique to such pages or use a conditional statement (an `if` statement) to handle special cases. For instance, to display Home instead of Index, amend the code in `title.php` like this:

```php
<?php
$title = basename($_SERVER['SCRIPT_FILENAME'], '.php');
$title = str_replace('_', ' ', $title);
if ($title == 'index') {
    $title = 'home';
}
$title = ucwords($title);
```

The first line of the conditional statement uses two equal signs to check the value of $title. The following line uses a single equal sign to assign the new value to $title. If the page is called anything other than `index.php`, the line inside the curly braces is ignored, and $title keeps its original value.

■ **Tip** PHP is case-sensitive, so this solution works only if "index" is all lowercase. To do a case-insensitive comparison, change the fourth line of the preceding code like this:

```
if (strtolower($title) == 'index') {
```

The function `strtolower()` converts a **str**ing **to lower**case—hence its name—and is frequently used to make case-insensitive comparisons. The conversion to lowercase is not permanent, because `strtolower($title)` isn't assigned to a variable; it's only used to make the comparison. To make a change permanent, you need to assign the result back to a variable, as on the final line, when `ucwords($title)` is assigned back to `$title`.

To convert a string to uppercase, use `strtoupper()`.

13. Save `title.php` and reload `index.php` into a browser. The page title now looks more natural, as shown in Figure 5-9.

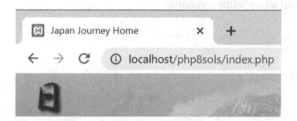

***Figure 5-9.** The conditional statement changes the title on index.php to Home*

14. Navigate back to `contact.php`, and you'll see that the page title is still derived correctly from the page name.

    You can check your code against `title.php` and updated versions of the other files in `index_03.php`, `blog_02.php`, `gallery_02.php`, and `contact_02.php` in the ch05 folder.

■ **Caution** The vast majority of PHP web sites are hosted on Linux servers, which treat filenames and directory (folder) names as case-sensitive. However, when developing locally on Windows or macOS, filenames and folder names are handled in a case-insensitive manner. To avoid broken paths when deploying files on a live server, I recommend using only lowercase when naming files and folders. If you want to use a mixture of uppercase and lowercase, make sure your spelling is consistent.

PHP Solution 5-5: Handling Missing Variables

There are many scenarios where an expected value is missing. For example, you might have misspelled a variable name, a value might not have been submitted from a form, or an include file is missing. So it's a good policy to check that a value from an external source exists before trying to use it. In this solution, you'll use two different approaches to this issue.

1. Continue using the same files as in the previous solution. Alternatively, copy index_03.php, blog_02.php, gallery_02.php, and contact_02.php from the ch05 folder to your site root. Also make sure that title.php, menu_02.php, and footer_01.php are in the includes folder. If using the files from the ch05 folder, remove the underscore and number from each filename.

2. In index.php, make the first letter of the variable in the `<title>` tag uppercase, changing it from $title to $Title. PHP variables are case-sensitive, so this no longer refers to the value generated by title.php.

3. Save the file, and load index.php into a browser. Right-click to view the source code. If you have error_reporting set to the level recommended in Chapter 2, you should see the result shown in Figure 5-10. The browser tab contains raw HTML that comes from a PHP warning about an undefined variable.

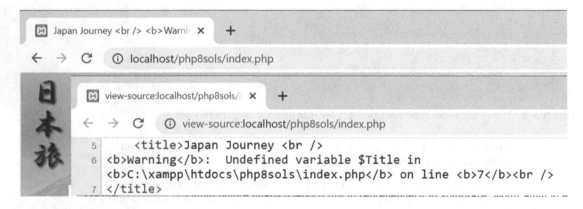

Figure 5-10. *Misspelling the variable generates a warning that appears in the browser tab*

■ **Note**   PHP 8 treats undefined variables as a more serious error than previous versions by generating a warning rather than a notice, which is the lowest error level.

---

4. The null coalescing operator (see "Setting a Default Value with the Null Coalescing Operator" in Chapter 4) handles this situation seamlessly. Change the PHP block in the `<title>` tag like this:

```
<?= $Title ?? 'default' ?>
```

5. Save and reload the page. The browser tab should now look like this:

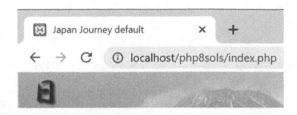

The undefined variable is ignored, and the value following the null coalescing operator is displayed without generating an error notice.

6. Delete the text between the quotes to leave an empty string like this:

```
<?= $Title ?? " ?>
```

7. Save and reload the page again. This time, the browser tab displays only the text that is in the HTML. The empty string simply suppresses the error notice.

8. Correct the variable name by making the first letter lowercase and test the page again. It now looks the same as at the end of the previous PHP solution (see Figure 5-9).

9. The null coalescing operator works fine for setting a default value when a variable doesn't exist; but you can't use it if you want to modify a variable. In this case, you need to use the isset() function to test for the variable's existence.

   Open blog.php and change the <title> tag like this:

```
<title>Japan Journey<?php if (isset($title)) {echo "&mdash;{$title}";}
    ?></title>
```

   Notice that the space between the HTML text and the opening PHP tag has been removed. Also, the opening PHP tag is no longer shorthand because the PHP block contains a conditional statement; it's not just displaying a value.

   The isset() function returns true if a variable exists. So, if $title has been defined, echo displays a double-quoted string containing an em dash (— is the HTML character entity) followed by the value of $title. I've wrapped the variable in curly braces because there's no space between the entity and $title. This is optional, but it makes the code easier to read.

■ **Tip** The isset() function returns true if the value is an empty string (a pair of quotes with no space between them). It checks that a variable has been defined and is not null. Use empty() to check for an empty string or zero value. PHP Solution 6–2 in the next chapter explains how to check that a string doesn't consist only of blank space characters.

---

10. Save `blog.php` and test it in a browser. The browser tab should look like this:

Because `$title` has a value, `isset()` returns `true` and displays the value preceded by an em dash.

11. Experiment with an undefined variable, such as `$Title`. The code inside the conditional statement will be ignored without triggering an error notice.

12. Use either `isset()` or the null coalescing operator to protect `gallery.php` and `contact.php` against the use of an undefined variable in the `<title>` tag.

You can check your code against `index_04.php`, `blog_03.php`, `gallery_03.php`, and `contact_03.php` in the `ch05` folder.

Creating Pages with Changing Content

So far, you've used PHP to generate different output depending on the page's filename. The next two solutions generate content that changes independently of the filename: a copyright notice that updates the year automatically on January 1 and a random image generator.

PHP Solution 5-6: Automatically Updating a Copyright Notice

The copyright notice in `footer.php` contains only static HTML. This PHP solution shows how to use the `date()` function to generate the current year automatically. The code also specifies the first year of copyright and uses a conditional statement to determine whether the current year is different. If it is, both years are displayed.

Continue working with the files from PHP Solution 5-5. Alternatively, use `index_04.php` and `footer_01.php` from the `ch05` folder, and remove the numbers from the filenames. If using the files from the `ch05` folder, make sure you have copies of `title.php` and `menu.php` in the `includes` folder.

1. Open `footer.php`. It contains the following HTML:

```
<footer>
    <p>&copy; 2006&ndash;2021 David Powers</p>
</footer>
```

The advantage of using an include file is that you can update the copyright notice throughout the site by changing this one file. However, it would be much more efficient to increment the year automatically.

2. The PHP date() function neatly takes care of this. Change the code in the paragraph like this:

```
<p>&copy; 2006&ndash;<?php echo date('Y'); ?> David Powers</p>
```

This replaces the second date and displays the current year using four digits. Make sure you pass an uppercase *Y* in quotes as the argument to date().

■ **Note** Table 16-4 in Chapter 16 lists the most frequently used characters that can be passed to the date() function to display date parts, such as month, day of the week, and so on.

---

3. Save footer.php and load index.php into a browser. The copyright notice at the foot of the page should look the same as before—unless, of course, you're reading this in 2022 or later, in which case the current year will be displayed.

4. Like most copyright notices, this covers a range of years, indicating when a site was first launched. Since the first date is in the past, it can be hard-coded. But if you're creating a new web site, you need only the current year. The range of years isn't needed until January 1.

   To display a range of years, you need to know the start year and the current year. If both years are the same, display only the current year; if they're different, display both with an en dash between them. It's a simple if. . .else situation. Change the code in the paragraph in footer.php like this:

```
<?php
$startYear = 2006;
$thisYear = date('Y');
if ($startYear == $thisYear) {
    $output = $startYear;
} else {
    $output = "{$startYear}&ndash;{$thisYear}";
}
?> <p>&copy; <?= $output ?> David Powers</p>
```

   As in PHP Solution 5-5, I've used curly braces around the variables in the else clause because they're in a double-quoted string that contains no whitespace.

5. Save footer.php and reload index.php in a browser. The copyright notice should look the same as before.

6. Change the argument passed to the date() function to a lowercase *y*, like this:

```
$thisYear = date('y');
```

7. Save footer.php and click the Reload button in your browser. The second year is displayed using only the last two digits, as shown in the following screenshot:

© 2006-21 David Powers

■ **Tip** This should serve as a reminder of the importance of case-sensitivity in PHP. Uppercase *Y* and lowercase *y* produce different results with the date() function. Forgetting about case-sensitivity is one of the most common causes of errors in PHP.

---

8. Change the argument passed to date() back to an uppercase *Y*. Set the value of $startYear to the current year and reload the page. This time, you should see only the current year displayed.

You now have a fully automated copyright notice. The finished code is in footer_02.php in the ch05 folder.

PHP Solution 5-7: Displaying a Random Image

All you need to display a random image is a list of available images, stored in an indexed array (see "Creating Arrays" in Chapter 4). Since indexed arrays are numbered from 0, you can select one of the images by generating a random number between 0 and one less than the length of the array. All this is accomplished by a few lines of code...

Continue using the same files. Alternatively, use index_04.php from the ch05 folder and rename it index.php. Since index_04.php uses title.php, menu.php, and footer.php, make sure all three files are in your includes folder. The images are already in the images folder.

1. Create a blank PHP page in the includes folder and name it random_image.php. Insert the following code (it's also in random_image_01.php in the ch05 folder):

```php
<?php
$images = ['kinkakuji', 'maiko', 'maiko_phone', 'monk', 'fountains',
    'ryoanji', 'menu', 'basin'];
$i = random_int(0, count($images)-1);
$selectedImage = "images/{$images[$i]}.jpg";
```

This is the complete script: an array of image names minus the .jpg filename extension (there's no need to repeat shared information—they're all JPEG), a random number generator, and a string that builds the correct path name for the selected file.

To generate a random number within a range, pass the minimum and maximum numbers as arguments to the random_int() function. Since there are eight images in the array, you need a number between 0 and 7. The simple way to do this would be to use random_int(0, 7)—simple, but inefficient. Every time you change the $images array, you need to count how many elements it contains and change the maximum number passed to random_int().

It's much easier to get PHP to do that for you with the count() function, which counts the number of elements in an array. You need a number one less than the number of elements in the array, so the second argument passed to random_int() becomes count($images)-1, and the result is stored in $i.

The random number is used on the final line to build the correct path name for the selected file. The variable $images[$i] is embedded in a double-quoted string with no whitespace separating it from surrounding characters, so it's enclosed in curly braces. Arrays start at 0, so if the random number is 1, $selectedImage is images/maiko.jpg.

If you're new to PHP, you may find it difficult to understand code like this:

```
$i = random_int(0, count($images)-1);
```

All that's happening is that the second argument passed to random_int() is an expression rather than a number. If it makes it easier for you to follow, rewrite the code like this:

```
$numImages = count($images); // $numImages is 8
$max = $numImages - 1;       // $max is 7
$i = random_int(0, $max);    // $i = random_int(0, 7)
```

2. Open index.php and include random_image.php by inserting the command in the same code block as title.php, like this:

```
<?php include './includes/title.php';
include './includes/random_image.php'; ?>
```

Since random_image.php doesn't send any direct output to the browser, it's safe to put it above the DOCTYPE.

3. Scroll down inside index.php, and locate the code that displays the image in the figure element. It looks like this:

```
<figure>
    <img src="images/maiko.jpg" alt="Maiko&mdash;trainee geishas in Kyoto"
        width="340" height="205" class="picBorder">
    <figcaption>Maiko&mdash;trainee geishas in Kyoto</figcaption>
</figure>
```

4. Instead of using images/maiko.jpg as a fixed image, replace it with $selectedImage. All the images have different dimensions, so delete the width and height attributes and use a generic alt attribute. Also remove the text in the figcaption element. The code in step 3 should now look like this:

```
<figure>
    <img src="<?= $selectedImage ?>" alt="Random image" class="picBorder">
    <figcaption></figcaption>
</figure>
```

■ **Note** The PHP block displays only a single value, so you can use the short echo tag <?=.

---

5. Save both random_image.php and index.php, and then load index.php into a browser. The image should now be chosen at random. Click the Reload button in your browser; you should see a variety of images, as shown in Figure 5-11.

Figure 5-11. *Storing image filenames in an indexed array makes it easy to display a random image*

You can check your code against `index_05.php` and `random_image_01.php` in the ch05 folder.

This is a simple and effective way of displaying a random image, but it would be much better if you could set the width and height for different-sized images dynamically, as well as add a caption to describe the image.

PHP Solution 5-8: Adding a Caption to the Random Image

This solution uses a multidimensional array—or an array of arrays—to store the filename and caption for each image. If you find the concept of a multidimensional array difficult to understand in abstract terms, think of it as a large box with a lot of envelopes inside, and inside each envelope is a photo and its caption. The box is the top-level array, and the envelopes inside are the subarrays.

The images are different sizes, but PHP conveniently provides a function called `getimagesize()`. Guess what it does.

This PHP solution builds on the previous one, so continue working with the same files.

1. Open random_image.php and change the code as follows:

```php
<?php
$images = [
    ['file'    => 'kinkakuji',
     'caption' => 'The Golden Pavilion in Kyoto'],
    ['file'    => 'maiko',
     'caption' => 'Maiko&mdash;trainee geishas in Kyoto'],
    ['file'    => 'maiko_phone',
     'caption' => 'Every maiko should have one&mdash;a mobile, of course'],
    ['file'    => 'monk',
     'caption' => 'Monk begging for alms in Kyoto'],
    ['file'    => 'fountains',
     'caption' => 'Fountains in central Tokyo'],
    ['file'    => 'ryoanji',
     'caption' => 'Autumn leaves at Ryoanji temple, Kyoto'],
    ['file'    => 'menu',
     'caption' => 'Menu outside restaurant in Pontocho, Kyoto'],
    ['file'    => 'basin',
     'caption' => 'Water basin at Ryoanji temple, Kyoto']
];
$i = random_int(0, count($images)-1);
$selectedImage = "images/{$images[$i]['file']}.jpg";
$caption = $images[$i]['caption'];
```

■ **Caution** You need to be careful with the code. Each subarray is enclosed in a pair of square brackets and is followed by a comma, which separates it from the next subarray. You'll find it easier to build and maintain multidimensional arrays if you align the array keys and values as shown.

Although the code looks complicated, it's an ordinary indexed array that contains eight items, each of which is an associative array containing definitions for 'file' and 'caption'. The definition of the multidimensional array forms a single statement, so there are no semicolons until line 19. The closing bracket on that line matches the opening one on line 2.

The variable used to select the image also needs to be changed, because $images[$i] no longer contains a string, but rather an array. To get the correct filename for the image, you need to use $images[$i]['file']. The caption for the selected image is contained in $images[$i]['caption'] and stored in a shorter variable.

2. You now need to amend the code in index.php to display the caption, like this:

```
<figure>
    <img src="<?= $selectedImage ?>" alt="Random image" class="picBorder">
    <figcaption><?= $caption ?></figcaption>
</figure>
```

3. Save index.php and random_image.php and load index.php into a browser. Most images will look fine, but there's an ugly gap to the right of the image of the trainee geisha with a mobile phone, as shown in Figure 5-12.

Eu fugiat nulla pariatur. Ut labore et dolore magna aliqua. Cupidatat non proident, quis nostrud exercitation ut enim ad minim veniam.

Consectetur adipisicing elit, duis aute irure dolor. Lorem ipsum dolor sit amet, ut enim ad minim veniam, consectetur adipisicing elit. Duis aute irure dolor ut aliquip ex ea commodo consequat.

Quis nostrud exercitation eu fugiat nulla pariatur. Ut **Every maiko should have one—a mobile, of course** labore et dolore magna aliqua. Sed do eiusmod tempor incididunt velit esse cillum dolore ullamco laboris nisi.

Figure 5-12. *The long caption protrudes beyond the image and shifts it too far left*

4. Add the following code at the end of random_image.php:

```
if (file_exists($selectedImage) && is_readable($selectedImage)) {
    $imageSize = getimagesize($selectedImage);
}
```

The if statement uses two functions, file_exists() and is_readable(), to make sure $selectedImage not only exists but also that it's accessible (it may be corrupted or have the wrong permissions). These functions return Boolean values (true or false), so they can be used directly as part of the conditional statement.

The single line inside the if statement uses the function getimagesize() that returns an array of information about the image, which is stored as $imageSize. You'll learn more about getimagesize() in Chapter 10. At the moment, you're interested in the following two pieces of information:

* $imageSize[0]: The width of the image in pixels

* $imageSize[3]: A string containing the image's height and width formatted for inclusion in an <img> tag

5. First of all, let's fix the code in the `<img>` tag. Change it like this:

```
<img src="<?= $selectedImage ?>" alt="Random image" class="picBorder"
   <?= $imageSize[3] ?>>
```

This inserts the correct `width` and `height` attributes inside the `<img>` tag.

6. Although this sets the dimensions for the image, you still need to control the width of the caption. You can't use PHP inside an external style sheet, but there's nothing stopping you from creating a `<style>` block in the `<head>` of `index.php`. Insert the following code just before the closing `</head>` tag.

```
<?php if (isset($imageSize)) { ?>
<style>
figcaption {
    width: <?= $imageSize[0] ?>px;
}
</style>
<?php } ?>
```

This code consists of only seven short lines, but it's an odd mix of PHP and HTML. Let's start with the first and final lines. If you strip away the PHP tags and replace the HTML `<style>` block with a comment, this is what you end up with:

```
if (isset($imageSize)) {
  // do something if $imageSize has been set
}
```

In other words, if the variable `$imageSize` hasn't been set (defined), the PHP engine ignores everything between the curly braces. It doesn't matter that most of the code between the braces is HTML and CSS. If `$imageSize` hasn't been set, the PHP engine skips to the closing brace, and the intervening code isn't sent to the browser.

■ **Tip** Many inexperienced PHP coders wrongly believe that they need to use `echo` or `print` to create HTML output inside a conditional statement. As long as the opening and closing braces match, you can use PHP to hide or display sections of HTML like this. It's a lot neater and involves a lot less typing than using `echo` all the time.

If `$imageSize` has been set, the `<style>` block is created, and `$imageSize[0]` is used to set the correct width for the paragraph that contains the caption.

7. Save `random_image.php` and `index.php`, and then reload `index.php` into a browser. Click the Reload button until the image of the trainee geisha with the mobile phone appears. This time, it should look like Figure 5-13. If you view the browser's source code, the style rule uses the correct width for the image.

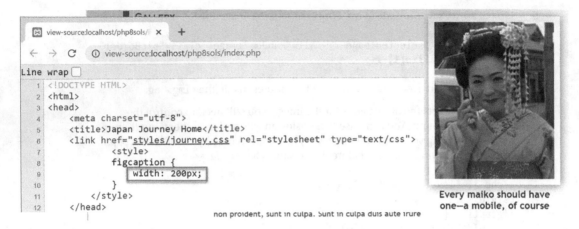

Every maiko should have one—a mobile, of course

Figure 5-13. *The ugly gap is removed by creating a style rule directly related to the image size*

■ **Note** If the caption still protrudes, make sure there's no gap between the closing PHP tag and px in the `<style>` block. CSS does not permit whitespace between the value and unit of measurement.

---

8. The code in `random_image.php` and the code you have just inserted prevent errors if the selected image can't be found, but the code that displays the image is devoid of similar checks. Temporarily change the name of one of the images, either in `random_image.php` or in the `images` folder. Reload `index.php` several times. Eventually, you should see two warnings like that in Figure 5-14. Not only is $imageSize undefined (and therefore null); you're trying to access an array offset (index) on a null object. It looks very unprofessional.

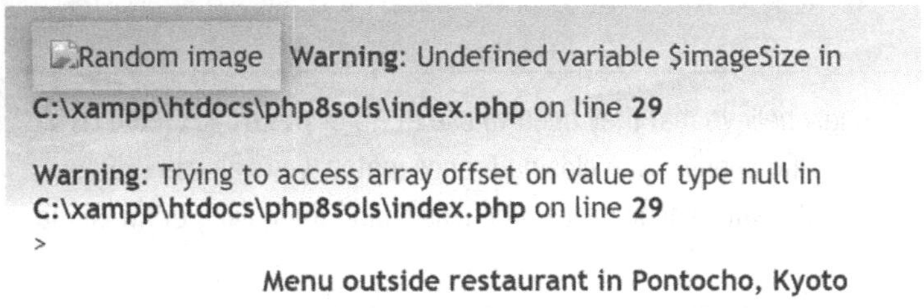

⬚Random image **Warning**: Undefined variable $imageSize in
C:\xampp\htdocs\php8sols\index.php on line **29**

Warning: Trying to access array offset on value of type null in
C:\xampp\htdocs\php8sols\index.php on line **29**
>
Menu outside restaurant in Pontocho, Kyoto

Figure 5-14. *An error in an include file can destroy the look of your page*

9. The conditional statement at the foot of `random_image.php` sets $imageSize only if the selected image both exists and is readable, so if $imageSize has been set, you know it's all systems go. Add the opening and closing blocks of a conditional statement around the figure element that displays the image in `index.php`, like this:

```php
<?php if (isset($imageSize)) { ?>
<figure>
    <img src="<?= $selectedImage ?>" alt="Random image" class="picBorder"
        <?= $imageSize[3] ?>>
    <figcaption><?= $caption ?></figcaption>
</figure>
<?php } ?>
```

Images that exist will display normally, but you'll avoid any embarrassing error messages in case of a missing or corrupt file—a much more professional look. Don't forget to restore the name of the image you changed in the previous step.

You can check your code against index_06.php and random_image_02.php in the ch05 folder.

Preventing Errors with Include Files

Pages that use a server-side technology such as PHP deal with a lot of unknowns, so it's wise to code defensively, checking values before using them. This section describes measures you can take to prevent and troubleshoot errors with include files.

Checking the Existence of Variables

The lesson that can be drawn from PHP Solutions 5-5 and 5-8 is that you should always use the null coalescing operator to set a default value or use isset() to verify the existence of a variable that comes from an include file and wrap any dependent code in a conditional statement. You can also use isset() with the logical Not operator (see Table 4-7 in Chapter 4) to assign a default value, like this:

```php
if (!isset($someVariable)) {
    $someVariable = default value;
}
```

You're likely to come across this structure for setting a default value in many scripts because the null coalescing operator has been available only since PHP 7. Neither is better than the other; but the null coalescing operator makes for shorter code.

Checking Whether a Function or Class Has Been Defined

Include files are frequently used to define custom functions or classes. Attempting to use a function or class that hasn't been defined triggers a fatal error. To check whether a function has been defined, pass the name of the function as a string to function_exists(). When passing the name of the function to function_exists(), omit the parentheses at the end of function name. For example, you check whether a function called doubleIt() has been defined like this:

```php
if (function_exists('doubleIt')) {
    // use doubleIt()
}
```

To check whether a class has been defined, use `class_exists()` in the same way, passing a string containing the class name as the argument:

```
if (class_exists('MyClass')) {
    // use MyClass
}
```

Assuming you want to use the function or class, a more practical approach is to use a conditional statement to include the definition file if the function or class hasn't already been defined. For example, the definition for `doubleIt()` is in a file called `utilities.php`:

```
if (!function_exists('doubleIt')) {
    require_once './includes/utilities.php';
}
```

Suppressing Error Messages on a Live Web Site

Assuming your include files are working normally on your remote server, the measures outlined in the previous sections are probably all the error checking you need. However, if your remote server displays error messages, you should take steps to suppress them. The following techniques hide all error messages, not only those related to include files.

Using the Error Control Operator

A rather crude technique is to use the PHP `error control operator` (@), which suppresses error messages associated with the line on which it's used. You place @ either at the beginning of the line or directly in front of the function or command that you think might generate an error, like this:

```
@ include './includes/random_image.php';
```

■ **Caution**   This won't work with `require` or `require_once` because attempting to load a missing or corrupted file with these commands generates a fatal error. The error control operator no longer suppresses fatal error messages in PHP 8.

The problem with the error control operator is that it hides errors rather than working around them. It's only one character, so it's easy to forget you have used it. Consequently, you can waste a lot of time looking for errors in the wrong part of your script. If you use the error control operator, the @ mark should be the first thing you remove when troubleshooting a problem.

The other drawback is that you need to use the error control operator on every line that might generate an error message, because it affects only the current line.

Turning Off display_errors in the PHP Configuration

A better way of suppressing error messages in a live web site is to turn off the `display_errors` directive in the web server's configuration. The most effective way to do this is to edit `php.ini` if your hosting company gives you control over its settings. Locate the `display_errors` directive and change `On` to `Off`.

If you don't have control of `php.ini`, many hosting companies allow you to change a limited range of configuration settings using a file called either `.htaccess` or `.user.ini`. The choice of file depends on how PHP was installed on the server, so check with your hosting company to find out which to use.

If your server supports `.htaccess` files, add the following command to the `.htaccess` file in the server root folder:

```
php_flag display_errors Off
```

In a `.user.ini` file, the command is simply this:

```
display_errors Off
```

Both `.htaccess` and `.user.ini` are plain-text files. Like `php.ini`, each command should be on a separate line. If the file doesn't already exist on your remote server, you can simply create it in a text editor. Make sure your editor doesn't automatically add `.txt` to the end of the filename. Then upload the file to your web site's server root folder.

■ **Tip** By default, macOS hides files with a name that begins with a dot. In macOS Sierra and later, use the keyboard shortcut Cmd+Shift+. (dot) to toggle the display of hidden files on and off.

Turning Off display_errors in an Individual File

If you don't have control over the server configuration, you can prevent error messages from being displayed by adding the following line at the top of any script:

```
<?php ini_set('display_errors', '0'); ?>
```

PHP Solution 5-9: Redirecting When an Include File Can't Be Found

All the techniques suggested so far only suppress error messages if an include file can't be found. If a page would be meaningless without the include file, you should redirect the user to an error page if the include file is missing.

One way to do so is to throw an exception, like this:

```
$file = './includes/menu.php';
if (file_exists($file) && is_readable($file)) {
    include $file;
} else {
    throw new Exception("$file can't be found");
}
```

When using code that might throw an exception, you need to wrap it in a `try` block and create a `catch` block to handle the exception (see "Handling Errors and Exceptions" in Chapter 4). This PHP solution shows how to do this, using the `catch` block to redirect users to a different page if an include file can't be found.

If you have designed and tested your site thoroughly, this technique should not be necessary on most pages that use include files. However, the following PHP solution is by no means a pointless exercise. It demonstrates several important features of PHP: how to throw and catch exceptions and how to redirect to another page. As you'll see from the following instructions, redirection isn't always straightforward. This PHP solution shows how to overcome the most common problem.

Continue working with `index.php` from PHP Solution 5-8. Alternatively, use `index_06.php` from the `ch05` folder.

1. Copy `error.php` from the `ch05` folder to the site root. Don't update the links in the page if your editing program prompts you to do so. This is a static page that contains a generic error message and links back to the other pages.

2. Open `index.php` in your editing program. The navigation menu is the most indispensable include file, so edit the `require` command in `index.php` like this:

```php
$file = './includes/menu.php';
if (file_exists($file) && is_readable($file)) {
    require $file;
} else {
    throw new Exception("$file can't be found");
}
```

■ **Tip** Storing the path of the include file in a variable like this avoids the need to retype it four times, reducing the likelihood of spelling mistakes.

---

3. To redirect the user to another page, use the `header()` function. Unless there's a syntax error, the PHP engine normally processes a page from the top, outputting the HTML until it reaches a problem. This means that output will have already begun by the time the PHP engine gets to this code. To prevent this from happening, start the `try` block before any output is generated. (This won't work on some setups, but bear with me, because it demonstrates an important point.)

Scroll to the top of the page and edit the opening PHP code block like this:

```php
<?php try {
    include './includes/title.php';
    include './includes/random_image.php'; ?>
```

This opens the `try` block.

4. Scroll down to the bottom of the page and add the following code after the closing `</html>` tag:

```php
<?php } catch (Exception $e) {
    header('Location: http://localhost/php8sols/error.php');
} ?>
```

This closes the `try` block and creates a `catch` block to handle the exception. The code in the `catch` block uses `header()` to redirect the user to `error.php`.

The `header()` function sends an HTTP header to the browser. It takes as its argument a string containing the header and its value separated by a colon.

In this case, it uses the Location header to redirect the browser to the page specified by the URL following the colon. Adjust the URL to match your own setup if necessary.

5. Save index.php and test the page in a browser. It should display as normal.

6. Change the value of $file, the variable you created in step 2, to point to a nonexistent include file, such as men.php.

7. Save index.php and reload it in your browser. If you're using XAMPP or the latest version of MAMP in your testing environment, you'll probably be correctly redirected to error.php. On some setups, though, you're likely to see the message in Figure 5-15.

Figure 5-15. The header() function won't work if output has already been sent to the browser

The error message in Figure 5-15 is probably responsible for more heads being banged against keyboards than any other. (I, too, bear the scars.) As mentioned earlier, the header() function cannot be used if output has been sent to the browser. So what's happened?

The answer is in the error message, but it's not immediately obvious. It says the error happened on line 55, which is where the header() function is called. What you really need to know is where the output was generated. That information is buried here:

```
(output started at C:\xampp\htdocs\php8sols\index.php:5)
```

The number 5 after the colon is the line number. So what's on line 5 of index.php? As you can see from the following screenshot, line 5 outputs the HTML DOCTYPE declaration.

```
1    <?php
2    try {
3    include './includes/title.php';
4    include './includes/random_image.php'; ?>
5    <!DOCTYPE HTML>
```

Because there's no error in the code up to this point, the PHP engine has already output the HTML. Once that has happened, header() can't redirect the page unless the output is stored in a buffer (the web server's memory).

■ **Note**   The reason you don't get this error message in many setups is because output buffering is commonly set to 4096, which means that 4 KB of output is stored in the buffer before the HTTP headers are sent to the browser. Although useful, this gives you a false sense of security because output buffering might not be enabled on your remote server. So keep reading even if you were correctly redirected.

---

8. Edit the code block at the top of index.php like this:

```
<?php ob_start();
try {
    include './includes/title.php';
    include './includes/random_image.php'; ?>
```

The ob_start() function turns on output buffering, preventing any output from being sent to the browser before the header() function is called.

9. The PHP engine automatically flushes the buffer at the end of the script, but it's better to do so explicitly. Edit the PHP code block at the foot of the page like this:

```
<?php } catch (Exception $e) {
    ob_end_clean();
    header('Location: http://localhost/php8sols/error.php');
}
ob_end_flush();
?>
```

Two different functions have been added here. When redirecting to another page, you don't want the HTML stored in the buffer. So, inside the catch block, a call is made to ob_end_clean(), which turns off the buffer and discards its contents.

However, if an exception isn't thrown, you want to display the contents of the buffer, so ob_end_flush() is called at the end of the page after both the try and catch blocks. This flushes the contents of the buffer and sends it to the browser.

10. Save index.php and reload it in a browser. This time, you should be redirected to the error page, as shown in Figure 5-16, regardless of whether buffering has been enabled in your server's configuration.

Figure 5-16. *Buffering the output enables the browser to redirect to the error page*

11. Change the value of $file back to ./includes/menu.php and save index.php. When you click the Home link on the error page, index.php should display normally.

You can compare your code with index_07.php in the ch05 folder.

Why Can't I Use Site Root–Relative Links with PHP Includes?

Well, you can and you can't. For the sake of clarity, I'll begin by explaining the distinction between links relative to the document and to the site root.

Document-Relative Links

Most web authoring tools specify the path to other files, such as style sheets, images, and other web pages, relative to the current document. If the target page is in the same folder, just the filename is used. If it's one level higher than the current page, the filename is preceded by ../. This is known as a **document-relative path** or link. If you have a site with many levels of folders, this type of link can be difficult to understand—at least for humans.

Links Relative to the Site Root

The other type of link used in web pages always begins with a forward slash, which is shorthand for the site root. The advantage of a **site root–relative path** is that it doesn't matter how deep the current page is in the site hierarchy. The forward slash at the beginning guarantees the browser will start looking from the top level of the site. Although site root-relative links are much easier to read, PHP include commands don't interpret them correctly. You must use a document-relative path or an absolute path or specify the includes folder in your include_path directive (see "Adjusting Your include_path" later in this chapter).

■ **Note**   It's only when the leading slash represents the site root that PHP include commands cannot locate the external file. An absolute path on Linux and macOS also begins with a forward slash. Absolute paths are unambiguous, so they present no problem.

You can convert a site root–relative path to an absolute one by concatenating the superglobal variable `$_SERVER['DOCUMENT_ROOT']` to the beginning of the path, like this:

```
require $_SERVER['DOCUMENT_ROOT'] . '/includes/filename.php';
```

Most servers support `$_SERVER['DOCUMENT_ROOT']`, but check the PHP Variables section at the bottom of the configuration details displayed by `phpinfo()` on your remote server to make sure.

Links Inside Include Files

This is the point that tends to confuse many people. PHP and browsers interpret paths that begin with a forward slash differently. So, although you can't use a site root–relative link to include a file, the links *inside* an include file should normally be relative to the site root. This is because an include file can be included at any level of the site hierarchy, so document-relative links break when a file is included at a different level.

■ **Note**   The navigation menu in `menu.php` uses document-relative links rather than ones relative to the site root. They have been deliberately left like that because, unless you have created a virtual host, the site root is `localhost`, not `php8sols`. This is a disadvantage of testing a site in a subfolder of the web server's document root. The Japan Journey site used throughout this book has only one level, so the document-relative links work. When developing a site that uses multiple levels of folders, use site root–relative links inside your include files and consider setting up a virtual host for testing.

Choosing Where to Locate Your Include Files

A useful feature of PHP include files is that they can be located anywhere, as long as the page with the include command knows where to find them. Include files don't even need to be inside your web server root. This means that you can protect include files that contain sensitive information, such as passwords, in a private directory (folder) that cannot be accessed through a browser.

■ **Tip**   If your hosting company provides a storage area outside your server root, you should seriously consider locating some, if not all, of your include files there.

Security Considerations with Includes

Include files are a very powerful feature of PHP. With that power come security risks. As long as the external file is accessible, PHP includes it and incorporates any code into the main script. Technically speaking, include files can even be on a different server. However, this is considered such a security risk that the configuration directive allow_url_include is disabled by default, so it's impossible to include files from a different server unless you have complete control over your server's configuration. Unlike include_path, the allow_url_include directive cannot be overridden except by the server administrator.

Even if you control both servers yourself, you should never include a file from a different server. It's possible for an attacker to spoof the address and try to execute a malicious script on your site.

Never include files that can be uploaded or overwritten by the public.

■ **Note** The remaining sections of this chapter are rather technical. They are provided primarily as a reference. Feel free to skip over them.

Adjusting Your include_path

An include command expects either a relative path or an absolute path. If neither is given, PHP automatically looks in the include_path specified in your PHP configuration. The advantage of locating include files in a folder specified in your web server's include_path is that you don't need to worry about getting the relative or absolute path correct. All you need is the filename. This can be very useful if you use a lot of includes or you have a site hierarchy several levels deep. There are three ways to change the include_path:

- **Edit the value in** php.ini: If your hosting company gives you access to php.ini, this is the best way to add a custom includes folder.

- **Use** .htaccess or .user.ini: If your hosting company allows changes to the configuration with an .htaccess or .user.ini file, this is a good alternative.

- **Use** set_include_path(): Use this only if the previous options are not available to you, because it affects the include_path only for the current file.

The value of the include_path for your web server is listed in the Core section of the configuration details when you run phpinfo(). It normally begins with a period, which indicates the current folder, and is followed by the absolute path of each folder to be searched. On Linux and macOS, each path is separated by a colon. On Windows, the separator is a semicolon. On a Linux or Mac server, your existing include_path directive might look like this:

```
.:/php/PEAR
```

On a Windows server, the equivalent would look like this:

```
.;C:\php\PEAR
```

Editing the include_path in php.ini or .user.ini

In php.ini, locate the include_path directive. To add a folder called includes in your own site, add a colon or semicolon—depending on your server's operating system—at the end of the existing value, followed by the absolute path to the includes folder.

On a Linux or Mac server, use a colon like this:

```
include_path=".:/php/PEAR:/home/mysite/includes"
```

On a Windows server, use a semicolon:

```
include_path=".;C:\php\PEAR;C:\sites\mysite\includes"
```

The commands are the same for a .user.ini file. The value in .user.ini overrides the default, so make sure you copy the existing value from phpinfo() and add the new path to it.

Using .htaccess to Change the include_path

The value in an .htaccess file overrides the default, so copy the existing value from phpinfo() and add the new path to it. On a Linux or Mac server, the value should be similar to this:

```
php_value include_path ".:/php/PEAR:/home/mysite/includes"
```

The command is the same on Windows, except that you separate the paths with a semicolon:

```
php_value include_path ".;C:\php\PEAR;C:\sites\mysite\includes"
```

■ **Caution**   In .htaccess, do not insert an equal sign between include_path and the list of path names.

Using set_include_path( )

Although set_include_path() affects only the current page, you can easily create a code snippet and paste it into pages in which you want to use it. PHP also makes it easy to get the existing include_path and combine it with the new one in a platform-neutral way.

Store the new path in a variable and then combine it with the existing value, like this:

```
$includes_folder = '/home/mysite/includes';
set_include_path(get_include_path() . PATH_SEPARATOR . $includes_folder);
```

It looks as though three arguments are being passed to set_include_path(), but it's only one; the three elements are joined by the concatenation operator (a period), not commas:

- get_include_path() gets the existing include_path.

- PATH_SEPARATOR is a PHP constant that automatically inserts a colon or semicolon depending on the operating system.

- $includes_folder adds the new path.

The problem with this approach is that the path to the new includes folder won't be the same on your remote and local testing servers. You can fix that with a conditional statement. The superglobal variable $_SERVER['HTTP_HOST'] contains the domain name of the web site. If your domain is www.example.com, you can set the correct path for each server like this:

```
if ($_SERVER['HTTP_HOST'] == 'www.example.com') {
    $includes_folder = '/home/example/includes';
} else {
```

```
    $includes_folder = 'C:/xampp/htdocs/php8sols/includes';
}
set_include_path(get_include_path() . PATH_SEPARATOR . $includes_folder);
```

Using set_include_path() is probably not worthwhile for small web sites that don't use many include files. However, you might find it useful on more complex projects.

Nesting Include Files

Once a file has been included in another, relative paths are calculated from the parent file, not from the included file. This presents problems for functions or class definitions in an external file that needs to include another external file.

If both external files are in the same folder, you include a nested file with just the filename, like this:

```
require_once 'Thumbnail.php';
```

In this case, the relative path should *not* begin with ./ because ./ means "start from this folder." With an include file, "this folder" means the parent file's folder, not the include file's folder, resulting in an incorrect path to the nested file.

When the include files are in different folders, you can build an absolute path to the target file using the PHP constant __DIR__. This constant returns the absolute path of the include file's directory (folder) without a trailing slash. Concatenating __DIR__, a forward slash, and a document-relative path converts the relative path into an absolute one. For example, let's say this is the relative path from one include file to another:

```
'../File/Upload.php'
```

You convert it into an absolute path like this:

```
__DIR__ . '/../File/Upload.php'
```

Adding the forward slash to the beginning of the document-relative path has the effect of finding the parent folder of the include file and then going up one level to find the correct path.

You'll see an example of this in use in Chapter 10, where an include file needs to include another file that's in a different folder.

Chapter Review

This chapter has plunged you headlong into the world of PHP, using includes, arrays, and multidimensional arrays. It has shown you how to extract the name of the current page, display a random image, and get the image's dimensions. You have also learned how to throw and catch exceptions and to redirect to a different page. There's a lot to absorb, so don't worry if it doesn't all sink in the first time. The more you use PHP, the more familiar you'll become with the basic techniques. In the next chapter, you'll learn how PHP processes input from online forms and will use that knowledge to send feedback from a web site to your email inbox.

CHAPTER 6

■ ■ ■

Bringing Forms to Life

Forms lie at the very heart of working with PHP. You use forms for logging in to restricted pages, registering new users, placing orders with online stores, entering and updating information in a database, sending feedback...and the list goes on. The same principles lie behind all these uses, so the knowledge you gain from this chapter will have practical value in most PHP applications. To demonstrate how to process information from a form, I'm going to show you how to gather feedback from visitors to your site and send it to your mailbox.

Unfortunately, user input can expose your site to malicious attacks. It's important to check data submitted from a form before accepting it. Although HTML5 form elements validate user input in modern browsers, you still need to check the data on the server. HTML5 validation helps legitimate users avoid submitting a form with errors, but malicious users can easily sidestep checks performed in the browser. Server-side validation is not optional, but essential. The PHP solutions in this chapter show you how to filter out or block anything suspicious or dangerous. No online application is completely hack-proof, but it doesn't take a lot of effort to keep all but the most determined marauders at bay. It's also a good idea to preserve user input and redisplay it if the form is incomplete or errors are discovered.

These solutions build a complete mail-processing script that can be reused in different forms, so it's important to read them in sequence.

In this chapter, you'll learn about the following:

- Understanding how user input is transmitted from an online form
- Displaying errors without losing user input
- Validating user input
- Sending user input by email

How PHP Gathers Information from a Form

Although HTML contains all the necessary tags to construct a form, it doesn't provide any means to process the form when submitted. For that, you need a server-side solution, such as PHP.

The Japan Journey web site contains a simple feedback form (see Figure 6-1). Other elements—such as radio buttons, check boxes, and drop-down menus—will be added later.

© David Powers 2022

D. Powers, *PHP 8 Solutions*, https://doi.org/10.1007/978-1-4842-7141-4_6

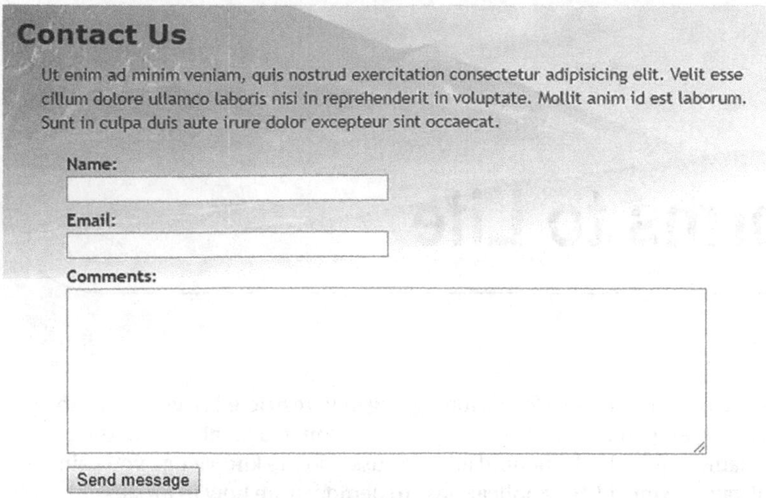

Contact Us

Ut enim ad minim veniam, quis nostrud exercitation consectetur adipisicing elit. Velit esse cillum dolore ullamco laboris nisi in reprehenderit in voluptate. Mollit anim id est laborum. Sunt in culpa duis aute irure dolor excepteur sint occaecat.

Name:

Email:

Comments:

Send message

***Figure 6-1.** Processing a feedback form is one of the most popular uses of PHP*

First, let's take a look at the HTML code for the form (it's in `contact_01.php` in the `ch06` folder):

```
<form method="post" action="">
    <p>
        <label for="name">Name:</label>
        <input name="name" id="name" type="text">
    </p>
    <p>
        <label for="email">Email:</label>
        <input name="email" id="email" type="text">
    </p>
    <p>
        <label for="comments">Comments:</label>
        <textarea name="comments" id="comments"></textarea>
    </p>
    <p>
        <input name="send" type="submit" value="Send message">
    </p>
</form>
```

The first two `<input>` tags and the `<textarea>` tag contain both `name` and `id` attributes set to the same value. The reason for this duplication is accessibility. HTML uses the `id` attribute to associate the `<label>` element with the correct `<input>` element. Form-processing scripts, however, rely on the `name` attribute. So, although the `id` attribute is optional in the Submit button, you *must* use the `name` attribute for each form element that you want to be processed.

■ **Note** The name attribute of a form input element shouldn't normally contain spaces. If you want to combine multiple words, join them with an underscore (PHP will do this automatically if you leave any spaces). Because the script developed later in this chapter converts the name attributes to PHP variables, don't use hyphens or any other characters that are invalid in PHP variable names.

Two other things to notice are the method and action attributes inside the opening <form> tag. The method attribute determines how the form sends data. It can be set to either post or get. The action attribute tells the browser where to send the data for processing when the Submit button is clicked. If the value is left empty, as here, the page attempts to process the form itself. However, an empty action attribute is invalid in HTML5, so that will need to be fixed.

■ **Note** I have deliberately avoided using any of the new HTML5 form features, such as type="email" and the required attribute. This makes it easier to test the PHP server-side validation scripts. After testing, you can update your forms to use the HTML5 validation features. Validation in the browser is mainly a courtesy to the user to prevent incomplete information from being submitted, so it's optional. Server-side validation should never be skipped.

Understanding the Difference Between post and get

The best way to demonstrate the difference between the post and get methods is with a real form. If you completed the previous chapter, you can continue working with the same files.

Otherwise, the ch06 folder contains a complete set of files for the Japan Journey site with all the code from Chapter 5 incorporated in them. Copy contact_01.php to the site root and rename it contact.php. Also copy footer.php, menu.php, and title.php of the ch06/includes folder to the includes folder in the site root.

1. Locate the opening <form> tag in contact.php and change the value of the method attribute from post to get, like this:

    ```
    <form method="get" action="">
    ```

2. Save contact.php and load the page in a browser. Type your name, email address, and a short message into the form. Then click Send message.

Name:

David

Email:

david@example.com

Comments:

Greetings :-)

Send message

3. Look in the browser address bar. You should see the contents of the form attached to the end of the URL, like this:

If you break up the URL, it looks like this:

```
http://localhost/php8sols/contact.php
?name=David
&email=david%40example.com
&comments=Greetings+%3A-%29
&send=Send+message
```

The data submitted by the form has been appended to the basic URL as a **query string** that begins with a question mark. The value from each field and the Submit button is identified by the name attribute of the form element, followed by an equal sign and the submitted data. The data from each input element is separated by an ampersand (&). URLs cannot contain spaces or certain characters (such as an exclamation mark or a smiley), so the browser replaces spaces with + and encodes other characters as hexadecimal values, a process known as **URL encoding** (for a full list of values, see www.degraeve.com/reference/urlencoding.php).

4. Go back into the code of contact.php and change method back to post, like this:

```
<form method="post" action="">
```

5. Save contact.php and reload the page in your browser, making sure you clear the query string from the end of the URL. Type another message and click Send message. Your message should disappear, but nothing else happens. It hasn't been lost, but you haven't done anything to process it yet.

6. In `contact.php`, add the following code immediately below the closing `</form>` tag:

```
<pre>
<?php if ($_POST) { print_r($_POST); } ?>
</pre>
```

This displays the contents of the $_POST superglobal array if any post data has been sent. As explained in Chapter 4, the print_r() function allows you to inspect the contents of arrays; the `<pre>` tags simply make the output easier to read.

7. Save the page and click the Refresh button in your browser. You'll probably see a warning similar to the following. This tells you that the data will be resent, which is exactly what you want. Confirm that you want to send the information again.

Confirm Form Resubmission

The page that you're looking for used information that you entered.
Returning to that page might cause any action you took to be repeated.
Do you want to continue?

[Continue]   [Cancel]

---

8. The code from step 6 should now display the contents of your message below the form, as shown in Figure 6-2. Everything has been stored in one of PHP's superglobal arrays, $_POST, which contains data sent using the post method. The name attribute of each form element is used as the array key, making it easy to retrieve the content.

```
           Array
(
    [name] => David
    [email] => david@example.com
    [comments] => Greetings :-)
    [send] => Send message
)
```

Figure 6-2. *The $_POST array uses the form's name attributes to identify each element of data*

As you have just seen, the get method sends your data appended to the URL, whereas the post method sends it with the HTTP headers so it's hidden from view. Some browsers limit the maximum length of a URL to about 2,000 characters, so the get method can be used only for small amounts of data. The post method can be used for much larger amounts of data. By default, PHP permits up to 8 MB of post data, although hosting companies may set a different limit.

However, the most important difference between the two methods is their intended use. The get method is designed to be used for requests that result in no change on the server no matter how many times they are made. Consequently, it's used mainly for database searches; bookmarking your search result is useful because all the search criteria are in the URL. On the other hand, the post method is designed for requests that result in changes on the server. So it's used to insert, update, or delete records in a database, upload files, or send an email.

We'll return to the get method later in the book. This chapter concentrates on the post method and its associated superglobal array, $_POST.

Getting Form Data with PHP Superglobals

The $_POST superglobal array contains data sent using the post method. It should come as no surprise that data sent by the get method is in the $_GET array.

To access values submitted by a form, just put the name attribute of the form element in quotes between square brackets after $_POST or $_GET, depending on the form's method attribute. So email becomes $_POST['email'] if sent by the post method and $_GET['email'] if sent by the get method. That's all there is to it.

You may come across scripts that use $_REQUEST, which avoids the need to distinguish between $_POST or $_GET. It's less secure. You should always know where user information comes from. $_REQUEST also includes the values of cookies, so you have no idea if you're dealing with a value submitted by the post method or one transmitted through the URL or injected by a cookie. Always use $_POST or $_GET.

You may come across old scripts that use $HTTP_POST_VARS and $HTTP_GET_VARS, which have the same meaning as $_POST and $_GET. These are obsolete and have been removed from PHP 8.

Processing and Validating User Input

The ultimate aim of this chapter is to send the input from the form in contact.php by email to your inbox. Using the PHP mail() function is relatively simple. It takes a minimum of three arguments: the address(es) the email is being sent to, a string containing the subject line, and a string containing the body of the message. You build the body of the message by concatenating (joining) the contents of the input fields into a single string.

Security measures implemented by most Internet service providers (ISPs) make it difficult if not impossible to test the mail() function in a local testing environment. Instead of jumping straight into the use of mail(), PHP Solutions 6-2 through 6-5 concentrate on validating user input to make sure required fields are filled in and displaying error messages. Implementing these measures makes your online forms more user-friendly and secure.

Using JavaScript or HTML5 form elements and attributes to check user input is called **client-side validation** because it happens on the user's computer (or client). It's useful because it's almost instantaneous and can alert the user to a problem without making an unnecessary round trip to the server. However, client-side validation is easy to sidestep. All a malicious user has to do is to submit data from a custom script, and your checks are rendered useless. It's vital to check user input with PHP, too.

■ **Tip** Client-side validation on its own is insufficient. Always verify the data from an external source using server-side validation with PHP.

Creating a Reusable Script

The ability to reuse the same script—perhaps with only a few edits—for multiple web sites is a great timesaver. However, sending the input data to a separate file for processing makes it difficult to alert users to errors without losing their input. To get around this problem, the approach taken in this chapter is to use what's known as a **self-processing form**.

When the form is submitted, the page reloads, and a conditional statement runs the processing script. If the server-side validation detects errors, the form can be redisplayed with error messages while preserving the user's input. Parts of the script specific to the form will be embedded above the DOCTYPE declaration. Generic, reusable parts will be in a separate file that can be included in any page that requires an email-processing script.

PHP Solution 6-1: Preventing Cross-Site Scripting in a Self-Processing Form

Leaving the `action` attribute of an opening form tag empty or omitting it altogether reloads the form when the data is submitted. However, an empty `action` attribute is invalid in HTML5. PHP has a very convenient superglobal variable (`$_SERVER['PHP_SELF']`) that contains the site root–relative path of the current file. Setting it as the value of the `action` attribute automatically inserts the correct value for a self-processing form—but using it on its own exposes your site to a malicious attack known as **cross-site scripting** (XSS). This PHP solution explains the risk and shows how to use `$_SERVER['PHP_SELF']` securely.

1. Load `bad_link.php` in the ch06 folder into a browser. It contains a single link to `form.php` in the same folder; but the link in the underlying HTML has been deliberately malformed to simulate an XSS attack.

■ **Note** The links in the exercise files for this PHP solution assume that they are in a folder called `php8sols/ch06` in your localhost server root. Adjust them if necessary to match your testing setup.

---

2. Click the link. In most browsers, you should see the JavaScript alert dialog shown in Figure 6-3.

Figure 6-3. *The malformed link embeds an XSS attack*

■ **Note**   Google Chrome and Microsoft Edge used to block suspected attacks with an XSS filter. However, this has been removed in favor of using a Content Security Policy (CSP). For details of CSPs, see `https://developer.mozilla.org/en-US/docs/Web/HTTP/CSP`.

---

3. Dismiss the JavaScript alert, and right-click to view the page source. Line 10 should look similar to this:

```
10    <form method="post"  action="/php8sols/ch06/form.php/"><script>alert('Gotcha!')</script><foo"">
```

The malformed link in bad_link.php has injected a snippet of JavaScript into the page immediately after the opening <form> tag. In this instance, it's a harmless JavaScript alert; but in a real XSS attack, it could try to steal cookies or other personal information. Such an attack would be silent, leaving the user unaware of what has happened unless they notice the script in the browser address bar.

This has happened because form.php uses $_SERVER['PHP_SELF'] to generate the value of the action attribute. The malformed link inserts the page location in the action attribute, closes the opening form tag, and then injects the <script> tag, which is executed immediately as the page loads.

4. A simple way to neutralize this type of XSS attack is to pass $_SERVER['PHP_SELF'] to the htmlentities() function like this:

```
<form method="post"  action="<?= htmlentities($_SERVER['PHP_SELF']) ?>">
```

This converts the angle brackets of the <script> tags to their HTML entity equivalents, preventing the script from being executed. Although it works, it leaves the malformed URL in the browser address bar, which could lead users to question the security of your site. I think a better solution is to redirect users to an error page when XSS is detected.

5. In form.php, create a PHP block above the DOCTYPE declaration, and define a variable with the site root–relative path to the current file like this:

```
<?php
$currentPage = '/php8sols/ch06/form.php';
?>
<!doctype html>
```

6. Now compare the value of $currentPage with $_SERVER['PHP_SELF']. If they're not identical, use the header() function to redirect the user to an error page and immediately exit the script like this:

```
if ($currentPage !== $_SERVER['PHP_SELF']) {
    header('Location: http://localhost/php8sols/ch06/missing.php');
    exit;
}
```

■ **Caution** The location passed to the header() function must be a fully qualified URL. If you use a document-relative link, the destination is appended to the malformed link, preventing the page from being redirected successfully.

---

7. Use $currentPage as the value of the action attribute in the opening form tag:

   ```
   <form method="post" action="<?= $currentPage ?>">
   ```

8. Save form.php, return to bad_link.php, and click the link again. This time you should be taken directly to missing.php.

9. Load form.php directly in the browser. It should load and work as expected.

   The finished version is in form_end.php in the ch06 folder. The file called bad_link_end.php links to the finished version if you just want to test the script.

This technique involves more code than simply passing $_SERVER['PHP_SELF'] to the htmlentities() function; but it has the advantage of guiding users seamlessly to an error page if they have followed a malicious link to your form. Obviously, the error page should link back to your main menu.

PHP Solution 6-2: Making Sure Required Fields Aren't Blank

When required fields are left blank, you don't get the information you need, and the user may never get a reply, particularly if contact details have been omitted.

Continue using the file from "Understanding the Difference Between post and get" earlier in this chapter. Alternatively, use contact_02.php from the ch06 folder and remove _02 from the filename.

1. The processing script uses two arrays called $errors and $missing to store details of errors and required fields that haven't been filled in. These arrays will be used to control the display of error messages alongside the form labels. There won't be any errors when the page first loads, so initialize $errors and $missing as empty arrays in the PHP code block at the top of contact.php, like this:

   ```
   <?php
   include './includes/title.php';
   $errors = [];
   $missing = [];
   ?>
   ```

2. The email-processing script should run only if the form has been submitted. Use a conditional statement to check the value of the superglobal variable $_SERVER['REQUEST_METHOD']. If it's POST (all in uppercase), you know the form has been submitted using the post method. Add the code highlighted in bold to the PHP block at the top of the page.

   ```
   <?php
   include './includes/title.php';
   $errors = [];
   $missing = [];
   ```

```
// check if the form has been submitted
if ($_SERVER['REQUEST_METHOD'] == 'POST') {
    // email processing script
}
?>
```

■ **Tip**   Checking that the value of $_SERVER['REQUEST_METHOD'] is POST is a generic condition that can be used with any form regardless of the name of the Submit button.

---

3.   Although you won't be sending the email just yet, define two variables to store the destination address and subject line of the email. The following code goes inside the conditional statement that you created in the previous step:

```
if ( $_SERVER['REQUEST_METHOD'] == 'POST') {
    // email processing script
    $to = 'david@example.com'; // use your own email address
    $subject = 'Feedback from Japan Journey';
}
```

4.   Next, create two arrays: one listing the name attribute of each field in the form and the other listing all *required* fields. For the sake of this demonstration, make the email field optional, so that only the name and comments fields are required. Add the following code inside the conditional block immediately after the code that defines the subject line:

```
    $subject = 'Feedback from Japan Journey';
    // list expected fields
    $expected = ['name', 'email', 'comments'];
    // set required fields
    $required = ['name', 'comments'];
}
```

■ **Tip**   The $expected array is to prevent an attacker from injecting other variables into the $_POST array in an attempt to overwrite your default values. By processing only those variables that you expect, your form is much more secure. Any spurious values are ignored.

---

5.   The next section of code is not specific to this form, so it should go in an external file that can be included in any email-processing script. Create a new PHP file called processmail.php in the includes folder. Then include it in contact.php immediately after the code you entered in the previous step, like this:

```
    $required = ['name', 'comments'];
    require './includes/processmail.php';
}
```

6. The code in processmail.php begins by checking the $_POST variables for required fields that have been left blank. Strip any default code inserted by your editor and add the following to processmail.php:

```php
<?php
foreach ($_POST as $key => $value) {
    // strip whitespace from $value if not an array
    if (!is_array($value)) {
        $value = trim($value);
    }
    if (!in_array($key, $expected)) {
        // ignore the value, it's not in $expected
        continue;
    }
    if (in_array($key, $required) && empty($value)) {
        // required value is missing
        $missing[] = $key;
        $$key = "";
        continue;
    }
    $$key = $value;
}
```

This foreach loop processes the $_POST array by stripping out leading and trailing whitespace from text fields and assigning the field's contents to a variable with a simplified name. As a result, $_POST['email'] becomes $email and so on. It also checks if required fields are left blank and adds them to the $missing array, setting the related variable to an empty string.

The $_POST array is an associative array, so the loop assigns the key and value of the current element to $key and $value, respectively. The loop begins by checking that the current value isn't an array, using the is_array() function with the logical Not operator (!). If it isn't, the trim() function strips leading and trailing whitespace and reassigns it to $value. Removing leading and trailing whitespace prevents anyone from pressing the space bar several times to avoid filling in a required field.

■ **Note** The form currently has only text input fields, but it will be expanded later to include <select> and check box elements that submit data as arrays. It's necessary to check whether the value of the current element is an array because passing an array to the trim() function triggers an error.

The next conditional statement checks whether the current key is not in the $expected array. If it isn't, the continue keyword forces the loop to stop processing the current element and move onto the next one. So anything not in the $expected array is ignored.

Next, we check if the current array key is in the $required array and if it has no value. If the condition returns true, the key is added to the $missing array, and a variable based on the key's name is created dynamically and its value is set to an empty string. Notice that $$key begins with two dollar signs in the following line:

```
$$key = "";
```

This means it's a variable variable (see "Creating New Variables Dynamically" in Chapter 4). So, if the value of $key is "name," $$key becomes $name.

Again, continue moves the loop onto the next element.

But, if we get all the way to the final line of the loop, we know that we're dealing with an element that needs to be processed, so a variable based on the key name is created dynamically and the current value is assigned to it.

7. Save processmail.php. You'll add more code to it later, but let's turn now to the main body of contact.php. The action attribute in the opening form tag is empty. For local testing purposes, just set its value to the name of the current page:

```
<form method="post" action="contact.php">
```

8. You need to display a warning if anything is missing. Add a conditional statement at the top of the page content between the <h2> heading and the first paragraph, like this:

```
<h2>Contact us</h2>
<?php if ($missing || $errors) { ?>
<p class="warning">Please fix the item(s) indicated.</p>
<?php } ?>
<p>Ut enim ad minim veniam . . . </p>
```

This checks $missing and $errors, which you initialized as empty arrays in step 1. As explained in "The Truth According to PHP" in Chapter 4, an empty array is treated as false, so the paragraph inside the conditional statement isn't displayed when the page first loads. However, if a required field hasn't been filled in when the form is submitted, its name is added to the $missing array. An array with at least one element is treated as true. The || means "or," so this warning paragraph will be displayed if a required field is left blank or if an error is discovered. (The $errors array comes into play in PHP Solution 6-4.)

9. To make sure it works so far, save contact.php and load it normally in a browser (don't click the Refresh button). The warning message is not displayed. Click Send message without filling in any of the fields. You should now see the message about missing items, as shown in the following screenshot:

Contact Us

Please fix the item(s) indicated.

10. To display a suitable message alongside each missing required field, use a PHP conditional statement to insert a `<span>` inside the `<label>` tag, like this:

```
<label for="name">Name:
<?php if (in_array('name', $missing)) { ?>
    <span class="warning">Please enter your name</span>
<?php } ?>
</label>
```

The condition uses the `in_array()` function to check if the `$missing` array contains the value `name`. If it does, the `<span>` is displayed. `$missing` is defined as an empty array at the top of the script, so the span won't be displayed when the page first loads.

11. Insert similar warnings for the `email` and `comments` fields like this:

```
<label for="email">Email:
<?php if (in_array('email', $missing)) { ?>
    <span class="warning">Please enter your email address</span>
<?php } ?>
</label>
<input name="email" id="email" type="text">
</p>
<p>
<label for="comments">Comments:
<?php if (in_array('comments', $missing)) { ?>
    <span class="warning">Please enter your comments</span>
<?php } ?>
</label>
```

The PHP code is the same except for the value you are looking for in the `$missing` array. It's the same as the `name` attribute for the form element.

12. Save `contact.php` and test the page again, first by entering nothing into any of the fields. The form labels should look like Figure 6-4.

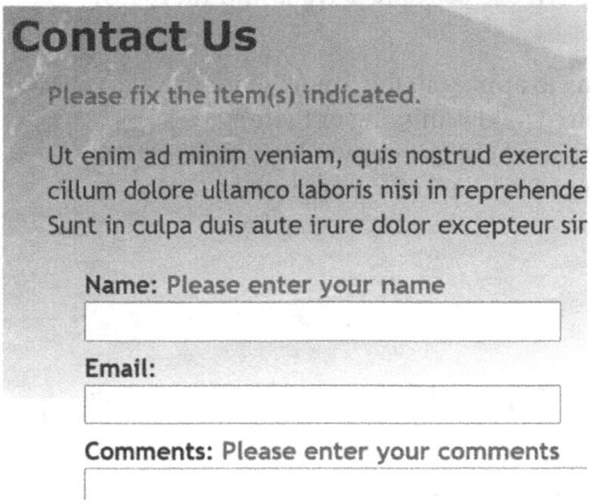

Figure 6-4. *By validating user input, you can display warnings about required fields*

Although you added a warning to the `<label>` for the email field, it's not displayed because email hasn't been added to the `$required` array. As a result, it's not added to the `$missing` array by the code in `processmail.php`.

13. Add email to the `$required` array in the code block at the top of `contact.php`, like this:

    ```
    $required = ['name', 'comments', 'email'];
    ```

14. Click Send message again without filling in any fields. This time, you'll see a warning message alongside each label.

15. Type your name in the Name field. In the Email and Comments fields, just press the spacebar several times, and then click Send message. The warning message alongside the Name field disappears, but the other two warning messages remain. The code in `processmail.php` strips whitespace from text fields, so it rejects attempts to bypass required fields by entering a series of spaces.

    If you have any problems, compare your code with `contact_03.php` and `includes/processmail_01.php` in the ch06 folder.

All that needs to be done to change the required fields is to change the names in the `$required` array and add a suitable alert inside the `<label>` tag of the appropriate input element inside the form. It's easy to do because you always use the name attribute of the form input element.

Preserving User Input When a Form Is Incomplete

Imagine you have spent 10 minutes filling in a form. You click the Submit button, and back comes the response that a required field is missing. It's infuriating if you have to fill in every field all over again. Since the content of each field is in the `$_POST` array, it's easy to redisplay it when an error occurs.

PHP Solution 6-3: Creating Sticky Form Fields

This PHP solution shows how to use a conditional statement to extract the user's input from the `$_POST` array and redisplay it in text input fields and text areas.

Continue working with the same files as before. Alternatively, use `contact_03.php` and `includes/processmail_01.php` from the ch06 folder.

1. When the page first loads, you don't want anything to appear in the input fields, but you *do* want to redisplay the content if a required field is missing or there's an error. That's the key: if the `$missing` or `$errors` array contains any values, the content of each field should be redisplayed. You set default text for a text input field with the `value` attribute of the `<input>` tag, so amend the `<input>` tag for name like this:

    ```
    <input name="name" id="name" type="text"
    <?php if ($missing || $errors) {
        echo 'value="' . htmlentities($name) . '"';
    } ?>>
    ```

The line inside the curly braces contains a combination of quotes and periods that might confuse you. The first thing to realize is that there's only one semicolon—right at the end—so the echo command applies to the whole line. As explained in Chapter 3, a period is called the concatenation operator, which joins strings and variables. You can break down the rest of the line into three sections, as follows:

- `'value="' .`

- `htmlentities($name)`

- `. '"'`

The first section outputs `value="` as text and uses the concatenation operator to join it to the next section, which passes $name to a function called htmlentities(). I'll explain why that's necessary in a moment, but the third section uses the concatenation operator again to join the final output, which consists solely of a double quote. So, if $missing or $errors contains any values and $_POST['name'] contains Joe, you'll end up with this inside the <input> tag:

```
<input name="name" id="name" type="text" value="Joe">
```

The $name variable contains the original user input, which was transmitted through the $_POST array. The foreach loop that you created in processmail.php in PHP Solution 6-2 processes the $_POST array and assigns each element to a variable with the same name. This allows you to access $_POST['name'] simply as $name.

So why do we need the htmlentities() function? As the function name suggests, it converts certain characters to their equivalent HTML character entities. The one you're concerned with here is the double quote. Let's say Eric "Slowhand" Clapton decides to send feedback through the form. If you use $name on its own, Figure 6-5 shows what happens when a required field is omitted and you don't use htmlentities().

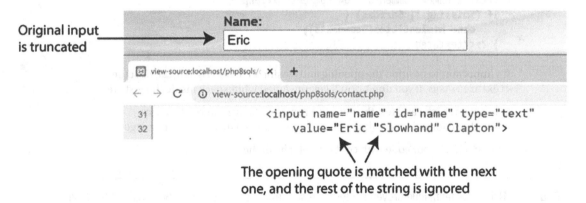

Figure 6-5. Quotes need special treatment before form fields can be redisplayed

Passing the content of the $_POST array element to the htmlentities(), however, converts the double quotes in the middle of the string to ". And, as Figure 6-6 shows, the content is no longer truncated.

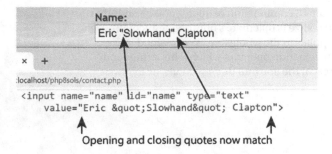

Figure 6-6. *Passing the value to htmlentities() before it's displayed solves the problem*

What's cool about this is that the character entity " is converted back to double quotes when the form is resubmitted. As a result, there's no need for further conversion before the email can be sent.

■ **Note** If htmlentities() corrupts your text, you can set the encoding directly in PHP 8 using a named argument (see "Using Named Arguments" in Chapter 4). For example, to set the encoding to Simplified Chinese, use htmlentities($name, encoding: 'GB2312').

---

2. Edit the email field the same way, using $email instead of $name.

3. The comments text area needs to be handled slightly differently because `<textarea>` tags don't have a value attribute. You must place the PHP block between the opening and closing tags of the text area, like this (new code is shown in bold):

```
<textarea name="comments" id="comments"><?php
  if ($missing || $errors) {
     echo htmlentities($comments);
  } ?></textarea>
```

It's important to position the opening and closing PHP tags right up against the `<textarea>` tags. If you don't, you'll get unwanted whitespace inside the text area.

4. Save contact.php and test the page in a browser. If any required fields are omitted, the form displays the original content along with any error messages.

You can check your code with contact_04.php in the ch06 folder.

■ **Caution** Using this technique prevents a form's reset button from resetting any fields that have been changed by the PHP script because it explicitly sets the value attribute of each field.

Filtering Out Potential Attacks

A particularly nasty exploit known as **email header injection** seeks to turn online forms into spam relays. The attacker tries to trick your script into sending HTML email with copies to many people. This is possible if you incorporate unfiltered user input in the additional headers that can be passed as the fourth argument to the mail() function. It's common to add the user's email address as a Reply-To header. If you detect spaces, new lines, carriage returns, or any of the strings "Content-Type:", "Cc:", or "Bcc:" in the submitted value, you're the target of an attack, so you should block the message.

PHP Solution 6-4: Blocking Email Addresses That Contain Suspect Content

This PHP solution checks the user's email address input for suspect content. If it's detected, a Boolean variable is set to true. This will be used later to prevent the email from being sent.

Continue working with the same page as before. Alternatively, use contact_04.php and includes/ processmail_01.php from the ch06 folder.

1. To detect the suspect phrases, we'll use a search pattern or **regular expression**. Add the following code at the top of processmail.php before the existing foreach loop:

```
// pattern to locate suspect phrases
$pattern = '/[\s\r\n]|Content-Type:|Bcc:|Cc:/i';
foreach ($_POST as $key => $value) {
```

The string assigned to $pattern will be used to perform a case-insensitive search for any of the following: a space, carriage return, newline feed, "Content-Type:", "Bcc:", or "Cc:". It's written in a format called Perl-compatible regular expression (PCRE). The search pattern is enclosed in a pair of forward slashes, and the i after the final slash makes the pattern case-insensitive.

■ **Tip** Regular expressions are an extremely powerful tool for matching text patterns. Admittedly, they're not easy to learn; but it's an essential skill if you're serious about working with programming languages such as PHP and JavaScript. Take a look at *Introducing Regular Expressions* by Jörg Krause (Apress, 2017, ISBN 978-1-4842-2508-0). It's aimed primarily at JavaScript developers, but there are only minor differences of implementation between JavaScript and PHP. The basic syntax is identical.

---

2. You can now use the PCRE stored in $pattern to detect any suspect user input in the submitted email address. Add the following code immediately after the $pattern variable from step 1:

```
// check the submitted email address
$suspect = preg_match($pattern, $_POST['email']);
```

The preg_match() function compares the regular expression passed as the first argument against the value in the second argument, in this case, the value from the Email field. It returns true if it finds a match. So, if any of the suspect content is found, $suspect will be true. But if there's no match, it will be false.

3. If suspect content is detected in the email address, there's no point in processing the $_POST array any further. Wrap the code that processes the $_POST variables in a conditional statement like this:

```
if (!$suspect) {
    foreach ($_POST as $key => $value) {
        // strip whitespace from $value if not an array
        if (!is_array($value)) {
            $value = trim($value);
        }
        if (!in_array($key, $expected)) {
            // ignore the value, it's not in $expected
            continue;
        }
        if (in_array($key, $required) && empty($value)) {
            // required value is missing
            $missing[] = $key;
            $$key = "";
            continue;
        }
    $$key = $value;
    }
}
```

This processes the variables in the $_POST array only if $suspect is not true.

Don't forget the extra curly brace to close the conditional statement.

4. Edit the PHP block after the <h2> heading in contact.php to add a new warning message above the form, like this:

```
<h2>Contact Us</h2>
<?php if ($_POST && $suspect) { ?>
    <p class="warning">Sorry, your mail could not be sent.
    Please try later.</p>
<?php } elseif ($missing || $errors) { ?>
  <p class="warning">Please fix the item(s) indicated.</p>
<?php } ?>
```

This sets a new condition that takes priority over the original warning message by being considered first. It checks if the $_POST array contains any elements—in other words, the form has been submitted—and if $suspect is true. The warning is deliberately neutral in tone. There's no point in provoking attackers.

5. Save contact.php and test the form by typing any of the suspect content in the Email field. You should see the new warning message, but your input won't be preserved.

You can check your code against contact_05.php and includes/processmail_02.php in the ch06 folder.

Sending Email

Before proceeding any further, it's necessary to explain how the PHP mail() function works, because it will help you understand the rest of the processing script.

The PHP mail() function takes up to five arguments, all of them strings, as follows:

- The address(es) of the recipient(s)
- The subject line
- The message body
- A list of other email headers (optional)
- Additional parameters (optional)

Email addresses in the first argument can be in either of the following formats:

```
'user@example.com'
'Some Guy <user2@example.com>'
```

To send to more than one address, use a comma-separated string like this:

```
'user@example.com, another@example.com, Some Guy <user2@example.com>'
```

The message body must be presented as a single string. This means that you need to extract the input data from the $_POST array and format the message, adding labels to identify each field. By default, the mail() function supports only plain text. New lines must use both a carriage return and newline character. It's also recommended to restrict the length of lines to no more than 78 characters. Although it sounds complicated, you can build the message body automatically with about 20 lines of PHP code, as you'll see in PHP Solution 6-6. Adding other email headers is covered in detail in the next section.

Many hosting companies now make the fifth argument a requirement. It ensures that the email is sent by a trusted user, and it normally consists of your own email address prefixed by -f (without a space in between), all enclosed in quotes. Check your hosting company's instructions to see whether this is required and the exact format it should take.

■ **Caution**   You should never incorporate user input into the fifth argument to the mail() function because it can be used to execute arbitrary script on the web server.

Using Additional Email Headers Safely

You can find a full list of email headers at www.faqs.org/rfcs/rfc2076, but some of the most well-known and useful ones enable you to send copies of an email to other addresses (Cc and Bcc) or to change the encoding. Each new header, except the final one, must be on a separate line terminated by a carriage return and newline character. In older versions of PHP, this meant using the \r and \n escape sequences in double-quoted strings (see Table 4-5 in Chapter 4).

■ **Tip**   Since PHP 7.2, the formatting of additional headers is handled automatically. Simply define an associative array using the header name as the key of each element and then pass the array as the fourth argument to the `mail()` function.

By default, `mail()` uses Latin1 (ISO-8859-1) encoding, which doesn't support accented characters. Web page editors these days frequently use Unicode (UTF-8), which supports most written languages, including the accents commonly used in European languages, as well as nonalphabetic scripts, such as Chinese and Japanese. To ensure that email messages aren't garbled, use the `Content-Type` header to set the encoding to UTF-8, like this:

```
$headers['Content-Type'] = 'text/plain; charset=utf-8';
```

You also need to add UTF-8 as the `charset` attribute in a `<meta>` tag in the `<head>` of your web pages like this:

```
<meta charset="utf-8">
```

Let's say you want to send copies to other departments, plus a copy to another address that you don't want the others to see. Email sent by `mail()` is often identified as coming from nobody@yourdomain (or whatever username is assigned to the web server), so it's a good idea to add a more user-friendly "From" address. This is how you build those additional headers:

```
$headers['From'] = 'Japan Journey<feedback@example.com>';
$headers['Cc'] = 'sales@example.com, finance@example.com';
$headers['Bcc'] = 'secretplanning@example.com';
```

After defining the array of headers you want to use, you pass the array to `mail()`, like this (assuming that the destination address, subject, and message body have already been stored in variables):

```
$mailSent = mail($to, $subject, $message, $headers);
```

Hard-coded additional headers like this present no security risk, but anything that comes from user input must be filtered before it's used. The biggest danger comes from a text field that asks for the user's email address. A widely used technique is to incorporate the user's email address into a `From` or `Reply-To` header, which enables you to reply directly to incoming messages by clicking the Reply button in your email program. It's very convenient, but attackers frequently try to pack an email input field with a large number of spurious headers. The previous PHP solution eliminated the headers most commonly used by attackers, but we need to check the email address further before incorporating it into the additional headers.

■ **Caution**   Although email fields are the prime target for attackers, the destination address and subject line are both vulnerable if you let users change the value. User input should always be regarded as suspect. Always hard-code the destination address and subject line. Alternatively, provide a drop-down menu of acceptable values and check the submitted value against an array of the same values.

PHP Solution 6-5: Adding Headers and Automating the Reply Address

This PHP solution adds three headers to the email: From, Content-Type (to set the encoding to UTF-8), and Reply-To. Before adding the user's email address to the final header, it uses a built-in PHP filter to verify that the submitted value conforms to the format of a valid email address.

Continue working with the same page as before. Alternatively, use contact_05.php and includes/processmail_02.php from the ch06 folder.

1. Headers are often specific to a particular web site or page, so the From and Content-Type headers will be added to the script in contact.php. Add the following code to the PHP block at the top of the page just before processmail. php is included:

```
$required = ['name', 'comments', 'email'];
// create additional headers
$headers['From'] = 'Japan Journey<feedback@example.com>';
$headers['Content-Type'] = 'text/plain; charset=utf-8';
require './includes/processmail.php';
```

2. The purpose of validating the email address is to make sure it's in a valid format, but the field might be empty because you decide not to make it required or because the user simply ignored it. If the field is required but empty, it will be added to the $missing array, and the warning you added in PHP Solution 6-2 will be displayed. If the field isn't empty, but the input is invalid, you need to display a different message.

   Switch to processmail.php and add this code at the bottom of the script:

```
// validate the user's email
if (!$suspect && !empty($email)) {
    $validemail = filter_input(INPUT_POST, 'email', FILTER_VALIDATE_EMAIL);
    if ($validemail) {
        $headers['Reply-To'] = $validemail;
    } else {
        $errors['email'] = true;
    }
}
```

   This begins by checking that no suspect content has been found and that the email field isn't empty. Both conditions are preceded by the logical Not operator, so they return true if $suspect and empty($email) are both false. The foreach loop you added in PHP Solution 6-2 assigns all expected elements in the $_POST array to simpler variables, so $email contains the same value as $_POST['email'].

   The next line uses filter_input() to validate the email address. The first argument is a PHP constant, INPUT_POST, which specifies that the value must be in the $_POST array. The second argument is the name of the element you want to test. The final argument is another PHP constant that specifies you want to check that the element conforms to the valid format for an email.

The `filter_input()` function returns the value being tested if it's valid. Otherwise, it returns `false`. So, if the value submitted by the user looks like a valid email address, `$validemail` contains the address. If the format is invalid, `$validemail` is `false`. The `FILTER_VALIDATE_EMAIL` constant accepts only a single email address, so any attempt to insert multiple email addresses will be rejected.

■ **Note** `FILTER_VALIDATE_EMAIL` checks the format, not whether the address is genuine.

If `$validemail` isn't `false`, it's safe to incorporate into a `Reply-To` email header. But if `$validemail` is `false`, `$errors['email']` is added to the `$errors` array.

3. You now need to amend the `<label>` for the email field in `contact.php`, like this:

```
<label for="email">Email:
<?php if (in_array('email', $missing)) { ?>
    <span class="warning">Please enter your email address</span>
<?php } elseif (isset($errors['email'])) { ?>
    <span class="warning">Invalid email address</span>
<?php } ?>
</label>
```

This adds an `elseif` clause to the first conditional statement and displays a different warning if the email address fails validation.

4. Save `contact.php` and test the form by leaving all fields blank and clicking Send message. You'll see the original error message. Test it again by entering a value that isn't an email address in the Email field or by entering two email addresses. You should see the invalid message.

■ **Note** If you put a space after the comma between multiple email addresses when testing the updated script, you won't see the new error message because the regular expression in PHP Solution 6–4 rejects values in the Email field that contain spaces. Either way, the attempted attack is foiled.

You can check your code with `contact_06.php` and `includes/processmail_03.php` in the ch06 folder.

PHP Solution 6-6: Building the Message Body and Sending the Mail

Many PHP tutorials show how to build the message body manually like this:

```
$message = "Name: $name\r\n\r\n";
$message .= "Email: $email\r\n\r\n";
$message .= "Comments: $comments";
```

This adds labels to identify which field the input comes from and inserts two carriage returns and newline characters between each one. This is fine for a small number of fields, but it soon becomes tedious with more fields. As long as you give your form fields meaningful name attributes, you can build the message body automatically with a `foreach` loop, which is the approach taken in this PHP solution.

Continue working with the same files as before. Alternatively, use contact_06.php and includes/ processmail_03.php from the ch06 folder.

1. Add the following code at the bottom of the script in processmail.php:

```
$mailSent = false;
```

This initializes a variable to redirect to a thank you page after the mail has been sent. It needs to be set to false until you know the mail() function has succeeded.

2. Now add the code that builds the message immediately after:

```
// go ahead only if not suspect, all required fields OK, and no errors
if (!$suspect && !$missing && !$errors) {
    // initialize the $message variable
    $message = '';
    // loop through the $expected array
    foreach($expected as $item) {
        // assign the value of the current item to $val
        if (isset($$item) && !empty($$item)) {
            $val = $$item;
        } else {
            // if it has no value, assign 'Not selected'
            $val = 'Not selected';
        }
        // if an array, expand as comma-separated string
        if (is_array($val)) {
            $val = implode(', ', $val);
        }
        // replace underscores in the label with spaces
        $item = str_replace('_', ' ', $item);
        // add label and value to the message body
        $message .= ucfirst($item).": $val\r\n\r\n";
    }
    // limit line length to 70 characters
    $message = wordwrap($message, 70);
    $mailSent = true;
}
```

This block of code begins by checking that $suspect, $missing, and $errors are all false. If they are, it builds the message body by looping through the $expected array, storing the result in $message as a series of label/value pairs.

The key to how it works lies in the following conditional statement:

```
if (isset($$item) && !empty($$item)) {
    $val = $$item;
}
```

This is another example of using a variable variable (see "Creating New Variables Dynamically" in Chapter 4). Each time the loop runs, $item contains the value of the current element in the $expected array. The first element is name, so $$item dynamically creates a variable called $name. In effect, the conditional statement becomes this:

```
if (isset($name) && !empty($name)) {
    $val = $name;
}
```

On the next pass, $$item creates a variable called $email and so on. PHP Solution 6–2 assigned the data submitted in each form field to a simple variable, so this conditional statement assigns the data from the current field to a temporary variable $val.

■ **Caution** This script builds the message body only from items in the $expected array. You must list the names of all form fields in the $expected array for it to work.

If a field not specified as required is left empty, its value is set to "Not selected." The code also processes values from multiple-choice elements, such as check-box groups and <select> lists, which are transmitted as subarrays of the $_POST array. The implode() function converts the subarrays into comma-separated strings. The first argument is the string you want to insert between each array element. The second argument is the array to be processed.

Each label is derived from the input field's name attribute in the current element of the $expected array. The first argument to str_replace() is an underscore. If an underscore is found in the name attribute, it's replaced by the second argument, a string consisting of a single space. The first letter is then set to uppercase by ucfirst(). Notice that the third argument to str_replace() is $item (with a single dollar sign), so this time it's an ordinary variable, not a variable variable. It contains the current value from the $expected array. The data from the current element followed by two carriage returns and newline characters is then concatenated to the label.

After the labels and field data have been combined into a single string, the wordwrap() function limits the line length to 70 characters.

The code that sends the email still needs to be added, but for testing purposes, $mailSent is set to true.

3. Save processmail.php. Locate this code block at the bottom of contact.php:

```
<pre>
<?php if ($_POST) {print_r($_POST);} ?>
</pre>
Change it to this:
<pre>
<?php if ($_POST && $mailSent) {
    echo htmlentities($message);
```

```
    foreach ($headers as $key => $value) {
        echo htmlentities("$key: $value") . '<br>';
    }
} ?>
</pre>
```

This checks that the form has been submitted and the mail is ready to send. It then displays the values in $message and the $headers array. All values are passed to htmlentities() to ensure they display correctly in the browser.

4. Save contact.php, and test the form by entering your name, email address, and a brief comment. When you click Send message, you should see the message body and headers displayed at the bottom of the page, as shown in Figure 6-7.

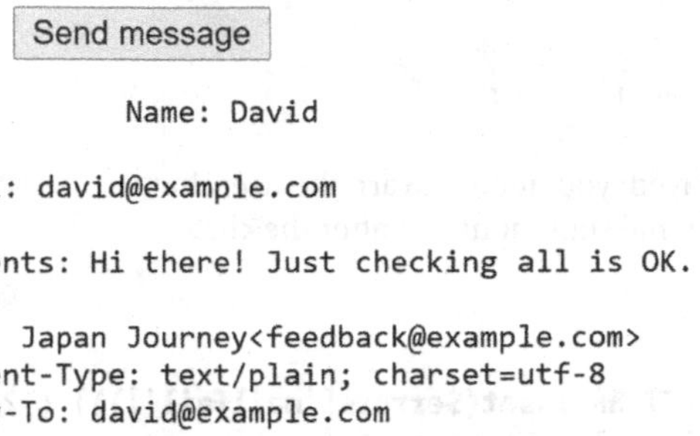

```
Send message

    Name: David

Email: david@example.com

Comments: Hi there! Just checking all is OK.

From: Japan Journey<feedback@example.com>
Content-Type: text/plain; charset=utf-8
Reply-To: david@example.com
```

Figure 6-7. *Verifying that the message body and headers are correctly formed*

Assuming the message body and headers display correctly at the bottom of the page, you're ready to add the code to send the email. If necessary, check your code against contact_07.php and includes/processmail_04.php in the ch06 folder.

5. In processmail.php, add the code to send the mail. Locate the following line:

```
$mailSent = true;
Change it to this:
$mailSent = mail($to, $subject, $message, $headers);
if (!$mailSent) {
    $errors['mailfail'] = true;
}
```

This passes the destination address, subject line, message body, and headers to the mail() function, which returns true if it succeeds in handing the email to the web server's mail transport agent (MTA). If it fails, $mailSent is set to false, and the conditional statement adds an element to the $errors array, allowing you to preserve the user's input when the form is redisplayed.

6. In the PHP block at the top of contact.php, add the following conditional statement immediately after the command that includes processmail.php:

```
require './includes/processmail.php';
if ($mailSent) {
    header('Location: http://www.example.com/thank_you.php');
    exit;
}
}
?>
```

You need to test this on your remote server, so replace www.example.com with your own domain name. This checks if $mailSent is true. If it is, the header() function redirects to thank_you.php, a page acknowledging the message has been sent. The exit command on the following line ensures the script is terminated after the page has been redirected.

There's a copy of thank_you.php in the ch06 folder.

7. If $mailSent is false, contact.php is redisplayed; you need to warn the user that the message couldn't be sent. Edit the conditional statement just after the <h2> heading, like this:

```
<h2>Contact Us </h2>
<?php if (($_POST && $suspect) || ($_POST && isset($errors['mailfail']))) { ?>
    <p class="warning">Sorry, your mail could not be sent. . . .
```

The original and new conditions have been wrapped in parentheses, so each pair is considered separately. The warning about the message not being sent is displayed if the form has been submitted and suspect phrases have been found *or* if the form has been submitted and $errors['mailfail'] has been set.

8. Delete the code block (including the <pre> tags) that displays the message body and headers at the bottom of contact.php.

9. Testing this locally is likely to result in the thank you page being shown, but the email never arriving. This is because most testing environments don't have an MTA. Even if you set one up, most mail servers reject mail from unrecognized sources. Upload contact.php and all related files, including processmail.php and thank_you.php, to your remote server and test the contact form there. Don't forget that processmail.php needs to be in a subfolder called includes.

You can check your code with contact_08.php and includes/processmail_05.php in the ch06 folder.

Troubleshooting mail()

It's important to understand that mail() isn't an email program. PHP's responsibility ends as soon as it passes the address, subject, message, and headers to the MTA. It has no way of knowing if the email is delivered to its intended destination. Normally, email arrives instantaneously, but network logjams can delay it by hours or even a couple of days.

■ **Tip** One of the most likely causes of failure when testing this script on a remote server is the version of PHP. If your remote server is running PHP 7.1 or earlier, the $headers array will need to be converted to a string with a carriage return and newline character between each header. Use implode() with "r\n" (double quotes) as the first argument.

If you're redirected to the thank you page after sending a message from contact.php, but nothing arrives in your inbox, check the following:

- Has the message been caught by a spam filter?

- Have you checked the destination address stored in $to? Try an alternative email address to see if it makes a difference.

- Have you used a genuine address in the From header? Using a fake or invalid address is likely to cause the mail to be rejected. Use a valid address that belongs to the same domain as your web server.

- Check with your hosting company to see if the fifth argument to mail() is required. If so, it should normally be a string composed of -f followed by your email address. For example, david@example.com becomes '-fdavid@example.com'.

If you still don't receive messages from contact.php, create a file with this script:

```php
<?php
ini_set('display_errors', '1');
$mailSent = mail('you@example.com', 'PHP mail test', 'This is a test email');
if ($mailSent) {
    echo 'Mail sent';
} else {
    echo 'Failed';
}
```

Replace you@example.com with your own email address. Upload the file to your web site and load the page into a browser.

If you see an error message about there being no From header, add one as a fourth argument to the mail() function, like this:

```php
$mailSent = mail('you@example.com', 'PHP mail test', 'This is a test email',
'From: me@example.com');
```

It's usually a good idea to use a different address from the destination address in the first argument. If your hosting company requires the fifth argument, adjust the code like this:

```php
$mailSent = mail('you@example.com', 'PHP mail test', 'This is a test email', null,
'-fme@example.com');
```

Using the fifth argument normally replaces the need to supply a From header, so using null (without quotes) as the fourth argument indicates that it has no value.

If you see "Mail sent" and no mail arrives or you see "Failed" after trying all five arguments, consult your hosting company for advice.

If you receive the test email from this script but not from `contact.php`, it means you have made a mistake in the code or that you have forgotten to upload `processmail.php`. Turn on the display of errors temporarily, as described in "Why Is My Page Blank?" in Chapter 3, to check `contact.php` is able to find `processmail.php`.

■ **Tip**   I was teaching at a university in England and couldn't work out why students' mails weren't being delivered, even though their code was perfect. It turned out the IT department had disabled Sendmail (the MTA) to prevent the server being used to deliver spam!

Handling Multiple-Choice Form Elements

The form in `contact.php` uses only text input fields and a text area. To work successfully with forms, you also need to know how to handle multiple-choice elements, namely:

- Radio buttons

- Check boxes

- Drop-down option menus

- Multiple-choice lists

The principle behind them is the same as the text input fields you have been working with: the `name` attribute of the form element is used as the key in the $_POST array. However, there are some important differences:

- Check-box groups and multiple-choice lists store selected values as an array, so you need to add an empty pair of square brackets at the end of the `name` attribute for these types of input. For example, for a check-box group called `interests`, the `name` attribute in each `<input>` tag should be `name="interests[]"`. If you omit the square brackets, only the last item selected is transmitted through the $_POST array.

- The values of selected items in a check-box group or multiple-choice list are transmitted as a subarray of the $_POST array. The code in PHP Solution 6-6 automatically converts these subarrays to comma-separated strings. However, when using a form for other purposes, you need to extract the values from the subarrays. You'll see how to do so in later chapters.

- Radio buttons, check boxes, and multiple-choice lists are *not* included in the $_POST array if no value is selected. Consequently, it's vital to use `isset()` to check for their existence before attempting to access their values when processing the form.

The remaining PHP solutions in this chapter show how to handle multiple-choice form elements. Rather than go through each step in detail, I'll just highlight the important points. Bear the following points in mind when working through the rest of this chapter:

- Processing these elements relies on the code in `processmail.php`.

- You must add the `name` attribute of each element to the $expected array for it to be added to the message body.

- To make a field required, add its name attribute to the $required array.
- If a field that's not required is left blank, the code in processmail.php sets its value to "Not selected."

Figure 6-8 shows contact.php with each type of input added to the original design.

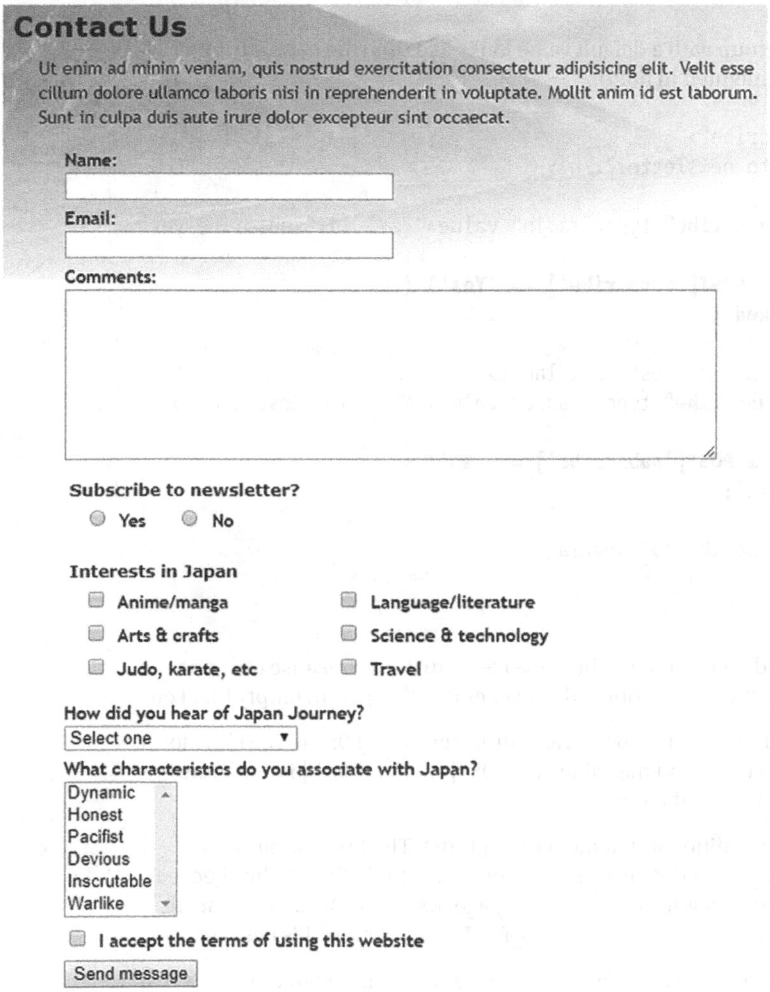

Contact Us

Ut enim ad minim veniam, quis nostrud exercitation consectetur adipisicing elit. Velit esse cillum dolore ullamco laboris nisi in reprehenderit in voluptate. Mollit anim id est laborum. Sunt in culpa duis aute irure dolor excepteur sint occaecat.

Name:

Email:

Comments:

Subscribe to newsletter?
○ Yes ○ No

Interests in Japan
☐ Anime/manga   ☐ Language/literature
☐ Arts & crafts   ☐ Science & technology
☐ Judo, karate, etc ☐ Travel

How did you hear of Japan Journey?
Select one ▼

What characteristics do you associate with Japan?
Dynamic
Honest
Pacifist
Devious
Inscrutable
Warlike

☐ I accept the terms of using this website
Send message

Figure 6-8. The feedback form with examples of multiple-choice form elements

■ **Tip** HTML5 form input elements all use the name attribute and send values as text or as a subarray of the $_POST array, so you should be able to adapt the code accordingly.

PHP Solution 6-7: Handling Radio Button Groups

Radio button groups let you pick only one value. Although it's common to set a default value in the HTML markup, it's not obligatory. This PHP solution shows how to handle both scenarios.

1. The simple way to deal with radio buttons is to make one of them the default. The radio group is always included in the $_POST array because a value is always selected.

   The code for a radio group with a default value looks like this (the name attributes and PHP code are highlighted in bold):

   ```
   <fieldset id="subscribe">
       <h2>Subscribe to newsletter?</h2>
       <p>
       <input name="subscribe" type="radio" value="Yes" id="subscribe-yes"
       <?php
       if ($_POST && $_POST['subscribe'] == 'Yes') {
           echo 'checked';
       } ?>>
       <label for="subscribe-yes">Yes</label>
       <input name="subscribe" type="radio" value="No" id="subscribe-no"
       <?php
       if (!$_POST || $_POST['subscribe'] == 'No') {
           echo 'checked';
       } ?>>
       <label for="subscribe-no">No</label>
       </p>
   </fieldset>
   ```

   All members of the radio group share the same name attribute. Because only one value can be selected, the name attribute does *not* end with a pair of empty brackets.

   The conditional statement related to the Yes button checks $_POST to see if the form has been submitted. If it has and the value of $_POST['subscribe'] is "Yes," the checked attribute is added to the <input> tag.

   In the No button, the conditional statement uses || (or). The first condition is !$_POST, which is true when the form hasn't been submitted. If true, the checked attribute is added as the default value when the page first loads. If false, it means the form has been submitted, so the value of $_POST['subscribe'] is checked.

2. When a radio button doesn't have a default value, it's not included in the $_POST array, so it isn't detected by the loop in processmail.php that builds the $missing array. To ensure that the radio button element is included in the $_POST array, you need to test for its existence after the form has been submitted. If it isn't included, you need to set its value to an empty string, like this:

   ```
   $required = ['name', 'comments', 'email', 'subscribe'];
   // set default values for variables that might not exist
   if (!isset($_POST['subscribe'])) {
       $_POST['subscribe'] = '';
   }
   ```

3. If the radio button group is required but not selected, you need to display an error message when the form reloads. You also need to change the conditional statements in the `<input>` tags to reflect the different behavior.

The following listing shows the `subscribe` radio button group from `contact_09.php`, with all the PHP code highlighted in bold:

```
<fieldset id="subscribe">
    <h2>Subscribe to newsletter?
    <?php if (in_array('subscribe', $missing)) { ?>
    <span class="warning">Please make a selection</span>
    <?php } ?>
    </h2>
    <p>
    <input name="subscribe" type="radio" value="Yes" id="subscribe-yes"
    <?php
    if ($_POST && $_POST['subscribe'] == 'Yes') {
        echo 'checked';
    } ?>>
    <label for="subscribe-yes">Yes</label>
    <input name="subscribe" type="radio" value="No" id="subscribe-no"
    <?php
    if ($_POST && $_POST['subscribe'] == 'No') {
        echo 'checked';
    } ?>>
    <label for="subscribe-no">No</label>
    </p>
</fieldset>
```

The conditional statement that controls the warning message in the `<h2>` tag uses the same technique as for the text input fields. The message is displayed if the radio group is a required item and it's in the `$missing` array.

The conditional statement surrounding the `checked` attribute is the same in both radio buttons. It checks if the form has been submitted and displays the checked attribute only if the value in `$_POST['subscribe']` matches.

PHP Solution 6-8: Handling Check-Box Groups

Check boxes can be used individually or in groups. The method of handling them is slightly different. This PHP solution shows how to deal with a check-box group called `interests`. PHP Solution 6-11 explains how to handle a single check box.

When used as a group, all check boxes in the group share the same `name` attribute, which needs to end with an empty pair of square brackets in order for PHP to transmit the selected values as an array. To identify which check boxes have been selected, each one needs a unique `value` attribute.

If no items are selected, the check-box group is not included in the `$_POST` array. After the form has been submitted, you need to check the `$_POST` array to see if it contains a subarray for the check-box group. If it doesn't, you need to create an empty subarray as the default value for the script in `processmail.php`.

1. To save space, just the first two check boxes of the group are shown. The name attribute and PHP sections of code are highlighted in bold:

```
<fieldset id="interests">
<h2>Interests in Japan</h2>
<div>
    <p>
        <input type="checkbox" name="interests[]" value="Anime/manga"
        id="anime"
        <?php
        if ($_POST && in_array('Anime/manga', $_POST['interests'])) {
            echo 'checked';
        } ?>>
        <label for="anime">Anime/manga</label>
    </p>
    <p>
        <input type="checkbox" name="interests[]" value="Arts & crafts"
        id="art"
        <?php
        if ($_POST && in_array('Arts & crafts', $_POST['interests'])) {
            echo 'checked';
        } ?>>
        <label for="art">Arts & crafts</label>
    </p>
    . . .
</div>
</fieldset>
```

Each check box shares the same name attribute, which ends with an empty pair of square brackets, so the data is treated as an array. If you omit the brackets, $_POST['interests'] contains the value of only the first check box selected. Also, $_POST['interests'] won't exist if no check box has been selected. You'll fix that in the next step.

■ **Note** Although the brackets must be added to the name attribute for multiple selections, the subarray of selected values is in $_POST['interests'], not $_POST['interests[]'].

The PHP code inside each check-box element performs the same role as in the radio button group, wrapping the checked attribute in a conditional statement. The first condition checks that the form has been submitted. The second condition uses the in_array() function to check whether the value associated with that check box is in the $_POST['interests'] subarray. If it is, it means the check box was selected.

2. After the form has been submitted, you need to check for the existence of $_POST['interests']. If it hasn't been set, you must create an empty array as the default value for the rest of the script to process. The code follows the same pattern as for the radio group:

```php
$required = ['name', 'comments', 'email', 'subscribe', 'interests'];
// set default values for variables that might not exist
if (!isset($_POST['subscribe'])) {
    $_POST['subscribe'] = '';
}
if (!isset($_POST['interests'])) {
    $_POST['interests'] = [];
}
```

3. To set a minimum number of required check boxes, use the count() function to confirm the number of values transmitted from the form. If it's less than the minimum required, add the group to the $errors array, like this:

```php
if (!isset($_POST['interests'])) {
    $_POST['interests'] = [];
}
// minimum number of required check boxes
$minCheckboxes = 2;
if (count($_POST['interests']) < $minCheckboxes) {
    $errors['interests'] = true;
}
```

The count() function returns the number of elements in an array, so this creates $errors['interests'] if fewer than two check boxes have been selected. You might be wondering why I have used a variable instead of the number like this:

```php
if (count($_POST['interests']) < 2) {
```

This certainly works and it involves less typing, but $minCheckboxes can be reused in the error message. Storing the number in a variable means this condition and the error message always remain in sync.

4. The error message in the body of the form looks like this:

```php
<h2>Interests in Japan
<?php if (isset($errors['interests'])) { ?>
    <span class="warning">Please select at least <?= $minCheckboxes ?></span>
<?php } ?>
</h2>
```

PHP Solution 6-9: Using a Drop-Down Option Menu

Drop-down option menus created with the <select> tag are similar to radio button groups in that they normally allow the user to pick only one option from several. Where they differ is one item is always selected in a drop-down menu, even if it's only the first item inviting the user to select one of the others. As a result, the $_POST array always contains an element referring to a <select> menu, whereas a radio button group is ignored unless a default value is preset.

1. The following code shows the first two items from the drop-down menu in
   contact_09.php, with the PHP code highlighted in bold. As with all multiple-
   choice elements, the PHP code wraps the attribute that indicates which item has
   been chosen. Although this attribute is called checked in both radio buttons and
   check boxes, it's called selected in <select> menus and lists. It's important to
   use the correct attribute to redisplay the selection if the form is submitted with
   required items missing. When the page first loads, the $_POST array contains no
   elements, so you can select the first <option> by testing for !$_POST. Once the
   form is submitted, the $_POST array always contains an element from a drop-
   down menu, so you don't need to test for its existence:

   ```php
   <p>
       <label for="howhear">How did you hear of Japan Journey?</label>
       <select name="howhear" id="howhear">
           <option value="No reply"
           <?php
           if (!$_POST || $_POST['howhear'] == 'No reply') {
               echo 'selected';
           } ?>>Select one</option>
           <option value="Apress"
           <?php
           if (isset($_POST && $_POST['howhear'] == 'Apress') {
               echo 'selected';
           } ?>>Apress</option>
           . . .
       </select>
   </p>
   ```

2. Even though an option is always selected in a drop-down menu, you might want
   to force users to make a selection other than the default. To do so, add the name
   attribute of the <select> menu to the $required array, and then set the value
   attribute and the $_POST array element for the default option to an empty string,
   like this:

   ```php
   <option value=""
   <?php
   if (!$_POST || $_POST['howhear'] == '') {
       echo 'selected';
   } ?>>Select one</option>
   ```

   The value attribute is not required in the <option> tag, but if you leave it out, the
   form uses the text between the opening and closing tags as the selected value.
   Therefore, it's necessary to set the value attribute explicitly to an empty string.
   Otherwise, "Select one" is transmitted as the selected value.

3. The code that displays a warning message if no selection has been made follows
   a familiar pattern:

```
<label for="select">How did you hear of Japan Journey?
<?php if (in_array('howhear', $missing)) { ?>
    <span class="warning">Please make a selection</span>
<?php } ?>
</label>
```

PHP Solution 6-10: Handling a Multiple-Choice List

Multiple-choice lists are similar to check-box groups: they allow the user to choose zero or more items, so the result is stored in an array. If no items are selected, the multiple-choice list is not included in the $_POST array, so you need to add an empty subarray in the same way as with a check-box group.

1. The following code shows the first two items from the multiple-choice list in contact_09.php, with the name attribute and PHP code highlighted in bold. The square brackets appended to the name attribute ensure that it stores the results as an array. The code works in an identical way to the check-box group in PHP Solution 6-8:

```
<p>
    <label for="characteristics">What characteristics do you associate with
    Japan?</label>
    <select name="characteristics[]" size="6" multiple="multiple"
    id="characteristics">
        <option value="Dynamic"
        <?php
        if ($_POST && in_array('Dynamic', $_POST['characteristics'])) {
            echo 'selected';
        } ?>>Dynamic</option>
        <option value="Honest"
        <?php
        if ($_POST && in_array('Honest', $_POST['characteristics'])) {
            echo 'selected';
        } ?>>Honest</option>
. . .
    </select>
</p>
```

2. In the code that processes the message, set a default value for a multiple-choice list in the same way as for an array of check boxes:

```
if (!isset($_POST['interests'])) {
  $_POST['interests'] = [];
}
if (!isset($_POST['characteristics'])) {
  $_POST['characteristics'] = [];
}
```

3. To make a multiple-choice list required and to set a minimum number of choices, use the same technique used for a check-box group in PHP Solution 6-8.

PHP Solution 6-11: Handling a Single Check Box

The way you handle a single check box is slightly different from a check-box group. With an individual check box, you don't append square brackets to the name attribute because it doesn't need to be processed as an array. Also, the value attribute is optional. If you don't set the value attribute, it defaults to "On" if the check box is selected. However, if the check box isn't selected, its name isn't included in the $_POST array, so you need to test for its existence.

This PHP solution shows how to add a single check box that seeks confirmation that the site's terms have been accepted. It assumes that selecting the check box is required.

1. This code shows the single check box, with the name attribute and PHP code highlighted in bold.

   ```
   <p>
       <input type="checkbox" name="terms" value="accepted" id="terms"
       <?php
       if ($_POST && !isset($errors['terms'])) {
           echo 'checked';
       } ?>>
       <label for="terms">I accept the terms of using this website
       <?php if (isset($errors['terms'])) { ?>
           <span class="warning">Please select the check box</span>
       <?php } ?></label>
   </p>
   ```

   The PHP block inside the <input> element inserts the checked attribute only if the $_POST array contains values and $errors['terms'] hasn't been set. This ensures that the check box is not selected when the page first loads. It also remains unchecked if the user submitted the form without confirming acceptance of the terms.

   The second PHP block displays an error message alongside the label if $errors['terms'] has been set.

2. In addition to adding terms to the $expected and $required arrays, you need to set a default value for $_POST['terms']; then set $errors['terms'] in the code that processes the data when the form is submitted:

   ```
   if (!isset($_POST['characteristics'])) {
       $_POST['characteristics'] = [];
   }
   if (!isset($_POST['terms'])) {
       $_POST['terms'] = '';
       $errors['terms'] = true;
   }
   ```

   You need to create $errors['terms'] only if the check box is required. For an optional check box, just set the value to an empty string if it's not included in the $_POST array.

Chapter Review

A lot of work has gone into building processmail.php, but the beauty of this script is that it works with any form. The only parts that need changing are the $expected and $required arrays and details specific to the form, such as the destination address, headers, and default values for multiple-choice elements that won't be included in the $_POST array if no value is selected.

I've avoided talking about HTML email because the mail() function is poorly equipped to handle it. The PHP online manual at www.php.net/manual/en/book.mail.php shows a way of sending HTML mail by adding an additional header. However, it's generally accepted that HTML mail should always contain an alternative text version for email programs that don't accept HTML. If you want to send HTML mail or attachments, try PHPMailer (https://github.com/PHPMailer/PHPMailer/).

As you'll see in later chapters, online forms lie at the heart of just about everything you do with PHP. They're the gateway between the browser and the web server. You'll come back time and again to the techniques that you have learned in this chapter.

CHAPTER 7

■■■

Using PHP to Manage Files

PHP has a huge range of functions designed to work with the server's file system, but finding the right one for the job isn't always easy. This chapter cuts through the tangle to show you some practical uses of these functions, such as reading and writing to text files to store small amounts of information without a database. Loops play an important role in inspecting the contents of the file system, so you'll also explore some of the Standard PHP Library (SPL) iterators that are designed to make loops more efficient.

As well as opening local files, PHP can read public files, such as news feeds, on other servers. News feeds are normally formatted as XML (Extensible Markup Language). In the past, extracting information from an XML file was a tortuous process, but the very aptly named SimpleXML makes it easy with PHP. In this chapter, you'll see how to create a drop-down menu that lists all images in a folder, to create a function to select files of a particular type from a folder, to pull in a live news feed from another server, and to prompt a visitor to download an image or PDF file rather than open it in the browser. As a bonus, you'll learn how to change the time zone of a date retrieved from another web site.

This chapter covers the following subjects:

- Reading and writing to files
- Listing the contents of a folder
- Inspecting files with the SplFileInfo class
- Controlling loops with SPL iterators
- Using SimpleXML to extract information from an XML file
- Consuming an RSS feed
- Creating a download link

Checking That PHP Can Open a File

Many of the PHP solutions in this chapter involve opening files for reading and writing, so it's important to make sure the correct permissions are set in your local testing environment and on your remote server. PHP is capable of reading and writing to files anywhere, as long as it has the correct permissions and knows where to find the file. So, for security, you should store files that you plan to read or write outside the web server root (typically called htdocs, public_html, or www). This prevents unauthorized people from reading your files or—worse—altering their content.

© David Powers 2022
D. Powers, *PHP 8 Solutions*, https://doi.org/10.1007/978-1-4842-7141-4_7

Most hosting companies use Linux or Unix servers, which impose strict rules about the ownership of files and directories. Check that the permissions on the directory where you store files outside the web server root have been set to 644 (this allows the owner to read and write to the directory; all other users can read only). If you still get the warning about permission being denied, consult your hosting company. If you are told to elevate any setting to 7, be aware that this gives permission for scripts to be executed, which could be exploited by a malicious attacker.

■ **Tip**   If you don't have access to a directory outside the site root, I recommend moving to a different hosting company. Files that are uploaded to a site other than by the site maintainer should always be checked before they are included in web pages. Storing them out of public view reduces any security risk.

Creating a Folder Outside the Server Root for Local Testing on Windows

For the following exercises, I suggest you create a folder called private at the top level of the C drive. There are no permissions issues on Windows, so that's all that you need to do.

Creating a Folder Outside the Server Root for Local Testing on macOS

Mac users might need to do a little more preparation because file permissions are similar to Linux. Create a folder called private in your home folder and follow the instructions in PHP Solution 7-1.

If everything goes smoothly, you won't need to do anything extra. But if you get a warning that PHP "failed to open stream," change the permissions for the private folder like this:

1.   Select private in the Mac Finder and select File ➤ Get Info (Cmd+I) to open its info panel.

2.   In Sharing & Permissions, click the padlock icon at the bottom right to unlock the settings, and then change the setting for everyone from Read only to Read & Write, as shown in the following screenshot:

3. Click the padlock icon again to preserve the new settings and close the info panel. You should now be able to use the private folder to continue with the rest of the chapter.

Configuration Settings That Affect File Access

Hosting companies can impose further restrictions on file access through php.ini. To find out what restrictions have been imposed, run phpinfo() on your web site and check the settings in the Core section. Table 7-1 lists the settings you need to check. Unless you run your own server, you normally have no control over these settings.

Table 7-1. *PHP configuration settings that affect file access*

Directive	Default value	Description
allow_url_fopen	On	Allows PHP scripts to open public files on the Internet
allow_url_include	Off	Controls the ability to include remote files

The settings in Table 7-1 both control access to files through a URL (as opposed to the local file system). The first one, allow_url_fopen, allows you to read remote files but not to include them in your scripts. This is generally safe, so the default is for it to be enabled.

On the other hand, `allow_url_include` lets you include remote files directly in your scripts. This is a major security risk, so the default is for `allow_url_include` to be disabled.

■ **Tip** If your hosting company has disabled `allow_url_fopen`, ask for it to be enabled. Otherwise, you won't be able to use PHP Solution 7-5. But don't get the names mixed up: `allow_url_include` should always be turned off in a hosting environment. Even if `allow_url_fopen` is disabled on your web site, you might still be able to access useful external data sources, such as news feeds and public XML documents using the Client URL Library (cURL). See `www.php.net/manual/en/book.curl.php` for more information.

Reading and Writing to Files

The ability to read and write to files has a wide range of applications. For example, you can open a file on another web site, read the contents into your server's memory, extract information using string and XML manipulation functions, and then write the results to a local file. You can also query a database on your own server and output the data as a text or CSV (comma-separated values) file. You can even generate files in Open Document Format or as Microsoft Excel spreadsheets. But first, let's look at the basic operations.

Reading Files in a Single Operation

PHP has three functions that read the contents of a text file in a single operation:

- **readfile()** opens a file and directly outputs its contents.
- **file_get_contents()** reads the whole contents of a file into a single string but doesn't generate direct output.
- **file()** reads each line into an array.

PHP Solution 7-1: Getting the Contents of a Text File

This PHP solution demonstrates the difference between using `readfile()`, `file_get_contents()`, and `file()` to access the contents of a file.

1. Copy `sonnet.txt` from the `ch07` folder to your `private` folder. It's a text file that contains Shakespeare's Sonnet 116.

2. Create a new folder called `filesystem` in your php8sols site root, and then create a PHP file called `get_contents.php` in the new folder. Insert the following code inside a PHP block (`get_contents_01.php` in the `ch07` folder shows the code embedded in a web page, but you can use just the PHP code for testing purposes):

   ```
   readfile('C:/private/sonnet.txt');
   ```

   If you're on a Mac, amend the path name like this, using your own Mac username:

   ```
   readfile('/Users/username/private/sonnet.txt');
   ```

If you're testing on Linux or on a remote server, amend the path name accordingly.

■ **Note** For brevity, the remaining examples in this chapter show only the Windows path name.

---

3. Save get_contents.php and view it in a browser. You should see something
   similar to the following screenshot. The browser ignores the line breaks in the
   original text and displays Shakespeare's sonnet as a solid block:

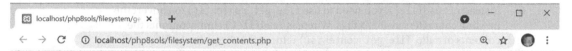

Let me not to the marriage of true minds Admit impediments; love is not love Which alters
when it alteration finds, Or bends with the remover to remove. Oh, no, it is an ever fixed
mark That looks on tempests and is never shaken; It is the star to every wand'ring bark,
Whose worth's unknown, although his height be taken. Love's not Time's fool, though rosy
lips and cheeks Within his bending sickle's compass come; Love alters not with his brief
hours and weeks, But bears it out even to the edge of Doom. If this be error and upon me
proved, I never writ, nor no man ever loved.

■ **Tip** If you see an error message, check that you typed the code correctly and that the correct file and folder
permissions have been set on a Mac or Linux.

---

4. PHP has a function called nl2br() that converts newline characters to
   tags (the trailing slash is for compatibility with XHTML and is valid in HTML5).
   Change the code in get_contents.php like this (it's in get_contents_02.php):

   ```
   nl2br(readfile('C:/private/sonnet.txt'));
   ```

5. Save get_contents.php and reload it in your browser. The output is still a
   solid block of text. When you pass one function as an argument to another one
   like this, the result of the inner function is normally passed to the outer one,
   performing both operations in a single expression. So you would expect the file's
   contents to be passed to nl2br() before being displayed in the browser. However,
   readfile() outputs the file's contents immediately. By the time it's finished,
   there's nothing for nl2br() to insert <br/> tags into. The text is already in the
   browser.

■ **Note**   When two functions are nested like this, the inner function is executed first, and the outer function processes the result. But the return value of the inner function needs to be meaningful as an argument to the outer function. The return value of readfile() is the number of bytes read from the file. Even if you add echo at the beginning of the line, all you get is 594 added to the end of the text. Nesting functions doesn't work in this case, but it's often a very useful technique, avoiding the need to store the result of the inner function in a variable before processing it with another function.

---

6. Instead of readfile(), you need to use file_get_contents() to convert the newline characters to <br/> tags. Whereas readfile() simply outputs the contents of a file, file_get_contents() returns the contents of a file as a single string. It's up to you to decide what to do with it. Amend the code like this (or use get_contents_03.php):

    ```
    echo nl2br(file_get_contents('C:/private/sonnet.txt'));
    ```

7. Reload the page in a browser. Each line of the sonnet is now on a line of its own:

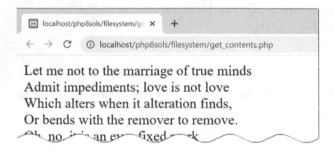

8. The advantage of file_get_contents() is that you can assign the file contents to a variable and process it in some way before deciding what to do with it. Change the code in get_contents.php like this (or use get_contents_04.php) and load the page into a browser:

    ```
    $sonnet = file_get_contents('C:/private/sonnet.txt');
    // replace new lines with spaces
    $words = str_replace("\r\n", ' ', $sonnet);
    // split into an array of words
    $words = explode(' ', $words);
    // extract the first nine array elements
    $first_line = array_slice($words, 0, 9);
    // join the first nine elements and display
    echo implode(' ', $first_line);
    ```

    This stores the contents of sonnet.txt in a variable called $sonnet, which is passed to str_replace(), which then replaces the carriage return and newline characters with a space and stores the result as $words.

■ **Note** See "Using Escape Sequences Inside Double Quotes" in Chapter 4 for an explanation of "\r\n". The text file was created in Windows, so line breaks are represented by a carriage return and newline character. Files created on macOS and Linux use only a newline character ("\n").

Then $words is passed to the explode() function. This alarmingly named function "blows apart" a string and converts it into an array, using the first argument to determine where to break the string. In this case a space is used, so the contents of the text file are split into an array of words.

The array of words is then passed to the array_slice() function, which takes a slice out of an array starting from the position specified in the second argument. The third argument specifies the length of the slice. PHP counts arrays from 0, so this extracts the first nine words.

Finally, implode() does the opposite of explode(), joining the elements of an array and inserting the first argument between each one. The result is displayed by echo, producing the following:

Let me not to the marriage of true minds

Instead of displaying the entire contents of the file, the script now displays only the first line. The full string is still stored in $sonnet.

9. However, if you want to process each line individually, it's simpler to use file(), which reads each line of a file into an array. To display the first line of sonnet. txt, the previous code can be simplified to this (see get_contents_05.php):

```
$sonnet = file('C:/private/sonnet.txt');
echo $sonnet[0];
```

10. In fact, if you don't need the full array, you can access a single line directly using a technique known as array dereferencing by adding its index number in square brackets after the call to the function. The following code displays the 11th line of the sonnet (see get_contents_06.php):

```
echo file('C:/private/sonnet.txt')[10];
```

Love alters not with his brief hours and weeks,

Of the three functions we've just explored, readfile() simply reads the content of a file and dumps it directly into the output. You can't manipulate the file content or extract information from it. However, a practical use of readfile() is to force a file to be downloaded, as you'll see later in this chapter.

The other two functions, file_get_contents() and file(), allow you to capture the contents in a variable that is ready for reformatting or extracting information. The only difference is that file_get_contents() reads the contents into a single string, whereas file() generates an array in which each element corresponds to a line in the file.

■ **Tip** The file() function preserves newline characters at the end of each array element. If you want to strip the newline characters, pass the constant FILE_IGNORE_NEW_LINES as the second argument to the function. You can also skip empty lines by using FILE_SKIP_EMPTY_LINES as the second argument. To remove newline characters and skip empty lines, separate the two constants with a vertical pipe, like this: FILE_IGNORE_NEW_LINES | FILE_SKIP_EMPTY_LINES.

Although we've tested file_get_contents() and file() only with a local text file, they can also retrieve the contents from public files on other domains. This makes them very useful for accessing information on other web pages, although extracting the information usually requires a solid understanding of string functions and the logical structure of documents as described by the Document Object Model or DOM (see www.w3.org/TR/WD-DOM/introduction.html).

The disadvantage of file_get_contents() and file() is that they read the whole file into memory. With very large files, it's preferable to use functions that process only a part of a file at a time. We'll look at those next.

Opening and Closing Files for Read/Write Operations

The functions we have looked at so far do everything in a single pass. However, PHP also has a set of functions that allow you to open a file, read it and/or write to it, and then close the file. The file can be either on the local file system or a publicly available file on a different domain.

The following are the most important functions used for this type of operation:

- fopen(): Opens a file

- fgets(): Reads the contents of a file, normally one line at a time

- fgetcsv(): Gets the current line from a CSV file and converts it into an array

- fread(): Reads a specified amount of a file

- fwrite(): Writes to a file

- feof(): Determines whether the end of the file has been reached

- rewind(): Moves the internal pointer back to the top of the file

- fseek(): Moves the internal pointer to a specific location in the file

- fclose(): Closes a file

The first of these, fopen(), offers a bewildering choice of options for how the file is to be used once it's open: fopen() has one read-only mode, four write-only modes, and five read/write modes. There are so many because they give you control over whether to overwrite the existing content or append new material. At other times, you may want PHP to create a file if it doesn't already exist.

Each mode determines where to place the internal pointer when it opens the file. It's like the cursor in a word processor: PHP starts reading or writing from wherever the pointer happens to be when you call fread() or fwrite().

Table 7-2 guides you through all the options.

Table 7-2. *Read/write modes used with fopen()*

Type	Mode	Description
Read-only	r	Internal pointer initially placed at the beginning of the file.
Write-only	w	Existing data deleted before writing. Creates a file if it doesn't already exist.
	a	Append mode. New data added at the end. Creates a file if it doesn't already exist.
	c	Existing content is preserved, but the internal pointer is placed at the beginning of the file. Creates a file if it doesn't already exist.
	x	Creates a file only if it doesn't already exist. Fails if there's already a file with the same name.
Read/write	r+	Read/write operations can take place in either order and begin wherever the internal pointer is at the time. Pointer is initially placed at the beginning of the file. File must already exist for operation to succeed.
	w+	Existing data deleted. Data can be read back after writing. Creates a file if it doesn't already exist.
	a+	Opens a file ready to add new data at the end of the file. Also permits data to be read back after internal pointer has been moved. Creates a file if it doesn't already exist.
	c+	Existing content is preserved, and the internal pointer is placed at the beginning of the file. Creates a new file if it doesn't already exist.
	x+	Creates a new file, but fails if a file of the same name already exists. Data can be read back after writing.

Choose the wrong mode, and you could end up deleting valuable data. You also need to be careful about the position of the internal pointer. If the pointer is at the end of the file and you try to read the contents, you end up with nothing. On the other hand, if the pointer is at the beginning of the file and you start writing, you overwrite the equivalent amount of existing data. "Moving the Internal Pointer" later in this chapter explains this in more detail.

You work with fopen() by passing it the following two arguments:

- The path to the file you want to open or URL if the file is on a different domain

- A string containing one of the modes listed in Table 7-2

The fopen() function returns a reference to the opened file, which can then be used with the other read/write functions. This is how you would open a text file for reading:

```
$file = fopen('C:/private/sonnet.txt', 'r');
```

Thereafter, you pass $file as the argument to other functions, such as fgets() and fclose(). Things should become clearer with a few practical demonstrations. Rather than building the files yourself, you'll probably find it easier to use the files in the ch07 folder. I'll run quickly through each mode.

■ **Note** Mac and Linux users need to adjust the path to the `private` folder in the example files to match their setup.

Reading a File with fopen( )

The file `fopen_read.php` contains the following code:

```php
// store the pathname of the file
$filename = 'C:/private/sonnet.txt';
// open the file in read-only mode
$file = fopen($filename, 'r');
// read the file and store its contents
$contents = fread($file, filesize($filename));
// close the file
fclose($file);
// display the contents with <br/> tags
echo nl2br($contents);
```

If you load this into a browser, you should see the following output:

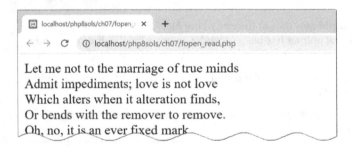

The result is identical to using `file_get_contents()` in `get_contents_03.php`. Unlike `file_get_contents()`, the function `fread()` needs to know how much of the file to read. You need to supply a second argument indicating the number of bytes. This can be useful if you want, say, only the first 100 or so characters from a very big file. However, if you want the whole file, you need to pass the file's path name to `filesize()` to get the correct figure.

The other way to read the contents of a file with `fopen()` is to use `fgets()`, which retrieves one line at a time. This means you need to use a `while` loop in combination with `feof()` to read right to the end of the file. The code in `fopen_readloop.php` looks like this:

```php
$filename = 'C:/private/sonnet.txt';
// open the file in read-only mode
$file = fopen($filename, 'r');
// create variable to store the contents
$contents = '';
// loop through each line until end of file
```

```
while (!feof($file)) {
    // retrieve next line, and add to $contents
    $contents .= fgets($file);
}
// close the file
fclose($file);
// display the contents
echo nl2br($contents);
```

The while loop uses fgets() to retrieve the contents of the file one line at a time—!feof($file) is the same as saying "until the end of $file"—and stores them in $contents.

Using fgets() is very similar to using the file() function in that it handles one line at a time. The difference is that you can break out of the loop with fgets() once you have found the information you're looking for. This is a significant advantage if you're working with a very large file. The file() function loads the entire file into an array, consuming memory.

PHP Solution 7-2: Extracting Data from a CSV File

Text files can be used as a flat-file database, where each record is stored in a single line with a comma, tab, or another delimiter between each field. This type of file is called a **CSV file**. Usually, CSV stands for comma-separated values, but it can also mean character-separated values when a tab or different delimiter is used. This PHP solution shows how to extract the values from a CSV file into a multidimensional associative array using fopen() and fgetcsv().

1. Copy weather.csv from the ch07 folder to your private folder. The file contains the following data as comma-separated values:

   ```
   city,temp
   London,11
   Paris,10
   Rome,12
   Berlin,8
   Athens,19
   ```

   The first line consists of titles for the data in the rest of the file. There are five lines of data, each containing the name of a city and a temperature.

■ **Caution** When storing data as comma-separated values, there should be no space after the comma. If you add a space, it's considered to be the first character of a data field. Each line in a CSV file must have the same number of items.

---

2. Create a file called getcsv.php in the filesystem folder and use fopen() to open weather.csv in read mode:

   ```
   $file = fopen('C:/private/weather.csv', 'r');
   ```

3. Use `fgetcsv()` to extract the first line from the file as an array, and then assign it to a variable called `$titles`:

```
$titles = fgetcsv($file);
```

This creates `$titles` as an array containing the values from the first line (city and temp).

The `fgetcsv()` function requires a single argument, the reference to the file you have opened. It also accepts up to four optional arguments:

- **The maximum length of the line**: The default value is 0, which means no limit.

- **The delimiter between fields**: Comma is the default.

- **The enclosure character**: If fields contain the delimiter as part of the data, they must be enclosed in quotes. Double quotes are the default.

- **The escape character**: The default is a backslash.

The CSV file that we're using doesn't require any of the optional arguments to be set.

4. On the next line, initialize an empty array for the values that will be extracted from the CSV data:

```
$cities = [];
```

5. After extracting values from a line, `fgetcsv()` moves to the next line. To get the remaining data from the file, you need to create a loop. Add the following code:

```
while (!(feof($file)) {
    $data = fgetcsv($file);
    $cities[] = array_combine($titles, $data);
}
```

The code inside the loop assigns the current line of the CSV file as an array to $data and then uses the `array_combine()` function to generate an associative array, which is added to the `$cities` array. This function requires two arguments, both of which must be arrays with the same number of elements. The two arrays are merged, drawing the keys for the resulting associative array from the first argument and the values from the second one.

6. Close the CSV file:

```
fclose($file);
```

7. To inspect the result, use `print_r()`. Surround it with <pre> tags to make the output easier to read:

```
echo '<pre>';
print_r($cities);
echo '</pre>';
```

8. Save getcsv.php and load it in a browser. You should see the result shown in Figure 7-1.

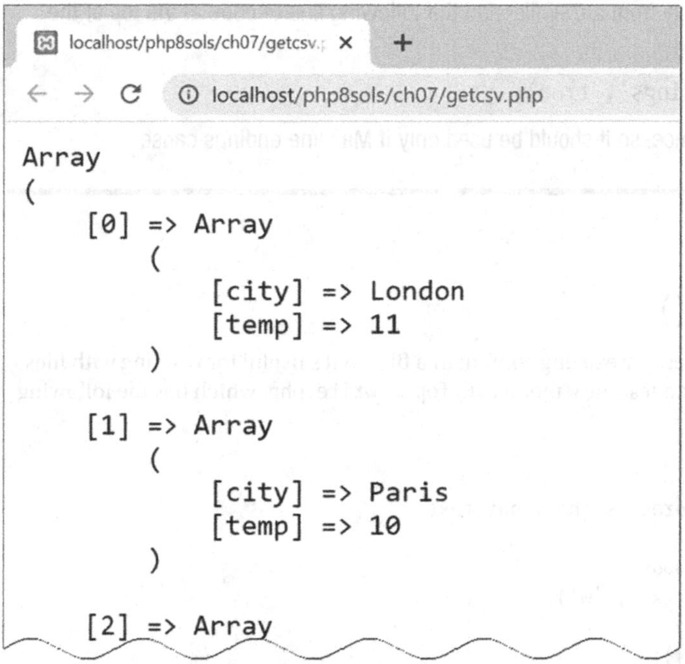

```
localhost/php8sols/ch07/getcsv.    ×    +

←  →  C    ⓘ  localhost/php8sols/ch07/getcsv.php

Array
(
    [0] => Array
        (
            [city] => London
            [temp] => 11
        )
    [1] => Array
        (
            [city] => Paris
            [temp] => 10
        )
    [2] => Array
```

Figure 7-1. The CSV data has been converted into a multidimensional associative array

9. This works well with weather.csv, but the script can be made more robust. If fgetcsv() encounters a blank line, it returns an array containing a single null element, which generates an error when passed as an argument to array_combine(). Amend the while loop by adding the conditional statement highlighted in bold:

```
while (!feof($file)) {
    $data = fgetcsv($file);
    if (empty($data[0])) {
        continue;
    }
    $cities[] = array_combine($titles, $data);
}
```

If fgetcsv() encounters a blank line, it returns an array containing a single element that is null. The conditional statement tests the first element in the $data array using the empty() function, which returns true if a variable doesn't exist or equates to false. If there's a blank line, the continue keyword returns to the top of the loop without executing the next line.

You can check your code against getcsv.php in the ch07 folder.

```
┌─────────────────────────────────────────────────────────────────────────┐
│                    CSV FILES CREATED ON MACOS                             │
└─────────────────────────────────────────────────────────────────────────┘
```

PHP often has difficulty detecting the line endings in CSV files created on Mac operating systems. If `fgetcsv()` fails to extract data correctly from a CSV file, add the following line of code at the top of the script:

```
ini_set('auto_detect_line_endings', true);
```

This has a marginal effect on performance, so it should be used only if Mac line endings cause problems with CSV files.

Replacing Content with fopen( )

The first of the write-only modes (w) deletes any existing content in a file, so it's useful for working with files that need to be updated frequently. You can test the w mode with fopen_write.php, which has the following PHP code above the DOCTYPE declaration:

```php
<?php
// if the form has been submitted, process the input text
if (isset($_POST['putContents'])) {
    // open the file in write-only mode
    $file = fopen('C:/private/write.txt', 'w');
    // write the contents
    fwrite($file, $_POST['contents']);
    // close the file
    fclose($file);
}
?>
```

When the form in the page is submitted, this code writes the value of $_POST['contents'] to a file called write.txt. The fwrite() function takes two arguments: the reference to the file and whatever you want to write to it.

■ **Note**   You may come across fputs() instead of fwrite(). The two functions are identical: fputs() is a synonym for fwrite().

If you load fopen_write.php into a browser, type something into the text area, and click Write to file. PHP creates write.txt and inserts whatever you typed into the text area. Since this is just a demonstration, I've omitted any checks to make sure that the file was successfully written. Open write.txt to verify that your text has been inserted. Now, type something different into the text area and submit the form again. The original content is deleted from write.txt and replaced with the new text.

Appending Content with fopen()

The append mode not only adds new content at the end, preserving any existing content, but it can also create a new file if it doesn't already exist. The code in fopen_append.php looks like this:

```
// open the file in append mode
$file = fopen('C:/private/append.txt', 'a');
// write the contents followed by a new line
fwrite($file, $_POST['contents'] . PHP_EOL);
// close the file
fclose($file);
```

Notice that I have concatenated PHP_EOL after $_POST['contents']. This is a PHP constant that represents a new line using the correct characters for the operating system. On Windows, it inserts a carriage return and newline character, but on Mac and Linux only a newline character.

If you load fopen_append.php into a browser, type some text, and submit the form. It creates a file called append.txt in the private folder and inserts your text. Type something else and submit the form again; the new text should be added to the end of the previous text, as shown in the following screenshot:

We'll come back to the append mode in Chapter 11.

Locking a File Before Writing

The purpose of using fopen() with c mode is to give you the opportunity to lock the file with flock() before modifying it.

The flock() function takes two arguments: the file reference and a constant specifying how the lock should operate. There are three types of operation:

- LOCK_SH acquires a shared lock for reading.

- LOCK_EX acquires an exclusive lock for writing.

- LOCK_UN releases the lock.

To lock a file before writing to it, open the file in c mode and immediately call flock(), like this:

```
// open the file in c mode
$file = fopen('C:/private/lock.txt', 'c');
// acquire an exclusive lock
flock($file, LOCK_EX);
```

This opens the file, or creates it if it doesn't already exist, and places the internal pointer at the beginning of the file. This means you need to move the pointer to the end of the file or delete the existing content before you can start writing with fwrite().

To move the pointer to the end of the file, use the fseek() function, like this:

```
// move to end of file
fseek($file, 0, SEEK_END);
```

Alternatively, delete the existing contents by calling ftruncate():

```
// delete the existing contents
ftruncate($file, 0);
```

After you have finished writing to the file, you must unlock it manually before calling fclose():

```
// unlock the file before closing
flock($file, LOCK_UN);
fclose($file);
```

■ **Caution**   If you forget to unlock the file before closing it, it remains locked to other users and processes, even if you can open it yourself.

Preventing Overwriting an Existing File

Unlike other write modes, x mode won't open an existing file. It only creates a new file ready for writing. If a file of the same name already exists, fopen() returns false, preventing you from overwriting it. The processing code in fopen_exclusive.php looks like this:

```
// create a file ready for writing only if it doesn't already exist
// error control operator prevents error message from being displayed
if ($file = @ fopen('C:/private/once_only.txt', 'x')) {
    // write the contents
    fwrite($file, $_POST['contents']);
    // close the file
    fclose($file);
} else {
    $error = 'File already exists, and cannot be overwritten.';
}
```

Attempting to write to an existing file in x mode generates a PHP warning and a fatal error. Wrapping the write and close operations in a conditional statement eliminates the fatal error, but fopen() still generates a warning. The error control operator (@) in front of fopen() suppresses the warning.

Load fopen_exclusive.php into a browser, type some text, and click Write to file. The content should be written to once_only.txt in your target folder.

If you try it again, the message stored in $error is displayed above the form.

Combined Read/Write Operations with fopen( )

By adding a plus sign (+) after any of the previous modes, the file is opened for both reading and writing. You can perform as many read or write operations as you like—and in any order—until the file is closed. The difference between the combined modes is as follows:

- r+: The file must already exist; a new one will not be automatically created. The internal pointer is placed at the beginning, ready for reading existing content.

- w+: Existing content is deleted, so there is nothing to read when the file is first opened.

- a+: The file is opened with the internal pointer at the end, ready to append new material, so the pointer needs to be moved back before anything can be read.

- c+: The file is opened with the internal pointer at the beginning.

- x+: Always creates a new file, so there's nothing to read when the file is first opened.

Reading is done with fread( ) or fgets( ) and writing with fwrite( ), exactly the same as before. What's important is to understand the position of the internal pointer.

Moving the Internal Pointer

Reading and writing operations always start wherever the internal pointer happens to be, so you normally want it to be at the beginning of the file for reading and at the end of the file for writing.

To move the pointer to the beginning, pass the file reference to rewind( ) like this:

```
rewind($file);
```

To move the pointer to the end of a file, use fseek( ) like this:

```
fseek($file, 0, SEEK_END);
```

You can also use fseek( ) to move the internal pointer to a specific position or relative to its current position. For details, see www.php.net/manual/en/function.fseek.

■ **Tip** In append mode (a or a+), content is always written to the end of the file regardless of the pointer's current position.

Exploring the File System

PHP's file system functions can also open directories (folders) and inspect their contents. From the web developer's point of view, practical uses of the file system functions include building drop-down menus that display the contents of a folder and creating a script that prompts a user to download a file, such as an image or PDF document.

Inspecting a Folder with scandir()

The scandir() function returns an array consisting of the files and folders within a specified folder. Just pass the path name of the folder (directory) as a string to scandir() and store the result in a variable like this:

```
$files = scandir('../images');
```

You can examine the result by using print_r() to display the contents of the array, as shown in the following screenshot (the code is in scandir.php in the ch07 folder):

```
Array
(
    [0] => .
    [1] => ..
    [2] => basin.jpg
    [3] => fountains.jpg
    [4] => fuji.jpg
    [5] => kinkakuji.jpg
    [6] => maiko.jpg
    [7] => maiko_phone.jpg
    [8] => menu.jpg
    [9] => monk.jpg
    [10] => ryoanji.jpg
    [11] => thumbs
)
```

The array returned by scandir() doesn't contain just files. The first two items are known as dot files, which represent the current and parent folders. The final item is a folder called thumbs.

The array contains only the names of each item. If you want more information about the contents of a folder, it's better to use the FilesystemIterator class.

Inspecting the Contents of a Folder with FilesystemIterator

The FilesystemIterator class lets you loop through the contents of a directory or folder. It's part of the Standard PHP Library (SPL), a core part of PHP. Among the main features of the SPL is a collection of specialized iterators that create sophisticated loops with very little code.

Because it's a class, you instantiate a FilesystemIterator object with the new keyword and pass the path of the folder you want to inspect to the constructor, like this:

```
$files = new FilesystemIterator('../images');
```

Unlike scandir(), this doesn't return an array of filenames, so you can't use print_r() to display its contents. Instead, it creates an object that gives you access to everything inside the folder. To display the filenames, use a foreach loop like this (the code is in iterator_01.php in the ch07 folder):

```
$files = new FilesystemIterator('../images');
foreach ($files as $file) {
    echo $file . '<br>';
}
```

This produces the following result:

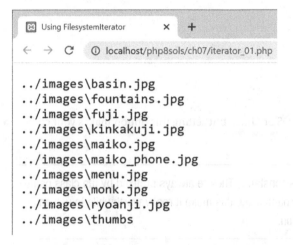

The following observations can be made about this output:

- The dot files representing the current and parent folders are omitted.

- The value displayed represents the relative path to the file rather than just the filename.

- Because the screenshot was taken on Windows, a backslash is used in the relative path.

In most circumstances, the backslash is unimportant, because PHP accepts either forward- or backslashes in Windows paths. However, if you want to generate URLs from the output of FilesystemIterator, there's an option to use Unix-style paths. One way to set the option is to pass a constant as the second argument to FilesystemIterator(), like this (see iterator_02.php):

```
$files = new FilesystemIterator('../images', FilesystemIterator::UNIX_PATHS);
```

Alternatively, you can invoke the setFlags() method on the FilesystemIterator object like this (see iterator_03.php):

```
$files = new FilesystemIterator('../images');
$files->setFlags(FilesystemIterator::UNIX_PATHS);
```

Both produce the output shown in the following screenshot:

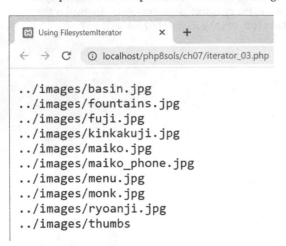

```
../images/basin.jpg
../images/fountains.jpg
../images/fuji.jpg
../images/kinkakuji.jpg
../images/maiko.jpg
../images/maiko_phone.jpg
../images/menu.jpg
../images/monk.jpg
../images/ryoanji.jpg
../images/thumbs
```

Of course, this won't make any difference on macOS or Linux, but setting this option makes your code more portable.

■ **Tip** The constants used by SPL classes are all class constants. They're always prefixed by the class name and the scope resolution operator (two colons). Lengthy names like this make it really worthwhile to use an editing program with PHP code hints and code completion.

Although it's useful to be able to display the relative paths of the folder's contents, the real value of using the FilesystemIterator class is that each time the loop runs, it gives you access to an SplFileInfo object. The SplFileInfo class has nearly 30 methods that can be used to extract useful information about files and folders. Table 7-3 lists a selection of the most useful SplFileInfo methods.

Table 7-3. *File information accessible through SplFileInfo methods*

Method	Returns
getFilename()	The name of the file
getPath()	The current object's relative path minus the filename, or minus the folder name if the current object is a folder
getPathName()	The current object's relative path, including the filename or folder name, depending on the current type
getRealPath()	The current object's full path, including filename if appropriate
getSize()	The size of the file or folder in bytes
isDir()	True, if the current object is a folder (directory)
isFile()	True, if the current object is a file
isReadable()	True, if the current object is readable
isWritable()	True, if the current object is writable

To access the contents of subfolders, use the RecursiveDirectoryIterator class. This burrows down through each level of the folder structure, but you need to use it in combination with the curiously named RecursiveIteratorIterator, like this (the code is in iterator_04.php):

```
$files = new RecursiveDirectoryIterator('../images');
$files->setFlags(RecursiveDirectoryIterator::SKIP_DOTS);
$files = new RecursiveIteratorIterator($files);
foreach ($files as $file) {
    echo $file->getRealPath() . '<br>';
}
```

■ **Note** By default, the RecursiveDirectoryIterator includes the dot files that represent the current and parent folders. To exclude them, you need to pass the class's SKIP_DOTS constant as the second argument to the constructor method or use the setFlags() method.

As the following screenshot shows, the RecursiveDirectoryIterator inspects the contents of all subfolders, revealing the contents of the thumbs folder, in a single operation:

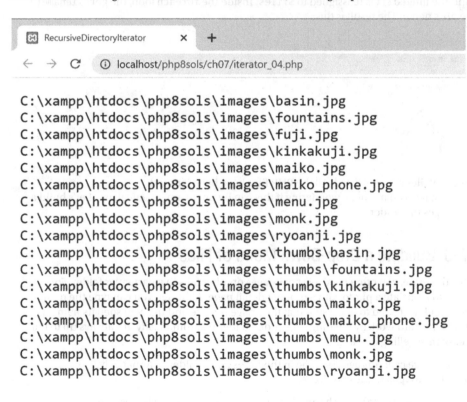

What if you want to find only certain types of files? Cue another iterator...

Restricting File Types with the RegexIterator

The RegexIterator acts as a wrapper to another iterator, filtering its contents using a regular expression (regex) as a search pattern. Let's say you want to find the text and CSV files in the ch07 folder. The regex used to search for .txt and .csv filename extensions looks like this:

```
'/\.(?:txt|csv)$/i'
```

This regex matches those two filename extensions in a case-insensitive manner. The code in iterator_05.php looks like this:

```
$files = new FilesystemIterator('.');
$files = new RegexIterator($files, '/\.(?:txt|csv)$/i');
foreach ($files as $file) {
    echo $file->getFilename() . '<br>';
}
```

The dot passed to the FilesystemIterator constructor tells it to inspect the current folder. The original $files object is then passed as the first argument to the RegexIterator constructor, with the regex as the second argument, and the filtered set is reassigned to $files. Inside the foreach loop, the getFilename() method retrieves the file's name. The result is this:

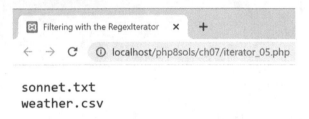

```
sonnet.txt
weather.csv
```

Only the text and CSV files are now listed. All the PHP files have been ignored.

I expect that by this stage, you might be wondering if this can be put to any practical use. Let's build a drop-down menu of images in a folder.

PHP Solution 7-3: Building a Drop-Down Menu of Files

When you work with a database, you often need a list of images or other files in a particular folder. For instance, you may want to associate a photo with a product detail page. Although you can type the name of the image into a text field, you need to make sure that the image is there and that you spell its name correctly. Get PHP to do the hard work by building a drop-down menu automatically. It's always up to date, and there's no danger of misspelling the name.

1. Create a PHP page called imagelist.php in the filesystem folder. Alternatively, use imagelist_01.php in the ch07 folder.

2. Create a form inside imagelist.php and insert a <select> element with just one <option>, like this (the code is already in imagelist_01.php):

```
<form method="post">
    <select name="pix" id="pix">
        <option value="">Select an image</option>
    </select>
</form>
```

3. This <option> is the only static element in the drop-down menu.

4. Amend the <select> element in the form like this:

```
<select name="pix" id="pix">
    <option value="">Select an image</option>
    <?php
    $files = new FilesystemIterator('../images');
    $images = new RegexIterator($files, '/\.(?:jpg|png|gif|webp)$/i');
    foreach ($images as $image) {
        $filename = $image->getFilename();
    ?>
        <option value="<?= $filename ?>"><?= $filename ?></option>
    <?php } ?>
</select>
```

Make sure that the path to the images folder is correct for your site's folder structure. The regex used as the second argument to the RegexIterator constructor matches case-insensitive files with the filename extensions .jpg, .png, .gif, and .webp.

The foreach loop simply gets the filename of the current image and inserts it into the <option> element.

Save imagelist.php and load it into a browser. You should see a drop-down menu listing all the images in your images folder, as shown in Figure 7-2.

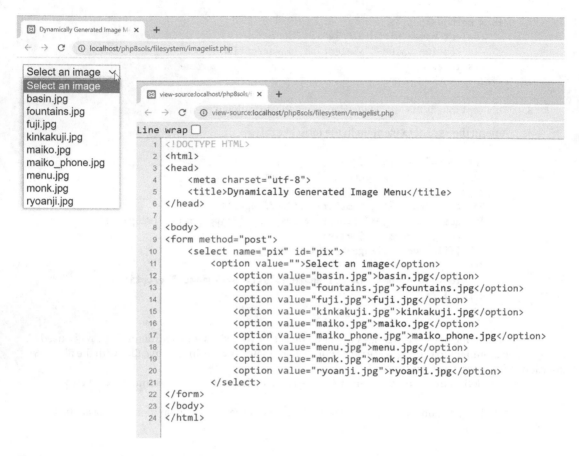

Figure 7-2. *PHP makes light work of creating a drop-down menu of images in a specific folder*

When incorporated into an online form, the filename of the selected image appears in the $_POST array and is identified by the name attribute of the <select> element—in this case, $_POST['pix']. That's all there is to it!

You can compare your code with imagelist_02.php in the ch07 folder.

PHP Solution 7-4: Creating a Generic File Selector

The previous PHP solution relies on an understanding of regular expressions. Adapting it to work with other filename extensions isn't difficult, but you need to be careful that you don't accidentally delete a vital character. Unless regexes are your specialty, it's probably easier to wrap the code in a function that can be used to inspect a specific folder and create an array of filenames of specific types. For example, you might want to create an array of PDF document filenames or one that contains both PDFs and Word documents. Here's how you do it.

1. Create a new file called buildlist.php in the filesystem folder. The file will contain only PHP code, so delete any HTML inserted by your editing program.

2. Add the following code to the file:

```php
function buildFileList(string $dir, string|array $extensions) {
    if (!is_dir($dir) && !is_readable($dir)) {
        return false;
    } else {
        if (is_array($extensions)) {
            $extensions = implode('|', $extensions);
        }
    }
}
```

3. This defines a function called `buildFileList()`, which takes two arguments:

- `$dir`: The path to the folder from which you want to get the list of filenames. This must be a string.

- `$extensions`: The function signature uses a union type declaration, which is new to PHP 8. It specifies that the argument can be either a string or an array. This should be a single filename extension or an array of filename extensions. To keep the code simple, the extensions should not include a leading period.

The function begins by checking whether `$dir` is a folder and is readable. If it isn't, the function returns `false`, and no more code is executed.

If `$dir` is okay, the `else` block is executed. It also begins with a conditional statement that checks whether `$extensions` is an array. If it is, it's passed to `implode()`, which joins the array elements with a vertical pipe (`|`) between each one. A vertical pipe is used in regexes to indicate alternative values. Let's say the following array is passed to the function as the second argument:

```php
['jpg', 'png', 'gif']
```

The conditional statement converts it to `jpg|png|gif`. So this looks for `jpg` or `png` or `gif`. However, if the argument is a string, it remains untouched.

4. You can now build the regex search pattern and pass both arguments to the `FilesystemIterator` and `RegexIterator`, like this:

```php
function buildFileList(string $dir, string|array $extensions) {
    if (!is_dir($dir) && !is_readable($dir)) {
        return false;
    } else {
        if (is_array($extensions)) {
            $extensions = implode('|', $extensions);
        }
        $pattern = "/\.(?:{$extensions})$/i";
        $folder = new FilesystemIterator($dir);
        $files = new RegexIterator($folder, $pattern);
    }
}
```

The regex pattern is built using a string in double quotes and wrapping $extensions in curly braces to make sure it's interpreted correctly by the PHP engine. Take care when copying the code. It's not exactly easy to read.

5. The final section of the code extracts the filenames to build an array, which is sorted and then returned. The finished function definition looks like this:

```php
function buildFileList(string $dir, string|array $extensions) {
    if (!is_dir($dir) && !is_readable($dir)) {
        return false;
    } else {
        if (is_array($extensions)) {
            $extensions = implode('|', $extensions);
        }
        $pattern = "/\.(?:{$extensions})$/i";
        $folder = new FilesystemIterator($dir);
        $files = new RegexIterator($folder, $pattern);
        $filenames = [];
        foreach ($files as $file) {
            $filenames[] = $file->getFilename();
        }
        natcasesort($filenames);
        return $filenames;
    }
}
```

This initializes an array and uses a foreach loop to assign the filenames to it with the getFilename() method. Finally, the array is passed to natcasesort(), which sorts it in a natural, case-insensitive order. What "natural" means is that strings that contain numbers are sorted in the same way as a person would. For example, a computer normally sorts img12.jpg before img2.jpg, because the 1 in 12 is lower than 2. Using natcasesort() results in img2.jpg preceding img12.jpg.

6. To use the function, use as arguments the path to the folder and the filename extensions of the files you want to find. For example, you could get all Word and PDF documents from a folder like this:

```php
$docs = buildFileList('folder_name', ['doc', 'docx', 'pdf']);
```

You can then loop through $docs in a foreach loop to build the option elements of a select list in the same way as in step 3 of PHP Solution 7-3.

The code for the buildFileList() function is in buildlist.php in the ch07 folder.

Accessing Remote Files

Reading, writing to, and inspecting files on your local computer or on your own web site are useful. But allow_url_fopen also gives you access to publicly available documents anywhere on the Internet. You can read the content, save it to a variable, and manipulate it with PHP functions before incorporating it in your own pages or saving the information to a database.

A word of caution: When extracting material from remote sources for inclusion in your own pages, there's a security risk. For example, a remote page might contain malicious scripts embedded in <script> tags or hyperlinks. Even if the remote page supplies data in a known format from a trusted source—such as product details from the Amazon.com database, weather information from a government meteorological office, or a news feed from a newspaper or broadcaster—you should always sanitize the content by passing it to htmlentities() (see PHP Solution 6-3). As well as converting double quotes to ", htmlentities() converts < to < and > to >. This displays tags in plain text, rather than treating them as HTML.

If you want to permit some HTML tags, use the strip_tags() function instead. If you pass a string to strip_tags(), it returns the string with all HTML tags and comments stripped out. It also removes PHP tags. A second, optional argument is a list of tags that you want preserved. For example, the following strips out all tags except paragraphs and first- and second-level headings:

```
$stripped = strip_tags($original, '<p><h1><h2>');
```

Consuming News and Other RSS Feeds

Some of the most useful remote sources of information that you might want to incorporate in your sites come from RSS feeds. RSS stands for Really Simple Syndication, and it's a dialect of XML. XML is similar to HTML in that it uses tags to mark up content. Instead of defining paragraphs, headings, and images, XML tags are used to organize data in a predictable hierarchy. XML is written in plain text, so it's frequently used to share information between computers that might be running on different operating systems.

Figure 7-3 shows the typical structure of an RSS 2.0 feed. The whole document is wrapped in a pair of <rss> tags. This is the root element, similar to the <html> tags of a web page. The rest of the document is wrapped in a pair of <channel> tags, which always contain the following three elements that describe the RSS feed: <title>, <description>, and <link>.

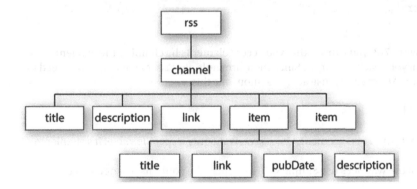

Figure 7-3. *The main contents of an RSS feed are in the item elements*

In addition to the three required elements, the <channel> can contain many other elements, but the interesting material is to be found in the <item> elements. In the case of a news feed, this is where the individual news items can be found. If you're looking at the RSS feed from a blog, the <item> elements normally contain summaries of the blog posts.

Each <item> element can contain several elements, but those shown in Figure 7-3 are the most common and usually the most interesting:

- <title>: The title of the item
- <link>: The URL of the item

- `<pubDate>`: Date of publication

- `<description>`: Summary of the item

This predictable format makes it easy to extract the information using SimpleXML.

■ **Note** You can find the full RSS specification at `www.rssboard.org/rss-specification`. Unlike most technical specifications, it's written in plain language and is easy to read.

Using SimpleXML

As long as you know the structure of an XML document, SimpleXML does what it says on the tin: it makes extracting information from XML simple. The first step is to pass the URL of the XML document to `simplexml_load_file()`. You can also load a local XML file by passing the path as an argument. For example, this gets the world news feed from the BBC:

```
$feed = simplexml_load_file('http://feeds.bbci.co.uk/news/world/rss.xml');
```

This creates an instance of the `SimpleXMLElement` class. All the elements in the feed can now be accessed as properties of the `$feed` object by using the names of the elements. With an RSS feed, the `<item>` elements can be accessed as `$feed->channel->item`.

To display the `<title>` of each `<item>`, create a `foreach` loop like this:

```
foreach ($feed->channel->item as $item) {
    echo $item->title . '<br>';
}
```

If you compare this with Figure 7-3, you can see that you access elements by chaining the element names with the `->` operator until you reach the target. Since there are multiple `<item>` elements, you need to use a loop to tunnel further down. Alternatively, use array notation, like this:

```
$feed->channel->item[2]->title
```

This gets the `<title>` of the third `<item>` element. Unless you want only a specific value, it's simpler to use a loop.

With that background out of the way, let's use SimpleXML to display the contents of a news feed.

PHP Solution 7-5: Consuming an RSS News Feed

This PHP solution shows how to extract the information from a live news feed using SimpleXML and then display it on a web page. It also shows how to format the `<pubDate>` element to a more user-friendly format and how to limit the number of items displayed using the `LimitIterator` class.

1. Create a new page called `newsfeed.php` in the `filesystem` folder. This page will contain a mixture of PHP and HTML.

2. The news feed chosen for this PHP solution is BBC World News. A condition of using most news feeds is that you acknowledge the source. So add The Latest from BBC News formatted as an `<h1>` heading at the top of the page.

■ **Note** For the terms and conditions of using a BBC news feed on your own site, see www.bbc.co.uk/
news/10628494#mysite and www.bbc.co.uk/usingthebbc/terms/can-i-share-things-from-
the-bbc/.

3. Create a PHP block below the heading and add the following code to load the feed:

```
$url = 'https://feeds.bbci.co.uk/news/world/rss.xml';
$feed = simplexml_load_file($url);
```

4. Use a foreach loop to access the <item> elements and display the <title> of
each one:

```
foreach ($feed->channel->item as $item) {
    echo htmlentities($item->title) . '<br>';
}
```

5. Save newsfeed.php and load the page in a browser. You should see a long list of
news items similar to Figure 7-4.

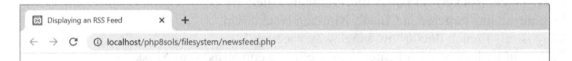

The Latest from BBC News

Israel-Gaza: Rockets hit Israel after militants killed
Uyghur imams targeted in China's Xinjiang crackdown
Why is this French doctor throwing away vaccines?
Tesla will no longer accept Bitcoin over climate concerns, says Musk
Liz Cheney: Republican ousted from leadership for challenging Trump election claims
Chinese county bans birthday parties in bid to be frugal

Figure 7-4. The news feed contains a large number of items

6. The normal feed often contains 30 or more items. That's fine for a news site, but
you probably want a shorter selection in your own site. Use another SPL iterator
to select a specific range of items. Amend the code like this:

```
$url = 'http://feeds.bbci.co.uk/news/world/rss.xml';
$feed = simplexml_load_file($url, 'SimpleXMLIterator');
$filtered = new LimitIterator($feed->channel->item, 0 , 4);
foreach ($filtered as $item) {
    echo htmlentities($item->title) . '<br>';
}
```

To use SimpleXML with an SPL iterator, you need to supply the name of the SimpleXMLIterator class as the second argument to simplexml_load_file(). You can then pass the SimpleXML element you want to affect to an iterator constructor.

In this case, $feed->channel->item is passed to the LimitIterator constructor. The LimitIterator takes three arguments: the object you want to limit, the starting point (counting from 0), and the number of times you want the loop to run. This code starts at the first item and limits the number of items to four.

The foreach loop now loops over the $filtered result. If you test the page again, you'll see just four titles, as shown in Figure 7-5. Don't be surprised if the selection of headlines is different from before. The BBC News web site is updated every minute.

Figure 7-5. *The LimitIterator restricts the number of items displayed*

7. Now that you have limited the number of items, amend the foreach loop to wrap the <title> elements in a link to the original article, and then display the <pubDate> and <description> items. The loop looks like this:

```
foreach ($filtered as $item) { ?>
    <h2><a href="<?= htmlentities($item->link) ?>">
        <?= htmlentities($item->title)?></a></h2>
    <p class="datetime"><?= htmlentities($item->pubDate) ?></p>
    <p><?= htmlentities($item->description) ?></p>
<?php } ?>
```

8. Save the page and test it again. The links take you directly to the relevant news story on the BBC web site. The news feed is now functional, but the <pubDate> format follows the format laid down in the RSS specification, as shown in the next screenshot:

Israel-Gaza: Rockets hit Israel after militants killed

Thu, 13 May 2021 06:27:48 GMT

9. To format the date and time in a more user-friendly way, pass $item->pubDate to the DateTime class constructor, and then use the DateTime format() method to display it. Change the code in the foreach loop, like this:

```
<p class="datetime"><?php $date = new DateTime($item->pubDate);
echo $date->format('M j, Y, g:ia'); ?></p>
```

This reformats the date as follows:

May 13, 2021, 6:27am

The mysterious PHP formatting strings for dates are explained in Chapter 16.

10. That looks a lot better, but the time is still expressed in GMT (London time). If most of your site's visitors live on the East Coast of the United States, you probably want to show the local time. That's no problem with a DateTime object. Use the setTimezone() method to change to New York time. You can even automate the display of EDT (Eastern Daylight Time) or EST (Eastern Standard Time) depending on whether daylight saving time is in operation. Amend the code like this:

```
<p class="datetime"><?php $date = new DateTime($item->pubDate);
$date->setTimezone(new DateTimeZone('America/New_York'));
$offset = $date->getOffset();
$timezone = ($offset == -14400) ? ' EDT' : ' EST';
echo $date->format('M j, Y, g:ia') . $timezone; ?></p>
```

To create a DateTimeZone object, pass to it as an argument one of the time zones listed at www.php.net/manual/en/timezones.php. This is the only place that the DateTimeZone object is needed, so it has been created directly as the argument to the setTimezone() method.

There isn't a dedicated method that tells you whether daylight saving time is in operation, but the getOffset() method returns the number of seconds the time is offset from Coordinated Universal Time (UTC). The following line determines whether to display EDT or EST:

```
$timezone = ($offset == -14400) ? ' EDT' : ' EST';
```

This uses the value of $offset with the ternary operator. In summer, New York is 4 hours behind UTC (–14440 seconds). So, if $offset is –14400, the condition equates to true, and EDT is assigned to $timezone. Otherwise, EST is used.

Finally, the value of $timezone is concatenated to the formatted time. The string used for $timezone has a leading space to separate the time zone from the time. When the page is loaded, the time is adjusted to the East Coast of the United States, like this:

May 13, 2021, 2:27am EDT

187

11. All the page needs now is smartening up with CSS. Figure 7-6 shows the finished news feed styled with newsfeed.css in the styles folder.

Figure 7-6. *The live news feed requires only a dozen lines of PHP code*

Although I have used the BBC news feed for this PHP solution, it should work with any RSS 2.0 feed. For example, you can try it locally with http://rss.cnn.com/rss/edition.rss. Using a CNN news feed in a public web site requires permission from CNN. Always check with the copyright holder for terms and conditions before incorporating a feed into a web site.

Creating a Download Link

A question that crops up regularly in online forums is "How do I create a link to an image (or PDF file) that prompts the user to download it?" The quick solution is to convert the file into a compressed format, such as ZIP. This frequently results in a smaller download, but the downside is that inexperienced users may not know how to unzip the file, or they may be using an older operating system that doesn't include an extraction facility. With PHP file system functions, it's easy to create a link that automatically prompts the user to download a file in its original format.

PHP Solution 7-6: Prompting a User to Download an Image

This PHP solution sends the necessary HTTP headers and uses readfile() to output the contents of a file as a binary stream, forcing the browser to download it.

1. Create a PHP file called download.php in the filesystem folder. The full listing is given in the next step. You can also find it in download.php in the ch07 folder.

2. Remove any default code created by your script editor and insert the following code:

```php
<?php
// define error page
$error = 'http://localhost/php8sols/error.php';
// define the path to the download folder
$filepath = 'C:/xampp/htdocs/php8sols/images/';
$getfile = NULL;
// block any attempt to explore the filesystem
if (isset($_GET['file']) && basename($_GET['file']) == $_GET['file']) {
    $getfile = $_GET['file'];
} else {
    header("Location: $error");
  exit;
}
if ($getfile) {
    $path = $filepath . $getfile;
    // check that it exists and is readable
    if (file_exists($path) && is_readable($path)) {
        // send the appropriate headers
        header('Content-Type: application/octet-stream');
        header('Content-Length: '. filesize($path));
        header('Content-Disposition: attachment; filename=' . $getfile);
        header('Content-Transfer-Encoding: binary');
        // output the file content
        readfile($path);
    } else {
        header("Location: $error");
    }
}
```

The only two lines that you need to change in this script are highlighted in bold. The first defines $error, a variable that contains the URL of your error page. The second line that needs to be changed defines the path to the folder where the download file is stored.

The script works by taking the name of the file to be downloaded from a query string appended to the URL and saving it as $getfile. Because query strings can be easily tampered with, $getfile is initially set to NULL. If you fail to do this, you could give a malicious user access to any file on your server.

The opening conditional statement uses basename() to make sure that an attacker cannot request a file, such as one that stores passwords, from another part of your file structure. As explained in Chapter 5, basename() extracts the filename component of a path, so if basename($_GET['file']) is different from $_GET['file'], you know there's an attempt to probe your server. You can then stop the script from going any further by using the header() function to redirect the user to the error page.

After checking that the requested file exists and is readable, the script sends the appropriate HTTP headers and uses readfile() to send the file to the output buffer. If the file can't be found, the user is redirected to the error page.

3. Test the script by creating another page; add a couple of links to download.php. Add a query string at the end of each link with file= followed by the name of a file to be downloaded. You'll find a page called getdownloads.php in the ch07 folder that contains the following two links:

```
<p><a href="download.php?file=fountains.jpg">Download fountains image</a></p>
<p><a href="download.php?file=monk.jpg">Download monk image</a></p>
```

4. Click one of the links. Depending on your browser settings, the file will either be downloaded to your default Downloads folder, or you will be presented with a dialog box asking you what to do with the file.

I've demonstrated download.php with image files, but it can be used for any type of file, as the headers send the file as a binary stream.

■ **Caution**   This script relies on header() to send the appropriate HTTP headers to the browser. It is vital to ensure that there are no new lines or whitespace ahead of the opening PHP tag. If you have removed all whitespace and still get an error message saying "headers already sent," your editor may have inserted invisible control characters at the beginning of the file. Some editing programs insert the byte order mark (BOM), which is known to cause problems with the header() function. Check your program preferences to make sure the option to insert the BOM is deselected.

Chapter Review

The file system functions aren't particularly difficult to use, but there are many subtleties that can turn a seemingly simple task into a complicated one. It's important to check that you have the right permissions. Even when handling files in your own web site, PHP needs permission to access any folder where you want to read files or write to them.

The SPL FilesystemIterator and RecursiveDirectoryIterator classes make it easy to examine the contents of folders. Used in combination with the SplFileInfo methods and the RegexIterator, you can quickly find files of a specific type within a folder or folder hierarchy.

When dealing with remote data sources, you need to check that allow_url_fopen hasn't been disabled. One of the most common uses of remote data sources is to extract information from RSS news feeds or XML documents, a task that takes only a few lines of code, thanks to SimpleXML.

Later in this book, we'll put some of the PHP solutions from this chapter to further practical use when working with images and building a simple user authentication system.

CHAPTER 8

■ ■ ■

Working with Arrays

Arrays are one of the most versatile data types in PHP. Their importance is reflected by the fact that there are more than 80 core functions dedicated to handling data stored in arrays. They can be generally categorized as for modifying, sorting, comparing, and extracting information from arrays. This chapter doesn't attempt to cover all of them. It focuses on some of the more interesting and useful applications of manipulating arrays.

This chapter covers

- Understanding various approaches to modifying the contents of an array
- Merging arrays
- Converting an array to a grammatical string
- Finding all permutations of an array
- Sorting arrays
- Automatically generating nested HTML lists from a multidimensional array
- Extracting data from JSON
- Assigning array elements to variables
- Unpacking arrays with the splat operator

Modifying Array Elements

Newcomers to PHP are frequently left scratching their head when they try to modify each element in an array. Say, for example, you want to perform a calculation with each element in an array of numbers. The simple way to do so appears to be to use a loop, perform the calculation inside the loop, and reassign the result to the current element, like this:

```
$numbers = [2, 4, 7];
foreach ($numbers as $number) {
    $number *= 2;
}
```

It looks as though it should work; but it doesn't. The values in the $numbers array remain unchanged. This happens because PHP works on a *copy* of the array inside a loop. The copy is discarded when the loop ends, and with it the results of the calculations. To change the original array, the value of each element needs to be passed by reference into the loop.

© David Powers 2022
D. Powers, *PHP 8 Solutions*, https://doi.org/10.1007/978-1-4842-7141-4_8

PHP Solution 8-1: Modify Array Elements with a Loop

This PHP solution shows how to modify each element in an array using a foreach loop. The technique is similar for both indexed and associative arrays.

1. Open modify_01.php in the ch08 folder. It contains the code in the previous section followed by print_r($numbers); between a pair of <pre> tags.

2. Load the page into a browser to verify that the values in the $numbers array are unchanged, as shown in the following screenshot:

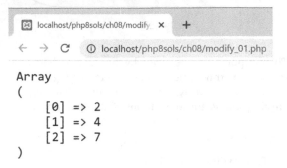

```
Array
(
    [0] => 2
    [1] => 4
    [2] => 7
)
```

3. Pass the value of each array element to the loop by reference by prefixing the temporary variable in the loop declaration with an ampersand like this:

    ```
    foreach ($numbers as &$number) {
    ```

4. When the loop ends, the temporary variable will still contain the recalculated value of the final array element. To avoid accidentally changing the value later, it's recommended to unset the temporary variable after the loop like this:

    ```
    foreach ($numbers as &$number) {
        $number *= 2;
    }
    unset($number);
    ```

5. Save the file and load it in a browser to test the amended code (it's in modify_02.php). Each number in the array should have been doubled, as the following screenshot shows:

```
Array
(
    [0] => 4
    [1] => 8
    [2] => 14
)
```

6. To modify the values of an associative array, you need to declare temporary variables for both the key and the value; but only the value should be passed by reference. The following code is in `modify_03.php`

```
:$book = [
    'author' => 'David Powers',
    'title' => 'PHP 8 Solutions'
];
foreach ($book as $key => &$value) {
    $book[$key] = strtoupper($value);
}
unset($value);
```

This produces the following output:

```
localhost/php8sols/ch08/modify    ×    +

←  →  C    ⓘ  localhost/php8sols/ch08/modify_03.php
```

```
Array
(
    [author] => DAVID POWERS
    [title] => PHP 8 SOLUTIONS
)
```

7. Let's say, however, that you want to modify the array keys. The logical approach would be to precede the key with an ampersand to pass it by reference like this:

```
foreach ($book as &$key => $value) {
```

However, if you attempt to do this, it triggers a fatal error. Array keys cannot be passed by reference. Only array values can.

8. To modify each key of an associative array, just modify it inside the loop in exactly the same way as outside a loop. The following code is in `modify_04.php`:

```
foreach ($book as $key => $value) {
    $book[ucfirst($key)] = $value;
}
```

It produces the following output:

```
localhost/php8sols/ch08/modify  ×  +

←  →  C   ⓘ localhost/php8sols/ch08/modify_04.php

Array
(
    [author] => David Powers
    [title] => PHP 8 Solutions
    [Author] => David Powers
    [Title] => PHP 8 Solutions
)
```

9. As the preceding screenshot shows, the original keys are preserved alongside the modified ones. If you want only the modified keys, you need to unset the original ones inside the loop like this (the code is in modify_05.php):

```
foreach ($book as $key => $value) {
    $book[ucfirst($key)] = $value;
    unset($book[$key]);
}
```

This preserves only the modified version of each key.

■ **Tip** If you want to convert array keys to uppercase or lowercase, the simple way to do so is to use the array_change_key_case() function as described in the following PHP solution.

PHP Solution 8-2: Modify Array Elements with array_walk()

An alternative to using a loop to modify array elements is to use the array_walk() function, which applies a callback function to each element of an array. The callback can be an anonymous function, an arrow function (see "Using the Concise Anonymous Syntax of Arrow Functions" in Chapter 4), or the name of a defined function. By default, array_walk() passes two arguments to the callback: the element's value and key—*in that order*. An optional third argument can also be used. This PHP solution explores the various ways that array_walk() can be used.

1. The main code in array_walk_01.php in the ch08 folder looks like this:

```
$numbers = [2, 4, 7];

array_walk($numbers, fn (&$val) => $val *= 2);
```

The first argument to array_walk() is the array that the callback function will be applied to. The second argument is the callback, in this case, an arrow function. As with a foreach loop, the value needs to be passed by reference, so the first argument to the callback function is preceded by an ampersand.

This example modifies an indexed array, so there is no need to pass the array key as the second argument to the callback function.

Applying `array_walk()` like this produces the same result as `modify_02.php` in the previous PHP solution: each value in the $numbers array is doubled.

2. When using array_walk() with an associative array, there's no need to pass the array key as an argument to the callback function if you only want to modify the value. The code in array_walk_02.php uses an arrow function to convert the value of each array element to an uppercase string like this:

```
$book = [
    'author' => 'David Powers',
    'title' => 'PHP 8 Solutions'
];
array_walk($book, fn (&$val) => $val = strtoupper($val));
```

This produces the same output as `modify_03.php` in the preceding PHP solution.

3. Instead of passing an anonymous or arrow function as the second argument to `array_walk()`, you can pass the name of a defined function as a string like this (the code is in `array_walk_03.php`):

```
array_walk($book, 'output');
function output (&$val) {
    return $val = strtoupper($val);
}
```

This produces the same output as the preceding example. If the function definition is in the same file, it doesn't matter whether it comes before or after the call to `array_walk()`. However, if the definition is in an external file, the file must be included before invoking `array_walk()`.

4. The callback function passed to `array_walk()` can take up to three arguments. The second argument must be the array key, whereas the final argument can be any other value that you want to use. When the third argument is used, it is also passed as the third argument to `array_walk()`. The following example in `array_walk_04.php` demonstrates its use:

```
array_walk($book, 'output', 'is');
function output (&$val, $key, $verb) {
    return $val = "The $key of this book $verb $val.";
}
```

This produces the following output:

```
Array
(
    [author] => The author of this book is David Powers.
    [title] => The title of this book is PHP 8 Solutions.
)
```

5. With array_walk(), you can't modify the array keys. If you simply want to
    change all keys to uppercase or lowercase, use array_change_key_case(). By
    default, it converts keys to lowercase. Unlike array_walk(), it doesn't modify
    the original array. It returns a new array with the modified keys, so you need to
    assign the result to a variable. In array_change_key_case_01.php, the array keys
    have been given an initial cap. The following code converts the keys to lowercase
    and reassigns the result to $book:

    ```php
    $book = [
        'Author' => 'David Powers',
        'Title' => 'PHP 8 Solutions'
    ];
    $book = array_change_key_case($book);
    ```

6. To convert the keys to uppercase, pass the PHP constant CASE_UPPER as the
    second argument to array_change_key_case() like this (the code is in array_
    change_key_case_02.php):

    ```php
    $book = array_change_key_case($book, CASE_UPPER);
    ```

PHP Solution 8-3: Modify Array Elements with array_map()

Passing array values by reference to a foreach loop or array_walk() modifies the original array. Often, this
is what you want. However, if you want to preserve the original array, consider using array_map(). This
applies a callback function to each array element and returns a new array with the modified elements. The
first argument to array_map() is the callback, as an anonymous function, an arrow function, or the name of a
defined function. The second argument is the array whose elements you want to modify.

If the callback takes more than one argument, the values for each one must be passed to array_map()
as arrays in the same order as required by the callback. Even if you want to use the same value each time for
a subsequent argument, it must be passed to array_map() as an array with the same number of elements as
the array being modified.

With an associative array, array_map() preserves the keys only when the callback takes a single
argument. If multiple arguments are passed to the callback, array_map() returns an indexed array.

1. The code in array_map_01.php shows a simple example of using array_map()
    to double numbers in an array using an arrow callback function. The code looks
    like this:

    ```php
    $numbers = [2, 4, 7];
    $doubled = array_map(fn ($num) => $num * 2}, $numbers);
    echo '<pre>';
    print_r($numbers);
    print_r($doubled);
    echo '</pre>';
    ```

    As the following screenshot shows, the values in the original $numbers array are
    unchanged. The $doubled array contains the results returned by the callback.

```
localhost/php8sols/ch08/array_n  ×  +

←  →  C  ⓘ localhost/php8sols/ch08/array_map_01.php

Array
(
    [0] => 2
    [1] => 4
    [2] => 7
)
Array
(
    [0] => 4
    [1] => 8
    [2] => 14
)
```

2. The next example in array_map_02.php uses a defined function to modify an associative array:

```php
$book = [
    'author' => 'David Powers',
    'title' => 'PHP 8 Solutions'
];
$modified = array_map('modify', $book);
function modify($val) {
    return strtoupper($val);
}
echo '<pre>';
print_r($book);
print_r($modified);
echo '</pre>';
```

As the following screenshot shows, the array keys are preserved in the modified array:

```
localhost/php8sols/ch08/array_n  ×  +

←  →  C  ⓘ localhost/php8sols/ch08/array_map_02.php

Array
(
    [author] => David Powers
    [title] => PHP 8 Solutions
)
Array
(
    [author] => DAVID POWERS
    [title] => PHP 8 SOLUTIONS
)
```

3. The code in array_map_03.php has been modified to demonstrate how to pass multiple arguments to the callback function:

```
$descriptions = ['British', 'the fifth edition'];
$modified = array_map('modify', $book, $descriptions);
function modify($val, $description) {
    return "$val is $description.";
}
```

A second parameter, $description, has been added to the modify() function. The values to be passed as arguments to the callback are stored in an array called $descriptions, which is passed as the third argument to array_map(). This produces the following result:

```
Array
(
    [author] => David Powers
    [title] => PHP 8 Solutions
)
Array
(
    [0] => David Powers is British.
    [1] => PHP 8 Solutions is the fifth edition.
)
```

Notice that the array keys have not been preserved in the modified array. Passing multiple arguments to the callback results in an indexed array.

4. The third and subsequent arguments passed to array_map() must contain the same number of elements as the array being modified. The code in array_map_04.php shows what happens if an argument contains too few elements. It looks like this:

```
$descriptions = ['British', 'the fifth edition'];
$label = ['Description'];
$modified = array_map('modify', $book, $descriptions, $label);
function modify($val, $description, $label) {
    return "$label: $val is $description.";
}
```

There's only one element in the $label array; but as the following screenshot shows, this doesn't result in the same value being reused.

```
   localhost/php8sols/ch08/array_n   ×   +

 ←  →  C   ⓘ localhost/php8sols/ch08/array_map_04.php

Array
(
    [author] => David Powers
    [title] => PHP 8 Solutions
)
Array
(
    [0] => Description: David Powers is British.
    [1] => ⓘ PHP 8 Solutions is the fifth edition.
)
```

When an array passed as an argument to array_map() has fewer elements than the first array (the one being modified), the shorter array is filled with empty elements. Consequently, the label is omitted from the second element in the modified array; but PHP doesn't trigger an error.

Merging Arrays

PHP offers several different ways of combining the elements of two or more arrays; but they don't always produce the same result. Understanding how each method works will avoid mistakes and confusion.

Using the Array Union Operator

The simplest way to merge arrays is with the array union operator, a plus sign (+). However, the results aren't what you might expect. The code in merge_01.php in the ch08 folder demonstrates what happens when you use the array union operator on two indexed arrays:

```
$first = ['PHP', 'JavaScript'];
$second = ['Java', 'R', 'Python'];
$languages = $first + $second;
echo '<pre>';
print_r($languages);
echo '</pre>';
```

Running this script produces the following output:

```
      localhost/php8sols/ch08/merge_   ×    +
    ←  →  C      ⓘ localhost/php8sols/ch08/merge_01.php

Array
(
    [0] => PHP
    [1] => JavaScript
    [2] => Python
)
```

Instead of five elements, the resulting array contains just three. This is because the array union operator doesn't concatenate the second array onto the end of the first one. With an indexed array, it ignores elements in the second array that have the same index as elements in the first. In this example, Java and R in the second array have the same indices (0 and 1) as PHP and JavaScript, so they're ignored. Only Python has an index (2) that doesn't exist in the first array, so it's added to the merged array.

The array union operator treats associative arrays similarly. The code in merge_02.php contains two associative arrays like this:

```
$first = ['PHP' => 'Rasmus Lerdorf', 'JavaScript' => 'Brendan Eich'];
$second = ['Java' => 'James Gosling', 'R' => 'Ross Ihaka', 'Python' => 'Guido van Rossum'];
$lead_developers = $first + $second;
```

Both arrays contain a unique set of keys, so the resulting array contains every element with its associated key, as the following screenshot shows:

```
      localhost/php8sols/ch08/merge_   ×    +
    ←  →  C      ⓘ localhost/php8sols/ch08/merge_02.php

Array
(
    [PHP] => Rasmus Lerdorf
    [JavaScript] => Brendan Eich
    [Java] => James Gosling
    [R] => Ross Ihaka
    [Python] => Guido van Rossum
)
```

However, when there's a duplicate key, the array union operator ignores the element in the second array, as demonstrated by the code in merge_03.php:

```
$first = ['PHP' => 'Rasmus Lerdorf', 'JavaScript' => 'Brendan Eich', 'R' => 'Robert
Gentleman'];
$second = ['Java' => 'James Gosling', 'R' => 'Ross Ihaka', 'Python' => 'Guido van Rossum'];
$lead_developers = $first + $second;
```

As the following screenshot shows, only Robert Gentleman is credited as lead developer of R. Ross Ihaka in the second array is ignored because he shares a duplicate key.

```
Array
(
    [PHP] => Rasmus Lerdorf
    [JavaScript] => Brendan Eich
    [R] => Robert Gentleman
    [Java] => James Gosling
    [Python] => Guido van Rossum
)
```

Ignoring duplicate indices or keys isn't always what you want, so PHP offers a couple of functions designed to produce a fully merged array of all elements.

Using array_merge() and array_merge_recursive()

The functions array_merge() and array_merge_recursive() concatenate two or more arrays to create a new array. The difference between them lies in the way they treat duplicate values in associative arrays.

With indexed arrays, array_merge() automatically renumbers each element's index and includes every value, including duplicates. This is demonstrated by the following code in merge_04.php:

```php
$first = ['PHP', 'JavaScript', 'R'];
$second = ['Java', 'R', 'Python', 'PHP'];
$languages = array_merge($first, $second);
```

As the following screenshot shows, the indices are numbered consecutively, and the repeated values (PHP and R) are preserved in the resulting array:

```
Array
(
    [0] => PHP
    [1] => JavaScript
    [2] => R
    [3] => Java
    [4] => R
    [5] => Python
    [6] => PHP
)
```

With associative arrays, the behavior of `array_merge()` depends on the existence of duplicate array keys. When there are no duplicates, `array_merge()` concatenates associative arrays in exactly the same way as using the array union operator. You can verify that by running the code in `merge_05.php`.

However, the presence of duplicate keys results in preserving only the last duplicate value. This is demonstrated by the following code in `merge_06.php`:

```
$first = ['PHP' => 'Rasmus Lerdorf', 'JavaScript' => 'Brendan Eich', 'R' => 'Robert
Gentleman'];
$second = ['Java' => 'James Gosling', 'R' => 'Ross Ihaka', 'Python' => 'Guido van Rossum'];
$lead_developers = array_merge($first, $second);
```

As the following screenshot shows, the value of R from the second array (Ross Ihaka) overwrites the value from the first array (Robert Gentleman):

■ **Caution**   The order in which the arrays are merged is different from the array union operator. The array union operator preserves the first duplicate value, whereas `array_merge()` preserves the last duplicate.

To preserve the values of duplicate keys, you need to use `array_merge_recursive()`. The code in `merge_07.php` merges the same arrays like this:

```
$lead_developers = array_merge_recursive($first, $second);
```

As the following screenshot shows, the values for the duplicate keys are merged into an indexed subarray:

```
Array
(
    [PHP] => Rasmus Lerdorf
    [JavaScript] => Brendan Eich
    [R] => Array
        (
            [0] => Robert Gentleman
            [1] => Ross Ihaka
        )

    [Java] => James Gosling
    [Python] => Guido van Rossum
)
```

Robert Gentleman's name is stored in the new array as $lead_developers['R'][0].

■ **Note** The array union operator, array_merge(), and array_merge_recursive() can be used with more than two arrays. The rules about duplicate keys and values are the same. With array_merge(), it's always the last duplicate that's preserved.

Merging Two Indexed Arrays into an Associative Array

The array_combine() function merges two indexed arrays to create an associative array by using the first array for keys and the second for values. Both arrays must have the same number of values. Otherwise, the function returns false and triggers a warning.

The following simple example in array_combine.php shows how it works:

```php
$colors = ['red', 'amber', 'green'];
$actions = ['stop', 'caution', 'go'];
$signals = array_combine($colors, $actions);
// $signals is ['red' => 'stop', 'amber' => 'caution', 'green' => 'go']
```

■ **Tip** See "PHP Solution 7-2: Extracting Data from a CSV File" for a practical use of array_combine().

Comparing Arrays

Table 8-1 lists PHP core functions that can be used to find the differences or intersections of arrays. All functions in the table accept two or more arrays as arguments. Where a callback function performs the comparison, the callback should be the final argument passed to the function.

Table 8-1. *PHP functions for comparing arrays*

Function	Description
array_diff()	Compares the first array with one or more others. Returns an array of values in the first array that are not present in the others.
array_diff_assoc()	Similar to array_diff(), but uses both the array keys and the values in the comparison.
array_diff_key()	Similar to array_diff(), but makes the comparison on the keys instead of the values.
array_diff_uassoc()	Same as array_diff_assoc(), but uses a user-supplied callback function to compare the keys.
array_diff_ukey()	Same as array_diff_key(), but uses a user-supplied callback function to compare the keys.
array_intersect()	Compares two or more arrays. Returns an array containing all values in the first array that are present in all the others. Keys are preserved.
array_intersect_assoc()	Similar to array_intersect(), but uses both the array keys and values in the comparison.
array_intersect_key()	Returns an array that contains all entries in the first array that have keys that are present in all the other arrays.
array_intersect_uassoc()	Same as array_intersect_assoc(), but uses a user-supplied callback function to compare the keys.
array_intersect_ukey()	Same as array_intersect_key(), but uses a user-supplied callback function to compare the keys.

I won't go into the details of each function, but let's take a look at the different results returned by comparing the following two arrays with array_diff_assoc() and array_diff_key():

```php
$first = [
    'PHP' => 'Rasmus Lerdorf',
    'JavaScript' => 'Brendan Eich',
    'R' => 'Robert Gentleman'];
$second = [
    'Java' => 'James Gosling',
    'R' => 'Ross Ihaka',
    'Python' => 'Guido van Rossum'];
$diff = array_diff_assoc($first, $second); // $diff is the same as $first
```

array_diff_assoc() (see array_diff_assoc.php in the ch08 folder) checks both keys and values, returning an array of elements that exist in the first array, but not in others. In this example, all three elements in the first array are returned, even though both arrays contain R as a key. This is because the values assigned to R are different.

```
$diff = array_diff_key($first, $second);
// $diff is ['PHP' => 'Rasmus Lerdorf','JavaScript' => 'Brendan Eich']
```

However, array_diff_key() (see array_diff_key.php in the ch08 folder) checks only the keys, ignoring the values. As a result, it returns the first two elements of the first array, but not the third because R exists as a key in the second array. The fact that the values assigned to R are different is irrelevant.

The ch08 folder contains simple examples of the other functions in Table 8-1 with brief explanatory comments. The *_uassoc() and *_ukey() versions require a callback function as the final argument to compare the key of each element. The callback must take two arguments and return an integer less than, equal to, or greater than zero if the first argument is, respectively, less than, equal to, or greater than the second. The examples in the ch08 folder use the built-in PHP strcasecmp() function to perform a case-insensitive comparison, which returns 0 if both strings are considered equal.

■ **Tip** The most efficient way of comparing two values is to use the spaceship operator. You'll see an example in "PHP Solution 8-5: Custom Sorting with the Spaceship Operator" later in this chapter.

Removing Duplicate Elements

To remove duplicate elements from a single array, use array_unique(), which takes an input array and returns a new array with the duplicate values removed. The code in unique_01.php in the ch08 folder contains the following simple example:

```
$original = ['John', 'john', 'Elton John', 'John', 'Elton John', 42, "42"];
$unique = array_unique($original);
print_r($unique);
```

This produces the output shown in the following screenshot:

Array ([0] => John [1] => john [2] => Elton John [5] => 42)

By default, array_unique() casts each value to a string and performs a strict comparison. As a result, both "John" and "john" are preserved because the comparison is case-sensitive. The last two items in the $original array are considered duplicates because the integer is cast as a string. As the screenshot shows, the original keys are preserved, indicating that the fourth and fifth elements have been deleted.

The `array_unique()` function also works with associative arrays. The example in `unique_02.php` looks like this:

```php
$tracks = [
    'The Beatles' => 'With a Little Help from my Friends',
    'Joe Cocker' => 'With A Little Help From My Friends',
    'Wet Wet Wet' => 'With a Little Help from my Friends',
    'Paul McCartney' => 'Yesterday'
];
$unique = array_unique($tracks);
echo '<pre>';
print_r($unique);
echo '</pre>';
```

This produces the following output:

```
localhost/php8sols/ch08/unique_   ×    +

←  →  C    ⓘ  localhost/php8sols/ch08/unique_02.php
```

```
Array
(
    [The Beatles] => With a Little Help from my Friends
    [Joe Cocker] => With A Little Help From My Friends
    [Paul McCartney] => Yesterday
)
```

The string comparison is case-sensitive, so Wet Wet Wet is excluded.

PHP Solution 8-4: Joining an Array with Commas

The built-in PHP `implode()` function joins all elements of an array with a user-supplied string. This PHP solution enhances the output by inserting "and" before the final element. It offers the option to limit the number of elements, replacing excess values by "and one other" or "and others."

1. Open `commas_01.php` in the ch08 folder. It contains a series of indexed arrays containing zero to five names of recording artists from the 1960s and 1970s. The final line uses `implode()` to join the last array with commas:

   ```php
   $too_many = ['Dave Dee', 'Dozy', 'Beaky', 'Mick', 'Tich'];
   echo implode(', ', $too_many);
   ```

2. Load the script into a browser. As the following screenshot shows, the output looks awkward without "and" before the final name:

Dave Dee, Dozy, Beaky, Mick, Tich

3. Delete the last line, and start defining a function like this:

```
function with_commas(array $array, int $max = 4) { }
```

The function signature takes two arguments: $array and $max. The type declarations specify that the first must be an array and the second an integer, so the function will trigger an error if any other type of data is passed to it. $max sets the maximum number of elements to be joined. It has a default value of 4, so it's an optional argument.

4. Inside the function, we can use a match expression (see "Using a match Expression for Decision Chains" in Chapter 4) to determine how to handle the output depending on the number of elements in the array:

```
$length = count($array);
$result = match ($length) {
    0 => '',
    1 => array_pop($array),
    2 => implode(' and ', $array),
    default => implode(', ', array_slice($array, 0, $length -1)) . '
    and ' . array_pop($array)
};
return $result;
```

First, we use count($array) to determine the number of elements in the array and assign the value to $length. This is then passed as the argument to the match expression, which stores the return value as $result.

If the array contains no elements, an empty string is returned. If there's just one, the array is passed to the array_pop() function. We need to do this because the function should return a string ready for display. If you just return $array, it's still an array that can't be displayed using echo or print. The array_pop() function removes the final element in an array and returns it.

If there are two elements in the array, the array is passed to the implode() function with the string "and" surrounded by a space on either side.

The default action uses implode() to join all but the final element of the array with a comma followed by a space. The second argument passed to implode() uses the array_slice() function to select the required elements. The array_slice() function takes three arguments: the array you want to extract elements from, the index of the element you want to start from, and the number of elements to extract. Arrays are counted from zero, so this begins at the start of the array and extracts $length-1 elements. Then the value of the last element (using array_pop() again) is concatenated to the comma-separated string preceded by "and" before the result is returned.

■ **Caution**   This script requires a minimum of PHP 8. For older versions of PHP, you need to use a switch statement as described in my *PHP 7 Solutions*.

---

5.   Save the script, and test it with each of the test arrays in turn. For example:

```
echo with_commas($fab_four);
```

6.   This joins the array elements with commas in a grammatical way:

John, Paul, George and Ringo

7.   Let's fix the situation where the number of array elements exceeds $max, starting with one in excess. Insert the following code immediately before default:

```
$max + 1 =>implode(', ', array_slice($array, 0, $max)) . ' and one other';
```

This passes `array_slice($array, 0, $max)` as the second argument to `implode()`. Then the string "and one other" is concatenated onto the result before returning it.

8.   Save the script and test it again. If you test it with $fab_four, you'll get the same result as in the preceding screenshot. Trying it with $too_many now produces the following result:

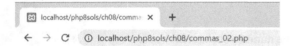

Dave Dee, Dozy, Beaky, Mick and one other

9.   Multiple elements in excess of $max are handled similarly. However, a match expression requires a slightly different approach to handle comparisons. Instead of passing $length as the argument to match(), you need to pass true and perform the comparison for each case. Amend the match expression like this:

```
$result = match (true) {
    $length === 0 => '',
    $length === 1 => array_pop($array),
    $length === 2 => implode(' and ', $array),
    $length === $max + 1 => implode(', ', array_slice($array, 0, $max)) .
    ' and one other',
    $length > $max + 1 => implode(', ', array_slice($array, 0, $max)) .
    ' and others',
    default => implode(', ', array_slice($array, 0, $length -1)) . ' and ' . array_
    pop($array)
};
```

10. Save the script and run it again. With $too_many, the result is unchanged. However, change the second argument to with_commas() to a smaller number like this:

```
echo with_commas($too_many, 3);
```

This changes the output as follows:

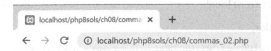

Dave Dee, Dozy, Beaky and others

11. You can check the completed code with commas_02.php in the ch08 folder.

Sorting Arrays

Table 8-2 lists the many built-in PHP functions for sorting arrays.

Table 8-2. *Array sort functions*

Function	Description
sort()	Sorts in ascending order (lowest to highest)
rsort()	Sorts in descending order (highest to lowest)
asort()	Sorts by values in ascending order, maintaining key to value relations
arsort()	Sorts by values in descending order, maintaining key to value relations
ksort()	Sorts in ascending order by keys, maintaining key to value relations
krsort()	Sorts in descending order by keys, maintaining key to value relations
natsort()	Sorts by values in a "natural order," maintaining key to value relations
natcasesort()	Sorts by values in a case-insensitive "natural order," maintaining key to value relations
usort()	Sorts by values using a callback comparison function
uasort()	Sorts by values using a callback comparison function, maintaining key to value relations
uksort()	Sorts by keys using a callback comparison function, maintaining key to value relations
array_multisort()	Sorts multiple or multidimensional arrays

All the functions in Table 8-2 affect the original array(s) and return only true or false depending on whether the operation was successful. The first six functions (down to and including krsort()) can take as an optional second argument the PHP constants listed in Table 8-3 to modify the sort order.

209

Table 8-3. *Constants that modify the sort order*

Constant	Description
SORT_REGULAR	Compares items without changing their types (default)
SORT_NUMERIC	Compares items as numbers
SORT_STRING	Compares items as strings
SORT_LOCALE_STRING	Compares items based on the current locale
SORT_NATURAL	Compares items in "natural order"
SORT_FLAG_CASE	Can be combined with SORT_STRING or SORT_NATURAL using a vertical pipe (|) to sort strings case-insensitively

The two functions and constant that sort values in a "natural order" sort strings that contain numbers in the same way as a human being. There's an example in natsort.php in the ch08 folder, which sorts the following array with both sort() and natsort():

```
$images = ['image10.jpg', 'image9.jpg', 'image2.jpg'];
```

The following screenshot shows the different results:

```
sort(): Array
(
    [0] => image10.jpg
    [1] => image2.jpg
    [2] => image9.jpg
)
natsort(): Array
(
    [1] => image2.jpg
    [2] => image9.jpg
    [0] => image10.jpg
)
```

With sort(), the order is not only counterintuitive, but the indices have been renumbered. With natsort(), the order is more human-friendly, and the original indices have been preserved.

■ **Tip** The natsort() and natcasesort() functions don't have reverse-order equivalents, but you can pass the result to the built-in array_reverse() function. This returns a new array with the elements in reverse order without sorting. Unlike the functions in Table 8-2, the original array is not changed. Associative array keys are preserved, but indexed arrays are renumbered. To prevent indexed arrays from being renumbered, pass the Boolean true as the second (optional) argument.

The callback comparison function used in usort(), uasort(), and uksort() must take two arguments and return an integer less than, equal to, or greater than zero if the first argument is, respectively, less than, equal to, or greater than the second argument. PHP Solution 8-5 shows how to do this with the spaceship operator.

PHP Solution 8-5: Custom Sorting with the Spaceship Operator

The first eight sort functions in Table 8-2 do a great job handling most sort operations. However, they can't cover every scenario. That's when the custom sort functions come in handy. This PHP solution shows how the spaceship operator simplifies custom sorting.

1. Open spaceship_01.php in the ch08 folder. It contains the following multidimensional array of a music playlist and a loop to display it as an unordered list:

```php
$playlist = [
    ['artist' => 'Jethro Tull', 'track' => 'Locomotive Breath'],
    ['artist' => 'Dire Straits', 'track' => 'Telegraph Road'],
    ['artist' => 'Mumford and Sons', 'track' => 'Broad-Shouldered Beasts'],
    ['artist' => 'Ed Sheeran', 'track' => 'Nancy Mulligan'],
    ['artist' => 'Dire Straits', 'track' => 'Sultans of Swing'],
    ['artist' => 'Jethro Tull', 'track' => 'Aqualung'],
    ['artist' => 'Mumford and Sons', 'track' => 'Thistles and Weeds'],
    ['artist' => 'Ed Sheeran', 'track' => 'Eraser']
];
echo '<ul>';
foreach ($playlist as $item) {
    echo "<li>{$item['artist']}: {$item['track']}</li>";
}
echo '</ul>';
```

2. Insert a line before the loop to sort the array using asort():

```php
asort($playlist);
```

3. Save the file, and load it into a browser. As Figure 8-1 shows, asort() has not only sorted the artists alphabetically; the tracks associated with each artist are also in alphabetical order.

211

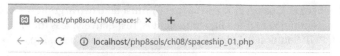

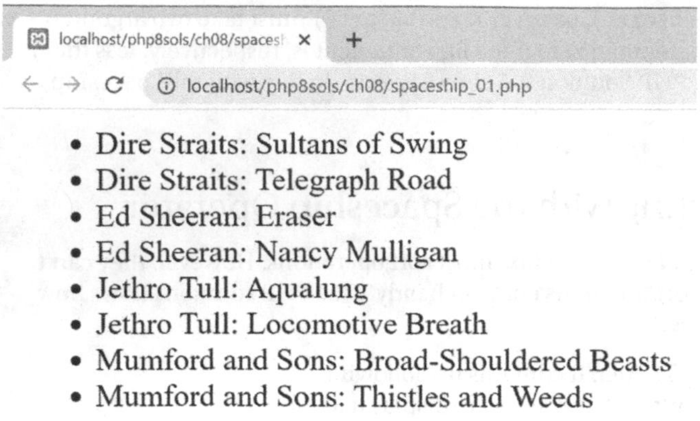

localhost/php8sols/ch08/spaces
localhost/php8sols/ch08/spaceship_01.php
• Dire Straits: Sultans of Swing
• Dire Straits: Telegraph Road
• Ed Sheeran: Eraser
• Ed Sheeran: Nancy Mulligan
• Jethro Tull: Aqualung
• Jethro Tull: Locomotive Breath
• Mumford and Sons: Broad-Shouldered Beasts
• Mumford and Sons: Thistles and Weeds

Figure 8-1. *The `asort()` function makes light work of sorting the values in a multidimensional associative array*

4. However, let's say you want to order the playlist alphabetically by track name. For that, you need a custom sort. Replace the line of code you inserted in step 2 with the following:

```
usort($playlist, fn ($a, $b) => $a['track'] <=> $b['track']);
```

   This uses the `usort()` function with an arrow callback function. The two arguments to the callback (`$a` and `$b`) represent the two array elements that you want to compare. The function compares the value of the current track element with the next one using the spaceship operator, which returns an integer less than, equal to, or greater than zero depending, respectively, on whether the operand on the left is less than, equal to, or greater than the operand on the right.

5. To make the results of the custom sort clearer to see, swap the order of artist and track displayed in each list item:

```
echo "<li>{$item['track']}: {$item['artist']}</li>";
```

6. Save the file and reload it in the browser. The tracks are now listed in alphabetical order (see Figure 8-2).

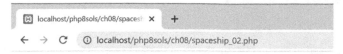

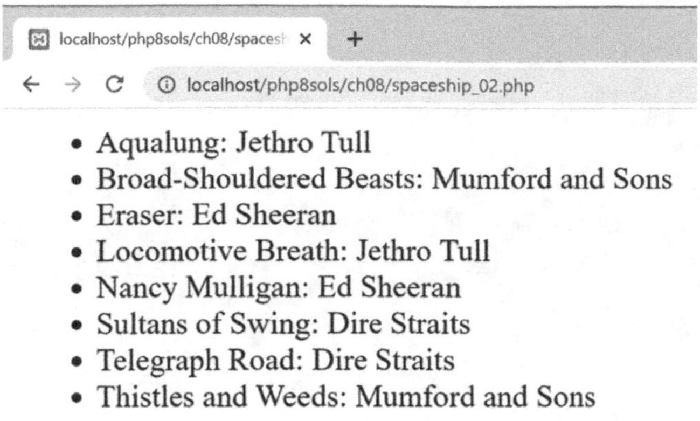

localhost/php8sols/ch08/spacesh
localhost/php8sols/ch08/spaceship_02.php
Aqualung: Jethro Tull
Broad-Shouldered Beasts: Mumford and Sons
Eraser: Ed Sheeran
Locomotive Breath: Jethro Tull
Nancy Mulligan: Ed Sheeran
Sultans of Swing: Dire Straits
Telegraph Road: Dire Straits
Thistles and Weeds: Mumford and Sons

Figure 8-2. *The playlist has now been sorted alphabetically by track name*

7. To reverse the order of the custom sort, swap the order of the operands on either side of the spaceship operator:

```
usort($playlist, fn ($a, $b) => $b['track'] <=> $a['track']);
```

8. You can check your code against `spaceship_02.php` in the `ch08` folder.

Complex Sorting with array_multisort()

The `array_multisort()` function serves two purposes, namely:

- To sort multiple arrays that you want to keep in sync
- To sort a multidimensional array by one or more dimensions

The code in `multisort_01.php` contains an example of arrays that need to be kept in sync when reordered. The `$states` array lists states in alphabetical order, while the `$population` array contains the population of each state listed in the same order:

```
$states = ['Arizona', 'California', 'Colorado', 'Florida', 'Maryland', 'New York',
'Vermont'];
$population = [7_151_502, 39_538_223, 5_773_714, 21_538_187, 6_177_224, 20_201_249,
643_077];
```

A loop then displays each state's name alongside its population:

```
echo '<ul>';
for ($i = 0, $len = count($states); $i < $len; $i++) {
    echo "<li>$states[$i]: $population[$i]</li>";
}
echo '</ul>';
```

Figure 8-3 shows the output.

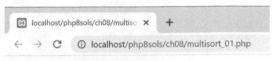

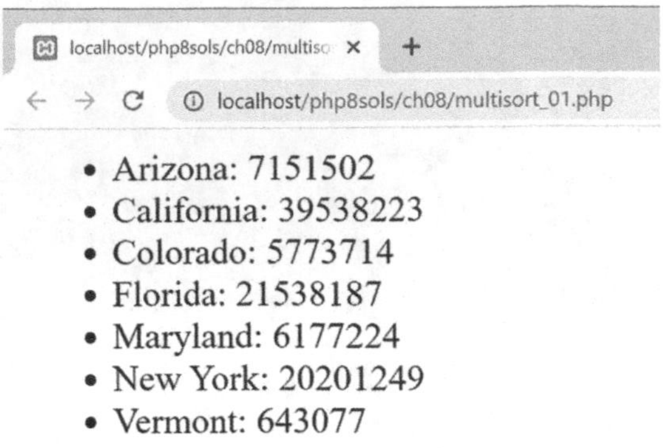

localhost/php8sols/ch08/multiso
localhost/php8sols/ch08/multisort_01.php
• Arizona: 7151502
• California: 39538223
• Colorado: 5773714
• Florida: 21538187
• Maryland: 6177224
• New York: 20201249
• Vermont: 643077

Figure 8-3. *Although the states and population figures are in different arrays, they're in the correct order*

■ **Note** The PHP engine strips out the underscores in the `$population` array when executing the script. The use of underscores in integers for readability was introduced in PHP 7.4.

However, if you want to reorder the population data in ascending or descending order, both arrays need to be kept in sync.

The code in `multisort_02.php` shows how this is done with `array_multisort()`:

```
array_multisort($population, SORT_ASC, $states);
```

The first argument to `array_multisort()` is the array that you want to sort first. It can be followed by two optional arguments: the sort direction using the constant `SORT_ASC` or `SORT_DESC` for ascending or descending, respectively, and the sort type using one of the constants listed in Table 8-3. The remaining arguments are the other arrays that you want to be sorted in sync with the first. Each subsequent array can also be followed by the optional arguments for sort direction and type.

In this example, the `$population` array is sorted in ascending order, and the `$states` array is reordered in sync with it. As Figure 8-4 shows, the correct relationship between the population data and the state names is maintained.

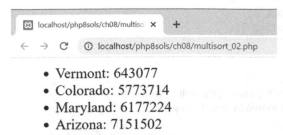

- Vermont: 643077
- Colorado: 5773714
- Maryland: 6177224
- Arizona: 7151502
- New York: 20201249
- Florida: 21538187
- California: 39538223

Figure 8-4. *The population numbers are now in ascending order, keeping the correct state names with them*

The next PHP solution shows an example of using `array_multisort()` to reorder a multidimensional array by multiple dimensions.

PHP Solution 8-6: Sorting a Multidimensional Array with array_multisort()

In the previous PHP solution, we used the spaceship operator to custom sort a multidimensional array by comparing the values assigned to a single key. In this solution, we'll use `array_multisort()` to perform a more complex sort operation.

1. The code in `multisort_03.php` contains an updated version of the `$playlist` multidimensional array from PHP Solution 8-5. A rating key has been added to each subarray like this:

```
$playlist = [
    ['artist' => 'Jethro Tull', 'track' => 'Locomotive Breath', 'rating' => 8],
    ['artist' => 'Dire Straits', 'track' => 'Telegraph Road', 'rating' => 7],
    ['artist' => 'Mumford and Sons', 'track' => 'Broad-Shouldered Beasts',
    'rating' => 9],
    ['artist' => 'Ed Sheeran', 'track' => 'Nancy Mulligan', 'rating' => 10],
    ['artist' => 'Dire Straits', 'track' => 'Sultans of Swing', 'rating' => 9],
    ['artist' => 'Jethro Tull', 'track' => 'Aqualung', 'rating' => 10],
    ['artist' => 'Mumford and Sons', 'track' => 'Thistles and Weeds', 'rating' => 6],
    ['artist' => 'Ed Sheeran', 'track' => 'Eraser', 'rating' => 8]
];
```

2. As the previous solution demonstrated, it's easy to sort the array alphabetically by track with `usort()` and the spaceship operator. We could also sort the array by rating; but sorting by both rating and track requires a different approach.

   The first step to sorting a multidimensional array by multiple criteria is to extract into separate arrays the values to be sorted. This is easily done using the `array_column()` function, which takes two arguments: the top-level array and the key you want to extract from each subarray. Add the following code after the `$playlist` array (it's in `multisort_04.php`):

```
$tracks = array_column($playlist, 'track');
$ratings = array_column($playlist, 'rating');
print_r($tracks);
print_r($ratings);
```

3. Save the file and test it in a browser. As Figure 8-5 shows, the values from the multidimensional array have been extracted to two indexed arrays.

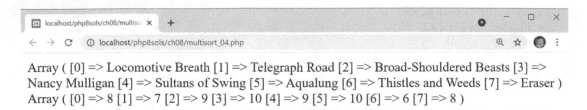

Array ([0] => Locomotive Breath [1] => Telegraph Road [2] => Broad-Shouldered Beasts [3] => Nancy Mulligan [4] => Sultans of Swing [5] => Aqualung [6] => Thistles and Weeds [7] => Eraser) Array ([0] => 8 [1] => 7 [2] => 9 [3] => 10 [4] => 9 [5] => 10 [6] => 6 [7] => 8)

Figure 8-5. *The values needed for sorting have been extracted to separate indexed arrays*

4. We don't need to inspect the contents of the $tracks and $ratings arrays anymore, so comment out or delete the two calls to print_r().

5. We can now use array_multisort() to sort the multidimensional array. The order of arguments passed to the function determines the priority that's assigned to the final sort. I want the playlist to be sorted by ratings in descending order and then by tracks alphabetically. So the first argument needs to be the $ratings array, followed by the sort direction; then the $tracks array, followed by the sort direction; and finally, $playlist, the multidimensional array.

   Add the following code to the bottom of the script:

   ```
   array_multisort($ratings, SORT_DESC, $tracks, SORT_ASC, $playlist);
   ```

6. The multidimensional array has now been resorted from the highest to the lowest ratings, with equally rated tracks in alphabetical order. We can verify that by looping through the $playlist array like this (the code is in multisort_05. php):

   ```
   echo '<ul>';
   foreach ($playlist as $item) {
       echo "<li>{$item['rating']} {$item['track']} by {$item['artist']}</li>";
   }
   echo '</ul>';
   ```

   Figure 8-6 shows proof that it worked.

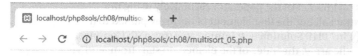

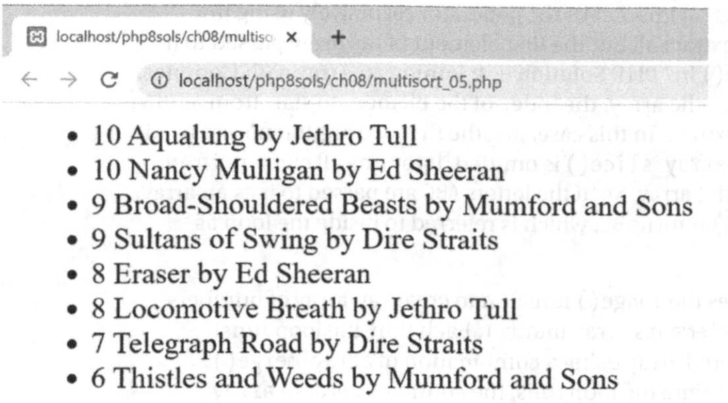

localhost/php8sols/ch08/multiso ×
localhost/php8sols/ch08/multisort_05.php
• 10 Aqualung by Jethro Tull
• 10 Nancy Mulligan by Ed Sheeran
• 9 Broad-Shouldered Beasts by Mumford and Sons
• 9 Sultans of Swing by Dire Straits
• 8 Eraser by Ed Sheeran
• 8 Locomotive Breath by Jethro Tull
• 7 Telegraph Road by Dire Straits
• 6 Thistles and Weeds by Mumford and Sons

Figure 8-6. *The multidimensional array has been sorted by multiple criteria*

■ **Note** In the preceding PHP solution, array_column() was used with associative subarrays, so the second argument was a string containing the key of values we wanted to extract. The function is also capable of extracting values from indexed subarrays. Just pass the index of the values you want to extract as the second argument. You'll see a practical example in "PHP Solution 9-6: Adapting the Class to Handle Multiple Uploads" in the next chapter.

PHP Solution 8-7: Finding All Permutations of an Array

This PHP solution is adapted from Python. It uses the `array_slice()` and `array_merge()` functions inside a recursive generator (see "Generators: A Special Type of Function That Keeps on Giving" in Chapter 4) to pull an array apart and merge back the elements in a different order. It's recursive because the generator calls itself repeatedly until it gets to the end of elements to process.

1. The definition of the generator looks like this (the code is in `permutations.php` in the `ch08` folder):

```
function permutations(array $elements) {
    $len = count($elements);
    if ($len <= 1) {
        yield $elements;
    } else {
        foreach(permutations(array_slice($elements, 1)) as $permutation) {
            foreach(range(0, $len - 1) as $i) {
                yield array_merge(
                    array_slice($permutation, 0, $i),
                    [$elements[0]],
                    array_slice($permutation, $i)
                );
            }
        }
    }
}
```

The `foreach` loop that begins on line 7 calls the generator recursively using the `array_slice()` function to extract all but the first element of the array passed to it. When we used `array_slice()` in "PHP Solution 8-4: Joining an Array with Commas," we passed it three arguments: the array, the index of the element to start from, and the number of elements to extract. In this case, just the first two arguments are used. When the final argument to `array_slice()` is omitted, it returns all elements from the start point to the end of the array. So, if the letters ABC are passed to it as an array, `array_slice($elements, 1)` returns BC, which is referred to inside the loop as `$permutation`.

The nested `foreach` loop uses the `range()` function to create an array of numbers from 0 to the length of the `$elements` array minus 1. Each time the loop runs, the generator yields a reordered array using a combination of `array_merge()` and `array_slice()`. The first time the loop runs, the counter `$i` is 0, so `array_slice($permutation, 0, 0)` extracts nothing from BC. `$elements[0]` is A, and `array_slice($permutation, 0)` is BC. As a result, the original array ABC is yielded.

The next time the loop runs, `$i` is 1, so B is extracted from `$permutation`, `$elements[0]` is still A, and `array_slice($permutation, 1)` is C, yielding BAC, and so on.

2. To use the `permutations()` generator, pass it an indexed array as an argument, and assign the generator to a variable like this:

```
$perms = permutations(['A', 'B', 'C']);
```

3. You can then use a `foreach` loop with the generator to get all permutations of the array (the code is in `permutations.php`):

```
foreach ($perms as $perm) {
    echo implode(' ', $perm) . '<br>';
}
```

This displays all permutations of ABC, as shown in the following screenshot:

A B C
B A C
B C A
A C B
C A B
C B A

Processing Array Data

In this section, we'll look at two PHP solutions for processing data stored in arrays: building HTML nested lists automatically from a multidimensional associative array and extracting data from a JSON feed.

PHP Solution 8-8: Building Nested Lists Automatically

This PHP solution revisits the `RecursiveIteratorIterator` from the Standard PHP Library (SPL) that we used in "Inspecting the Contents of a Folder with FilesystemIterator" in Chapter 7 to burrow down the file system. A useful feature of classes like the `RecursiveIteratorIterator` is that you can adapt them to your own needs by extending them. When you extend a class, the **subclass**—often referred to as the **child class**—inherits all public and protected methods and properties of its parent. You can add new methods and properties or change how the parent class's methods work by overriding them. The `RecursiveIteratorIterator` exposes several public methods that can be overridden to inject HTML tags between array keys and values while looping over a multidimensional associative array.

■ **Note**   Classes can declare methods and properties to be public, protected, or private. Public means they can be accessed outside the class definition. Protected means they can be accessed only inside the class definition or in a child class. Private means they can be accessed only inside the class definition and not in a child class.

Before building the PHP script, let's examine the structure of nested lists in HTML. The following illustration shows a simple nested list:

- Label 1
  - Item 1
  - Item 2

The HTML code looks like this:

```
<ul>
    <li>Label 1
        <ul>
            <li>Item 1</li>
            <li>Item 2</li>
        </ul>
    </li>
</ul>
```

The important point to note is that the indented list is nested inside the top-level list item. The closing </li> tag for Label 1 comes after the closing </ul> tag of the nested list. Hand-coding HTML nested lists is prone to error because it can be difficult to keep track of where list items open and close. We need to bear in mind this structure when automating nested lists with PHP.

1. Create a file called ListBuilder.php in the ch08 folder. If you just want to study the completed code, it's in ListBuilder_end.php complete with comments.

2. Define a class called ListBuilder to extend RecursiveIteratorIterator and create two protected properties for the array to be processed and for the output HTML:

    ```
    class ListBuilder extends RecursiveIteratorIterator
    {
        protected $array;
        protected $output = '';
    }
    ```

3. Most classes have a constructor method to initialize them and accept any arguments. The ListBuilder class needs to take an array as its argument and prepare it for use. Add the following code to the class definition (all the ListBuilder code needs to go before the closing curly brace of the code in step 2):

    ```
    public function __construct(array $array) {
        $this->array = new RecursiveArrayIterator($array);
        // Call the RecursiveIteratorIterator parent constructor
        parent::__construct($this->array, parent::SELF_FIRST);
    }
    ```

    The name of the constructor method is the same for all classes, and it begins with two underscores. This constructor takes a single argument: the array that will be converted into nested unordered lists.

    To use an array with an SPL iterator, it must first be converted to an iterator, so the first line inside the constructor creates a new instance of RecursiveArrayIterator and assigns it to the ListBuilder's $array property.

    Because we're overriding the RecursiveIteratorIterator constructor, we need to invoke the parent constructor and pass it the $array property as the first argument. Calling parent::SELF_FIRST as the second argument gives access to both the keys and values of the array being processed. Without this second argument, we wouldn't have access to the keys.

■ **Tip** You'll learn more about classes and extending them in Chapters 9 and 10.

---

4. An HTML unordered list begins and ends with opening and closing <ul> tags. RecursiveIteratorIterator has public methods that are called automatically at the beginning and end of a loop, so we can override them to add the necessary tags to the $output property with the combined concatenation operator like this:

    ```
    public function beginIteration() {
        $this->output .= '<ul>';
    }
    public function endIteration() {
        $this->output .= '</ul>';
    }
    ```

5. Two public methods are also called automatically at the beginning and end of each subarray. We can use these to insert the opening `<ul>` tag of a nested list and to close the nested list and its parent list item:

```
public function beginChildren() {
    $this->output .= '<ul>';
}
public function endChildren() {
    $this->output .= '</ul></li>';
}
```

6. To process each array element, we can override the `nextElement()` public method that's called automatically... Yes, you've guessed it. This is slightly more complex because we need to check whether the current element has a subarray. If it has, we need to add an opening `<li>` tag and the subarray's key. Otherwise, we need to add the current value between a pair of `<li>` tags like this:

```
public function nextElement() {
    // Check whether there's a subarray
    if (parent::callHasChildren()) {
        // Display the subarray's key
        $this->output .= '<li>' . self::key();
    } else {
        // Display the current array element
        $this->output .= '<li>' . self::current() . '</li>';
    }
}
```

Most of this code is self-explanatory. The condition calls the parent's—in other words, RecursiveIteratorIterator's—callHasChildren() method. This returns true if the current element has child elements—in other words, a subarray. If it has, an opening `<li>` tag is concatenated onto the $output property, followed by self::key(). This calls the ListBuilder's key() method, which is inherited from RecursiveIteratorIterator, to get the value of the current key. There's no closing `</li>` tag because that won't be added until the subarray has been processed.

The else clause is executed if the current element doesn't have any children. It calls the current() method to get the value of the current element, which is sandwiched between a pair of `<li>` tags.

7. To display the nested lists, we need to iterate over the array and return the $output property. We can use the magic __toString() method. Define it like this:

```
public function __toString() {
    // Generate the list
    $this->run();
    return $this->output;
}
```

8. To complete the ListBuilder class, define the run() method like this:

```
protected function run() {
    self::beginIteration();
    while (self::valid()) {
        self::next();
    }
    self::endIteration();
}
```

This simply calls four methods that are inherited from RecursiveIteratorIterator. They call beginIteration(), then run the array through a while loop, and end the iteration.

9. To test the ListBuilder, open multidimensional_01.php in the ch08 folder. It contains a multidimensional associative array called $wines. Include the ListBuilder definition, and then generate the output and display it by adding the following code (the completed code is in multidimensional_02.php):

```
require './ListBuilder.php';
echo new ListBuilder($wines);
```

Figure 8-7 shows the result.

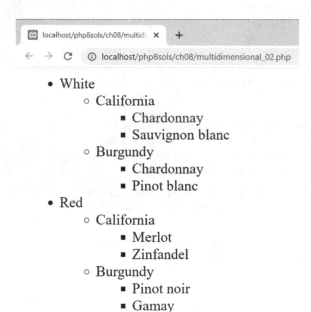

Figure 8-7. *ListBuilder extends RecursiveIteratorIterator to automate building nested lists from a multidimensional associative array*

PHP Solution 8-9: Extracting Data from JSON

In the previous chapter, we used SimpleXML to digest an RSS news feed. The disadvantage of RSS and other forms of XML to distribute data is that the tags used to wrap the data make it verbose. JavaScript Object Notation (JSON) is increasingly being used to distribute data online because it's more succinct. While the succinct format makes JSON faster to download and consumes less bandwidth, the disadvantage is that it's less easy to read.

This PHP solution accesses a JSON feed from San Francisco Open Data (https://datasf.org/opendata/), converts it to an array, builds a multidimensional associative array of the data, and then filters it to extract the desired information. It sounds like a lot of hard work, but it involves relatively little code.

1. The JSON data feed for this PHP solution is in film_locations.json in the ch08/data folder. Alternatively, you can obtain the most up-to-date version from https://data.sfgov.org/api/views/yitu-d5am/rows. json?accessType=DOWNLOAD. If you access the online version, save it as a .json file on your local hard disk to avoid the need to keep accessing the remote feed.

2. The feed consists of data compiled by the San Francisco Film Commission of locations around the city where movies have been shot. One of the challenges of working with JSON is locating the information you want because there's no common naming convention. Although this feed is formatted on separate lines and indented, JSON is frequently devoid of whitespace to make it more compact. Converting it to a multidimensional associative array simplifies the identification process. Create a PHP file called json.php in the ch08 folder, and add the following code (it's in json_01.php):

```php
$json = file_get_contents('./data/film_locations.json');
$data = json_decode($json, true);
echo '<pre>';
print_r($data);
echo '</pre>';
```

This grabs the raw JSON from the data file using file_get_contents(), converts it to a multidimensional associative array, and then displays it. Passing true as the second argument to json_decode() converts JSON objects into PHP associative arrays.

3. Save the file and run the script in a browser. The $data array is huge. It contains details of more than 3,400 movies. Wrapping <pre> tags around print_r() makes it easy to inspect the structure to identify where the interesting data is located. As Figure 8-8 shows, the top-level array is called meta. Nested inside is a subarray called view, which in turn contains a subarray called columns.

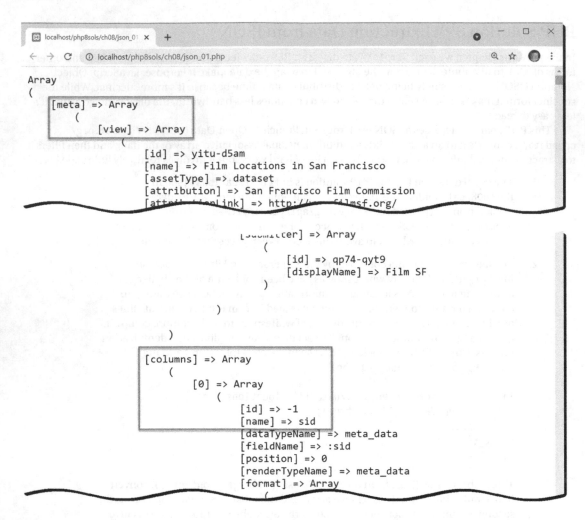

Figure 8-8. *Converting the JSON feed to an associative array simplifies identifying the location of data*

The columns subarray contains an indexed array; and inside the first element is yet another array with a key called name. The significance of this becomes clear when you scroll further down to find an array called data (see Figure 8-9).

■ **Tip** Because the JSON file is so big, use the browser's Find utility to search for [data].

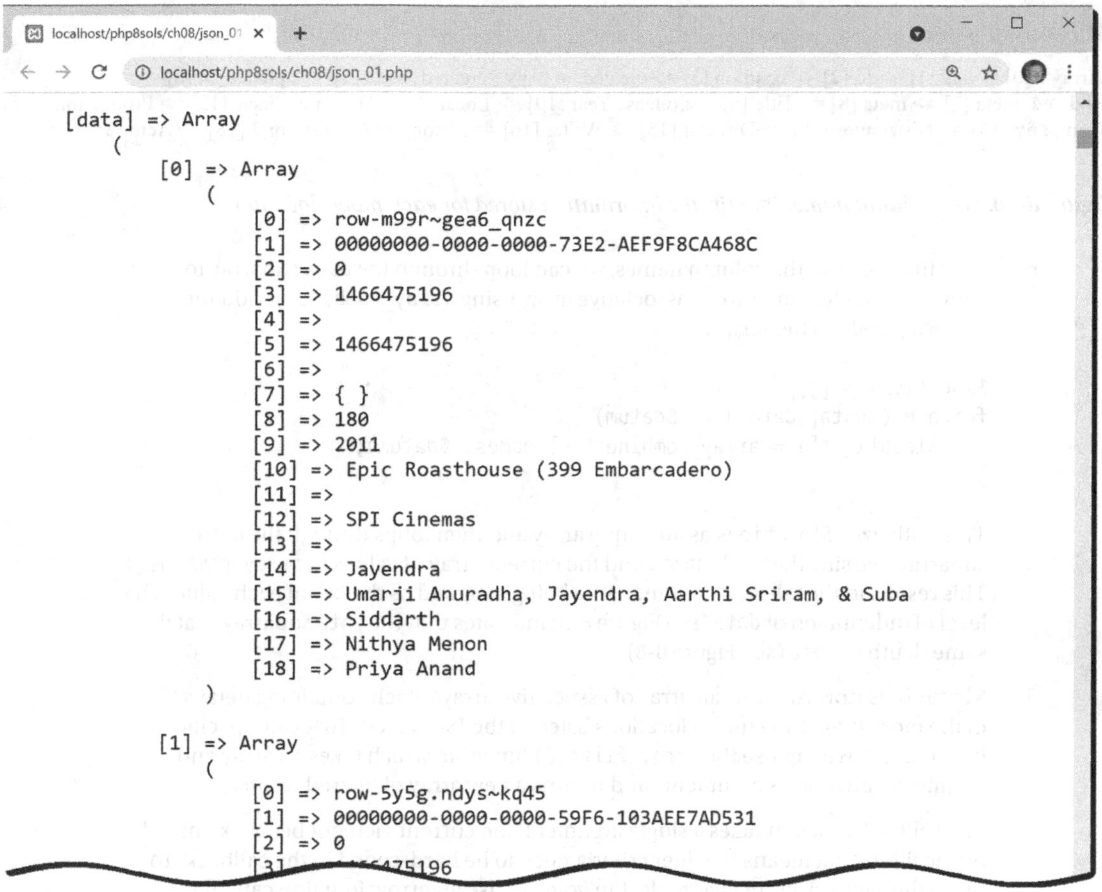

```
[data] => Array
    (
        [0] => Array
            (
                [0] => row-m99r~gea6_qnzc
                [1] => 00000000-0000-0000-73E2-AEF9F8CA468C
                [2] => 0
                [3] => 1466475196
                [4] =>
                [5] => 1466475196
                [6] =>
                [7] => { }
                [8] => 180
                [9] => 2011
                [10] => Epic Roasthouse (399 Embarcadero)
                [11] =>
                [12] => SPI Cinemas
                [13] =>
                [14] => Jayendra
                [15] => Umarji Anuradha, Jayendra, Aarthi Sriram, & Suba
                [16] => Siddarth
                [17] => Nithya Menon
                [18] => Priya Anand
            )

        [1] => Array
            (
                [0] => row-5y5g.ndys~kq45
                [1] => 00000000-0000-0000-59F6-103AEE7AD531
                [2] => 0
                [3] => 1466475196
```

Figure 8-9. The movie data is stored in indexed arrays for compactness

This is where all the interesting information is stored. It contains an indexed subarray with more than 3,400 elements, each of which contains another indexed array with 19 elements. Instead of repeating the column names thousands of times, the data is mapped to the array of names identified in Figure 8-8. To extract the information we want, it's necessary to build an associative array for each movie in this data array.

4. We can obtain the column names using the array_column() function that we encountered in "PHP Solution 8-6: Sorting a Multidimensional Array with array_multisort()." However, the name element is buried deep within the top-level array that was stored as $data in step 2. The indentation in Figure 8-8 helps find the correct subarray to pass as the first argument. Add the following code to the script (it's in json_02.php):

```
$col_names = array_column($data['meta']['view']['columns'], 'name');
```

225

5. Use `print_r()` to check that you have extracted the correct values, as shown in Figure 8-10.

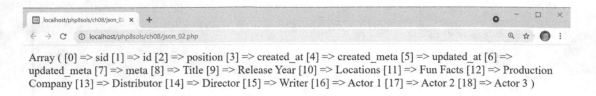

Array ([0] => sid [1] => id [2] => position [3] => created_at [4] => created_meta [5] => updated_at [6] => updated_meta [7] => meta [8] => Title [9] => Release Year [10] => Locations [11] => Fun Facts [12] => Production Company [13] => Distributor [14] => Director [15] => Writer [16] => Actor 1 [17] => Actor 2 [18] => Actor 3)

Figure 8-10. *The column names identify the information stored for each movie location*

6. Now that we have the column names, we can loop through the `data` subarray to convert each element into an associative array using `array_combine()`. Add the following code to the script:

```
$locations = [];
foreach ($data['data'] as $datum) {
    $locations[] = array_combine($col_names, $datum);
}
```

This initializes `$locations` as an empty array and then loops through the `data` subarray, passing the `$col_names` and the current array of values to `array_combine()`. This results in the relevant column name being assigned as the key of each value. The level of indentation of `data` (see Figure 8-9) indicates that the `data` subarray is at the same depth as `meta` (see Figure 8-8).

7. `$locations` now contains an array of associative arrays, each containing details of the more than 3,400 movie locations listed in the JSON feed. To locate specific information, we can use the `array_filter()` function, which takes an array and a callback function as arguments and returns a new array of filtered results.

The callback function takes a single argument, the current element being examined by the filter. That means the filter criteria need to be hard-coded in the callback. To make the callback more adaptable, I'm going to use an arrow function capable of inheriting a variable from the global scope. Define the search term and the callback function like this:

```
$search = 'Pier 7';
$getLocation = fn($location) => str_contains($location['Locations'],
$search);
```

The arrow function is assigned to a variable. It takes a single argument, `$location`, which represents the current array element. The callback function performs a case-sensitive search for the search term in the `Locations` element of the current array using the `str_contains()` function, which is new to PHP 8. If the search term is found, the result will be `true`.

8. We can now filter the `$locations` array and display the results like this (the finished code is in `json_03.php`):

```
$filtered = array_filter($locations, $getLocation);
echo '<ul>';
foreach ($filtered as $item) {
    echo "<li>{$item['Title']} ({$item['Release Year']}) filmed at
    {$item['Locations']}</li>";
}
echo '</ul>';
```

9. Save the script and test it in a browser. You should see the results displayed as in Figure 8-11.

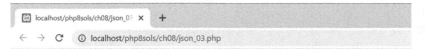

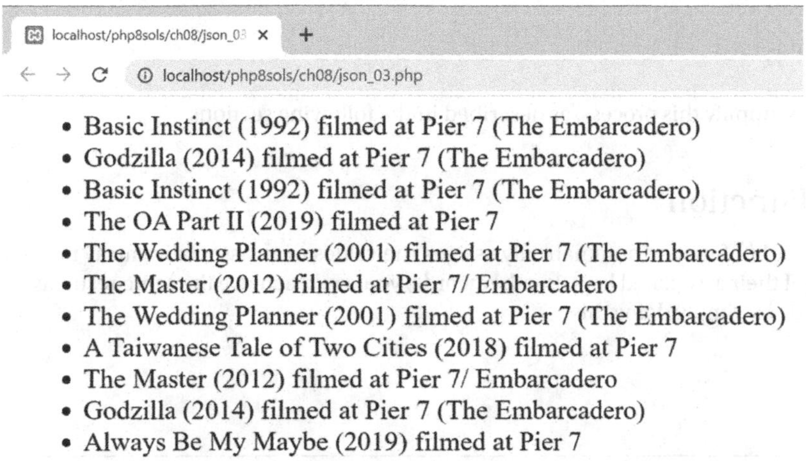

- Basic Instinct (1992) filmed at Pier 7 (The Embarcadero)
- Godzilla (2014) filmed at Pier 7 (The Embarcadero)
- Basic Instinct (1992) filmed at Pier 7 (The Embarcadero)
- The OA Part II (2019) filmed at Pier 7
- The Wedding Planner (2001) filmed at Pier 7 (The Embarcadero)
- The Master (2012) filmed at Pier 7/ Embarcadero
- The Wedding Planner (2001) filmed at Pier 7 (The Embarcadero)
- A Taiwanese Tale of Two Cities (2018) filmed at Pier 7
- The Master (2012) filmed at Pier 7/ Embarcadero
- Godzilla (2014) filmed at Pier 7 (The Embarcadero)
- Always Be My Maybe (2019) filmed at Pier 7

Figure 8-11. The information has been filtered from more than 3,400 entries in the JSON feed

10. Some movies are listed more than once in the JSON file. To remove the duplicates, amend the code by creating an empty array and amending the foreach loop like this:

```
$duplicates = [];
foreach ($filtered as $item) {
    if (in_array($item['Title'], $duplicates)) continue;
    echo "<li>{$item['Title']} ({$item['Release Year']}) filmed at
{$item['Locations']}</li>";
    $duplicates[] = $item['Title'];
}
```

The conditional statement inside the loop uses the in_array() function to check whether $**item['Title']** is in the $duplicates array. If it is, the function returns true, and the continue keyword skips the current iteration of the loop. After the result is displayed, $item['Title'] is added to the $duplicates array. The updated code is in json_04.php.

11. Run the script again. This time, the duplicates are omitted.

12. Change the value of $search to the names of other locations in San Francisco, such as Presidio or Alcatraz, to see the names of movies shot there.

Automatically Assigning Array Elements to Variables

There's no doubt that associative arrays are extremely useful, but they have the disadvantage of being laborious to type and embed in double-quoted strings. Consequently, it's common to assign associative array elements to simple variables like this:

```
$name = $_POST['name'];
$email = $_POST['email'];
$message = $_POST['message'];
```

However, there are ways to simplify this process, as described in the following sections.

Using the extract() Function

In its most basic form, the extract() function automatically assigns the values of an associative array to variables based on the names of their associated keys. In other words, you *could* achieve the same result as the preceding three lines of code by simply doing this:

```
extract($_POST);
```

■ **Caution**   Using extract() to process unfiltered data from user input, such as the $_POST or $_GET array, is considered a major security risk. A malicious attacker could try to inject variables that overwrite values that you have already defined.

Used in its simplest form, the extract() function is a blunt tool. Unless you know exactly which keys are in the associative array, you run the risk of overwriting existing variables. To overcome this problem, the function can take two optional arguments: one of eight PHP constants that determine what to do in case of naming conflicts and a string that can be used to prefix the variable names. You can find details of these options in the online documentation at www.php.net/manual/en/function.extract.php.

Although the optional arguments refine the behavior of extract(), the need to use them reduces the convenience the function offers. There's also another drawback to extract(): it can't cope with keys that contain characters that are invalid in variable names. For example, the following is a perfectly valid associative array:

```
$author = ['first name' => 'David', 'last name' => 'Powers'];
```

Even though the keys contain spaces, $author['first name'] and $author['last name'] are valid. However, passing the $author array to extract() results in no variables being created.

These limitations greatly reduce the value of extract().

Using list()

Although the parentheses make list() look like a function, technically speaking, it isn't; it's a PHP language construct that assigns a list of variables to an array of values in a single operation. It has been available since PHP 4, but it has been considerably enhanced in PHP 7.1.

Prior to PHP 7.1, list() works only with indexed arrays. You list the variable names that you want to assign the array values to in the same order as they appear in the array. The following example in list_01. php shows how it works:

```
$person = ['David', 'Powers', 'London'];
list($first_name, $last_name, $city) = $person;
// Displays "David Powers lives in London."
echo "$first_name $last_name lives in $city.";
```

In PHP 7.1 and later, list() can also be used with associative arrays. The syntax is similar to that for creating a literal associative array. The associative array key is assigned to a variable using the double arrow operator. Because each array key identifies its associated value, they don't need to be listed in the same order as in the array, nor do all keys have to be used, as the following example in list_02.php shows:

```
$person = [
    'first name' => 'David',
    'last name' => 'Powers',
    'city' => 'London',
    'country' => 'the UK'];
list('country' => $country,
    'last name' => $surname,
    'first name' => $name) = $person;
// Displays "David Powers lives in the UK."
echo "$name $surname lives in $country.";
```

Using Array Shorthand Syntax for list()

Another enhancement in PHP 7.1 is the use of array shorthand syntax for list(). The assignment of variables in the previous two examples can be simplified like this (the full code is in list_03.php and list_04.php):

```
[$first_name, $last_name, $city] = $person;
['country' => $country, 'last name' => $surname, 'first name' => $name] = $person;
```

PHP Solution 8-10: Using a Generator to Process a CSV File

This PHP solution adapts the script in "PHP Solution 7-2: Extracting Data from a CSV File" to use a generator to process a CSV file and assign the values from the array yielded by each line to variables with list() array shorthand.

1. Open csv_processor.php in the ch08 folder. It contains the following definition of a generator called csv_processor():

```
// generator that yields each line of a CSV file as an array
function csv_processor($csv_file) {
    if (@!$file = fopen($csv_file, 'r')) {
        echo "Can't open $csv_file.";
        return;
    }
    while (($data = fgetcsv($file)) !== false) {
        yield $data;
    }
    fclose($file);
}
```

The generator takes a single argument, the name of a CSV file. It uses the file manipulation functions described in Chapter 7 to open the file in read mode. The error control operator (@) suppresses any PHP error messages if the file can't be opened, displays a custom message, and returns, preventing any further attempt to process the file.

Assuming the file is opened successfully, the while loop passes one line at a time to the fgetcsv() function, which returns the data as an array that's yielded by the generator. When the loop comes to an end, the file is closed.

This is a handy utility function that can be used to process any CSV file.

2. Create a file called csv_list.php in the ch08 folder and include csv_processor.php:

```
require_once './csv_processor.php';
```

3. In the ch08/data folder, scores.csv contains the following data stored as comma-separated values:

```
Home team,Home score,Away team,Away score
Arsenal,2,Newcastle United,0
Tottenham Hotspur,2,Crystal Palace,0
Watford,4,Fulham,1
Manchester City,2,Cardiff City,0
Southampton,1,Liverpool,3
Wolverhampton Wanderers,2,Manchester United,1
```

4. Load the data in the CSV file by creating an instance of the csv_processor() generator like this:

```
$scores = csv_processor('./data/scores.csv');
```

5. The easiest way to use a generator is with a foreach loop. Each time the loop runs, the generator yields the current line of the CSV file as an indexed array. Use list() array shorthand to assign the array values to variables, and then display them with echo like this:

```
foreach ($scores as $score) {
    [$home, $hscore, $away, $ascore] = $score;
    echo "$home $hscore:$ascore $away<br>";
}
```

6. Save the file and run the script by loading it into a browser. Alternatively, use `csv_list_01.php` in the `ch08` folder. As Figure 8-12 shows, the output includes the row of column titles from the CSV file.

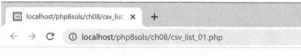

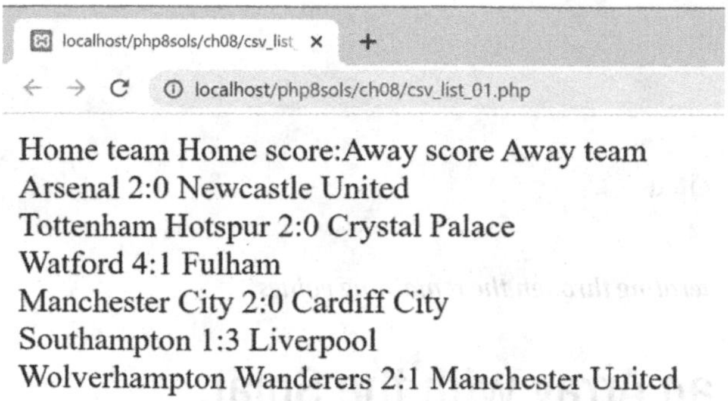

localhost/php8sols/ch08/csv_list
localhost/php8sols/ch08/csv_list_01.php
Home team Home score:Away score Away team
Arsenal 2:0 Newcastle United
Tottenham Hotspur 2:0 Crystal Palace
Watford 4:1 Fulham
Manchester City 2:0 Cardiff City
Southampton 1:3 Liverpool
Wolverhampton Wanderers 2:1 Manchester United

Figure 8-12. *The generator processes every line of the CSV file, including the column titles*

7. The problem with using a `foreach` loop is that it processes every line in the CSV file. We could increment a counter each time the loop runs and use it to skip the first line with the `continue` keyword. However, generators have built-in methods that allow us to move through the values to be yielded and to retrieve the current value. Edit the code in step 5 like this (the changes are highlighted in bold):

```
$scores->next();
    while ($scores->valid()) {
    [$home, $hscore, $away, $ascore] = $scores->current();
    echo "$home $hscore:$ascore $away<br>";
    $scores->next();
}
```

Instead of a `foreach` loop, the revised code uses a `while` loop that invokes the generator's `valid()` method. This returns `true` as long as there is at least one more value for the generator to yield. So this has the effect of looping over every line in the CSV file that's being processed.

To skip the first line, the `next()` method is called before the loop begins. As the name suggests, this moves the generator to the next available value. Inside the loop, the `current()` method returns the current value, and the `next()` method moves to the next value ready for the loop to run again.

8. Save the file and run the script again (the code is in `csv_list_02.php`). This time only the scores are displayed, as shown in Figure 8-13.

Arsenal 2:0 Newcastle United
Tottenham Hotspur 2:0 Crystal Palace
Watford 4:1 Fulham
Manchester City 2:0 Cardiff City
Southampton 1:3 Liverpool
Wolverhampton Wanderers 2:1 Manchester United

Figure 8-13. *The first line has been skipped before iterating through the remaining values*

Unpacking Arguments from an Array with the Splat Operator

The splat operator (. . .) that was introduced briefly in Chapter 4 has two roles, namely:

- When used in a function definition, it converts multiple arguments into an array that can be used inside the function.

- When invoking a function, it unpacks an array of arguments treating them as if they were passed individually to a function.

The following PHP solution shows a simple example of how this can be of practical value.

PHP Solution 8-11: Processing a CSV File with the Splat Operator

The fgetcsv() function returns the data from a CSV file as an indexed array. This PHP solution shows how the splat operator can be used to pass the array directly to a function that requires multiple arguments without the need to separate the individual elements. It also uses the csv_processor() generator described in the previous PHP solution.

1. Create a file called csv_splat.php in the ch08 folder and include csv_processor.php:

   ```
   require_once './csv_processor.php';
   ```

2. In the ch08/data folder, weather.csv contains the following data:

   ```
   City,temp
   London,11
   Paris,10
   Rome,12
   Berlin,8
   Athens,19
   ```

   The temperatures are in degrees Celsius. For the benefit of people who believe that water freezes at 32° rather than 0°, we need to process this data in a user-friendly way.

3. In `csv_splat.php`, add the following function definition (the code is in `csv_splat_01.php`):

```
function display_temp($city, $temp) {
    $tempF = round($temp/5*9+32);
    return "$city: $temp&deg;C ($tempF&deg;F)";
}
```

The function takes two arguments: the name of a city and a temperature. The temperature is converted to Fahrenheit using the standard formula (divide by 5, multiply by 9, and add 32) and rounded to the nearest integer.

The function then returns a string consisting of the city name and temperature in degrees Celsius followed by the Fahrenheit equivalent in parentheses.

4. The CSV file containing the data begins with a row of column titles, so we need to skip the first row using the same technique as in the previous solution. Load the data into the `csv_processor()` generator and skip the first line like this:

```
$cities = csv_processor('./data/weather.csv');
$cities->next();
```

5. Use a while loop to process the remaining lines of data with the `display_temp()` function and splat operator like this:

```
while ($cities->valid()) {
    echo display_temp(...$cities->current()) . '<br>';
    $cities->next();
}
```

As in the previous solution, the generator's `current()` method returns the current line of data as an array. However, this time, instead of assigning each array element to a variable, the splat operator unpacks the array and assigns the values as arguments in the same order as they appear in the array.

If you find this code difficult to understand, assign the return value from the `current()` method to a variable first like this:

```
$data = $cities->current();
echo display_temp(...$data) . '<br>';
```

Preceding the array passed as the argument to the function with the splat operator has exactly the same effect as this (the code is in `csv_splat_02.php`):

```
[$city, $temp] = $cities->current();
echo display_temp($city, $temp) . '<br>';
```

Figure 8-14 shows the result of using either technique.

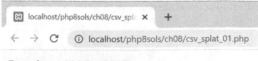

localhost/php8sols/ch08/csv_spl
localhost/php8sols/ch08/csv_splat_01.php
London: 11°C (52°F)
Paris: 10°C (50°F)
Rome: 12°C (54°F)
Berlin: 8°C (46°F)
Athens: 19°C (66°F)

Figure 8-14. *Each data array has been processed by passing it directly to the function with the splat operator*

Using the splat operator to unpack an array of arguments has the advantage of conciseness, but shorter code isn't always the most readable, which can make it difficult to debug when you don't get the results you expected. Personally, I think that assigning array elements to variables and then passing them explicitly as arguments is a safer approach. But even if you don't use a particular technique, it's useful to understand how it works in case you need to work with other people's code.

Chapter Review

Working with arrays is one of the most common tasks in PHP, particularly when working with a database. Nearly all results from a database query are returned as an associative array, so it's important to understand how to process them. In this chapter, we've looked at modifying arrays, merging them, sorting, and extracting data. The main point to remember about using an array in a loop is that PHP always works on a copy of the array unless you pass the values into the loop by reference. By contrast, the functions that sort arrays work on the original array.

You can find full details of all array-related functions in the PHP online documentation at `www.php.net/manual/en/ref.array.php`. This chapter has shown practical examples of using roughly half of them, putting you well on the way to becoming an expert in handling arrays in PHP.

CHAPTER 9

■ ■ ■

Uploading Files

PHP's ability to handle forms isn't restricted to text. It can also be used to upload files to a server. For instance, you could build a real estate web site for clients to upload pictures of their properties or a site for all your friends and relatives to upload their holiday photos. However, just because you can do it doesn't necessarily mean that you should. Allowing others to upload material to your web site could expose you to all sorts of problems. You need to make sure that images are the right size, that they're of suitable quality, and that they don't contain any illegal material. You also need to ensure that uploads don't contain malicious scripts. In other words, you need to protect your web site just as carefully as your own computer.

PHP makes it relatively simple to restrict the type and size of files accepted. What it cannot do is check the suitability of the content. Think carefully about security measures, such as restricting uploads to registered and trusted users by placing the upload form in a password-protected area.

Until you learn how to restrict access to pages with PHP in Chapters 11 and 19, use the PHP solutions in this chapter only in a password-protected directory if deployed on a public web site. Most hosting companies provide simple password protection through the site's control panel.

The first part of this chapter is devoted to understanding the mechanics of file uploads, which will make it easier to understand the code that follows. This is a fairly intense chapter, not a collection of quick solutions. But by the end of the chapter, you will have built a PHP class capable of handling single and multiple file uploads. You can then use the class in any form by writing only a few lines of code.

You'll learn about the following:

- Understanding the $_FILES array
- Restricting the size and type of uploads
- Preventing files from being overwritten
- Handling multiple uploads

How PHP Handles File Uploads

The term upload means moving a file from one computer to another, but as far as PHP is concerned, all that's happening is that a file is being moved from one location to another. This means you can test all the scripts in this chapter on your local computer without the need to upload files to a remote server.

PHP supports file uploads by default, but hosting companies can restrict the size of uploads or disable them altogether. Before proceeding, it's a good idea to check the settings on your remote server.

© David Powers 2022
D. Powers, *PHP 8 Solutions*, https://doi.org/10.1007/978-1-4842-7141-4_9

Checking Whether Your Server Supports Uploads

All the information you need is displayed on the main PHP configuration page that you can display by running `phpinfo()` on your remote server, as described in Chapter 2. Scroll down until you find `file_uploads` in the Core section.

If the local value is On, you're ready to go, but you should also check the other configuration settings listed in Table 9-1.

Table 9-1. *PHP configuration settings that affect file uploads*

Directive	Default value	Description
max_execution_time	30	The maximum number of seconds that a PHP script can run. If the script takes longer, PHP generates a fatal error.
max_file_uploads	20	The maximum number of files that can be uploaded simultaneously. Excess files are silently ignored.
max_input_time	–1	The maximum number of seconds that a PHP script is allowed to parse the $_POST and $_GET arrays and file uploads. The default setting is –1, which uses the same value as max_execution_time. Very large uploads are likely to run out of time. Setting the value to 0 allows unlimited time.
post_max_size	8M	The maximum permitted size of all $_POST data, *including* file uploads. Although the default is 8M (8 megabytes), hosting companies may impose a smaller limit.
upload_tmp_dir	NULL	This is where PHP stores uploaded files until your script moves them to a permanent location. If no value is defined in php.ini, PHP uses the system default temporary directory (C:\Windows\Temp or /tmp on Mac/Linux).
upload_max_filesize	2M	The maximum permitted size of a single upload file. The default is 2M (megabytes), but hosting companies may impose a smaller limit. An integer indicates the number of bytes. K means kilobytes, M stands for megabytes, and G for gigabytes.

In theory, PHP can handle uploads of very large files, but the limits are determined by the settings in Table 9-1. The value of `post_max_size` includes everything in the $_POST array, so the total size of files that can be uploaded simultaneously on a typical server is less than 8 MB, with no single file greater than 2 MB. The server administrator can change these defaults, so it's important to check the limits set by your hosting company. If you exceed those limits, an otherwise perfect script will fail.

If the local value of `file_uploads` is Off, uploads have been disabled. There is nothing you can do about it, other than ask your hosting company if it offers a package with file uploading enabled. Your only alternatives are to move to a different host or to use a different solution, such as uploading files by FTP.

■ **Tip** After using `phpinfo()` to check your remote server's settings, remove the script or put it in a password-protected directory.

Adding a File Upload Field to a Form

Adding a file upload field to an HTML form is easy. Just add enctype="multipart/form-data" to the opening <form> tag and set the type attribute of an <input> element to file. The following code is a simple example of an upload form (it's in file_upload_01.php in the ch09 folder):

```
<form action="file_upload.php" method="post" enctype="multipart/form-data">
    <p>
        <label for="image">Upload image:</label>
        <input type="file" name="image" id="image">
    </p>
    <p>
        <input type="submit" name="upload" value="Upload">
    </p>
</form>
```

Although this is standard HTML, how it's rendered in a web page depends on the browser. Most modern browsers display a Choose File or Browse button with a status message or the name of the selected file on the right (see Figure 9-1). Some older browsers display a text input field and launch a file selection panel as soon as you click inside the field. These differences don't affect the operation of an upload form, but you need to take them into account when designing the layout.

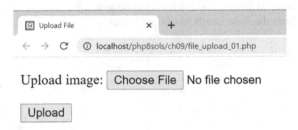

Figure 9-1. *Most browsers display a button to open a file selection panel*

Understanding the $_FILES Array

What confuses many people is that their file seems to vanish after it has been uploaded. This is because, even though the upload form uses the post method, PHP transmits the details of uploaded files in a separate superglobal array called $_FILES. Moreover, files are uploaded to a temporary folder and are deleted unless you explicitly move them to the desired location. This allows you to subject the file to security checks before accepting the upload.

Inspecting the $_FILES Array

The best way to understand how the $_FILES array works is to see it in action. You can test everything in a local test environment on your computer. It works in the same way as uploading a file to a remote server.

1. Create a folder called uploads in the php8sols site root. Create a file called file_upload.php in the uploads folder and insert the code from the previous section. Alternatively, copy file_upload_01.php from the ch09 folder and rename the file file_upload.php.

2. Insert the following code right after the closing `</form>` tag (it's also in `file_upload_02.php`):

```
</form>
<pre>
<?php
if (isset($_POST['upload'])) {
    print_r($_FILES);
}
?>
</pre>
</body>
```

This uses `isset()` to check whether the $_POST array contains upload, the name attribute of the Submit button. If it does, you know the form has been submitted, so you can use `print_r()` to inspect the $_FILES array. The `<pre>` tags make the output easier to read.

3. Save `file_upload.php` and load it into a browser.

4. Click the Browse (or Choose File) button and select a local file. Click Open (or Choose on a Mac) to close the selection dialog box, and then click Upload. You should see something like Figure 9-2.
$_FILES is a multidimensional array—an array of arrays. The top level contains a single element that gets its key (or index) from the name attribute of the file input field, in this case, image.

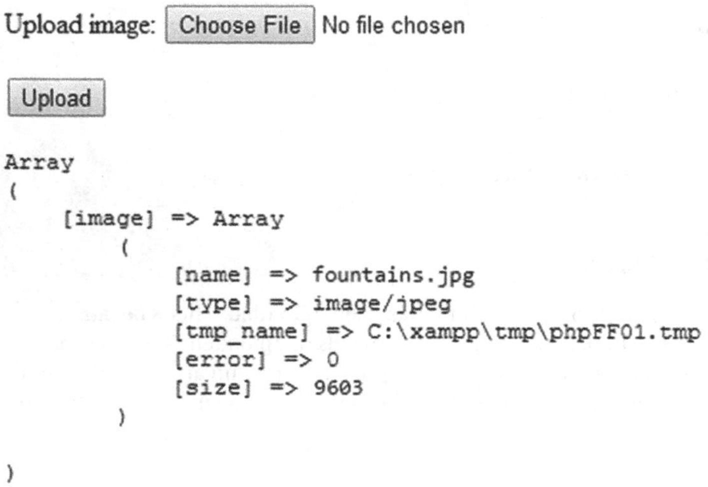

Upload image: | Choose File | No file chosen

| Upload |

```
Array
(
    [image] => Array
        (
            [name] => fountains.jpg
            [type] => image/jpeg
            [tmp_name] => C:\xampp\tmp\phpFF01.tmp
            [error] => 0
            [size] => 9603
        )

)
```

Figure 9-2. The $_FILES array contains the details of an uploaded file

The top-level image array contains a subarray consisting of five elements, namely:

- name: The original name of the uploaded file

- type: The uploaded file's MIME type

- `tmp_name`: The location of the uploaded file
- `error`: An integer indicating the status of the upload
- `size`: The size of the uploaded file in bytes

Don't waste time searching for the temporary file indicated by `tmp_name`: it won't be there. If you don't save it immediately, PHP discards it.

■ **Note** A MIME type is a standard used by browsers to determine a file's format and how to handle it. See `https://developer.mozilla.org/en-US/docs/Web/HTTP/Basics_of_HTTP/MIME_types` for more information.

---

5. Click Upload without selecting a file. The `$_FILES` array should look like Figure 9-3.

Upload image: [Choose File] No file chosen

[Upload]

```
Array
(
    [image] => Array
        (
            [name] =>
            [type] =>
            [tmp_name] =>
            [error] => 4
            [size] => 0
        )

)
```

Figure 9-3. *The $_FILES array still exists when no file is uploaded*

An error level of 4 indicates that no file was uploaded; 0 means the upload succeeded. Table 9-2 later in this chapter lists all the error codes.

6. Select a program file and click the Upload button. In many cases, the form will happily try to upload the program and will display its type as application/zip, application/octet-stream, or something similar. This should serve as a warning that it's important to check what type of file is being uploaded.

Establishing an Upload Directory

For security, files uploaded through an online form shouldn't be publicly accessible through a browser. In other words, they shouldn't be inside the site root (typically `htdocs`, `public_html`, or `www`). On your remote server, create a directory for uploads outside the site root and set the permissions to 644 (owner can read and write; others can read only).

Creating an Upload Folder for Local Testing on Windows

For the following exercises, I suggest you create a folder called `upload_test` at the top level of the C drive. There are no permissions issues on Windows, so that's all that you need to do.

Creating an Upload Folder for Local Testing on macOS

Mac users might need to do a little more preparation because file permissions are similar to Linux. Create a folder called `upload_test` in your home folder and follow the instructions in PHP Solution 9-1.

If everything goes smoothly, you won't need to do anything extra. But if you get a warning that PHP "failed to open stream," change the permissions for the `upload_test` folder like this:

1. Select `upload_test` in the Mac Finder and select File ➤ Get Info (Cmd+I) to open its info panel.

2. In Sharing & Permissions, click the padlock icon at the bottom right to unlock the settings, and then change the setting for everyone from Read only to Read & Write, as shown in the following screenshot:

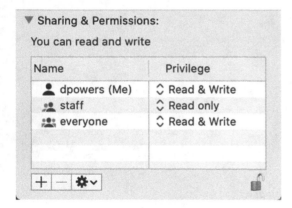

3. Click the padlock icon again to preserve the new settings and close the info panel. You should now be able to use the `upload_test` folder to continue with the rest of the chapter.

Uploading Files

Before building the file upload class, it's a good idea to create a simple file upload script to make sure that your system handles uploads correctly.

Moving the Temporary File to the Upload Folder

The temporary version of an uploaded file has only a fleeting existence. If you don't do anything with the file, it's discarded immediately. You need to tell PHP where to move it and what to call it. You do this with the move_uploaded_file() function, which takes the following two arguments:

- The name of the temporary file
- The full path name of the file's new location, including the filename itself

Obtaining the name of the temporary file itself is easy: it's stored in the $_FILES array as tmp_name. Because the second argument requires a full path name, it gives you the opportunity to rename the file. For the moment, let's keep things simple and use the original filename, which is stored in the $_FILES array as name.

PHP Solution 9-1: Creating a Basic File Upload Script

Continue working with the same file as in the previous exercise. Alternatively, use file_upload_03.php from the ch09 folder. The final script for this PHP solution is in file_upload_04.php.

1. If you are using the file from the previous exercise, delete the code highlighted in bold between the closing </form> and </body> tags:

```
</form>
<pre>
<?php
if (isset($_POST['upload'])) {
    print_r($_FILES);
}
?>
</pre>
</body>
```

2. In addition to the automatic limits set in the PHP configuration (see Table 9-1), you can specify a maximum size for an upload file in your HTML form. Add the following line highlighted in bold immediately before the file input field:

```
<label for="image">Upload image:</label>
<input type="hidden" name="MAX_FILE_SIZE" value="<?= $max ?>">
<input type="file" name="image" id="image">
```

This is a hidden form field, so it won't be displayed onscreen. However, it's vital to place it *before* the file input field; otherwise, it won't work. The name attribute, MAX_FILE_SIZE, is fixed and case-sensitive. The value attribute sets the maximum size of the upload file in bytes.

Instead of specifying a numeric value, I have used a variable called $max. This value will also be used in the server-side validation of the file upload, so it makes sense to define it once, avoiding the possibility of changing it in one place but forgetting to change it elsewhere.

The advantage of using MAX_FILE_SIZE is that PHP abandons the upload if the file is bigger than the stipulated value, avoiding unnecessary delays if the file is too big. Unfortunately, users can get around this restriction by faking the value submitted by the hidden field, so the script you'll develop in the rest of this chapter will check the size on the server side, too.

3. Define the value of $max in a PHP block above the DOCTYPE declaration, like this:

```php
<?php
// set the maximum upload size in bytes
$max = 51200;
?>
<!DOCTYPE HTML>
```

This sets the maximum upload size to 50 KB (51,200 bytes).

4. The code that moves the uploaded file from its temporary location to its permanent one needs to be run after the form has been submitted. Insert the following code in the PHP block you have just created at the top of the page:

```php
$max = 51200;
if (isset($_POST['upload'])) {
    // define the path to the upload folder
    $path = '/path/to/upload_test/';
    // move the file to the upload folder and rename it
    move_uploaded_file($_FILES['image']['tmp_name'],
        $path . $_FILES['image']['name']);
}
?>
```

Although the code is quite short, there's a lot going on. The conditional statement executes the code only if the Upload button has been clicked by checking to see if its key is in the $_POST array.

The value of $path depends on your operating system and the location of the upload_test folder.

- If you are using Windows and you created the upload_test folder at the top level of the C drive, it should look like this:

  `$path = 'C:/upload_test/';`

  Note that I have used forward slashes instead of the Windows convention of backslashes. You can use either, but if you use backslashes, the final one needs to be escaped by another backslash, like this (otherwise, the backslash escapes the quote):

  `$path = 'C:\upload_test\\';`

- On a Mac, if you created the upload_test folder in your home folder, it should look like this (replace *username* with your Mac username):

  `$path = '/Users/username/upload_test/';`

- On a remote server, you need the fully qualified file path as the second argument. On Linux, it will probably be something like this:

```
$path = '/home/user/private/upload_test/';
```

The final line inside the `if` statement moves the file with the `move_uploaded_file()` function. The function takes two arguments: the name of the temporary file and the full path to where the file is to be saved.

`$_FILES` is a multidimensional array that takes its name from the file input field. So `$_FILES['image']['tmp_name']` is the temporary file, and `$_FILES['image']['name']` contains the name of the original file. The second argument, `$path . $_FILES['image']['name']`, stores the uploaded file under its original name inside the upload folder.

■ **Caution**   You may come across scripts that use `copy()` instead of `move_uploaded_file()`. Without other checks in place, `copy()` can expose your web site to serious security risks. For example, a malicious user could try to trick your script into copying files that it should not have access to, such as password files. Always use `move_uploaded_file()`; it's much more secure.

---

5. Save `file_upload.php`, and load it into your browser. Click the Browse or Choose File button and select a file from the `images` folder in the `php8sols` site. If you choose one from elsewhere, make sure it's less than 50 KB. Click Open (Choose on a Mac) to display the filename in the form. Click the Upload button. If you're testing locally, the form input field should clear almost instantly.

6. Navigate to the `upload_test` folder and confirm that a copy of the image you selected is there. If it isn't, check your code against `file_upload_04.php`. Also check that the correct permissions have been set on the upload folder, if necessary.

■ **Note**   The download files use `C:/upload_test/`. Adjust this to your own setup.

If you get no error messages and cannot find the file, make sure that the image didn't exceed `upload_max_filesize` (see Table 9-1). Also check that you didn't leave the trailing slash off the end of `$path`. Instead of `myfile.jpg` in the `upload_test` folder, you may find `upload_testmyfile.jpg` one level higher in your disk structure.

7. Change the value of `$max` to 3000, save `file_upload.php`, and test it again by selecting a file bigger than 2.9 KB to upload (any file in the images folder will do). Click the Upload button and check the `upload_test` folder. The file shouldn't be there.

8. If you're in the mood for experimentation, move the `MAX_FILE_SIZE` hidden field below the file input field, and try it again. Make sure you choose a different file from the one you used in step 6, because `move_uploaded_file()` overwrites existing files of the same name. You'll learn later how to give files unique names.

This time the file should be copied to your upload folder. The hidden field must come before the file input element for `MAX_FILE_SIZE` to have any effect. Move the hidden field back to its original position before continuing.

Creating a PHP File Upload Class

As you have just seen, it takes just a few lines of code to upload a file, but this is not enough on its own to call the job complete. You need to make the process more secure by implementing the following steps:

- Check the error level.

- Verify on the server that the file doesn't exceed the maximum permitted size.

- Check that the file is of an acceptable type.

- Remove spaces from the filename.

- Rename files that have the same name as an existing one to prevent overwriting.

- Handle multiple file uploads automatically.

- Inform the user of the outcome.

You need to implement these steps every time you want to upload files, so it makes sense to build a script that can be easily reused. That's why I have chosen to use a custom class. Building PHP classes is generally regarded as an advanced subject, but don't let that put you off. If you need to study the basics of working with classes and namespaces, see "Building Custom Classes" in Chapter 4.

If you're in a hurry, the finished class is in the ch09/Php8Solutions folder. Even if you don't build the script yourself, read through the descriptions so you have a clear understanding of how it works.

PHP Solution 9-2: Creating the Basic File Upload Class

In this PHP solution, you'll create the basic definition for a class called Upload to handle file uploads. You'll also create an instance of the class (an Upload object) and use it to upload an image. Give yourself plenty of time to go through the following steps. They're not difficult, but they introduce concepts that might be unfamiliar if you have never worked with PHP classes.

1. Create a subfolder called Php8Solutions in the php8sols site root folder. Use the same combination of uppercase and lowercase letters in the folder name.

2. Create a subfolder called File (with an uppercase F) in the Php8Solutions folder.

3. In the new Php8Solutions/File folder, create a file called Upload.php. Again, use the same combination of uppercase and lowercase letters in the filename. Then insert the following code:

```php
<?php
namespace Php8Solutions\File;
class Upload {
}
```

All the remaining code goes between the curly braces. This file will contain only PHP code, so you don't need a closing PHP tag.

■ **Note** Although the class is adapted from the version in the third and fourth editions of this book, it changes the signature of the constructor function made possible through new features in PHP. Consequently, I am using a different namespace from the previous editions. An important principle of object-oriented programming is that the user interface should remain the same even if the internal structure of a class changes. Using a different namespace indicates that the Upload class is not simply an updated version that can be slotted into an existing script.

---

4. PHP classes hide their inner workings by declaring some variables and functions as protected. If you prefix a variable or function with the keyword protected, it can be accessed only inside the class or a subclass. This prevents values from being changed accidentally.

   The Upload class needs protected variables for the following items:

   - Path to the upload folder

   - Maximum file size

   - Permitted MIME types

   - Messages to report the status of uploads

   Create variables for the permitted MIME types and messages by adding them inside the curly braces, like this:

   ```
   class Upload {
       protected $permitted = [
           'image/gif',
           'image/jpeg',
           'image/pjpeg',
           'image/png',
           'image/webp'
       ];
       protected $messages = [];
   }
   ```

   These properties can be accessed elsewhere in the class using $this->, which refers to the current object. For example, inside the class definition, you access $permitted as $this->permitted.

■ **Note** When you first declare a property inside a class, it begins with a dollar sign like any other variable. However, you omit the dollar sign from the property name after the -> operator.

   Both protected properties have been given a default value:

   - $permitted contains an array of image MIME types.

   - $messages is an empty array.

5. When you create an object, the class definition file automatically calls the class's constructor method, which initializes the object. The constructor method for all classes is called __construct() (with two underscores). Unlike the properties you defined in the previous step, the constructor needs to be accessible outside the class, so you precede its definition with the public keyword.

The constructor for the Upload class takes three arguments:

- The name of the file field in the upload form

- The path to the folder where you want to upload the file

- The maximum permitted file size (this will have a default value, making it optional)

The second and third arguments will create protected properties using the constructor property promotion feature that is new to PHP 8 (see "Using Constructor Property Promotion" in Chapter 4). Add the following code after the list of protected properties, making sure it's before the closing curly brace of the class definition:

```
public function __construct(
    string $field,
    protected string $path,
    protected int $max = 51200
) {
    if (!is_dir($this->path) && !is_writable($this->path)) {
        throw new \Exception("$this->path must be a valid, writable
        directory.");
    } else {
        $this->path = rtrim($this->path, '/\\') . DIRECTORY_
        SEPARATOR;
        if ($this->checkFile($_FILES[$field])) {
            $this->moveFile($_FILES[$field]);
        }
    }
}
```

Each argument is preceded by a type declaration, specifying that the first two must be strings and the third one an integer. The second and third parameters are preceded by a visibility declaration, making their values accessible through the rest of the class definition using $this.

The conditional statement inside the constructor passes the $path protected property to the is_dir() and is_writable() functions, which check that the value submitted is a valid directory (folder) that is writable. If it isn't, the constructor throws an exception.

■ **Note** Classes can define their own exceptions, and because the Upload class is defined within a namespace, it's ambiguous whether the constructor should use a custom exception or the Exception class that's a core part of PHP. To access core commands inside a namespace, you prefix them with a backslash. That's why there's a backslash in front of Exception. We're using the core Exception class, not a custom one.

If the value is a valid, writable directory, the rtrim() function removes any whitespace and slashes from the end of $path and then concatenates the correct directory separator for the operating system. This ensures that the path ends with a slash regardless of whether it's added by the user when creating an Upload object. When just one argument is passed to rtrim(), it removes only whitespace. The second, optional argument is a string containing all other characters to be stripped. Two backslashes are required to escape the closing quote.

The nested conditional statement passes $_FILES[$field] to two internal methods that we'll define next. The value of $field comes from the first argument passed to the constructor, so this will contain the name of the file input field.

■ **Tip** $_FILES is one of PHP's superglobal arrays, so it's available in all parts of a script. That's why there's no need to pass it as an argument to the class constructor method.

---

6. The nested conditional statement calls checkFile() using the $this keyword. The $this keyword is also used to call functions (methods) defined within the class. For the time being, we'll assume that the file is okay, so checkFile() will simply return true. Add the following code to the class definition:

```
protected function checkFile($file) {
    return true;
}
```

Preceding the definition with the protected keyword means this method can be accessed only inside the class. We'll return to checkFile() in PHP Solution 9-3 to add a series of tests before uploading the file.

■ **Tip**   The order of function (method) definitions inside a class doesn't matter, as long as they're within the curly braces that enclose the class. However, it's my preference to keep all public methods together at the top, with protected methods at the bottom.

---

7. If the file passes the series of tests, the conditional statement in the upload() method passes the file to another internal method called moveFile(), which is basically a wrapper for the move_uploaded_file() function that we used in PHP Solution 9-1. The code looks like this:

```
protected function moveFile($file) {
    $success = move_uploaded_file($file['tmp_name'],
        $this->destination . $file['name']);
    if ($success) {
        $result = $file['name'] . ' was uploaded successfully';
        $this->messages[] = $result;
    } else {
        $this->messages[] = 'Could not upload ' . $file['name'];
    }
}
```

If the upload succeeds, move_uploaded_file() returns true. Otherwise, it returns false. By storing the return value in $success, an appropriate message is stored in the $messages array. If $success is true, the message is initially assigned to $result, whereas on failure, it's assigned directly to the $messages array. That's because more information will be added later to the successful message if the file needs to be renamed.

8. Since $messages is a protected property, you need to create a public method to retrieve the contents of the array:

```
public function getMessages() {
    return $this->messages;
}
```

This simply returns the contents of the $messages array. Since that's all it does, why not make the array public in the first place? Public properties can be accessed—and changed—outside the class definition. Protecting $messages ensures that the contents of the array cannot be altered, so you know the message has been generated by the class. This might not seem like such a big deal with a message like this, but it becomes very important when you start working with more complex scripts or in a team.

9. Save Upload.php and switch to file_upload.php.

10. At the top of file_upload.php, import the Upload class by adding the following line immediately after the opening PHP tag:

```
use Php8Solutions\File\Upload;
```

■ **Caution**   You must import namespaced classes in the top level of a script, even if the class definition is loaded later. Putting use inside a conditional statement generates a parse error.

---

11. Inside the conditional statement, delete the code that calls the move_uploaded_file() function, and then use require_once to include the Upload class definition:

```
if (isset($_POST['upload'])) {
    // define the path to the upload folder
    $path = 'C:/upload_test/';
    require_once '../Php8Solutions/File/Upload.php';
}
```

12. We can now create an instance of the Upload class, but because it might throw an exception, it's best to create a try/catch block (see "Handling Errors and Exceptions" in Chapter 4). Add the following code immediately after the code you inserted in the previous step:

```
try {
    $loader = new Upload('image', $path);
    $result = $loader->getMessages();
} catch (Throwable $t) {
    echo $t->getMessage();
}
```

This creates an instance of the Upload class, called $loader, by passing it the name of the file input field and path to the upload_test folder. Then, it calls the getMessages() method, storing the result in $result.

The catch block will catch both internal errors and exceptions, so the type declaration is Throwable rather than Exception. There's no need to prefix Throwable with a backslash because the script in file_upload.php is not in a namespace. Only the class definition is in a namespace.

■ **Caution** The Upload class has a getMessages() method, while the exception uses getMessage(). That extra "s" makes a difference.

---

13. Add the following PHP code block above the form to display any messages returned by the $loader object:

```
<body>
<?php
if (isset($result)) {
    echo '<ul>';
    foreach ($result as $message) {
        echo "<li>$message</li>";
    }
echo '</ul>';
}
?>
<form action="file_upload.php" method="post" enctype="multipart/form-data">
```

This is a simple foreach loop that displays the contents of $result as an unordered list. When the page first loads, $result isn't set, so this code runs only after the form has been submitted.

14. Save file_upload.php and test it in a browser. As long as you choose an image that's less than 50 KB, you should see confirmation that the file was uploaded successfully, as shown in Figure 9-4.

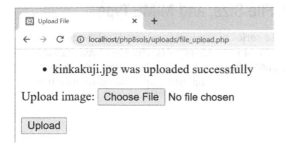

Figure 9-4. The Upload class reports a successful upload

You can compare your code with `file_upload_05.php` and `Php8Solutions/File/Upload_01.php` in the ch09 folder.

The class does exactly the same as PHP Solution 9-1: it uploads a file, but it requires a lot more code to do so. However, you have laid the foundation for a class that's going to perform a series of security checks on uploaded files. This is code that you'll write once. When you use the class, you won't need to write this code again.

If you haven't worked with objects and classes before, some of the concepts might seem strange. Think of the `$loader` object simply as a way of accessing the functions (methods) you have defined in the `Upload` class. You often create separate objects to store different values, for example, when working with `DateTime` objects. In this case, a single object is sufficient to handle the file upload.

Checking Upload Errors

As it stands, the `Upload` class uploads any type of file indiscriminately. Even the 50 KB limit can be circumvented, because the only check is made in the browser. Before handing the file to the `moveFile()` method, the `checkFile()` method needs to run a series of tests. One of the most important is to inspect the error level reported by the `$_FILES` array. Table 9-2 shows a full list of error levels.

Table 9-2. *Meaning of the different error levels in the $_FILES array*

Error level	Meaning
0	Upload successful.
1	File exceeds maximum upload size specified in `php.ini` (default 2 MB).
2	File exceeds size specified by `MAX_FILE_SIZE` (see PHP Solution 9-1).
3	File only partially uploaded.
4	Form submitted with no file specified.
6	No temporary folder.
7	Cannot write file to disk.
8	Upload stopped by an unspecified PHP extension.

Error level 5 is currently not defined.

PHP Solution 9-3: Testing the Error Level, File Size, and MIME Type

This PHP solution updates the `checkFile()` method to call a series of internal (protected) methods to verify that the file is okay to accept. If a file fails for any reason, an error message reports why. Continue working with `Upload.php`. Alternatively, use `Upload_01.php` in the ch09/Php8Solutions/File folder, move it to `Php8Solutions/File` at the top level of the php8sols site, and rename it `Upload.php`. (Always remove the underscore and number from partially completed files.)

1. The checkFile() method needs to run three tests: on the error level, the size of the file, and the file's MIME type. Update the method definition like this:

```
protected function checkFile($file) {
    $errorCheck = $this->getErrorLevel($file);
    $sizeCheck = $this->checkSize($file);
    $typeCheck = $this->checkType($file);
    return $errorCheck && $sizeCheck && $typeCheck;
}
```

The argument passed to the checkFile() method is the top-level element in the $_FILES array. The upload field in the form we're using is called image, so $file is the equivalent of $_FILES['image'].

Originally, checkFile() simply returned true. Now, it runs a series of internal methods that you'll define in a moment. Each of the methods will return true if the file passes the test. Otherwise, it will return false and append an appropriate error message to the $messages array if it finds a problem with the uploaded file. When each set of checks is complete, checkFile() returns the combined result of the checks. If any of the tests fails, it returns false and prevents the file from being uploaded. Otherwise, it returns true, allowing the file to be uploaded.

2. The getErrorLevel() method uses a match statement to check the error levels listed in Table 9-2. If the error level is 0, it means the file was uploaded successfully, so it returns true. Otherwise, it creates a suitable message to add to the $messages array and returns $result. The code looks like this:

```
protected function getErrorLevel($file) {
    $result = match($file['error']) {
        0 => true,
        1, 2 => $file['name'] . ' is too big: (max: ' .
        $this->getMaxSize() . ').',
        3 => $file['name'] . ' was only partially uploaded.',
        4 => 'No file submitted.',
        default => 'Sorry, there was a problem uploading ' .
        $file['name']
    };
    return $result;
}
```

Part of the message for error levels 1 and 2 is created by a method called getMaxSize(), which converts the value of $max from bytes to kilobytes. You'll define getMaxSize() shortly.

Only the first four error levels have descriptive messages. The default keyword catches other error levels, including any that might be added in the future, and adds a generic reason.

3. Because the match statement in getErrorLevel() returns an error message if there's a problem, we need to add it to the $messages property. Amend the checkFile() method to handle the return value like this:

```
$errorCheck = $this->getErrorLevel($file);
if ($errorCheck !== true) {
    $this->messages[] = $errorCheck;
    $errorCheck = false;
}
$sizeCheck = $this->checkSize($file);
```

This uses the not identical comparison operator to check the return value. If it's not a Boolean true, the error message returned by the match statement in getErrorLevel() is added to the $messages property, and $errorCheck is reset to false.

4. The checkSize() method looks like this:

```
protected function checkSize($file) {
    if ($file['error'] == 1 || $file['error'] == 2 ) {
        return false;
    } elseif ($file['size'] == 0) {
        $this->messages[] = $file['name'] . ' is an empty file.';
        return false;
    } elseif ($file['size'] > $this->max) {
        $this->messages[] = $file['name'] . ' exceeds the maximum size
            for a file (' . $this->getMaxSize() . ').';
        return false;
    }
    return true;
}
```

The conditional statement starts by checking the error level. If it's 1 or 2, the file is too big, so the method simply returns false. The appropriate error message has already been set by the getErrorLevel() method.

The next condition checks if the reported size is zero. Although this happens if the file is too big or no file was selected, those scenarios have already been covered by the getErrorLevel() method. So the assumption is that the file is empty. An appropriate message is generated, and the method returns false.

Next, the reported size is compared with the value stored in the $max property. Although files that are too big should trigger error level 2, you still need to make this comparison in case the user has managed to sidestep MAX_FILE_SIZE. The error message also uses getMaxSize() to display the maximum size and then returns false.

If the size is okay, the method returns true.

5. The third test checks the MIME type. Add the following code to the class definition:

```
protected function checkType($file) {
    if (!in_array($file['type'], $this->permitted)) {
        $this->messages[] = $file['name'] . ' is not a permitted type of file.';
        return false;
    }
    return true;
}
```

The conditional statement uses the in_array() function with the logical Not operator to check the type reported by the $_FILES array against the array stored in the $permitted property. If it's not in the array, the reason for rejection is added to the $messages array, and the method returns false. Otherwise, it returns true.

6. The getMaxSize() method used by getErrorLevel() and checkSize() converts the raw number of bytes stored in $max into a friendlier format. Add the following definition to the class file:

```
public function getMaxSize() {
    return number_format($this->max/1024, 1) . ' KB';
}
```

This uses the number_format() function, which normally takes two arguments: the value you want to format and the number of decimal places you want the number to have. The first argument is $this->max/1024, which divides $max by 1024 (the number of bytes in a kilobyte). The second argument is 1, so the number is formatted to one decimal place. The . ' KB' at the end concatenates KB to the formatted number.

The getMaxSize() method has been declared public in case you want to display the value in another part of a script that uses the Upload class.

7. Save Upload.php and test it again with file_upload.php. With images smaller than 50 KB, it works the same as before. But if you try uploading a file that's too big and of the wrong MIME type, you get a result similar to Figure 9-5.

You can check your code against Upload_02.php in the ch09/Php8Solutions/File folder.

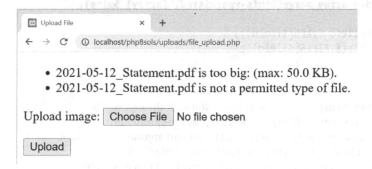

Figure 9-5. The class now reports errors with invalid size and MIME types

Changing Protected Properties

The $permitted property allows only images to be uploaded, and the $max property limits files to no more than 50 KB, but these limits might be too restrictive. You can change $max by using the optional third argument to the Upload constructor. Let's add another optional argument for the $permitted property.

PHP Solution 9-4: Allowing Different Types and Sizes to Be Uploaded

This PHP solution shows you how to allow other types of files to be uploaded as well as change the maximum permitted size. You'll also see how to use a named argument to avoid the need to supply all arguments when you don't want to change all optional ones.

Continue working with Upload.php from the previous PHP solution. Alternatively, use Upload_02.php in the ch09/Php8Solutions/File folder.

1. To make the Upload class more flexible, add another optional parameter to the constructor signature like this:

```
public function __construct(
        string $field,
        protected string $path,
        protected int $max = 51200,
        string|array|null $mime = null
    ) {
```

The $mime parameter is preceded by a union type declaration (see "Specifying Multiple Data Types" in Chapter 4), permitting a string, an array, or null. The default is null.

2. Edit the else block in the constructor method to add new MIME types to the $permitted property like this:

```
} else {
    $this->path = rtrim($this->path, '/\\') . DIRECTORY_SEPARATOR;
    if (!is_null($mime)) {
        $this->permitted = array_merge($this->permitted, (array) $mime);
    }
        if ($this->checkFile($_FILES[$field])) {
            $this->moveFile($_FILES[$field]);
        }
    }
```

The nested conditional statement uses the is_null() function with the logical Not operator to check whether $mime is null. If it isn't, the array_merge() function appends $mime to the array in the $permitted property. The second argument to array_merge() is preceded by the array casting operator (see Table 4-1 in Chapter 4). This converts $mime to an array if a single MIME type has been passed to the constructor as a string.

3. Save Upload.php and test file_upload.php again. It should continue to upload images smaller than 50 KB, as before.

4. Amend file_upload.php to add a named argument for the $mime optional parameter to the Upload constructor like this:

```
$loader = new Upload('image', $path, mime: 'application/pdf');
```

Named arguments use the name of the parameter stripped of the leading $ sign and followed by a colon. They allow you to skip other optional arguments if you don't want to change their value.

5. Test `file_upload.php` again to upload a PDF file. If it's smaller than 50 KB, it should work correctly. However, if the file exceeds 50 KB, you should see something similar to Figure 9-6.

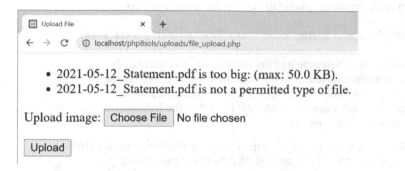

- 2021-05-12_Statement.pdf is too big: (max: 50.0 KB).
- 2021-05-12_Statement.pdf is not a permitted type of file.

Figure 9-6. There appears to be an error in checking the MIME type

What's happening is that the file isn't being uploaded because its size exceeds `MAX_FILE_SIZE`. As a result, the `type` element of the `$_FILES` array has no value. When that happens, there's no point in trying to check the MIME type.

6. Amend the `checkFile()` method to wrap the call to `checkType()` in a conditional statement like this:

```
protected function checkFile($file) {
    $errorCheck = $this->getErrorLevel($file);
    if ($errorCheck !== true) {
        $this->messages[] = $errorCheck;
        $errorCheck = false;
    }
    $sizeCheck = $this->checkSize($file);
    $typeCheck = false;
    if (!empty($file['type'])) {
        $typeCheck = $this->checkType($file);
    }
    return $errorCheck && $sizeCheck && $typeCheck;
}
```

This uses the `empty()` function with the logical Not operator to verify that the `type` element of the `$_FILES` array is not empty. However, `$typeCheck` will be an undefined variable if the check on the MIME type is not performed, so it needs to be initialized to `false` before the conditional statement. If the type is OK, `$typeCheck` will be reset to `true` by the `checkType()` method.

7. If you test the upload form with a large PDF file again, the false error message should no longer display.

8. Change the value of $max at the top of upload_file.php sufficiently to upload the large PDF (the code is just before the conditional statement that processes the upload). You also need to pass $max to the constructor in the try block. Normally, it should be the third argument, but one advantage of using named arguments is they can be in any order. Amend the call to the constructor like this:

```
$loader = new Upload('image', $path, mime: 'application/pdf', max: $max);
```

9. By changing the value of $max and passing it to the constructor, you affect both MAX_FILE_SIZE in the form's hidden field and the maximum value stored inside the class. Save file_upload.php and reload it in the browser before testing it again. This is necessary to refresh the value of MAX_FILE_SIZE in the hidden form field. Everything should now work correctly.

You can check your class definition against Upload_03.php in the ch09/Php8Solutions/File folder. There's an updated version of the upload form in file_upload_06.php in the ch09 folder.

By now I hope you're getting the idea of building a PHP class from functions (methods) dedicated to doing a single job. Fixing the incorrect error message about the PDF not being a permitted type was made easier by the fact that the message could only have come from the checkType() method. Most of the code used in the method definitions relies on built-in PHP functions. Once you learn which functions are best suited to the task at hand, building a class—or any other PHP script—becomes much easier.

PHP Solution 9-5: Renaming Files

By default, PHP overwrites existing files if the uploaded file has the same name as one already in the upload folder. This PHP solution improves the Upload class by adding the option to insert a number before the filename extension if there's a conflict of names. It also replaces spaces in filenames with underscores because spaces can occasionally cause problems.

Continue working with Upload.php from the previous PHP solution. Alternatively, use Upload_03.php in the ch09/Php8Solutions/File folder.

1. Add a new protected property to the existing ones at the top of the class definition in Upload.php:

```
protected $newName;
```

This will be used to store the file's new name if it is changed.

2. Add a fifth optional parameter to the constructor signature to control the renaming of duplicates like this:

```
public function __construct(
        string $field,
        protected string $path,
        protected int $max = 51200,
        string|array|null $mime = null,
        bool $rename = true
    ) {
```

This makes the renaming of files the default.

3. We need to check the filename after it has passed the other tests run by the checkFile() method. Add the following line highlighted in bold to the final conditional statement in the constructor method:

```
if ($this->checkFile($_FILES[$field]) {
    $this->checkName($_FILES[$field], $rename);
    $this->moveFile($_FILES[$field]);
}
```

You don't need to check the filename if the file has failed any of the previous tests, so the code highlighted in bold calls a new method checkName() only if checkFile() returns true.

4. Define checkName() as a protected method. The first part of the code looks like this:

```
protected function checkName($file, $rename) {
    $this->newName = null;
    $nospaces = str_replace(' ', '_', $file['name']);
    if ($nospaces != $file['name']) {
        $this->newName = $nospaces;
    }
}
```

The method begins by setting the $newName property to null (in other words, no value). The class will eventually be capable of handling multiple file uploads. Consequently, the property needs to be reset each time.

Then, the str_replace() function replaces spaces in the filename with underscores and assigns the result to $nospaces. The str_replace() function was described in PHP Solution 5-4.

The value of $nospaces is compared with $file['name']. If they're not the same, $nospaces is assigned as the value of the $newName property.

That deals with spaces in filenames. Before handling duplicate filenames, let's fix the code that moves the uploaded file to its destination.

5. If the name has been changed, the moveFile() method needs to use the amended name when saving the file. Update the beginning of the moveFile() method like this:

```
protected function moveFile($file) {
    $filename = $this->newName ?? $file['name'];
    $success = move_uploaded_file($file['tmp_name'], $this->path .
    $filename);
    if ($success) {
```

The new first line uses the null coalescing operator (see "Setting a Default Value with the Null Coalescing Operator" in Chapter 4) to assign a value to $filename. If the $newName property has been set by the checkName() method, the new name is used. Otherwise, $file['name'], which contains the original value from the $_FILES array, is assigned to $filename.

On the second line, $filename replaces the value concatenated to the $path property. So, if the name has been changed, the new name is used to store the file. But if no change has been made, the original name is used.

6. It's a good idea to let the user know if the filename has been changed. Make the following change to the conditional statement in moveFile() that creates the message if the file has been successfully uploaded:

```
if ($success) {
    $result = $file['name'] . ' was uploaded successfully';
    if (!is_null($this->newName)) {
        $result .= ', and was renamed ' . $this->newName;
    }
    $this->messages[] = $result;
}
```

If the $newName property is not null, you know the file has been renamed, and that information is added to the message stored in $result using the combined concatenation operator (.=).

7. Save Upload.php and test uploading files that have spaces in their names. The spaces should be replaced by underscores, as shown in Figure 9-7.

Figure 9-7. *The spaces have been replaced by underscores*

8. Next, add the code for renaming duplicate files to the checkName() method. Insert the following code just before the method's closing curly brace:

```
if ($rename) {
    $name = $this->newName ?? $file['name'];
        if (file_exists($this->path . $name)) {
        // rename file
        $basename = pathinfo($name, PATHINFO_FILENAME);
        $extension = pathinfo($name, PATHINFO_EXTENSION);
        $this->newName = $basename . '_' . time() . ".$extension";
    }
}
```

The conditional statement checks whether $rename is true or false. The code inside the braces is executed only if it's true.

The first line of code inside the conditional block uses the null coalescing operator to set the value of $name. This is the same technique used in the moveFile() method. If the $newName property has a value, that value is assigned to $name. Otherwise, the original name is used.

We can then check whether a file with the same name already exists by concatenating $name onto the $path property to get the full path and passing it to the file_exists() function. This returns true if there's already a file with that name in the upload directory.

If a file with the same name already exists, the next two lines use pathinfo() to split the filename into its base name and extension using the constants PATHINFO_FILENAME and PATHINFO_EXTENSION, respectively. Now that we've got both the base name and the extension stored in separate variables, it's easy to build a new name by inserting a number between the base name and the extension. Ideally, the numbers should run incrementally from 1. However, on a busy site, this would consume a lot of resources and doesn't guarantee against a race condition where two people are uploading a file with the same name simultaneously. I've opted for a simpler solution that inserts an underscore followed by the current Unix timestamp between the base name and extension. The time() function returns the current time expressed as the number of seconds since midnight UTC (Coordinated Universal Time) at the beginning of January 1, 1970.

9. Save Upload.php and test the revised class in file_upload.php. Start by adding a named argument for rename and setting it to false in the call to the Upload constructor, like this:

```
$loader = new Upload('image', $path, mime: 'application/pdf', max:
$max, rename: false);
```

10. Upload the same file several times. You should receive a message that the upload has been successful, but when you check the contents of the upload_test folder, there should be only one copy of the file. It has been overwritten each time.

11. Remove the final argument from the call to the constructor:

```
$loader = new Upload('image', $path, mime: 'application/pdf', max:
$max);
```

12. Save file_upload.php and repeat the test, uploading the same file several times. Each time you upload the file, you should see a message that it has been renamed.

13. Check the results by inspecting the contents of the upload_test folder. You should see something similar to Figure 9-8.

Check your code, if necessary, against `Upload_04.php` in the `ch09/Php8Solutions/File` folder.

Figure 9-8. *The class removes spaces from filenames and prevents files from being overwritten.*

■ **Tip**   In this PHP Solution, using named arguments wasn't strictly necessary because the first two optional arguments are always used, although not in the same order as in the constructor signature. The value of named arguments lies in the ability to skip optional arguments while setting others that are listed later in the function signature. Named arguments are available only in PHP 8 and later.

Uploading Multiple Files

You now have a flexible class for file uploads, but it can handle only one file at a time. Adding the `multiple` attribute to the file field's `<input>` tag permits the selection of multiple files in an HTML5-compliant browser.

The final stage in building the `Upload` class is to adapt it to handle multiple files. To understand how the code works, you need to see what happens to the `$_FILES` array when a form allows for multiple uploads.

How the $_FILES Array Handles Multiple Files

Since `$_FILES` is a multidimensional array, it's capable of handling multiple uploads. In addition to adding the `multiple` attribute to the `<input>` tag, you need to add an empty pair of square brackets to the `name` attribute, like this:

```
<input type="file" name="image[]" id="image" multiple>
```

As you learned in Chapter 6, adding square brackets to the `name` attribute submits multiple values as an array. You can examine how this affects the `$_FILES` array by using `multi_upload.php` in the `ch09` folder. Figure 9-9 shows the result of selecting three files in a browser that supports the `multiple` attribute.

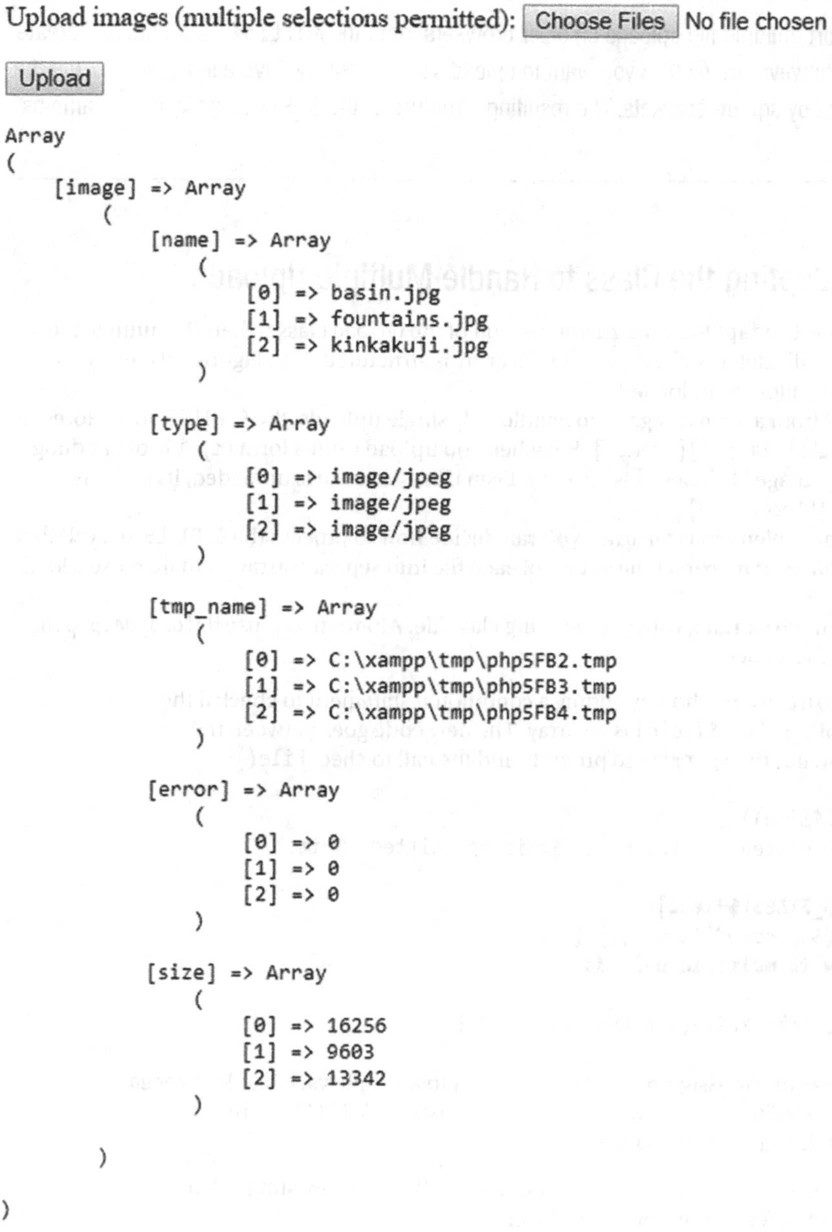

Upload images (multiple selections permitted): | Choose Files | No file chosen

| Upload |

```
Array
(
    [image] => Array
        (
            [name] => Array
                (
                    [0] => basin.jpg
                    [1] => fountains.jpg
                    [2] => kinkakuji.jpg
                )

            [type] => Array
                (
                    [0] => image/jpeg
                    [1] => image/jpeg
                    [2] => image/jpeg
                )

            [tmp_name] => Array
                (
                    [0] => C:\xampp\tmp\php5FB2.tmp
                    [1] => C:\xampp\tmp\php5FB3.tmp
                    [2] => C:\xampp\tmp\php5FB4.tmp
                )

            [error] => Array
                (
                    [0] => 0
                    [1] => 0
                    [2] => 0
                )

            [size] => Array
                (
                    [0] => 16256
                    [1] => 9603
                    [2] => 13342
                )

        )

)
```

Figure 9-9. *The $_FILES array can upload multiple files in a single operation*

Although this structure is not as convenient as having the details of each file stored in a separate subarray, the numeric keys keep track of the details that refer to each file. For example, $_FILES['image']['name'][2] relates directly to $_FILES['image']['tmp_name'][2], and so on.

261

■ **Tip** If you need to support multiple file uploads on older browsers, omit the `multiple` attribute and create separate file input fields for however many files you want to upload simultaneously. Give each `<input>` tag the same name attribute followed by square brackets. The resulting structure of the `$_FILES` array is the same as in Figure 9-9.

PHP Solution 9-6: Adapting the Class to Handle Multiple Uploads

This PHP solution shows how to adapt the constructor method of the `Upload` class to handle multiple file uploads. The class automatically detects when the `$_FILES` array is structured as in Figure 9-9 and uses a loop to handle however many files are uploaded.

When you upload a file from a form designed to handle only single uploads, the `$_FILES` array stores the filename as a string in `$_FILES['image']['name']`. But when you upload from a form capable of handling multiple uploads, `$_FILES['image']['name']` is an array. Even if only one file is uploaded, its name is stored as `$_FILES['image']['name'][0]`.

So, by detecting if the name element is an array, you can decide how to process the `$_FILES` array. If the name element is an array, you need to extract the details of each file into separate arrays and then use a loop to process each one.

With that in mind, continue working with your existing class file. Alternatively, use `Upload_04.php` in the `ch09/Php8Solutions/File` folder.

1. Amend the constructor method by adding a conditional statement to check if the name element of `$_FILES[$field]` is an array. The new code goes between the section that updates the `$permitted` property and the call to `checkFile()`:

```
if (!is_null($mime)) {
    $this->permitted = array_merge($this->permitted, $mime);
}
$uploaded = $_FILES[$field];
if (is_array($uploaded['name'])) {
    // deal with multiple uploads
} else {
    if ($this->checkFile($_FILES[$field])) {
```

The new code begins by assigning `$_FILES[$field]` to a simple variable, `$uploaded`. This avoids the need to use nested array references, such as `$_FILES[$field]['name']`, in code that will be added later.

If `$uploaded['name']` is an array, it needs special handling. The existing call to `checkFile()` now goes inside a new `else` block.

2. In order to deal with multiple uploads, the challenge is to gather the five values associated with a single file (name, type, etc.) before passing them to the `checkFile()`, `checkName()`, and `moveFile()` methods.

If you refer to Figure 9-9, each element in the `$uploaded` array is an indexed array. So the name of the first file is at index 0 of the name subarray, its type is at index 0 of the type subarray, and so on. We can use a loop to extract each value at index 0 and combine the values with the relevant keys.

First, we need to find out how many files have been uploaded. That's easily done by passing the name subarray to the count() function. Add the following code after the multiple uploads comment like this:

```
// deal with multiple uploads
$numFiles = count($uploaded['name']);
```

3. Next, extract the subarray keys by adding the following code on the next line:

```
$keys = array_keys($uploaded);
```

This creates an array consisting of name, type, tmp_file, and so on.

4. Now we can create a loop to build an array of the details of each file. Add the following code after the code you have just inserted:

```
for ($i = 0; $i < $numFiles; $i++) {
    $values = array_column($uploaded, $i);
    $currentfile = array_combine($keys, $values);
    print_r($currentfile);
}
```

The loop reorganizes the contents of the $_FILES array so that the details of each file are available as if they had been uploaded individually. In other words, instead of all the name, type, and other elements being grouped together, $currentfile contains an associative array of a single file's details that can be processed using the methods we've already defined in the Upload class.

It achieves this with just two lines of code. So let's examine what's going on. The array_column() function extracts from a multidimensional array all elements in subarrays that have the same key or index passed to it as the second argument. In this case, the second argument is the counter $i. When the loop first runs, $i is 0. So it extracts the value at index 0 in each subarray of $uploaded (in other words $_FILES['image']). The fact that each subarray has a different key (name, type, etc.) is irrelevant; array_column() searches only for matching keys or indexes inside each subarray. In effect, it gets the details of the first file that has been uploaded.

The array_combine() function then builds an array, assigning each value to its related key. So the value at index 0 of the name subarray becomes $currentfile['name'], the value at index 0 of the type subarray becomes $currentfile['type'], and so on.

The next time the loop runs, $i is incremented, building an array of the second file's details. The loop keeps on running until the details of all files have been processed. Because this can be difficult to grasp conceptually, I've added print_r() to inspect the results.

5. Save Upload.php. To test it, update file_upload.php by adding a pair of square brackets at the end of the name attribute in the file field and insert the multiple attribute, like this:

```
<input type="file" name="image[]" id="image" multiple>
```

You don't need to make any changes to the PHP code above the DOCTYPE declaration. The code is the same for both single and multiple uploads.

6. Save file_upload.php and reload it in your browser. Test it by selecting multiple files. When you click Upload, the details of each file should be displayed in separate arrays. Right-click to view the browser's source code. You should see something like Figure 9-10.

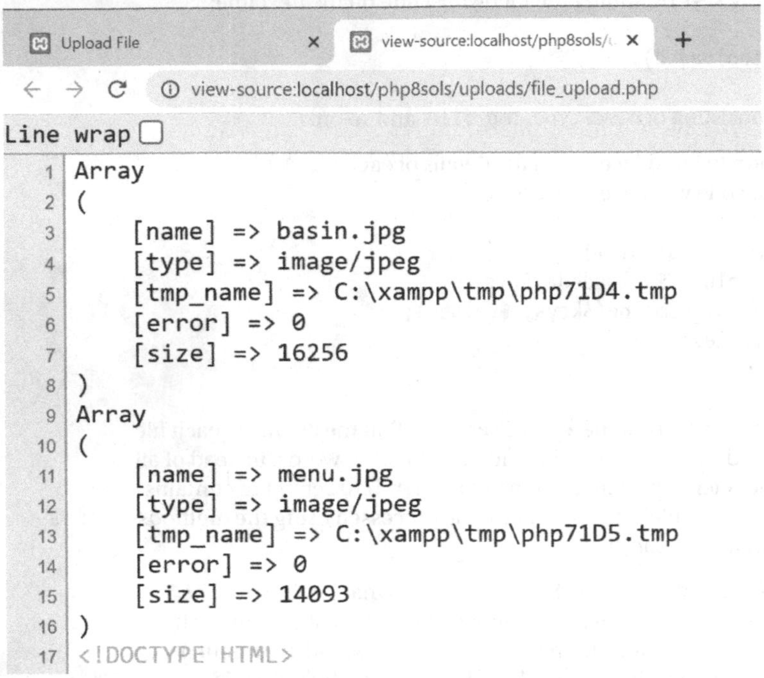

```
1  Array
2  (
3      [name] => basin.jpg
4      [type] => image/jpeg
5      [tmp_name] => C:\xampp\tmp\php71D4.tmp
6      [error] => 0
7      [size] => 16256
8  )
9  Array
10 (
11     [name] => menu.jpg
12     [type] => image/jpeg
13     [tmp_name] => C:\xampp\tmp\php71D5.tmp
14     [error] => 0
15     [size] => 14093
16 )
17 <!DOCTYPE HTML>
```

Figure 9-10. The details of each uploaded file are now in separate arrays.

7. Now that we have an individual array of details for each file, we can process them the same way as before. The simple way to do this would be to copy the following block of code from the else block and paste it into the for loop in place of the call to print_r() (changing all instances of $_FILES[$field] to $currentfile):

```
if ($this->checkFile($_FILES[$field])) {
    $this->checkName($_FILES[$field], $rename);
    $this->moveFile($_FILES[$field]);
}
```

It's only four lines of code, so repeating it doesn't seem a big deal. However, you might need to edit the code in the future, perhaps to add in further checks. You would then need to make the same changes to both blocks—and that's where code errors begin to creep in. This is now a separate routine that should be in a dedicated internal method.

Instead of copying this section of code, cut it to your clipboard.

8. Create a new protected method inside the Upload class definition and paste the code you have just cut into it. Change $_FILES[$field] to $uploaded to match the first parameter in the function signature. The new method looks like this:

```php
protected function processUpload($uploaded, $rename) {
    if ($this->checkFile($uploaded)) {
        $this->checkName($uploaded, $renameDuplicates);
        $this->moveFile($uploaded);
    }
}
```

9. Invoke this new method in the for loop and the else block. The complete updated version of the constructor method now looks like this:

```php
public function __construct(
    string $field,
    protected string $path,
    protected int $max = 51200,
    string|array|null $mime = null,
    bool $rename = true
) {
    if (!is_dir($this->path) && !is_writable($this->path)) {
        throw new \Exception("$this->path must be a valid, writable directory.");
    } else {
        $this->path = rtrim($this->path, '/\\') . DIRECTORY_SEPARATOR;
        if (!is_null($mime)) {
            $this->permitted = array_merge($this->permitted, (array) $mime);
        }
        $uploaded = $_FILES[$field];
        if (is_array($uploaded['name'])) {
            // deal with multiple uploads
            $numFiles = count($uploaded['name']);
            $keys = array_keys($uploaded);
            for ($i = 0; $i < $numFiles; $i++) {
                $values = array_column($uploaded, $i);
                $currentfile = array_combine($keys, $values);
                $this->processUpload($currentfile, $rename);
            }
        } else {
            $this->processUpload($_FILES[$field], $rename);
        }
    }
}
```

10. Save Upload.php and try uploading multiple files. You should see messages relating to each file. Files that meet your criteria are uploaded. Those that are too big or of the wrong type are rejected. The class also works with single files.

You can check your code against Upload_05.php in the ch09/Php8Solutions/File folder.

Using the Upload Class

The Upload class is simple to use—just import the namespace, include the class definition in your script, and create an Upload object by passing the input field name and file path to the upload folder, like this:

```
$path = 'C:/upload_test/';
$loader = new Upload('image', $path);
```

■ **Tip**   The trailing slash at the end of the path to the upload folder is optional.

By default, the class permits only images to be uploaded; it limits the maximum size to 50 KB; and it renames files that have spaces in their name or that already exist in the upload folder. The defaults can be overridden by submitting values for the following optional arguments:

- $size: An integer to change the default maximum file size in bytes (default 51200, equivalent to 50 KB).

- $permitted: A string of a single MIME type or an array of multiple types to allow files other than images to be uploaded.

- $rename: Setting this to false overwrites files with the same name in the upload folder.

The class has two public methods, namely:

- getMessages(): Returns an array of messages reporting the status of uploads.

- getMaxSize(): Returns the maximum permitted size formatted as kilobytes rounded to one decimal place.

Points to Watch with File Uploads

The basic script in PHP Solution 9-1 shows that uploading files from a web form is fairly straightforward with PHP. The main causes of failure are not setting the correct permissions on the upload directory or folder and forgetting to move the uploaded file to its target destination before the end of the script. The problem with the basic script is that it lets just about anything to be uploaded. That's why this chapter has devoted so much effort to building a more robust solution. Even with the extra checks performed in the Upload class, you should consider security carefully.

Letting other people upload files to your server exposes you to risk. In effect, you're allowing visitors the freedom to write to your server's hard disk. It's not something you would allow strangers to do on your own computer, so you should guard access to your upload directory with the same degree of vigilance.

Ideally, uploads should be restricted to registered and trusted users, so the upload form should be in a password-protected part of your site. Registration enables you to block people who misuse your trust. Also, the upload folder does not need to be inside your site root, so locate it in a private directory whenever possible. Uploaded images might contain hidden scripts, so they shouldn't be located in a folder that has execute permissions. Remember there is no way PHP can check that material is legal or decent, so immediate public display entails risks that go beyond the merely technical. You should also bear the following security points in mind:

- Set a maximum size for uploads both in the web form and on the server side.

- Restrict the types of uploaded files by inspecting the MIME type in the $_FILES array.

- Replace spaces in filenames with underscores or hyphens.

- Inspect your upload folder on a regular basis. Make sure there's nothing in there that shouldn't be, and do some housekeeping from time to time. Even if you limit file upload sizes, you may run out of your allocated space without realizing it.

Chapter Review

This chapter has introduced you to creating a PHP class. If you're new to PHP or programming, you might have found it tough going. Don't be disheartened. The Upload class contains more than 150 lines of code, some of it complex, although I hope the descriptions have explained what the code is doing at each stage. Even if you don't understand all the code, the Upload class will save you a lot of time. It implements the main security measures necessary for file uploads, yet using it involves fewer than a dozen lines of code:

```
use Php8Solutions\File\Upload;
if (isset($_POST['upload'])) {
    require_once 'Php8Solutions/File/Upload.php'; // use correct path
    try {
        $loader = new Upload('image', 'C:/upload_test/');  // field name and destination
        folder as arguments
        $result = $loader->getMessages();
    } catch (Throwable $t) {
        echo $t->getMessage();
    }
}
```

If you found this chapter to be a struggle, come back to it later when you have more experience, and you should find the code easier to understand.

In the next chapter, you'll learn how to use PHP's image manipulation functions to generate thumbnails from larger images. You'll also extend the Upload class from this chapter to upload and resize images in a single operation.

■ ■ ■

CHAPTER 10

Generating Thumbnail Images

PHP has an extensive range of functions designed to work with images. You've already met one of them, getimagesize(), in Chapter 5. As well as providing useful information about an image's dimensions, PHP can manipulate images by resizing or rotating them. It can also add text dynamically without affecting the original and can even create images on the fly.

To give you just a taste of PHP image manipulation, I'm going to show you how to generate a smaller copy of an uploaded image. Most of the time you'll want to use a dedicated graphics program, such as Adobe Photoshop, to generate thumbnail images because it will give you much better quality control. However, automatic thumbnail generation with PHP can be very useful if you want to allow registered users to upload images while ensuring they conform to a maximum size. You can save just the resized copy or the copy along with the original.

In the previous chapter, you built a PHP class to handle file uploads. In this chapter you'll create two classes: one to generate thumbnail images and the other to upload and resize images in a single operation. Rather than build the second class from scratch, you'll base it on the Upload class from Chapter 9. A great advantage of using classes is that they're **extensible**—a class based on another can inherit the functionality of its parent class. Building the classes to upload images and generate thumbnails from them involves a lot of code. But once you have defined the classes, using them involves only a few lines of script. If you're in a rush or if writing a lot of code makes you break out in a cold sweat, you can just use the finished classes. Come back later to learn how the code works. It uses many basic PHP functions that you'll find useful in other situations.

In this chapter, you'll learn about the following:

- Scaling an image
- Saving a rescaled image
- Automatically resizing and renaming uploaded images
- Creating a subclass by extending an existing one

Checking Your Server's Capabilities

Working with images in PHP relies on the gd extension. The all-in-one PHP packages recommended in Chapter 2 support gd by default, but you need to make sure the gd extension has also been enabled on your remote web server. As in previous chapters, run phpinfo() on your web site to check the server's configuration. Scroll down until you reach the section shown in the following screenshot (it should be about halfway down the page):

© David Powers 2022

D. Powers, *PHP 8 Solutions*, https://doi.org/10.1007/978-1-4842-7141-4_10

gd

GD Support	enabled
GD Version	bundled (2.1.0 compatible)
FreeType Support	enabled
FreeType Linkage	with freetype
FreeType Version	2.9.1
GIF Read Support	enabled
GIF Create Support	enabled
JPEG Support	enabled
libJPEG Version	9 compatible
PNG Support	enabled
libPNG Version	1.6.34
WBMP Support	enabled
XPM Support	enabled
libXpm Version	30512
XBM Support	enabled
WebP Support	enabled
BMP Support	enabled
TGA Read Support	enabled

Directive	Local Value	Master Value
gd.jpeg_ignore_warning	1	1

If you can't find this section, the gd extension isn't enabled, so you won't be able to use any of the scripts in this chapter on your web site. Ask for it to be enabled or move to a different host.

Don't forget to delete the file that runs `phpinfo()` unless it's in a password-protected directory.

Manipulating Images Dynamically

The gd extension allows you to generate images entirely from scratch or work with existing images. Either way, the underlying process always follows four basic steps:

1. Create a resource for the image in the server's memory while it's being processed.

2. Process the image.

3. Display and/or save the image.

4. Remove the image resource from the server's memory.

This process means that you are always working on an image in memory only and not on the original. Unless you save the image to disk before the script terminates, any changes are discarded. Working with images typically requires a lot of memory, so it's vital to destroy the image resource as soon as it's no longer needed. If a script runs slowly or crashes, it probably indicates that the original image is too large.

Making a Smaller Copy of an Image

The aim of this chapter is to show you how to resize images automatically on upload. This involves extending the Upload class from Chapter 9. However, to make it easier to understand how to work with PHP's image manipulation functions, I propose to start by using images already on the server and then create a separate class to generate the thumbnail images.

Getting Ready

The starting point is the following simple form, which uses PHP Solution 7-3 to create a drop-down menu of the photos in the images folder. You can find the code in create_thumb_01.php in the ch10 folder. Copy it to a new folder called gd in the php8sols site root and rename it create_thumb.php.

The form in the body of the page looks like this:

```
<form method="post" action="create_thumb.php">
    <p>
        <select name="pix" id="pix">
            <option value="">Select an image</option>
            <?php
            $files = new FilesystemIterator('../images');
            $images = new RegexIterator($files, '/\.(?:jpg|png|gif|webp)$/i');
            foreach ($images as $image) { ?>
                <option value="<?= $image->getRealPath() ?>">
                    <?= $image->getFilename() ?></option>
            <?php } ?>
        </select>
    </p>
    <p>
        <input type="submit" name="create" value="Create Thumbnail">
    </p>
</form>
```

When loaded into a browser, the drop-down menu should display the names of the photos in the images folder. This makes it easier to pick images quickly for testing. The fully qualified path for each image is inserted in the value attribute of the <option> tag by calling the SplFileInfo getRealPath() method.

Inside the upload_test folder that you created in Chapter 9, create a new folder called thumbs, making sure it has the necessary permissions for PHP to write to it. Refer to "Establishing an Upload Directory" in the previous chapter if you need to refresh your memory.

Building the Thumbnail Class

To generate a thumbnail image, the class needs to execute the following steps:

1. Get the dimensions of the original image.

2. Get the image's MIME type.

3. Calculate the scaling ratio.

4. Create an image resource of the correct MIME type for the original image.

5. Create an image resource for the thumbnail.

6. Create the resized copy.

7. Save the resized copy to the destination folder using the correct MIME type.

8. Destroy the image resources to free memory.

In addition to generating a thumbnail image, the class automatically inserts _thb before the filename extension, but an optional argument to the constructor method allows you to alter this value. Another optional argument sets the maximum size of the thumbnail. To keep the calculations simple, the maximum size controls only the larger of the thumbnail's dimensions.

To avoid naming conflicts, the Thumbnail class will use a namespace. Because it's exclusively for images, we'll create a new folder called Image in the Php8Solutions folder and use Php8Solutions\Image as the namespace.

There's a lot to do, so I'll break up the code into sections. They're all part of the same class definition, but presenting the script this way should make it easier to understand, particularly if you want to use some of the code in a different context.

PHP Solution 10-1: Getting the Image Details

This PHP solution describes how to get the dimensions and MIME type of the original image.

1. Create a new folder called Image in the Php8Solutions folder. Then create a page called Thumbnail.php inside the folder. The file will contain only PHP, so strip out any HTML code inserted by your editing program.

2. Declare the namespace at the top of the new file:

```
namespace Php8Solutions\Image;
```

3. The class needs to keep track of quite a few properties. Begin the class definition by listing them, like this:

```
class Thumbnail {
    protected $original;
    protected $originalWidth;
    protected $originalHeight;
    protected $basename;
    protected $imageType;
    protected $messages = [];
}
```

As in the Upload class, all the properties have been declared as protected, which means they can't be changed accidentally outside the class definition. The names are descriptive, so they need little explanation.

4. The constructor takes four arguments, two of them optional. The first two required arguments are the path to the image and the path to the folder where the thumbnail is to be created. The two optional arguments set the maximum size of the thumbnail's longer dimension and the suffix to be added to the filename. The last three arguments use PHP 8's constructor property promotion to set them as protected properties. Add the constructor definition after the list of properties defined in the previous step, but inside the closing curly brace:

```
public function __construct(
    string $image,
    protected string $path,
    protected int $max = 120,
    protected string $suffix = '_thb'
```

```
) {
  if (is_file($image) && is_readable($image)) {
      $dimensions = getimagesize($image);
  } else {
      throw new \Exception("Cannot open $image.");
  }
  if (!is_array($dimensions)) {
      throw new \Exception("$image doesn't appear to be an image.");
  } else {
      if ($dimensions[0] == 0) {
          throw new \Exception("Cannot determine size of $image.");
      }
      // check the MIME type
      if (!$this->checkType($dimensions['mime'])) {
          throw new \Exception('Cannot process that type of file.');
      }
  }
  if (is_dir($path) && is_writable($path)) {
      $this->path = rtrim($path, '/\\') . DIRECTORY_SEPARATOR;
  } else {
      throw new \Exception("Cannot write to $path.");
  }
  $this->original = $image;
  $this->originalWidth = $dimensions[0];
  $this->originalHeight = $dimensions[1];
  $this->basename = pathinfo($image, PATHINFO_FILENAME);
  $this->max = abs($max);
  if ($suffix != '_thb') {
      $this->suffix = $this->setSuffix($suffix) ?? '_thb';
  }
}
```

The constructor begins with a conditional statement that checks that $image is a file and is readable. If it is, it's passed to getimagesize(), and the result is stored in $dimensions. Otherwise, an exception is thrown. As in the previous chapter, Exception is preceded by a backslash to indicate that we want to use the core Exception class rather than a custom one for this namespaced class.

When you pass an image to getimagesize(), it returns an array containing the following elements:

- 0: Width (in pixels)

- 1: Height

- 2: An integer indicating the type of image

- 3: A string containing the correct width and height attributes ready for insertion in an <img> tag

- mime: The image's MIME type

- channels: 3 for RGB and 4 for CMYK images

- bits: The number of bits for each color

273

If the value passed as an argument to getimagesize() isn't an image, it returns false. Consequently, if $dimensions isn't an array, an exception is thrown reporting that the file doesn't appear to be an image. But if $dimensions is an array, it looks as though we're dealing with an image. But the else block makes two further checks before proceeding.

If the value of the first element in the $dimensions array is 0, there's something wrong with the image, so an exception is thrown reporting that the image's size can't be determined. The next check passes the reported MIME type to an internal method called checkType() that will be defined in the next step. If checkType() returns false, another exception is thrown.

The next conditional statement uses the same technique as in PHP Solution 9-2 to check that the folder where the thumbnail will be created exists and is writable, removing any trailing slashes and concatenating the appropriate directory separator for the operating system.

This series of exceptions prevents any further processing if there's a problem with the image or folder. Assuming the script gets this far, the image's path is stored in the $original property, and its width and height are stored in $originalWidth and $originalHeight, respectively.

The file's name without the filename extension is extracted using pathinfo() with the PATHINFO_FILENAME constant in the same way as in PHP Solution 9-5. This is stored in the $basename property and will be used to build the thumbnail's name with the suffix.

The value of $max is passed to the abs() function before it's assigned to the $max property. The type declaration in the constructor signature ensures that only an integer will be accepted, but passing the value to abs() converts it to a positive number in the event of it being negative.

The final conditional statement checks whether the argument supplied as $suffix is different from the default. If it is, it's passed to the setSuffix() method that we'll define shortly. This returns either a string or null. If the return value is a string, it's assigned to the $suffix property. But if it's null, the null coalescing operator (See "Setting a Default Value with the Null Coalescing Operator" in Chapter 4) reassigns the default value to the property.

5. The checkType() method compares the MIME type with an array of acceptable image types. If it finds a match, it stores the type in the $imageType property and returns true. Otherwise, it returns false. The method is used internally, so it needs to be declared as protected. Add the following code to the class definition:

```
protected function checkType($mime) {
    $mimetypes = ['image/jpeg', 'image/png', 'image/gif', 'image/webp'];
    if (in_array($mime, $mimetypes)) {
        // extract the characters after '/'
        $this->imageType = substr($mime, strpos($mime, '/')+1);
        return true;
    }
    return false;
}
```

JPEG, PNG, and GIF are universally supported by browsers; I have also included WebP because support is now widespread. All image MIME types begin with image/. To make the value easier to use later, the substr() function extracts the characters after the slash and stores them in the $imageType property. When used with two arguments, substr() starts at the position (counting from 0) specified in the second argument and returns the rest of the string. Rather than use a fixed number as the second argument, I have used the strpos() function to find the position of the slash and added 1. This makes the code more generic because some proprietary image formats begin with application/ rather than image/. The first argument to strpos() is the entire string you're searching in, and the second is the string you're searching for.

6. The setSuffix() method needs to make sure the value doesn't contain any special characters. The code looks like this:

```
protected function setSuffix($suffix) {
    if (preg_match('/^\w+$/', $suffix)) {
        if (!str_starts_with($suffix, '_')) {
            return '_' . $suffix;
        } else {
            return $suffix;
        }
    }
}
```

This uses preg_match(), which takes a regular expression as its first argument and searches for a match in the value passed as the second argument. Regular expressions need to be wrapped in a pair of matching delimiter characters—normally forward slashes, as used here. Stripped of the delimiters, the regex looks like this:

```
^\w+$
```

In this context, the caret (^) tells the regex to start at the beginning of the string. The \w is a regex token that matches any alphanumeric character or an underscore. The + means match the preceding token or character one or more times, and the $ means match the end of the string. In other words, the regex matches a string that contains only alphanumeric characters and underscores. If the string contains spaces or special characters, it won't match.

If the match fails, the default $suffix property remains unchanged. Otherwise, this conditional statement is executed:

```
if (!str_starts_with($suffix, '_') ) {
```

The condition equates to true if the first character of $suffix is *not* an underscore. It uses the str_starts_with() function, which is new to PHP 8. As the name suggests, it checks the first character of a string. So, if the suffix doesn't begin with an underscore, one is added. Otherwise, the original value is preserved. In either case, the value is returned.

However, if the argument supplied to the constructor contains any characters other than alphanumeric ones and the underscore, the conditional statement fails, and the method returns nothing—in other words, `null`.

7. It's a good idea to test your code as you build the class. Catching errors early is much easier than hunting for a problem in a long script. To test the code, create a new public method called `test()` inside the class definition.

It doesn't matter in which order your methods appear inside the class definition, but it's common practice to keep all public methods together after the constructor and to put protected methods at the bottom of the file. This makes the code easier to maintain.

Insert the following definition between the constructor and the `checkType()` definition:

```
public function test() {
    $values = <<<END
    <pre>
    File: $this->original
    Original width: $this->originalWidth
    Original height: $this->originalHeight
    Base name: $this->basename
    Image type: $this->imageType
    Max: $this->max
    Path: $this->path
    Suffix: $this->suffix
    </pre>
    END;
    echo $values;
    if ($this->messages) {
        print_r($this->messages);
    }
}
```

This uses echo with heredoc syntax (see "Avoiding the Need to Escape Quotes with Heredoc Syntax" in Chapter 4) and `print_r()` to display the value of the properties. Although there are no quotes in the output, using heredoc syntax with <pre> tags makes both the code and the output easier to read.

8. To test the class definition so far, save `Thumbnail.php` and add the following code to the PHP block above the `DOCTYPE` declaration in `create_thumb.php` (the code can be found in `create_thumb_02.php` in the `ch10` folder):

```
use Php8Solutions\Image\Thumbnail;
    if (isset($_POST['create'])) {
        require_once('../Php8Solutions/Image/Thumbnail.php');
        try {
            $thumb = new Thumbnail($_POST['pix'] ,
                'C:/upload_test/thumbs', suffix: '$%^');
            $thumb->test();
```

```
    } catch (Throwable $t) {
        echo $t->getMessage();
    }
}
```

This imports the Thumbnail class from the Php8Solutions\Image namespace and then adds the code that is to be executed when the form is submitted.

The name attribute of the Submit button in create_thumb.php is create, so this code runs only when the form has been submitted. It includes the Thumbnail class definition; creates an instance of the class, passing the selected value from the form and the path to the thumbs folder (adjust as necessary to match your own setup), as well as a named argument for suffix that has deliberately used nonalphanumeric characters; and then calls the test() method.

The catch block uses Throwable as the type declaration, so it will handle both internal PHP errors and exceptions thrown by the Thumbnail class.

9. Save create_thumb.php and load it into a browser. Select an image and click Create Thumbnail. This produces output similar to Figure 10-1.

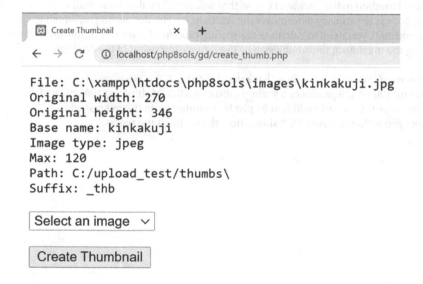

Figure 10-1. Displaying the details of the selected image confirms the code is working

---

■ **Note** Figure 10–1 was taken on Windows, so the DIRECTORY_SEPARATOR constant has appended a backslash to the path. This makes no difference because PHP accepts both forward- and backslashes in Windows paths.

Notice that the default suffix has been substituted for the one that contained nonalphanumeric characters.

10. Test the script again with different values for the suffix, using only alphanumeric characters and beginning with and without an underscore. Also try a different size for the $max property.

   If necessary, check your code against Thumbnail_01.php in the ch10/Php8Solutions/Images folder.

■ **Caution** The value of $_POST['pix'] is being passed directly to the test() method because it's coming directly from our own form. In a production environment, you should always check values received from a form. For example, use basename() to extract just the filename and specify allowable directories.

Although some properties have default values, you need to provide options to change the maximum size of the thumbnail image and the suffix applied to the base of the filename. You also need to tell the class where to create the thumbnail.

PHP Solution 10-2: Calculating the Thumbnail's Dimensions

This PHP solution adds a protected method to the Thumbnail class that will calculate the thumbnail's dimensions. The value set in the $maxSize property determines the width or height, depending on which is larger. To avoid distorting the thumbnail, you need to calculate the scaling ratio for the shorter dimension. The ratio is calculated by dividing the maximum thumbnail size by the larger dimension of the original image.

For example, the original image of the Golden Pavilion (kinkakuji.jpg) is 270 × 346 pixels. If the maximum size is set at 120, dividing 120 by 346 produces a scaling ratio of 0.3468. Multiplying the width of the original image by this ratio fixes the thumbnail's width at 94 pixels (rounded up to the nearest whole number), maintaining the correct proportions. Figure 10-2 shows how the scaling ratio works.

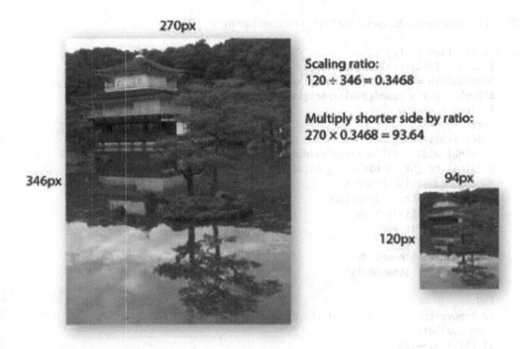

Figure 10-2. Working out the scaling ratio for a thumbnail image

Continue working with your existing class definition. Alternatively, use Thumbnail_01.php in the ch10/Php8Solutions/Image folder.

1. Calculating the thumbnail dimensions doesn't require any further user input, so it can be handled by a protected method. Add the following code to the class definition.

    ```php
    protected function calculateRatio() {
        if ($this->originalWidth <= $this->max &&
            $this->originalHeight <= $this->max) {
            return 1;
        } elseif ($this->originalWidth > $this->originalHeight) {
            return $this->max/$this->originalWidth;
        } else {
            return $this->max/$this->originalHeight;
        }
    }
    ```

    The conditional statement begins by checking if the width and height of the original image are less than or equal to the maximum size. If they are, the image doesn't need to be resized, so the method returns a scaling ratio of 1.

    The elseif block checks if the width is greater than the height. If it is, the width is used to calculate the scaling ratio. The else block is invoked if the height is greater or both sides are equal. In either case, the height is used to calculate the scaling ratio.

279

2. To test the new method, amend the `test()` method like this:

```
public function test() {
    $ratio = $this->calculateRatio();
    $thumbWidth = round($this->originalWidth * $ratio);
    $thumbHeight = round($this->originalHeight * $ratio);
    $values = <<<END
<pre>
File: $this->original
Original width: $this->originalWidth
Original height: $this->originalHeight
Base name: $this->basename
Image type: $this->imageType
Destination: $this->path
Max size: $this->maxSize
Suffix: $this->suffix
Thumb width: $thumbWidth
Thumb height: $thumbHeight
</pre>
END;
    // Remove the indentation of the preceding line in < PHP 7.3
    echo $values;
    if ($this->messages) {
        print_r($this->messages);
    }
}
```

This calls the new method. The resulting scaling ratio is then used to calculate the width and height of the thumbnail. The calculation is passed to the `round()` function to convert the result to the nearest integer. The calculations will need to be moved out of the `test()` method, but it's important to check first that we're getting the expected results.

3. Test the updated class by selecting an image in `create_thumb.php` and clicking `Create Thumbnail`. You should see the values displayed onscreen, as shown in Figure 10-3. Experiment with different values for the maximum size of the thumbnail.

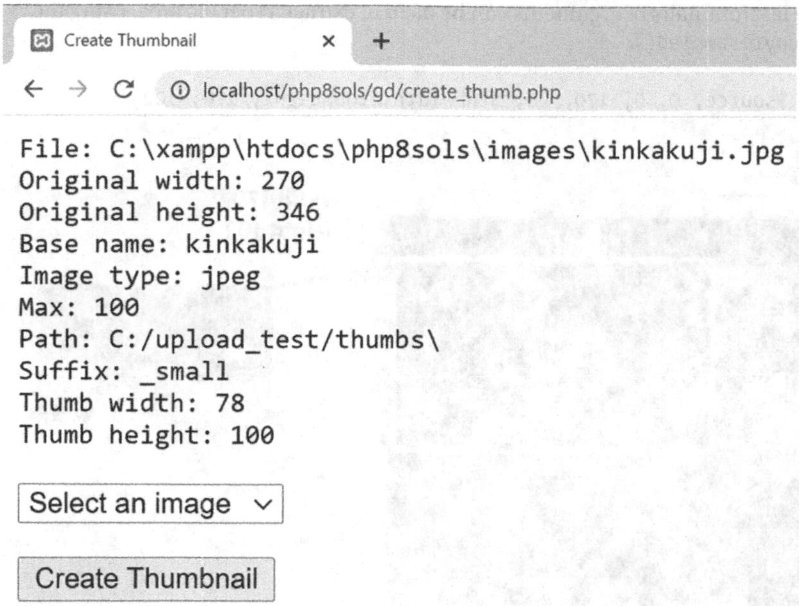

```
File: C:\xampp\htdocs\php8sols\images\kinkakuji.jpg
Original width: 270
Original height: 346
Base name: kinkakuji
Image type: jpeg
Max: 100
Path: C:/upload_test/thumbs\
Suffix: _small
Thumb width: 78
Thumb height: 100
```

Figure 10-3. *The class is now generating all the values needed to create the thumbnail image*

If necessary, check your code against Thumbnail_02.php in the ch10 folder.

Using gd Functions to Create a Scaled Copy of an Image

After you have gathered all the necessary information, you can generate a thumbnail image from a larger one. This involves creating image resources for both the original image and the thumbnail. For the original image, you need to use a function that matches the image's MIME type. Each of the following functions takes a single argument—the path to the file:

- imagecreatefromjpeg()

- imagecreatefrompng()

- imagecreatefromgif()

- imagecreatefromwebp()

Because the thumbnail doesn't yet exist, you use a different function, imagecreatetruecolor(), which takes two arguments—the width and height (in pixels).

Yet another function creates a resized copy of an image: imagecopyresampled(). This takes no fewer than ten arguments—all of them required. The arguments fall into five pairs, as follows:

- References to the two image resources—copy first, original second

- The x and y coordinates of where to position the top-left corner of the copied image

- The x and y coordinates of the top-left corner of the original

- The width and height of the copy

- The width and height of the area to copy from the original

Figure 10-4 shows how the last four pairs of arguments can be used to extract a specific area, using the following arguments to `imagecopyresampled()`:

```
imagecopyresampled($thumb, $source, 0, 0, 170, 20, $thbwidth,$thbheight, 170, 102);
```

Figure 10-4. *The imagecopyresampled() function allows you to copy part of an image*

The x and y coordinates of the area to copy are measured in pixels from the top left of the image. The x and y axes begin at 0 at the top left and increase to the right and down. By setting the width and height of the area to copy to 170 and 102, respectively, PHP extracts the area outlined in white.

So now you know how web sites manage to crop uploaded images. They calculate the coordinates dynamically using JavaScript or some other technology. For the `Thumbnail` class, you'll use the whole of the original image to generate the thumbnail.

After creating the copy with `imagecopyresampled()`, you need to save it, again using a function specific to the MIME type, namely:

- `imagejpeg()`
- `imagepng()`
- `imagegif()`
- `imagewebp()`

Each function takes as its first two arguments the image resource and the path to where you want to save it.

The `imagejpeg()`, `imagepng()`, and `imagewebp()` functions take an optional third argument to set the image quality. For `imagejpeg()` and `imagewebp()`, you set the quality by specifying a number in the range from 0 (worst) to 100 (best). If you omit the argument, the default is 75 for `imagejpeg()` and 80 for `imagewebp()`. For `imagepng()`, the range is 0–9. Confusingly, 0 produces the best quality (no compression).

Finally, once you have saved the thumbnail, you need to destroy the image resources by passing them to `imagedestroy()`. In spite of its destructive name, this function has no effect on the original image or the thumbnail. It simply frees the server memory by destroying the image resources required during processing.

PHP Solution 10-3: Generating the Thumbnail Image

This PHP solution completes the Thumbnail class by creating the image resources, copying the thumbnail, and saving it in the destination folder.

Continue working with your existing class definition. Alternatively, use Thumbnail_02.php in the ch10/Php8Solutions/Image folder.

1. Now that we have verified that the class is calculating the correct values to generate a thumbnail image, we can rename the test() method and delete the code that displayed the results. Change the method's name to create() and delete everything except the first three lines. You should be left with this:

```php
public function create() {
    $ratio = $this->calculateRatio();
    $thumbWidth = round($this->originalWidth * $ratio);
    $thumbHeight = round($this->originalHeight * $ratio);
}
```

2. The image resource for the original image needs to be specific to its MIME type, so create an internal method to select the correct type. Add the following code to the class definition:

```php
protected function createImageResource() {
    switch ($this->imageType) {
        case 'jpeg':
            return imagecreatefromjpeg($this->original);
        case 'png':
            return imagecreatefrompng($this->original);
        case 'gif':
            return imagecreatefromgif($this->original);
        case 'webp':
            return imagecreatefromwebp($this->original);
    }
}
```

The checkType() method that you created in PHP Solution 10-1 stores the MIME type as jpeg, png, gif, or webp. So the switch statement checks the MIME type, matches it to the appropriate function, and passes the original image as an argument. The method then returns the resulting image resource.

3. The create() method needs two image resources: one for the original image and the other for the thumbnail. Update the create() method like this:

```php
public function create() {
    $ratio = $this->calculateRatio();
    $thumbWidth = round($this->originalWidth * $ratio);
    $thumbHeight = round($this->originalHeight * $ratio);
    $resource = $this->createImageResource();
    $thumb = imagecreatetruecolor($thumbWidth, $thumbHeight);
}
```

This calls the `createImageResource()` method that you created in step 2 and then creates an image resource for the thumbnail, passing the thumbnail's width and height to `imagecreatetruecolor()`.

4. The next stage in creating the thumbnail involves passing both image resources to `imagecopyresampled()` and setting the coordinates and dimensions. Add the following line of code to the `create()` method:

```
imagecopyresampled($thumb, $resource, 0, 0, 0, 0, $thumbWidth, $thumbHeight,
$this->originalWidth, $this->originalHeight);
```

The first two arguments are the image resources you have just created for the thumbnail and original image. The next four arguments set the x and y coordinates for both the copy and the original to the top-left corner. Next come the width and height calculated for the thumbnail, followed by the original image's width and height. Setting arguments 3–6 to the top-left corner and both sets of dimensions to the full amounts copies the whole original image to the whole of the thumbnail. In other words, it creates a smaller copy of the original.

You don't need to assign the result of `imagecopyresampled()` to a variable. The scaled-down image is now stored in $thumb, but you still need to save it.

5. Complete the definition of `create()` like this:

```
public function create() {
    $ratio = $this->calculateRatio();
    $thumbWidth = round($this->originalWidth * $ratio);
    $thumbHeight = round($this->originalHeight * $ratio);
    $resource = $this->createImageResource();
    $thumb = imagecreatetruecolor($thumbWidth, $thumbHeight);
    imagecopyresampled($thumb, $resource, 0, 0, 0, 0, $thumbWidth,
        $thumbHeight, $this->originalWidth, $this->originalHeight);
    $newname = $this->basename . $this->suffix;
    switch ($this->imageType) {
        case 'jpeg':
            $newname .= '.jpg';
            $success = imagejpeg($thumb, $this->path . $newname);
            break;
        case 'png':
            $newname .= '.png';
            $success = imagepng($thumb, $this->path . $newname);
            break;
        case 'gif':
            $newname .= '.gif';
            $success = imagegif($thumb, $this->path . $newname);
            break;
        case 'webp':
            $newname .= '.webp';
            $success = imagewebp($thumb, $this->path . $newname);
            break;
    }
```

```
    if ($success) {
        $this->messages[] = "$newname created successfully.";
    } else {
        $this->messages[] = "Couldn't create a thumbnail for " .
            basename($this->original);
    }
    imagedestroy($resource);
    imagedestroy($thumb);
}
```

The first line of new code concatenates the suffix to the filename stripped of its filename extension. So, if the original file is called menu.jpg and the default _thb suffix is used, $newname becomes menu_thb.

The switch statement checks the image's MIME type and appends the appropriate filename extension. In the case of menu.jpg, $newname becomes menu_thb.jpg. The scaled-down image is then passed to the appropriate function to save it, using the destination folder and $newname as the path for where it is saved. I have omitted the optional quality argument for JPEG, PNG, and WebP images. The default quality should be sufficient for thumbnail images.

The result of the save operation is stored in $success. Depending on the outcome, $success is either true or false, and an appropriate message is added to the $messages property. The message is created using the basename() function rather than the $basename property because the filename extension has been stripped from the property, whereas the function preserves it.

Finally, imagedestroy() frees the server memory by destroying the resources used to create the thumbnail image.

6. Up to now, you have used the test() method to display error messages. Create a public method to get the messages:

```
public function getMessages() {
    return $this->messages;
}
```

7. Save Thumbnail.php. In create_thumb.php, replace the call to the test() method with a call to create(). Also call getMessages() and assign the result to a variable, like this:

```
$thumb->create();
    $messages = $thumb->getMessages();
```

8. Add a PHP code block just after the opening <body> tag to display any messages:

```
<?php
if (!empty($messages)) {
    echo '<ul>';
    foreach ($messages as $message) {
        echo "<li>$message</li>";
    }
    echo '</ul>';
}
?>
```

You've seen this code in previous chapters, so it needs no explanation.

Save create_thumb.php, load it in a browser, and test it by selecting an image from the list and clicking Create Thumbnail. If all goes well, you should see a message reporting the creation of the thumbnail, and you can confirm its existence in the thumbs subfolder of upload_test, as shown in Figure 10-5.

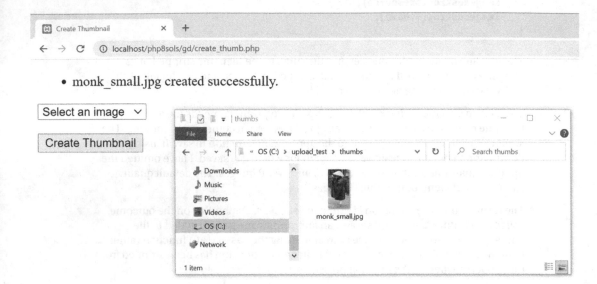

Figure 10-5. *The thumbnail has been successfully created in the destination folder*

9. If the thumbnail isn't created, the error message generated by the Thumbnail class should help you detect the source of the problem. Also, check your code carefully against Thumbnail_03.php in the ch10/Php8Solutions/Image folder. If the tests in the previous PHP solutions worked, the error is likely in the create(), createImageResource(), or createThumbnail() method definition. The other place to check is, of course, your PHP configuration. The class depends on the gd extension being enabled. Although gd is widely supported, it's not always on by default.

Resizing an Image Automatically on Upload

Now that you have a class that creates a thumbnail from a larger image, it's relatively simple to adapt the Upload class from Chapter 9 to generate a thumbnail from an uploaded image—in fact, not only from a single image but also from multiple images.

Instead of changing the code in the Upload class, it's more efficient to extend the class and create a subclass. You then have the choice of using the original class to perform uploads of any type of file or the subclass to create thumbnail images on upload. The subclass also needs to provide the option to save or discard the larger image after the thumbnail has been created.

Before diving into the code, let's take a quick look at how you create a subclass.

Extending a Class

We saw an example of extending a built-in class, RecursiveIteratorIterator, in "PHP Solution 8-8: Building Nested Lists Automatically." The advantage of extending a class is that the new **subclass** or **child class** inherits all the features of its parent, including both properties and methods, but can adapt (or **override**) some of them and acquire new ones of its own. This simplifies the process of creating a class to perform a more specialized task. The Upload class you created in Chapter 9 performs basic file uploads. In this chapter, you'll extend it to create a child class called ThumbnailUpload that uses the basic upload features of its parent but adds specialized features that create thumbnail images. The subclass will be created in the Php8Solutions/Image folder, so it will use Php8Solutions\Image as its namespace.

Like all children, a child class often needs to borrow from its parent. This frequently happens when you override a method in the child class but need to use the original version as well. To refer to the parent version, you prefix it with the parent keyword followed by two colons, like this:

```
parent::originalMethod();
```

You'll see how this works in PHP Solution 10-4, because the child class defines its own constructor to add extra arguments but also needs to use the parent constructor.

Let's create a class capable of uploading images and generating thumbnails at the same time.

PHP Solution 10-4: Creating the ThumbnailUpload Class

This PHP solution extends the Upload class from Chapter 9 and uses it in conjunction with the Thumbnail class to upload and resize images. It demonstrates how to create a child class and override parent methods. To create the child class, you need Upload.php from Chapter 9 and Thumbnail.php from this chapter. There's a copy of these files in the ch09/Php8Solutions/File and ch10/Php8Solutions/Image folders, respectively.

1. Create a new file called ThumbnailUpload.php in the Php8Solutions/Image folder. It will contain only PHP code, so strip out any HTML inserted by your script editor and add the following code:

    ```php
    <?php
    namespace Php8Solutions\Image;
    use Php8Solutions\File\Upload;
    require_once __DIR__ . '/../File/Upload.php';
    require_once 'Thumbnail.php';
    class ThumbnailUpload extends Upload {
    }
    ```

    This declares the Php8Solutions\Image namespace and imports the Upload class from the Php8Solutions\File namespace before including the definitions of the Upload and Thumbnail classes.

■ **Note** When used in an include file, __DIR__ returns the directory of the included file without a trailing slash. Adding the slash at the beginning of the relative path to Upload.php allows PHP to build a complete path, moving back up one level to find it in the Php8Solutions/File folder. Thumbnail.php is in the same folder as ThumbnailUpload.php, so it's included using only the filename. See "Nesting Include Files" in Chapter 5.

The ThumbnailUpload class then declares that it extends Upload. Although Upload is in a different namespace, you can refer to it simply as Upload because it has been imported. All subsequent code needs to be inserted between the curly braces of the class definition.

2. When you extend a class, the only time you need to define a constructor method is when you want to change how the constructor works. The ThumbnailUpload class takes a total of seven arguments, most of them optional. When testing locally, a Thumbnail object can access the original image on your own hard drive. However, generating the thumbnail is a server-side operation, so it won't work on a web site without first uploading the original image to the server. So the first three arguments to the constructor are the same as for the Upload class: the image input field ($field), the path to the location where the image is uploaded ($path), and the maximum file size of the uploaded image ($max). The remaining parameters set values related to the thumbnail. All parameters are preceded by a visibility declaration, using PHP 8's constructor property promotion to automatically make them protected class properties. The constructor looks like this:

```php
public function __construct(
    protected string $field,
    protected string $path,
    protected int $max = 51200,
    protected int $maxDimension = 120,
    protected string $suffix = '_thb',
    protected ?string $thumbPath = null,
    protected bool $deleteOriginal = false,
) {
    $this->thumbPath = $thumbPath ?? $path;
    if (is_dir($this->thumbPath) && is_writable($this->thumbPath)) {
        $this->thumbPath = rtrim($this->thumbPath, '/\\') .
            DIRECTORY_SEPARATOR;
    } else {
        throw new \Exception("$this->thumbPath must be a valid,
            writable directory.");
    }
    parent::__construct(
        $this->field,
        $this->path,
        $this->max
    );
}
```

The last five parameters all have default values, so they're optional arguments. The value of $maxDimension sets the maximum size of the larger dimension of the thumbnail. This value is also set in the Thumbnail class. It's repeated here so you can override it when uploading an image and generating the thumbnail in a single operation. The same is true of the $suffix parameter.

The $thumbPath parameter is preceded by a nullable type declaration, which means the value must be either a string or null. The first line in the body of the constructor uses the null coalescing operator (??) to assign the value to the $thumbPath property.

If the value passed to the constructor is null, the value of $path is used instead, creating the thumbnail in the same directory as the uploaded image.

The final parameter, $deleteOriginal, is a Boolean that determines whether the full-size image should be deleted after the thumbnail is created. By default, it's set to false, preserving the image.

The conditional statement in the constructor body uses the same technique as in PHP Solution 9–2 to check that the folder where the thumbnail will be created exists and is writable, removing any trailing slashes and concatenating the appropriate directory separator for the operating system.

Finally, the constructor calls the Upload constructor using the parent keyword, passing it the name of the file input field, the path to the upload folder, and the maximum upload size. In effect, the constructor of the extended class initializes all the class properties needed to upload the full-size image and generate the thumbnail before calling the parent constructor to upload the full-size version.

3. In the parent class, the moveFile() method saves an uploaded file to its target destination. The thumbnail needs to be generated from the original image, so you need to override the parent's moveFile() method and use it to call a new protected method called createThumbnail() that you'll define shortly. Copy the moveFile() method from Upload.php and amend it by adding the code highlighted in bold:

```
protected function moveFile($file) {
    $filename = $this->newName ?? $file['name'];
    $success = move_uploaded_file($file['tmp_name'],
        $this->path . $filename);
    if ($success) {
        // add a message only if the original image is not deleted
        if (!$this->deleteOriginal) {
            $result = $file['name'] . ' was uploaded successfully';
            if (!is_null($this->newName)) {
                $result .= ', and was renamed ' . $this->newName;
            }
            $this->messages[] = $result;
        }
        // create a thumbnail from the uploaded image
        $this->createThumbnail($this->path . $filename);
        // delete the uploaded image if required
        if ($this->deleteOriginal) {
            unlink($this->path . $filename);
        }
    } else {
        $this->messages[] = 'Could not upload ' . $file['name'];
    }
}
```

If the original image has been uploaded successfully, the new code adds a conditional statement to generate the message only if $deleteOriginal is false. It then calls the createThumbnail() method, passing it the uploaded image as the argument. Finally, if $deleteOriginal has been set to true, it uses unlink() to delete the uploaded image, leaving only the thumbnail.

4. The protected method to generate the thumbnail looks like this:

```
protected function createThumbnail($image) {
    $thumb = new Thumbnail($image, $this->thumbPath,
        $this->maxDimension, $this->suffix);
    $thumb->create();
    $messages = $thumb->getMessages();
    $this->messages = array_merge($this->messages, $messages);
}
```

This takes a single argument, the path to an image, and creates a Thumbnail object, passing all four arguments to the Thumbnail constructor: the path to the image, the path to where the thumbnail should be created, the maximum size of the larger dimension, and the suffix to be appended to the filename. It then calls the create() and getMessages() methods on the Thumbnail object to generate the new image and get any messages created as a result.

The final line uses array_merge() to merge the messages generated by the Thumbnail object with the $messages property of the ThumbnailUpload class. Although the ThumbnailUpload class doesn't define a $messages property of its own, the child class automatically inherits it from its parent.

5. Save ThumbnailUpload.php. To test it, copy create_thumb_upload_01.php from the ch10 folder to the gd folder and save it as create_thumb_upload.php. The file contains a simple form with a file field and a PHP block that displays messages. Add the following PHP code block above the DOCTYPE declaration:

```
<?php
use Php8Solutions\Image\ThumbnailUpload;
if (isset($_POST['upload'])) {
    require_once('../Php8Solutions/Image/ThumbnailUpload.php');
    try {
        $loader = new ThumbnailUpload('image', 'C:/upload_test/',
            thumbPath: 'C:/upload_test/thumbs');
        $messages = $loader->getMessages();
    } catch (Throwable $t) {
        echo $t->getMessage();
    }
}
?>
```

This example supplies three arguments to the ThumbnailUpload constructor. The first two are required: the file input field name and the path to the folder where the full-size image is to be uploaded. The final argument is a PHP 8 named argument that specifies the path to the folder for the thumbnail file, skipping the intervening parameters and using the default settings. Adjust the paths in the constructor, if necessary.

6. Save create_thumb_upload.php and load it in a browser. Click the Browse or Choose Files button and select multiple images. When you click the Upload button, you should see messages informing you of the successful upload and creation of the thumbnails. Check the destination folders, as shown in Figure 10-6.

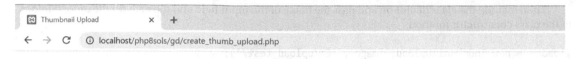

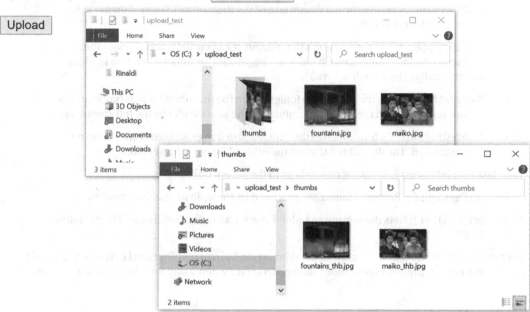

- fountains.jpg was uploaded successfully
- fountains_thb.jpg created successfully.
- maiko.jpg was uploaded successfully
- maiko_thb.jpg created successfully.

Upload images to create thumbnails: Choose Files No file chosen

Upload

Figure 10-6. *The thumbnails are created at the same time as the images are uploaded*

7. Test the ThumbnailUpload class by uploading the same images again. This time, the original images and thumbnails should be renamed in the same way as in Chapter 9 through the addition of a number before the filename extension.

8. Try different tests, changing the suffix inserted into the thumbnail names or deleting the original image after the thumbnail has been created. If you run into problems, check your code against ThumbnailUpload.php in the ch10/ Php8Solutions/Image folder.

Using the ThumbnailUpload Class

The ThumbnailUpload class is easy to use. Because it uses a namespace, import the class at the top level of your file like this:

```
use Php8Solutions\Image\ThumbnailUpload;
```

Then include the class definition and pass the name of the input field and the path for the upload folder to the class constructor method:

```
$loader = new ThumbnailUpload('image', 'C:/upload_test/');
```

By default, the thumbnail is created in the same folder as the full-size image; but you can change various defaults using five optional arguments, either by passing them in the correct order or by using named arguments. The following options can be used as named arguments:

- max: Sets the maximum size of the full-size image in bytes. The default is 51200, which is the equivalent of 50 KB.

- maxDimension: Specifies the maximum size of the thumbnail's larger dimension in pixels. The default is 120.

- suffix: Appended to the thumbnail's filename. It can contain only alphanumeric characters and the underscore. If it doesn't begin with an underscore, one is added automatically. The default is '_thb'.

- thumbPath: Specifies the path to the folder where the thumbnail is to be created. The default is null, which creates the thumbnail in the same folder as the full-size image.

- deleteOriginal: Determines whether the full-size image is deleted after creating the thumbnail. The default is false, so the original image is preserved.

The class also inherits the following methods from the parent Upload class:

- getMessages(): Retrieves messages generated by the upload and the thumbnail.

- getMaxSize(): Gets the maximum upload size for an individual image. The default is 50 KB.

Because the ThumbnailUpload class is dependent on the Upload and Thumbnail classes, you need to upload all three class definition files to your remote web server when using this class on a live web site.

Chapter Review

This has been another intense chapter, showing not only how to generate thumbnails from larger images but also introducing you to extending an existing class and overriding inherited methods. Designing and extending classes can be confusing at first, but it becomes less intimidating if you concentrate on what each method is doing. A key principle of class design is to break large tasks down into small, manageable units. Ideally, a method should perform a single task, such as creating the image resource for the original image.

The real advantage of using classes is the time and effort they save once you have defined them. Instead of typing dozens of lines of code each time you want to add file or thumbnail upload functionality to a web site, calling the class involves just a few simple lines. Also, don't think of the code in this chapter as being exclusively for creating and uploading thumbnail images. Many of the subroutines in the class files could be adapted for use in other situations.

In the next chapter, you'll learn all about PHP sessions, which preserve information related to a specific user and play a vital role in password-protecting web pages.

■ ■ ■

CHAPTER 11

Pages That Remember: Simple Login and Multipage Forms

The Web is a brilliant illusion. When you visit a well-designed web site, you get a great feeling of continuity, as though flipping through the pages of a book or a magazine. Everything fits together as a coherent entity. The reality is quite different. Each part of an individual page is stored and handled separately by the web server. Apart from needing to know where to send the relevant files, the server has no interest in who you are. Each time a PHP script runs, the variables exist only in the server's memory and are normally discarded as soon as the script finishes. Even variables in the $_POST and $_GET arrays have only a brief lifespan. Their value is passed once to the next script and then removed from memory unless you do something with it, such as storing the information in a hidden form field. Even then, it persists only if the form is submitted.

To get around these problems, PHP uses **sessions**. After briefly describing how sessions work, I'll show you how you can use session variables to create a simple, file-based login system and pass information from one page to another without the need to use hidden form fields.

In this chapter, you'll learn about the following:

- Understanding what sessions are and how to create them
- Creating a file-based login system
- Checking password strength with a custom-built class
- Setting a time limit for sessions
- Using sessions to keep track of information over multiple pages

What Sessions Are and How They Work

A session ensures continuity by storing a random identifier—the session ID—on the web server and as a cookie on the visitor's computer. The web server uses the cookie to recognize that it's communicating with the same person (or, to be more precise, with the same computer). Figures 11-1 to 11-3 show the details of a simple session created in my local testing environment.

As Figure 11-1 shows, the cookie stored in the browser is called PHPSESSID, and the content is a jumble of letters and numbers. This random string is the session's ID.

© David Powers 2022
D. Powers, *PHP 8 Solutions*, https://doi.org/10.1007/978-1-4842-7141-4_11

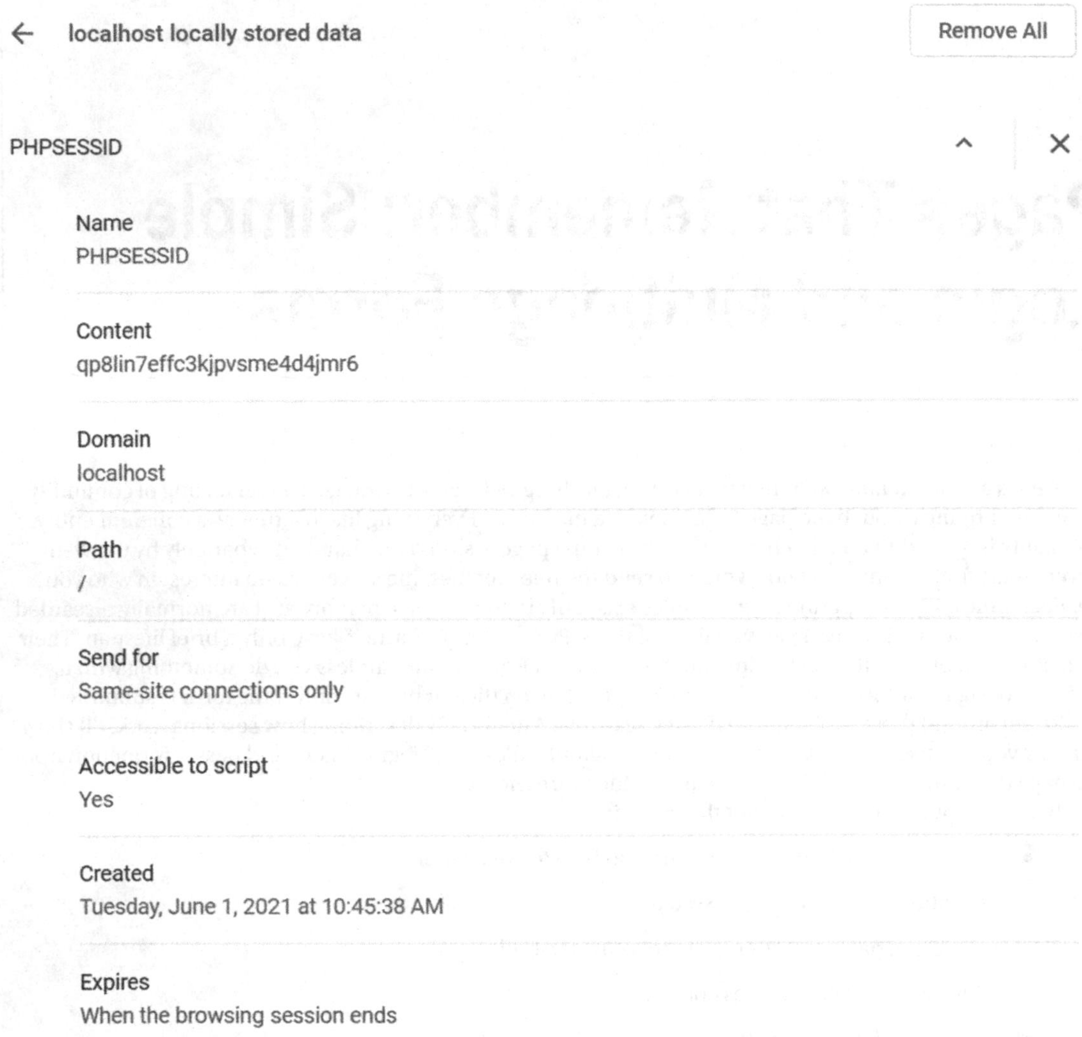

←   localhost locally stored data   [Remove All]

PHPSESSID   ^   ✕

Name
PHPSESSID

Content
qp8lin7effc3kjpvsme4d4jmr6

Domain
localhost

Path
/

Send for
Same-site connections only

Accessible to script
Yes

Created
Tuesday, June 1, 2021 at 10:45:38 AM

Expires
When the browsing session ends

Figure 11-1. PHP sessions store a unique identifier as a cookie in the browser

A matching file, which contains the same jumble of letters and numbers as part of its filename, is created on the web server, as shown in Figure 11-2.

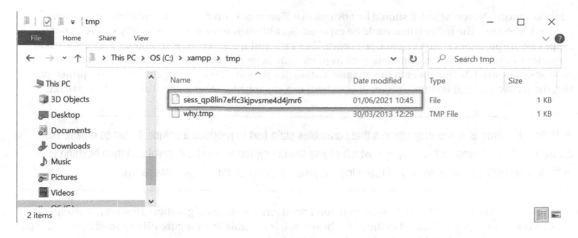

Figure 11-2. *The content of the cookie identifies the session data stored on the web server*

When a session is initiated, the server stores information in session variables that can be accessed by other pages as long as the session remains active (normally until the browser is closed). Because the session ID is unique to each visitor, the information stored in session variables cannot be seen by anyone else. This means sessions are ideal for user authentication, although they can be used for any situation where you want to preserve information for the same user when passing from one page to the next, such as with a multipage form or a shopping cart.

The only information stored on the user's computer is the cookie that contains the session ID, which is meaningless by itself. This means private information cannot be exposed simply by examining the content of this cookie.

The session variables and their values are stored on the web server. Figure 11-3 shows the contents of a simple session file. As you can see, it's in plain text, and the content isn't difficult to decipher. The session shown in the figure has one variable: name. The variable's name is followed by a vertical pipe, then the letter "s," a colon, a number, another colon, and the variable's value in quotes. The "s" stands for string, and the number indicates how many characters the string contains. So this session variable contains my name as a string that is five characters long.

Figure 11-3. *The details of the session are stored on the server in plain text*

This setup has several implications. The cookie containing the session ID normally remains active until the browser is closed. So, if several people share the same computer, they all have access to each other's sessions unless they always close the browser before handing over to the next person, something over which you have no control. So it's important to provide a logout mechanism to delete both the cookie and the session variables, keeping your site secure. You can also create a timeout mechanism, which automatically prevents anyone from regaining access after a certain period of inactivity.

Storing session variables in plain text on the web server is not, in itself, a cause for concern. As long as the server is correctly configured, the session files cannot be accessed through a browser. Inactive files are also routinely deleted by PHP (in theory, the lifetime is 1,440 seconds—24 minutes—but this cannot be relied upon). Nevertheless, it should be obvious that if an attacker manages to compromise the server or hijack a session, the information could be exposed. So, although sessions are generally secure enough for password-protecting parts of a web site or working with multipage forms, you should never use session variables to store sensitive information, such as passwords or credit card details. As you'll see in "Using Sessions to Restrict Access" later in this chapter, although a password is used to gain access to a protected site, the password itself is stored (preferably hashed) in a separate location and not as a session variable.

■ **Note**   Hashing is a one-way process that scrambles plain text to produce a unique message digest. It's frequently confused with encryption, which allows the encrypted text to be decrypted. When hashing is executed correctly, there is no way of reversing the process to reveal the original password.

Sessions are supported by default, so you don't need any special configuration. However, sessions won't work if cookies are disabled in the user's browser. It is possible to configure PHP to send the session ID through a query string, but this is considered a security risk.

Creating PHP Sessions

Just put the following command in every PHP page that you want to use in a session:

```
session_start();
```

This command should be called only once in each page, and it must be called before the PHP script generates any output, so the ideal position is immediately after the opening PHP tag. If any output is generated before the call to `session_start()`, the command fails, and the session won't be activated for that page. (See "The 'Headers Already Sent' Error" section later for an explanation.)

Creating and Destroying Session Variables

You create a session variable by adding it to the `$_SESSION` superglobal array in the same way you would assign an ordinary variable. Say you want to store a visitor's name and display a greeting. If the name is submitted in a login form as `$_POST['name']`, you assign it like this:

```
$_SESSION['name'] = $_POST['name'];
```

`$_SESSION['name']` can now be used in any page that begins with `session_start()`. Because session variables are stored on the server, you should get rid of them as soon as they are no longer required by your script or application. Unset a session variable like this:
```
unset($_SESSION['name']);
```

To unset all session variables—for instance, when you're logging someone out—set the `$_SESSION` superglobal array to an empty array, like this:

```
$_SESSION = [];
```

■ **Caution**   Do not be tempted to try unset($_SESSION). It works all right—but it's a little too effective. It not only clears the current session but also prevents any further session variables from being stored.

Destroying a Session

By itself, unsetting all the session variables effectively prevents any of the information from being reused, but you should also invalidate the session cookie like this:

```
if (isset($_COOKIE[session_name()])) {
    setcookie(session_name(), ", time()-86400, '/');
}
```

This uses the function session_name() to get the name of the session dynamically and resets the session cookie to an empty string and to expire 24 hours ago (86,400 is the number of seconds in a day). The final argument ('/') applies the cookie to the whole domain.

Finally, close the session with the following command:

```
session_destroy();
```

This function is rather poorly named. It simply closes the session. It doesn't destroy any of the session variables or unset the session cookie. It's important to invalidate the session cookie and close a session to avoid the risk of an unauthorized person gaining access either to a restricted part of the site or to any information exchanged during the session. However, a visitor may forget to log out, so it's not always possible to guarantee that the session will be properly closed, which is why it's so important not to store sensitive information in a session variable.

■ **Note**   PHP 8 doesn't support session_register() or session_unregister() often found in old scripts.

Regenerating the Session ID

When a user changes status, such as after logging in, it's recommended as a security measure to regenerate the session ID. This changes the random string of letters and numbers that identify the session but preserves all the information stored in session variables. In *Pro PHP Security, Second Edition* (Apress, 2010, ISBN 978-1-4302-3318-3), Chris Snyder and Michael Southwell explain that "the goal of generating a fresh session ID is to remove the possibility, however slight, that an attacker with knowledge of the low-level security session might be able to perform high-security tasks."

To regenerate the session ID, simply call session_regenerate_id() and redirect the user to another page or reload the same one.

The "Headers Already Sent" Error

Although using PHP sessions is very easy, there's one problem that causes beginners a great deal of head banging. Instead of everything working the way you expect, you see the following message:

```
Warning: Cannot add header information - headers already sent
```

I've mentioned this problem several times before in conjunction with the header() function. It affects session_start() and setcookie() as well. In the case of session_start(), the solution is simple: make sure that you put it immediately after the opening PHP tag (or very soon thereafter), and check that there's no whitespace before the opening tag.

Sometimes the problem occurs even if there is no whitespace ahead of the PHP tag. This is usually caused by editing software inserting the byte order mark (BOM) at the beginning of the script. If this happens, open your script editor's preferences and disable the use of the BOM in PHP pages.

When using setcookie() to destroy the session cookie, however, it's quite likely that you may need to send output to the browser before calling the function. In this case, PHP lets you save the output in a buffer using ob_start(). You then flush the buffer with ob_end_flush() after setcookie() has done its job. You'll see how to do this in PHP Solution 11-2.

Using Sessions to Restrict Access

The first words that probably come to mind when thinking about restricting access to a web site are "username" and "password." Although these generally unlock entry to a site, neither is essential to a session. You can store any value as a session variable and use it to determine whether to grant access to a page. For instance, you could create a variable called $_SESSION['status'] and give visitors access to different parts of the site depending on its value or no access at all if it hasn't been set.

A little demonstration should make everything clear and will show you how sessions work in practice.

PHP Solution 11-1: A Simple Session Example

This should take only a few minutes to build, but you can also find the complete code in session_01.php, session_02.php, and session_03.php, in the ch11 folder.

1. Create a page called session_01.php in a new folder called sessions in the php8sols site root. Insert a form with a text field called name and a Submit button. Set the method to post and action to session_02.php. The form should look like this:

    ```
    <form method="post" action="session_02.php">
        <p>
            <label for="name">Enter your name:</label>
            <input type="text" name="name" id="name">
        </p>
        <p>
            <input type="submit" name="Submit" value="Submit">
        </p>
    </form>
    ```

2. In another page called session_02.php, insert this above the DOCTYPE declaration:

    ```php
    <?php
    // initiate session
    session_start();
    // check that form has been submitted and that name is not empty
    if ($_POST && !empty($_POST['name'])) {
        // set session variable
    ```

```
        $_SESSION['name'] = $_POST['name'];
    }
    ?>
```

The inline comments explain what's going on. The session is started, and as long as $_POST['name'] isn't empty, its value is assigned to $_SESSION['name'].

3. Insert the following code between the <body> tags in session_02.php:

```php
<?php
// check session variable is set
if (isset($_SESSION['name'])) {
    // if set, greet by name
    echo 'Hi there, ' . htmlentities($_SESSION['name']) . '. <a
        href="session_03.php">Next</a>';
} else {
    // if not set, send back to login
    echo 'Who are you? <a href="session_01.php">Please log in</a>';
}
?>
```

If $_SESSION['name'] has been set, a welcome message is displayed along with a link to session_03. php. Otherwise, the page tells the visitor that it doesn't recognize who's trying to gain access and provides a link back to the first page.

■ **Caution**   Take care when typing the following line:

```
echo 'Hi there, ' . htmlentities($_SESSION['name']) . '. <a href="session03.
php">Next</a>';
```

The first two periods (surrounding htmlentities($_SESSION['name'])) are the PHP concatenation operator. The third period (immediately after a single quote) is an ordinary period that will be displayed as part of the string.

---

4. Create session_03.php. Type the following above the DOCTYPE to initiate the session:

```php
<?php session_start(); ?>
```

5. Insert the following code between the <body> tags of session_03.php:

```php
<?php
// check whether session variable is set
if (isset($_SESSION['name'])) {
    // if set, greet by name
    echo 'Hi, ' . htmlentities($_SESSION['name']) . '. See, I remembered
        your name!<br>';
    // unset session variable
```

```
        unset($_SESSION['name']);
        // invalidate the session cookie
        if (isset($_COOKIE[session_name()])) {
            setcookie(session_name(), '', time()-86400, '/');
        }
        // end session
        session_destroy();
        echo '<a href="session_02.php">Back to page 2</a>';
    } else {
        // display if not recognized
        echo "Sorry, I don't know you.<br>";
        echo '<a href="session_01.php">Please log in</a>';
    }
    ?>
```

If $_SESSION['name'] has been set, the page displays it, then unsets it, and invalidates the current session cookie. By placing session_destroy() at the end of the first code block, the session and its associated variables cease to be available.

6. Load session_01.php into a browser, type your name in the text field, and click Submit.

7. You should see something like the following screenshot. At this stage, there is no apparent difference between what happens here and in an ordinary form:

Hi there, David. <u>Next</u>

8. When you click Next, the power of sessions begins to show. The page remembers your name, even though the $_POST array is no longer available to it. In most cases, you'll probably see something similar to the following screenshot:

Hi, David. See, I remembered your name!
<u>Back to page 2</u>

However, on some servers, you might get the following warning message that header information cannot be modified because headers have already been sent:

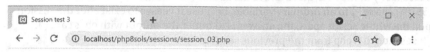

Hi, David. See, I remembered your name!

Warning: Cannot modify header information - headers already sent by (output started at C:\xampp\htdocs\php8sols\sessions\session_03.php:4) in **C:\xampp\htdocs\php8sols\sessions\session_03.php** on line **21**
Back to page 2

■ **Note**   As explained in Chapter 5, servers don't produce the warning about headers if they're configured to buffer the first 4 KB of output. However, not all servers buffer output, so it's important to fix this problem.

---

9.   Click the link to page 2 (if you got an error message, it's just below the message). The session has been destroyed, so this time session_02.php has no idea who you are:

Who are you? Please log in

10.   Type the address of session_03.php in the browser address bar and load it. It, too, has no recollection of the session and displays an appropriate message:

Sorry, I don't know you.
Please log in

Even if you didn't get the warning message in step 8, you need to prevent it from happening when you deploy pages that rely on sessions to other servers. The error message not only looks bad, but it also means setcookie() can't invalidate the session cookie. Even though session_start() comes immediately after the opening PHP tag in session_03.php, the warning message is triggered by the DOCTYPE declaration, the <head>, and other HTML being output before setcookie().

PHP Solution 11-2: Buffering the Output with ob_start( )

Although you could put setcookie() in the PHP block above the DOCTYPE declaration, you would also need to assign the value of $_SESSION['name'] to an ordinary variable, because it ceases to exist after the session is destroyed. Rather than pull the whole script apart, the answer is to buffer the output with ob_start().

Continue working with session_03.php from the previous section.

1. Amend the PHP block above the DOCTYPE declaration like this:

```php
<?php
session_start();
ob_start();
?>
```

   This turns on output buffering and prevents output from being sent to the browser until the end of the script or until you specifically flush the output with ob_end_flush().

2. Flush the output immediately after invalidating the session cookie, like this:

```php
// invalidate the session cookie
if (isset($_COOKIE[session_name()])) {
    setcookie(session_name(), '', time()-86400, '/');
}
ob_end_flush();
```

3. Save session_03.php and test the sequence again. This time there should be no warning. More important, the session cookie is no longer valid. (The updated code is in session_04.php.)

Using File-Based Authentication

As you have just seen, the combination of session variables and conditional statements lets you present completely different pages to a visitor depending on whether a session variable has been set. All you need to do is add a password-checking system, and you have a basic user authentication system.

Before diving into the code, let's consider the important question of secure passwords.

Making Passwords Secure

Passwords should never be stored in a publicly accessible location. In other words, if you're using a file-based authentication system, the file must be outside the web server's document root. Moreover, the passwords should not be kept in plain text. For greater security, it's advisable to hash passwords. For many years, it was recommended to use the MD5 or SHA-1 algorithm to hash passwords as a 32- or 40-digit hexadecimal number. One of their original strengths, speed, has turned out to be a major weakness. Automated scripts can process huge numbers of calculations per second in a brute-force attack to determine the original value—not so much guessing as trying every possible combination.

The current recommendation is to use two functions: password_hash() and password_verify(), which offer a much more robust system of hashing and verifying passwords. To hash a password, just pass it to the password_hash() function, like this:

```php
$hashed = password_hash($password, PASSWORD_DEFAULT);
```

The second argument to password_hash() is a constant that leaves the encryption method up to PHP, allowing you to keep up to date with what is considered the most secure method at the time.

■ **Note** The password_hash() function has other options for advanced users. For details, see www.php. net/manual/en/function.password-hash.php. There's also a FAQ (frequently asked questions) page about safe password hashing at www.php.net/manual/en/faq.passwords.php.

Using password_hash() scrambles plain text passwords in a way that makes it impossible to reverse. This means that even if your password file is exposed, no one will be able to work out what the passwords are. It also means that you have no way of converting a password back to its original value. In one respect, this is unimportant: when a user logs in, password_verify() checks the submitted value against the hashed version. The disadvantage is that there is no way that you can send users password reminders if they forget them; a new password must be created. Nevertheless, good security demands hashing passwords.

Hashing is no protection against the most common problem with passwords: ones that are easy to guess or that use common words. Many registration systems now enforce the use of stronger passwords by requiring a mixture of alphanumeric characters and symbols.

So the first task is to create a user registration form that checks the following:

- That the password and username contain a minimum number of characters

- That the password matches minimum strength criteria, such as containing a mixture of numbers, uppercase and lowercase characters, and symbols

- That the password matches a second entry in a confirmation field

- That the username isn't already in use

PHP Solution 11-3: Creating a Password Strength Checker

This PHP solution shows how to create a class that checks whether a password meets certain requirements, such as the use of spaces, a minimum number of characters, and a combination of different types of characters. By default, the class checks only that the password has only single spaces, no spaces at the beginning or end, and contains a minimum number of characters. Optional methods allow you to set tougher conditions, such as using a combination of uppercase and lowercase characters, numbers, and nonalphanumeric symbols.

This PHP solution starts by building the user registration form that will also be used in PHP Solution 11-4.

1. Create a page called register.php in the sessions folder and insert a form with three text input fields and a Submit button. Lay out the form and name the input elements as shown in the following screenshot. If you want to save time, use register_01.php in the ch11 folder:

2. As always, you want the processing script to run only if the form has been submitted, so everything needs to be enclosed in a conditional statement that checks whether the name attribute of the Submit button is in the $_POST array. Then you need to check that the input meets your minimum requirements. Insert the following code in a PHP block above the DOCTYPE declaration:

```php
if (isset($_POST['register'])) {
    $username = trim($_POST['username']);
    $password = trim($_POST['pwd']);
    $retyped = trim($_POST['conf_pwd']);
    require_once '../Php8Solutions/Authenticate/CheckPassword.php';
}
```

The code inside the conditional statement passes the input from the three text fields to trim() to remove whitespace from the beginning and end, and it assigns the results to simple variables. Then it includes the file that will contain the class that checks the password, which you'll define next.

■ **Note** At this stage, the code doesn't check whether $password and $retyped are the same. Not comparing them now simplifies testing the class.

---

3. Create a new folder called Authenticate in the Php8Solutions folder. Then create a file called CheckPassword.php inside the new folder. It will contain only PHP script, so strip out any HTML and add the following code:

```php
<?php
namespace Php8Solutions\Authenticate;

class CheckPassword {
    const MIN_LENGTH = 8;
    protected array $errors = [];
```

```
public function __construct(
    protected string $password,
    protected int ?$minChars = null,
    protected bool $mixedCase = false,
    protected int $minNums = 0,
    protected int $minSymbols = 0
) {
    if (!isset($this->minChars) || $this->minChars <
        self::MIN_LENGTH) {
        $this->minChars = self::MIN_LENGTH;
    }
    $this->check();
}

}
```

This defines the basic CheckPassword class, which initially checks only whether the password contains multiple spaces, begins or ends with a space, and has the required minimum number of characters. You'll add the other features shortly.

The file begins by declaring Php8Solutions\Authenticate as its namespace and then defines the CheckPassword class with a constant MIN_LENGTH set to 8. This determines the minimum number of characters in the password. There's also a protected property called $errors that is initialized as an empty array. This will be used to store all error messages if the password fails any of the checks.

The constructor method has five parameters, all of which are preceded by the protected visibility declaration, so PHP 8's constructor property promotion automatically converts them to class properties. Only the first argument is required: the password to be checked, which must be a string. The remaining parameters all have default values, so they become optional arguments.

The $minChars parameter accepts either an integer or null. By default, it is null. Setting a value for this argument allows you to change the minimum number of characters in the password. However, the conditional statement in the body of the constructor checks if a value has been supplied and is greater than the MIN_LENGTH constant using the self keyword with the scope resolution operator (::). If both parts of the condition equate to false, the value of MIN_LENGTH is used. Otherwise, the value passed to the constructor is used. This prevents a value lower than the minimum specified in the constant from being used.

The other parameters set defaults for other requirements: a mixture of uppercase and lowercase characters, a minimum of numeric characters, and a minimum of nonalphanumeric characters. The defaults for all three are negative.

The constructor finally calls an internal method called check(), which we'll define next.

4. Insert the following code after the constructor definition:

```
protected function check() {
    if (preg_match('/\s{2,}/', $this->password)) {
        $this->errors[] = 'Password can contain only single
        spaces.';
    }
    if (strlen($this->password) < $this->minChars) {
    $this->errors[] = "Password must be at least
        $this->minChars characters.";
    }
}
```

The check() method contains two conditional statements. The first uses preg_match() with a regular expression that searches for two or more consecutive whitespace characters inside the password. The other conditional statement uses strlen() to determine the length of the password string and compares the result with the $minChars property.

If the password fails either of these tests, the $errors property will contain at least one element. So we can use that to determine whether to accept or reject the password.

5. The getErrors() public method simply returns the array of error messages, and it looks like this:

```
public function getErrors() {
    return $this->errors;
}
```

6. Add the getErrors() method to the class definition, save CheckPassword.php, and switch to register.php.

7. In register.php, add the following line immediately after the opening PHP tag to import the CheckPassword class:

```
use Php8Solutions\Authenticate\CheckPassword;
```

■ **Caution** You must always import namespaced classes at the top level of a script. Attempting to import the class in a conditional statement generates a parse error.

---

8. Inside the conditional statement that executes the code after the form has been submitted, create a CheckPassword object, passing $password as the argument. Then call the getErrors() method like this:

```
require_once '../Php8Solutions/Authenticate/CheckPassword.php';
$checkPwd = new CheckPassword($password);
$errors = $checkPwd->getErrors();
}
```

Only the first argument to the CheckPassword constructor is required. At this stage, the class is capable only of checking for multiple spaces and the length of the password. So the only other argument that would have any effect is setting the minimum number of characters. Leaving it out sets the minimum to the default 8.

9. Add the following PHP code block just above the form in the body of the page:

```
<h1>Register User</h1>
<?php
if (isset($errors)) {
    echo '<ul>';
    if (empty($errors)) {
            echo '<li>Password OK</li>';
    } else {
        foreach ($errors as $error) {
            echo "<li>$error</li>";
```

```
            }
        }
        echo '</ul>';
    }
?>
<form action="register.php" method="post">
```

This checks whether $errors has been defined. If it has, we know that the form has been submitted, so a conditional statement checks whether $errors is empty. If it is, we know the password passed the tests; and we display an appropriate message. Otherwise, the foreach loop displays the error messages.

10. Save register.php and load it in a browser. Test the CheckPassword class by clicking the Register button without filling in any of the fields. You should see a message informing you that the password requires a minimum of eight characters.

11. Try it with a password that contains eight characters. You should see Password OK.

■ **Tip** Only the value entered in the password field is being checked, so there's no need to fill in the other fields at this stage.

---

12. Try a password with at least eight characters, but insert a space in the middle. You should see Password OK.

13. Put two consecutive spaces in the middle. You'll be warned that only single spaces are permitted.

14. Try one with fewer than eight characters and multiple consecutive spaces in the middle. You'll see the following warnings:

Register User

- Password can contain only single spaces.
- Password must be at least 8 characters.

Username: [   ]

Password: [   ]

Retype Password: [   ]

[Register]

15. Change the code in register.php to pass the optional second argument to the CheckPassword constructor, setting the minimum number of characters to 10:

```
$checkPwd = new CheckPassword($password, 10);
```

16. Save and test the page again. If you encounter any problems, compare your code with register_02.php in the ch11 folder and CheckPassword_01.php in the ch11/Php8Solutions/Authenticate folder.

17. Assuming that your code is working, amend the check() method to add tests for a mixture of uppercase and lowercase characters, a minimum number of numeric characters, and a minimum number of nonalphanumeric characters. The updated code looks like this:

```
public function check() {
    if (preg_match('/\s{2,}/', $this->password)) {
        $this->errors[] = 'Password can contain only single spaces.';
    }
    if (strlen($this->password) < $this->minChars) {
        $this->errors[] = "Password must be at least
            $this->minChars characters.";
    }
    if ($this->mixedCase) {
        $pattern = '/(?=.*\p{Ll})(?=.*\p{Lu})/u';
        if (!preg_match($pattern, $this->password)) {
            $this->errors[] = 'Password should include uppercase
                and lowercase characters.';
        }
    }
    if ($this->minNums > 0) {
        $pattern = '/\d/';
        $found = preg_match_all($pattern, $this->password, $matches);
        if ($found < $this->minNums) {
            $this->errors[] = "Password should include at least
                $this->minNums number(s).";
        }
    }
    if ($this->minSymbols > 0) {
        $pattern =  '/[\p{S}\p{P}]/u';
        $found = preg_match_all($pattern, $this->password, $matches);
        if ($found < $this->minSymbols) {
            $this->errors[] = "Password should include at least
                $this->minSymbols nonalphanumeric character(s).";
        }
    }
}
```

Each of the three new conditional statements is run only if the equivalent optional argument is passed to the class constructor. Each one stores a regular expression as $pattern and then uses preg_match() or preg_match_all() to test the password.

If the $mixedCase property is set to true, the regular expression and password are passed to preg_match() to look for at least one lowercase letter and one uppercase letter in any position in the password. The regular expression uses Unicode category metacharacters for lowercase and uppercase, so permitted characters are not restricted to the unaccented characters A–Z. The lowercase *u* after the closing delimiter is a modifier that treats the pattern and subject strings as UTF-8.

The $minNums and $minSymbols properties are set to 0 by default. If they're reset to a positive number, the regular expression and password are passed to the preg_match_all() function to find how many times the regex matches. The function requires three arguments: the regex, the string to be searched, and a variable to store the matches; it returns the number of matches found. In this case, all you're interested in is the number of matches. The variable that stores the matches is discarded.

The $pattern in the last conditional statement uses the Unicode category metacharacters for math symbols, currency signs, punctuation, and other symbols together with the UTF-8 modifier.

18. Save CheckPassword.php and test the updated class by passing the optional arguments to the class constructor in register.php. You can either pass them in the same order as in the constructor signature or by using named arguments. For example, the following requires the password to have at least two numbers and one nonalphanumeric symbol:

```
$checkPwd = new CheckPassword($password, minNums: 2,
    minSymbols: 1);
```

Use a variety of combinations to enforce different strengths of password.

If necessary, check your code against register_03.php in the ch11 folder and CheckPassword_02.php in the ch11/Php8Solutions/Authenticate folder.

Now that we can check the password strength, we can build a simple user registration system.

PHP Solution 11-4: Creating a File-Based User Registration System

This PHP solution creates a simple user registration system that hashes passwords with the password_hash() function. It uses the CheckPassword class from PHP Solution 11-3 to enforce minimum strength requirements. Further checks ensure that the username contains a minimum number of characters and that the user has retyped the password correctly in a second field.

The user credentials are stored in a plain-text file, which must be outside the web server's document root. The instructions assume you have set up a private folder that PHP has write access to, as described in Chapter 7. It's also assumed that you're familiar with the "Appending Content with fopen()" section in that chapter.

Continue working with the files from the preceding PHP solution. Alternatively, use register_03.php in the ch11 folder and CheckPassword_02.php in the ch11/Php8Solutions/Authenticate folder.

1. Create a file called register_user_csv.php in the includes folder and strip out any HTML inserted by your script editor.

2. When using a namespaced class, the import statement must be in the same file as where the class is used, even if it's an include file. Cut the following line from the top of register.php and paste it into register_user_csv.php:

```
use Php8Solutions\Authenticate\CheckPassword;
```

3. Cut the following code from register.php and paste it into register_user_csv. php after the import statement (it doesn't matter if your password strength settings are different):

```
require_once '../Php8Solutions/Authenticate/CheckPassword.php';
$checkPwd = new CheckPassword($password, minNums: 2,
    minSymbols: 1);
$errors = $checkPwd->getErrors();
```

4. At the end of the remaining script above the DOCTYPE declaration in register.
php, create a variable for the location of the text file that will be used to store the
user credentials; include register_user_csv.php. The code in the PHP block at
the top of register.php should now look like this:

```
if (isset($_POST['register'])) {
    $username = trim($_POST['username']);
    $password = trim($_POST['pwd']);
    $retyped = trim($_POST['conf_pwd']);
    $userfile = 'C:/private/hashed.csv';
    require_once '../includes/register_user_csv.php';
}
```

The CSV file for the user credentials doesn't exist yet. It will be created automatically when the first user
is registered. Amend the path to the private folder to match your own setup if necessary.

5. In register_user_csv.php, paste the code you cut from register.php in step 3
and amend the command that includes the class definition, like this:

```
require_once __DIR__ .
    '/../Php8Solutions/Authenticate/CheckPassword.php';
```

You need to adapt the relative path because register_user_csv.php is also an
include file (see "Nesting Include Files" in Chapter 5).

6. Insert the code highlighted in bold immediately after the include command:

```
require_once __DIR__ .
    '/../Php8Solutions/Authenticate/CheckPassword.php';
$usernameMinChars = 6;
$formErrors = [];
if (strlen($username) < $usernameMinChars) {
    $formErrors[] = "Username must be at least $usernameMinChars characters.";
}
if (!preg_match('/^[-_\p{L}\d]+$/ui', $username)) {
    $formErrors[] = 'Only alphanumeric characters, hyphens, and underscores
        are permitted in username.';
}
if ($password != $retyped) {
    $formErrors[] = "Your passwords don't match.";
}
$checkPwd = new CheckPassword($password, minNums: 2,
    minSymbols: 1);
```

The first two lines of new code specify the minimum number of characters in the username and
initialize an empty array for error messages from the registration form. The rest of the new code checks
the length of the username with strlen() and tests whether it contains any characters other than letters,

numbers, hyphens, and underscores. The regular expression that checks the username accepts all UTF-8 letters, including accented characters. While this allows a very wide range of characters to be used, it prevents users from registering a name that could be used to inject malicious code. The final conditional statement checks that both password fields contain the same values.

■ **Note**   It's debatable whether it's worth checking the password strength if the value entered in the second password field doesn't match the first. However, I've decided that alerting the user to an inadequate password is a good idea even if the fields don't match.

---

7. Amend the code at the bottom of register_user_csv.php like this:

    ```
    $errors = array_merge($formErrors, $checkPwd->getErrors());
    ```

    Instead of simply assigning the result of calling the getErrors() method to $errors, both arrays of error messages are merged using the array_merge() function.

8. Save register_user_csv.php and register.php, and then test the form again. Leave all the fields blank and click Register. You should see a series of error messages similar to this (the password-related ones depend on the options set in the class constructor):

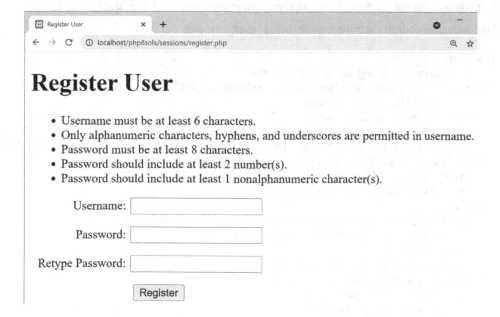

Try a variety of tests to make sure your validation code is working.

If you have problems, compare your code with register_user_csv_01.php and register_04.php in the ch11 folder.

Assuming that your code is working, you're ready to create the registration part of the script. Let's pause to consider what the main script needs to do. First, you need to hash the password. Then, before writing the details to a CSV file, you must check whether the username is unique. This presents a problem regarding which mode to use with fopen().

■ **Note** The various fopen() modes are described in Chapter 7.

Ideally, you want the internal pointer at the beginning of the file so that you can loop through existing records. The r+ mode does this, but the operation fails unless the file already exists. You can't use w+, because it deletes existing content. You can't use x+ either, because it fails if a file of the same name already exists.

That leaves a+ and c+ as the only options with the flexibility you need: both create the file if necessary and let you read and write. They differ in where the internal pointer is placed when you open the file: a+ puts it at the end, whereas c+ puts it at the beginning. This makes c+ more useful for checking existing records, but a+ has the advantage of always appending new content at the end of the file. This avoids the danger of accidentally overwriting existing values. We'll open the CSV file in a+ mode.

The file is empty the first time you run the script (you can tell because the filesize() function returns 0), so you can go ahead and write the details using fputcsv(). This is the counterpart of fgetcsv(), which was described in Chapter 7. Whereas fgetcsv() extracts the data from a CSV file one line at a time, fputcsv() creates a CSV record. It has two required arguments: the file reference and an array of values to be inserted as a CSV record. It also accepts optional arguments to set the delimiter and enclosure characters (see the online documentation at www.php.net/manual/en/function.fputcsv.php).

If filesize() doesn't return 0, you need to reset the internal pointer and loop through the records to see if the username is already registered. If there's a match, you break out of the loop and prepare an error message. If there isn't a match by the end of the loop, you know it's a new username that needs to be added to the file. Now that you understand the flow of the script, you can insert it into register_user_csv.php.

9. Add the following code at the bottom of register_user_csv.php:

```php
if (!$errors) {
    // hash password using default algorithm
    $password = password_hash($password, PASSWORD_DEFAULT);
    // open the file in append mode
    $file = fopen($userfile, 'a+');
    // if filesize is zero, no names yet registered
    // so just write the username and password to file as CSV
    if (filesize($userfile) === 0) {
        fputcsv($file, [$username, $password]);
        $result = "$username registered.";
    } else {
        // if filesize is greater than zero, check username first
        // move internal pointer to beginning of file
        rewind($file);
        // loop through file one line at a time
        while (!feof($file)) {
            $data = fgetcsv($file);
            // skip empty lines
        if (!$data) continue;
            if ($data[0] == $username) {
                $result = "$username taken - choose a different username.";
                break;
            }
        }
```

```
        // if $result not set, username is OK
        if (!isset($result)) {
            // insert new CSV record
            fputcsv($file, [$username, $password]);
            $result = "$username registered.";
        }
        // close the file
        fclose($file);
    }
}
```

The preceding explanation and inline comments should help you follow the script.

10. The registration script stores the outcome in $result or the $errors array.
    Amend the code in the body of register.php to display the result or the error
    messages, as follows:

```
        <?php
        if (isset($errors) || isset($result)) {
            echo '<ul>';
                if (empty($errors)) {
                    echo "<li>$result</li>";
                } else {
                    foreach ($errors as $error) {
                        echo "<li>$error</li>";
                    }
                }
            echo '</ul>';
        }
        ?>
```

This displays the value of $result as a single bulleted item. Otherwise, it loops through the $errors
array if it's not empty.

11. Save both register_user_csv.php and register.php and test the registration
    system. Try registering the same username more than once. You should see a
    message informing you that the username is taken and asking you to choose
    another.

12. Open hashed.csv. You should see the usernames in plain text, but the passwords
    should have been hashed. Even if you choose the same password for two
    different users, the hashed version is different because password_hash() adds a
    random value known as a **salt** to the password before encrypting it. Figure 11-4
    shows two users that were both registered with the password chapter11*.

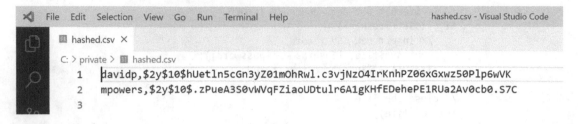

***Figure 11-4.** Using a salt produces completely different hashes of the same password*

If necessary, check your code against register_user_csv_02.php and register_05.php in the ch11 folder.

■ **Tip** Most of the code in register_user_csv.php is generic. All you need to do to use it with any registration form is to define $username, $password, $retyped, and $userfile before including it and capture the results using $errors and $result. The only changes you might need to make to the external file are in setting the minimum number of characters in the username and setting parameters for the password strength. Those settings are defined at the top of the file, so they're easy to access and adjust.

Checking Hashed Passwords with password_verify( )

The password_verify() function does exactly what you expect: it verifies passwords that have been hashed with password_hash(). It takes just two arguments, the submitted password and the hashed version. If the submitted password is correct, the function returns true. Otherwise, it returns false.

PHP Solution 11-5: Building the Login Page

This PHP solution shows how to submit a username and password through the post method and then check the submitted values against those stored in an external text file. If a match is found, the script sets a session variable and then redirects the user to another page.

1. Create a file called login.php in the sessions folder, and then insert a form with text input fields for username and password, plus a Submit button named login, like this (alternatively, use login_01.php in the ch11 folder):

    ```
    <form method="post" action="login.php">
        <p>
            <label for="username">Username:</label>
            <input type="text" name="username" id="username">
        </p>
        <p>
            <label for="pwd">Password:</label>
            <input type="password" name="pwd" id="pwd">
        </p>
        <p>
            <input name="login" type="submit" value="Log in">
        </p>
    </form>
    ```

It's a simple form, nothing fancy:

2. Add the following code in a PHP block above the DOCTYPE declaration:

```php
$error = '';
if (isset($_POST['login'])) {
    session_start();
    $username = $_POST['username'];
    $password = $_POST['pwd'];
    // location of usernames and passwords
    $userlist = 'C:/private/hashed.csv';
    // location to redirect on success
    $redirect = 'http://localhost/php8sols/sessions/menu.php';
    require_once '../includes/authenticate.php';
}
```

This initializes a variable called $error as an empty string. If the login fails, this will be used to display an error message informing the user of the reason for failure.

The conditional statement then checks whether the $_POST array contains an element named login. If it does, the form has been submitted, and the code inside the curly braces initiates a PHP session and stores the values passed through the $_POST array in $username and $password. Then it creates $userlist, which defines the location of the file that contains the registered usernames and passwords, and $redirect, the URL of the page the user will be sent to after successfully logging in.

Finally, the code inside the conditional statement includes authenticate.php, which you'll create next.

■ **Note** Adjust the value of $userlist to match the location in your own setup.

---

3. Create a file called authenticate.php in the includes folder. It will contain only PHP code, so strip out any HTML inserted by your script editor and insert the following code:

```php
<?php
if (!file_exists($userlist) || !is_readable($userlist)) {
    $error = 'Login facility unavailable. Please try later.';
} else {
    $file = fopen($userlist, 'r');
    while (!feof($file)) {
        $data = fgetcsv($file);
        // ignore if the first element is empty
```

```php
        if (empty($data[0])) {
            continue;
        }
        // if username and password match, create session variable,
        // regenerate the session ID, and break out of the loop
        if ($data[0] == $username && password_verify($password, $data[1])) {
            $_SESSION['authenticated'] = 'Jethro Tull';
            session_regenerate_id();
            break;
        }
    }
    fclose($file);
}
```

This adapts the code that you used in getcsv.php in PHP Solution 7-2. The conditional statement checks for a nonexistent file or one that can't be read. If there's a problem with $userlist, the error message is created immediately.

Otherwise, the main code in the else block extracts the content of the CSV file by opening the file in read mode and using the fgetcsv() function to return an array of the data in each line. The CSV file containing usernames and hashed passwords doesn't have column titles, so the while loop examines the data in each line.

If $data[0] is empty, it probably means the current line is blank, so it's skipped.

The first array element of each line ($data[0]) contains the stored username. It's compared with the submitted value, $username.

The password submitted through the login form is stored in $password, and the hashed version is stored in $data[1]. Both are passed as arguments to password_verify(), which returns true if there's a match.

If both username and password match, the script creates a variable called $_SESSION['authenticated'] and assigns it the name of one of the great folk-rock bands of the 1970s. There's nothing magic about either of these (apart from Jethro Tull's music); I've chosen the name and value of the variable arbitrarily. All that matters is a session variable is created. As soon as a match is found, the session ID is regenerated, and break exits the loop.

4. If the login is successful, the header() function needs to redirect the user to the URL stored in $redirect and then exit the script. Otherwise, an error message needs to be created, informing the user that the login failed. The complete script looks like this:

```php
<?php
if (!file_exists($userlist) || !is_readable($userlist)) {
    $error = 'Login facility unavailable. Please try later.';
} else {
    $file = fopen($userlist, 'r');
    while (!feof($file)) {
        $data = fgetcsv($file);
        // ignore if the first element is empty
        if (empty($data[0])) {
            continue;
        }
        // if username and password match, create session variable,
        // regenerate the session ID, and break out of the loop
        if ($data[0] == $username && password_verify($password, $data[1])) {
            $_SESSION['authenticated'] = 'Jethro Tull';
```

```
                    session_regenerate_id();
                    break;
            }
        }
        fclose($file);
        // if the session variable has been set, redirect
        if (isset($_SESSION['authenticated'])) {
            header("Location: $redirect");
            exit;
        } else {
            $error = 'Invalid username or password.';
        }

    }
```

5. In login.php, add the following short code block just after the opening <body>
    tag to display any error messages:

```
<body>
<?php
if ($error) {
    echo "<p>$error</p>";
}
?>
<form method="post" action="login.php">
```

The completed code is in authenticate.php and login_02.php in the ch11 folder. Before you can test
login.php, you need to create menu.php and restrict access with a session.

PHP Solution 11-6: Restricting Access to a Page with a Session

This PHP solution demonstrates how to restrict access to a page by checking for the existence of a session
variable that indicates the user's credentials have been authenticated. If the variable hasn't been set, the
header() function redirects the user to the login page.

1. Create two pages in the sessions folder called menu.php and secretpage.php. It
    doesn't matter what they contain, as long as they link to each other. Alternatively,
    use menu_01.php and secretpage_01.php in the ch11 folder.

2. Protect access to each page by inserting the following above the DOCTYPE
    declaration:

```
<?php
session_start();
// if session variable not set, redirect to login page
if (!isset($_SESSION['authenticated'])) {
    header('Location: http://localhost/php8sols/sessions/login.php');
    exit;
}
?>
```

After starting the session, the script checks if $_SESSION['authenticated'] has been set. If it hasn't been, it redirects the user to login.php and exits. That's all there is to it! The script doesn't need to know the value of $_SESSION['authenticated'], although you could make doubly sure by amending line 4 like this:

```
if (!isset($_SESSION['authenticated']) || $_SESSION['authenticated']
    != 'Jethro Tull') {
```

This now also rejects a visitor if $_SESSION['authenticated'] has the wrong value.

3. Save menu.php and secretpage.php, and then try to load either of them into a browser. You should always be redirected to login.php.

4. Enter a valid username and password from those you registered in hashed.csv (the values are case-sensitive) in login.php, and then click Log in. You should be redirected immediately to menu.php, and the link to secretpage.php should also work.

You can check your code against menu_02.php and secretpage_02.php in the ch11 folder.

All you need to do to protect any page on your site is to add the eight lines of code in step 2 above the DOCTYPE declaration.

PHP Solution 11-7: Creating a Reusable Logout Button

As well as logging in to a site, users should be able to log out. This PHP solution shows how to create a logout button that can be inserted in any page.

Continue working with the files from the preceding section.

1. Create a logout button in the <body> of menu.php by inserting the following form:

```
<form method="post">
    <input name="logout" type="submit" value="Log out">
</form>
```

The page should look similar to the following screenshot:

Restricted area

Go to another secret page

Log out

2. You now need to add the script that runs when the logout button is clicked. Amend the code above the DOCTYPE declaration like this (the code is in menu_02. php):

```php
<?php
session_start();
// if session variable not set, redirect to login page
if (!isset($_SESSION['authenticated'])) {
    header('Location: http://localhost/php8sols/sessions/login.php');
    exit;
}
// run this script only if the logout button has been clicked
if (isset($_POST['logout'])) {
    // empty the $_SESSION array
    $_SESSION = [];
    // invalidate the session cookie
    if (isset($_COOKIE[session_name()])) {
        setcookie(session_name(), '', time()-86400, '/');
    }
    // end session and redirect
    session_destroy();
    header('Location: http://localhost/php8sols/sessions/login.php');
    exit;
}
?>
```

This is the same code as in "Destroying a Session" earlier in the chapter. The only differences are that it's enclosed in a conditional statement so that it runs only when the logout button is clicked and it uses header() to redirect the user to login.php.

3. Save menu.php and test it by clicking Log out. You should be redirected to login. php. Any attempt to return to menu.php or secretpage.php will bring you back to login.php.

4. You can put the same code in every restricted page, but PHP is all about saving work, not making it. It makes sense to turn this into an include file. Create a new file called logout.php in the includes folder. Cut and paste the new code from steps 1 and 2 into the new file, like this (it's in logout.php in the ch11 folder):

```php
<?php
// run this script only if the logout button has been clicked
if (isset($_POST['logout'])) {
    // empty the $_SESSION array
    $_SESSION = array();
    // invalidate the session cookie
    if (isset($_COOKIE[session_name()])) {
        setcookie(session_name(), ", time()-86400, '/');
    }
    // end session and redirect
    session_destroy();
```

```
        header('Location: http://localhost/php8sols/sessions/login.php');
        exit;
    }
    ?>
    <form method="post">
        <input name="logout" type="submit" value="Log out">
    </form>
```

Because the form will be included in different pages, you can't set the action attribute to a specific page. However, omitting it simply results in the current page being reloaded, so the logout script will be available in every page that includes logout.php.

5. At the same point in menu.php from which you cut the code for the form, include the new file, as follows:

```
<?php include '../includes/logout.php'; ?>
```

Including the code from an external file like this means that there will be output to the browser before the calls to setcookie() and header(). So you need to buffer the output, as shown in PHP Solution 11-2.

6. Add ob_start(); immediately after the call to session_start() at the top of menu.php. There's no need to use ob_end_flush() or ob_end_clean(). PHP automatically flushes the buffer at the end of the script if you haven't already explicitly done so.

7. Save menu.php and test the page. It should look and work exactly the same as before.

8. Repeat steps 5 and 6 with secretpage.php. You now have a simple, reusable logout button that can be incorporated into any restricted page.

You can check your code against menu_04.php, secretpage_03.php, and logout.php in the ch11 folder.

PHP Solutions 11-3 to 11-7 build a simple yet effective user authentication system that doesn't require a database backend. However, it does have its limitations. Above all, it's essential that the CSV file containing the usernames and passwords be located outside the server root. Also, once you get more than a few records, querying a database is usually much faster than looping through a CSV file line by line. Chapter 19 covers user authentication with a database.

Keeping the Hashing Algorithm Up to Date

The major advantage of using password_hash() and password_verify() is that they're designed to keep abreast of improvements in cryptography. Instead of specifying a particular hashing algorithm, using PASSWORD_DEFAULT as the second argument to password_hash() ensures that new registrations always use whatever is considered to be the most secure method at the time. Even if the default changes, existing passwords can still be verified by the password_verify() function because the hashed password contains information that identifies how it was hashed.

There's also a function called password_needs_rehash() that checks whether the hashed password needs to be updated to the current standard. It's designed to be used when a user logs in to the site. The following code assumes that the submitted password is stored in $password, that the hashed one is in $hashed, and that you're using the PHP default method of hashing:

```
if (password_verify($password, $hashed) {
    if (password_needs_rehash($hashed, PASSWORD_DEFAULT)) {
        $hashed = password_hash($password, PASSWORD_DEFAULT);
        // store the updated version of $hashed
    }
}
```

It's debatable whether performing this check every time a user logs in is overkill. PHP's policy is to change the default encryption only upon a full release, such as 8.1.0 or 8.2.0. The only exception to this is in an emergency when a critical security flaw is found in the current default. If you keep abreast of PHP developments, you can create a script that updates all stored passwords in a single operation whenever the default changes. However, using password_needs_rehash() every time someone logs in is imperceptibly fast on most servers and may be worth adding to your login routine to keep your site secure.

Setting a Time Limit on Sessions

By default, PHP sets the lifetime of the session cookie on the user's computer to 0, which keeps the session active until the user logs out or the browser is closed. You can make the session timeout earlier through a call to ini_set(), the function that allows you to change some PHP configuration directives on the fly. As soon as the session starts, pass the directive session.cookie_lifetime as the first argument and a string containing the number of seconds you want the cookie to remain active as the second argument. For example, you could limit the session cookie's lifetime to 10 minutes like this:

```
session_start();
ini_set('session.cookie_lifetime', '600');
```

Although this is effective, it has two drawbacks. First, the expiration is set relative to the time on the server, not the user's computer. If the user's computer clock is wrong, the cookie might be out of date immediately, or it might persist much longer than you anticipate. The other problem is that the user might be automatically logged out without explanation. The next PHP solution offers an approach that is more user-friendly.

PHP Solution 11-8: Ending a Session After a Period of Inactivity

This PHP solution shows how to end a session if a user doesn't do anything within a specified period that triggers a page to load. When the session first starts, typically when the user logs in, the current time is stored in a session variable. Each time the user loads a page, the session variable is compared with the current time. If the difference is greater than a predetermined limit, the session and its variables are destroyed. Otherwise, the variable is updated to the current time.

These instructions assume you have set up the login system in PHP Solutions 11-3 to 11-7.

1. You need to store the current time after the user's credentials have been authenticated but before the script redirects the user to the restricted part of the site. Locate the following section of code in authenticate.php (around lines 14–18) and insert the new code highlighted in bold as follows:

```
if ($data[0] == $username && password_verify($password, $data[1])) {
    $_SESSION['authenticated'] = 'Jethro Tull';
    $_SESSION['start'] = time();
    session_regenerate_id();
    break;
}
```

The time() function returns a current timestamp. By being stored in $_SESSION ['start'], it becomes available to every page that begins with session_start().

2. When a session times out, just dumping a user unceremoniously back at the login screen isn't very friendly, so it's a good idea to explain what's happened. In login.php, add the code highlighted in bold to the PHP block immediately after the opening <body> tag (around lines 22–27):

```
<?php
if ($error) {
    echo "<p>$error</p>";
} elseif (isset($_GET['expired'])) { ?>
    <p>Your session has expired. Please log in again.</p>
<?php } ?>
```

The message is shown if the URL contains a parameter called expired in a query string.

3. Open menu.php, cut the code in the PHP block above the DOCTYPE declaration, and paste it into a new blank file.

4. Save the file as session_timeout.php in the includes folder, and then edit the code like this:

```
<?php
session_start();
ob_start();
// set a time limit in seconds
$timelimit = 15;
// get the current time
$now = time();
// where to redirect if rejected
$redirect = 'http://localhost/php8sols/sessions/login.php';
// if session variable not set, redirect to login page
if (!isset($_SESSION['authenticated'])) {
    header("Location: $redirect");
    exit;
} elseif ($now > $_SESSION['start'] + $timelimit) {
    // if timelimit has expired, destroy session and redirect
    $_SESSION = [];
    // invalidate the session cookie
    if (isset($_COOKIE[session_name()])) {
        setcookie(session_name(), '', time()-86400, '/');
    }
    // end session and redirect with query string
    session_destroy();
```

```
    header("Location: {$redirect}?expired=yes");
    exit;
} else {
    // if it's got this far, it's OK, so update start time
    $_SESSION['start'] = time();
}
```

The inline comments explain what is going on, and you should recognize most of the elseif clause from PHP Solution 11-5. PHP measures time in seconds, and I've set $timelimit (on line 5) to a ridiculously short 15 seconds purely to demonstrate the effect. To set a more reasonable limit of, say, 15 minutes, change this later, like this:

```
$timelimit = 15 * 60; // 15 minutes
```

You could, of course, set $timelimit to 900, but why bother when PHP can do the hard work for you?

If the sum of $_SESSION['start'] plus $timelimit is less than the current time (stored as $now), you end the session and redirect the user to the login page. The line that performs the redirect adds a query string to the end of the URL, as follows:

```
http://localhost/php8sols/sessions/login.php?expired=yes
```

The code in step 2 takes no notice of the value of expired; adding yes as the value just makes it look more user-friendly in the browser address bar.

If the script gets as far as the final else, it means that $_SESSION ['authenticated'] has been set and that the time limit hasn't been reached, so $_ SESSION['start'] is updated to the current time, and the page displays as normal.

5. Include session_timeout.php above the DOCTYPE declaration in menu.php. The include command should be the only code in the PHP block:

```
<?php require_once '../includes/session_timeout.php'; ?>
<!DOCTYPE HTML>
```

6. Replace the code above the DOCTYPE declaration in secretpage.php in the same way.

7. Save all the pages you have edited and load either menu.php or secretpage.php into a browser. If the page displays, click Log out. Then log back in and navigate back and forth between menu.php and secretpage.php. Once you have verified that the links work, wait 15 seconds or more and try to navigate back to the other page. You should be automatically logged out and presented with the following screen:

Your session has expired. Please log in again.

Username: [   ]

Password: [   ]

[Log in]

If necessary, check your code against authenticate_02.php, login_04.php, session_timeout.php, menu_05.php, and secretpage_04.php in the ch11 folder.

Passing Information Through Multipage Forms

Variables passed through the $_POST and $_GET arrays have only a fleeting existence. Once they have been passed to a page, they're gone, unless you save their values in some way. A common method of preserving information that's passed from one form to another is to extract its value from the $_POST array and store it in a hidden field in HTML, like this:

```
<input type="hidden" name="address" id="address" value="<?= htmlentities($_POST['address']) ?>">
```

As their name suggests, hidden fields are part of a form's code, but nothing is displayed onscreen. Hidden fields are fine for one or two items, but say you have a survey that's spread over four pages. If you have 10 items on a page, you need a total of 60 hidden fields (10 on the second page, 20 on the third, and 30 on the fourth). Session variables can save you all that coding. They can also make sure that visitors always start on the right page of a multipage form.

PHP Solution 11-9: Using Sessions for a Multipage Form

In this PHP solution, you'll build a script for use in multipage forms that gathers data from the $_POST array and assigns it to session variables. The script automatically redirects the user to the first page of the form if an attempt is made to access any other part of the form first.

1. Copy multiple_01.php, multiple_02.php, multiple_03.php, and multiple_04.php from the ch11 folder to the sessions folder. The first three pages contain simple forms that ask for the user's name, age, and address. The action attribute of each <form> tag is set to the current page, so the forms are self-processing, but they don't yet contain any processing script. The final page is where the data from the first three pages will eventually be displayed.

2. Add the following code in a PHP block above the DOCTYPE declaration in multiple_01.php:

    ```
    if (isset($_POST['next'])) {
        session_start();
        // set a variable to control access to other pages
        $_SESSION['formStarted'] = true;
        // set required fields
        $required = 'first_name';
        $firstPage = 'multiple_01.php';
        $nextPage = 'multiple_02.php';
        $submit = 'next';
        require_once '../includes/multiform.php';
    }
    ```

The name attribute of the Submit button is next, so the code in this block runs only if the form has been submitted. It initiates a session and creates a session variable that will be used to control access to the other form pages.

Next come four variables that will be used by the script that processes the multipage form:

- $required: This is an array of the name attributes of required fields in the current page. If only one field is required, a string can be used instead of an array. If no fields are required, it can be omitted.

- $firstPage: The filename of the first page of the form.

- $nextPage: The filename of the next page in the form.

- $submit: The name of the Submit button in the current page.

Finally, the code includes the script that processes the multipage form.

3. Create a file called multiform.php in the includes folder. Delete any HTML markup and insert the following code:

```php
<?php
if (!isset($_SESSION)) {
    session_start();
}
$filename = basename($_SERVER['SCRIPT_FILENAME']);
$current = 'http://' . $_SERVER['HTTP_HOST'] .
    $_SERVER['PHP_SELF'];
```

Each page of the multipage form needs to call session_start(), but calling it twice on the same page generates an error, so the conditional statement first checks whether the $_SESSION superglobal variable is accessible. If it isn't, it initiates the session for the page.

After the conditional statement, $_SERVER['SCRIPT_FILENAME'] is passed to the basename() function to extract the filename of the current page. This is the same technique that you used in PHP Solution 5-3.

$_SERVER['SCRIPT_FILENAME'] contains the path of the parent file, so when this script is included in multiple_01.php, the value of $filename will be multiple_01.php, *not* multiform.php.

The next line builds the URL for the current page from the string http:// and the values of $_SERVER['HTTP_HOST'], which contains the current domain name, and $_SERVER['PHP_SELF'], which contains the path of the current file minus the domain name. If you're testing locally, when the first page of the multipage form loads, $current is http://localhost/php8sols/sessions/multiple_01.php.

4. Now that you have both the name of the current file and its URL, you can use str_replace() to create the URLs for the first and next pages, like this:

```php
$redirectFirst = str_replace($filename, $firstPage, $current);
$redirectNext = str_replace($filename, $nextPage, $current);
```

The first argument is the string you want to replace, the second is the replacement string, and the third is the target string. In step 2, you set $firstPage to multiple_01.php and $nextPage to multiple_02.php. As a result, $redirectFirst becomes http://localhost/php8sols/sessions/multiple_01.php, and $redirectNext is http://localhost/php8sols/sessions/multiple_02.php.

5. To prevent users from accessing the multipage form without starting at the beginning, add a conditional statement that checks the value of $filename. If it's not the same as the first page, and $_SESSION['formStarted'] hasn't been created, the header() function redirects to the first page, like this:

```php
if ($filename != $firstPage && !isset($_SESSION['formStarted'])) {
    header("Location: $redirectFirst");
    exit;
}
```

6. The rest of the script loops through the $_POST array, checking for required fields that are blank and adding them to a $missing array. If nothing is missing, the header() function redirects the user to the next page of the multipage form. The complete script for multiform.php looks like this:

```php
<?php
if (!isset($_SESSION)) {
    session_start();
}
$filename = basename($_SERVER['SCRIPT_FILENAME']);
$current = 'http://' . $_SERVER['HTTP_HOST'] .
    $_SERVER['PHP_SELF'];
$redirectFirst = str_replace($filename, $firstPage, $current);
$redirectNext = str_replace($filename, $nextPage, $current);
if ($filename != $firstPage && !isset($_SESSION['formStarted'])) {
    header("Location: $redirectFirst");
    exit;
}
if (isset($_POST[$submit])) {
    // create empty array for any missing fields
    $missing = [];
    // create $required array if not set
    if (!isset($required)) {
        $required = [];
    } else {
        // using casting operator to turn single string to array
        $required = (array) $required;
    }
    // process the $_POST variables and save them in the $_SESSION array
    foreach ($_POST as $key => $value) {
        // skip submit button
        if ($key == $submit) continue;
        // strip whitespace if not an array
        if (!is_array($value)) {
            $value = trim($value);
        }
        // if empty and required, add to $missing array
        if (in_array($key, $required) && empty($value)) {
            $missing[] = $key;
            continue;
        }
```

```
        // otherwise, assign to a session variable of the same name as $key
        $_SESSION[$key] = $value;
    }
    // if no required fields are missing, redirect to next page
    if (!$missing) {
        header("Location: $redirectNext");
        exit;
    }
}
```

The code is very similar to that used in Chapter 6 to process the feedback form, so the inline comments should be sufficient to explain how it works. The conditional statement wrapped around the new code uses $_POST[$submit] to check if the form has been submitted. I have used a variable rather than hard-coding the name of the Submit button to make the code more flexible. Although this script is included in the first page only after the form has been submitted, it's included directly in the other pages, so it's necessary to add the conditional statement here.

The name and value of the Submit button are always included in the $_POST array, so the foreach loop uses the continue keyword to skip to the next item if the key is the same as the Submit button's name. This avoids adding the unwanted value to the $_SESSION array. See "Breaking Out of a Loop" in Chapter 4 for a description of continue.

7. Add the following code in a PHP block above the DOCTYPE declaration in multiple_02.php:

```
$firstPage = 'multiple_01.php';
$nextPage = 'multiple_03.php';
$submit = 'next';
require_once '../includes/multiform.php';
```

This sets the values of $firstPage, $nextPage, and $submit and includes the processing script you have just created. The form on this page contains only one field, which is optional, so the $required variable isn't needed. The processing script automatically creates an empty array if it isn't set in the main page.

8. In multiple_03.php, add the following in a PHP code block above the DOCTYPE declaration:

```
// set required fields
$required = ['city', 'country'];
$firstPage = 'multiple_01.php';
$nextPage = 'multiple_04.php';
$submit = 'next';
require_once '../includes/multiform.php';
```

Two fields are required, so their name attributes are listed as an array and assigned to $required. The other code is the same as in the previous page.

9. Add the following code above the `<form>` tag in `multiple_01.php`, `multiple_02.php`, and `multiple_03.php`:

```php
<?php if (isset($missing)) { ?>
<p> Please fix the following required fields:</p>
    <ul>
    <?php
    foreach ($missing as $item) {
        echo "<li>$item</li>";
    }
    ?>
    </ul>
<?php } ?>
```

This displays a list of required items that haven't yet been filled in.

10. In `multiple_04.php`, add the following code in a PHP block above the DOCTYPE declaration to redirect users to the first page if they didn't enter the form from there:

```php
session_start();
if (!isset($_SESSION['formStarted'])) {
    header('Location: http://localhost/php8sols/sessions/multiple_01.php');
    exit;
}
```

11. In the body of the page, add the following code to the unordered list to display the results:

```php
<ul>
<?php
$expected = ['first_name', 'family_name', 'age',
            'address', 'city', 'country'];
// unset the formStarted variable
unset($_SESSION['formStarted']);
foreach ($expected as $key) {
    echo "<li>$key: " . htmlentities($_SESSION[$key] ) . '</li>';
    // unset the session variable
    unset($_SESSION[$key]);
}
?>
</ul>
```

This lists the name attributes of the form fields as an array and assigns the array to $expected. This is a security measure to ensure you don't process bogus values that might have been injected into the $_POST array by a malicious user.

The code then unsets $_SESSION['formStarted'] and loops through the $expected array using each value to access the relevant element of the $_SESSION array and display it in the unordered list. The session variable is then deleted. Deleting the session variables individually leaves intact any other session-related information.

12. Save all the pages, then try to load one of the middle pages of the form, or the last one, into a browser. You should be taken to the first page. Click Next without filling in either field. You'll be asked to fill in the `first_name` field. Fill in the required fields and click Next on each page. The results should be displayed on the final page, as shown in Figure 11-5.

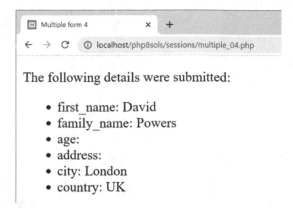

Figure 11-5. *The session variables preserved the input from multiple pages*

You can check your code against `multiple_01_done.php`, `multiple_02_done.php`, `multiple_03_done.php`, `multiple_04_done.php`, and `multiform.php` in the `ch11` folder.

This is just a simple demonstration of a multipage form. In a real-world application, you would need to preserve the user input when required fields are left blank.

The script in `multiform.php` can be used with any multipage form by creating `$_SESSION['formStarted']` on the first page after the form has been submitted and by using `$required`, `$firstPage`, `$nextPage`, and `$submit` on each page. Use the `$missing` array to handle required fields that aren't filled in.

Chapter Review

If you started this book with little or no knowledge of PHP, you're no longer in the beginners' league, but rather are leveraging the power of PHP in a lot of useful ways. Hopefully, by now you'll have begun to appreciate that the same or similar techniques crop up again and again. Instead of just copying code, you should start to recognize techniques that you can adapt to your needs and then experiment on your own.

The rest of this book continues to build on your knowledge but brings a new factor into play: the MySQL relational database (and its drop-in replacement, MariaDB), which will take your PHP skills to a higher level. The next chapter offers an introduction to MySQL and shows you how to set it up for the remaining chapters.

■ ■ ■

CHAPTER 12

Getting Started with a Database

Dynamic web sites take on a whole new meaning in combination with a database. Drawing content from a database allows you to present material in ways that would be impractical—if not impossible—with a static web site. Examples that spring to mind are online stores, such as Amazon.com; news sites, such as the BBC (www.bbcnews.com); and the big search engines, including Google and Bing. Database technology allows these web sites to present thousands, often millions, of unique pages. Even if your ambitions are nowhere near as grandiose, a database can increase your web site's richness of content with relatively little effort.

PHP supports all major databases, including Microsoft SQL Server, Oracle, and PostgreSQL, but it's most frequently used in conjunction with the open source MySQL database. According to DB-Engines (https://db-engines.com/en/ranking), MySQL ranked as the second most widely used database in mid-2021, a position it has held for many years. However, controversy surrounds the future of MySQL, which Google and Wikimedia have abandoned in favor of MariaDB (https://mariadb.org/), which stands at 12 in the DB-Engines ranking. Several leading Linux distributions have also replaced MySQL with MariaDB. This chapter begins with a brief discussion of the implications of the rivalry between these two databases.

In this chapter, you'll learn about the following:

- Understanding how a database stores information

- Choosing a graphical interface to interact with a database

- Creating user accounts

- Defining a database table with the appropriate data types

- Backing up and transferring data to another server

MySQL or MariaDB?

MySQL was originally developed as a free, open source database by MySQL AB in Sweden. It rapidly gained popularity among individual developers and was also adopted by major players, such as Wikipedia and BBC News. However, MySQL AB was sold to Sun Microsystems in 2008, which in turn was acquired 2 years later by Oracle, a major commercial database supplier. Many regarded this as a threat to MySQL's continued survival as a free, open source database. Oracle is on record as saying "MySQL is integral to Oracle's complete, open and integrated strategy." But this did little to impress one of MySQL's original creators, Michael "Monty" Widenius, who accused Oracle of removing features from MySQL and of being slow to fix security issues.

Because the MySQL code is open source, Widenius forked it to create MariaDB, which is described as "an enhanced, drop-in replacement for MySQL." Since then, MariaDB has started to implement new features of its own. In spite of the break, the two database systems are virtually interchangeable. The MariaDB executable uses the same name as MySQL (mysqld on macOS and Linux, mysqld.exe on Windows). The main privileges table is also called mysql, and the default storage engine identifies itself as InnoDB, even though it's actually a fork of InnoDB called Percona XtraDB.

As far as the code in this book is concerned, it should make no difference whether you use MariaDB or MySQL. MariaDB understands all the MySQL-specific PHP code. It's also supported by the phpMyAdmin graphical interface for MySQL that I'll be using in the remaining chapters.

■ **Note** To avoid constant repetition, you should assume that all references to MySQL apply equally to MariaDB, except where I make a specific reference to MariaDB.

How a Database Stores Information

All the data in a relational database, such as MySQL, is stored in tables, very much in the same way as in a spreadsheet, with information organized into rows and columns. Figure 12-1 shows the database table that you will build later in this chapter, as displayed in phpMyAdmin.

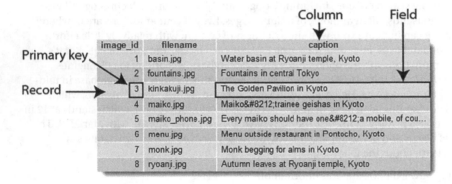

Figure 12-1. *A database table stores information in rows and columns like in a spreadsheet*

Each **column** has a name (image_id, filename, and caption) indicating what it stores.

The rows aren't labeled, but the first column (image_id) contains a unique value known as a **primary key**, which identifies the data associated with the row. Each row contains an individual **record** of related data.

The intersection of a row and a column, where the data is stored, is called a **field**. For instance, the caption field for the third record in Figure 12-1 contains the value "The Golden Pavilion in Kyoto," and the primary key for that record is 3.

■ **Note** The terms "field" and "column" are often used interchangeably, particularly in older versions of phpMyAdmin. A field holds one piece of information for a single record, whereas a column contains the same field for all records.

How Primary Keys Work

Although Figure 12-1 shows `image_id` as a consecutive sequence from 1 to 8, they're not row numbers. Figure 12-2 shows the same table with the captions sorted in alphabetical order. The field highlighted in Figure 12-1 has moved to the seventh row, but it still has the same `image_id` and `filename`.

image_id	filename	caption ▲
8	ryoanji.jpg	Autumn leaves at Ryoanji temple, Kyoto
5	maiko_phone.jpg	Every maiko should have one—a mobile, of cou...
2	fountains.jpg	Fountains in central Tokyo
4	maiko.jpg	Maiko—trainee geishas in Kyoto
6	menu.jpg	Menu outside restaurant in Pontocho, Kyoto
7	monk.jpg	Monk begging for alms in Kyoto
3	kinkakuji.jpg	The Golden Pavilion in Kyoto
1	basin.jpg	Water basin at Ryoanji temple, Kyoto

Now in the seventh row, but image_id → remains unchanged

Figure 12-2. *The primary key identifies the row even when the table is sorted in a different order*

Although the primary key is rarely displayed, it identifies the record and all the data stored in it. Once you know the primary key of a record, you can update it, delete it, or use it to display data in a separate page. Don't worry about how you find the primary key. It's easily done using **Structured Query Language** (SQL), the standard means of communicating with all major databases. The important thing to remember is to assign a primary key to every record.

■ **Tip** Some people pronounce SQL like the word "sequel." Others spell it out as "ess-queue-ell." The official pronunciation of MySQL is "My-ess-queue-ell."

- A primary key doesn't need to be a number, but *it must be unique.*

- Product numbers make good primary keys. They may consist of numbers, letters, and other characters, but are always unique. Social Security and staff ID numbers are also unique, but could lead to personal data breaches because primary keys are appended to query strings when retrieving or updating data.

- MySQL can generate a primary key for you automatically.

- Once a primary key has been assigned, it should never repeat and never be changed.

Because a primary key must be unique, MySQL doesn't normally reuse the number when a record is deleted. Although this leaves gaps in the sequence, it's unimportant. The purpose of the primary key is to identify the record. Any attempt to close the gaps puts the integrity of the database at serious risk.

■ **Tip** Some people want to remove gaps in the sequence to keep track of the number of records in a table. It's not necessary, as you'll discover in the next chapter.

Linking Tables with Primary and Foreign Keys

Unlike a spreadsheet, most databases store data in several smaller tables, rather than in one huge table. This prevents duplication and inconsistency. Let's say you're building a database of your favorite quotations. Instead of typing out the name of the author each time, it's more efficient to put the authors' names in a separate table and store a reference to an author's primary key with each quotation. As you can see in Figure 12-3, every record in the left-hand table identified by author_id 32 is a quotation from William Shakespeare.

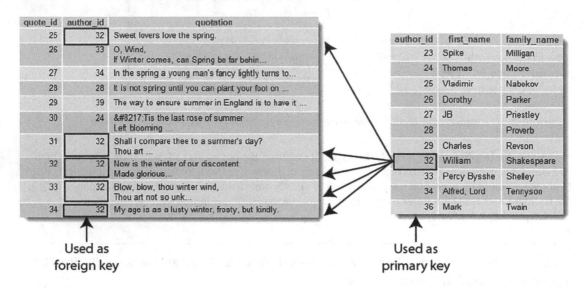

Figure 12-3. *Foreign keys are used to link information stored in separate tables*

Because the name is stored in only one place, it guarantees that it's always spelled correctly. And if you do make a spelling mistake, just a single correction is all that's needed to ensure that the change is reflected throughout the database.

Storing a primary key from one table within another table is known as creating a **foreign key**. Using foreign keys to link information in different tables is one of the most powerful aspects of a relational database. It can also be difficult to grasp in the early stages, so we'll work with single tables until Chapters 17 and 18, which cover foreign keys in detail. In the meantime, bear the following points in mind:

- When used as the primary key of a table, the value must be unique within the column. So each author_id in the table on the right of Figure 12-3 is used only once.

- When used as a foreign key, there can be multiple references to the same value. So 32 appears several times in the author_id column in the table on the left.

Breaking Down Information into Small Chunks

You may have noticed that the table on the right in Figure 12-3 has separate columns for each author's first name and family name. This is an important principle of a relational database: *break down complex information into its component parts, and store each part separately.*

It's not always easy to decide how far to go with this process. In addition to first and last names, you might want separate columns for titles (Mr., Mrs., Ms., Dr., etc.) and for middle names or initials. Addresses are best broken down into street, town, county, state, zip code, and so on. Although it may be a nuisance to break down information into small chunks, you can always use SQL and/or PHP to join them together again. However, once you have more than a handful of records, it's a major undertaking to try to separate complex information that is stored in a single field.

Checkpoints for Good Database Design

There is no *right* way to design a database—each one is different. However, the following guidelines should point you in the right direction:

- Give each record in a table a unique identifier (primary key).

- Put each group of associated data in a table of its own.

- Cross-reference related information by using the primary key from one table as the foreign key in other tables.

- Store only one item of information in each field.

- Stay DRY (don't repeat yourself).

In the early stages, you are likely to make design mistakes that you later come to regret. Try to anticipate future needs, and make your table structure flexible. You can add new tables at any time to respond to new requirements.

That's enough theory for the moment. Let's move on to something more practical by building a database for the Japan Journey web site from Chapters 5 and 6.

Using a Graphical Interface

The traditional way to interact with MySQL databases is through a Command Prompt window or Terminal. But it's a lot easier to use a third-party graphic interface, such as phpMyAdmin, a browser-based front end to MySQL (see Figure 12-4).

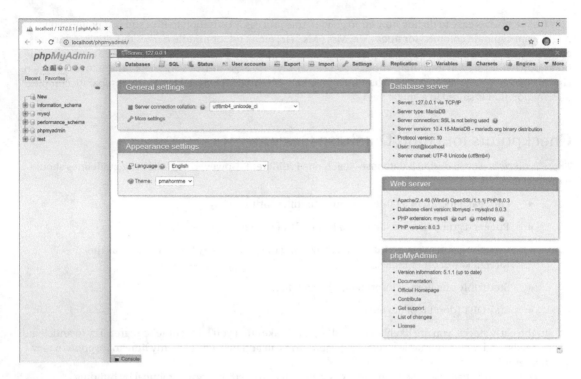

Figure 12-4. *phpMyAdmin is a free graphical interface to MySQL that runs in your browser*

Because phpMyAdmin (www.phpmyadmin.net) is installed automatically with XAMPP, MAMP, and most other free all-in-one packages, it's the UI chosen for this book. It's easy to use and has all the basic functionality required for setting up and administering MySQL databases. It works on Windows, macOS, and Linux. Many hosting companies provide it as the standard interface to MySQL.

If you work with databases on a regular basis, you may want to eventually explore the other graphical interfaces. One that's worthy of note is Navicat (www.navicat.com/en/), a paid-for product available for Windows, macOS, and Linux. The Navicat Cloud service also lets you administer databases from an iPhone or iPad. Navicat is particularly popular among web developers because it's capable of performing scheduled backups of databases from a remote server to your local computer. Navicat for MySQL supports both MySQL and MariaDB.

Launching phpMyAdmin

If you're running XAMPP on Windows, there are three ways to launch phpMyAdmin:

- Enter http://localhost/phpMyAdmin/ in the browser address bar.

- Click the MySQL Admin button in the XAMPP control panel.

- Click the phpMyAdmin link under Tools in the XAMPP administration page (http://localhost/xampp/).

If you installed MAMP on macOS, click Tools ➤ phpMyAdmin in the menu at the top of the MAMP start page (click WebStart in the MAMP control widget).

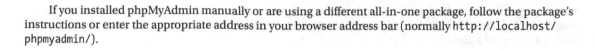

If you installed phpMyAdmin manually or are using a different all-in-one package, follow the package's instructions or enter the appropriate address in your browser address bar (normally http://localhost/phpmyadmin/).

■ **Tip**   If you get a message saying that the server is not responding or that the socket is not correctly configured, make sure that the MySQL server is running.

If you installed XAMPP, you might be presented with a screen asking for a username and password. If so, log in to phpMyAdmin as the root superuser. Enter root as the username and use the password you created for root when setting up XAMPP.

■ **Caution**   When accessing phpMyAdmin on a remote server, always use a secure connection (https). Anyone eavesdropping on an unsecure connection would be able to gain control over your precious data, stealing it, corrupting it, or even deleting it completely.

Setting Up the phpsols Database

In a local testing environment, there's no limit to the number of databases that you can create in MySQL, and you can call them whatever you like. I am going to assume that you are working in a local testing environment and so will show you how to set up a database called phpsols, together with two user accounts called psread and pswrite.

■ **Note**   On shared hosting, you may be limited to just one database set up by the hosting company. If you're testing on a remote server and don't have the freedom to set up a new database and user accounts, substitute the name and username allocated by your hosting company for phpsols and pswrite, respectively.

MySQL Naming Rules

The basic MySQL naming rules for databases, tables, and columns are as follows:

- Names can be up to 64 characters long.
- Legal characters are numbers, letters, the underscore, and $.
- Names can begin with a number but cannot consist exclusively of numbers.

Some hosting companies seem blissfully ignorant of these rules and assign clients databases that contain one or more hyphens (an illegal character) in their name. If a database, table, or column name contains spaces or illegal characters, you must always surround it by backticks (`) in SQL queries. Note that this is not a single quote ('), but rather is a separate character. On my Windows keyboard, it's directly above the Tab key. On my Mac keyboard, it's next to the left Shift key on the same key as the tilde (~).

When choosing names, you might accidentally choose one of MySQL's many reserved words (https://dev.mysql.com/doc/refman/8.0/en/keywords.html), such as date or time. One technique to avoid this is

337

to use compound words, such as arrival_date, arrival_time, and so on. Alternatively, surround all names with backticks. phpMyAdmin does this automatically, but you need to do this manually when writing your own SQL in a PHP script.

■ **Note** Because so many people have used date, text, time, and timestamp as column names, MySQL permits their use without backticks. However, you should avoid using them. It's bad practice and is unlikely to work if you migrate your data to a different database system.

Case Sensitivity of Names

Windows and macOS treat MySQL names as case-insensitive. However, Linux and Unix servers respect case sensitivity. To avoid problems when transferring databases and PHP code from your local computer to a remote server, I strongly recommend that you use lowercase exclusively in database, table, and column names. When building names from more than one word, join them with an underscore.

Using phpMyAdmin to Create a New Database

Creating a new database in phpMyAdmin is easy.

■ **Note** phpMyAdmin has a frequent release cycle, which often results in minor changes to the user interface. Occasionally, the changes are more significant. These instructions and the accompanying screenshots are based on phpMyAdmin 5.1.1. Although there might be differences with the version you're using, the basic process should be broadly the same.

---

1. Launch phpMyAdmin and select the Databases tab at the top of the main window.

2. Type the name of the new database (phpsols) into the first field under Create database. The drop-down menu to the right of the field sets the **collation** for the database. Collation determines the order data is sorted. As the following screenshot shows, the default setting on my installation is utf8mb4_general_ci. This supports virtually every human language and should be suitable unless you have specific needs for your own language. The ci indicates that the sort order is case-insensitive. On older versions of phpMyAdmin, the default is latin1_ swedish_ci. This reflects MySQL's Swedish origins. English uses the same sort order. Then click Create:

Databases

Create database

phpsols | utf8mb4_general_ci ⌄ | Create

3. Confirmation that the database has been created should flash up onscreen, followed by a screen that invites you to create a table:

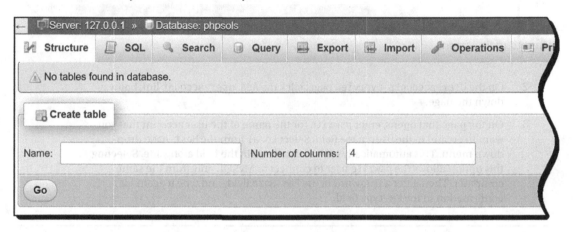

4. Before creating tables in a new database, it's a good idea to create user accounts for it. Leave phpMyAdmin open, as you'll continue using it in the next section.

Creating Database-Specific User Accounts

A new installation of MySQL normally has only one registered user—the superuser account called "root," which has complete control over everything. (XAMPP also creates a user account called "pma," which phpMyAdmin uses for advanced features not covered by this book.) The root user should *never* be used for anything other than top-level administration, such as the creation and removal of databases, creating user accounts, and exporting and importing data. Each individual database should have at least one—preferably two—dedicated user account with limited privileges.

When you put a database online, you should grant users the fewest privileges they need and no more. There are four important privileges—all named after the equivalent SQL commands:

- SELECT: Retrieves records from database tables

- INSERT: Inserts records into a database

- UPDATE: Changes existing records

- DELETE: Deletes records but not tables or databases (the command for that is DROP)

339

Most of the time, visitors only need to retrieve information, so the psread user account will have just the SELECT privilege and will be read-only. However, for user registration or site administration, you need all four privileges. These will be made available to the pswrite account.

Granting User Privileges

1. In phpMyAdmin, return to the main screen by clicking the little house icon at the top left of the screen. Then click the User accounts tab (on older versions of phpMyAdmin, it's called Users):

Return to main screen

2. On the User accounts overview page, click the Add user account link halfway down the page.

3. On the page that opens, enter pswrite (or the name of the user account that you want to create) in the User name field. Select Local from the Host name drop-down menu. This automatically enters localhost in the field alongside. Selecting this option allows the pswrite user to connect to MySQL only from the same computer. Then enter a password in the Password field, and type it again for confirmation in the Re-type field.

■ **Note** In the example files for this book, I've used 0Ch@Nom1$u as the password. MySQL passwords are case-sensitive.

---

4. Beneath the Login Information table are sections labeled Database for user account and Global privileges. Ignore both of them. Scroll down to the bottom of the page and click the Go button.

5. This presents you with confirmation that the user has been created and offers options to edit the user's privileges. Click the Database button above Edit privileges:

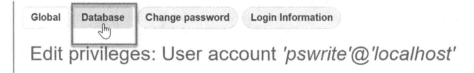

Edit privileges: User account *'pswrite'@'localhost'*

6. Under Database-specific privileges, select phpsols from the list (if necessary, activate the drop-down menu labeled Add privileges on the following database(s)) and click Go:

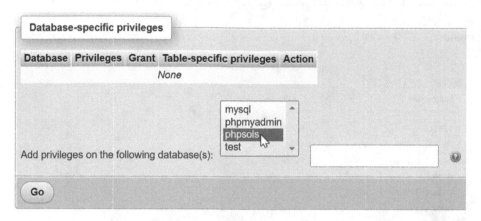

■ **Note** MySQL has three default databases: information_schema, a read-only, virtual database that contains details of all other databases on the same server; mysql, which contains details of all user accounts and privileges; and test, which is empty. You should never edit the mysql database directly unless you're sure what you're doing.

---

7. The next screen allows you to set the privileges for this user on just the phpsols database. You want pswrite to have all four privileges listed earlier, so click the check boxes next to SELECT, INSERT, UPDATE, and DELETE.

If you hover your mouse pointer over each option, phpMyAdmin displays a tooltip describing the option's use, as shown. After selecting the four privileges, click Go:

Database	Table	Routine	Login Information

Edit privileges: User account *'pswrite'@'localhost'* - Database *phpsols*

Database-specific privileges ⊟ **Check all**

Note: MySQL privilege names are expressed in English.

☑ **Data**	☐ **Structure**	☐ **Administration**
☑ SELECT	☐ CREATE	☐ GRANT
☑ INSERT	☐ ALTER	☐ LOCK TABLES
☑ UPDATE ⎯ Allows inserting and replacing data.		☐ REFERENCES
☑ DELETE	☐ DROP	
	☐ CREATE TEMPORARY TABLES	
	☐ SHOW VIEW	
	☐ CREATE ROUTINE	
	☐ ALTER ROUTINE	
	☐ EXECUTE	
	☐ CREATE VIEW	
	☐ EVENT	
	☐ TRIGGER	

Go

■ **Caution**   Many screens in phpMyAdmin have more than one Go button. Always click the button at the foot of or alongside the section with the options you want to set.

---

8. phpMyAdmin presents you with confirmation that the privileges have been updated for the pswrite user account; the page displays the Database-specific privileges table again, in case you need to change anything. Click the User accounts tab at the top of the page to return to the User accounts overview.

9. Click Add user account and repeat steps 3 through 8 to create a second user account called psread. This user will have much more restricted privileges, so when you get to step 7, check only the SELECT option. The password used for psread in the example files is K1yoMizu^dera.

Creating a Database Table

Now that you have a database and dedicated user accounts, you can begin creating tables. Let's begin by creating a table to hold the details of images, as shown in Figure 12-1 at the beginning of this chapter. Before you can start entering data, you need to define the table structure. This involves deciding the following:

- The name of the table
- How many columns it will have
- The name of each column
- What type of data will be stored in each column
- Whether the column must always have data in each field
- Which column contains the table's primary key

If you look at Figure 12-1, you can see that the table contains three columns: image_id (primary key), filename, and caption. Because it contains details of images, that's a good name to use for the table. There's not much point in storing a filename without a caption, so every column must contain data. Great! Apart from the data type, all the decisions have been made. I'll explain the data types as we go along.

Defining the Images Table

These instructions show how to define a table in phpMyAdmin. If you prefer to use Navicat or a different UI for MySQL, use the settings in Table 12-1.

1. Launch phpMyAdmin, if it's not already open, and select phpsols from the list of databases on the left of the screen. This opens the Structure tab, which reports that no tables have been found in the database.

2. In the Create table section, type the name of the new table (images) in the Name field and enter 3 in the Number of columns field. Then click the Go button.

3. The next screen is where you define the table. There are a lot of options, but not all of them need to be filled in. Table 12-1 lists the settings for the images table.

Table 12-1. *Settings for the images table*

Field	Type	Length/Values	Attributes	Null	Index	A_I
image_id	INT		UNSIGNED	Deselected	PRIMARY	Selected
filename	VARCHAR	25		Deselected		
caption	VARCHAR	120		Deselected		

The first column, image_id, is defined as type INT, which stands for integer. Its attribute is set to UNSIGNED, which means that only positive numbers are allowed. When you select PRIMARY from the Index drop-down, phpMyAdmin opens a modal panel where you can specify advanced options. Accept the default setting, and click Go to dismiss the panel. Then, select the A_I (AUTO_INCREMENT) check box. This tells MySQL to insert the next available number (starting at 1) in this column whenever a new record is inserted.

The next column, filename, is defined as type VARCHAR with a length of 25. This means it accepts up to 25 characters of text.

343

The final column, caption, is also VARCHAR with a length of 120, so it accepts up to 120 characters of text.

The Null check box for all columns is deselected, so they must always contain something. However, that "something" can be as little as an empty string. I'll describe the column types in more detail in the "Choosing the Right Data Type in MySQL" section later in this chapter.

The following screenshot shows the options after they have been set in phpMyAdmin (the columns to the right of A_I have been left out because they don't need to be filled in):

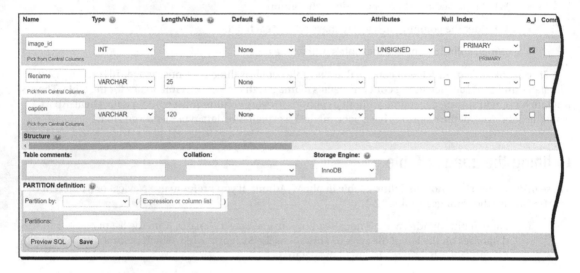

Toward the bottom of the screen is an option for Storage Engine. This determines the format used internally to store the database files. InnoDB has been the default since MySQL 5.5. Prior to that MyISAM was the default. I'll explain the differences between these storage engines in Chapter 17. In the meantime, use InnoDB. Converting from one storage engine to another is very simple.

When you have finished, click the Save button at the bottom of the screen.

■ **Tip** If you click Go instead of Save, phpMyAdmin adds an extra column for you to define. If this happens, just click Save. As long as you don't enter values into the fields, phpMyAdmin ignores the extra column.

---

4. The next screen displays the details of the table you have just created (if you don't see this screen, click the Structure tab):

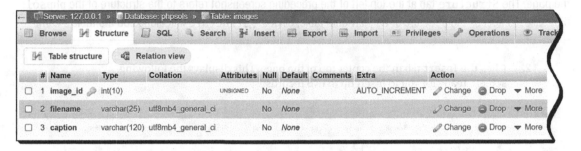

The gold key to the right of image_id indicates that it's the table's primary key. To edit any settings, click Change in the appropriate row. This opens the previous screen and allows you to change the values.

■ **Tip** If you made a complete mess and want to start again, click the Operations tab at the top of the screen. Then, in the Delete data or table section, click Delete the table (DROP) and confirm that you want to drop the table. (In SQL, *delete* refers only to records. You *drop* a column, table, or database.)

Inserting Records into a Table

Now that you have a table, you need to put some data into it. Eventually, you'll need to build your own content management system using HTML forms, PHP, and SQL, but the quick and easy way to do it is with phpMyAdmin.

Using phpMyAdmin to Insert Records Manually

These instructions show how to add records to the images table through the phpMyAdmin interface.

1. If phpMyAdmin is still displaying the structure of the images table as at the end of the previous section, skip to step 2. Otherwise, launch phpMyAdmin and select the phpsols database from the list on the left. Then click Structure to the right of images, as shown in the following screenshot:

> ■ **Tip** The breadcrumb trail at the top of the main frame provides the context for the tabs across the head of the page. The Structure tab at the top left of the preceding screenshot refers to the structure of the phpsols database. To access the structure of an individual table, click the Structure link alongside the table's name.

2. Click the Insert tab in the center top of the page. This displays the following screen, ready for you to insert up to two records:

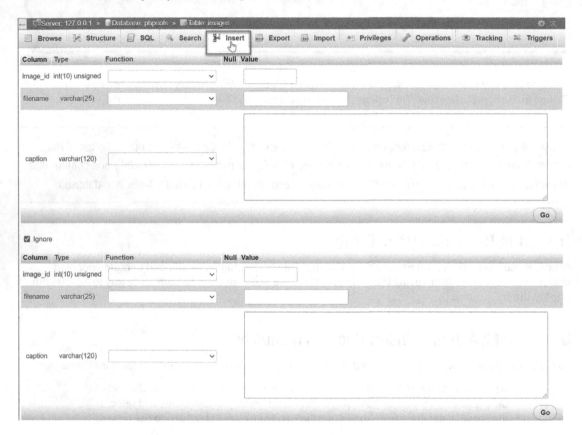

3. The forms display the names and details of each column. You can ignore the Function fields. MySQL has a large number of functions that you can apply to the values being stored in your table. You'll learn more about them in the following chapters. The Value field is where you enter the data you want to insert in the table.

Because you have defined image_id as AUTO_INCREMENT, MySQL inserts the next available number automatically. So you *must* leave the image_id Value field blank. Fill in the next two Value fields as follows:

- filename: basin.jpg

- caption: Water basin at Ryoanji temple, Kyoto

4. In the second form, leave the Value field for image_id blank and fill in the next two fields like this:

    - filename: fountains.jpg

    - caption: Fountains in central Tokyo

    Normally, the Ignore check box is automatically deselected when you add values to the second form, but deselect it if necessary.

5. Click the Go button at the bottom of the second form. The SQL used to insert the records is displayed at the top of the page. I'll explain the basic SQL commands in the remaining chapters, but studying the SQL that phpMyAdmin displays is a good way to learn how to build your own queries. SQL is closely based on human language, so it isn't all that difficult to learn.

6. Click the Browse tab at the top left of the page. You should now see the first two entries in the images table, as shown here:

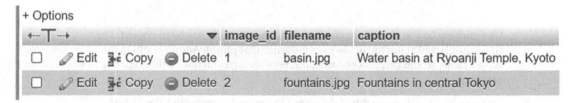

As you can see, MySQL has inserted 1 and 2 in the image_id fields.

You could continue typing out the details of the remaining six images, but let's speed things up a bit by using an SQL file that contains all the necessary data.

Loading the Images Records from an SQL File

Because the primary key of the images table has been set to AUTO_INCREMENT, it's necessary to drop the table and all its data. The SQL file does this automatically and builds the table from scratch. These instructions assume that phpMyAdmin is open to the page in step 6 of the previous section.

1. If you're happy to overwrite the data in the images table, skip to step 2. However, if you have entered data that you don't want to lose, copy your data to a different table. Click the Operations tab at the top of the page (depending on the size of your screen, Operations might be hidden inside More at the far right of the row of tabs), type the name of the new table in the blank field in the section titled Copy table to (database.table), and click Go. The following screenshot shows the settings for copying the structure and data of the images table to images_backup within the phpsols database:

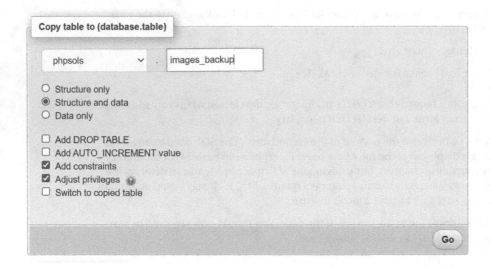

After clicking Go you should see confirmation that the table has been copied. The breadcrumb trail at the top of the page indicates that phpMyAdmin is still in the images table, so you can proceed to step 2, even though you have a different page onscreen.

2. Click the Import tab at the top of the page. On the next screen, click the Browse (or Choose File) button in File to import, and then navigate to images.sql in the ch12 folder. Leave all options at their default setting, and click Go at the foot of the page:

Importing into the table "images"

File to import:

File may be compressed (gzip, bzip2, zip) or uncompressed.
A compressed file's name must end in **.[format].[compression]**. Example: **.sql.zip**

Browse your computer: [Choose File] images.sql (Max: 40MiB)

You may also drag and drop a file on any page.

Character set of the file: [utf-8 ▾]

Partial import:

☑

Allow the interruption of an import in case the script detects it is close to the PHP timeout limit. *(This might be a good way to import large files, however it can break transactions.)*

Skip this number of queries (for SQL) starting from the first one: [0]

Other options:

☑ Enable foreign key checks

Format:

[SQL ▾]

Format-specific options:

SQL compatibility mode: [NONE ▾]

☑ Do not use AUTO_INCREMENT for zero values

(Go)

3. phpMyAdmin drops the original table, creates a new version, and inserts all the records. When you see confirmation that the file has been imported, click the Browse button at the top left of the page. You should now see the same data as shown in Figure 12-1 at the beginning of the chapter.

If you open `images.sql` in a text editor, you'll see that it contains the SQL commands that create the images table and populate it with data. This is how the table is built:

```
DROP TABLE IF EXISTS `images`;
CREATE TABLE `images` (
  `image_id` int(10) UNSIGNED NOT NULL AUTO_INCREMENT,
  `filename` varchar(25) NOT NULL,
  `caption` varchar(120) NOT NULL,
) ENGINE=InnoDB DEFAULT CHARSET=utf8mb4;
```

The primary key is set in a separate SQL command. Importing data from an SQL file like this is how you transfer data from your local testing environment to the remote server where your web site is located. Assuming that your hosting company provides phpMyAdmin for you to administer your remote database, all you need to do to transfer the data is to launch the version of phpMyAdmin on your remote server, click the Import tab, select the SQL file on your local computer, and click Go.

The next section describes how to create the SQL file.

Creating an SQL File for Backup and Data Transfer

MySQL doesn't store your database in a single file that you can simply upload to your web site. Even if you find the right files, you're likely to damage them unless the MySQL server is turned off. Anyway, most hosting companies won't permit you to upload the raw files because it would also involve shutting down their server, causing a great deal of inconvenience for everyone.

Nevertheless, moving a database from one server to another is easy. All it involves is creating a backup **dump** of the data and loading it into the other database using phpMyAdmin or any other database administration program. The dump is a text file that contains all the SQL commands needed to populate an individual table or even an entire database. phpMyAdmin can create backups of your entire MySQL server, individual databases, selected tables, or individual tables.

■ **Tip**   You don't need to read the details of how to create a dump file until you're ready to transfer data to another server or create a backup.

To keep things simple, these instructions show how to back up only a single database.

1. In phpMyAdmin, select the `phpsols` database from the list on the left. If the database was already selected, click the `Database: phpsols` breadcrumb at the top of the screen, as shown here:

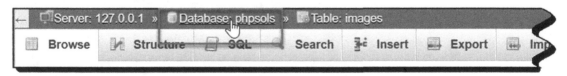

2. Select Export from the tabs along the top of the screen.

3. There are two export methods: Quick and Custom. The Quick method has only one option for the format of the export file. The default is SQL, so all you have to do is click Go, and phpMyAdmin creates the SQL dump file and saves it to your browser's default Downloads folder. The file has the same name as the database, so for the phpsols database, it's called phpsols.sql.

4. The Quick method is okay for exporting a small amount of data, but you normally need more control over the export options; select the Custom radio button. There are a lot of options, so let's take a look at them section by section.

5. The Format section defaults to SQL but offers a range of other formats, including CSV, JSON, and XML.

6. The Table(s) section lists all the tables in your database. By default all are selected, but you can choose which to export by deselecting the check boxes of the options you don't want. In the following screenshot, only the images table structure and data have been selected, so images_backup won't be exported:

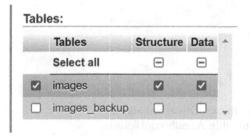

■ **Tip**   It's often a good idea to back up individual tables rather than an entire database because most PHP servers are configured to limit uploads to 2 MB. Compressing dump files, as described in the next step, also helps get around size restrictions.

---

7. The Output section has several useful options.

    Selecting the check box labeled Rename exported databases/tables/columns launches a modal panel where you can assign the new names.

    The Use LOCK TABLES statement check box adds commands that prevent anyone else from inserting, updating, or deleting records while the dump file is being used to import data and/or structure.

    There are also radio buttons that give you the option of either saving the SQL dump to a file (this is the default) or viewing the output as text. Viewing as text can be useful if you want to check the SQL that's being generated before you create the file:

Output:

☐   Rename exported databases/tables/columns

☐   Use `LOCK TABLES` statement

◉   Save output to a file

      File name template: 🔵 | @DATABASE@ | ☑ use this for future exports

      Character set of the file: | utf-8 ˅ |

      Compression: | None ˅ |

      ☐   Export tables as separate files

○   View output as text

Skip tables larger than | | MiB

The File name template contains a value between @ marks. This automatically generates the filename from the server, database, or table. A really cool feature is that you can use PHP `strftime()` formatting characters (see `www.php.net/manual/en/function.strftime.php`) to enhance the template. For example, you can add the current date automatically to the filename just before the filename extension, like this:

`@DATABASE@_%Y-%m-%d`

The default value of `Character set of the file` is utf-8. You need to change this only if your data is stored in a specific regional format.

By default dump files are not compressed, but the drop-down menu offers the option to use zipped or gzipped compression. This can greatly reduce the size of the dump file, speeding up the transfer of data. When importing a compressed file, phpMyAdmin automatically detects the compression type and unzips it.

The final option allows you to skip files larger than a specified number of MB.

8. In `Format-specific options`, the choices are determined by the format selected in step 5. For SQL, you can opt to display comments in the dump file and enclose the export in a transaction. The value of using a transaction is that the database is rolled back to its previous state if an error causes the import to be abandoned.

    Other options include disabling foreign key checks, exporting views as tables, and exporting metadata. Finally, you have the option to maximize compatibility with different database systems or older versions of MySQL. Normally, the value should be set to the default: `NONE`.

9. The `Object creation options` section lets you fine-tune the SQL for creating databases and tables. The following screenshot shows the default settings:

Object creation options

Add statements:

☐ Add `CREATE DATABASE` / `USE` statement

☐ Add `DROP TABLE` / `VIEW` / `PROCEDURE` / `FUNCTION` / `EVENT` / `TRIGGER` statement

☑ Add `CREATE TABLE` statement

    ☐ `IF NOT EXISTS` (less efficient as indexes will be generated during table creation)

    ☑ `AUTO_INCREMENT` value

☑ Add `CREATE VIEW` statement

    ☐ Use simple view export

    ☐ Exclude definition of current user

    ☐ `OR REPLACE` view

☐ Add `CREATE PROCEDURE` / `FUNCTION` / `EVENT` statement

☑ Add `CREATE TRIGGER` statement

☑ Enclose table and column names with backquotes *(Protects column and table names formed with special characters or keywords)*

> When creating a backup, it's usually a good idea to select the Add `DROP TABLE` / `VIEW` / `PROCEDURE` / `FUNCTION` / `EVENT` / `TRIGGER` statement check box, because a backup is normally used to replace existing data that has become corrupted.
>
> The final check box, which is selected by default, wraps table and column names in backquotes (backticks) to avoid problems with names that contain invalid characters or use reserved words. I suggest always leaving this selected.

10. The `Data creation options` section controls how data is inserted into tables. In most cases, the default settings are fine. However, you may be interested in changing the first four, which are shown in the following screenshot:

Data creation options

☐ Truncate table before insert

    ☐ `INSERT DELAYED` statements

    ☐ `INSERT IGNORE` statements

Function to use when dumping data: `INSERT ∨`

> The first check box allows you to truncate the table before inserting the data. This is useful if you want to replace the existing data, perhaps if it has been corrupted.

The other two check boxes affect how INSERT commands are executed. INSERT DELAYED doesn't work with the default InnoDB tables. Moreover, it is deprecated as of MySQL 5.6.6, so it's probably best to avoid it.

INSERT IGNORE skips errors, such as duplicate primary keys. Personally, I think it's best to be alerted to errors, so I don't recommend using it.

The drop-down menu labeled Function to use when dumping data lets you choose INSERT, UPDATE, or REPLACE. The default is to insert new records with INSERT. If you select UPDATE, only existing records are updated. REPLACE updates where necessary and inserts new records if they don't already exist.

11. When you have made all your selections, click Go at the bottom of the page. You now have a backup that can be used to transfer the contents of your database to another server.

■ **Tip** By default, the file created by phpMyAdmin contains the SQL commands only to create and populate the database tables. It does not include the command to create the database unless you select the custom option to do so. This means you can import the tables into any database. It does not need to have the same name as the one in your local testing environment.

Choosing the Right Data Type in MySQL

You may have received a bit of a shock when selecting Type for the image_id column. phpMyAdmin lists all available data types—there are more than 40 in MySQL 8 and MariaDB 10. Rather than confuse you with unnecessary details, I'll explain just those most commonly used.

You can find full details of all data types in the MySQL documentation at https://dev.mysql.com/doc/refman/8.0/en/data-types.html.

Storing Text

The difference between the main text data types boils down to the maximum number of characters that can be stored in an individual field, the treatment of trailing spaces, and whether you can set a default value.

- CHAR: A fixed-length string. You must specify the required length in the Length/Values field. The maximum permitted value is 255. Internally, strings are right-padded with spaces to the specified length, but the trailing spaces are stripped when you retrieve the value. You can define a default.

- VARCHAR: A variable-length string. You must specify the maximum number of characters you plan to use (in phpMyAdmin, enter the number in the Length/Values field). The maximum number of characters is 65,535. If a string is stored with trailing spaces, they are preserved on retrieval. Accepts a default value.

- TEXT: Stores text up to a maximum of 65,535 characters (approximately 50% longer than this chapter). Cannot define a default value.

TEXT is convenient because you don't need to specify a maximum size (in fact, you can't). Although the maximum size for VARCHAR and TEXT is 65,535 characters, the effective amount is less because the maximum amount that can be stored across all columns in a row is 65,535 bytes.

■ **Tip** Keep it simple: use VARCHAR for short text items and TEXT for longer ones. VARCHAR and TEXT columns take only the amount of disk space needed to store the values entered in them. CHAR columns always allocate the full amount of space declared as the required length, even when empty.

Storing Numbers

The most frequently used numeric column types are as follows:

- INT: Any whole number (integer) between –2,147,483,648 and 2,147,483,647. If the column is declared as UNSIGNED, the range is from 0 to 4,294,967,295.

- FLOAT: A floating-point number. You can optionally specify two comma-separated numbers to limit the range. The first number specifies the maximum number of digits, and the second specifies how many of those digits should come after the decimal point. Since PHP will format numbers after calculation, I recommend that you use FLOAT without the optional parameters.

- DECIMAL: A number with a fraction; contains a fixed number of digits after the decimal point. When defining the table, you need to specify the maximum number of digits and how many of those digits should come after the decimal point. In phpMyAdmin, enter the numbers separated by a comma in the Length/Values field. For example, 6,2 permits numbers in the range from –9999.99 to 9999.99. If you don't specify the size, the decimal fraction is truncated when values are stored in this type of column.

The difference between FLOAT and DECIMAL is accuracy. Floating-point numbers are treated as approximate values and are subject to rounding errors (for a detailed explanation, see https://dev.mysql.com/doc/refman/8.0/en/problems-with-float.html).

Use DECIMAL to store currencies.

■ **Caution** Don't use commas or spaces as the thousands separator. Apart from numerals, the only characters permitted in numbers are the negative operator (–) and the decimal point (.).

Storing Dates and Times

MySQL stores dates in one format only: YYYY-MM-DD. It's the standard approved by the ISO (International Organization for Standardization) and avoids the ambiguity inherent in different national conventions. I'll return to the subject of dates in Chapter 16. The most important column types for dates and times are as follows:

- DATE: A date stored as YYYY-MM-DD. The range is 1000-01-01 to 9999-12-31.

- DATETIME: A combined date and time displayed in the format YYYY-MM-DD HH:MM:SS.

- TIMESTAMP: A timestamp (normally generated automatically by the computer). Legal values range from the beginning of 1970 to partway through January 2038.

■ **Caution**   MySQL timestamps use the same format as DATETIME, meaning they are incompatible with Unix and PHP timestamps, which are based on the number of seconds since January 1, 1970. Don't mix them.

Storing Predefined Lists

MySQL lets you store two types of predefined lists that could be regarded as the database equivalents of radio button and check-box states:

- ENUM: This column type stores a single choice from a predefined list, such as "yes, no, don't know" or "100–110 V, 220–240 V." The maximum number of items that can be stored in the predefined list is a mind-boggling 65,535—some radio button group!

- SET: This column type stores zero or more choices from a predefined list. The list can hold a maximum of 64 choices.

While ENUM is quite useful, SET tends to be less so, mainly because it violates the principle of storing only one piece of information in each field. The type of situation in which it can be useful is when recording optional extras on a car or multiple choices in a survey.

Storing Binary Data

Storing binary data, such as images, isn't a good idea. It bloats your database, and you can't display images directly from a database. However, the following column types are designed for binary data:

- TINYBLOB: Up to 255 bytes

- BLOB: Up to 64 KB

- MEDIUMBLOB: Up to 16 MB

- LONGBLOB: Up to 4 GB

With such whimsical names, it's a bit of a letdown to discover that BLOB stands for **binary large object**.

Chapter Review

Much of this chapter has been devoted to theory, explaining the basic principles of good database design. Instead of putting all the information you want to store in a single, large table like a spreadsheet, you need to plan the structure of your database carefully, moving repetitive information into separate tables. As long as you give each record in a table a unique identifier—its primary key—you can keep track of information and link it to related records in other tables through the use of foreign keys. The concept of using foreign keys can be difficult to understand at the outset, but it should become clearer by the end of this book.

You have also learned how to create MySQL user accounts with limited privileges, as well as how to define a table and import and export data using an SQL file. In the next chapter, you'll use PHP to connect to the phpsols database in order to display the data stored in the images table.

■ ■ ■

CHAPTER 13

Connecting to a Database with PHP and SQL

PHP 8 offers two ways to connect to and interact with a MySQL database: MySQL Improved (MySQLi) and PHP Data Objects (PDO). Which one you choose is an important decision, because they use incompatible code. You can't mix them in the same database connection. It's also important not to confuse MySQLi with the original MySQL extension, which is no longer supported. In most cases, the only difference in the names of MySQLi functions is the addition of the letter *i* (e.g., mysqli_query() instead of mysql_query()). However, the order of arguments is usually different, so converting an old script involves more than just inserting an *i* into the function name.

As its name suggests, MySQLi is designed specifically to work with MySQL. It's also fully compatible with MariaDB. PDO, on the other hand, is database system–neutral. In theory, at least, you can switch your web site from MySQL to Microsoft SQL Server or a different database system by changing only a couple of lines of PHP code. In practice, you normally need to rewrite at least some of your SQL queries because each database vendor adds custom functions on top of the standard SQL.

My personal preference is to use PDO; but for the sake of completeness, the remaining chapters cover both MySQLi and PDO. If you want to concentrate on only one of them, just ignore the sections that relate to the other. Although you use PHP to connect to the database and store any results, the database queries need to be written in SQL. This chapter teaches you the basics of retrieving information stored in a table.

In this chapter, we'll cover the following:

- Connecting to MySQL and MariaDB with MySQLi and PDO

- Counting the number of records in a table

- Using SELECT queries to retrieve data and display it on a web page

- Keeping data secure with prepared statements and other techniques

Checking Your Remote Server Setup

XAMPP and MAMP support both MySQLi and PDO, but you need to check the PHP configuration of your remote server to verify the degree of support it offers. Run phpinfo() on your remote server, scroll down the configuration page, and look for the following sections. They're listed alphabetically, so you'll need to scroll down a long way to find them:

D. Powers, *PHP 8 Solutions*, https://doi.org/10.1007/978-1-4842-7141-4_13

mysqli		
Mysqli Support	**enabled**	
Client API library version	mysqlnd 8.0.3	
Active Persistent Links	0	
Inactive Persistent Links	0	
Active Links	0	

Directive	Local Value	Master Value
mysqli.allow_local_infile	Off	Off
mysqli.allow_persistent	On	On
mysqli.default_host	*no value*	*no value*
		3306
pcre.jit	1	
pcre.recursion_limit	100000	100000

PDO		
PDO support	**enabled**	
PDO drivers	mysql, sqlite	

pdo_mysql		
PDO Driver for MySQL	**enabled**	
	nlnd 8.0.3	

All hosting companies should have the first section (`mysqli`). If only `mysql` (without the final *i*) is listed, you're on a server that's dangerously out of date. Get your hosting company to move you to a server running an up-to-date version of PHP 8.x as soon as possible (you can check which versions of PHP are currently supported at `https://php.net/supported-versions.php`). If you plan to use PDO, you not only need to check that PDO is enabled, but you must also make sure that `pdo_mysql` is listed. PDO requires a different driver for each type of database.

How PHP Communicates with a Database

Regardless of whether you use MySQLi or PDO, the process always follows this sequence:

1. Connect to the database using the hostname, username, password, and database name.

2. Prepare an SQL query.

3. Execute the query and save the result.

4. Extract the data from the result (usually with a loop).

Username and password are the usernames and passwords of the accounts you created in Chapter 12 or of the account given to you by your hosting company. But what about hostname? In a local testing environment, it's `localhost`. What comes as a surprise is that it's often `localhost` even on a remote server. This is because in many cases the database server is located on the same server as your web site. In other words, the web server that displays your pages and the database server are local to each other. However, if the database server is on a separate machine, your hosting company will tell you the address to use. The important point is that the hostname is *not* usually the same as your web site's domain name.

Let's take a quick look at how you connect to a database with each of the methods.

Connecting with the MySQL Improved Extension

MySQLi has two interfaces: procedural and object-oriented. The procedural interface is designed to ease the transition from the original MySQL functions. Since the object-oriented version is more compact, that's the version adopted here.

To connect to MySQL or MariaDB, you create a mysqli object by passing four arguments to the constructor method: the hostname, username, password, and name of the database. This is how you connect to the phpsols database:

```
$conn = new mysqli($hostname, $username, $password, 'phpsols');
```

This stores the connection object as $conn.

If your database server uses a nonstandard port, you need to pass the port number as a fifth argument to the mysqli constructor.

■ **Tip**　MAMP uses a socket connection to MySQL, so there's no need to add the port number even if MySQL is listening on port 8889. This applies to both MySQLi and PDO.

Connecting with PDO

PDO requires a slightly different approach. The most important difference is that PDO throws an exception if the connection fails. If you don't catch the exception, the debugging information displays all the connection details, including your username and password. Consequently, you need to wrap the code in a try block and catch the exception to prevent sensitive information from being displayed.

The first argument to the PDO constructor method is a **data source name** (DSN). This is a string that consists of the PDO driver name followed by a colon, followed by PDO driver–specific connection details.

To connect to MySQL or MariaDB, the DSN needs to be in the following format:

```
'mysql:host=hostname;dbname=databaseName'
```

If your database server is using a nonstandard port, the DSN should also contain the port number, like this:

```
'mysql:host=hostname;port=portNumber;dbname=databaseName'
```

After the DSN, you pass the username and password to the PDO() constructor method. So the code to connect to the phpsols database looks like this:

```
try {
 $conn = new PDO("mysql:host=$hostname;dbname=phpsols", $username, $password);
} catch (PDOException $e) {
 echo $e->getMessage();
}
```

Using echo to display the message generated by the exception is acceptable during testing, but when you deploy the script on a live web site, you need to redirect the user to an error page, as described in PHP Solution 5-9.

■ **Tip**   The DSN is the only part of the PHP code that you need to change in order to connect to a different database system. All the remaining PDO code is completely database-neutral. Details of how to create the DSN for PostgreSQL, Microsoft SQL Server, SQLite, and other database systems can be found at www.php.net/manual/en/pdo.drivers.php.

PHP Solution 13-1: Making a Reusable Database Connector

Connecting to a database is a routine chore that needs to be performed in every page from now on. This PHP solution creates a simple function stored in an external file that connects to the database. It's designed mainly for testing the different MySQLi and PDO scripts in the remaining chapters without the need to retype the connection details each time or to switch between different connection files.

1. Create a file called connection.php in the includes folder and insert the following code (there's a copy of the completed script in the ch13 folder):

```php
<?php
function dbConnect($usertype, $connectionType = 'mysqli') {
    $host = 'localhost';
    $db = 'phpsols';
    if ($usertype == 'read') {
        $user = 'psread';
        $pwd = 'K1yoMizu^dera';
    } elseif ($usertype == 'write') {
        $user = 'pswrite';
        $pwd = 'OCh@Nom1$u';
    } else {
        exit('Unrecognized user');
    }
    // Connection code goes here
}
```

The function takes two arguments: the user type and the connection type. The second argument defaults to mysqli. If you want to concentrate on using PDO, set the default value of the second argument to pdo.

The first two lines inside the function store the names of the host server and the database that you want to connect to.

The conditional statement checks the value of the first argument and switches between the psread and pswrite username and password as appropriate. If the user account is unrecognized, the exit() function halts the script and displays Unrecognized user.

2. Replace the Connection code goes here comment with the following:

```php
if ($connectionType == 'mysqli') {
    $conn = @ new mysqli($host, $user, $pwd, $db);
    if ($conn->connect_error) {
        exit($conn->connect_error);
    }
```

```
        return $conn;
    } else {
        try {
            return new PDO("mysql:host=$host;dbname=$db", $user, $pwd);
        } catch (PDOException $e) {
            echo $e->getMessage();
        }
    }
```

If the second argument is set to mysqli, a MySQLi connection object called $conn is created. The error control operator (@) prevents the constructor method from displaying error messages. If the connection fails, the reason is stored in the object's connect_error property. If it's empty, it's treated as false, so the next line is skipped, and the $conn object is returned. But if there's a problem, exit() displays the value of connect_error and brings the script to a halt.

Otherwise, the function returns a PDO connection object. There's no need to use the error control operator with the PDO constructor because it throws a PDOException if there's a problem. The catch block uses the exception's getMessage() method to display the cause of the problem.

■ **Tip**   If your database server uses a nonstandard port, don't forget to add the port number as the fifth argument to the mysqli() constructor and to include it in the PDO DSN, as described in the preceding sections. This isn't necessary if the database uses a socket connection, which is common on macOS and Linux.

---

3. Create a file called connection_test.php in the phpsols site root folder and insert the following code:

    ```php
    <?php
    require_once './includes/connection.php';
    if ($conn = dbConnect('read')) {
        echo 'Connection successful';
    }
    ```

    This includes the connection script and tests it with the psread user account and MySQLi.

4. Save the page and load it in a browser. If you see Connection successful, all is well. If you get an error message, consult the troubleshooting hints in the next section.

5. Test the connection with the pswrite user and MySQLi:

    ```php
    if ($conn = dbConnect('write')) {
        echo 'Connection successful';
    }
    ```

6. Test both user accounts with PDO by adding 'pdo' as the second argument to dbConnect().

7. Assuming all went well, you're ready to start interacting with the phpsols database. If you ran into problems, check out the next section.

Troubleshooting Database Connection Problems

The most common cause of failure when connecting to a database is getting the username or password wrong. Passwords and usernames are case-sensitive. Check the spelling carefully. For example, the following screenshot shows what happens if you change psread to Psread:

Access denied for user 'Psread'@'localhost' (using password: YES)

Access has been denied because there's no such user. The initial cap in the username makes all the difference. But even if the username is right, you may get the same error message, like this:

Access denied for user 'psread'@'localhost' (using password: YES)

This totally confuses many people. The error message confirms that you're using a password. So why is access denied? It's the wrong password. That's why.

If the error message says using password: NO, it means you've forgotten to supply the password. The phrase using password is a clue that the problem is related to login credentials.

When the phrase is missing, it indicates a different problem, as shown in the next screenshot:

Access denied for user 'psread'@'localhost' to database 'phpsoles'

The problem here is that the name of the database is incorrect. If you misspell the host, you'll get a message that no such host is known.

The screenshots in this section were generated by MySQLi. PDO generates the same messages, but includes error numbers and codes as well.

Sanitizing Text Results from a Database

When displaying results of an SQL query, you can be confident that values stored in certain types of columns will be in a specific format. For example, numeric column types can store only numbers. Similarly, date- and time-related columns store values only in the ISO date-time format. However, text-related columns can store any type of string, including HTML, JavaScript, and other executable code. When outputting values from a text-related column, you should always sanitize them to prevent arbitrary code from being executed.

The simple way to sanitize text output is to pass it to htmlspecialchars(). This function is related to htmlentities(), but it converts a more restricted range of characters to their equivalent HTML character entities. Specifically, it converts ampersands, quotes, and angle brackets; but it leaves periods (dots) untouched. This has the effect of neutralizing attempts to execute code when displayed in a browser because the angle brackets of <script> and PHP tags are converted. It's important not to convert dots because they're used in the names of files that we want to display.

The drawback with htmlspecialchars() is that by default it double encodes existing character entities. As a result, & is converted to &. You can turn off this default behavior by passing the named argument double_encode to htmlspecialchars() and setting its value to false.

Typing out the named argument every time you want to invoke htmlspecialchars() is tedious. So I have defined the following custom function in a file called utility_funcs.php in the ch13 folder:

```
function safe($text) {
    return htmlspecialchars($text, double_encode: false);
}
```

This simply passes $text to htmlspecialchars(), setting the optional argument, and returns the result. Copy utility_funcs.php to the includes folder, and include it in scripts that output text from the database.

As an alternative to htmlspecialchars(), you can pass text values to strip_tags(), which allows you to specify permitted HTML tags (see "Accessing Remote Files" in Chapter 7).

Querying the Database and Displaying the Results

Before you attempt to display the results of a database query, it's a good idea to find out how many results there are. If there aren't any results, you'll have nothing to display. It's also necessary for creating a navigation system for paging through a long set of results (you'll learn how to do that in the next chapter). In user authentication (covered in Chapter 19), no results when searching for a username and password mean that the login should fail.

MySQLi and PDO use different approaches to counting and displaying results. The next two PHP solutions show how to do it with MySQLi. For PDO, skip ahead to PHP Solution 13-4.

PHP Solution 13-2: Counting Records in a Result Set (MySQLi)

This PHP solution shows how to submit an SQL query that selects all the records in the images table and stores the result in a MySQLi_Result object. The object's num_rows property contains the number of records retrieved by the query.

1. Create a new folder called mysqli in the php8sols site root, and then create a new file called mysqli.php inside the folder. The page will eventually be used to display a table, so it should have a DOCTYPE declaration and an HTML skeleton.

2. Include the connection file in a PHP block above the DOCTYPE declaration, and connect to the phpsols database using the account with read-only privileges like this:

```
require_once '../includes/connection.php';
$conn = dbConnect('read');
```

3. Next, prepare the SQL query. Add this code immediately after the previous step (but before the closing PHP tag):

```
$sql = 'SELECT * FROM images';
```

    This means "select everything from the images table." The asterisk (*) is shorthand for "all columns."

4. Now execute the query by calling the query() method on the connection object and passing the SQL query as an argument, like this:

```
$result = $conn->query($sql);
```

    The result is stored in a variable, which I have imaginatively named $result.

5. If there's a problem, $result will be false. To find out what the problem is, we need to get the error message, which is stored as the error property of the mysqli connection object. Add the following conditional statement after the previous line:

```
if (!$result) {
    $error = $conn->error;
}
```

6. Assuming there's no problem, $result now holds a MySQLi_Result object, which has a property called num_rows. To get the number of records found by the query, add an else block to the conditional statement and assign the value to a variable, like this:

```
if (!$result) {
    $error = $conn->error;
} else {
    $numRows = $result->num_rows;
}
```

7. You can now display the result in the body of the page like this:

```
<?php
if (isset($error)) {
    echo "<p>$error</p>";
} else {
    echo "<p>A total of $numRows records were found.</p>";
}
?>
```

If there's a problem, $error will have been set, so it's displayed. Otherwise, the else block shows the number of records found. Both strings embed variables, so they're enclosed in double quotes.

8. Save mysqli.php and load it into a browser. You should see the following result:

A total of 8 records were found.

Check your code, if necessary, with mysqli_01.php in the ch13 folder.

PHP Solution 13-3: Displaying the Images Table Using MySQLi

The most common way to display the results of a SELECT query is to use a loop to extract one row from the result set at a time. MySQLi_Result has a method called fetch_assoc() that retrieves the current row as an associative array ready for display on the web page. Each element in the array is named after the corresponding column in the table.

This PHP solution shows how to loop through a MySQLi_Result object to display the results of a SELECT query. Continue using the file from PHP Solution 13-2.

1. Copy utility_funcs.php from the ch13 folder to the includes folder, and include it at the top of the script:

    ```
    require_once '../includes/connection.php';
    require_once '../includes/utility_funcs.php';
    ```

2. Remove the closing curly brace at the end of the else block in the body of the page (it should be around line 24). Although most of the code to display the images table is HTML, it needs to be inside the else block.

3. Insert a blank line after the closing PHP tag and add the closing brace on the next line in a separate PHP block. The revised code should look like this:

    ```
            } else {
    echo "<p>A total of $numRows records were found.</p>";
            ?>
    <?php } ?>
            </body>
    ```

4. Add the following table between the two PHP blocks in the main body of mysqli. php so that it's controlled by the else block. The reason for doing this is to prevent errors if the SQL query fails. The PHP code that displays the result set is highlighted in bold:

    ```
    <table>
        <tr>
            <th>image_id</th>
            <th>filename</th>
    ```

365

```
            <th>caption</th>
        </tr>
    <?php while ($row = $result->fetch_assoc()) { ?>
        <tr>
            <td><?= $row['image_id'] ?></td>
            <td><?= safe($row['filename']) ?></td>
            <td><?= safe($row['caption']) ?></td>
        </tr>
    <?php } ?>
    </table>
```

■ **Tip** The while loop iterates through the database result, using the fetch_assoc() method to extract each record into $row. Each element of $row is displayed in a table cell. The loop continues until fetch_assoc() comes to the end of the result set.

It's not necessary to sanitize the value of image_id because it's in a column that stores only integers.

5. Save mysqli.php and view it in a browser. You should see the contents of the images table displayed as shown in the following screenshot:

A total of 8 records were found.

image_id	filename	caption
1	basin.jpg	Water basin at Ryoanji temple, Kyoto
2	fountains.jpg	Fountains in central Tokyo
3	kinkakuji.jpg	The Golden Pavilion in Kyoto
4	maiko.jpg	Maiko—trainee geishas in Kyoto
5	maiko_phone.jpg	Every maiko should have one—a mobile, of course
6	menu.jpg	Menu outside restaurant in Pontocho, Kyoto
7	monk.jpg	Monk begging for alms in Kyoto
8	ryoanji.jpg	Autumn leaves at Ryoanji temple, Kyoto

You can compare your code, if necessary, with mysql_02.php in the ch13 folder.

MySQLi Connection Crib Sheet

Table 13-1 summarizes the basic details of connection and database queries for MySQLi.

Table 13-1. *Connection to MySQL/MariaDB with the MySQL Improved object-oriented interface*

Action	Usage	Comments
Connect	`$conn = new mysqli($h,$u,$p,$d);`	All arguments are optional; first four always needed in practice: hostname, username, password, database name. Creates connection object.
Choose DB	`$conn->select_db('dbName');`	Used to select a different database.
Submit query	`$result = $conn->query($sql);`	Returns result object.
Count results	`$numRows = $result->num_rows;`	Returns number of rows in result object.
Extract record	`$row = $result->fetch_assoc();`	Extracts current row from result object as associative array.
Extract record	`$row = $result->fetch_row();`	Extracts current row from result object as indexed (numbered) array.

PHP Solution 13-4: Counting Records in a Result Set (PDO)

PDO doesn't have a direct equivalent to the MySQLi num_rows property. With most databases you need to execute an SQL query to count the number of items in the table and then fetch the result. However, the PDO rowCount() method fulfills a dual purpose with both MySQL and MariaDB. Normally, it reports only the number of rows affected by inserting, updating, or deleting records, but with MySQL and MariaDB, it also reports the number of records found by a SELECT query.

1. Create a new folder called pdo in the php8sols site. Then create a file called pdo.php in the folder you have just created. The page will eventually be used to display a table, so it should have a DOCTYPE declaration and an HTML skeleton.

2. Include the connection file in a PHP block above the DOCTYPE declaration, and then create a PDO connection to the phpsols database using the read-only account, like this:

```
require_once '../includes/connection.php';
$conn = dbConnect('read', 'pdo');
```

3. Next, prepare the SQL query:

```
$sql = 'SELECT * FROM images';
```

This means "select every record in the images table." The asterisk (*) is shorthand for "all columns."

4. Now execute the query and store the result in a variable, like this:

```
$result = $conn->query($sql);
```

5. To check if there's a problem with the query, you can get an array of error information from the database using the connection object's errorInfo() method. The third element of the array contains a brief description of the problem if something goes wrong. Add the following code:

```php
$error = $conn->errorInfo()[2];
```

We're interested only in the third element, so we can use the array dereferencing technique we encountered in PHP Solution 7-1 ("Getting the Contents of a Text File") by adding the array index in a pair of square brackets immediately after the call to $conn->errorInfo() and assigning the value to $error.

6. If the query is executed successfully, $error will be null, which PHP treats as false. So, if there's no error, we can get the number of rows in the result set by calling the rowCount() method on the $result object, like this:

```php
if (!$error) {
    $numRows = $result->rowCount();
}
```

7. You can now display the outcome of the query in the body of the page, as follows:

```php
<?php
if ($error) {
    echo "<p>$error</p>";
} else {
    echo "<p>A total of $numRows records were found.</p>";
}
?>
```

8. Save the page and load it into a browser. You should see the same result as shown in step 8 of PHP Solution 13-2. Check your code, if necessary, with pdo_01.php.

Counting Records with PDO in Other Databases

Using the PDO rowCount() to report the number of items found by a SELECT query works with both MySQL and MariaDB, but it cannot be guaranteed to work on all other databases. If rowCount() doesn't work, use the following code instead:

```php
// prepare the SQL query
$sql = 'SELECT COUNT(*) FROM images';
// submit the query and capture the result
$result = $conn->query($sql);
$error = $conn->errorInfo()[2];
if (!$error) {
    // find out how many records were retrieved
    $numRows = $result->fetchColumn();
    // free the database resource
    $result->closeCursor();
}
```

This uses the SQL COUNT() function with an asterisk to count all items in the table. There's only one result, so it can be retrieved with the fetchColumn() method, which gets the first column from a database result. After storing the result in $numRows, you must call the closeCursor() method to free the database resource for any further queries.

PHP Solution 13-5: Displaying the Images Table Using PDO

To display the results of a SELECT query with PDO, you can use the query() method in a foreach loop to extract the current row as an associative array. Each element in the array is named after the corresponding column in the table.

Continue working with the same file as in the previous PHP solution.

1. Copy utility_funcs.php from the ch13 folder to the includes folder, and include it at the top of the script:

    ```
    require_once '../includes/connection.php';
    require_once '../includes/utility_funcs.php';
    ```

2. Remove the closing curly brace at the end of the else block in the body of the page (it should be around line 26). Although most of the code to display the images table is HTML, it needs to be inside the else block.

3. Insert a blank line after the closing PHP tag, and then add the closing brace on the next line in a separate PHP block. The revised code should look like this:

    ```
            } else {
        echo "<p>A total of $numRows records were found.</p>";
    ?>
    <?php } ?>
                    </body>
    ```

4. Add the following table between the two PHP blocks in the main body of pdo.php so that it's controlled by the else block. This is to prevent errors if the SQL query fails. The PHP code that displays the result set is displayed in bold:

    ```
    <table>
        <tr>
            <th>image_id</th>
            <th>filename</th>
            <th>caption</th>
        </tr>
      <?php foreach ($conn->query($sql) as $row) { ?>
            <tr>
                <td><?= $row['image_id'] ?></td>
                <td><?= safe($row['filename']) ?></td>
                <td><?= safe($row['caption']) ?></td>
            </tr>
      <?php } ?>
    </table>
    ```

5. Save the page and view it in a browser. It should look like the screenshot in PHP Solution 13-3. You can compare your code against pdo_02.php in the ch13 folder.

PDO Connection Crib Sheet

Table 13-2 summarizes the basic details of connection and database queries with PDO. Some commands will be used in later chapters, but are included here for ease of reference.

Table 13-2. *Database connection with PDO*

Action	Usage	Comments
Connect	`$conn = new PDO($DSN,$u,$p);`	In practice, requires three arguments: data source name (DSN), username, password. Must be wrapped in try/catch block.
Submit SELECT query	`$result = $conn->query($sql);`	Returns results as a PDOStatement object.
Extract records	`foreach($conn->query($sql) as $row) {`	Submits SELECT query and gets current row as associative array in a single operation.
Count results	`$numRows = $result->rowCount()`	In MySQL/MariaDB, returns number of results from SELECT. Not supported in most other databases.
Get single result	`$item = $result->fetchColumn();`	Gets first record in first column of result. To get result from other columns, use column number (counting from 0) as argument.
Get next record	`$row = $result->fetch();`	Gets next row from result set as associative array.
Release DB resources	`$result->closeCursor();`	Frees up connection to allow new query.
Submit non-SELECT query	`$affected = $conn->exec($sql);`	Although query() can be used for non-SELECT queries, exec() returns the number of affected rows.

Using SQL to Interact with a Database

As you have just seen, PHP connects to the database, sends the query, and receives the results, but the query itself needs to be written in SQL. Although SQL is a common standard, there are many dialects of SQL. Each database vendor, including MySQL, has added extensions to the standard language. These improve efficiency and functionality, but are usually incompatible with other databases. The SQL in this book works with MySQL 5.1 or later and with MariaDB, but it won't necessarily transfer to Microsoft SQL Server, Oracle, or another database.

Writing SQL Queries

SQL syntax doesn't have many rules, and all of them are quite simple.

SQL Keywords Are Case-Insensitive

The query that retrieves all records from the images table looks like this:

```
SELECT * FROM images
```

The words in uppercase are SQL keywords. This is purely a convention. The following are all equally correct:

```
SELECT * FROM images
select * from images
SeLEcT * fRoM images
```

Although SQL keywords are case-insensitive, the same *doesn't* apply to database column names. The advantage of using uppercase for keywords is that it makes SQL queries easier to read. You're free to choose whichever style suits you best, but the ransom-note style of the last example is probably best avoided.

Whitespace Is Ignored

This allows you to spread SQL queries over several lines for increased readability. The one place where whitespace is *not* allowed is between a function name and the opening parenthesis. The following generates an error:

```
SELECT COUNT (*) FROM images /* BAD EXAMPLE */
```

The space needs to be closed up like this:

```
SELECT COUNT(*) FROM images /* CORRECT */
```

As you probably gathered from these examples, you can add comments to SQL queries by putting them between /* and */.

Strings Must Be Quoted

All strings must be quoted in an SQL query. It doesn't matter whether you use single or double quotes, as long as they are in matching pairs. However, it's normally better to use MySQLi or PDO prepared statements, as explained later in this chapter.

Handling Numbers

As a general rule, numbers should not be quoted, as anything in quotes is a string. However, MySQL accepts numbers enclosed in quotes and treats them as their numeric equivalent. Be careful to distinguish between a real number and any other data type made up of numbers. For instance, a date is made up of numbers but should be enclosed in quotes and stored in a date-related column type. Similarly, telephone numbers should be enclosed in quotes and stored in a text-related column type.

■ **Note** SQL queries normally end with a semicolon, which is an instruction to the database to execute the query. When using PHP, the semicolon must be omitted from the SQL. Consequently, stand-alone examples of SQL are presented throughout this book without a concluding semicolon.

Refining the Data Retrieved by a SELECT Query

The only SQL query you have run so far retrieves all records from the images table. Much of the time, you want to be more selective.

Selecting Specific Columns

Using an asterisk to select all columns is a convenient shortcut, but you should normally specify only those columns you need. List the column names separated by commas after the SELECT keyword. For example, this query selects only the filename and caption fields for each record:

```
SELECT filename, caption FROM images
```

You can test this in mysqli_03.php and pdo_03.php in the ch13 folder.

Changing the Order of Results

To control the sort order, add an ORDER BY clause with the name(s) of the column(s) in order of precedence. Separate multiple columns by commas. The following query sorts the captions from the images table in alphabetical order (the code is in mysqli_04.php and pdo_04.php):

```
$sql = 'SELECT * FROM images ORDER BY caption';
```

■ **Note** This semicolon is part of the PHP statement, not part of the SQL query.

The preceding query produces this output:

A total of 8 records were found.

image_id	filename	caption
8	ryoanji.jpg	Autumn leaves at Ryoanji temple, Kyoto
5	maiko_phone.jpg	Every maiko should have one—a mobile, of course
2	fountains.jpg	Fountains in central Tokyo
4	maiko.jpg	Maiko—trainee geishas in Kyoto
6	menu.jpg	Menu outside restaurant in Pontocho, Kyoto
7	monk.jpg	Monk begging for alms in Kyoto
3	kinkakuji.jpg	The Golden Pavilion in Kyoto
1	basin.jpg	Water basin at Ryoanji temple, Kyoto

To reverse the sort order, add the DESC (for "descending") keyword like this (there are examples in mysqli_05.php and pdo_05.php):

```
$sql = 'SELECT * FROM images ORDER BY caption DESC';
```

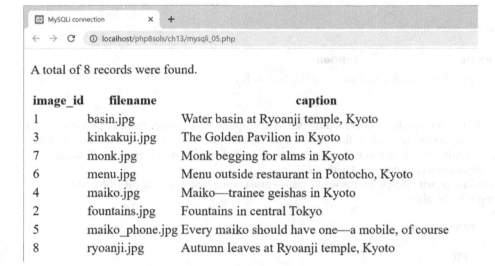

A total of 8 records were found.

image_id	filename	caption
1	basin.jpg	Water basin at Ryoanji temple, Kyoto
3	kinkakuji.jpg	The Golden Pavilion in Kyoto
7	monk.jpg	Monk begging for alms in Kyoto
6	menu.jpg	Menu outside restaurant in Pontocho, Kyoto
4	maiko.jpg	Maiko—trainee geishas in Kyoto
2	fountains.jpg	Fountains in central Tokyo
5	maiko_phone.jpg	Every maiko should have one—a mobile, of course
8	ryoanji.jpg	Autumn leaves at Ryoanji temple, Kyoto

There is also an ASC (for "ascending") keyword. It's the default sort order, so is normally omitted.

However, specifying ASC increases clarity when columns in the same table are sorted in a different order. For example, if you publish multiple articles every day, you could use the following query to display titles in alphabetical order, but ordered by the date of publication with the most recent ones first:

```
SELECT * FROM articles
ORDER BY published DESC, title ASC
```

Searching for Specific Values

To search for specific values, add a WHERE clause to the SELECT query. The WHERE clause follows the name of the table. For example, the query in mysqli_06.php and pdo_06.php looks like this:

```
$sql = 'SELECT * FROM images
WHERE image_id = 6';
```

■ **Note**   SQL uses one equal sign to test for equality, unlike PHP, which uses two.

It produces the following result:

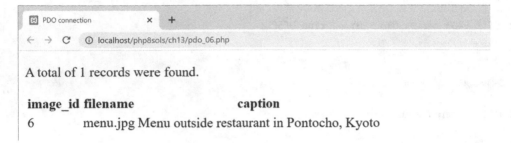

A total of 1 records were found.

image_id filename	caption
6 menu.jpg Menu outside restaurant in Pontocho, Kyoto	

In addition to testing for equality, a WHERE clause can use comparison operators, such as greater than (>) and less than (<). Rather than go through all the options now, I'll introduce others as needed. Chapter 15 has a comprehensive roundup of the four main SQL commands, SELECT, INSERT, UPDATE, and DELETE, including a list of the main comparison operators used with WHERE.

If used in combination with ORDER BY, the WHERE clause must come first. For example (the code is in mysqli_07.php and pdo_07.php):

```
$sql = 'SELECT * FROM images
WHERE image_id > 5
ORDER BY caption DESC';
```

This selects the three images that have an image_id greater than 5 and sorts them by their captions in reverse order.

Searching for Text with Wildcard Characters

In SQL, the percentage sign (%) is a wildcard character that matches anything or nothing. It's used in a WHERE clause in conjunction with the LIKE keyword.

The query in mysqli_08.php and pdo_08.php looks like this:

```
$sql = 'SELECT * FROM images
WHERE caption LIKE "%Kyoto%"';
```

It searches for all records in the images table where the caption column contains "Kyoto" and produces the following result:

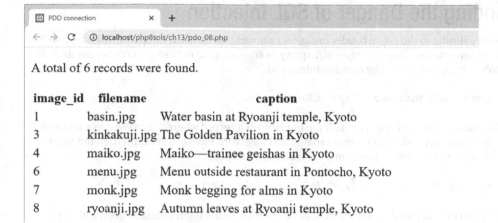

A total of 6 records were found.

image_id	filename	caption
1	basin.jpg	Water basin at Ryoanji temple, Kyoto
3	kinkakuji.jpg	The Golden Pavilion in Kyoto
4	maiko.jpg	Maiko—trainee geishas in Kyoto
6	menu.jpg	Menu outside restaurant in Pontocho, Kyoto
7	monk.jpg	Monk begging for alms in Kyoto
8	ryoanji.jpg	Autumn leaves at Ryoanji temple, Kyoto

As the preceding screenshot shows, it finds six records out of the eight in the images table. All the captions end with "Kyoto," so the wildcard character at the end is matching nothing, whereas the wildcard at the beginning matches the rest of each caption.

If you omit the leading wildcard ("Kyoto%"), the query searches for captions that begin with "Kyoto." None of them do, so you get no results from the search.

The query in mysqli_09.php and pdo_09.php looks like this:

```
$sql = 'SELECT * FROM images
WHERE caption LIKE "%maiko%"';
```

It produces the following result:

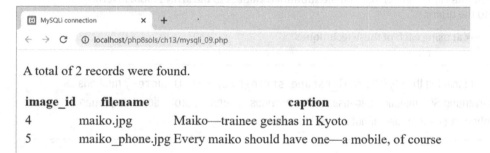

A total of 2 records were found.

image_id	filename	caption
4	maiko.jpg	Maiko—trainee geishas in Kyoto
5	maiko_phone.jpg	Every maiko should have one—a mobile, of course

The query spells "maiko" all in lowercase, but the query also finds it with an initial capital. Searches with LIKE are case-insensitive.

To perform a case-sensitive search, you need to add the BINARY keyword like this (the code is in mysqli_10.php and pdo_10.php):

```
$sql = 'SELECT * FROM images
WHERE caption LIKE BINARY "%maiko%"';
```

All the examples you have seen so far have been hard-coded, but most of the time, the values used in SQL queries need to come from user input. Unless you're careful, this puts you at risk of a malicious exploit known as SQL injection. The rest of this chapter explains this danger and how to avoid it.

Understanding the Danger of SQL Injection

SQL injection is very similar to the email header injection I warned you about in Chapter 6. An injection attack tries to insert spurious conditions into an SQL query in an attempt to expose or corrupt your data. The meaning of the following query should be easy to understand:

```
SELECT * FROM users WHERE username = 'xyz' AND pwd = 'abc'
```

It's the basic pattern for a login application. If the query finds a record where username is xyz and pwd is abc, you know that a correct combination of username and password has been submitted, so the login succeeds. All an attacker needs to do is inject an extra condition like this:

```
SELECT * FROM users WHERE username = 'xyz' AND pwd = 'abc' OR 1 = 1
```

The OR means that only one of the conditions needs to be true, so the login succeeds even without a correct username and password. SQL injection relies on quotes and other control characters not being properly escaped when part of the query is derived from a variable or user input.

There are several strategies you can adopt to prevent SQL injection, depending on the situation:

- If the variable is an integer (e.g., the primary key of a record), use is_numeric() and the (int) casting operator to ensure it's safe to insert in the query.

- Use a **prepared statement**. In a prepared statement, placeholders in the SQL query represent values that come from user input. The PHP code automatically wraps strings in quotes and escapes embedded quotes and other control characters. The syntax is different for MySQLi and PDO.

- None of the preceding strategies is suitable for column names, which must not be enclosed in quotes. To use a variable for column names, create an array of acceptable values and check that the submitted value is in the array before inserting it into the query.

Let's take a look at using each of these techniques.

■ **Note**   I have not included the MySQLi real_escape_string() or the PDO quote() methods as techniques for preventing SQL injection because neither provides bulletproof protection. Use prepared statements to embed values from user input into SQL queries.

PHP Solution 13-6: Inserting an Integer from User Input into a Query

This PHP solution shows how to sanitize a variable from user input to make sure it contains only an integer before inserting the value into an SQL query. The technique is the same for both MySQLi and PDO.

1. Copy either mysqli_integer_01.php or pdo_integer_01.php from the ch13 folder to the mysqli or pdo folder, and remove the _01 from the filename. Each file contains an SQL query that selects the image_id and filename columns from the images table. In the body of the page, there's a form with a drop-down menu that is populated by a loop that runs through the results of the SQL query. The MySQLi version looks like this:

```
<form action="mysqli_integer.php" method="get">
    <select name="image_id">
    <?php while ($row = $images->fetch_assoc()) { ?>
        <option value="<?= $row['image_id'] ?>"
        <?php if (isset($_GET['image_id']) &&
            $_GET['image_id'] == $row['image_id']) {
            echo 'selected';
        } ?>
        ><?= safe($row['filename']) ?></option>
    <?php } ?>
    </select>
    <input type="submit" name="go" value="Display">
</form>
```

The form uses the get method and assigns the image_id to the value attribute of the <option> tags. If $_GET['image_id'] has the same value as $row['image_id'], the current image_id is the same as that passed through the page's query string, so the selected attribute is added to the opening <option> tag. The value of $row['filename'] is inserted between the opening and closing <option> tags.

The PDO version is identical apart from the fact that it runs the query directly in a foreach loop using the PDO fetch() method.

If you load the page into a browser, you'll see a drop-down menu that lists the files in the images folder like this:

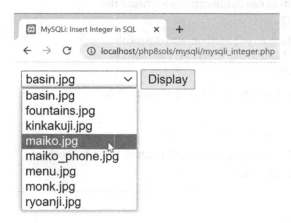

2. Insert the following code immediately after the closing </form> tag. The code is the same for both MySQLi and PDO, apart from one line (this is the MySQLi version):

```
<?php
if (isset($_GET['image_id'])) {
    $image_id = (int) $_GET['image_id'];
    $error = ($image_id === 0) ? true : false;
    if (!$error) {
        $sql = "SELECT filename, caption FROM images
```

```
                 WHERE image_id = $image_id";
                 $result = $conn->query($sql);
                 $row = $result->fetch_assoc();
                 ?>
                 <figure><img src="../images/<?= safe($row['filename']) ?>">
                     <figcaption><?= safe($row['caption']) ?></figcaption>
                 </figure>
             <?php }
             if ($error) {
                 echo '<p>Image not found</p>';
           }
     } ?>
```

The conditional statement checks whether image_id has been sent through the
$_GET array. If it has, it's assigned to $image_id using the (int) casting operator.
Using the casting operator serves two purposes: it prevents attempts to probe
your script for error messages by submitting a floating-point number, and it
converts non-numeric values to 0.

The next line uses the ternary operator to set $error to true or false depending
on whether $image_id is 0.

If $error is false, the script queries the database and displays the selected
image and caption. Since you know $image_id is an integer, it's safe to insert
directly in the SQL query. Because it's a number, it doesn't need to be wrapped in
quotes, but the string assigned to $sql needs to use double quotes to ensure the
value of $image_id is inserted into the query.

The new query is submitted to MySQL by the query() method, and the result
is stored in $row. Finally, $row['filename'] and $row['caption'] are used to
display the image and its caption in the page.

However, if $error is true, the final conditional statement displays "Image not
found."

■ **Tip** I opted for a separate conditional statement to display "Image not found" because I plan to check for
another error later and I want to use the same error message for both.

---

3. If you are using the PDO version, locate this line:

    ```
    $row = $result->fetch_assoc();
    ```

    Change it to this:

    ```
    $row = $result->fetch();
    ```

4.   Save the page and load it into a browser. When the page first loads, only the drop-down menu is displayed.

5.   Select a filename from the drop-down menu and click Display. The image of your choice should be displayed, as shown in the following screenshot:

Maiko—trainee geishas in Kyoto

If you encounter problems, check your code against mysqli_integer_02.php or pdo_integer_02.php in the ch13 folder.

6.   Edit the query string in the browser, changing the value of image_id to a string. You should see "Image not found." However, if the string begins with a number between 1 and 8, you'll see the image and caption related to that number.

7.   Try a floating-point number between 1.0 and 8.9. The relevant image is displayed normally.

8.   Try a number outside the range of 1–8. In older versions of PHP, no error messages are displayed because there's nothing wrong with the query. It's simply looking for a value that doesn't exist. However, in PHP 8, you'll get a warning message like this if you have set error_reporting in php.ini to the level recommended in Chapter 2:

Warning: Trying to access
array offset on value of type
null in
C:\xampp\htdocs\php8sols\mysqli\mysqli_integer.php
on line 52

9. To avoid this, you should check the number of rows returned by the query, using the num_rows property with MySQLi or the rowCount() method with PDO.

    Change the code like this for MySQLi:

    ```php
    $result = $conn->query($sql);
    if ($result->num_rows) {
        $row = $result->fetch_assoc();
    ?>
        <figure><img src="../images/<?= safe($row['filename']) ?>">
            <figcaption><?= safe($row['caption']) ?></figcaption>
        </figure>
    <?php } else { ?>
        $error = true;
        }
    }
    if ($error) {
        echo '<p>Image not found</p>';
    }
    } ?>
    ```

    For PDO, use $result->rowCount() in place of $result->num_rows.

    If no rows are returned by the query, 0 is treated by PHP as implicitly false, so the condition fails, and the else clause is executed instead, setting $error to true.

    The conditional statement that displays "Image not found" could be moved into an else block, but this script has several nested conditions. Keeping it separate makes it easier to read the script and follow the conditional logic.

10. Test the page again. When you select an image from the drop-down menu, it displays normally as before. But if you try entering an out-of-range value in the query string, you see the error message instead.

The amended code is in mysqli_integer_03.php and pdo_integer_03.php in the ch13 folder.

Using Prepared Statements for User Input

Both MySQLi and PDO support prepared statements, which offer important security features. A prepared statement is a template for an SQL query that contains a placeholder for each value that is changeable. This not only makes it easier to embed variables in your PHP code but also prevents SQL injection attacks as quotes and other characters are automatically escaped before the query is executed.

Other advantages of using prepared statements are that they're more efficient when the same query is used more than once. Also, you can bind the results from each column of a SELECT query to named variables, making it easier to display the output.

Both MySQLi and PDO use question marks as anonymous placeholders, like this:

```
$sql = 'SELECT image_id, filename, caption FROM images WHERE caption LIKE ?';
```

PDO also supports the use of named placeholders. A named placeholder begins with a colon followed by an identifier, like this:

```
$sql = 'SELECT image_id, filename, caption FROM images WHERE caption LIKE :search';
```

■ **Note**   Placeholders are not wrapped in quotes, even when the value they represent is a string. This makes it a lot easier to build an SQL query because there's no need to worry about getting the correct combination of single and double quotes.

Placeholders can be used only for column values. They can't be used for other parts of an SQL query, such as column names or operators. This is because values that contain non-numeric characters are automatically escaped and wrapped in quotes when the SQL is executed. Column names and operators cannot be in quotes.

Prepared statements involve slightly more code than just submitting the query directly, but placeholders make the SQL easier to read and write, and the process is more secure.

The syntax for MySQLi and PDO is different, so the following sections deal with them separately.

Embedding Variables in MySQLi Prepared Statements

Using a MySQLi prepared statement involves several stages.

Initialize the Statement

To initialize the prepared statement, call the stmt_init() method on the database connection and store it in a variable, as follows:

```
$stmt = $conn->stmt_init();
```

Prepare the Statement

You then pass the SQL query to the statement's prepare() method. This checks that you haven't used question mark placeholders in the wrong place and that when everything is put together, the query is valid SQL.

If there are any mistakes, the `prepare()` method returns `false`, so it's common to enclose the next steps in a conditional statement to ensure they run only if everything is still okay.

Error messages can be accessed through the statement's `error` property.

Bind Values to the Placeholders

Replacing the question marks with the actual values held in the variables is technically known as **binding the parameters**. It's this step that protects your database from SQL injection.

Pass the variables to the statement's `bind_param()` method in the same order as you want them inserted into the SQL query, together with a first argument specifying the data type of each variable, again in the same order as the variables. The data type must be specified by one of the following four characters:

- b: Binary (such as an image, Word document, or PDF file)

- d: Double (floating-point number)

- i: Integer (whole number)

- s: String (text)

The number of variables passed to `bind_param()` must be exactly the same as the number of question mark placeholders. For example, to pass a single value as a string, use this:

```
$stmt->bind_param('s', $_GET['words']);
```

To pass two values, the `SELECT` query needs two question marks as placeholders, and both variables need to be bound with `bind_param()`, like this:

```
$sql = 'SELECT * FROM products WHERE price < ? AND type = ?';
$stmt = $conn->stmt_init();
$stmt->prepare($sql);
$stmt->bind_param('ds', $_GET['price'], $_GET['type']);
```

The first argument to `bind_param()`, `'ds'`, specifies `$_GET['price']` as a floating-point number and `$_GET['type']` as a string.

Execute the Statement

Once the statement has been prepared and the values have been bound to the placeholders, call the statement's `execute()` method. The result of a `SELECT` query can then be fetched from the statement object. With other types of queries, this is the end of the process.

Binding the Results (Optional)

Optionally, you can bind the results of a `SELECT` query to variables with the `bind_result()` method. This avoids the need to extract each row and then access the results as `$row['column_name']`.

To bind the results, you must name each column specifically in the `SELECT` query. List the variables you want to use in the same order and pass them as arguments to `bind_result()`. For example, let's say your SQL looks like this:

```
$sql = 'SELECT image_id, filename, caption FROM images WHERE caption LIKE ?';
```

To bind the results of the query, use this code:

```
$stmt->bind_result($image_id, $filename, $caption);
```

This allows you to access the results directly as $image_id, $filename, and $caption.

Store the Result (Optional)

When you use a prepared statement for a SELECT query, the results are unbuffered. This means that they remain on the database server until you fetch them. This has the advantage of requiring less memory, particularly if the result set contains a large number of rows. However, unbuffered results impose the following restrictions:

- Once the results are fetched, they're no longer stored in memory. Consequently, you can't use the same result set more than once.

- You can't run another query on the same database connection until all of the results have been fetched or cleared.

- You can't use the num_rows property to find out how many rows are in the result set.

- You can't use data_seek() to move to a specific row in the result set.

To avoid these restrictions, you can optionally store the result set using the statement's store_result() method. However, if you simply want to display the result immediately without reusing later, there's no need to store it first.

■ **Note**   To clear an unbuffered result, call the statement's free_result() method.

Fetch the Result

To loop through the results of a SELECT query that has been executed with a prepared statement, use the fetch() method. If you have bound the results to variables, do it like this:

```
while ($stmt->fetch()) {
 // display the bound variables for each row
}
```

If you haven't bound the results to variables, use $row = $stmt->fetch() and access each variable as $row['column_name'].

Close the Statement

When you have finished with a prepared statement, the close() method frees the memory used.

PHP Solution 13-7: Using a MySQLi Prepared Statement in a Search

This PHP solution shows how to use a MySQLi prepared statement with a SELECT query; it also demonstrates binding the result to named variables.

1. Copy mysqli_prepared_01.php from the ch13 folder and save it in the mysqli folder as mysqli_prepared.php. The file contains a search form and a table for displaying the results.

2. In a PHP code block above the DOCTYPE declaration, create a conditional statement to include connection.php and utility_funcs.php, and create a read-only connection when the search form is submitted. The code looks like this:

```php
if (isset($_GET['go'])) {
    require_once '../includes/connection.php';
    require_once '../includes/utility_funcs.php';
    $conn = dbConnect('read');
}
```

3. Next, add the SQL query inside the conditional statement. The query needs to name the three columns you want to retrieve from the images table. Use a question mark as the placeholder for the search term, like this:

```php
$sql = 'SELECT image_id, filename, caption FROM images
            WHERE caption LIKE ?';
```

4. Before passing the user-submitted search term to the bind_param() method, you need to add the wildcard characters to it and assign it to a new variable, like this:

```php
$searchterm = '%'. $_GET['search'] .'%';
```

5. You can now create the prepared statement. The finished code in the PHP block above the DOCTYPE declaration looks like this:

```php
if (isset($_GET['go'])) {
    require_once '../includes/connection.inc.php';
    $conn = dbConnect('read');
    $sql = 'SELECT image_id, filename, caption FROM images
                WHERE caption LIKE ?';
    $searchterm = '%'. $_GET['search'] .'%';
    $stmt = $conn->stmt_init();
    if ($stmt->prepare($sql)) {
        $stmt->bind_param('s', $searchterm);
        $stmt->execute();
        $stmt->bind_result($image_id, $filename, $caption);
        $stmt->store_result();
        $numRows = $stmt->num_rows;
    } else {
        $error = $stmt->error;
    }
}
```

This initializes the prepared statement and assigns it to $stmt. The SQL query is then passed to the prepare() method, which checks the validity of the query's syntax. If there's a problem with the syntax, the else block assigns the error message to $error. If there are no mistakes in the syntax, the rest of the script inside the conditional statement is executed.

The first line inside the conditional statement binds $searchterm to the SELECT query, replacing the question mark placeholder. The first argument tells the prepared statement to treat it as a string.

After the prepared statement is executed, the next line binds the results of the SELECT query to $image_id, $filename, and $caption. These need to be in the same order as in the query. I have named the variables after the columns they represent, but you can use any variables you want.

Then the result is stored. Note that you store the result simply by calling the statement object's store_result() method. Unlike using query(), you don't assign the return value of store_result() to a variable. If you do, it's simply true or false, depending on whether the result was stored successfully.

Finally, the number of rows retrieved by the query is obtained from the statement object's num_rows property and stored in $numRows.

6. Add a conditional statement after the opening <body> tag to display the error message if a problem has occurred:

```php
<?php
if (isset($error)) {
    echo "<p>$error</p>";
}
?>
```

7. Add the following code after the search form to display the result:

```php
<?php if (isset($numRows)) { ?>
    <p>Number of results for <b><?= safe($_GET['search']) ?></b>:
        <?= $numRows ?></p>
    <?php if ($numRows) { ?>
        <table>
            <tr>
                <th>image_id</th>
                <th>filename</th>
                <th>caption</th>
            </tr>
            <?php while ($stmt->fetch()) { ?>
                <tr>
                    <td><?= $image_id ?></td>
                    <td><?= safe($filename) ?></td>
                    <td><?= safe($caption) ?></td>
                </tr>
            <?php } ?>
        </table>
    <?php }
} ?>
```

The first conditional statement is wrapped around the paragraph and table, preventing them from being displayed if $numRows doesn't exist, which happens when the page is first loaded. If the form has been submitted, $numRows will have been set, so the search term is redisplayed, and the value of $numRows reports the number of matches.

If the query returns no results, $numRows is 0, which is treated as false, so the table is not displayed. If $numRows contains anything other than 0, the table is displayed. The while loop that displays the results calls the fetch() method on the prepared statement. There's no need to store the current record as $row, because the values from each column have been bound to $image_id, $filename, and $caption.

8. Save the page and load it into a browser. Enter some text in the search field and click Search. The number of results is displayed together with any captions that contain the search term, as shown in the following screenshot:

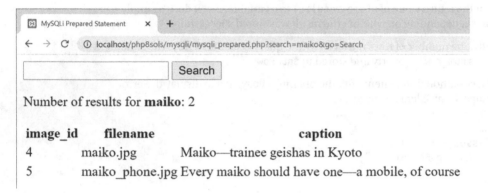

You can compare your code with mysqli_prepared_02.php in the ch13 folder.

Embedding Variables in PDO Prepared Statements

PDO prepared statements offer the choice of anonymous and named placeholders.

Using Anonymous Placeholders

Anonymous placeholders use question marks in exactly the same way as MySQLi:

```
$sql = 'SELECT image_id, filename, caption FROM images WHERE caption LIKE ?';
```

Using Named Placeholders

Named placeholders begin with a colon, like this:

```
$sql = 'SELECT image_id, filename, caption FROM images WHERE caption LIKE :search';
```

Using named placeholders makes the code a lot easier to understand, particularly if you choose names that are based on the variables that contain the values to be embedded in the SQL.

Preparing the Statement

Preparing and initializing a statement is done in a single step (unlike with MySQLi, which requires two). You pass the SQL with placeholders directly to the connection object's prepare() method, which returns the prepared statement, like this:

```
$stmt = $conn->prepare($sql);
```

Binding Values to the Placeholders

There are several different ways to bind values to placeholders. When using anonymous placeholders, the simplest way is to create an array of values in the same order as the placeholders and then to pass the array to the statement's execute() method. Even if there's only one placeholder, you must use an array. For example, to bind $searchterm to a single anonymous placeholder, you must enclose it in a pair of square brackets, like this:

```
$stmt->execute([$searchterm]);
```

You can also bind values to named placeholders in a similar way, but the argument passed to the execute() method must be an associative array, using the named placeholder as the key of each value. So the following binds $searchterm to the :search named placeholder:

```
$stmt->execute([':search' => $searchterm]);
```

Alternatively, you can use the statement's bindParam() and bindValue() methods to bind the values before calling the execute() method. When used with anonymous placeholders, the first argument to both methods is a number, counting from 1, representing the placeholder's position in the SQL. With named placeholders, the first argument is the named placeholder as a string. The second argument is the value you want to insert in the query.

However, there's a subtle difference between the two methods:

- With bindParam(), the second argument *must* be a variable. It cannot be a string, number, or any other type of expression.

- With bindValue(),the second argument should be a string, number, or expression. But it can also be a variable.

Because bindValue() accepts any type of value, bindParam() might seem redundant. The difference is that the value of the argument passed to bindValue() must already be known because it binds the actual value, whereas bindParam() binds only the variable. Consequently, the value can be assigned to the variable later.

To illustrate the difference, let's use the SELECT query in "Using Named Placeholders." The :search placeholder follows the LIKE keyword, so the value needs to be combined with wildcard characters. Trying to do the following generates an error:

```
// This will NOT work
$stmt->bindParam(':search', '%'. $_GET['search'] .'%');
```

You cannot concatenate the wildcard characters to the variable with bindParam(). The wildcard characters need to be added before the variable is passed as an argument, like this:

```
$searchterm = '%'. $_GET['search'] .'%';
$stmt->bindParam(':search', $searchterm);
```

Alternatively, you can build the expression as an argument to bindValue():

```
// This WILL work
$stmt->bindValue(':search', '%'. $_GET['search'] .'%');
```

The bindParam() and bindValue() methods accept an optional third argument: a constant specifying the data type. The main constants are as follows:

- PDO::PARAM_INT: Integer (whole number)
- PDO::PARAM_LOB: Binary (such as an image, Word document, or PDF file)
- PDO::PARAM_STR: String (text)
- PDO::PARAM_BOOL: Boolean (true or false)
- PDO::PARAM_NULL: Null

PDO::PARAM_NULL is useful if you want to set the value of a database column to null. For example, if a primary key is auto-incremented, you need to pass null as the value when inserting new records. This is how you set a named parameter called :id to null with bindValue():

```
$stmt->bindValue(':id', NULL, PDO::PARAM_NULL);
```

■ **Note** There isn't a PDO constant for floating-point numbers.

Executing the Statement

If you bind the values to placeholders using bindParam() or bindValue(), you simply call the execute() method without arguments:

```
$stmt->execute();
```

Otherwise, pass an array of values as described in the previous section. In both cases, the result of the query is stored in $stmt.

Error messages can be accessed in the same way as with a PDO connection. However, instead of calling the errorInfo() method on the connection object, use it on the PDO statement, like this:

```
$error = $stmt->errorInfo()[2];
```

If there's no error, $error will be null. Otherwise, it will contain a string describing the problem.

Binding the Results (Optional)

To bind the results of a SELECT query to variables, each column needs to be bound separately using the bindColumn() method, which takes two arguments. The first argument can be either the name of the column or its number counting from 1. The number comes from its position in the SELECT query, not the order in which it appears in the database table. So, to bind the result from the filename column to $filename in the SQL example we've been using, either of the following is acceptable:

```
$stmt->bindColumn('filename', $filename);
$stmt->bindColumn(2, $filename);
```

Because each column is bound separately, you don't need to bind all of them. However, it's more convenient to do so because it avoids the need to assign the result of the fetch() method to an array.

Fetching the Result

To fetch the results of a SELECT query, call the statement's fetch() method. If you have used bindColumn() to bind the output to variables, you can use the variables directly. Otherwise, it returns an array of the current row indexed both by column name and a zero-indexed column number.

■ **Note**   You can control the PDO fetch() method's type of output by passing it a constant as an argument. See www.php.net/manual/en/pdostatement.fetch.php.

PHP Solution 13-8: Using a PDO Prepared Statement in a Search

This PHP solution shows how to embed the user-submitted value from a search form into a SELECT query with a PDO prepared statement. It uses the same search form as that in the MySQLi version in PHP Solution 13-7.

1. Copy pdo_prepared_01.php from the ch13 folder and save it in the pdo folder as pdo_prepared.php.

2. Add the following code in a PHP block above the DOCTYPE declaration:

```
if (isset($_GET['go'])) {
    require_once '../includes/connection.php';
    require_once '../includes/utility_funcs.php';
    $conn = dbConnect('read', 'pdo');
    $sql = 'SELECT image_id, filename, caption FROM images
                WHERE caption LIKE :search';
    $stmt = $conn->prepare($sql);
    $stmt->bindValue(':search', '%' . $_GET['search'] . '%');
    $stmt->execute();
    $error = $stmt->errorInfo()[2];
    if (!$error) {
        $stmt->bindColumn('image_id', $image_id);
        $stmt->bindColumn('filename', $filename);
        $stmt->bindColumn(3, $caption);
        $numRows = $stmt->rowCount();
    }
}
```

When the form is submitted, this includes the connection file and creates a PDO read-only connection. The prepared statement uses :search as a named parameter in place of the user-submitted value.

The % wildcard characters are concatenated with the search term at the same time as binding it to the prepared statement. So `bindValue()` is used instead of `bindParam()`.

After the statement is executed, the statement's `errorInfo()` method is called to see if an error message has been generated and stored in `$errorInfo[2]`.

If there are no problems, the results are bound to `$image_id`, `$filename`, and `$caption` using the `bindColumn()` method. The first two use the column names, but the `caption` column is referred to by its position (counting from 1) in the `SELECT` query.

3. The code that displays the results is identical to that in steps 6 and 7 in PHP Solution 13-7. You can check the finished code in `pdo_prepared_02.php` in the `ch13` folder.

PHP Solution 13-9: Debugging a PDO Prepared Statement

Occasionally, a database query doesn't produce the result you expect. When that happens, it's useful to see exactly what your script sent to the database server. With MySQLi, there isn't a simple way to examine the values inserted into an SQL query by a prepared statement. But with PDO, it couldn't be easier. This functionality was introduced in PHP 7.2.

1. Continue using `pdo_prepared.php` from the previous PHP solution. Alternatively, copy `pdo_prepared_02.php` from the `ch13` folder to the `pdo` folder, and rename it `pdo_prepared.php`.

2. Amend the code after the closing `</table>` tag like this:

```
</table>
 <?php }
 echo '<pre>';
 $stmt->debugDumpParams();
 echo '</pre>';
 }
 ?>
```

This inserts a pair of `<pre>` tags to make the output of the call to the `debugDumpParams()` method of the `PDOStatement` object more readable.

3. Save the file, load it into a browser, and conduct a search. In addition to the results of the search, you should see output similar to the following screenshot:

```
PDO Prepared Statement        ×    +

←  →  C    ⓘ  localhost/php8sols/pdo/pdo_prepared.php?search=temp&go=Search
```

| | Search |

Number of results for temp: 2

image_id	filename	caption
1	basin.jpg	Water basin at Ryoanji temple, Kyoto
8	ryoanji.jpg	Autumn leaves at Ryoanji temple, Kyoto

```
SQL: [94] SELECT image_id, filename, caption FROM images
                WHERE caption LIKE :search
Sent SQL: [95] SELECT image_id, filename, caption FROM images
                WHERE caption LIKE '%temp%'
Params:  1
Key: Name: [7] :search
paramno=-1
name=[7] ":search"
is_param=1
param_type=2
```

The SQL query is displayed twice. The first time shows the query as it appears in the PHP code—in this case, including the named parameter :search. The second time, it displays the actual value that was sent to the database server.

In this case, the search for "temp" returned two captions that contain "temple." That's fine if that's what you expect. But let's say you wanted only an exact match. Seeing the % wildcard characters would explain the rogue result, making it easier to debug problems with prepared statements that don't produce the results you anticipate.

You can compare your code with pdo_prepared_03.php in the ch13 folder.

■ **Caution**   It's important to call the execute() method before invoking debugDumpParams().

PHP Solution 13-10: Changing Column Options Through User Input

This PHP solution shows how to change the name of SQL keywords in a SELECT query through user input. SQL keywords cannot be wrapped in quotes, so using prepared statements won't work. Instead, you need to ensure that the user input matches an array of expected values. If no match is found, use a default value instead. The technique is identical for MySQLi and PDO.

1. Copy either mysqli_order_01.php or pdo_order_01.php from the ch13 folder and save it in the mysqli or pdo folder. Both versions select all records from the images table and display the results in a table. The pages also contain a form that allows the user to select the name of a column by which to sort the results in either ascending or descending order. In its initial state, the form is inactive. The pages display the details sorted by image_id in ascending order, like this:

MySQLi: Order by User Input	×	+		
← → C	ⓘ localhost/php8sols/mysqli/mysqli_order.php			

Order by: [image_id ∨] [Ascending ∨] [Change]

image_id	filename	caption
1	basin.jpg	Water basin at Ryoanji temple, Kyoto
2	fountains.jpg	Fountains in central Tokyo
3	kinkakuji.jpg	The Golden Pavilion in Kyoto
4	maiko.jpg	Maiko—trainee geishas in Kyoto
5	maiko_phone.jpg	Every maiko should have one—a mobile, of course
6	menu.jpg	Menu outside restaurant in Pontocho, Kyoto
7	monk.jpg	Monk begging for alms in Kyoto
8	ryoanji.jpg	Autumn leaves at Ryoanji temple, Kyoto

2. Amend the code in the PHP block above the DOCTYPE declaration like this (the following listing shows the PDO version, but the changes highlighted in bold are the same for MySQLi):

```
require_once '../includes/connection.php';
require_once '../includes/utility_funcs.php';
// connect to database
$conn = dbConnect('read', 'pdo');
// set default values
$col = 'image_id';
$dir = 'ASC';
// create arrays of permitted values
$columns = ['image_id', 'filename', 'caption'];
$direction = ['ASC', 'DESC'];
// if the form has been submitted, use only expected values
if (isset($_GET['column']) && in_array($_GET['column'], $columns)) {
    $col = $_GET['column'];
}
if (isset($_GET['direction']) && in_array($_GET['direction'], $direction)) {
    $dir = $_GET['direction'];
}
// prepare the SQL query using sanitized variables
$sql = "SELECT * FROM images
            ORDER BY $col $dir";
```

```
// submit the query and capture the result
$result = $conn->query($sql);
$error = $conn->errorInfo()[2];
```

The new code defines two variables, $col and $dir, that are embedded directly in the SELECT query. Because they have been assigned default values, the query displays the results sorted by the image_id column in ascending order when the page first loads.

Two arrays, $columns and $direction, then define permitted values: the column names and the ASC and DESC keywords. These arrays are used by the conditional statements that check the $_GET array for column and direction. The submitted values are reassigned to $col and $dir only if they match a value in the $columns and $direction arrays, respectively. This prevents any attempt to inject illegal values into the SQL query.

3. Edit the <option> tags in the drop-down menus so they display the selected values for $col and $dir, like this:

```
<select name="column" id="column">
    <option <?php if ($col == 'image_id') echo 'selected'; ?>
        >image_id</option>
    <option <?php if ($col == 'filename') echo 'selected'; ?>
        >filename</option>
    <option <?php if ($col == 'caption') echo 'selected'; ?>
        >caption</option>
</select>
<select name="direction" id="direction">
    <option value="ASC" <?php if ($dir == 'ASC') echo 'selected'; ?>
        >Ascending</option>
    <option value="DESC" <?php if ($dir == 'DESC') echo 'selected'; ?>
        >Descending</option>
</select>
```

4. Save the page and test it in a browser. You can change the sort order of the display by selecting the values in the drop-down menus and clicking Change. However, if you try to inject an illegal value through the query string, the page uses the default values of $col and $dir to display the results sorted by image_id in ascending order.

You can check your code against mysqli_order_02.php and pdo_order_02.php in the ch13 folder.

Chapter Review

PHP 8 provides two methods of communicating with MySQL:

- **The MySQL Improved (MySQLi) extension:** This is recommended for all new MySQL projects. It's more efficient than the original MySQL extension that is no longer supported. It has the added safety of prepared statements and is fully compatible with MariaDB.

- **The PHP Data Objects (PDO) abstraction layer, which is database-neutral:** This
  is my preferred method of communicating with a database. Not only is it database-
  neutral; it has the advantage of using named parameters for prepared statements,
  making the code easier to read and understand. Moreover, debugging prepared
  statements is trivially easy. Although the code is database-neutral, PDO requires
  the correct driver to be installed for your chosen database. The driver for MySQL
  is fully compatible with MariaDB and is commonly installed. Other drivers are less
  common. However, if the correct driver is installed, only the data source name (DSN)
  in the connection string needs to be changed to switch from one database to another.

Although PHP communicates with the database and stores the results, queries need to be written
in SQL, the standard language used to query a relational database. This chapter showed how to retrieve
information stored in a database table using a SELECT statement, refining the search with a WHERE clause,
and changing the sort order with ORDER BY. You also learned several techniques to protect queries from SQL
injection, including prepared statements, which use placeholders instead of embedding variables directly in
a query.

In the next chapter, you'll put this knowledge to practical use by creating an online photo gallery.

CHAPTER 14

■ ■ ■

Creating a Dynamic Photo Gallery

The previous chapter concentrated mainly on extracting the contents of the images table as text. This chapter builds on those techniques to develop the mini photo gallery shown in Figure 14-1.

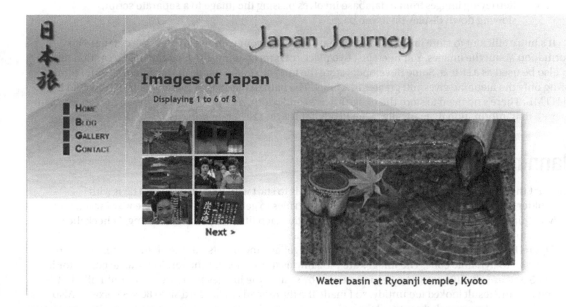

Figure 14-1. *This mini photo gallery is driven by pulling information from a database*

The gallery also demonstrates some cool features that you'll want to incorporate into text-driven pages. For instance, the grid of thumbnail images on the left displays two images per row. Just by changing two numbers, you can make the grid as many columns wide and as many rows deep as you like. Clicking one of the thumbnails replaces the main image and caption. It's the same page that reloads, but exactly the same technique is used to create online catalogs that take you to another page with more details about a product. The Next link at the foot of the thumbnail grid shows you the next set of photographs, using exactly the same technique as you use to page through a long set of search results. This gallery isn't just a pretty face or two... This chapter covers

- Understanding why storing images in a database is a bad idea and what you should do instead

- Planning the layout of a dynamic gallery

- Displaying a fixed number of results in a table row

© David Powers 2022

D. Powers, *PHP 8 Solutions*, https://doi.org/10.1007/978-1-4842-7141-4_14

- Limiting the number of records retrieved at a time

- Paging through a long set of results

Why Not Store Images in a Database?

The images table contains filenames and captions, but not the images themselves. Even though you can store binary objects, such as images, in a database, I don't intend to do so for the simple reason that it's usually more trouble than it's worth. The main problems are as follows:

- Images can't be indexed or searched without storing textual information separately.

- Images are usually large, bloating the size of tables. If there's a limit on the amount of storage in your database, you risk running out of space.

- Table fragmentation affects performance if images are deleted frequently.

- Retrieving images from a database involves passing the image to a separate script, slowing down display on a web page.

It's more efficient to store images in an ordinary folder on your web site and use the database for information about the images. You need just two pieces of information—the filename and a caption that can also be used as alt text. Some developers store the full path to the image in the database, but I think storing only the filename gives you greater flexibility. The path to the images folder will be embedded in the HTML. There's no need to store the image's height and width. As you saw in Chapters 5 and 10, you can generate that information dynamically using PHP's getimagesize() function.

Planning the Gallery

I find that the best way to design a database-driven site is to start with a static page and fill it with placeholder text and images. I then create my CSS style rules to get the page looking the way I want, and finally I replace each placeholder element with PHP code. Each time I replace something, I check the page in a browser to make sure everything is still holding together.

Figure 14-2 shows the static mockup I made of the gallery and points out the elements that need to be converted to dynamic code. The images are the same as those used for the random image generator in Chapter 5 and are all different sizes. I experimented by scaling the images to create the thumbnails, but decided that the result looked too untidy, so I made the thumbnails a standard size (80 × 54 pixels). Also, to make life easy, I gave each thumbnail the same name as the larger version and stored them in a separate subfolder of the images folder called thumbs.

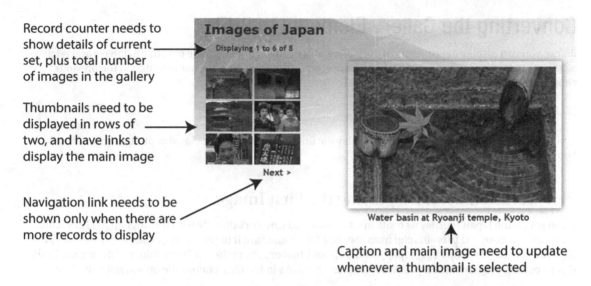

Record counter needs to show details of current set, plus total number of images in the gallery

Thumbnails need to be displayed in rows of two, and have links to display the main image

Navigation link needs to be shown only when there are more records to display

Images of Japan

Displaying 1 to 6 of 8

Next >

Water basin at Ryoanji temple, Kyoto

Caption and main image need to update whenever a thumbnail is selected

Figure 14-2. *Working out what needs to be done to convert a static gallery to a dynamic one*

In the previous chapter, displaying the contents of the images table was easy. You created a single table row, with the contents of each field in a separate table cell. By looping through the result set, each record was displayed on a row of its own, simulating the column structure of the database table. This time, the two-column structure of the thumbnail grid no longer matches the database structure. You need to count how many thumbnails have been inserted in a row before creating the next row.

Once I had worked out what needed to be done, I stripped out the code for thumbnails 2–6 and for the navigation link. The following listing shows what was left in the <main> element of gallery.php, with the elements that need to be converted to PHP code highlighted in bold (you can find the code in gallery_01. php in the ch14 folder):

```
<main>
    <h2>Images of Japan</h2>
    <p id="picCount">Displaying 1 to 6 of 8</p>
    <div id="gallery">
        <table id="thumbs">
            <tr>
                <!-- This row needs to be repeated -->
                <td><a href="gallery.php"><img src="images/thumbs/basin.jpg" alt=""
                    width="80" height="54"></a></td>
            </tr>
            <!-- Navigation link needs to go here -->
        </table>
        <figure id="main_image">
            <img src="images/basin.jpg" alt="" width="350" height="237">
            <figcaption>Water basin at Ryoanji temple, Kyoto</figcaption>
        </figure>
    </div>
</main>
```

Converting the Gallery Elements to PHP

Before you can display the contents of the gallery, you need to connect to the phpsols database and retrieve all the records stored in the images table. The procedure for doing so is the same as that in the previous chapter, using the following simple SQL query:

```
SELECT filename, caption FROM images
```

You can then use the first record to display the first image and its associated caption and thumbnail. You don't need image_id.

PHP Solution 14-1: Displaying the First Image

If you set up the Japan Journey web site in Chapter 5, you can work directly with the original gallery.php. Alternatively, copy gallery_01.php from the ch14 folder and save it in the php8sols site root as gallery. php. You also need to copy title.php, menu.php, and footer.php to the includes folder of the php8sols site. If your editing program asks if you want to update the links in the files, choose the option not to update.

1. Load gallery.php into a browser to make sure that it displays correctly. The main part of the page should look like Figure 14-3, with one thumbnail image and a larger version of the same image.

Water basin at Ryoanji temple, Kyoto

Figure 14-3. *The stripped-down version of the static gallery ready for conversion*

2. The gallery depends on a connection to the database, so include connection.php, create a read-only connection to the phpsols database, and define the SQL query. Add the following code just before the closing PHP tag above the DOCTYPE declaration in gallery.php (new code is highlighted in bold):

```
include './includes/title.php';
require_once './includes/connection.php';
require_once './includes/utility_funcs.php';
$conn = dbConnect('read');
$sql = 'SELECT filename, caption FROM images';
```

If you are using PDO, add 'pdo' as the second argument to dbConnect().

3. The code for submitting the query and extracting the first record from the results depends on which method of connection you are using. For MySQLi, use this:

```
// submit the query
$result = $conn->query($sql);
if (!$result) {
    $error = $conn->error;
} else {
    // extract the first record as an array
    $row = $result->fetch_assoc();
}
```

For PDO, use this:

```
// submit the query
$result = $conn->query($sql);
// get any error messages
$error = $conn->errorInfo()[2];
if (!$error) {
    // extract the first record as an array
    $row = $result->fetch();
}
```

To display the first image when the page loads, you need to retrieve the first result before creating a loop that will eventually display the grid of thumbnails. The code for both MySQLi and PDO submits the query, extracts the first record, and stores it in $row.

4. You now have the details of the first record image stored as $row['filename'] and $row['caption']. In addition to the filename and caption, you need the dimensions of the large version so that you can display it in the main body of the page. Add the following code inside the else block immediately after the code that fetches the first result:

```
// get the name and caption for the main image
$mainImage = safe($row['filename']);
$caption = safe($row['caption']);
// get the dimensions of the main image
$imageSize = getimagesize('images/'.$mainImage)[3];
```

The text values from the database are sanitized using the safe() function that was defined in the previous chapter.

As explained in Chapter 10, getimagesize() returns an array, the fourth element of which contains a string with the width and height of an image ready for insertion into an <img> tag. We're interested only in the fourth element, so we can use the array dereferencing technique introduced in Chapter 7. Adding [3] after the closing parenthesis of getimagesize() returns only the fourth element of the array, which is assigned to $imageSize.

5. You can now use this information to dynamically display the thumbnail, main image, and caption. The main image and thumbnail have the same name, but you eventually want to display all thumbnails by looping through the full result set. Consequently, the dynamic code that goes in the table cell needs to refer to the current record—in other words, to $row['filename'] and $row['caption'], rather than to $mainImage and $caption. They also need to be sanitized by passing them to the safe() function. You'll see later why I've assigned the values from the first record to separate variables. Amend the code in the table like this:

```
            <td><a href="gallery.php">
<img src="images/thumbs/<?= safe($row['filename']); ?>"
                alt="<?= safe($row['caption']); ?>" width="80"
                height="54"></a></td>
```

6. In case there's a problem with the query, you need to check if $error equates to true and prevent the gallery from being displayed. Add a PHP block containing the following conditional statement immediately after the <h2> Images of Japan heading:

```
<?php if (isset($error)) {
    echo "<p>$error</p>";
    } else {
?>
```

■ **Tip** Although the PDO version of the script in step 3 assigns a value to $error, you can use isset($error) here because the value is null if the query is executed successfully. Passing null to isset() returns false.

---

7. Insert a new line immediately before the closing </main> tag (around line 55) and add a PHP block with the else block's closing curly brace:

```
<?php } ?>
```

8. Save gallery.php and view it in a browser. It should look the same as Figure 14-3. The only difference is that the thumbnail and its alt text are dynamically generated. You can verify this by looking at the source code. The original static version had an empty alt attribute, but as the following screenshot shows, it now contains the caption from the first record:

```
28          <tr>
29              <!--This row needs to be repeated-->
30              <td><a href="gallery.php">
31                      <img src="images/thumbs/basin.jpg"
32                          alt="Water basin at Ryoanji temple, Kyoto"
33                          width="80" height="54"></a></td>
34          </tr>
```

If things go wrong, make sure there's no gap between the static and dynamically generated text in the image's src attribute. Also check that you're using the right code for the type of connection you have created with the database. You can check your code against gallery_mysqli_02.php or gallery_pdo_02.php in the ch14 folder.

9. Once you have confirmed that you're picking up the details from the database, you can convert the code for the main image. Amend it like this (new code is in bold):

```
<figure id="main_image">
    <img src="images/<?= $mainImage ?>" alt="<?= $caption ?>"
        <?= $imageSize ?>></p>
    <figcaption><?= $caption ?></figcaption>
</figure>
```

$mainImage and $caption don't need to be passed to the safe() function because they were already sanitized in step 4.

$imageSize inserts a string containing the correct width and height attributes for the main image.

10. Test the page again. It should look the same as in Figure 14-3, but the images and captions are being drawn dynamically from the database, and getimagesize() is calculating the correct dimensions for the main image. You can check your code against gallery_mysqli_03.php or gallery_pdo_03.php in the ch14 folder.

Building the Dynamic Elements

The first task after converting the static page is to display all the thumbnails and then build dynamic links that will enable you to display the large version of any thumbnail that has been clicked. Displaying all the thumbnails is easy—just loop through them (we'll work out how to display them in rows of two later). Activating the link for each thumbnail requires a little more thought. You need a way of telling the page which large image to display.

Passing Information Through a Query String

In the last section, you used $mainImage to identify the large image, so you need a way of changing its value whenever a thumbnail is clicked. The solution is to add the image's filename to a query string at the end of the URL in the link, like this:

```
<a href="gallery.php?image=filename">
```

You can then check whether the $_GET array contains an element called image. If it does, change the value of $mainImage. If it doesn't, leave $mainImage as the filename from the first record in the result set.

PHP Solution 14-2: Activating the Thumbnails

Continue working with the same file as in the previous section. Alternatively, copy gallery_mysqli_03.php or gallery_pdo_03.php to the php8sols site root, and save it as gallery.php

1. Locate the opening <a> tag of the link surrounding the thumbnail. It looks like this:

```
<a href="gallery.php">
```

Change it to this:

```
<a href="gallery.php?image=<?= safe($row['filename']) ?>">
```

This adds a query string to the end of the href attribute, assigning the current filename to a variable called image. It's important that there are no spaces surrounding ?image=.

2. Save the page and load it into a browser. Hover your mouse pointer over the thumbnail and check the URL displayed in the status bar. It should look like this:

```
http://localhost/php8sols/gallery.php?image=basin.jpg
```

If nothing is shown in the status bar, click the thumbnail. The page shouldn't change, but the URL in the address bar should now include the query string. Check that there are no gaps in the URL or query string.

3. To show all the thumbnails, you need to wrap the table cell in a loop. Insert a new line after the HTML comment about repeating the row and create the first half of a do... while loop like this (see Chapter 4 for details of the different types of loops):

```
<!-- This row needs to be repeated -->
<?php do { ?>
```

4. You already have the details of the first record in the result set, so the code to get subsequent records needs to go after the closing </td> tag. Create some space between the closing </td> and </tr> tags, and insert the following code. It's slightly different for each method of database connection.

For MySQLi, use this:

```
</td>
    <?php } while ($row = $result->fetch_assoc()); ?>
</tr>
```

For PDO, use this:

```
</td>
    <?php } while ($row = $result->fetch()); ?>
</tr>
```

This fetches the next row in the result set and sends the loop back to the top. Because $row['filename'] and $row['caption'] have different values, the next thumbnail and its associated alt text are inserted into a new table cell. The query string is also updated with the new filename.

5. Save the page and test it in a browser. You should now see all eight thumbnails in a single row across the top of the gallery, as shown in the following screenshot:

Water basin at Ryoanji temple, Kyoto

Hover your mouse pointer over each thumbnail, and you should see the query string displaying the name of the file. You can check your code against gallery_ mysqli_04.php or gallery_pdo_04.php.

6. Clicking the thumbnails still doesn't do anything, so you need to create the logic that changes the main image and its associated caption. Locate this section of code in the block above the DOCTYPE declaration:

```
// get the name and caption for the main image
$mainImage = safe($row['filename']);
$caption = safe($row['caption']);
```

Highlight the line that defines $caption and cut it to your clipboard. Wrap the other line in a conditional statement like this:

```
// get the name for the main image
if (isset($_GET['image'])) {
    $mainImage = safe($_GET['image']);
} else {
    $mainImage = safe($row['filename']);
}
```

The $_GET array contains values passed through a query string, so if $_GET['image'] has been set (defined), it takes the filename from the query string and stores it as $mainImage. If $_GET['image'] doesn't exist, the value is taken from the first record in the result set, as before.

7. Finally, you need to get the caption for the main image. It's no longer going to be the same every time, so you need to move it to the loop that displays the thumbnails in the thumbs table. It goes right after the opening curly brace of the loop (around line 48). Position your cursor after the brace and insert a couple of lines, and then paste the caption definition that you cut in the previous step. You want the caption to match the main image, so if the current record's filename is the same as $mainImage, that's the one you're after. Wrap the code that you have just pasted in a conditional statement, like this:

```
<?php
do {
    // set caption if thumbnail is same as main image
    if ($row['filename'] == $mainImage) {
        $caption = safe($row['caption']); // this is the line you pasted
    }
?>
```

8. Save the page and reload it in your browser. This time, when you click a thumbnail, the main image and caption will change. Don't worry about some images and captions being hidden by the footer. That will correct itself when the thumbnails move to the left of the main image.

■ **Note**   Passing information through a query string like this is an important aspect of working with PHP and database results. Although form information is normally passed through the $_POST array, the $_GET array is frequently used to pass details of a record that you want to display, update, or delete. It's also commonly used for searches because the query string can easily be bookmarked.

---

9. There's no danger of SQL injection in this case. But if someone changes the value of the filename passed through the query string, you'll get ugly error messages if the image can't be found and display_errors is on. Before calling getimagesize(), let's find out if the image exists. Wrap it in a conditional statement like this:

```
if (file_exists('images/'.$mainImage)) {
    // get the dimensions of the main image
    $imageSize = getimagesize('images/'.$mainImage)[3];
} else {
    $error = 'Image not found.';
}
```

10. Try changing the value of image in the query string to any value except that of an existent file. When you load the page, you should see Image not found.

Check your code, if necessary, against gallery_mysqli_05.php or gallery_pdo_05.php.

Creating a Multicolumn Table

With only eight images, the single row of thumbnails across the top of the gallery doesn't look too bad. However, it's useful to be able to build a table dynamically by using a loop that inserts a specific number of table cells in a row before moving to the next row. This is achieved by keeping count of how many cells have been inserted. When the limit is reached for the row, the code needs to insert a closing tag for the current row and, if more thumbnails remain, also insert an opening tag for the next row. What makes it easy to implement is the modulus operator, %, which returns the remainder of a division.

This is how it works. Let's say you want two cells in each row. After the first cell is inserted, the counter is set to 1. If you divide 1 by 2 with the modulus operator (1 % 2), the result is 1. When the next cell is inserted, the counter is increased to 2. The result of 2 % 2 is 0. The next cell produces this calculation: 3 % 2, which results in 1. But the fourth cell produces 4 % 2, which is again 0. So, every time that the calculation results in 0, you know—or to be more exact, PHP knows—you're at the end of a row.

So how do you know if there are any more rows left? By putting the code that inserts the closing and opening <tr> tags at the top of the loop, there must always be at least one image left. However, the first time the loop runs, the remainder is also 0, so the issue is that you need to prevent the tags from being inserted until at least one image has been displayed. Phew… Let's try it.

PHP Solution 14-3: Looping Horizontally and Vertically

This PHP solution shows how to control a loop so as to display a specific number of columns in a table. The number of columns is controlled by setting a constant. Continue working with the files from the preceding section. Alternatively, use gallery_mysqli_05.php or gallery_pdo_05.php.

1. You may decide at a later stage that you want to change the number of columns in the table, so it's a good idea to create a constant at the top of the script where it's easy to find, rather than burying the figures deep in your code. Insert the following code just before creating the database connection:

```
// define number of columns in table
define('COLS', 2);
```

A **constant** is similar to a variable, except that its value cannot be changed by another part of the script. You create a constant with the define() function, which takes two arguments: the name of the constant and its value. By convention, constants are always in uppercase and are case-sensitive. Unlike variables, they do not begin with a dollar sign.

2. You need to initialize the cell counter outside the loop. Also create a variable that indicates whether it's the first row. Add the following code immediately after the constant you have just defined:

```
define('COLS', 2);
// initialize variables for the horizontal looper
$pos = 0;
$firstRow = true;
```

3. The code that keeps count of the columns goes inside the PHP block at the start of the loop that displays the thumbnails. Amend the code like this:

```
<?php do {
    // set caption if thumbnail is same as main image
    if ($row['filename'] == $mainImage) {
        $caption = safe($row['caption']);
    }
    // if remainder is 0 and not first row, close row and start new one
    if ($pos++ % COLS === 0 && !$firstRow) {
        echo '</tr><tr>';
    }
    // once loop begins, this is no longer true
    $firstRow = false;
?>
```

Because the increment operator (++) is placed after $pos, its value is divided by the number of columns before being incremented by 1. The first time the loop runs, the remainder is 0, but $firstRow is true, so the conditional statement fails. However, $firstRow is reset to false after the conditional statement. On future iterations of the loop, the conditional statement closes the current table row and starts a new one each time the remainder is 0.

4. If there are no more records, you need to check if you have an incomplete row at the bottom of the table. Add a while loop after the existing do . . . while loop. In the MySQLi version, it looks like this:

```
<?php } while ($row = $result->fetch_assoc());
    while ($pos++ % COLS) {
        echo '<td> </td>';
    }
?>
```

The new code is identical in the PDO version. The only difference is that the preceding line uses $result->fetch() instead of $result->fetch_assoc().

The second loop continues incrementing $pos while $pos++ % COLS produces a remainder (which is interpreted as true) and inserts an empty cell.

■ **Caution**   This second loop is not nested inside the first. It runs only after the first loop has ended.

---

5. Save the page and reload it in a browser. The single row of thumbnails across the top of the gallery should now be neatly lined up two by two, as shown in Figure 14-4.

Images of Japan

Displaying 1 to 6 of 8

Water basin at Ryoanji temple, Kyoto

Figure 14-4. *The thumbnails are now in neat columns*

Try changing the value of COLS and reloading the page. The main image will be displaced because the page has been designed for only two columns, but you can see how easy it is to control the number of cells in each row by changing just one number. You can check your code against gallery_mysqli_06.php or gallery_pdo_06.php.

Paging Through a Long Set of Records

The grid of eight thumbnails fits quite comfortably in the gallery, but what if you have 28 or 48? The answer is to limit the number of results displayed on each page and then build a navigation system that lets you page back and forth through the results. You've seen this technique countless times when using a search engine; now you're going to learn how to build it yourself. The task can be broken down into the following two stages:

1. Selecting a subset of records to display

2. Creating the navigation links to page through the subsets

Both stages are relatively easy to implement, although they involve applying a little conditional logic. Keep a cool head, and you'll breeze through it.

Selecting a Subset of Records

Limiting the number of results on a page is simple—just add the LIMIT keyword to the SQL query like this:

```
SELECT filename, caption FROM images LIMIT startPosition, maximum
```

The LIMIT keyword can be followed by one or two numbers. If you use just one number, it sets the maximum number of records to be retrieved. That's useful, but it's not suitable for a paging system. For that, you need to use two numbers: the first indicates which record to start from, and the second stipulates the maximum number of records to be retrieved. MySQL counts records from 0, so to display the first six images, you need the following SQL:

```
SELECT filename, caption FROM images LIMIT 0, 6
```

To show the next set, the SQL needs to change to this:

```
SELECT filename, caption FROM images LIMIT 6, 6
```

There are only eight records in the images table, but the second number is only a maximum, so this retrieves records 7 and 8.

To build the navigation system, you need a way of generating these numbers. The second number never changes, so let's define a constant called SHOWMAX. Generating the first number (call it $startRecord) is pretty easy, too. Start numbering the pages from 0, and multiply the second number by the current page number. So, if you call the current page $curPage, the formula looks like this:

```
$startRecord = $curPage * SHOWMAX;
```

And for the SQL, it becomes this:

```
SELECT filename, caption FROM images LIMIT $startRecord, SHOWMAX
```

If $curPage is 0, $startRecord is also 0 (0 × 6), but when $curPage increases to 1, $startRecord changes to 6 (1 × 6), and so on.

Since there are only eight records in the images table, you need a way of finding out the total number of records so as to prevent the navigation system from retrieving empty result sets. In the last chapter, you used the MySQLi num_rows property and rowCount() in PDO. However, that won't work this time, because you want to know the total number of records, not how many there are in the *current* result set. The answer is to use the SQL COUNT() function like this:

```
SELECT COUNT(*) FROM images
```

When used like this in combination with an asterisk, COUNT() gets the total number of records in the table. So, to build a navigation system, you need to run both SQL queries: one to find the total number of records and the other to retrieve the required subset. These are simple queries, so the result is almost instantaneous.

I'll deal with the navigation links later. Let's begin by limiting the number of thumbnails on the first page.

PHP Solution 14-4: Displaying a Subset of Records

This PHP solution shows how to select a subset of records in preparation for creating a navigation system that pages through a longer set. It also demonstrates how to display the numbers of the current selection, as well as the total number of records.

Continue working with the same file as before. Alternatively, use gallery_mysqli_06.php or gallery_pdo_06.php.

1. Define SHOWMAX and the SQL query to find the total number of records in the table. Amend the code toward the top of the page like this (new code is shown in bold):

```
// initialize variables for the horizontal looper
$pos = 0;
$firstRow = true;
// set maximum number of records
define('SHOWMAX', 6);
$conn = dbConnect('read');
// prepare SQL to get total records
$getTotal = 'SELECT COUNT(*) FROM images';
```

2. You now need to run the new SQL query. The code goes immediately after the code in the preceding step but differs according to the type of MySQL connection.

   For MySQLi, use this:

```
// submit query and store result as $totalPix
$total = $conn->query($getTotal);
$totalPix = $total->fetch_row()[0];
```

   This submits the query and then uses the fetch_row() method, which gets a single row from a MySQLi_Result object as an indexed array. There's only one column in the result, so we can get the total count of records in the images table using array dereferencing by adding 0 in square brackets after the call to fetch_row().

   For PDO, use this:

```
// submit query and store result as $totalPix
$total = $conn->query($getTotal);
$totalPix = $total->fetchColumn();
```

   This submits the query and then uses fetchColumn() to get a single result, which is stored in $totalPix.

3. Next, set the value of $curPage. The navigation links that you'll create later will pass the value of the required page through a query string, so you need to check whether curPage is in the $_GET array. If it is, use that value, but make sure it's an integer by preceding it with the (int) casting operator. Otherwise, set the current page to 0. Insert the following code immediately after the code in the previous step:

```
// set the current page
$curPage = (isset($_GET['curPage'])) ? (int) $_GET['curPage'] : 0;
```

4. You now have all the information that you need to calculate the start row and to build the SQL query to retrieve a subset of records. Add the following code immediately after the code in the preceding step:

```
// calculate the start row of the subset
$startRow = $curPage * SHOWMAX;
```

5. But there's a problem. The value of $curPage comes from the query string. If someone changes the number manually in the browser address bar, $startRow might be greater than the number of records in the database. If the value of $startRow exceeds $totalPix, you need to reset both $startRow and $curPage to 0. Add this conditional statement after the code in the preceding step:

```
if ($startRow > $totalPix) {
    $startRow = 0;
    $curPage = 0;
}
```

6. The original SQL query should now be on the next line. Amend it like this:

```
// prepare SQL to retrieve subset of image details
$sql = "SELECT filename, caption FROM images LIMIT $startRow," . SHOWMAX;
```

I've used double quotes this time, because I want PHP to process $startRow. Unlike variables, constants aren't processed inside double-quoted strings. So SHOWMAX is added to the end of the SQL query with the concatenation operator (a period). The comma inside the closing quotes is part of the SQL, separating the two arguments of the LIMIT clause.

7. Save the page and reload it into a browser. Instead of eight thumbnails, you should see just six, as shown in Figure 14-5.

Water basin at Ryoanji temple, Kyoto

Figure 14-5. *The number of thumbnails is limited by the SHOWMAX constant*

Change the value of SHOWMAX to see a different number of thumbnails.

8. The text above the thumbnail grid doesn't update because it's still hard-coded, so let's fix that. Locate the following line of code in the main body of the page:

```
<p id="picCount">Displaying 1 to 6 of 8</p>
```

Replace it with this:

```php
<p id="picCount">Displaying <?php echo $startRow+1;
if ($startRow+1 < $totalPix) {
    echo ' to ';
    if ($startRow+SHOWMAX < $totalPix) {
        echo $startRow+SHOWMAX;
    } else {
        echo $totalPix;
    }
}
echo " of $totalPix";
?></p>
```

Let's take this line by line. The value of $startRow is zero-based, so you need to add 1 to get a more user-friendly number. So $startRow+1 displays 1 on the first page and 7 on the second page.

In the second line, $startRow+1 is compared with the total number of records. If it's less, that means the current page is displaying a range of records, so the third line displays the text "to" with a space on either side.

You then need to work out the top number of the range, so a nested if ... else conditional statement adds the value of the start row to the maximum number of records to be shown on a page. If the result is less than the total number of records, $startRow+SHOWMAX gives you the number of the last record on the page. However, if it's equal to or greater than the total, you display $totalPix instead.

Finally, you exit both conditional statements and display "of" followed by the total number of records.

9. Save the page and reload it in a browser. You still get only the first subset of thumbnails, but you should see the second number change dynamically whenever you alter the value of SHOWMAX. Check your code, if necessary, against gallery_mysqli_07.php or gallery_pdo_07.php.

Navigating Through Subsets of Records

As I mentioned in step 3 of the preceding section, the value of the required page is passed to the PHP script through a query string. When the page first loads, there is no query string, so the value of $curPage is set to 0. Although a query string is generated when you click a thumbnail to display a different image, it includes only the filename of the main image, so the original subset of thumbnails remains unchanged. To display the next subset, you need to create a link that increases the value of $curPage by 1. It follows, therefore, that to return to the previous subset, you need another link that reduces the value of $curPage by 1.

That's simple enough, but you also need to make sure that these links are displayed only when there is a valid subset to navigate to. For instance, there's no point in displaying a back link on the first page, because there isn't a previous subset. Similarly, you shouldn't display a forward link on the page that displays the last subset, because there's nothing to navigate to.

Both issues are easily solved by using conditional statements. There's one final thing that you need to take care of. You must also include the value of the current page in the query string generated when you click a thumbnail. If you fail to do so, $curPage is automatically set back to 0, and the first set of thumbnails is displayed instead of the current subset.

PHP Solution 14-5: Creating the Navigation Links

This PHP solution shows how to create the navigation links to page back and forth through each subset of records. Continue working with the same file as before. Alternatively, use gallery_mysqli_07.php or gallery_pdo_07.php.

1. I have placed the navigation links in an extra row at the bottom of the thumbnail table. Insert this code between the placeholder comment and the closing </table> tag:

```php
<!-- Navigation link needs to go here -->
<tr><td>
<?php
// create a back link if current page greater than 0
if ($curPage > 0) {
    echo '<a href="gallery.php?curPage=' . ($curPage-1) . '"> < Prev</a>';
} else {
    // otherwise leave the cell empty
    echo ' ';
}
?>
</td>
<?php
// pad the final row with empty cells if more than 2 columns
if (COLS-2 > 0) {
    for ($i = 0; $i < COLS-2; $i++) {
        echo '<td> </td>';
    }
}
?>
<td>
<?php
// create a forward link if more records exist
if ($startRow+SHOWMAX < $totalPix) {
    echo '<a href="gallery.php?curPage=' . ($curPage+1) . '"> Next ></a>';
} else {
    // otherwise leave the cell empty
    echo ' ';
}
?>
</td></tr>
</table>
```

It looks like a lot, but the code breaks down into three sections: the first creates a back link if $curPage is greater than 0; the second pads the final table row with empty cells if there are more than two columns; and the third uses the same formula as before ($startRow+SHOWMAX < $totalPix) to determine whether to display a forward link.

Make sure you get the combination of quotes right in the links. The other point to note is that the $curPage-1 and $curPage+1 calculations are enclosed in parentheses to avoid the period after the number being misinterpreted as a decimal point. It's used here as the concatenation operator to join the various parts of the query string.

2. You now need to add the value of the current page to the query string in the link surrounding the thumbnail. Locate this section of code (around line 96):

```
<a href="gallery.php?image=<?= safe($row['filename']) ?>">
```

Change it like this:

```
<a href="gallery.php?image=<?= safe($row['filename']) ?>&amp;curPage=<?= $curPage ?>">
```

You want the same subset to be displayed when clicking a thumbnail, so you just pass the current value of $curPage through the query string.

■ **Caution** All the code *must* be on the same line with no space between the closing PHP tag and &. This code creates the URL and query string, which must have no spaces in it.

---

3. Save the page and test it. Click the Next link, and you should see the remaining subset of thumbnails, as shown in Figure 14-6. There are no more images to be displayed, so the Next link disappears, but there's a Prev link at the bottom left of the thumbnail grid. The record counter at the top of the gallery now reflects the range of thumbnails being displayed, and if you click the right thumbnail, the same subset remains onscreen while displaying the appropriate large image. You're done!

Monk begging for alms in Kyoto

Figure 14-6. *The page navigation system is now complete*

You can check your code against `gallery_mysqli_08.php` or `gallery_pdo_08.php`.

Chapter Review

In just a few pages, you have turned a boring list of filenames into a dynamic online gallery, complete with a page navigation system. All that's necessary is to create a thumbnail for each major image, upload both images to the appropriate folders, and add the filename and a caption to the `images` table in the database. As long as the database is kept up to date with the contents of the `images` and `thumbs` folders, you have a dynamic gallery. Not only that, you've learned how to select subsets of records, link to related information through a query string, and build a page navigation system.

The more you use PHP, the more you realize that the skill doesn't lie so much in remembering how to use lots of obscure functions but in working out the logic needed to get PHP to do what you want. It's a question of if this, do that; if something else, do something different. Once you can anticipate the likely eventualities of a situation, you can normally build the code to handle it.

So far, you've concentrated on extracting records from a simple database table. In the next chapter, I'll show you how to insert, update, and delete material.

CHAPTER 15

■ ■ ■

Managing Content

Although you can use phpMyAdmin for a lot of database administration, you might want to set up areas where clients can log in to update some data without giving them full rein of your database. To do so, you need to build your own forms and create customized content management systems.

At the heart of every content management system lies what is sometimes called the CRUD—Create, Read, Update, and Delete—cycle, which utilizes just four SQL commands: INSERT, SELECT, UPDATE, and DELETE. To demonstrate the basic SQL commands, this chapter shows you how to build a simple content management system for a table called blog.

Even if you don't want to build your own content management system, the four commands covered in this chapter are essential for just about any database-driven page, such as user login, user registration, search form, search results, and so on.

In this chapter, you'll learn about the following:

- Inserting new records in a database table
- Displaying a list of existing records
- Updating existing records
- Asking for confirmation before a record is deleted

Setting Up a Content Management System

Managing the content in a database table involves four stages, which I normally assign to four separate but interlinked pages: one each for inserting, updating, and deleting records, plus a list of existing records. The list of records serves two purposes: to identify what's stored in the database and, more important, to link to the update and delete scripts by passing the record's primary key through a query string.

The blog table contains a series of titles and text articles to be displayed in the Japan Journey site, as shown in Figure 15-1. In the interests of keeping things simple, the table contains just five columns: article_id (primary key), title, article, created, and updated.

© David Powers 2022
D. Powers, *PHP 8 Solutions*, https://doi.org/10.1007/978-1-4842-7141-4_15

Creating the Blog Database Table

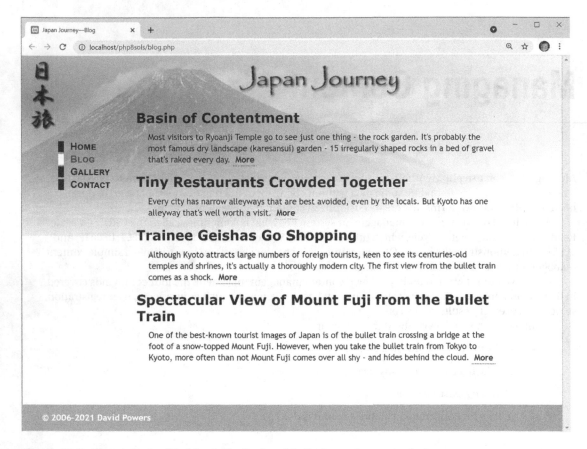

Figure 15-1. *The contents of the blog table displayed in the Japan Journey web site*

If you just want to get on with studying the content management pages, import the table structure and data from `blog.sql` from the `ch15` folder. Open phpMyAdmin, select the `phpsols` database, and import the table in the same way as in Chapter 12. The SQL file creates the table and populates it with four short articles.

If you would prefer to create everything yourself from scratch, open phpMyAdmin, select the `phpsols` database, and click the `Structure` tab if it's not already selected. In the `Create table` section, type **blog** in the `Name` field and **5** in the `Number of columns` field. Then click `Go`. Use the settings shown in the following screenshot and Table 15-1:

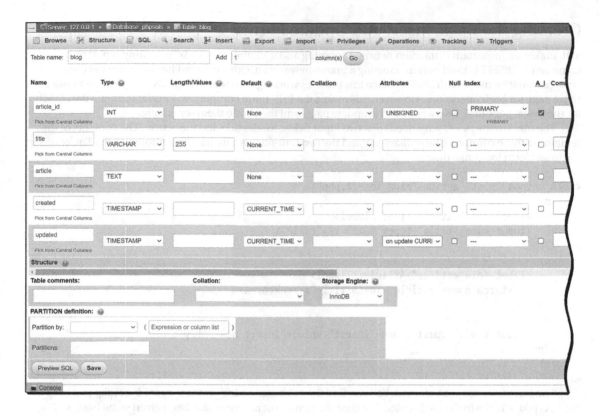

Table 15-1. *Column definitions for the blog table*

Field	Type	Length/Values	Default	Attributes	Null	Index	A_I
article_id	INT			UNSIGNED	Deselected	PRIMARY	Selected
title	VARCHAR	255			Deselected		
article	TEXT				Deselected		
created	TIMESTAMP		CURRENT_ TIMESTAMP		Deselected		
updated	TIMESTAMP		CURRENT_ TIMESTAMP	on update CURRENT_ TIMESTAMP	Deselected		

The default value of the created and updated columns is set to CURRENT_TIMESTAMP. So both columns get the same value when a record is first entered. The Attributes column for updated is set to on update CURRENT_TIMESTAMP. This means it will be updated whenever a change is made to a record. To keep track of when a record was originally created, the value in the created column is never updated.

417

Creating the Basic Insert and Update Forms

SQL makes an important distinction between inserting and updating records by providing separate commands. INSERT is used only for creating a brand-new record. Once a record has been inserted, any changes must be made with UPDATE. Since this involves working with identical fields, it is possible to use the same page for both operations. However, this makes the PHP more complex, so I prefer to create the HTML for the insert page first, save a copy as the update page, and then code them separately.

The form in the insert page needs just two input fields: for the title and the article. The contents of the remaining three columns (the primary key and the two timestamps) are handled automatically. The code for the insert form looks like this:

```
<form method="post" action="blog_insert.php">
    <p>
        <label for="title">Title:</label>
        <input name="title" type="text" id="title">
    </p>
    <p>
        <label for="article">Article:</label>
        <textarea name="article" id="article"></textarea>
    </p>
    <p>
        <input type="submit" name="insert" value="Insert New Entry">
    </p>
</form>
```

The form uses the post method. You can find the full code in blog_insert_mysqli_01.php and blog_insert_pdo_01.php in the ch15 folder. The content management forms have been given some basic styling with admin.css, which is in the styles folder. When viewed in a browser, the form looks like this:

Insert New Blog Entry

Title:

[   ]

Article:

[   ]

[Insert New Entry]

The update form is identical except for the heading and Submit button. The button code looks like this (the full code is in blog_update_mysqli_01.php and blog_update_pdo_01.php):

```
<input type="submit" name="update" value="Update Entry">
```

I've given the title and article input fields the same names as the columns in the blog table. This makes it easier to keep track of variables when coding the PHP and SQL later.

■ **Tip** As a security measure, some developers recommend using different names from the database columns because anyone can see the names of input fields just by looking at the form's source code. Using different names makes it more difficult to break into the database. This shouldn't be a concern in a password-protected part of a site. However, you may want to consider the idea for publicly accessible forms, such as those used for user registration or login.

Inserting New Records

The basic SQL for inserting new records into a table looks like this:

```
INSERT [INTO] table_name (column_names)
VALUES (values)
```

The INTO is in square brackets, which means that it's optional. It's purely there to make the SQL read a little more like human language. The column names can be in any order you like, but the values in the second set of parentheses must be in the same order as the columns they refer to.

Although the code is very similar for MySQLi and PDO, I'll deal with each one separately to avoid confusion.

■ **Note** Many of the scripts in this chapter use a technique known as "setting a flag." A flag is a Boolean variable that is initialized to either true or false and used to check whether something has happened. For instance, if $OK is initially set to false and reset to true only when a database query executes successfully, it can be used as the condition controlling another code block.

PHP Solution 15-1: Inserting a New Record with MySQLi

This PHP solution shows how to insert a new record into the blog table using a MySQLi prepared statement. Using a prepared statement avoids problems with escaping quotes and control characters. It also protects your database against SQL injection (see Chapter 13).

1. Create a folder called admin in the php8sols site root. Copy blog_insert_mysqli_01.php from the ch15 folder, and save it as blog_insert_mysqli.php in the new folder.

2. The code that inserts a new record should be run only if the form has been submitted, so it's enclosed in a conditional statement that checks for the name attribute of the Submit button (insert) in the $_POST array. Put the following above the DOCTYPE declaration:

```php
<?php
if (isset($_POST['insert'])) {
    require_once '../includes/connection.php';
    // initialize flag
    $OK = false;
    // create database connection
    // initialize prepared statement
    // create SQL
    // bind parameters and execute statement
    // redirect if successful or display error
}
?>
```

After including the connection function, the code sets $OK to false. This is reset to true only if there are no errors. The five comments at the end map out the remaining steps that we'll fill in next.

3. Create a connection to the database as the user with read and write privileges, initialize a prepared statement, and create the SQL with placeholders for data that will be derived from the user input like this:

```php
// create database connection
$conn = dbConnect('write');
// initialize prepared statement
$stmt = $conn->stmt_init();
// create SQL
$sql = 'INSERT INTO blog (title, article)
        VALUES(?, ?)';
```

The values that will be derived from $_POST['title'] and $_POST['article'] are represented by question mark placeholders. The other columns will be populated automatically. The article_id column is the primary key, which uses AUTO_INCREMENT, and the default for the created and updated columns is CURRENT_TIMESTAMP.

■ **Note** The code is in a slightly different order from Chapter 13. The script will be developed further in Chapter 17 to run a series of SQL queries, so the prepared statement is initialized first.

---

4. The next stage is to replace the question marks with the values held in the variables—a process called **binding the parameters**. Insert the following code:

```php
if ($stmt->prepare($sql)) {
    // bind parameters and execute statement
    $stmt->bind_param('ss', $_POST['title'], $_POST['article']);
    $stmt->execute();
    if ($stmt->affected_rows > 0) {
        $OK = true;
    }
}
```

This is the section that protects your database from SQL injection. Pass the variables to the bind_param() method in the same order as you want them inserted into the SQL query, together with a first argument that specifies the data type of each variable, once again in the same order as the variables. Both are strings, so this argument is 'ss'.

Once the values have been bound to the placeholders, call the execute() method.

The affected_rows property records how many rows were affected by an INSERT, UPDATE, or DELETE query.

■ **Caution**   If the query triggers a MySQL error, affected_rows returns –1. Unlike some computing languages, PHP treats –1 as true. So you need to check that affected_rows is greater than zero to be sure that the query succeeded. If it is greater than zero, $OK is reset to true.

---

5. Finally, redirect the page to a list of existing records or display any error message. Add this code after the previous step:

```
// redirect if successful or display error
    if ($OK) {
        header('Location:
            http://localhost/php8sols/admin/blog_list_mysqli.php');
        exit;
    } else {
        $error = $stmt->error;
    }
}
?>
```

6. Add the following code block in the body of the page to display the error message if the insert operation fails:

```
<h1>Insert New Blog Entry</h1>
<?php if (isset($error)) {
    echo "<p>Error: $error</p>";
    } ?>
<form method="post" action="blog_insert_mysqli.php">
```

The completed code is in blog_insert_mysqli_02.php in the ch15 folder.

That completes the insert page, but before testing it, create blog_list_mysqli. php, which is described in PHP Solution 15-3.

■ **Note**   To focus on the code that interacts with the database, the scripts in this chapter don't validate the user input. In a real-world application, you should use the techniques described in Chapter 6 to check the data submitted from the form and redisplay it if errors are detected.

PHP Solution 15-2: Inserting a New Record with PDO

This PHP solution shows how to insert a new record in the blog table using a PDO prepared statement. If you haven't already done so, create a folder called admin in the php8sols site root.

1. Copy blog_insert_pdo_01.php to the admin folder and save it as blog_insert_pdo.php.

2. The code that inserts a new record should be run only if the form has been submitted, so it's enclosed in a conditional statement that checks for the name attribute of the Submit button (insert) in the $_POST array. Put the following in a PHP block above the DOCTYPE declaration:

```php
if (isset($_POST['insert'])) {
    require_once '../includes/connection.php';
    // initialize flag
    $OK = false;
    // create database connection
    // create SQL
    // prepare the statement
    // bind the parameters and execute the statement
    // redirect if successful or display error
}
```

After including the connection function, the code sets $OK to false. This is reset to true only if there are no errors. The five comments at the end map out the remaining steps.

3. Create a PDO connection to the database as the user with read and write privileges, and build the SQL like this:

```php
// create database connection
$conn = dbConnect('write', 'pdo');
// create SQL
$sql = 'INSERT INTO blog (title, article)
VALUES(:title, :article)';
```

The values that will be derived from variables are represented by named placeholders consisting of the column name preceded by a colon (:title and :article). The value for the other columns will be generated by the database. The article_id primary key is incremented automatically, and the created and updated columns have their default values set to CURRENT_TIMESTAMP.

4. The next stage is to initialize the prepared statement and bind the values from the variables to the placeholders—a process known as **binding the parameters**. Add the following code:

```php
// prepare the statement
$stmt = $conn->prepare($sql);
// bind the parameters and execute the statement
$stmt->bindParam(':title', $_POST['title'], PDO::PARAM_STR);
$stmt->bindParam(':article', $_POST['article'], PDO::PARAM_STR);
```

```
// execute and get number of affected rows
$stmt->execute();
$OK = $stmt->rowCount();
```

This begins by passing the SQL query to the prepare() method of the database connection ($conn) and storing a reference to the statement as a variable ($stmt).

Next, the values in the variables are bound to the placeholders in the prepared statement, and the execute() method runs the query.

When used with an INSERT, UPDATE, or DELETE query, the PDO rowCount() method reports the number of rows affected by the query. If the record is inserted successfully, $OK is 1, which PHP treats as true. Otherwise, it's 0, which is treated as false.

5. Finally, redirect the page to a list of existing records or display any error message. Add this code after the previous step:

```
// redirect if successful or display error
    if ($OK) {
        header('Location: http://localhost/php8sols/admin/blog_list_pdo.php');
        exit;
    } else {
        $error = $stmt->errorInfo()[2];
    }
}
?>
```

The error message, if any, is stored as the third element of the array returned by $stmt->errorInfo() and is accessed using array dereferencing.

6. Add a PHP code block in the body of the page to display any error message:

```
<h1>Insert New Blog Entry</h1>
<?php if (isset($error)) {
    echo "<p>Error: $error</p>";
} ?>
<form method="post" action="blog_insert_pdo.php">
```

The completed code is in blog_insert_pdo_02.php in the ch15 folder.

That completes the insert page, but before testing it, create blog_list_pdo.php, which is described next.

Linking to the Update and Delete Pages

Before you can update or delete a record, you need to find its primary key. A practical way of doing this is to query the database to select all records. You can use the results of this query to display a list of all records, complete with links to the update and delete pages. By adding the value of article_id to a query string in each link, you automatically identify the record to be updated or deleted. As Figure 15-2 shows, the URL displayed in the browser status bar (bottom left) identifies the article_id of the article Tiny Restaurants Crowded Together as 3.

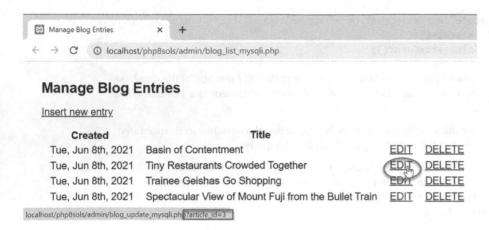

Figure 15-2. *The EDIT and DELETE links contain the record's primary key in a query string*

The update page uses this to display the correct record ready for updating. The same information is conveyed in the DELETE link to the delete page.

To create a list like this, you need to start with an HTML table that contains two rows and as many columns as you want to display, plus two extra columns for the EDIT and DELETE links. The first row is used for column headings. The second row is wrapped in a PHP loop to display all the results. The table in blog_list_mysqli_01.php in the ch15 folder looks like this (the version in blog_list_pdo_01.php is the same, except that the links in the last two table cells point to the PDO versions of the update and delete pages):

```
<table>
    <tr>
        <th>Created</th>
        <th>Title</th>
        <th> </th>
        <th> </th>
    </tr>
    <tr>
        <td></td>
        <td></td>
        <td><a href="blog_update_mysqli.php">EDIT</a></td>
        <td><a href="blog_delete_mysqli.php">DELETE</a></td>
    </tr>
</table>
```

PHP Solution 15-3: Creating the Links to the Update and Delete Pages

This PHP solution shows how to create a page to manage the records in the blog table by displaying a list of all records and linking to the update and delete pages. There are only minor differences between the MySQLi and PDO versions, so these instructions describe both.

Copy blog_list_mysqli_01.php or blog_list_pdo_01.php to the admin folder and save it as blog_list_mysqli.php or blog_list_pdo.php, depending on which method of connection you plan to use. The different versions link to the appropriate insert, update, and delete files.

1. You need to connect to the database and create the SQL query. Add the following code in a PHP block above the DOCTYPE declaration:

```
require_once '../includes/connection.php';
require_once '../includes/utility_funcs.php';
// create database connection
$conn = dbConnect('read');
$sql = 'SELECT * FROM blog ORDER BY created DESC';
```

   If you're using PDO, add 'pdo' as the second argument to dbConnect().

2. Submit the query by adding the following code before the closing PHP tag.

   For MySQLi, use this:

```
$result = $conn->query($sql);
if (!$result) {
    $error = $conn->error;
}
```

   For PDO, use this:

```
$result = $conn->query($sql);
$error = $conn->errorInfo()[2];
```

3. Add a conditional statement just before the table to display any error message, and wrap the table in the else block. The code before the table looks like this:

```
<?php if (isset($error)) {
    echo "<p>$error</p>";
} else { ?>
```

   The closing curly brace goes in a separate PHP block after the closing </table> tag.

4. You now need to enclose the second table row in a loop and retrieve each record from the result set. The following code goes between the closing </tr> tag of the first row and the opening <tr> tag of the second row.

   For MySQLi, use this:

```
</tr>
    <?php while($row = $result->fetch_assoc()) { ?>
<tr>
```

   For PDO, use this:

```
</tr>
    <?php while ($row = $result->fetch()) { ?>
<tr>
```

   This is the same as in the previous chapter, so it should need no explanation.

5. Display the `created` and `title` fields for the current record in the first two cells of the second row, like this:

```
<td><?= $row['created'] ?></td>
<td><?= safe($row['title']) ?></td>
```

The `created` column stores a `TIMESTAMP` data type, which is a fixed format, so it doesn't need sanitizing. But the `title` column is text-related, so it needs to be passed to the `safe()` function defined in Chapter 13.

6. In the next two cells, add the query string and value of the `article_id` field for the current record to both URLs, as follows (although the links are different, the highlighted code is the same for the PDO version):

```
<td><a href="blog_update_mysqli.php?article_id=<?= $row['article_id'] ?>"
    >EDIT</a></td>
<td><a href="blog_delete_mysqli.php?article_id=<?= $row['article_id'] ?>"
    >DELETE</a></td>
```

What you're doing here is adding `?article_id=` to the URL and then using PHP to display the value of `$row['article_id']`. The `article_id` column stores only integers, so the value doesn't need to be sanitized. It's important that you don't leave any spaces that might break the URL or the query string. After the PHP has been processed, the opening `<a>` tag should look like this when viewing the page's source code in a browser (although the number will vary according to the record):

```
<a href="blog_update_mysqli.php?article_id=2">
```

7. Finally, close the loop surrounding the second table row with a curly brace, like this:

```
</tr>
    <?php } ?>
</table>
```

8. Save `blog_list_mysqli.php` or `blog_list_pdo.php` and load the page into a browser. Assuming that you loaded the contents of `blog.sql` into the phpsols database earlier, you should see a list of four items, as shown in Figure 15-2. You can now test `blog_insert_mysqli.php` or `blog_insert_pdo.php`. After inserting an item, you should be returned to the appropriate version of `blog_list.php`, and the date and time of creation, together with the title of the new item, should be displayed at the top of the list. Check your code against `blog_list_mysqli_02.php` or `blog_list_pdo_02.php` in the ch15 folder if you encounter any problems.

■ **Tip** This code assumes that there will always be some records in the table. As an exercise, use the technique in PHP Solution 13-2 (MySQLi) or 13-4 (PDO) to count the number of results, and use a conditional statement to display a message if no records are found. The solution is in `blog_list_norec_mysqli.php` and `blog_list_norec_pdo.php`.

Updating Records

An update page needs to perform two separate processes, as follows:

1. Retrieve the selected record, and display it ready for editing

2. Update the edited record in the database

The first stage uses the $_GET superglobal array to retrieve the primary key from the URL and then uses it to select and display the record in the update form, as shown in Figure 15-3.

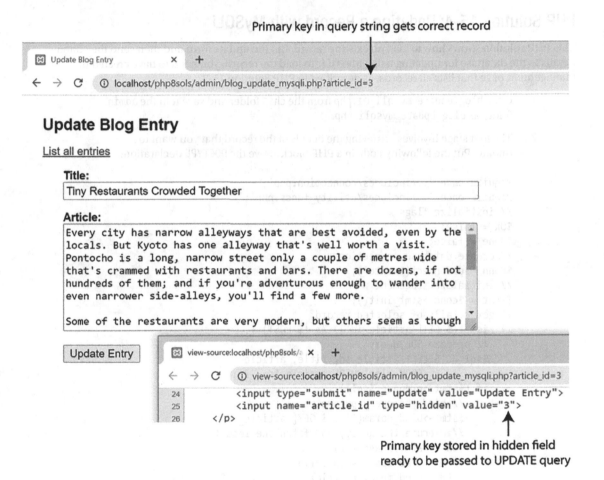

Figure 15-3. *The primary key keeps track of a record during the update process*

The primary key is stored in a hidden field in the update form. After you have edited the record in the update page, you submit the form using the post method to pass all the details, including the primary key, to an UPDATE command.

The basic syntax of the SQL UPDATE command looks like this:

```
UPDATE table_name SET column_name = value, column_name = value
WHERE condition
```

The condition when updating a specific record is the primary key. So, when updating article_id 3 in the blog table, the basic UPDATE query looks like this:

```
UPDATE blog SET title = value, article = value
WHERE article_id = 3
```

Although the basic principle is the same for both MySQLi and PDO, the code differs sufficiently to warrant separate instructions.

PHP Solution 15-4: Updating a Record with MySQLi

This PHP solution shows how to load an existing record into the update form and then send the edited details to the database for updating using MySQLi. To load the record, you need to have created the management page that lists all records, as described in PHP Solution 15-3.

1. Copy blog_update_mysqli_01.php from the ch15 folder and save it in the admin folder as blog_update_mysqli.php.

2. The first stage involves retrieving the details of the record that you want to update. Put the following code in a PHP block above the DOCTYPE declaration:

```
require_once '../includes/connection.php';
require_once '../includes/utility_funcs.php';
// initialize flags
$OK = false;
$done = false;
// create database connection
$conn = dbConnect('write');
// initialize statement
$stmt = $conn->stmt_init();
// get details of selected record
if (isset($_GET['article_id']) && !$_POST) {
    // prepare SQL query
    $sql = 'SELECT article_id, title, article
            FROM blog WHERE article_id = ?';
    if ($stmt->prepare($sql)) {
        // bind the query parameter
        $stmt->bind_param('i', $_GET['article_id']);
        // execute the query, and fetch the result
        $OK = $stmt->execute();
        // bind the results to variables
        $stmt->bind_result($article_id, $title, $article);
        $stmt->fetch();
    }
}
// redirect if $_GET['article_id'] not defined
if (!isset($_GET['article_id'])) {
    $url = 'http://localhost/php8sols/admin/blog_list_mysqli.php';
    header("Location: $url");
    exit;
}
```

```
// get error message if query fails
if (isset($stmt) && !$OK && !$done) {
    $error = $stmt->error;
}
```

Although this is very similar to the code used for the insert page, the first few lines are *outside* the conditional statements. Both stages of the update process require the database connection and a prepared statement, so this avoids the need to duplicate the same code later. Two flags are initialized: $OK to check the success of retrieving the record and $done to check whether the update succeeds.

The first conditional statement makes sure that $_GET['article_id'] exists and that the $_POST array is empty. So the code inside the braces is executed only when the query string is set, but the form hasn't been submitted.

You prepare the SELECT query in the same way as for an INSERT command, using a question mark as a placeholder for the variable. However, note that instead of using an asterisk to retrieve all columns, the query specifies three columns by name like this:

```
$sql = 'SELECT article_id, title, article
            FROM blog WHERE article_id = ?';
```

This is because a MySQLi prepared statement lets you bind the result of a SELECT query to variables, and to be able to do this, you must specify the column names and the order you want them to be in.

First, you need to initialize the prepared statement and bind $_GET['article_id'] to the query with $stmt->bind_param(). Because the value of article_id must be an integer, you pass 'i' as the first argument.

The code executes the query and then binds the result to variables in the same order as the columns specified in the SELECT query before fetching the result.

The next conditional statement redirects the page to blog_list_mysqli.php if $_GET['article_id'] hasn't been defined. This prevents anyone from trying to load the update page directly in a browser. The redirect location has been assigned to a variable because a query string will be added to it later if the update is successful.

The final conditional statement stores an error message if the prepared statement has been created but both $OK and $done remain false. You haven't added the update script yet, but if the record is retrieved or updated successfully, one of them will be switched to true. So if both remain false, you know there was something wrong with one of the SQL queries.

3. Now that you have retrieved the contents of the record, you need to display them in the update form. If the prepared statement succeeded, $article_id should contain the primary key of the record to be updated, because it's one of the variables you bound to the result set with the bind_result() method.

However, if there's an error, you need to display the message onscreen. But if someone alters the query string to an invalid number, $article_id will be set to 0, so there is no point in displaying the update form. Add the following conditional statements immediately before the opening <form> tag:

```
<p><a href="blog_list_mysqli.php">List all entries </a></p>
<?php if (isset($error)) {
    echo "<p class='warning'>Error: $error</p>";
}
if($article_id == 0) { ?>
    <p class="warning">Invalid request: record does not exist.</p>
<?php } else { ?>
<form method="post" action="blog_update_mysqli.php">
```

The first conditional statement displays any error message reported by the MySQLi prepared statement. The second wraps the update form in an else block, so the form will be hidden if $article_id is 0.

4. Add the closing curly brace of the else block immediately after the closing </form> tag, like this:

```
</form>
        <?php } ?>
</body>
```

5. If $article_id is not 0, you know that $title and $article also contain valid values and can be displayed in the update form without further testing. However, you need to pass text values to safe() to avoid problems with quotes and executable code. Display $title in the value attribute of the title input field like this:

```
<input name="title" type="text" id="title" value="<?= safe($title) ?>">
```

6. Do the same for the article text area. Because text areas don't have a value attribute, the code goes between the opening and closing <textarea> tags like this:

```
<textarea name="article" id="article"><?= safe($article) ?></textarea>
```

Make sure there is no space between the opening and closing PHP and <textarea> tags. Otherwise, you'll get unwanted spaces in your updated record.

7. The UPDATE command needs to know the primary key of the record you want to change. You need to store the primary key in a hidden field so that it is submitted in the $_POST array with the other details. Because hidden fields are not displayed onscreen, the following code can go anywhere inside the form:

```
<input name="article_id" type="hidden" value="<?= $article_id ?>">
```

8. Save the update page and test it by loading blog_list_mysqli.php into a browser and selecting the EDIT link for one of the records. The contents of the record should be displayed in the form fields, as shown in Figure 15-3.

The Update Entry button doesn't do anything yet. Just make sure that everything is displayed correctly, and confirm that the primary key is registered in the hidden field. You can check your code, if necessary, against blog_update_mysqli_02.php.

9. The name attribute of the Submit button is update, so all the update processing code needs to go in a conditional statement that checks for the presence of update in the $_POST array. Place the following code, highlighted in bold, immediately above the code in step 1 that redirects the page:

```
$stmt->fetch();
    }
}
// if form has been submitted, update record
if (isset($_POST ['update'])) {
    // prepare update query
    $sql = 'UPDATE blog SET title = ?, article = ?
                WHERE article_id = ?';
    if ($stmt->prepare($sql)) {
        $stmt->bind_param('ssi', $_POST['title'], $_POST['article'],
            $_POST['article_id']);
        $done = $stmt->execute();
    }
}
// redirect page on success or if $_GET['article_id']) not defined
if ($done || !isset($_GET['article_id'])) {
    $url = 'http://localhost/php8sols/admin/blog_list_mysqli.php';
    if ($done) {
        $url .= '?updated=true';
    }
    header("Location: $url");
    exit;
}
```

The UPDATE query is prepared with question mark placeholders where values are to be supplied from variables. The prepared statement has already been initialized in the code outside the conditional statement, so you can pass the SQL to the prepare() method and bind the variables with $stmt->bind_param(). The first two variables are strings, and the third is an integer, so the first argument is 'ssi'.

If the UPDATE query succeeds, the execute() method returns true, resetting the value of $done. Unlike an INSERT query, using the affected_rows property has little meaning because it returns 0 if the user decides to click the Update Entry button without making any changes, so we won't use it here. You need to add $done || to the condition in the redirect script. This ensures that the page is redirected if either the update succeeds or someone tries to access the page directly.

If the update succeeds, a query string is appended to the redirect location.

10. Edit the PHP block above the table in blog_list_mysqli.php to display a message that the record has been updated like this:

```
<?php if (isset($error)) {
    echo "<p>$error</p>";
} else {
```

```
        if (isset($_GET['updated'])) {
            echo '<p>Record updated</p>';
        }
    ?>
    <table>
```

This conditional statement is nested inside the existing else block; it's not an elseif statement. So it will be displayed with the table of database records after a record has been updated.

11. Save blog_update_mysqli.php and test it by loading blog_list_mysqli. php, selecting one of the EDIT links, and making changes to the record that is displayed. When you click Update Entry, you should be taken back to blog_ list_mysqli.php, and "Record updated" should appear above the list. You can verify that your changes were made by clicking the same EDIT link again. Check your code, if necessary, with blog_update_mysqli_03.php and blog_list_ mysqli_03.php.

PHP Solution 15-5: Updating a Record with PDO

This PHP solution shows how to load an existing record into the update form and then send the edited details to the database for updating using PDO. To load the record, you need to have created the management page that lists all records, as described in PHP Solution 15-3.

1. Copy blog_update_pdo_01.php from the ch15 folder and save it in the admin folder as blog_update_pdo.php.

2. The first stage involves retrieving the details of the record that you want to update. Put the following code in a PHP block above the DOCTYPE declaration:

```
require_once '../includes/connection.php';
require_once '../includes/utility_funcs.php';
// initialize flags
$OK = false;
$done = false;
// create database connection
$conn = dbConnect('write', 'pdo');
// get details of selected record
if (isset($_GET['article_id']) && !$_POST) {
    // prepare SQL query
    $sql = 'SELECT article_id, title, article FROM blog
                WHERE article_id = ?';
    $stmt = $conn->prepare($sql);
    // pass the placeholder value to execute() as a single-element array
    $OK = $stmt->execute([$_GET['article_id']]);
    // bind the results
    $stmt->bindColumn(1, $article_id);
    $stmt->bindColumn(2, $title);
    $stmt->bindColumn(3, $article);
    $stmt->fetch();
}
```

```
// redirect if $_GET['article_id'] not defined
if (!isset($_GET['article_id'])) {
    $url = 'http://localhost/php8sols/admin/blog_list_pdo.php';
    header("Location: $url");
    exit;
}
if (isset($stmt)) {
    // get error message (will be null if no error)
    $error = $stmt->errorInfo()[2];
}
```

Although this is very similar to the code used for the insert page, the first few lines are *outside* the first conditional statement. Both stages of the update process require the database connection, so this avoids the need to duplicate the same code later. Two flags are initialized: $OK to check the success of retrieving the record and $done to check whether the update succeeds.

The first conditional statement checks that $_GET['article_id'] exists and that the $_POST array is empty. This makes sure that the code inside is executed only when the query string is set, but the form hasn't yet been submitted.

When preparing the SQL query for the insert form, you used named placeholders for the variables. This time, let's use a question mark, like this:

```
$sql = 'SELECT article_id, title, article FROM blog
        WHERE article_id = ?';
```

There's only one variable that needs to be bound to the anonymous placeholder, so pass it directly to the execute() method as a single-element array, like this:

```
$OK = $stmt->execute([$_GET['article_id']]);
```

■ **Caution**   This code uses the array shorthand syntax, so $_GET['article_id'] is wrapped in a pair of square brackets. Don't forget the array's closing square bracket.

The results are then bound to $article_id, $title, and $article with the bindColumn() method. This time, I have used numbers (counting from 1) to indicate which column to bind each variable to.

There's only one record to fetch in the result, so the fetch() method is called immediately.

The next conditional statement redirects the page to blog_list_pdo.php if $_GET['article_id'] hasn't been defined. This prevents anyone from trying to load the update page directly in a browser. The redirect location has been assigned to a variable because a query string will be added to it later if the update is successful.

The last conditional statement retrieves any error message from the prepared statement. It's separate from the rest of the prepared statement code because it will also be used for a second prepared statement that you'll add later.

3. Now that you have retrieved the contents of the record, you need to display them in the update form. If the prepared statement succeeded, $article_id should contain the primary key of the record to be updated, because it's one of the variables you bound to the result set with the bindColumn() method.

   However, if there's an error, you need to display that message onscreen. But if someone alters the query string to an invalid number, $article_id will be set to 0, so there is no point in displaying the update form. Add the following conditional statements immediately before the opening <form> tag:

```
<p><a href="blog_list_pdo.php">List all entries </a></p>
<?php if (isset($error)) {
    echo "<p class='warning'>Error: $error</p>";
}
if($article_id == 0) { ?>
    <p class="warning">Invalid request: record does not exist.</p>
<?php } else { ?>
<form method="post" action="blog_update_pdo.php">
```

   The first conditional statement displays any error message reported by the PDO prepared statement. The second wraps the update form in an else block, so the form will be hidden if $article_id is 0.

4. Add the closing curly brace of the else block immediately after the closing </form> tag, like this:

```
</form>
        <?php } ?>
</body>
```

5. If $article_id is not 0, you know that $title and $article also exist and can be displayed in the update form without further testing. However, you need to pass text values to safe() to avoid problems with quotes and executable code. Display $title in the value attribute of the title input field like this:

```
<input name="title" type="text" id="title" value="<?= safe($title) ?>">
```

6. Do the same for the article text area. Because text areas don't have a value attribute, the code goes between the opening and closing <textarea> tags like this:

```
<textarea name="article" id="article"><?= safe($article) ?></textarea>
```

   Make sure there is no space between the opening and closing PHP and <textarea> tags. Otherwise, you will get unwanted spaces in your updated record.

7. The UPDATE command needs to know the primary key of the record you want to change. You need to store the primary key in a hidden field so that it is submitted in the $_POST array with the other details. Because hidden fields are not displayed onscreen, the following code can go anywhere inside the form:

```
<input name="article_id" type="hidden" value="<?= $article_id ?>">
```

8. Save the update page and test it by loading blog_list_pdo.php into a browser and selecting the EDIT link for one of the records. The contents of the record should be displayed in the form fields, as shown in Figure 15-3.

   The Update Entry button doesn't do anything yet. Just make sure that everything is displayed correctly, and confirm that the primary key is registered in the hidden field. You can check your code, if necessary, against blog_update_pdo_02.php.

9. The name attribute of the Submit button is update, so all the update processing code needs to go in a conditional statement that checks for the presence of update in the $_POST array. Place the following code, highlighted in bold, immediately above the code in step 1 that redirects the page:

```php
$stmt->fetch();
}
// if form has been submitted, update record
if (isset($_POST['update'])) {
    // prepare update query
    $sql = 'UPDATE blog SET title = ?, article = ?
                WHERE article_id = ?';
    $stmt = $conn->prepare($sql);
    // execute query by passing array of variables
    $done = $stmt->execute([$_POST['title'], $_POST['article'],
        $_POST['article_id']]);
}
// redirect page on success or $_GET['article_id'] not defined
if ($done || !isset($_GET['article_id'])) {
    $url = 'http://localhost/php8sols/admin/blog_list_pdo.php';
    if ($done) {
        $url .= '?updated=true';
    }
    header("Location: $url");
    exit;
}
```

Again, the SQL query is prepared using question marks as placeholders for values to be derived from variables. This time, there are three placeholders, so the corresponding variables need to be passed as an array to the execute() method. Needless to say, the array must be in the same order as the placeholders.

If the UPDATE query succeeds, the execute() method returns true, resetting the value of $done. You can't use the rowCount() method here to get the number of affected rows because it returns 0 if the Update Entry button is clicked without making any changes. You'll notice we have added $done || to the condition in the redirect script. This ensures the page is redirected if either the update succeeds or someone tries to access the page directly. If the record has been updated, a query string is appended to the redirect location.

10. Edit the PHP block above the table in `blog_list_pdo.php` to display a message that the record has been updated like this:

```php
<?php if (isset($error)) {
    echo "<p>$error</p>";
} else {
    if (isset($_GET['updated'])) {
        echo '<p>Record updated</p>';
    }
}
?>
<table>
```

This conditional statement is nested inside the existing `else` block; it's not an `elseif` statement. So it will be displayed with the table of database records after a record has been updated.

11. Save `blog_update_pdo.php` and test it by loading `blog_list_pdo.php`, selecting one of the EDIT links, and making changes to the record that is displayed. When you click Update Entry, you should be taken back to `blog_list_pdo.php`, and "Record updated" should appear above the list. You can verify that your changes were made by clicking the same EDIT link again. Check your code, if necessary, against `blog_update_pdo_03.php` and `blog_list_pdo_03.php`.

Deleting Records

Deleting a record in a database is similar to updating one. The basic `DELETE` command looks like this:

```
DELETE FROM table_name WHERE condition
```

What makes the `DELETE` command potentially dangerous is that it is final. Once you have deleted a record, there's no going back—it's gone forever. There's no Recycle Bin or Trash to fish it out from. Even worse, the `WHERE` clause is optional. If you omit it, every single record in the table is irrevocably sent into cyber-oblivion. Consequently, it's a good idea to display details of the record to be deleted and ask the user to confirm or cancel the process (see Figure 15-4).

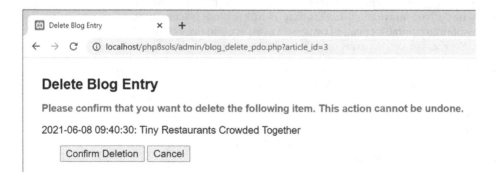

Figure 15-4. Deleting a record is irreversible, so get confirmation before going ahead

Building and scripting the delete page is almost identical to the update page, so I won't give step-by-step instructions. However, here are the main points:

- Retrieve the details of the selected record.

- Display sufficient details, such as the title, for the user to confirm that the correct record has been selected.

- Give the Confirm Deletion and Cancel buttons different name attributes, and use each name attribute with isset() to control the action taken.

- Instead of wrapping the entire form in the else block, use conditional statements to hide the Confirm Deletion button and the hidden field.

The code that performs the deletion for each method follows.

```
For MySQLi:if (isset($_POST['delete'])) {
    $sql = 'DELETE FROM blog WHERE article_id = ?';
    if ($stmt->prepare($sql)) {
        $stmt->bind_param('i', $_POST['article_id']);
        $stmt->execute();
        if ($stmt->affected_rows > 0) {;
            $deleted = true;
        } else {
            $error = 'There was a problem deleting the record.';
        }
    }
}
```

For PDO:

```
if (isset($_POST['delete'])) {
    $sql = 'DELETE FROM blog WHERE article_id = ?';
    $stmt = $conn->prepare($sql);
    $stmt->execute([$_POST['article_id']]);
    // get number of affected rows
    $deleted = $stmt->rowCount();
    if (!$deleted) {
        $error = 'There was a problem deleting the record.';
        $error .= $stmt->errorInfo()[2];
    }
}
```

You can find the finished code in blog_delete_mysqli.php and blog_delete_pdo.php in the ch15 folder. To test the delete script, copy the appropriate file to the admin folder.

Reviewing the Four Essential SQL Commands

Now that you have seen SELECT, INSERT, UPDATE, and DELETE in action, let's review the basic syntax for MySQL and MariaDB. This is not an exhaustive listing, but it concentrates on the most important options, including some that have not yet been covered.

I have used the same typographic conventions as the MySQL online manual at `https://dev.mysql.com/doc/refman/8.0/en/` (which you may also want to consult):

- Anything in uppercase is an SQL command.

- Expressions in square brackets are optional.

- Lowercase italics represent variable input.

- A vertical pipe (|) separates alternatives.

Although some expressions are optional, they must appear in the order listed. For example, in a SELECT query, WHERE, ORDER BY, and LIMIT are all optional, but LIMIT can never come before WHERE or ORDER BY.

SELECT

SELECT is used for retrieving records from one or more tables. Its basic syntax is as follows:

```
SELECT [DISTINCT] select_list
FROM table_list
[WHERE where_expression]
[ORDER BY col_name | formula] [ASC | DESC]
[LIMIT [skip_count,] show_count]
```

The DISTINCT option tells the database you want to eliminate duplicate rows from the results.

The *select_list* is a comma-separated list of columns that you want included in the result. To retrieve all columns, use an asterisk (*). If the same column name is used in more than one table, the references must be unambiguous, using the syntax *table_name.column_name*. Chapters 17 and 18 explain in detail about working with multiple tables.

The *table_list* is a comma-separated list of tables from which the results are to be drawn. All tables that you want to be included in the results *must* be listed.

The WHERE clause specifies search criteria, for example:

```
WHERE quotations.family_name = authors.family_name
WHERE article_id = 2
```

WHERE expressions can use comparison, arithmetic, logical, and pattern-matching operators. The most important ones are listed in Table 15-2.

Table 15-2. *The main operators used in MySQL WHERE expressions*

Comparison		Arithmetic	
<	Less than	+	Addition
<=	Less than or equal to	-	Subtraction
=	Equal to	*	Multiplication
!=	Not equal to	/	Division
<>	Not equal to	DIV	Integer division
>	Greater than	%	Modulus
>=	Greater than or equal to		
IN()	Included in list		
BETWEEN *min* AND *max*	Between (and including two values)		
Logical		**Pattern matching**	
AND	Logical and	LIKE	Case-insensitive match
&&	Logical and	NOT LIKE	Case-insensitive nonmatch
OR	Logical or	LIKE BINARY	Case-sensitive match
||	Logical or (best avoided)	NOT LIKE BINARY	Case-sensitive nonmatch

Of the two operators that mean "not equal to," <> is standard SQL. Not all databases support !=.

DIV is the counterpart of the modulus operator. It produces the result of division as an integer with no fractional part, whereas modulus produces only the remainder:

```
5 / 2       /* result 2.5 */
5 DIV 2     /* result 2   */
5 % 2       /* result 1   */
```

I suggest you avoid using || because it's actually used as the string concatenation operator in standard SQL. By not using it with MySQL, you avoid confusion if you ever work with a different relational database. To join strings, MySQL uses the CONCAT() function (see https://dev.mysql.com/doc/refman/8.0/en/string-functions.html#function_concat).

IN() evaluates a comma-separated list of values inside the parentheses and returns true if one or more of the values is found. Although BETWEEN is normally used with numbers, it also applies to strings. For instance, BETWEEN 'a' AND 'd' returns true for *a, b, c,* and *d* (but not their uppercase equivalents). Both IN() and BETWEEN can be preceded by NOT to perform the opposite comparison.

LIKE, NOT LIKE, and the related BINARY operators are used for text searches in combination with the following two wildcard characters:

- %: Matches any sequence of characters or none

- _ (an underscore): Matches exactly one character

So the following WHERE clause matches Dennis, Denise, and so on, but not Aiden:

```
WHERE first_name LIKE 'den%'
```

To match Aiden, put % at the front of the search pattern. Because % matches any sequence of characters or none, '%den%' still matches Dennis and Denise. To search for a literal percentage sign or underscore, precede it with a backslash (\% or _).

Conditions are evaluated from left to right but can be grouped in parentheses if you want a set of conditions to be considered together.

ORDER BY specifies the sort order of the results. This can be specified as a single column, a comma-separated list of columns, or an expression such as RAND(), which randomizes the order. The default sort order is ascending (a–z, 0–9), but you can specify DESC (descending) to reverse the order.

LIMIT followed by one number stipulates the maximum number of records to return. If two numbers are given separated by a comma, the first tells the database how many rows to skip (see "Selecting a Subset of Records" in Chapter 14).

See https://dev.mysql.com/doc/refman/8.0/en/select.html for more details on SELECT.

INSERT

The INSERT command is used to add new records to a database. The general syntax is as follows:

```
INSERT [INTO] table_name (column_names)
VALUES (values)
```

The word INTO is optional; it simply makes the command read a little more like human language. The column names and values are comma-delimited lists, and both must be in the same order. So, to insert the forecast for New York (blizzard), Detroit (smog), and Honolulu (sunny) into a weather database, this is how you would do it:

```
INSERT INTO forecast (new_york, detroit, honolulu)
VALUES ('blizzard', 'smog', 'sunny')
```

The reason for this syntax is to allow you to insert more than one record at a time. Each subsequent record is in a separate set of parentheses, with each set separated by a comma:

```
INSERT numbers (x,y)
VALUES (10,20),(20,30),(30,40),(40,50)
```

You'll use this multiple insert syntax in Chapter 18. Any columns omitted from an INSERT query are set to their default value. *Never set an explicit value for the primary key where the column is set to* AUTO_INCREMENT; leave the column name out of the INSERT statement.

For more details, see https://dev.mysql.com/doc/refman/8.0/en/insert.html.

UPDATE

This command is used to change existing records. The basic syntax looks like this:

```
UPDATE table_name
SET col_name = value [, col_name = value]
[WHERE where_expression]
```

The WHERE expression tells MySQL which record or records you want to update (or perhaps in the case of the following example, dream about):

```
UPDATE sales SET q4_2021 = 25000
WHERE title = 'PHP 8 Solutions, Fifth Edition'
```

See https://dev.mysql.com/doc/refman/8.0/en/update.html for more details on UPDATE.

DELETE

DELETE can be used to delete single records, multiple records, or the entire contents of a table. The general syntax for deleting from a single table is as follows:

```
DELETE FROM table_name [WHERE where_expression]
```

Although phpMyAdmin prompts you for confirmation before deleting a record, databases take you at your word and perform the deletion immediately. DELETE is totally unforgiving—once the data is deleted, it is gone *forever*. The following query will delete all records from a table called subscribers where the date in expiry_date has already passed:

```
DELETE FROM subscribers
WHERE expiry_date < NOW()
```

For more details, see https://dev.mysql.com/doc/refman/8.0/en/delete.html.

■ **Caution**   Although the WHERE clause is optional in both UPDATE and DELETE, you should be aware that if you leave WHERE out, the entire table is affected. This means that a careless slip with either of these commands could result in every single record being identical—or wiped out.

Security and Error Messages

When developing a web site with PHP and a database, it's essential to display error messages so that you can debug your code if anything goes wrong. However, raw error messages look unprofessional in a live web site. They can also reveal clues about your database structure to potential attackers. Therefore, before deploying your scripts live on the Internet, you should replace the error messages generated by the database with a neutral message of your own, such as "Sorry, the database is unavailable."

Chapter Review

Content management with a database involves inserting, selecting, updating, and deleting records. Each record's primary key plays a vital role in the update and delete processes. Most of the time, generating the primary key is handled automatically by the database when a record is first created. Thereafter, finding a record's primary key is simply a matter of using a SELECT query, either by displaying a list of all records or by searching for something you know about the record, such as a title or words in an article.

MySQLi and PDO prepared statements make database queries more secure by removing the need to ensure that quotes and control characters are properly escaped. They also speed up your application if the same query needs to be repeated during a script using different variables. Instead of validating the SQL every time, the script needs to do it only once with the placeholders.

Although this chapter has concentrated on content management, the same basic techniques apply to most interaction with a database. Of course, there's a lot more to SQL—and to PHP. In the next chapter, I'll address some of the most common problems, such as displaying only the first sentence or so of a long text field and handling dates. Then in Chapter 17 we'll explore working with more than one table in a database.

■ ■ ■

Formatting Text and Dates

We have some unfinished business left over from the previous chapter. Figure 15-1 in Chapter 15 shows content from the blog table with just the first two sentences of each article displayed and a link to the rest of the article. However, I didn't show you how it was done. There are several ways to extract a shorter piece of text from the beginning of a longer one. Some are rather crude and usually leave you with a broken word at the end. In this chapter, you'll learn how to extract complete sentences.

The other unfinished business is that the full list of articles in blog_list_mysqli.php and blog_list_pdo.php displays the MySQL timestamp in its raw state, which isn't very elegant. You need to reformat the date to look more user-friendly. Handling dates can be a major headache because MySQL and MariaDB store them in a completely different way from PHP. This chapter guides you through the minefield of storing and displaying dates in a PHP/MySQL context. You'll also learn about PHP date and time features that make complex date calculations, such as finding the second Tuesday of each month, child's play.

In this chapter, you'll learn about the following:

- Extracting the first section of a longer text item

- Using an alias in an SQL query

- Displaying text retrieved from a database as paragraphs

- Formatting dates with MySQL

- Selecting records based on temporal criteria

- Using the PHP DateTime, DateTimeZone, DateInterval, and DatePeriod classes

Displaying a Text Extract

There are many ways to extract the first few lines or characters from a longer piece of text. Sometimes you need just the first 20 or 30 characters to identify an item. At other times, it's preferable to show complete sentences or paragraphs.

Extracting a Fixed Number of Characters

You can extract a fixed number of characters from the beginning of a text item either with the PHP substr() function or with the LEFT() function in an SQL query.

© David Powers 2022
D. Powers, *PHP 8 Solutions*, https://doi.org/10.1007/978-1-4842-7141-4_16

■ **Note**   The following examples pass the text to the safe() function defined in Chapter 13. This sanitizes text from external sources by converting ampersands, double quotes, and angle brackets to their HTML character entity equivalents, but prevents existing entities from being double encoded. The function definition is included in the file utility_funcs.php.

Using the PHP substr() Function

The substr() function extracts a substring from a longer string. It takes three arguments: the string you want to extract the substring from, the starting point (counted from 0), and the number of characters to extract. The following code displays the first 100 characters of $row['article']:

```
echo safe(substr($row['article'], 0, 100));
```

The original string remains intact. If you omit the third argument, substr() extracts everything to the end of the string. This makes sense only if you choose a starting point other than 0.

Using the LEFT() Function in an SQL Query

The LEFT() function extracts characters from the beginning of a column. It takes two arguments: the column name and the number of characters to extract. The following retrieves article_id, title, and the first 100 characters from the article column of the blog table:

```
SELECT article_id, title, LEFT(article, 100)
FROM blog ORDER BY created DESC
```

Whenever you use a function in an SQL query like this, the column name no longer appears in the result set as article, but as LEFT(article, 100) instead. So it's a good idea to assign an **alias** to the affected column using the AS keyword. You can either reassign the column's original name as the alias or use a descriptive name as in the following example (the code is in blog_left_mysqli.php and blog_left_pdo. php in the ch16 folder):

```
SELECT article_id, title, LEFT(article, 100) AS first100
FROM blog ORDER BY created DESC
```

If you process each record as $row, the extract is in $row['first100']. To retrieve both the first 100 characters and the full article, simply include both in the query like this:

```
SELECT article_id, title, LEFT(article, 100) AS first100, article
FROM blog ORDER BY created DESC
```

Taking a fixed number of characters produces a crude result, as Figure 16-1 shows.

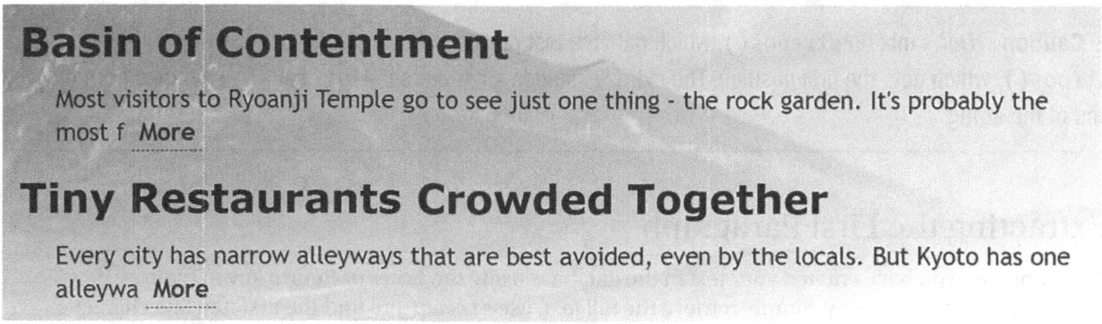

Basin of Contentment

Most visitors to Ryoanji Temple go to see just one thing - the rock garden. It's probably the most f **More**

Tiny Restaurants Crowded Together

Every city has narrow alleyways that are best avoided, even by the locals. But Kyoto has one alleywa **More**

Figure 16-1. *Selecting the first 100 characters from an article chops many words in half*

Ending an Extract on a Complete Word

To end an extract on a complete word, you need to find the final space and use that to determine the length of the substring. So, if you want the extract to be a maximum of 100 characters, use either of the preceding methods to start with, and store the result in $extract. Then you can use the PHP string functions strrpos() and substr() to find the last space and end the extract like this (the code is in blog_word_mysqli.php and blog_word_pdo.php):

```
$extract = $row['first100'];
// find position of last space in extract
$lastSpace = strrpos($extract, ' ');
// use $lastSpace to set length of new extract and add ...
echo safe(substr($extract, 0, $lastSpace)) . '... ';
```

This produces the more elegant result shown in Figure 16-2. It uses strrpos(), which finds the last position of a character or substring within another string. Since you're looking for a space, the second argument is a pair of quotes with a single space between them. The result is stored in $lastSpace, which is passed as the third argument to substr(), finishing the extract on a complete word. Finally, add a string containing three dots and a space, and join the two with the concatenation operator (a period or dot).

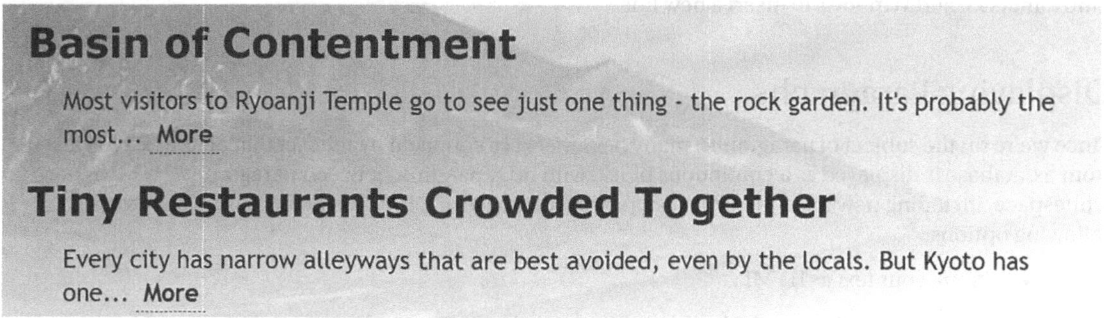

Basin of Contentment

Most visitors to Ryoanji Temple go to see just one thing - the rock garden. It's probably the most... **More**

Tiny Restaurants Crowded Together

Every city has narrow alleyways that are best avoided, even by the locals. But Kyoto has one... **More**

Figure 16-2. *Ending the extract on a complete word produces a more elegant result*

■ **Caution** Don't mix up strrpos(), which gets the last position of a character or substring, with strpos(), which gets the first position. The extra "r" stands for "reverse"—strrpos() searches from the end of the string.

Extracting the First Paragraph

Assuming that you have entered your text in the database using the Enter or Return key to indicate new paragraphs, this is very easy. Simply retrieve the full text, use strpos() to find the first newline character, and use substr() to extract the first section of text up to that point.

The following SQL query is used in blog_para_mysqli.php and blog_para_pdo.php:

```
SELECT article_id, title, article
FROM blog ORDER BY created DESC
```

The following code is used to display the first paragraph of article:

```
<?= safe(substr($row['article'], 0, strpos($row['article'], PHP_EOL))) ?>
```

Let's break it up and take a look at the third argument on its own:

```
strpos($row['article'], PHP_EOL)
```

This locates the first end of line character in $row['article'] in a cross-platform way using the PHP_EOL constant (see "Appending Content with fopen()" in Chapter 7). You could rewrite the code like this:

```
$newLine = strpos($row['article'], PHP_EOL);
echo safe(substr($row['article'], 0, $newLine));
```

Both sets of code do exactly the same thing, but PHP lets you nest a function as an argument passed to another function. As long as the nested function returns a valid result, you can frequently use shortcuts like this.

Using the PHP_EOL constant eliminates the problem of dealing with the different characters used by Linux, macOS, and Windows to insert a new line.

Displaying Paragraphs

Since we're on the subject of paragraphs, many beginners are confused by the fact that all the text retrieved from a database is displayed as a continuous block, with no separation between paragraphs. HTML ignores whitespace, including new lines. To get text stored in a database displayed as paragraphs, you have the following options:

- Store your text as HTML.
- Convert new lines to <br/> tags.
- Create a custom function to replace new lines with paragraph tags.

Storing Database Records as HTML

The first option involves installing an HTML editor, such as CKEditor (https://ckeditor.com/) or TinyMCE (www.tiny.cloud/), in your content management forms. Mark up your text as you insert or update it. The HTML is stored in the database, and the text displays as intended. Installing one of these editors is beyond the scope of this book.

■ **Note**   If you store text as HTML in a database, you can't use the `safe()` function to display it because the HTML tags will be displayed as part of the text. Instead, use `strip_tags()` and specify which tags are permitted (see "Accessing Remote Files" in Chapter 7 and www.php.net/manual/en/function.strip-tags.php).

Converting New Lines to
 Tags

The simplest option is to pass your text to the `nl2br()` function before displaying it, like this:

```
echo nl2br(safe($row['article']));
```

Voilà! Paragraphs. Well, not really. The `nl2br()` function converts newline characters to `<br/>` tags (the closing slash is for compatibility with XHTML and is valid in HTML5). As a result, you get fake paragraphs. It's a quick and dirty solution, but not ideal.

■ **Tip**   Using `nl2br()` is a suboptimal solution. But if you decide to use it, you must sanitize the text before passing it to `nl2br()`. Otherwise, the angle brackets of the `<br />` tags will be converted to HTML character entities, resulting in them being displayed in your text rather as tags in the underlying HTML.

Creating a Function to Insert <p> Tags

To display text retrieved from a database as genuine paragraphs, wrap the database result in a pair of paragraph tags, and then use the `preg_replace()` function to convert consecutive newline characters to a closing `</p>` tag, immediately followed by an opening `<p>` tag, like this:

```
<p><?= preg_replace('/[\r\n]+/', "</p>\n<p>", safe($row['article'])); ?></p>
```

The regular expression used as the first argument matches one or more carriage returns and/or newline characters. You can't use the `PHP_EOL` constant here because you need to match all consecutive newline characters and replace them with a single pair of paragraph tags. The pair of `<p>` tags is in double quotes, with `\n` between them to add a newline character, in order to make the HTML code easier to read. Remembering the pattern for a regex can be difficult, so you can easily convert this into a custom function, like this:

```
function convertToParas($text) {
    $text = trim($text);
    $text = htmlspecialchars($text, double_encode: false);
    return '<p>' . preg_replace('/[\r\n]+/', "</p>\n<p>", $text) . "</p>\n";
}
```

This trims whitespace, including newline characters, from the beginning and end of the text, which it then sanitizes by passing it to the htmlspecialchars() function with the double_encode named argument to prevent the ampersand of HTML entities from being converted to &. The second line of code inside the function is the same as in the safe() function that was defined in Chapter 13. The final line adds a <p> tag at the beginning, replaces internal sequences of newline characters with closing and opening tags, and appends a closing </p> tag and newline character at the end.

You can then use the function like this:

```
<?= convertToParas($row['article']); ?>
```

The code for the function definition is in an updated version of utility_funcs.php in the ch16 folder. You can see it being used in blog_ptags_mysqli.php and blog_ptags_pdo.php.

■ **Note** Although the updated version of utility_funcs.php contains both the safe() and convertToParas() function definitions, I decided against calling the safe() function inside convertToParas() because it would have created a potentially unstable dependency. If, at some stage in the future, you decided to employ a different way of sanitizing text and deleted the safe() function definition, invoking convertToParas() would trigger a fatal error because it relies on a custom function that would no longer exist.

Extracting Complete Sentences

PHP has no concept of what constitutes a sentence. Counting periods means you ignore all sentences that end with an exclamation point or a question mark. You also run the risk of breaking a sentence on a decimal point or cutting off a closing quote after a period. To overcome these problems, I have devised a PHP function called getFirst() that identifies the punctuation at the end of a normal sentence:

- A period, question mark, or exclamation point

- Optionally followed by a single or double quote

- Followed by one or more spaces

The getFirst() function takes two arguments: the text from which you want to extract the first section and the number of sentences you want to extract. The second argument is optional; if it's not supplied, the function extracts the first two sentences. The code looks like this (it's in utility_funcs.php):

```
function getFirst($text, $number=2) {
    // use regex to split into sentences
    $sentences = preg_split('/([.?!]["\']?\s)/', $text, $number+1,
        PREG_SPLIT_DELIM_CAPTURE);
    if (count($sentences) > $number * 2) {
        $remainder = array_pop($sentences);
    } else {
        $remainder = '';
    }
    $result = [];
    $result[0] = implode('', $sentences);
```

```
$result[1] = $remainder;
return $result;
}
```

This function returns an array containing two elements: the extracted sentences and any text that's left over. You can use the second element to create a link to a page containing the full text.

The line highlighted in bold uses a regex to identify the end of each sentence—a period, question mark, or exclamation point, optionally followed by a double or single quotation mark and a space. This is passed as the first argument to preg_split(), which uses the regex to split the text into an array. The second argument is the target text. The third argument determines the maximum number of chunks to split the text into. You want one more than the number of sentences to be extracted. Normally, preg_split() discards the characters matched by the regex, but using PREG_SPLIT_DELIM_CAPTURE as the fourth argument together with a pair of capturing parentheses in the regex preserves them as separate array elements. In other words, the elements of the $sentences array consist alternately of the text of a sentence followed by the punctuation and space, like this:

```
$sentences[0] = '"Hello, world';
$sentences[1] = '!" ';
```

It's impossible to know in advance how many sentences there are in the target text, so you need to find out if there's anything remaining after extracting the desired number of sentences. The conditional statement uses count() to ascertain the number of elements in the $sentences array and compares the result with $number multiplied by 2 (because the array contains two elements for each sentence). If there's more text, array_pop() removes the last element of the $sentences array and assigns it to $remainder. If there's no further text, $remainder is an empty string.

The final stage of the function uses implode() with an empty string as its first argument to stitch the extracted sentences back together and then returns a two-element array containing the extracted text and anything that's left over.

Don't worry if you found that explanation hard to follow. The code is quite advanced. It took a lot of experimentation to build the function, and I have improved it gradually over the years.

PHP Solution 16-1: Displaying the First Two Sentences of an Article

This PHP solution shows how to display an extract from each article in the blog table using the getFirst() function described in the preceding section. If you created the Japan Journey site earlier in the book, use blog.php. Alternatively, use blog_01.php from the ch16 folder and save it as blog.php in the php8sols site root. You also need footer.php, menu.php, title.php, and connection.php in the includes folder. There are copies of these files in the ch16 folder if you don't already have them in the includes folder.

1. Copy the updated version of utility_funcs.php from the ch16 folder to the includes folder, and include it in blog.php in the PHP code block above the DOCTYPE declaration. Also include connection.php and create a connection to the database. This page needs read-only privileges, so use read as the argument passed to dbConnect(), like this:

```
require_once './includes/connection.php';
require_once './includes/utility_funcs.php';
// create database connection
$conn = dbConnect('read');
```

Add 'pdo' as the second argument to dbConnect() if you're using PDO.

2. Prepare an SQL query to retrieve all records from the blog table and then submit it, like this:

```
$sql = 'SELECT * FROM blog ORDER BY created DESC';
$result = $conn->query($sql);
```

3. Add the code to check for a database error.

```
For MySQLi, use this:if (!$result) {
    $error = $conn->error;
}
```

For PDO, call the errorInfo() method and check for the existence of the third array element, like this:

```
$errorInfo = $conn->errorInfo();
if (isset($errorInfo[2])) {
    $error = $errorInfo[2];
}
```

4. Delete all the static HTML inside the <main> element in the body of the page, and add the code to display the error message if a problem arises with the query:

```
<main>
<?php if (isset($error)) {
    echo "<p>$error</p>";
} else {
}
?>
</main>
```

5. Create a loop inside the else block to display the results:

```
while ($row = $result->fetch_assoc()) {
    echo "<h2>{$row['title']}</h2>";
    $extract = getFirst($row['article']);
    echo '<p>' . safe($extract[0]);
    if ($extract[1]) {
        echo '<a href="details.php?article_id=' . $row['article_id'] . '">
            More</a>';
    }
    echo '</p>';
}
```

The code is the same for PDO, except for this line:

```
while ($row = $result->fetch_assoc()) {
```

Replace it with this:

```
while ($row = $result->fetch()) {
```

450

The getFirst() function processes $row['article'] and stores the result in $extract. The first two sentences of article in $extract[0] are immediately displayed. If $extract[1] contains anything, it means there is more to display. So the code inside the if block displays a link to details.php, with the article's primary key in a query string.

6. Save the page and test it in a browser. You should see the first two sentences of each article displayed as shown in Figure 16-3.

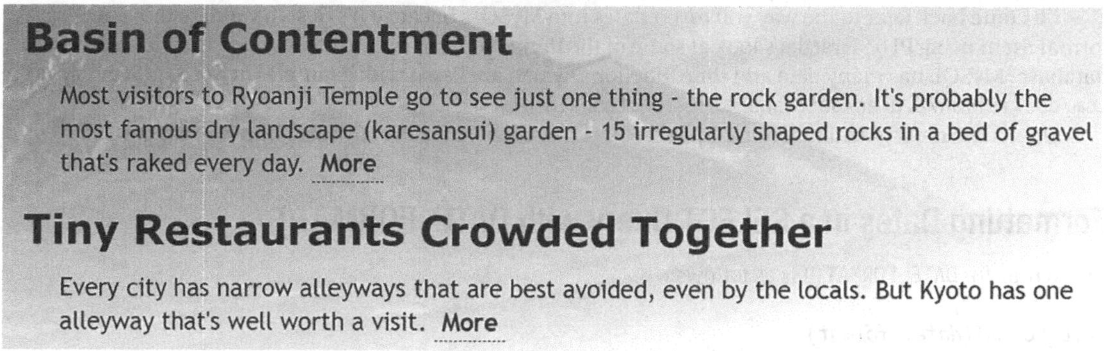

Basin of Contentment

Most visitors to Ryoanji Temple go to see just one thing - the rock garden. It's probably the most famous dry landscape (karesansui) garden - 15 irregularly shaped rocks in a bed of gravel that's raked every day. More

Tiny Restaurants Crowded Together

Every city has narrow alleyways that are best avoided, even by the locals. But Kyoto has one alleyway that's well worth a visit. More

Figure 16-3. *The first two sentences have been extracted cleanly from the longer text*

7. Test the function by adding a number as a second argument to getFirst(), like this:

```
$extract = getFirst($row['article'], 3);
```

This displays the first three sentences. If you increase the number so that it equals or exceeds the number of sentences in an article, the More link won't be displayed.

You can compare your code with blog_mysqli.php and blog_pdo.php in the ch16 folder.

We'll look at details.php in Chapter 17. Before that, let's tackle the minefield presented by using dates in a dynamic web site.

Let's Make a Date

Dates and time are so fundamental to modern life that we rarely pause to think how complex they are. There are 60 seconds to a minute and 60 minutes to an hour, but 24 hours to a day. Months range between 28 and 31 days, and a year can be either 365 or 366 days. The confusion doesn't stop there, because 7/4 means July 4 to an American or Japanese person, but 7 April to a European. To add to the confusion, PHP handles dates differently from MySQL. Time to bring order to chaos...

■ **Note**   MariaDB handles dates the same way. To avoid unnecessary repetition, I'll refer only to MySQL.

How MySQL Handles Dates

In MySQL, dates and time are always expressed in descending order from the largest unit to the smallest: year, month, date, hour, minutes, seconds. Hours are always measured using the 24-hour clock, with midnight expressed as 00:00:00. Even if this seems unfamiliar to you, it's the recommendation laid down by the International Organization for Standardization (ISO).

MySQL allows considerable flexibility about the separator between the units (any punctuation symbol is acceptable), but there is no argument about the order—it's fixed. If you attempt to store a date in any other format than year, month, date, MySQL inserts 0000-00-00 in the database.

I'll come back later to the way you insert dates into MySQL, because it's best to validate them and format them using PHP. First, let's look at some of the things you can do with dates once they're stored in a database. MySQL has many date and time functions, which are listed with examples at `https://dev.mysql.com/doc/refman/8.0/en/date-and-time-functions.html`.

One of the most useful functions is `DATE_FORMAT()`, which does exactly what its name suggests.

Formatting Dates in a SELECT Query with DATE_FORMAT()

The syntax for `DATE_FORMAT()` is as follows:

```
DATE_FORMAT(date, format)
```

Normally, *date* is the table column to be formatted, and *format* is a string composed of formatting specifiers and any other text you want to include. Table 16-1 lists the most common specifiers, all of which are case-sensitive.

Table 16-1. *Frequently used MySQL date format specifiers*

Period	Specifier	Description	Example
Year	%Y	Four-digit format	2021
	%y	Two-digit format	21
Month	%M	Full name	January, September
	%b	Abbreviated name, three letters	Jan, Sep
	%m	Number with leading zero	01, 09
	%c	Number without leading zero	1, 9
Day of month	%d	With leading zero	01, 25
	%e	Without leading zero	1, 25
	%D	With English text suffix	1st, 25th
Weekday name	%W	Full text	Monday, Thursday
	%a	Abbreviated name, three letters	Mon, Thu

(*continued*)

Table 16-1. *(continued)*

Period	Specifier	Description	Example
Hour	%H	24-hour clock with leading zero	01, 23
	%k	24-hour clock without leading zero	1, 23
	%h	12-hour clock with leading zero	01, 11
	%l (lowercase "L")	12-hour clock without leading zero	1, 11
Minutes	%i	With leading zero	05, 25
Seconds	%S	With leading zero	08, 45
AM/PM	%p		

As explained earlier, when using a function in an SQL query, assign the result to an alias using the AS keyword. Referring to Table 16-1, you can format the date in the created column of the blog table in a common US style and assign it to an alias, like this:

```
DATE_FORMAT(created, '%c/%e/%Y') AS date_created
```

To format the same date in the European style, reverse the first two specifiers, like this:

```
DATE_FORMAT(created, '%e/%c/%Y') AS date_created
```

■ **Tip** When using DATE_FORMAT(), don't use the original column name as the alias, because the values are converted to strings, which plays havoc with the sort order. Choose a different alias, and use the original column name to sort the results.

PHP Solution 16-2: Formatting a MySQL Date or Timestamp

This PHP solution formats the dates in the blog entry management page from Chapter 15.

1. Open blog_list_mysqli.php or blog_list_pdo.php in the admin folder and locate the SQL query. It looks like this:

   ```
   $sql = 'SELECT * FROM blog ORDER BY created DESC';
   ```

2. Change it like this:

   ```
   $sql = 'SELECT article_id, title,
   DATE_FORMAT(created, "%a, %b %D, %Y") AS date_created
               FROM blog ORDER BY created DESC';
   ```

   I used single quotes around the whole SQL query, so the format string inside DATE_FORMAT() needs to be in double quotes.

   Make sure there is no gap before the opening parenthesis of DATE_FORMAT().

The format string begins with %a, which displays the first three letters of the weekday name. If you use the original column name as the alias, the ORDER BY clause sorts the dates in reverse alphabetical order: Wed, Thu, Sun, and so on. Using a different alias ensures that the dates are still ordered chronologically.

3. In the first table cell in the body of the page, change $row['created'] to $row['**date**_created'] to match the alias in the SQL query.

4. Save the page and load it into a browser. The dates should now be formatted as shown in Figure 16-4. Experiment with other specifiers to suit your preferences.

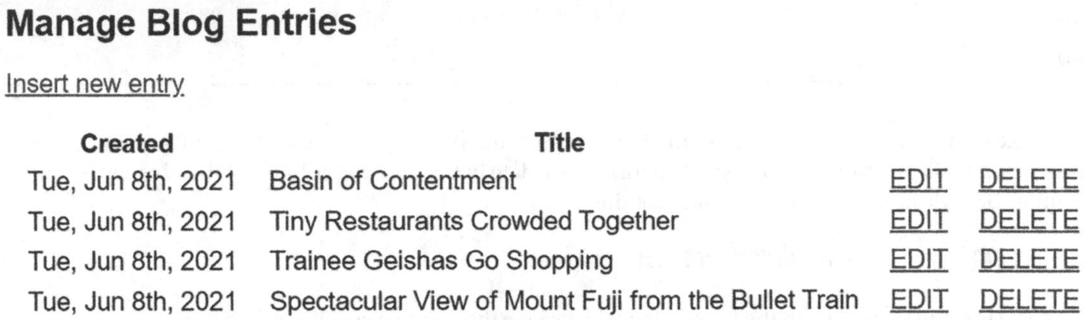

Manage Blog Entries

Insert new entry

Created	Title		
Tue, Jun 8th, 2021	Basin of Contentment	EDIT	DELETE
Tue, Jun 8th, 2021	Tiny Restaurants Crowded Together	EDIT	DELETE
Tue, Jun 8th, 2021	Trainee Geishas Go Shopping	EDIT	DELETE
Tue, Jun 8th, 2021	Spectacular View of Mount Fuji from the Bullet Train	EDIT	DELETE

Figure 16-4. The MySQL timestamps are now nicely formatted

Updated versions of blog_list_mysqli.php and blog_list_pdo.php are in the ch16 folder.

Adding to and Subtracting from Dates

When working with dates, it's often useful to add or subtract a specific time period. For instance, you may want to display items that have been added to the database within the past 7 days or stop displaying articles that haven't been updated for 3 months. MySQL makes this easy with DATE_ADD() and DATE_SUB(). Both functions have synonyms called ADDDATE() and SUBDATE(), respectively.

The basic syntax is the same for all of them and looks like this:

```
DATE_ADD(date, INTERVAL value interval_type)
```

When using these functions, *date* can be the column containing the date you want to alter, a string containing a particular date (in YYYY-MM-DD format), or a MySQL function, such as NOW(). INTERVAL is a keyword followed by a value and an interval type, the most common of which are listed in Table 16-2.

Table 16-2. *Most frequently used interval types with DATE_ADD() and DATE_SUB()*

Interval type	Meaning	Value format
DAY	Days	Number
DAY_HOUR	Days and hours	String presented as 'DD hh'
WEEK	Weeks	Number
MONTH	Months	Number
QUARTER	Quarters	Number
YEAR	Years	Number
YEAR_MONTH	Years and months	String presented as 'YY-MM'

The interval types are constants, so do *not* add "S" to the end of DAY, WEEK, and so on to make them plural.

One of the most useful applications of these functions is to display only the most recent items in a table.

PHP Solution 16-3: Displaying Items Updated Within the Past Week

This PHP solution shows how to limit the display of database results according to a specific time interval. Use blog.php from PHP Solution 16-1.

1. Locate the SQL query in blog.php. It looks like this:

    ```
    $sql = 'SELECT * FROM blog ORDER BY created DESC';
    ```

2. Change it like this:

    ```
    $sql = 'SELECT * FROM blog
    WHERE updated > DATE_SUB(NOW(), INTERVAL 1 WEEK)
                ORDER BY created DESC';
    ```

    This tells MySQL that you want only items that have been updated in the past week.

3. Save and reload the page in your browser. Depending on when you last updated an item in the blog table, you should see either nothing or a limited range of items. If necessary, change the interval type to DAY or HOUR to test that the time limit is working.

4. Open blog_list_mysqli.php or blog_list_pdo.php, select an item that isn't displayed in blog.php, and edit it. Reload blog.php. The item that you have just updated should now be displayed.

You can compare your code with blog_limit_mysqli.php and blog_limit_pdo.php in the ch16 folder.

Inserting Dates into MySQL

MySQL's requirement for dates to be formatted as YYYY-MM-DD presents a headache for online forms that allow users to input dates. As you saw in Chapter 15, the current date and time can be inserted automatically by using a TIMESTAMP column. You can also use the MySQL NOW() function to insert the current date in a DATE or DATETIME column. It's when you need any other date that problems arise.

The HTML5 date input type should, in theory, have solved the problem. Browsers that support date input fields usually display a date picker when the field gets focus and insert the date in the local format. There's an example in date_test.php in the ch16 folder. Figure 16-5 shows how Google Chrome displays the date on my computer in the correct European format; but when the form is submitted, the value is converted to the ISO format. Although the vast majority of browsers in current use now support date input fields, it's wise to treat date input fields with caution.

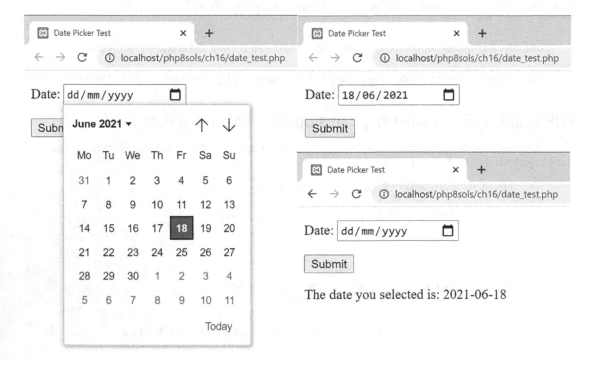

Figure 16-5. *HTML5 date input fields display dates in local format, but submit them in the ISO format*

Using a single input field for a date relies on the user's browser supporting HTML5 date input correctly or trusting the user to follow a set pattern for inputting dates, such as MM/DD/YYYY. If everybody complies, you can use the explode() function to rearrange the date parts, like this:

```
if (isset($_POST['theDate'])) {
    $date = explode('/', $_POST['theDate']);
    $mysqlFormat = "$date[2]-$date[0]-$date[1]";
}
```

If someone deviates from the format, you end up with invalid dates in your database.

Consequently, the most reliable method of gathering dates from an online form remains the use of separate input fields for month, day, and year.

PHP Solution 16-4: Validating and Formatting Dates for MySQL Input

This PHP solution concentrates on checking the validity of a date and converting it to MySQL format. It's designed to be incorporated in an insert or update form of your own.

1. Create a page called date_converter.php and insert a form containing the following code (or use date_converter_01.php in the ch16 folder):

```
<form method="post" action="date_converter.php">
    <p>
        <label for="month">Month:</label>
        <select name="month" id="month">
            <option value=""></option>
        </select>
        <label for="day">Date:</label>
        <input name="day" type="number" required id="day" max="31" min="1"
            maxlength="2">
        <label for="year">Year:</label>
        <input name="year" type="number" required id="year" maxlength="4">
    </p>
    <p>
        <input type="submit" name="convert" id="convert" value="Convert">
    </p>
</form>
```

This creates a drop-down menu called month and two input fields called day and year. The drop-down menu doesn't have any values at the moment, but it will be populated by a PHP loop. The day and year fields use the HTML5 number type and required attribute. The day field also has the max and min attributes so as to restrict the range to between 1 and 31. Browsers that support the new HTML5 form elements display number steppers alongside the fields and restrict the type and range of input. Other browsers render them as ordinary text input fields. For the benefit of older browsers, both have maxlength attributes that limit the number of characters accepted.

2. Amend the section that builds the drop-down menu, like this:

```
<select name="month" id="month">
    <?php
    $months = ['Jan','Feb','Mar','Apr','May','Jun',
        'Jul','Aug', 'Sep', 'Oct', 'Nov','Dec'];
    $thisMonth = date('n');
    for ($i = 1; $i <= 12; $i++) { ?>
        <option value="<?= $i ?>"
            <?php
            if ((!$_POST && $i == $thisMonth) ||
                (isset($_POST['month']) && $i == $_POST['month'])) {
                echo ' selected';
            } ?>>
            <?= $months[$i - 1] ?>
        </option>
    <?php } ?>
</select>
```

457

This creates an array of month names and uses the date() function to find the number of the current month (the meaning of the argument passed to date() is explained later in this chapter).

A for loop then populates the menu's <option> tags. I have set the initial value of $i to 1, because I want to use it for the value of the month. Inside the loop, the conditional statement checks two sets of conditions, both of which are enclosed in parentheses to ensure they're evaluated in the correct sequence. The first set checks that the $_POST array is empty and the values of $i and $thisMonth are the same. But if the form has been submitted, $_POST['month'] will have been set, so the alternative set of conditions checks whether $i is the same as $_POST['month']. As a result, when the form is first loaded, selected is inserted into the <option> tag for the current month. But if the form has already been submitted, the month selected by the user is displayed again.

The name of the month is displayed between the <option> tags by drawing it from the $months array. Because indexed arrays begin at 0, you need to subtract 1 from the value of $i to get the right month.

3. Also populate the fields for the day and year with the current date or the value selected after the form has been submitted:

```
<label for="day">Date:</label>
<input name="day" type="number" required id="day" max="31" min="1"
    maxlength="2" value="<?php if (!$_POST) {
            echo date('j');
        } elseif (isset($_POST['day'])) {
            echo safe($_POST['day']);
        } ?>">
<label for="year">Year:</label>
<input name="year" type="number" required id="year" maxlength="4"
        value="<?php if (!$_POST) {
            echo date('Y');
        } elseif (isset($_POST['year'])) {
            echo safe($_POST['year']);
        }
} ?>">
```

4. Save the page and test it in a browser. It should display the current date and look similar to Figure 16-6.

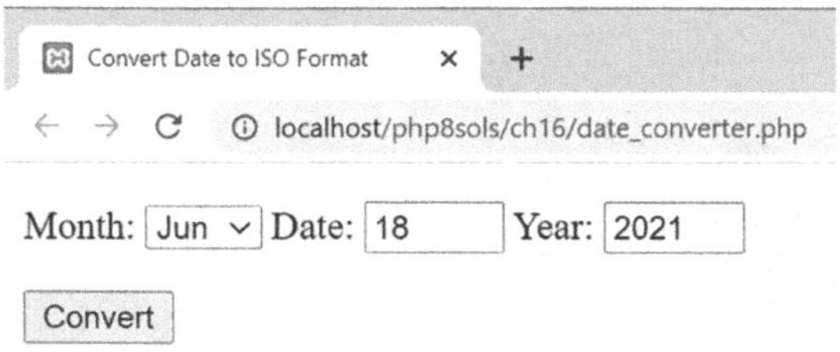

Figure 16-6. Using separate input fields for date parts helps eliminate errors

If you test the input fields, in most browsers the Date field should accept no more than two characters and the Year field a maximum of four. Even though this reduces the possibility of mistakes, you still need to validate the input and format the date correctly.

5. The code that performs all the checks is a custom function in `utility_funcs.php`. It looks like this:

```
function convertDateToISO(int $month, int $day, int $year) {
    $month = trim($month);
    $day = trim($day);
    $year = trim($year);
    if (empty($month) || empty($day) || empty($year)) {
        throw new Exception('Please fill in all fields');
    } elseif (($month < 1 || $month > 12) || ($day < 1 || $day > 31) || ($year
    < 1000 ||
        $year > 9999)) {
        throw new Exception('Please use numbers within the correct range');
    } elseif (!checkdate($month,$day,$year)) {
        throw new Exception('You have used an invalid date');
    }
    return sprintf('%d-%02d-%02d', $year, $month, $day);
}
```

The function takes three arguments: month, day, and year. By using type declarations, the function will silently cast the arguments to integers if the wrong type of input is used. The first three lines of code trim any whitespace from either end of the input.

The series of conditional statements checks the input values to see if they are empty, are not within acceptable ranges, or form an invalid date. Even though the form is prepopulated with values, there's no guarantee that the input will come from your form. It could come from an automated script, which is why these checks are necessary.

The range for years is dictated by the legal range for MySQL. In the unlikely event that you need a year out of that range, you must choose a different column type to store the data.

If the input has survived the first two tests, it's subjected to the PHP function `checkdate()`, which is smart enough to know when it's a leap year and prevents mistakes such as September 31.

Any error causes the function to throw an exception. But if the input has passed all these tests, it's returned after being rebuilt in the correct format for insertion into MySQL using the `sprintf()` function. This takes as its first argument a formatting string, in which %d represents an integer and %02d represents a two-digit integer padded with a leading zero if necessary. The hyphens are treated literally. The following three arguments are the values to be slotted into the formatting string. This produces the date in ISO format, with leading zeros on the month and day.

■ **Note** See www.php.net/manual/en/function.sprintf.php for sprintf() details.

---

6. For testing purposes, add this code just below the form in the main body of the page:

```
if (isset($_POST['convert'])) {
    try {
        $converted = convertDateToISO($_POST['month'], $_POST['day'],
            $_POST['year']);
        echo 'Valid date: ' . $converted;
    } catch (Throwable $t) {
        echo 'Error: ' . $t->getMessage() . '<br>';
        echo 'Input was: ' . $months[$_POST['month'] - 1] . ' ' .
            safe($_POST['day']) . ', ' . safe($_POST['year']);
    }
}
```

This checks whether the form has been submitted. If it has been, it passes the form values to the convertDateToISO() function, saving the result in $converted. Because the function might throw an Exception, the code is embedded in a try/catch structure.

If the input and date are valid, the formatted date is displayed. If the date cannot be converted to ISO format, the catch block displays the error message stored in the Exception, together with the original input. To display the correct value for the month, 1 is subtracted from the value of $_POST['month'], and the result is used as the key for the $months array. The values of $_POST['day'] and $_POST['year'] are passed to the safe() function as a precaution against the form being used for a remote exploit.

7. Save the page and test it by entering a date and clicking Convert. If the date is valid, you should see it converted to ISO format, as shown in Figure 16-7.

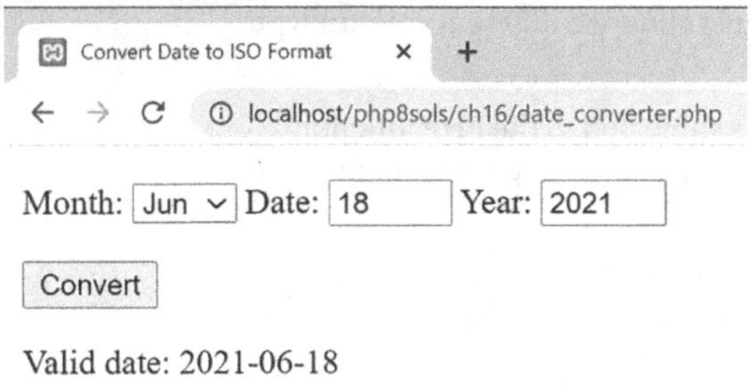

Figure 16-7. The date has been validated and converted to ISO format

8. If you enter an invalid date, you should see an appropriate message instead (see Figure 16-8).

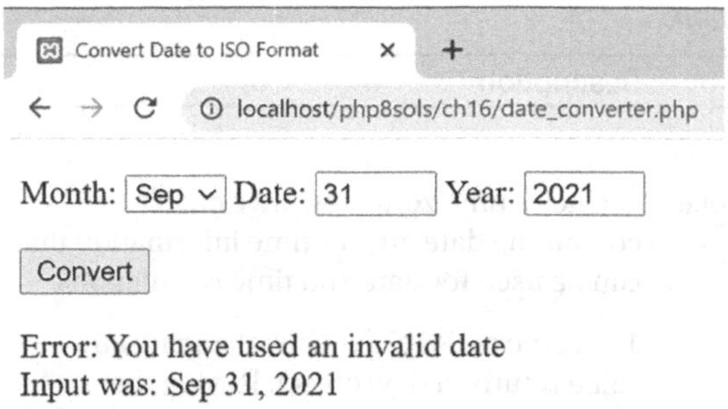

Figure 16-8. *The convertDateToISO() function rejects invalid dates*

You can compare your code with date_converter_02.php in the ch16 folder.

When creating a form for a table that requires a date from user input, add three fields for month, day, and year in the same way as in date_converter.php. Before inserting the form input into the database, include utility_funcs.php (or wherever you decide to store the function), and use the convertDateToISO() function to validate the date and format it for insertion into the database:

```
require_once 'utility_funcs.php';
try {
    $date = convertDateToMySQL($_POST['month'], $_POST['day'], $_POST['year']);
} catch(Throwable $t) {
    $errors[] = $t->getMessage();
}
```

If your $errors array has any elements, abandon the insert or update process and display the errors. Otherwise, $date is safe to insert in the SQL query.

■ **Note**   The rest of this chapter is devoted to handling dates in PHP. It's an important but complex subject. I suggest that you skim through each section to familiarize yourself with PHP's date-handling functionality and return to this section when you need to implement a particular feature.

Working with Dates in PHP

PHP, in common with other computer languages, handles the complexities of dates and time by calculating in seconds from the Unix epoch, midnight UTC (Coordinated Universal Time) on January 1, 1970. Fortunately, PHP does most of the hard work in the background through its DateTime, DateTimeZone, DateInterval, and DatePeriod classes. Basic operations are handled by simple functions.

The range of available dates depends on how PHP has been compiled. The DateTime and related classes store date and time information internally as a 64-bit number, making it possible to represent dates from about 292 billion years in the past to the same number of years in the future. However, if PHP is compiled on a 32-bit processor, the functions in the second half of Table 16-3 are restricted to a range of approximately 1901 to January 2038.

Table 16-3 summarizes the main date- and time-related classes and functions in PHP.

Table 16-3. PHP date- and time-related classes and functions

	Name	Arguments	Description
Class			
	DateTime	Date string, DateTimeZone object	Creates a time zone–sensitive object containing date and/or time information that can be used for date and time calculations.
	DateTimeImmutable	Same as DateTime	The same as DateTime, but changing any value returns a new object, leaving the original unmodified.
	DateTimeZone	Time zone string	Stores time zone information for use with DateTime objects.
	DateInterval	Interval specification	Represents a fixed amount of time in years, months, hours, etc.
	DatePeriod	Start, interval, end/recurrence, options	Calculates recurring dates over a set period or number of recurrences.
Function			
	time()	None	Generates a Unix timestamp for the current date and time.
	mktime()	Hour, minute, second, month, date, year	Generates a Unix timestamp for the specified date/time.
	strtotime()	Date string, timestamp	Attempts to generate a Unix timestamp from an English textual description, such as "next Tuesday." The returned value is relative to the second argument, if supplied.
	date()	Format string, timestamp	Formats a date in English using the specifiers listed in Table 16-4. If the second argument is omitted, the current date and time are used.
	strftime()	Format string, timestamp	Same as date(), but uses the language specified by the system locale.

Setting the Default Time Zone

All date and time information in PHP is stored according to the server's default time zone setting. It's common for web servers to be located in a different time zone from your target audience, so it's useful to know how to change the default.

The server's default time zone should normally be set in the date.timezone directive in php.ini, but if your hosting company forgets to do so or you want to use a different time zone, you need to set it yourself.

If your hosting company gives you control over your own version of php.ini, change the value of date.timezone there. That way, it's automatically set for all your scripts.

If your server supports .htaccess or .user.ini files, you can change the time zone by adding the appropriate command in the site root. For .htaccess, use this:

```
php_value date.timezone 'timezone'
```

For .user.ini, the command looks like this:

```
date.timezone=timezone
```

Replace *timezone* with the correct setting for your location. You can find a full list of valid time zones at www.php.net/manual/en/timezones.php.

If none of those options is available to you, add the following at the beginning of any script that uses date or time functions (replacing *timezone* with the appropriate value):

```
ini_set('date.timezone', 'timezone');
```

Creating a DateTime Object

To create a DateTime object, just use the new keyword followed by DateTime(), like this:

```
$now = new DateTime();
```

This creates an object that represents the current date and time according to the web server's clock and default time zone setting.

The DateTime() constructor also takes two optional arguments: a string containing a date and/or time and a DateTimeZone object. The date/time string for the first argument can be in any of the formats listed at www.php.net/manual/en/datetime.formats.php. Unlike MySQL, which accepts only one format, PHP goes to the opposite extreme. For example, to create a DateTime object for Christmas Day 2021, all the following formats are valid:

```
'12/25/2021'
'25-12-2021'
'25 Dec 2021'
'Dec 25 2021'
'25-XII-2021'
'25.12.2021'
'2021/12/25'
'2021-12-25'
'December 25th, 2021'
```

This is not an exhaustive list. It's just a selection of valid formats. Where the potential confusion arises is in the use of separators. For example, the forward slash is permitted in American-style (12/25/2021) and ISO (2021/12/25) dates, but not when the date is presented in European order or when the month is represented by Roman numerals. To present the date in European order, the separator must be a dot, tab, or dash.

Dates can also be specified using relative expressions, such as "next Wednesday," "tomorrow," or "last Monday." However, there's potential for confusion here, too. Some people use "next Wednesday" to mean "Wednesday next week." PHP interprets the expression literally. If today is Tuesday, "next Wednesday" means the following day.

You can't use echo on its own to display the value stored in a DateTime object. In addition to echo, you need to tell PHP how to format the output using the format() method.

Formatting Dates in PHP

The DateTime class's format() method uses the same format characters as the date() function. Although this makes for continuity, the format characters are often difficult to remember and seem to have no obvious reasoning behind them. Table 16-4 lists the most useful date and time format characters.

The DateTime class and date() function display the names of weekdays and months in English only, but the strftime() function uses the language specified by the server's locale. So, if the server's locale is set to Spanish, a DateTime object and date() display Saturday, but strftime() displays sábado. In addition to the format characters used by both the DateTime class and the date() function, Table 16-4 lists the equivalent characters used by strftime(). Not all formats have an equivalent in strftime().

Table 16-4. *The main date and time format characters*

Unit	DateTime/date()	strftime()	Description	Example
Day	D	%d	Day of the month with leading zero	01–31
	J	%e*	Day of the month without leading zero	1–31
	S		English ordinal suffix for day of the month	st, nd, rd, or th
	D	%a	First three letters of day name	Sun, Tue
	l (lowercase "L")	%A	Full name of day	Sunday, Tuesday
Month	M	%m	Number of month with leading zero	01–12
	N		Number of month without leading zero	1–12
	M	%b	First three letters of month name	Jan, Jul
	F	%B	Full name of month	January, July
Year	Y	%Y	Year displayed as four digits	2014
	y	%y	Year displayed as two digits	14
Hour	g		Hour in 12-hour format without leading zero	1–12
	h	%I	Hour in 12-hour format with leading zero	01–12
	G		Hour in 24-hour format without leading zero	0–23
	H	%H	Hour in 24-hour format with leading zero	01–23
Minutes	i	%M	Minutes with leading zero if necessary	00–59
Seconds	s	%S	Seconds with leading zero if necessary	00–59
AM/PM	a		Lowercase	am
AM/PM	A	%p	Uppercase	PM

Note: %e is not supported on Windows.

You can combine these format characters with punctuation to display the current date on your web pages according to your own preferences.

To format a `DateTime` object, pass the format string as an argument to the `format()` method like this (the code is in date_format_01.php in the ch16 folder):

```php
<?php
$now = new DateTime();
$xmas2021 = new DateTime('12/25/2021');
?>
<p>It's now <?= $now->format('g.ia') ?> on <?= $now->format('l, F jS, Y') ?></p>
<p>Christmas 2021 falls on a <?= $xmas2021->format('l') ?></p>
```

In this example, two `DateTime` objects are created: one for the current date and time and the other for December 25, 2021. Using the format characters from Table 16-4, various date parts are extracted from the two objects, producing the output shown in the following screenshot:

The code in date_format_02.php produces the same output by using the `date()` and `strtotime()` functions, like this:

```php
<?php $xmas2021 = strtotime('12/25/2021') ?>
<p>It's now <?= date('g.ia') ?> on <?= date('l, F jS, Y') ?></p>
<p>Christmas 2021 falls on a <?= date('l', $xmas2021) ?></p>
```

The first line uses `strtotime()` to create a timestamp for December 25, 2021. There's no need to create a timestamp for the current date and time, because `date()` defaults to them when used without a second argument.

If the timestamp for Christmas Day isn't used elsewhere in the script, the first line can be omitted, and the last call to `date()` can be rewritten like this (see date_format_03.php):

```php
date('l', strtotime('12/25/2021'))
```

Creating a DateTime Object from a Custom Format

You can specify a custom input format for a `DateTime` object using the format characters in Table 16-4. Instead of creating the object with the `new` keyword, you use the `createFromFormat()` static method, like this:

```php
$date = DateTime::createFromFormat(format_string, input_date, timezone);
```

The third argument, *timezone*, is optional. If included, it should be a `DateTimeZone` object.

A **static method** belongs to the whole class, rather than to a particular object. You call a static method using the class name followed by the scope resolution operator (a double colon) and the method name.

■ **Tip**   Internally, the scope resolution operator is called PAAMAYIM_NEKUDOTAYIM, which is Hebrew for "double colon." Why Hebrew? The Zend Engine that powers PHP was originally developed by Zeev Suraski and Andi Gutmans when they were students at the Technion—Israel Institute of Technology. Apart from earning points in a geek trivia quiz, knowing the meaning of PAAMAYIM_NEKUDOTAYIM could save you a lot of head-scratching when you see it in a PHP error message.

For example, you can use the createFromFormat() method to accept a date in the European format of day, month, year, separated by slashes, like this (the code is in date_format_04.php):

```
$xmas2021 = DateTime::createFromFormat('d/m/Y', '25/12/2021');
echo $xmas2021->format('l, jS F Y');
```

This produces the following output:

Saturday, 25th December 2021

■ **Caution**   Attempting to use 25/12/2021 as the input to the DateTime constructor triggers a fatal error because the DD/MM/YYYY is not supported. If you want to use a format not supported by the DateTime constructor, you must use the createFromFormat() static method.

Although the createFromFormat() method is useful, it can be used only in circumstances where you know the date will always be in a specific format.

Choosing Between date() and the DateTime Class

When it comes to displaying a date, it's always a two-step process with the DateTime class. You need to instantiate the object before you can call the format() method. With the date() function, you can do it in a single pass. Since they both use the same format characters, date() wins hands down when dealing with the current date and/or time.

■ **Tip**   Technically speaking, you can call the format() method at the same time as instantiating a DateTime object by wrapping the creation of the object in a pair of parentheses. But using date() is much simpler. You can compare the two methods of displaying a date in date_format_05.php.

For simple tasks like displaying the current date, time, or year, use date(). Where the DateTime class comes into its own is when working with date-related calculations and time zones using the methods listed in Table 16-5.

Table 16-5. *The main DateTime methods*

Method	Arguments	Description
format()	Format string	Formats the date/time using the format characters in Table 16-4.
setDate()	Year, month, day	Changes the date. The arguments should be separated by commas. Months or days in excess of the permitted range are added to the resulting date, as described in the main text.
setTime()	Hours, minutes, seconds	Resets the time. Arguments are comma-separated values. Seconds are optional. Values in excess of the permitted range are added to the resulting date/time.
modify()	Relative date string	Changes the date/time using a relative expression, such as '+2 weeks'.
getTimestamp()	None	Returns the Unix timestamp for the date/time.
setTimestamp()	Unix timestamp	Sets the date/time according to the Unix timestamp.
setTimezone()	DateTimeZone object	Changes the time zone.
getTimezone()	None	Returns a DateTimeZone object representing the DateTime object's time zone.
getOffset()	None	Returns the time zone offset from UTC, expressed in seconds.
add()	DateInterval object	Increments the date/time by the set period.
sub()	DateInterval object	Deducts the set period from the date/time.
diff()	DateTime object, Boolean	Returns a DateInterval object representing the difference between the current DateTime object and the one passed as an argument. Using true as the optional second argument converts negative values to their positive equivalent.

Adding out-of-range values with setDate() and setTime() results in the excess being added to the resulting date or time. For example, using 14 as the month sets the date to February of the following year. Setting the hour to 26 results in 2 AM on the following day.

A useful trick with setDate() allows you to set the date to the last day of any month by setting the month value to the following month and the day to 0. The code in setDate.php demonstrates this with the last day of February 2022 and 2024 (a leap year):

```php
<?php
$format = 'F j, Y';
$date = new DateTime();
$date->setDate(2022, 3, 0);
?>
<p>Non-leap year: <?= $date->format($format) ?>.</p>
<p>Leap year: <?php $date->setDate(2024, 3, 0);
    echo $date->format($format); ?>.</p>
```

The preceding example produces the following output:

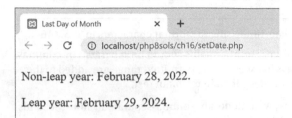

Non-leap year: February 28, 2022.

Leap year: February 29, 2024.

Handling Overflows with Relative Dates

The modify() method accepts a relative date string, which can produce unexpected results. For example, if you add one month to a DateTime object that represents January 31, 2022, the resulting value is not the last day of February, but March 3.

This happens because adding one month to the original date results in February 31, but February has only 28 days in a non-leap year. So the out-of-range value is added to the month, resulting in March 3. If you subsequently subtract one month from the same DateTime object, it brings you back to February 3, not to the original starting date. The code in date_modify_01.php illustrates this point, as Figure 16-9 shows:

```php
<?php
$format = 'F j, Y';
$date = new DateTime('January 31, 2022');
?>
<p>Original date: <?= $date->format($format) ?>.</p>
<p>Add one month: <?php
$date->modify('+1 month');
echo $date->format($format);
$date->modify('-1 month');
?>
<p>Subtract one month: <?= $date->format($format) ?>
```

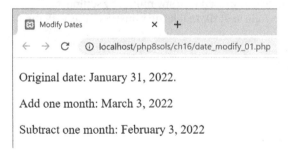

Figure 16-9. *Adding and subtracting months can lead to unexpected results*

The way to avoid this problem is to use 'last day of' in the relative expression, like this (the code is in date_modify_02.php):

```php
<?php
$format = 'F j, Y';
$date = new DateTime('January 31, 2022');
?>
<p>Original date: <?= $date->format($format) ?>.</p>
<p>Add one month: <?php
    $date->modify('last day of +1 month');
    echo $date->format($format);
    $date->modify('last day of -1 month');
    ?>
<p>Subtract one month: <?= $date->format($format) ?>
```

As Figure 16-10 shows, this now produces the desired result.

Original date: January 31, 2022.

Add one month: February 28, 2022

Subtract one month: January 31, 2022

Figure 16-10. *Using 'last day of' in the relative expression eliminates the problem*

Using the DateTimeZone Class

A DateTime object automatically uses the web server's default time zone unless you have reset the time zone using one of the methods described earlier. However, you can set the time zone of individual DateTime objects either through the optional second argument of the constructor or by using the setTimezone() method. In both cases, the argument must be a DateTimeZone object.

To create a DateTimeZone object, pass one of the supported time zones listed at www.php.net/manual/en/timezones.php as an argument to the constructor like this:

```php
$UK = new DateTimeZone('Europe/London');
$USeast = new DateTimeZone('America/New_York');
$Hawaii = new DateTimeZone('Pacific/Honolulu');
```

When checking the list of supported time zones, it's important to realize that they're based on geographic regions and cities rather than on official time zones. This is because PHP automatically takes daylight saving time into account. Arizona, which doesn't use daylight saving time, is covered by America/Phoenix.

The organization of time zones into geographic regions produces some surprises. America doesn't mean the United States, but the continents of North and South America and the Caribbean. As a result, Honolulu is not listed in America, but as a Pacific time zone. Europe also means the European continent, including the British Isles and Ireland but excluding other islands. So Reykjavik and Madeira are listed as Atlantic time zones, and Longyearbyen on the Norwegian island of Svalbard has the exclusive privilege of being the only Arctic time zone.

The code in `timezones.php` creates DateTimeZone objects for London, New York, and Honolulu and then initializes a DateTime object using the first one, like this:

```
$now = new DateTime('now', $UK);
```

After displaying the date and time using echo and the format() method, the time zone is changed using the setTimezone() method, like this:

```
$now->setTimezone($USeast);
```

The next time $now is displayed, it shows the date and time in New York. Finally, setTimezone() is used again to change the time zone to Honolulu, producing the following output:

In London, it's now Saturday, June 19th, 2021 3.49pm.

In New York, it's Saturday, June 19th, 2021 10.49am.

In Hawaii, it's Saturday, June 19th, 2021 4.49am.

■ **Caution** The accuracy of time zone conversions depends on the time zone database compiled into PHP being up to date.

To find the time zone of your server, you can either check php.ini or use the getTimezone() method with a DateTime object. The getTimezone() method returns a DateTimeZone object, not a string containing the time zone. To get the value of the time zone, you need to use the DateTimeZone object's getName() method, like this (the code is in timezone_display.php):

```
$now = new DateTime();
$timezone = $now->getTimezone();
echo $timezone->getName();
```

The DateTimeZone class has several other methods that expose information about a time zone. For the sake of completeness, they're listed in Table 16-6, but the main use of the DateTimeZone class is to set the time zone for DateTime objects.

Table 16-6. *DateTimeZone methods*

Method	Arguments	Description
getLocation()	None	Returns an associative array containing the country code, latitude, longitude, and comments about the time zone.
getName()	None	Returns a string containing the geographic area and city of the time zone.
getOffset()	DateTime object	Calculates the offset from UTC (in seconds) of the DateTime object passed as an argument.
getTransitions()	Start, end	Returns a multidimensional array containing historical and future dates and times of switching to and from daylight saving time. Accepts two timestamps as optional arguments to limit the range of results.
listAbbreviations()	None	Generates a large multidimensional array containing the UTC offsets and names of time zones supported by PHP.
listIdentifiers()	DateTimeZone constant, country code	Returns an array of all PHP time zone identifiers, such as Europe/London, America/New_York, and so on. Accepts two optional arguments to limit the range of results. Use as the first argument one of the DateTimeZone constants listed at www.php.net/manual/en/class.datetimezone.php. If the first argument is DateTimeZone::PER_COUNTRY, a two-letter country code can be used as the second argument.

The last two methods in Table 16-6 are static methods. Call them directly on the class by using the scope resolution operator, like this:

```
$abbreviations = DateTimeZone::listAbbreviations();
```

Adding and Subtracting Set Periods with the DateInterval Class

The DateInterval class is used to specify the period to be added or subtracted from a DateTime object using the add() and sub() methods. It's also used by the diff() method, which returns a DateInterval object. Using the DateInterval class feels rather odd to begin with, but it's relatively simple to understand.

To create a DateInterval object, you need to pass to the constructor a string that specifies the length of the interval; this string must be formatted according to the ISO 8601 standard. The string always begins with the letter P (for period), followed by one or more pairs of integers and letters known as **period designators**. If the interval includes hours, minutes, or seconds, the time element is preceded by the letter T. Table 16-7 lists the valid period designators.

Table 16-7. *ISO 8601 period designators used by the DateInterval class*

Period designator	Meaning
Y	Years
M	Months
W	Weeks—cannot be combined with days
D	Days—cannot be combined with weeks
H	Hours
M	Minutes
S	Seconds

The following examples should clarify how to specify an interval:

```
$interval1 = new DateInterval('P2Y');             // 2 years
$interval2 = new DateInterval('P5W');             // 5 weeks
$interval3 = new DateInterval('P37D');            // 5 weeks 2 days
$interval4 = new DateInterval('PT6H20M');         // 6 hours 20 minutes
$interval5 = new DateInterval('P1Y2DT3H5M50S');   // 1 year 2 days 3 hours 5 min 50 sec
```

Note that `$interval3` needs to specify the total number of days because weeks are automatically converted to days, so W and D cannot be combined in the same interval definition.

To use a `DateInterval` object with the `add()` or `sub()` method of the `DateTime` class, pass the object as an argument. For example, this adds 12 days to the date for Christmas Day 2021:

```
$xmas2021 = new DateTime('12/25/2021');
$interval = new DateInterval('P12D');
$xmas2021->add($interval);
```

If you don't need to reuse the interval, you can pass the `DateInterval` constructor directly as the argument to `add()` like this:

```
$xmas2021 = new DateTime('12/25/2021');
$xmas2021->add(new DateInterval('P12D'));
```

The result of this calculation is demonstrated in `date_interval_01.php`, which produces the following output:

Twelfth Night falls on Thursday, January 6th, 2022.

An alternative to using the period designators listed in Table 16-7 is to use the static `createFromDateString()` method, which takes as an argument an English relative date string in the same way as `strtotime()` does. Using `createFromDateString()`, the preceding example can be rewritten like this (the code is in `date_interval_02.php`):

```
$xmas2021 = new DateTime('12/25/2021');
$xmas2021->add(DateInterval::createFromDateString('+12 days'));
```

This produces exactly the same result.

■ **Caution**   Adding and subtracting months with `DateInterval` has the same effect as described earlier. If the resulting date is out of range, the extra days are added. For example, adding one month to January 31 results in March 3 or 2, depending on whether it's a leap year. To get the last day of the month, use the technique described earlier in "Handling Overflows with Relative Dates."

Finding the Difference Between Two Dates with the diff() Method

To find the difference between two dates, create a `DateTime` object for both dates, and pass the second object as the argument to the first object's `diff()` method. The result is returned as a `DateInterval` object. To extract the result from the `DateInterval` object, you need to use the object's `format()` method, which uses the format characters listed in Table 16-8. These are different from the format characters used by the `DateTime` class. Fortunately, most of them are easy to remember.

Table 16-8. *Format characters used by the DateInterval format() method*

Format character	Description	Examples
%Y	Years. At least two digits, with leading zero if necessary	12, 01
%y	Years, no leading zero	12, 1
%M	Months with leading zero	02, 11
%m	Months, no leading zero	2, 11
%D	Days with leading zero	03, 24
%d	Days, no leading zero	3, 24
%a	Total number of days	15, 231
%H	Hours with leading zero	03, 23
%h	Hours, no leading zero	3, 23
%I	Minutes with leading zero	05, 59
%i	Minutes, no leading zero	5, 59
%S	Seconds with leading zero	05, 59
%s	Seconds, no leading zero	5, 59
%R	Display minus when negative, plus when positive	-, +
%r	Display minus when negative, no sign when positive	-
%%	Percentage sign	%

The following example in date_interval_03.php shows how to get the difference between the current date and the American Declaration of Independence using diff() and displaying the result with the format() method:

```php
<p><?php
$independence = new DateTime('7/4/1776');
$now = new DateTime();
$interval = $now->diff($independence);
echo $interval->format('%Y years %m months %d days'); ?>
since American Declaration of Independence.</p>
```

If you load date_interval_03.php into a browser, you should see something similar to the following screenshot (of course, the actual period will be different):

244 years 11 months 15 days since American Declaration of Independence.

The format characters follow a logical pattern. Uppercase characters always produce at least two digits with a leading zero if necessary. Lowercase characters have no leading zero.

■ **Caution**   With the exception of %a, which represents the total number of days, the format characters represent only specific parts of the overall interval. For example, if you change the format string to $interval->format('%m months'), it shows only the number of whole months that have elapsed since last July 4. It does not show the total number of months since July 4, 1776.

Calculating Recurring Dates with the DatePeriod Class

Working out recurring dates, such as the second Tuesday of each month, is now remarkably easy, thanks to the DatePeriod class. It works in conjunction with a DateInterval.

The DatePeriod constructor is unusual in that it accepts arguments in three different ways. The first way of creating a DatePeriod object is to supply the following arguments:

- A DateTime object representing the start date
- A DateInterval object representing the recurring interval
- An integer representing the number of recurrences
- The DatePeriod::EXCLUDE_START_DATE constant (optional)

Once you have created a DatePeriod object, you can display the recurring dates in a foreach loop using the DateTime format() method.

The code in date_interval_04.php displays the second Tuesday of each month in 2022:

```
$start = new DateTime('12/31/2021');
$interval = DateInterval::createFromDateString('second Tuesday of next month');
$period = new DatePeriod($start, $interval, 12, DatePeriod::EXCLUDE_START_DATE);
foreach ($period as $date) {
   echo $date->format('l, F jS, Y') . '<br>';
}
```

It produces the output shown in Figure 16-11.

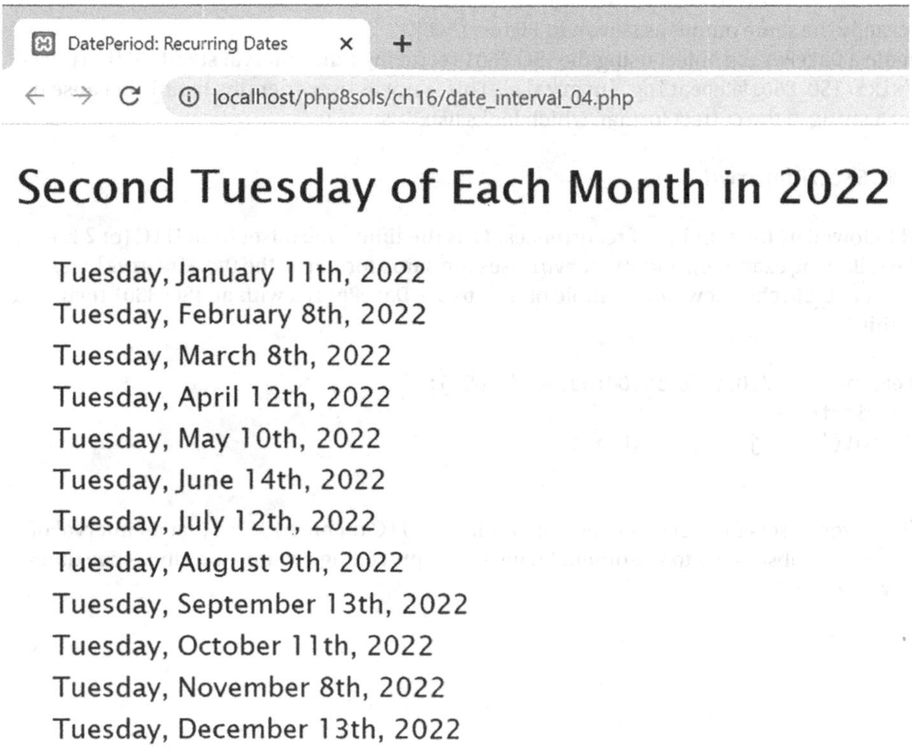
DatePeriod: Recurring Dates
localhost/php8sols/ch16/date_interval_04.php
Second Tuesday of Each Month in 2022
Tuesday, January 11th, 2022
Tuesday, February 8th, 2022
Tuesday, March 8th, 2022
Tuesday, April 12th, 2022
Tuesday, May 10th, 2022
Tuesday, June 14th, 2022
Tuesday, July 12th, 2022
Tuesday, August 9th, 2022
Tuesday, September 13th, 2022
Tuesday, October 11th, 2022
Tuesday, November 8th, 2022
Tuesday, December 13th, 2022

Figure 16-11. *Calculating a recurring date is remarkably easy with the DatePeriod class*

The first line of PHP code sets the start date as December 31, 2021. The next line uses the `DateInterval` static method `createFromDateString()` to set the interval at the second Tuesday of next month. Both values are passed to the `DatePeriod` constructor, together with 12 as the number of recurrences and the `DatePeriod::EXCLUDE_START_DATE` constant. The constant's name is self-explanatory. Finally, a `foreach` loop displays the resulting dates using the `DateTime format()` method.

The second way of creating a DatePeriod object is to replace the number of recurrences in the third argument with a DateTime object representing the end date. The code in date_interval_05.php has been amended like this:

```
$start = new DateTime('12/31/2021');
$interval = DateInterval::createFromDateString('second Tuesday of next month');
$end = new DateTime('12/31/2022');
$period = new DatePeriod($start, $interval, $end, DatePeriod::EXCLUDE_START_DATE);
foreach ($period as $date) {
    echo $date->format('l, F jS, Y') . '<br>';
}
```

This produces exactly the same output as shown in Figure 16-11.

You can also create a DatePeriod object using the ISO 8601 recurring time-interval standard (https:// en.wikipedia.org/wiki/ISO_8601#Repeating_intervals). This is not as user-friendly, mainly because of the need to construct a string in the correct format, which looks like this:

R*n*/YYYY-MM-DDTHH:MM:SS*tz*/P*interval*

R*n* is the letter R followed by the number of recurrences; *tz* is the time zone offset from UTC (or Z for UTC, as shown in the following example); and P*interval* uses the same format as the DateInterval class. The code in date_interval_06.php shows an example of how to use DatePeriod with an ISO 8601 recurring interval. It looks like this:

```
$period = new DatePeriod('R4/2021-06-19T00:00:00Z/P10D');
foreach ($period as $date) {
    echo $date->format('l, F j, Y') . '<br>';
}
```

The ISO recurring interval sets four recurrences from midnight UTC on June 19, 2021, at an interval of 10 days. The recurrences are subsequent to the original date, so the preceding example produces five dates, as shown in the following output:

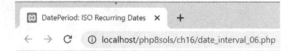

Saturday, June 19, 2021
Tuesday, June 29, 2021
Friday, July 9, 2021
Monday, July 19, 2021
Thursday, July 29, 2021

Chapter Review

A large part of this chapter has been devoted to the powerful date and time classes. I haven't covered the DateTimeImmutable class because it's identical to DateTime in every respect except one. A DateTimeImmutable object never modifies itself. Instead, it always returns a new object with the modified values. This can be useful if you have a date, such as a person's date of birth, which never changes. Using the setDate() or add() method with this type of object returns a new object, preserving the original details and providing a new object for the updated ones, such as start of employment, marriage, pensionable age, and so on.

You probably don't need the date- and time-related classes every day, but they're extremely useful. MySQL's date and time functions also make it easy to format dates and execute queries based on temporal criteria.

Perhaps the biggest problem with dates is deciding whether to use SQL or PHP to handle the formatting and/or calculations. A useful feature of the PHP DateTime class is that the constructor accepts a date stored in the ISO format, so you can use an unformatted date or timestamp from your database to create DateTime objects. However, unless you need to perform further calculations, it's more efficient to use the DATE_FORMAT() function as part of a SELECT query.

This chapter has also provided you with three functions for formatting text and dates. In the next chapter, you'll learn how to store and retrieve related information in multiple database tables.

■ ■ ■

Pulling Data from Multiple Tables

As I explained in Chapter 13, one of the major strengths of a relational database is the ability to link data in different tables by using the primary key from one table as a foreign key in another table. The phpsols database has two tables: images and blog. It's time to add some more and join them, so that you can assign categories to blog entries and associate images with individual articles.

You don't physically join multiple tables, but rather do so through SQL. Often, you can join tables by identifying a direct relationship between primary and foreign keys. In some cases, though, the relationship is more complex and needs to go through a third table that acts as a cross-reference between the other two.

In this chapter, you'll learn how to establish the relationship between tables and how to insert the primary key from one table as a foreign key in another table. Although it sounds difficult conceptually, it's actually quite easy—you use a database query to look up the primary key in the first table, save the result, and use that result in another query to insert it in the second table.

In particular, you'll learn about the following:

- Understanding the different types of table relationships

- Using a cross-reference table for many-to-many relationships

- Altering a table's structure to add new columns or an index

- Storing a primary key as a foreign key in another table

- Linking tables with INNER JOIN and LEFT JOIN

Understanding Table Relationships

The simplest type of relationship is **one-to-one** (often represented as **1:1**). This type of relationship is often found in databases that contain information only certain people should see. For example, companies often store details of employees' salaries and other confidential information in a table separate from the more widely accessible staff list. Storing the primary key of each staff member's record as a foreign key in the salaries table establishes a direct relationship between the tables, allowing the accounts department to see the full range of information while restricting others to only the public information.

There's no confidential information in the phpsols database, but you might create a one-to-one relationship between a single photo in the images table with an article in the blog table, as illustrated by Figure 17-1.

© David Powers 2022
D. Powers, *PHP 8 Solutions*, https://doi.org/10.1007/978-1-4842-7141-4_17

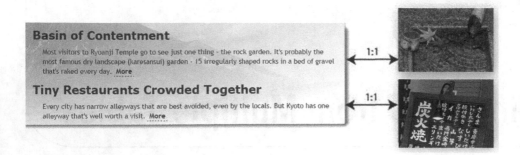

Figure 17-1. *A one-to-one relationship links one record directly with another*

This is the simplest way of creating a relationship between the two tables, but it's not ideal. As more articles are added, the nature of the relationship is likely to change. The photo associated with the first article in Figure 17-1 shows maple leaves floating on the water, so it might be suitable for illustrating an article about the changing seasons or autumn hues. The crystal-clear water, bamboo water scoop, and bamboo pipe also suggest other themes that the photo could be used to illustrate. So you could easily end up with the same photo being used for several articles, or a **one-to-many** (or **1:n**) relationship, as represented by Figure 17-2.

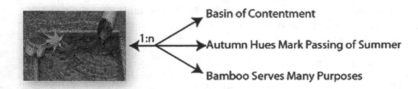

Figure 17-2. *A one-to-many relationship links one record with several others*

As you have already learned, a primary key must be unique. So, in a 1:n relationship, you store the primary key from the table on the 1 side of the relationship (the **primary** or **parent table**) as a foreign key in the table on the n side (the **secondary** or **child table**). In this case, the image_id from the images table needs to be stored as a foreign key in the blog table. What's important to understand about a 1:n relationship is that it's also a collection of 1:1 relationships. Reading Figure 17-2 from right to left, each article has a relationship with a single image. Without this one-on-one relationship, you wouldn't be able to identify which image is associated with a particular article.

What happens if you want to associate more than one image to each article? You could create several columns in the blog table to hold the foreign keys, but this rapidly becomes unwieldy. You might start off with image1, image2, and image3, but if most articles have only one image, two columns are redundant much of the time. And are you going to add an extra column for that extra-special article that requires four images?

When faced with the need to accommodate **many-to-many** (or **n:m**) relationships, you need a different approach. The images and blog tables don't contain sufficient records to demonstrate n:m relationships, but you could add a categories table to tag individual articles. Most articles are likely to belong to multiple categories, and each category will be related with several articles.

The way to resolve complex relationships is through a **cross-reference table** (sometimes called a **linking table**), which establishes a series of one-to-one relationships between related records. This is a special table containing just two columns, both of which are declared a joint primary key. Figure 17-3 shows how this works. Each record in the cross-reference table stores details of the relationship between individual articles in the blog and categories tables. To find all articles that belong to the Kyoto category, you match cat_id 1 in the categories table with cat_id 1 in the cross-reference table. This identifies the records in the blog table with the article_id 2, 3, and 4 as being associated with Kyoto.

Figure 17-3. *A cross-reference table resolves many-to-many relationships as 1:1*

Establishing relationships between tables through foreign keys has important implications for how you update and delete records. If you're not careful, you end up with broken links. Ensuring that dependencies aren't broken is known as maintaining **referential integrity**. We'll tackle this important subject in the next chapter. First, let's concentrate on retrieving information stored in separate tables linked through a foreign-key relationship.

Linking an Image to an Article

To demonstrate how to work with multiple tables, let's begin with the straightforward scenarios outlined in Figures 17-1 and 17-2: relations that can be resolved as 1:1 through the storage of the primary key from one table (the parent table) as a foreign key in a second table (the child or dependent table). This involves adding an extra column in the child table to store the foreign key.

Altering the Structure of an Existing Table

Ideally, you should design your database structure before populating it with data. However, relational databases, such as MySQL, are flexible enough to let you add, remove, or change columns in tables even when they already contain records. To associate an image with individual articles in the phpsols database, you need to add an extra column to the blog table to store image_id as a foreign key.

PHP Solution 17-1: Adding an Extra Column to a Table

This PHP solution shows how to add an extra column to an existing table using phpMyAdmin. It assumes that you created the blog table in the phpsols database in Chapter 15.

1. In phpMyAdmin, select the phpsols database and click the Structure link for the blog table.

2. Below the blog table structure is a form that allows you to add extra columns. You want to add only one column, so the default value in the Add column(s) text box is fine. It's normal practice to put foreign keys immediately after the table's primary key, so select after article_id from the drop-down menu, as shown in the following screenshot. Then click Go:

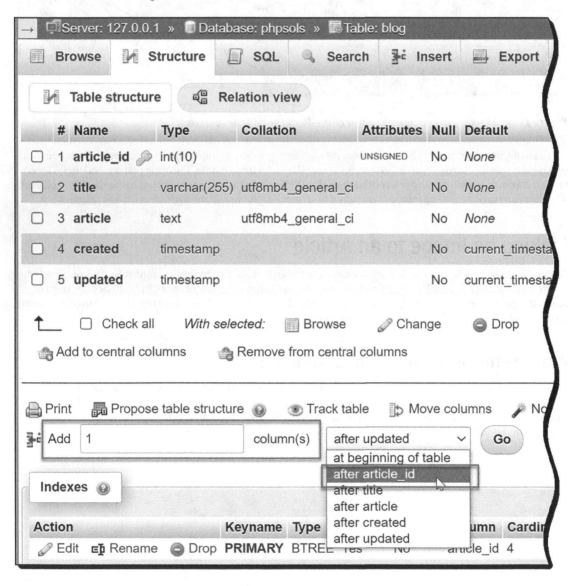

3. This opens the screen for you to define column attributes. Use the following settings:

   - Name: image_id
   - Type: INT
   - Attributes: UNSIGNED
   - Null: Selected

- Index: INDEX (there's no need to give it a name in the modal dialog that pops up)

   Do *not* select the A_I (AUTO_INCREMENT) check box. You don't want image_id to be incremented automatically. Its value will be inserted from the images table.

   The Null check box has been selected because not all articles will be associated with an image. Click Save.

4. Select the Structure tab and check that the blog table structure now looks like this:

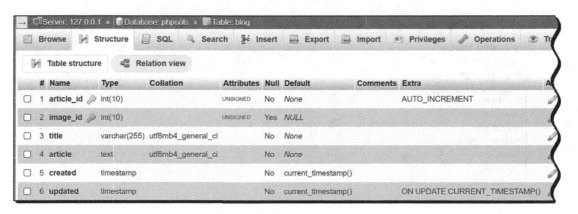

5. If you click the Browse tab at the top left of the screen, you will see that the value of image_id is NULL in each record. The challenge now is to insert the correct foreign keys without the need to look up the numbers manually. We'll tackle that next.

Inserting a Foreign Key in a Table

The basic principle behind inserting a foreign key in another table is quite simple: you query the database to find the primary key of the record that you want to link to the other table. You can then use an INSERT or UPDATE query to add the foreign key to the target record.

To demonstrate the basic principle, you'll adapt the update form from Chapter 15 (blog_update_mysqli.php or blog_update_pdo.php) to add a drop-down menu that lists images already registered in the images table (see Figure 17-4).

Figure 17-4. *A dynamically generated drop-down menu inserts the appropriate foreign key*

The menu is dynamically generated by a loop that displays the results of a SELECT query. Each image's primary key is stored in the value attribute of the <option> tag. When the form is submitted, the selected value is incorporated into the UPDATE query as the foreign key.

PHP Solution 17-2: Adding the Image Foreign Key (MySQLi)

This PHP solution shows how to update records in the blog table by adding the primary key of a selected image as a foreign key. It adapts admin/blog_update_mysqli.php from Chapter 15. Use the version that you created in Chapter 15. Alternatively, copy blog_update_mysqli_03.php from the ch15 folder to the admin folder and remove _03 from the filename.

1. The existing SELECT query that retrieves details of the article to be updated needs to be amended so that it includes the foreign key, image_id, and the result needs to be bound to a new result variable, $image_id. You then need to run a second SELECT query to get the details of the images table. Before you can do so, you need to free the database resources by calling the prepared statement's free_result() method. Add the following code highlighted in bold to the existing script:

484

```
if (isset($_GET['article_id']) && !$_POST) {
    // prepare SQL query
    $sql = 'SELECT article_id, image_id, title, article FROM blog
        WHERE article_id = ?';
    if ($stmt->prepare($sql)) {
        // bind the query parameter
        $stmt->bind_param('i', $_GET['article_id']);
        // execute the query
        $OK = $stmt->execute();
        // bind the results to variables and fetch
        $stmt->bind_result($article_id, $image_id, $title, $article);
        $stmt->fetch();
        // free the database resources for the second query
        $stmt->free_result();
    }
}
```

You can free the result immediately after calling the fetch() method because there's only one record in the result set, and the value in each column has been bound to a variable.

2. Inside the form, you need to display the filenames stored in the images table. Since the second SELECT statement doesn't rely on external data, it's simpler to use the query() method instead of a prepared statement. Add the following code after the article text area (it's all new code, but the PHP sections are highlighted in bold for ease of reference):

```
<p>
    <label for="image_id">Uploaded image:</label>
    <select name="image_id" id="image_id">
        <option value="">Select image</option>
        <?php
        // get the list images
        $getImages = 'SELECT image_id, filename
                        FROM images ORDER BY filename';
        $images = $conn->query($getImages);
        while ($row = $images->fetch_assoc()) {
            ?>
            <option value="<?= $row['image_id'] ?>"
                <?php
                if ($row['image_id'] == $image_id) {
                    echo 'selected';
                }
                ?>><?= safe($row['filename']) ?></option>
        <?php } ?>
    </select>
</p>
```

The first <option> tag is hard-coded with the label Select image, and its value is set to an empty string. The remaining <option> tags are populated by a while loop that extracts each record to an array called $row.

485

A conditional statement checks whether the current image_id is the same as the one already stored in the articles table. If it is, selected is inserted into the <option> tag so that it displays the correct value in the drop-down menu.

Make sure you don't omit the third character in the following line:

```
?>><?= safe($row['filename']) ?></option>
```

It's the closing angle bracket of the <option> tag, sandwiched between two PHP tags.

3. Save the page and load it into a browser. You should be automatically redirected to blog_list_mysqli.php. Select one of the EDIT links and make sure that your page looks like Figure 17-4. Check the browser source code view to verify that the value attributes of the <option> tags contain the primary key of each image.

■ **Tip** If the <select> menu doesn't list the images, there's almost certainly an error with the SELECT query in step 2. Add echo $conn->error; immediately after the call to the query() method, and reload the page. You'll need to view the browser source code to see the error message. If the message is "Commands out of sync; you can't run this command now," the problem lies with failing to free the database resources with free_result() in step 1.

---

4. The final stage is to add the image_id to the UPDATE query. Because some blog entries might not be associated with an image, you need to create alternative prepared statements, like this:

```
// if form has been submitted, update record
if (isset($_POST ['update'])) {
    // prepare update query
    if (!empty($_POST['image_id'])) {
        $sql = 'UPDATE blog SET image_id = ?, title = ?, article = ?
                WHERE article_id = ?';
        if ($stmt->prepare($sql)) {
            $stmt->bind_param('issi', $_POST['image_id'], $_POST['title'],
                $_POST['article'], $_POST['article_id']);
            $done = $stmt->execute();
        }
    } else {
        $sql = 'UPDATE blog SET image_id = NULL, title = ?, article = ?
                WHERE article_id = ?';
        if ($stmt->prepare($sql)) {
            $stmt->bind_param('ssi', $_POST['title'], $_POST['article'],
                $_POST['article_id']);
            $done = $stmt->execute();
        }
    }
}
```

If $_POST['image_id'] has a value, you add it to the SQL as the first parameter with a placeholder question mark. Since it must be an integer, you add i to the beginning of the first argument of bind_param().

However, if $_POST['image_id'] doesn't contain a value, you need to create
a different prepared statement to set the value of image_id to NULL in the SQL
query. Because it has an explicit value, you don't add it to bind_param().

5. Test the page again, select a filename from the drop-down menu, and click
Update Entry. You can verify whether the foreign key has been inserted into the
articles table by refreshing Browse in phpMyAdmin or by selecting the same
article for updating. This time, the correct filename should be displayed in the
drop-down menu.

Check your code against blog_update_mysqli_04.php in the ch17 folder, if necessary.

PHP Solution 17-3: Adding the Image Foreign Key (PDO)

This PHP solution uses PDO to update records in the blog table by adding the primary key of a selected
image as a foreign key. The main difference from MySQLi is that PDO can bind a null value to a placeholder
using the bindValue() method. These instructions adapt admin/blog_update_pdo.php from Chapter 15.
Use the version that you created in Chapter 15. Alternatively, copy blog_update_pdo_03.php from the ch15
folder to the admin folder and remove _03 from the filename.

1. Add image_id to the SELECT query that retrieves details of the article to be
updated, and bind the result to $image_id. This involves renumbering the
columns passed as the first argument to bindColumn() for $title and $article.
The revised code looks like this:

```php
if (isset($_GET['article_id']) && !$_POST) {
    // prepare SQL query
    $sql = 'SELECT article_id, image_id, title, article FROM blog
            WHERE article_id = ?';
    $stmt = $conn->prepare($sql);
    // pass the placeholder value to execute() as a single-element array
    $OK = $stmt->execute([$_GET['article_id']]);
    // bind the results
    $stmt->bindColumn(1, $article_id);
    $stmt->bindColumn(2, $image_id);
    $stmt->bindColumn(3, $title);
    $stmt->bindColumn(4, $article);
    $stmt->fetch();
}
```

2. Inside the form, you need to display the filenames stored in the images table.
Since the second SELECT statement doesn't rely on external data, it's simpler to
use the query() method instead of a prepared statement. Add the following code
after the article text area (it's all new code, but the PHP sections are highlighted
in bold for ease of reference):

```php
<p>
    <label for="image_id">Uploaded image:</label>
    <select name="image_id" id="image_id">
        <option value="">Select image</option>
        <?php
```

```php
                // get the list images
                $getImages = 'SELECT image_id, filename
                            FROM images ORDER BY filename';
                foreach ($conn->query($getImages) as $row) {
                    ?>
                    <option value="<?= $row['image_id'] ?>"
                        <?php
                        if ($row['image_id'] == $image_id) {
                            echo 'selected';
                        }
                        ?>><?= safe($row['filename']) ?></option>
                <?php } ?>
        </select>
</p>
```

The first <option> tag is hard-coded with the label Select image, and its value is set to an empty string. The remaining <option> tags are populated by a foreach loop that executes the $getImages SELECT query and extracts each record to an array called $row.

A conditional statement checks whether the current image_id is the same as the one already stored in the articles table. If it is, selected is inserted into the <option> tag so that it displays the correct value in the drop-down menu.

Make sure you don't omit the third character in the following line:

```php
?>><?= safe($row['filename']) ?></option>
```

It's the closing angle bracket of the <option> tag, sandwiched between two PHP tags.

3. Save the page and load it into a browser. You should be automatically redirected to blog_list_pdo.php. Select one of the EDIT links, and make sure that your page looks like Figure 17-4. Check the browser source code view to verify that the value attributes of the <option> tags contain the primary key of each image.

4. The final stage is to add the image_id to the UPDATE query. When a blog entry isn't associated with an image, you need to enter null in the image_id column. This involves changing the way the values are bound to the anonymous placeholders in the prepared statement. Instead of passing them as an array to the execute() method, you need to use bindValue() and bindParam(). The revised code looks like this:

```php
// if form has been submitted, update record
if (isset($_POST['update'])) {
    // prepare update query
    $sql = 'UPDATE blog SET image_id = ?, title = ?, article = ?
                WHERE article_id = ?';
    $stmt = $conn->prepare($sql);
    if (empty($_POST['image_id'])) {
        $stmt->bindValue(1, NULL, PDO::PARAM_NULL);
```

```
    } else {
        $stmt->bindParam(1, $_POST['image_id'], PDO::PARAM_INT);
    }
    $stmt->bindParam(2, $_POST['title'], PDO::PARAM_STR);
    $stmt->bindParam(3, $_POST['article'], PDO::PARAM_STR);
    $stmt->bindParam(4, $_POST['article_id'], PDO::PARAM_INT);
    // execute query
    $done = $stmt->execute();
}
```

The values are bound to the anonymous placeholders using numbers, counting from 1, to identify which placeholder they should be applied to. A conditional statement checks whether $_POST['image_id'] is empty. If it is, bindValue() sets the value to null, using the keyword NULL as the second argument and a PDO constant as the third argument. As explained in "Embedding Variables in PDO Prepared Statements" in Chapter 13, you need to use bindValue() when the value being bound is anything other than a variable.

The remaining values are all variables, so they're bound using bindParam(). I've used the PDO constants for integer and string for the remaining values. This isn't strictly necessary, but it makes the code clearer.

Finally, the array of values has been removed from between the parentheses of the execute() method.

5. Test the page again, select a filename from the drop-down menu, and click Update Entry. You can verify whether the foreign key has been inserted into the articles table by refreshing Browse in phpMyAdmin or by selecting the same article for updating. This time, the correct filename should be displayed in the drop-down menu.

Check your code against blog_update_pdo_04.php in the ch17 folder, if necessary.

Selecting Records from Multiple Tables

There are several ways to link tables in a SELECT query, but the most common is to list the table names, separated by INNER JOIN. On its own, INNER JOIN produces all possible combinations of rows (a Cartesian join). To select only related values, you need to specify the primary-key/foreign-key relationship. For example, to select articles and their related images from the blog and images tables, you can use a WHERE clause, like this:

```
SELECT title, article, filename, caption
FROM blog INNER JOIN images
WHERE blog.image_id = images.image_id
```

The title and article columns exist only in the blog table. Likewise, filename and caption exist only in the images table. They're unambiguous and don't need to be qualified. However, image_id exists in both tables, so you need to prefix each reference with the table name and a period.

For many years, it was common practice to use a comma in place of INNER JOIN, like this:

```
SELECT title, article, filename, caption
FROM blog, images
WHERE blog.image_id = images.image_id
```

■ **Caution**   Using a comma to join tables can result in SQL syntax errors because of changes made to the way joins are handled since MySQL 5.0.12. Use INNER JOIN instead.

Instead of a WHERE clause, you can use ON, like this:

```
SELECT title, article, filename, caption
FROM blog INNER JOIN images ON blog.image_id = images.image_id
```

When both columns have the same name, you can use the following syntax, which is my personal preference:

```
SELECT title, article, filename, caption
FROM blog INNER JOIN images USING (image_id)
```

■ **Note**   The column name after USING must be in parentheses.

PHP Solution 17-4: Building the Details Page

This PHP solution shows how to join the blog and images tables to display a selected article with its associated photo. The code for MySQLi and PDO is almost identical, so this solution covers both.

1. Copy details_01.php from the ch17 folder to the php8sols site root and rename it details.php. Do not update the links if your editing environment prompts you to do so. Make sure that footer.php and menu.php are in the includes folder, and load the page in a browser. It should look like Figure 17-5.

Figure 17-5. The details page contains a placeholder image and text

2. Load `blog_list_mysqli.php` or `blog_list_pdo.php` into a browser and update the following three articles by assigning the image filename as indicated:

    •   Basin of Contentment: `basin.jpg`

    •   Tiny Restaurants Crowded Together: `menu.jpg`

    •   Trainee Geishas Go Shopping: `maiko.jpg`

3. Navigate to the `blog` table in phpMyAdmin and click the `Browse` tab to check that the foreign keys have been registered. At least one article should have `NULL` as the value for `image_id`, as shown in Figure 17-6.

article_id	image_id	title	article
1	NULL	Spectacular View of Mount Fuji from the Bullet Tra...	One of the b... known tour... of Japan is o...
2	4	Trainee Geishas Go Shopping	Although Kyo... attracts larg... numbers of... t...
3	6	Tiny Restaurants Crowded Together	Every city ha... alleyways t... best avoi...
4	1	Basin of Contentment	Most visitors to... Ryoanji Tem... see just one...

Figure 17-6. The foreign key of the article not associated with an image is set to NULL

4. Before attempting to display an image, we need to make sure that it comes from where we expect and that it is actually an image. Create a variable at the top of details.php to store the relative path to the images directory (complete with trailing slash) like this:

```
// Relative path to image directory
$imageDir = './images/';
```

5. Next, include utility_funcs.php from the previous chapter (if necessary, copy it from the ch16 folder to the includes folder). Then include the database connection file, create a read-only connection, and prepare the SQL query inside a PHP code block above the DOCTYPE declaration, like this:

```
require_once './includes/utility_funcs.php';
require_once './includes/connection.php';
// connect to the database
$conn = dbConnect('read');  // add 'pdo' if necessary
// check for article_id in query string
$article_id = isset($_GET['article_id']) ? (int) $_GET['article_id'] : 0;
$sql = "SELECT title, article,DATE_FORMAT(updated, '%W, %M %D, %Y') AS updated,
            filename, caption
            FROM blog INNER JOIN images USING (image_id)
            WHERE blog.article_id = $article_id";
$result = $conn->query($sql);
$row = $result->fetch_assoc();  // for PDO use $result->fetch();
```

The code checks for article_id in the URL query string using the ternary operator. The condition tests for its existence with isset(). If that returns true, the value is assigned to $article_id using the (int) casting operator to make sure it's an integer. Otherwise, $article_id is set to 0. You could choose a default article instead, but leave it at 0 for the moment because I want to illustrate an important point.

The SELECT query retrieves the title, article, and updated columns from the blog table and the filename and caption columns from the images table. The value of updated is formatted using the DATE_FORMAT() function and an alias, as described in Chapter 16. Because only one record is being retrieved, using the original column name as the alias doesn't cause a problem with the sort order.

The tables are joined using INNER JOIN and a USING clause that matches the values in the image_id columns in both tables. The WHERE clause selects the article identified by $article_id. Since the data type of $article_id has been checked, it's safe to use in the query. There's no need to use a prepared statement.

Note that the query is wrapped in double quotes so that the value of $article_id is interpreted. To avoid conflicts with the outer pair of quotes, single quotes are used around the format string passed as an argument to DATE_FORMAT().

6. Now that we have queried the database, we can check the image. To make sure that it's where we expect, pass the value of $row['filename'] to the basename() function and concatenate the result to the relative path to the images directory. We can then check that the file exists and is readable. If it is, get its width and height using getimagesize(). Add the following code immediately after the code you inserted in the previous step:

```php
if ($row && !empty($row['filename'])) {
    $image = $imageDir . basename($row['filename']);
    if (file_exists($image) && is_readable($image)) {
        $imageSize = getimagesize($image)[3];
    }
}
```

As explained in PHP Solution 10-1 in Chapter 10, `getimagesize()` returns an array of information about an image, including at index 3 a string containing the correct width and height attributes ready for insertion in an `<img>` tag. Here, we're using array dereferencing to assign it directly to `$imageSize`.

7. The rest of the code displays the results of the SQL query in the main body of the page. Replace the placeholder text in the `<h2>` tags like this:

```php
<h2><?php if ($row) {
        echo safe($row['title']);
    } else {
        echo 'No record found';
    }
    ?>
</h2>
```

If the `SELECT` query finds no results, `$row` will be empty, which PHP interprets as `false`. So this displays the title or "No record found" if the result set is empty.

8. Replace the placeholder date like this:

```php
<p><?php if ($row) { echo $row['updated']; } ?></p>
```

9. Immediately following the date paragraph is a `<figure>` element containing a placeholder image. Not all articles are associated with an image, so the `<figure>` needs to be wrapped in a conditional statement that checks that `$imageSize` contains a value. Amend the `<figure>` like this:

```php
<?php if (!empty($imageSize)) { ?>
    <figure>
        <img src="<?= $image ?>" alt="<?= safe($row['caption']) ?>"
        <?= $imageSize ?>>
    </figure>
<?php } ?>
```

10. Finally, you need to display the article. Delete the paragraph of placeholder text, and add the following code between the closing curly brace and closing PHP tag at the end of the final code block in the previous step:

```php
<?php } if ($row) { echo convertToParas($row['article']); } ?>
```

This uses the `convertToParas()` function in `utility_funcs.php` to wrap the blog entry in `<p>` tags and replace sequences of newline characters with closing and opening tags (see "Displaying Paragraphs" in Chapter 16).

11. Save the page and load `blog.php` into a browser. Click the More link for an article that has an image assigned through a foreign key. You should see `details.php` with the full article and image laid out as shown in Figure 17-7.

    Check your code, if necessary, with `details_mysqli_01.php` or `details_pdo_01.php` in the ch17 folder.

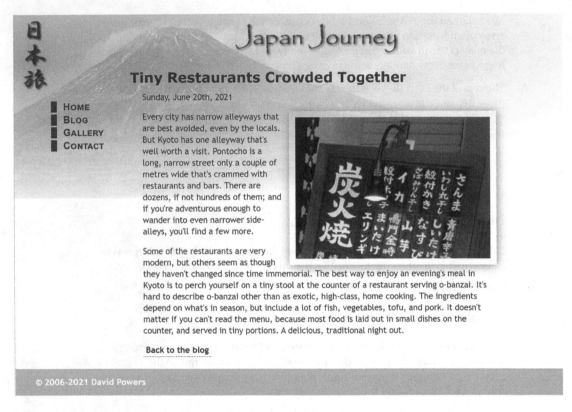

Figure 17-7. *The details page pulls the article from one table and the image from another*

12. Click the link back to `blog.php` and test the other items. Each article that has an image associated with it should display correctly. Click the More link for the article that doesn't have an image. This time you should see the result shown in Figure 17-8.

Figure 17-8. *The lack of an associated image causes the SELECT query to fail*

You know that the article is in the database because the first two sentences wouldn't be displayed in blog.php otherwise. To understand this sudden "disappearance," refer to Figure 17-6. The value of image_id is NULL for the record that doesn't have an image associated with it. Because all the records in the images table have a primary key, the USING clause can't find a match. The next section explains how to deal with this type of situation.

Finding Records That Don't Have a Matching Foreign Key

Copy the SELECT query from PHP Solution 17-4 and remove the condition that searches for a specific article, which leaves this:

```
SELECT title, article, DATE_FORMAT(updated, '%W, %M %D, %Y') AS updated, filename, caption
FROM blog INNER JOIN images USING (image_id)
```

If you run this query in the SQL tab of phpMyAdmin, it produces the result shown in Figure 17-9.

title	article	updated	filename	caption
Trainee Geishas Go Shopping	Although Kyoto attracts large numbers of foreign t...	Sunday, June 20th, 2021	maiko.jpg	Maiko—trainee geishas in Kyoto
Tiny Restaurants Crowded Together	Every city has narrow alleyways that are best avoi...	Sunday, June 20th, 2021	menu.jpg	Menu outside restaurant in Pontocho, Kyoto
Basin of Contentment	Most visitors to Ryoanji Temple go to see just one...	Sunday, June 20th, 2021	basin.jpg	Water basin at Ryoanji temple, Kyoto

Figure 17-9. *INNER JOIN finds only records that have a match in both tables*

With INNER JOIN, the SELECT query succeeds in finding only those records where there's a complete match. One of the articles doesn't have an image associated with it, so the value of image_id in the articles table is NULL, which doesn't match anything in the images table.

In this type of situation, you need to use LEFT JOIN instead of INNER JOIN. With LEFT JOIN, the result includes records that have a match in the left table, but not in the right one. Left and right refer to the order in which you perform the join. Rewrite the SELECT query like this:

```
SELECT title, article, DATE_FORMAT(updated, '%W, %M %D, %Y') AS updated, filename, caption
FROM blog LEFT JOIN images USING (image_id)
```

When you run it in phpMyAdmin, you get all four articles, as shown in Figure 17-10.

title	article	updated	filename	caption
Spectacular View of Mount Fuji from the Bullet Tra...	One of the best-known tourist images of Japan is o...	Sunday, June 20th, 2021	*NULL*	*NULL*
Trainee Geishas Go Shopping	Although Kyoto attracts large numbers of foreign t...	Sunday, June 20th, 2021	maiko.jpg	Maiko—trainee geishas in Kyoto
Tiny Restaurants Crowded Together	Every city has narrow alleyways that are best avoi...	Sunday, June 20th, 2021	menu.jpg	Menu outside restaurant in Pontocho, Kyoto
Basin of Contentment	Most visitors to Ryoanji Temple go to see just one...	Sunday, June 20th, 2021	basin.jpg	Water basin at Ryoanji temple, Kyoto

Figure 17-10. *LEFT JOIN includes records that don't have a match in the right table*

As you can see, the empty fields from the right table (images) are displayed as NULL.
If the column names are not the same in both tables, use ON like this:

```
FROM table_1 LEFT JOIN table_2 ON table_1.col_name = table_2.col_name
```

So now you can rewrite the SQL query in details.php like this:
```
$sql = "SELECT title, article, DATE_FORMAT(updated, '%W, %M %D, %Y') AS updated,
        filename, caption
        FROM blog LEFT JOIN images USING (image_id)
        WHERE blog.article_id = $article_id";
```

If you click the More link to view the article that doesn't have an associated image, you should now see the article correctly displayed as shown in Figure 17-11. The other articles should still display correctly, too. The finished code can be found in details_mysqli_02.php and details_pdo_02.php.

Figure 17-11. *LEFT JOIN also retrieves articles that don't have a matching foreign key*

Creating an Intelligent Link

The link at the bottom of details.php goes straight back to blog.php. That's fine with only four items in the blog table, but once you start getting more records in a database, you need to build a navigation system, as I showed you in Chapter 14. The problem with a navigation system is that you need a way to return visitors to the same point in the result set that they came from.

PHP Solution 17-5: Returning to the Same Point in a Navigation System

This PHP solution checks whether the visitor arrived from an internal or an external link. If the referring page was within the same site, the link returns the visitor to the same place. If the referring page was an external site or if the server doesn't support the necessary superglobal variables, the script substitutes a standard link. It is shown here in the context of details.php, but it can be used on any page.

The code is not database-dependent, so it's identical for both MySQLi and PDO.

1. Locate the back link in the main body of details.php. It looks like this:

    ```
    <p><a href="blog.php">Back to the blog</a></p>
    ```

2. Place your cursor immediately to the right of the first quotation mark, and insert the following code highlighted in bold:

    ```
    <p><a href="
    <?php
    // check that browser supports $_SERVER variables
    if (isset($_SERVER['HTTP_REFERER']) && isset($_SERVER['HTTP_HOST'])) {
        $url = parse_url($_SERVER['HTTP_REFERER']);
        // find if visitor was referred from a different domain
        if ($url['host'] == $_SERVER['HTTP_HOST']) {
            // if same domain, use referring URL
            echo $_SERVER['HTTP_REFERER'];
        }
    } else {
        // otherwise, send to main page
        echo 'blog.php';
    } ?>">Back to the blog</a></p>
    ```

$_SERVER['HTTP_REFERER'] and $_SERVER['HTTP_HOST'] are superglobal variables that contain the URL of the referring page and the current hostname. You need to check their existence with isset() because not all servers support them. Also, the browser might block the URL of the referring page.

The parse_url() function creates an array containing each part of a URL, so $url['host'] contains the hostname. If it matches $_SERVER['HTTP_HOST'], you know that the visitor was referred by an internal link, so the full URL of the internal link is inserted in the href attribute. This includes any query string, so the link sends the visitor back to the same position in a navigation system. Otherwise, an ordinary link is created to the target page.

The finished code is in details_mysqli_03.php and details_pdo_3.php in the ch17 folder.

Chapter Review

Retrieving information stored in multiple tables is relatively simple with INNER JOIN and LEFT JOIN. The key to working successfully with multiple tables lies in structuring the relationship between them so that complex relationships can always be resolved as 1:1, if necessary through a cross-reference (or linking) table. The next chapter continues the exploration of working with multiple tables, showing you how to deal with foreign-key relationships when inserting, updating, and deleting records.

CHAPTER 18

■ ■ ■

Managing Multiple Database Tables

The previous chapter showed you how to use INNER JOIN and LEFT JOIN to retrieve information stored in multiple tables. You also learned how to link existing tables by adding an extra column to the child table and updating each record individually to insert a foreign key. However, most of the time you'll want to insert data simultaneously in both tables. That presents a challenge, because INSERT commands can operate on only one table at a time. You need to handle the insert operations in the correct sequence, starting with the parent table, so that you can get the new record's primary key and insert it in the child table at the same time as other details. Similar considerations also need to be taken into account when updating and deleting records. The code involved isn't difficult, but you need to keep the sequence of events clearly in mind as you build the scripts.

This chapter guides you through the process of inserting new articles in the blog table, optionally selecting a related image or uploading a new one, and assigning the article to one or more categories, all in a single operation. Then you'll build the scripts to update and delete articles without destroying the referential integrity of related tables.

You'll also learn about processing multiple queries as a batch using a transaction, rolling the database back to its original state if any part of the batch fails, as well as about foreign-key constraints, which control what happens if you try to delete records that still have a foreign-key relationship in another table. Not all databases support transactions and foreign-key constraints, so it's important to check whether your remote server does. This chapter also explains what measures you can take to preserve the integrity of your data if your server doesn't support foreign-key constraints.

In particular, you'll learn about the following:

- Inserting, updating, and deleting records in related tables

- Finding the primary key of a record immediately after it has been created

- Processing multiple queries as a single batch and rolling back if any part fails

- Converting a table's storage engine

- Establishing foreign-key constraints between InnoDB tables

Maintaining Referential Integrity

With single tables, it doesn't matter how often you update a record or how many records you delete; the impact on other records is zero. Once you store the primary key of a record as a foreign key in a different table, you create a dependency that needs to be managed. For example, Figure 18-1 shows the second article from the blog table ("Trainee Geishas Go Shopping") linked to the Kyoto and People categories through the article2cat cross-reference table.

© David Powers 2022
D. Powers, *PHP 8 Solutions*, https://doi.org/10.1007/978-1-4842-7141-4_18

Figure 18-1. You need to manage foreign-key relations to avoid orphaned records

If you delete the article, but fail to delete the entries for article_id 2 in the cross-reference table, a query that looks for all articles in the Kyoto or People category tries to match a nonexistent record in the blog table. Similarly, if you decide to delete one of the categories without also deleting matching records in the cross-reference table, a query that looks for the categories associated with an article tries to match a nonexistent category.

Before long, your database is littered with orphaned records. Fortunately, maintaining referential integrity is not difficult. SQL does it through the establishment of rules known as foreign-key constraints that tell the database what to do when you update or delete a record that has dependent records in another table.

Support for Transactions and Foreign-key Constraints

Transactions and foreign-key constraints are supported by InnoDB, the default storage engine in MySQL 5.5 and later. The equivalent storage engine in MariaDB is Percona XtraDB, but it identifies itself as InnoDB and has the same features. Even if your remote server is running the latest version of MySQL or MariaDB, there's no guarantee that InnoDB is supported, because your hosting company may have disabled it.

If your server is running an older version of MySQL, the default storage engine is MyISAM, which doesn't support transactions or foreign-key constraints. However, you might still have access to InnoDB, because it has been an integral part of MySQL since version 4.0. Converting MyISAM tables to InnoDB is very simple and takes only a few seconds.

If you don't have access to InnoDB, you need to maintain referential integrity by building the necessary rules into your PHP scripts. This chapter shows both approaches.

■ **Note** MyISAM tables have the advantage of being very fast. They require less disk space and are ideal for storing large amounts of data that isn't changed very often. However, the MyISAM engine is no longer being actively developed, so it's not recommended to use it for new projects.

PHP Solution 18-1: Checking Whether InnoDB Is Supported

This PHP solution explains how to check whether your remote server supports the InnoDB storage engine.

1. If your hosting company provides phpMyAdmin to administer your database(s), launch phpMyAdmin on your remote server and click the Engines tab at the top of the screen, if it's available. This displays a list of storage engines similar to Figure 18-2.

Storage Engine	Description
CSV	Stores tables as CSV files
MRG_MyISAM	Collection of identical MyISAM tables
MEMORY	Hash based, stored in memory, useful for temporary tables
Aria	Crash-safe tables with MyISAM heritage. Used for internal temporary tables and privilege tables
MyISAM	Non-transactional engine with good performance and small data footprint
SEQUENCE	Generated tables filled with sequential values
InnoDB	Supports transactions, row-level locking, foreign keys and encryption for tables
PERFORMANCE_SCHEMA	Performance Schema

Figure 18-2. *Checking storage engine support through phpMyAdmin*

■ **Note**   The screenshot in Figure 18–2 was taken on a MariaDB server. You are likely to see a different selection of storage engines on a MySQL server, but both MySQL and MariaDB should normally offer at least InnoDB and MyISAM. The Aria storage engine is MariaDB's improved version of MyISAM. It's not covered in this book because it's not available on MySQL nor does it support transactions or foreign-key constraints.

---

2. The list displays all storage engines, including those that are not supported. Unsupported or disabled storage engines are grayed out. If you're not sure of the status of InnoDB, click its name in the list.

3. If InnoDB is not supported, you'll see a message telling you so. If, on the other hand, you see a list of variables similar to Figure 18-3, you're in luck—InnoDB is supported.

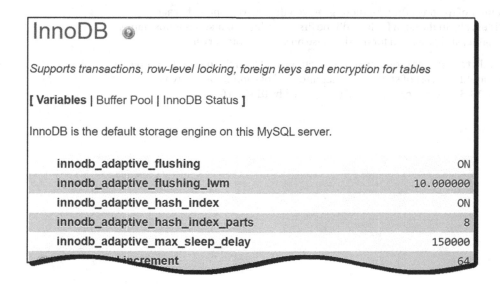

Figure 18-3. *Confirmation that InnoDB is supported*

4. If there's no `Engines` tab in phpMyAdmin, select any table in your database and click the `Operations` tab at the top right of the screen. In the `Table options` section, click the down arrow to the right of the `Storage engine` field to display the available options (see Figure 18-4). If InnoDB is listed, it's supported.

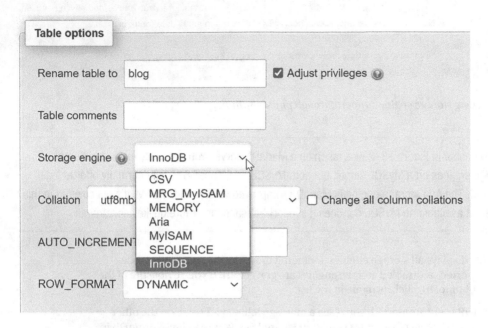

Figure 18-4. *The available storage engines are listed in Table options*

5. If neither of the preceding methods gives you the answer, open `storage_engines.php` in the `ch18` folder. Edit the first three lines to insert the hostname, username, and password for the database on your remote server.

6. Upload `storage_engines.php` to your web site and load the page into a browser. You should see a list of storage engines and level of support, as shown in Figure 18-5. In some cases, `NO` will be replaced by `DISABLED`.

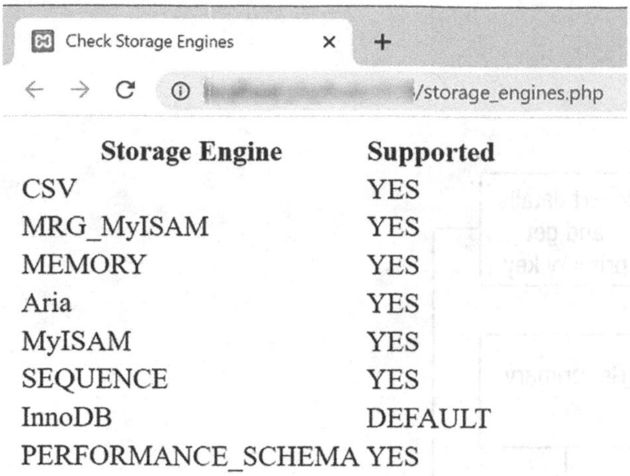

Storage Engine	Supported
CSV	YES
MRG_MyISAM	YES
MEMORY	YES
Aria	YES
MyISAM	YES
SEQUENCE	YES
InnoDB	DEFAULT
PERFORMANCE_SCHEMA	YES

Figure 18-5. The SQL query in storage_engines.php reports which ones are supported

As Figure 18-5 shows, a typical installation supports several storage engines. What may come as a surprise is that you can use different storage engines within the same database. In fact, it's recommended that you do. Even if your remote server supports InnoDB, it's usually more efficient to use MyISAM or Aria for tables that don't require transactions or have a foreign-key relationship. Use InnoDB for tables that require transactions or have foreign-key relationships.

I'll explain how to convert tables to InnoDB later in this chapter. Before that, let's look at how to establish and use foreign-key relationships regardless of the storage engine being used.

Inserting Records into Multiple Tables

An INSERT query can insert data into only one table. Consequently, when working with multiple tables, you need to plan your insert scripts carefully to ensure that all the information is stored and that the correct foreign-key relationships are established.

PHP Solutions 17-2 (MySQLi) and 17-3 (PDO) in the previous chapter showed how to add the correct foreign key for an image that is already registered in the database. However, when inserting a new blog entry, you need to be able to select an existing image, upload a new image, or choose to have no image at all. This means that your processing script needs to check whether an image has been selected or uploaded and execute the relevant commands accordingly. In addition, tagging a blog entry with zero or more categories increases the number of decisions the script needs to make. Figure 18-6 shows the decision chain.

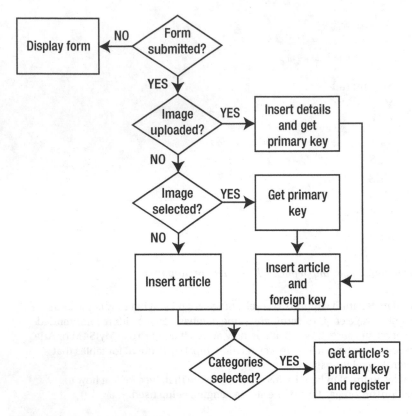

Figure 18-6. *The decision chain for inserting a new blog article with an image and categories*

When the page first loads, the form hasn't been submitted, so the page simply displays the insert form. Both the existing images and categories are listed in the insert form by querying the database in the same way as was done for the images in the update form in PHP Solutions 17-2 and 17-3.

After the form has been submitted, the processing script goes through the following steps:

1. If an image has been uploaded, the upload is processed, the details of the image are stored in the images table, and the script gets the primary key of the new record.

2. If no image has been uploaded, but an existing image has been selected, the script gets its foreign key from the value submitted through the $_POST array.

3. In either case, the new blog article is inserted in the blog table along with the image's primary key as a foreign key. However, if an image has neither been uploaded nor selected from the existing ones, the article is inserted in the blog table without a foreign key.

4. Finally, the script checks whether any categories have been selected. If they have, the script gets the new article's primary key and combines it with the primary keys of the selected categories in the article2cat table.

If there's a problem at any stage, the script needs to abandon the rest of the process and redisplay the user's input. The script is quite long, so I'll break it up into several sections. The first stage is to create the article2cat cross-reference table.

Creating a Cross-reference Table

When dealing with many-to-many relationships in a database, you need to build a cross-reference table like the one in Figure 18-1. A cross-reference table consists of just two columns, which are jointly declared as the table's primary key (known as a **composite primary key**). If you look at Figure 18-7, you'll see that the article_id and cat_id columns both contain the same number several times—something that's unacceptable in a primary key, which must be unique. However, in a composite primary key, it's the combination of both values that is unique. The first two combinations, 1,3 and 2,1, are not repeated anywhere else in the table, nor are any of the others.

article_id	cat_id
1	3
2	1
2	2
3	1
3	4
4	1
4	3
4	5

Figure 18-7. *In a cross-reference table, both columns together form a composite primary key*

Setting Up the Categories and Cross-Reference Tables

In the ch18 folder, you'll find categories.sql, which contains the SQL to create the categories table and the cross-reference table, article2cat, together with some sample data. In phpMyAdmin, select the phpsols database, and use the Import tab to load categories.sql to create the tables and data. The settings for the tables are listed in Tables 18-1 and 18-2. Both database tables have just two columns.

Table 18-1. *Settings for the categories table*

Name	Type	Length/Values	Attributes	Null	Index	A_I
cat_id	INT		UNSIGNED	Deselected	PRIMARY	Selected
category	VARCHAR	20		Deselected		

Table 18-2. *Settings for the article2cat cross-reference table*

Name	Type	Length/Values	Attributes	Null	Index	A_I
article_id	INT		UNSIGNED	Deselected	PRIMARY	
cat_id	INT		UNSIGNED	Deselected	PRIMARY	

The important point about the definition for a cross-reference table is that both columns are set as primary key and that the A_I (AUTO_INCREMENT) check box is not selected for either column.

■ **Caution** To create a composite primary key, you must declare both columns to be primary keys at the same time. If, by mistake, you declare only one as the primary key, the database prevents you from adding the second one later. You must delete the primary-key index from the single column and then reapply it to both. It's the combination of the two columns that is treated as the primary key.

Getting the Filename of an Uploaded Image

The script makes use of the Upload class from Chapter 9, but the class needs slight tweaking because the filenames of uploaded files are incorporated into the $messages property.

PHP Solution 18-2: Improving the Upload Class

This PHP solution adapts the Upload class from Chapter 9 by creating a new protected property to store the names of successfully uploaded files, together with a public method to retrieve the array of names.

1. Open Upload.php in the Php8Solutions/File folder. Alternatively, copy Upload. php from the ch18/Php8Solutions/File folder and save it in Php8Solutions/ File in the php8sols site root.

2. Add the following line to the list of properties at the top of the file:

    ```php
    protected $filenames = [];
    ```

    This initializes a protected property called $filenames as an empty array.

3. Amend the moveFile() method to add the amended filename to the $filenames property if the file is successfully uploaded. The new code is highlighted in bold:

    ```php
    protected function moveFile($file) {
        $filename = $this->newName ?? $file['name'];
        $success = move_uploaded_file($file['tmp_name'], $this->destination .
    $filename);
        if ($success) {
            // add the amended filename to the array of uploaded files
            $this->filenames[] = $filename;
            $result = $file['name'] . ' was uploaded successfully';
            if (!is_null($this->newName)) {
                $result .= ', and was renamed ' . $this->newName;
            }
            $this->messages[] = $result;
        } else {
            $this->messages[] = 'Could not upload ' . $file['name'];
        }
    }
    ```

    The name is added to the $filenames array only if the file is successfully moved to the destination folder.

4. Add a public method to return the values stored in the $filenames property. The code looks like this:

```
public function getFilenames() {
    return $this->filenames;
}
```

It doesn't matter where you put this code in the class definition, but it's common practice to keep all public methods together.

5. Save Upload.php. If you need to check your code, compare it with Upload_01.php in the ch18/Php8Solutions/File folder.

Adapting the Insert Form to Deal with Multiple Tables

The insert form for blog articles that you created in Chapter 15 already contains the code needed to insert most of the details in the blog table. Rather than start again from scratch, it makes sense to adapt the existing page. As it stands, the page contains only a text input field for the title and a text area for the article.

You need to add a multiple-choice <select> list for categories and a drop-down <select> menu for existing images.

To prevent a user from selecting an existing image at the same time as uploading a new one, a check box and JavaScript control the display of the relevant input fields. Selecting the check box disables the drop-down menu for existing images and displays the input fields for a new image and caption. Deselecting the check box hides and disables the file and caption fields and re-enables the drop-down menu. If JavaScript is disabled, the options for uploading a new image and captions are hidden.

■ **Note**   To save space, most of the remaining PHP solutions in this chapter give detailed instructions only for MySQLi. The structure and PHP logic for the PDO version are the same. The only differences lie in the commands used to submit the SQL queries and to display the results. Fully commented PDO files are in the ch18 folder.

PHP Solution 18-3: Adding the Category and Image Input Fields

This PHP solution begins the process of adapting the blog entry insert form from Chapter 15 by adding the input fields for categories and images.

1. In the admin folder, find and open the version of blog_insert_mysqli.php that you created in Chapter 15. Alternatively, copy blog_insert_mysqli_01.php from the ch18 folder to the admin folder and remove _01 from the filename.

2. The <select> elements for the categories and existing images need to query the database when the page first loads, so you need to move the connection script and database connection outside the conditional statement that checks if the form has been submitted. Locate the lines highlighted in bold:

```
if (isset($_POST['insert'])) {
    require_once '../includes/connection.php';
    // initialize flag
```

```
    $OK = false;
    // create database connection
$conn = dbConnect('write');
```

Move them outside the conditional statement and include utility_funcs.php, like this:

```
require_once '../includes/connection.php';
require_once '../includes/utility_funcs.php';
// create database connection
$conn = dbConnect('write');
if (isset($_POST['insert'])) {
    // initialize flag
    $OK = false;
```

3. The form in the body of the page needs to be capable of uploading a file, so you need to add the enctype attribute to the opening <form> tag, like this:

```
<form method="post" action="blog_insert_mysqli.php"
enctype="multipart/form-data">
```

4. If an error occurs when trying to upload a file—for example, if it's too big or is not an image file—the insert operation will be halted. Amend the existing text input field and text area to redisplay the values, using the same technique as shown in Chapter 6. The text input field looks like this:

```
<input name="title" type="text" id="title" value="<?php if (isset($error)) {
    echo safe($_POST['title']);
} ?>">
```

The text area looks like this:

```
<textarea name="article" id="article"><?php if (isset($error)) {
    echo safe($_POST['article']);
} ?></textarea>
```

Make sure there's no gap between the opening and closing PHP tags and the HTML. Otherwise, you'll add unwanted whitespace inside the text input field and text area.

5. The new form elements go between the text area and the Submit button. First, add the code for the multiple-choice <select> list for categories. The code looks like this:

```
<p>
    <label for="category">Categories:</label>
    <select name="category[]" size="5" multiple id="category">
        <?php
        // get categories
        $getCats = 'SELECT cat_id, category FROM categories ORDER BY category';
        $categories = $conn->query($getCats);
```

```
    while ($row = $categories->fetch_assoc()) {
        ?>
        <option value="<?= $row['cat_id'] ?>" <?php
        if (isset($_POST['category']) && in_array($row['cat_id'],
            $_POST['category'])) { echo 'selected';
        } ?>><?= safe($row['category']) ?></option>
    <?php } ?>
    </select>
</p>
```

To allow the selection of multiple values, the multiple attribute has been added to the <select> tag, and the size attribute has been set to 5. The values need to be submitted as an array, so a pair of square brackets has been appended to the name attribute.

The SQL queries the categories table, and a while loop populates the <option> tags with the primary keys and category names. The conditional statement in the while loop adds selected to the <option> tag to redisplay selected values if the insert operation fails.

6. Save blog_insert_mysqli.php and load the page into a browser. The form should now look like Figure 18-8.

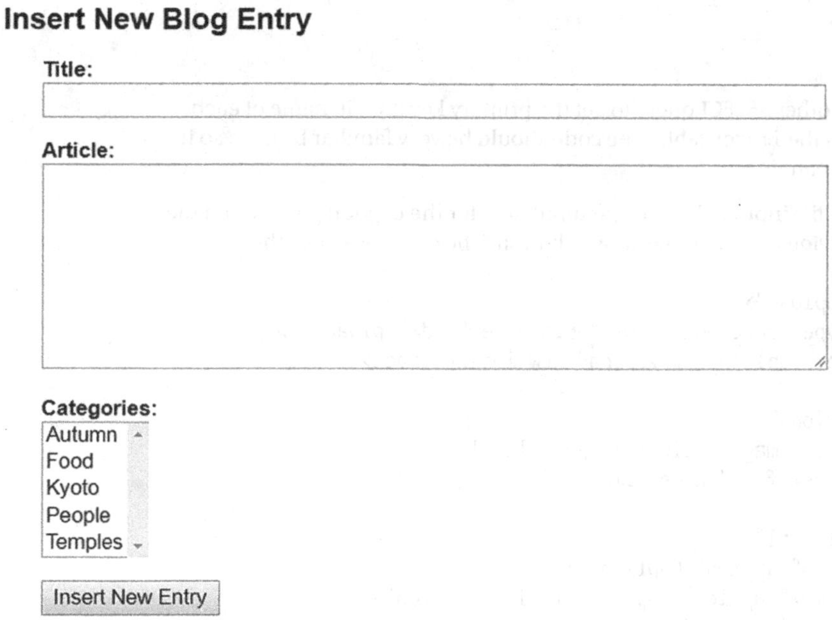

Insert New Blog Entry

Title:

Article:

Categories:
Autumn
Food
Kyoto
People
Temples

Insert New Entry

Figure 18-8. *The multiple-choice <select> list pulls the values from the categories table*

7. View the page's source code to verify that the primary key of each category is correctly embedded in the value attribute of each <option> tag. You can compare your code with blog_insert_mysqli_02.php in the ch18 folder.

8. Next, create the `<select>` drop-down menu to display the images already registered in the database. Add this code immediately after the code you inserted in step 5:

```
<p>
    <label for="image_id">Uploaded image:</label>
    <select name="image_id" id="image_id">
        <option value="">Select image</option>
        <?php
        // get the list of images
        $getImages = 'SELECT image_id, filename
                        FROM images ORDER BY filename';
        $images = $conn->query($getImages);
        while ($row = $images->fetch_assoc()) {
            ?>
            <option value="<?= $row['image_id'] ?>"
                <?php
                if (isset($_POST['image_id']) && $row['image_id'] ==
                    $_POST['image_id']) {
                    echo 'selected';
                }
                ?>><?= safe($row['filename']) ?></option>
        <?php } ?>
    </select>
</p>
```

This creates another SELECT query to get the primary key and filename of each image stored in the images table. The code should be very familiar by now, so it needs no explanation.

9. The check box, file input field, and text input field for the caption go between the code in the previous step and the Submit button. The code looks like this:

```
<p id="allowUpload">
    <input type="checkbox" name="upload_new" id="upload_new">
    <label for="upload_new">Upload new image</label>
</p>
<p class="optional">
    <label for="image">Select image:</label>
    <input type="file" name="image" id="image">
</p>
<p class="optional">
    <label for="caption">Caption:</label>
    <input name="caption" type="text" id="caption">
</p>
```

The paragraph that contains the check box has been given the ID allowUpload, and the two other paragraphs have been assigned a class called optional. The style rules in admin.css set the display property of these three paragraphs to none.

10. Save blog_insert_mysqli.php and load the page in a browser. The images
    <select> drop-down menu is displayed below the categories list, but the three
    form elements you inserted in step 9 are hidden. This is what will be displayed
    if JavaScript is disabled in the browser. Users will have the option to select
    categories and an existing image but not to upload a new image.

    If necessary, check your code against blog_insert_mysqli_03.php in the ch18
    folder.

11. Copy toggle_fields.js from the ch18 folder to the admin folder. The file
    contains the following JavaScript:

    ```
    const cbox = document.getElementById('allowUpload');
    cbox.style.display = 'block';
    const uploadImage = document.getElementById('upload_new');
    uploadImage.onclick = function () {
        const image_id = document.getElementById('image_id');
        const image = document.getElementById('image');
        const caption = document.getElementById('caption');
        const sel = uploadImage.checked;
        image_id.disabled = sel;
        image.parentNode.style.display = sel ? 'block' : 'none';
        caption.parentNode.style.display = sel ? 'block' : 'none';
        image.disabled = !sel;
        caption.disabled = !sel;
    }
    ```

    This uses the IDs of the elements inserted in step 8 to control their display. If
    JavaScript is enabled, the check box is automatically displayed when the page
    loads, but the file input field and text input field for the caption remain hidden.
    If the check box is checked, the drop-down menu of existing images is disabled,
    and the hidden elements are displayed. If the check box is subsequently
    unchecked, the drop-down menu is re-enabled, and the file input field and
    caption field are hidden again.

12. Link toggle_fields.js to blog_insert_mysqli.php with a <script> tag just
    before the closing </body> tag, like this:

    ```
    </form>
        <script src="toggle_fields.js"></script>
    </body>
    ```

    Adding the JavaScript at the bottom of the page speeds up downloading and
    display. The code in toggle_fields.js won't work correctly if you add it to the
    <head>.

13. Save blog_insert_mysqli.php and load the page in a browser. In a JavaScript-
    enabled browser, the check box should be displayed between the <select>
    drop-down menu and the Submit button. Select the check box to disable the
    drop-down menu and display the hidden fields, as shown in Figure 18-9.

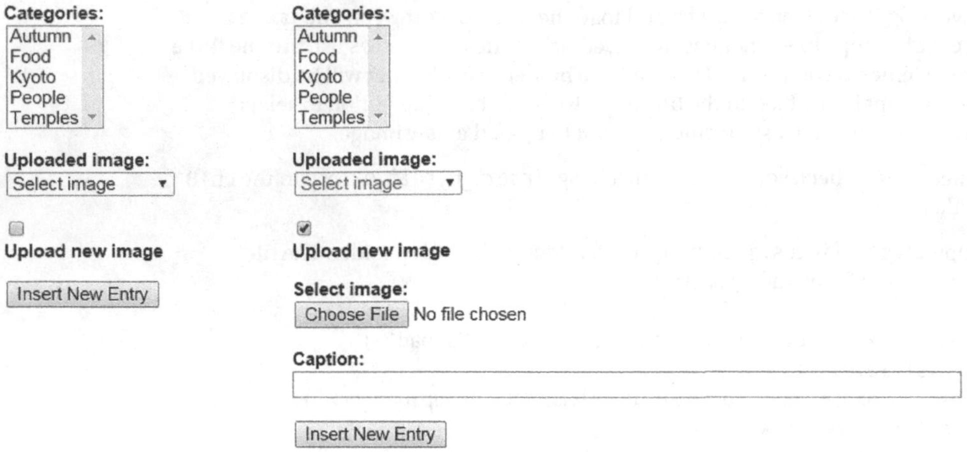

Categories:
```
Autumn  ▲
Food
Kyoto
People
Temples ▼
```

Uploaded image:
```
Select image      ▼
```

☐
Upload new image

[Insert New Entry]

Categories:
```
Autumn  ▲
Food
Kyoto
People
Temples ▼
```

Uploaded image:
```
Select image      ▼
```

☑
Upload new image

Select image:
[Choose File] No file chosen

Caption:
```
[                                                        ]
```

[Insert New Entry]

Figure 18-9. *The check box controls the display of the file and caption input fields*

14. Deselect the check box. The file and caption input fields are hidden, and the drop-down menu is re-enabled. You can check your code, if necessary, with `blog_insert_mysqli_04.php` and `toggle_fields.js` in the ch18 folder.

I used JavaScript rather than PHP to control the display of the file and caption input fields because PHP is a server-side language. After the PHP engine has sent the output to the browser, it has no further interaction with the page unless you send another request to the web server. JavaScript, on the other hand, works in the browser, so it's able to manipulate the content of the page locally. JavaScript can also be used in conjunction with PHP to send requests to the web server in the background, and it can use the result to refresh part of the page without reloading it—a technique known as Ajax, which is beyond the scope of this book.

The updated insert form now has input fields for categories and images, but the processing script still handles only the text input field for the title and the text area for the blog entry.

PHP Solution 18-4: Inserting Data into Multiple Tables

This PHP solution adapts the existing script in `blog_insert_mysqli.php` to upload a new image (if required) and then insert data into the `images`, `blog`, and `article2cat` tables following the decision chain outlined in Figure 18-6. It assumes you have set up the `article2cat` cross-reference table and have completed PHP Solutions 18-2 and 18-3.

Don't attempt to rush through this section. The code is quite long, but it brings together many of the techniques you have learned previously.

■ **Note** If you're using PDO, a separate section after this PHP solution describes the main differences in the code.

---

1. The `Upload` class that you updated in PHP Solution 18-2 uses a namespace, so you need to import it at the top level of the script. Add this line immediately after the opening PHP tag at the top of `blog_insert_mysqli.php`:

```
use Php8Solutions\File\Upload;
```

2. Immediately after the prepared statement has been initialized, insert the following conditional statement to process the image if one has been uploaded or selected:

```
// initialize prepared statement
$stmt = $conn->stmt_init();
// if a file has been uploaded, process it
if(isset($_POST['upload_new']) && $_FILES['image']['error'] == 0) {
    $imageOK = false;
    require_once '../Php8Solutions/File/Upload.php';
    $loader = new Upload('image', '../images/');
    $names = $loader->getFilenames();
    // $names will be an empty array if the upload failed
    if ($names) {
        $sql = 'INSERT INTO images (filename, caption) VALUES (?, ?)';
        if ($stmt->prepare($sql)) {
            $stmt->bind_param('ss', $names[0], $_POST['caption']);
            $stmt->execute();
            $imageOK = $stmt->affected_rows;
        }
    }
    // get the image's primary key or find out what went wrong
    if ($imageOK) {
        $image_id = $stmt->insert_id;
    } else {
        $imageError = implode(' ', $loader->getMessages());
    }
} elseif (!empty($_POST['image_id'])) {
    // get the primary key of a previously uploaded image
    $image_id = $_POST['image_id'];
}
// create SQL
$sql = 'INSERT INTO blog (title, article) VALUES(?, ?)';
```

This begins by checking if $_POST['upload_new'] has been set. As explained in Chapter 6, a check box is included in the $_POST array only if it has been selected. So, if the check box hasn't been selected, the condition fails, and the elseif clause at the bottom is tested instead. The elseif clause checks for the existence of $_POST['image_id']. If it exists and is not empty, it means that an existing image has been selected from the drop-down menu, and the value is stored in $image_id.

If both tests fail, an image has neither been uploaded nor selected from the drop-down menu. The script later takes this into account when preparing the INSERT query for the blog table, allowing you to create a blog entry without an image.

However, if $_POST['upload_new'] exists, the check box has been selected, and an image has probably been uploaded. To make sure, the conditional statement also checks the value of $_FILES['image']['error']. As you learned in Chapter 9, the error code 0 indicates a successful upload. Any other error code means the upload failed or that no file was selected.

Assuming a file has been successfully uploaded from the form, the conditional statement includes the Upload class definition and creates an object called $loader, passing it the name of the file input field and setting the destination folder to images. To avoid complicating the code, I'm not using the three optional arguments to the Upload constructor. So the default maximum size and MIME types will be used, and images with duplicate filenames will be renamed.

The changes you made to the Upload class in PHP Solution 18-2 add the name of an uploaded file to the $filenames property only if the file was moved successfully to the destination folder. The getFilenames() method retrieves the contents of the $filenames property and assigns the result to $names.

If the file was moved successfully, its filename is stored as the first element of the $names array. So if $names contains a value, you can safely proceed with the INSERT query, which binds the values of $names[0] and $_POST['caption'] as strings to the prepared statement.

After the statement has been executed, the affected_rows property resets the value of $imageOK. If the INSERT query succeeded, $imageOK is 1, which is treated as true.

If the image details were inserted in the images table, the prepared statement's insert_id property retrieves the primary key of the new record and stores it in $image_id. The insert_id property must be accessed before running any other SQL queries because it contains the primary key of the most recent query.

However, if $imageOK is still false, the else block calls the upload object's getMessages() method and assigns the result to $imageError. The getMessages() method returns an array, so the implode() function is used to join the array elements as a single string. The most likely cause of failure is a file that's too big or that's of the wrong MIME type.

3. As long as the image upload didn't fail, the next stage in the process is to insert the blog entry into the blog table. The form of the INSERT query depends on whether an image is associated with the blog entry. If it is, $image_id exists and needs to be inserted in the blog table as a foreign key. Otherwise, the original query can be used.

Amend the original query like this:

```
// insert blog details only if there hasn't been an image upload error
if (!isset($imageError)) {
    // if $image_id has been set, insert it as a foreign key
    if (isset($image_id)) {
        $sql = 'INSERT INTO blog (image_id, title, article) VALUES(?, ?, ?)';
        if ($stmt->prepare($sql)) {
            $stmt->bind_param('iss', $image_id, $_POST['title'],
            $_POST['article']);
            $stmt->execute();
        }
    } else {
        // create SQL
        $sql = 'INSERT INTO blog (title, article)
                VALUES(?, ?)';
```

```
        if ($stmt->prepare($sql)) {
            // bind parameters and execute statement
            $stmt->bind_param('ss', $_POST['title'], $_POST['article']);
            $stmt->execute();
        }
    }
    if ($stmt->affected_rows > 0) {
        $OK = true;
    }
}
```

This whole section of code is wrapped in a conditional statement that checks whether $imageError exists. If it does, there's no point in inserting the new blog entry, so the entire code block is ignored.

However, if $imageError doesn't exist, the nested conditional statement prepares different INSERT queries depending on whether $image_id exists and then executes whichever one has been prepared.

The conditional statement that checks the affected_rows property is moved out of the else block so that it applies to either INSERT query.

4. The next stage of the process inserts values into the article2cat cross-reference table. The code follows immediately after the code in the previous step and looks like the following:

```
// if the blog entry was inserted successfully, check for categories
if ($OK && isset($_POST['category'])) {
    // get the article's primary key
    $article_id = $stmt->insert_id;
    foreach ($_POST['category'] as $cat_id) {
        if (is_numeric($cat_id)) {
            $values[] = "($article_id, " . (int) $cat_id . ')';
        }
    }
    if ($values) {
        $sql = 'INSERT INTO article2cat (article_id, cat_id)
                VALUES ' . implode(',', $values);
        // execute the query and get error message if it fails
        if (!$conn->query($sql)) {
            $catError = $conn->error;
        }
    }
}
```

The value of $OK is determined by the affected_rows property from the query that inserted the data in the blog table, and the multiple-choice <select> list is included in the $_POST array only if any categories are selected. So this code block is run only if the data was successfully inserted in the blog table and at least one category was selected in the form. It begins by obtaining the primary key of the insert operation from the prepared statement's insert_id property and assigning it to $article_id.

The form submits the category values as an array. The foreach loop checks each value in $_POST['category']. If the value is numeric, the following line is executed:

```
$values[] = "($article_id, " . (int) $cat_id . ')';
```

This creates a string with the two primary keys, $article_id and $cat_id, separated by a comma and wrapped in a pair of parentheses. The (int) casting operator makes sure that $cat_id is an integer. The result is assigned to an array called $values. For example, if $article_id is 10 and $cat_id is 4, the resulting string assigned to the array is (10, 4).

If $values contains any elements, implode() converts it to a comma-separated string and appends it to the SQL query. For example, if categories 2, 4, and 5 are selected, the resulting query looks like this:

```
INSERT INTO article2cat (article_id, cat_id)
VALUES (10, 2),(10, 4),(10, 5)
```

As explained in "Reviewing the Four Essential SQL Commands" in Chapter 15, this is how you insert multiple rows with a single INSERT query.

Because $article_id comes from a reliable source and the data type of $cat_id has been checked, it's safe to use these variables directly in an SQL query without using a prepared statement. The query is executed with the query() method. If it fails, the connection object's error property is stored in $catError.

5. The final section of code handles the redirect on success and error messages. The amended code looks like this:

```
// redirect if successful or display error
if ($OK && !isset($imageError) && !isset($catError)) {
    header('Location: http://localhost/php8sols/admin/blog_list_mysqli.php');
    exit;
} else {
    $error = $stmt->error;
    if (isset($imageError)) {
        $error .= ' ' . $imageError;
    }
    if (isset($catError)) {
        $error .= ' ' . $catError;
    }
}
```

The condition controlling the redirect now ensures that $imageError and $catError don't exist. If either does, the value is concatenated to the original $error, which contains any error message from the prepared statement object.

6. Save blog_insert_mysqli.php and test it in a browser. Try uploading an image that's too big or a file of the wrong MIME type. The form should be redisplayed with an error message and the blog details preserved. Also try inserting blog entries both with and without images and/or categories. You now have a versatile insert form.

If you don't have suitable images to upload, use the images in the `phpsols images` folder. The `Upload` class renames them to avoid overwriting the existing files.

You can check your code against `blog_insert_mysqli_05.php` in the `ch18` folder.

Main Differences in the PDO Version

The final PDO version can be found in `blog_insert_pdo_05.php` in the `ch18` folder. It follows the same basic structure and logic as the MySQLi version, but has some important differences in the way values are inserted in the database.

The code in step 2 follows the MySQLi version closely but uses named placeholders instead of anonymous ones. To get the number of affected rows, PDO uses the `rowCount()` method on the statement object. The primary key of the most recent insert operation is obtained using the `lastInsertId()` method on the connection object. Like the MySQLi `insert_id` property, you need to access it immediately after the INSERT query has been executed.

The biggest changes are in the code in step 3 that inserts the details into the blog table. Because PDO can insert a `null` value into a column using `bindValue()`, only one prepared statement is needed. The PDO code for step 3 looks like this:

```
// insert blog details only if there hasn't been an image upload error
if (!isset($imageError)) {
    // create SQL
    $sql = 'INSERT INTO blog (image_id, title, article)
            VALUES(:image_id, :title, :article)';
    // prepare the statement
    $stmt = $conn->prepare($sql);
    // bind the parameters
    // if $image_id exists, use it
    if (isset($image_id)) {
        $stmt->bindParam(':image_id', $image_id, PDO::PARAM_INT);
    } else {
        // set image_id to NULL
        $stmt->bindValue(':image_id', NULL, PDO::PARAM_NULL);
    }
    $stmt->bindParam(':title', $_POST['title'], PDO::PARAM_STR);
    $stmt->bindParam(':article', $_POST['article'], PDO::PARAM_STR);
    // execute and get number of affected rows
    $stmt->execute();
    $OK = $stmt->rowCount();
}
```

If an image has been uploaded, the conditional statement highlighted in bold binds the value of `$image_id` to the named `:image_id` placeholder. But if no image has been uploaded, `bindValue()` sets the value to NULL.

In step 4, the PDO version uses `exec()` instead of `query()` to insert the values into the `article2cat` table. The `exec()` method executes an SQL query and returns the number of rows affected, so it should be used with INSERT, UPDATE, and DELETE queries when a prepared statement is not required.

The other important difference is in the code that builds the error message if there's a problem. Because creating and preparing a statement is a one-step process in PDO, the statement object might not exist if a problem arises. If there's no statement, the call to `errorInfo()` will be null. So the code uses the

517

null coalescing operator to get the error message from the database connection object instead. It's also necessary to initialize $error as an empty string to concatenate the various messages to it, like this:

```
// redirect if successful or display error
if ($OK && !isset($imageError) && !isset($catError)) {
    header('Location: http://localhost/php8sols/admin/blog_list_pdo.php');
    exit;
} else {
    $error = ";
    $error .= $stmt->errorInfo()[2] ?? $conn->errorInfo()[2];
    if (isset($imageError)) {
        $error .= ' ' . $imageError;
    }
    if (isset($catError)) {
        $error .= ' ' . $catError;
    }
}
```

Updating and Deleting Records in Multiple Tables

The addition of the categories and article2cat tables means that the changes to blog_update_mysqli. php and blog_update_pdo.php in PHP Solutions 17-2 and 17-3 in the previous chapter no longer adequately cover the foreign-key relationships in the phpsols database. In addition to amending the update form, you also need to create scripts to delete records without destroying the database's referential integrity.

Updating Records in a Cross-Reference Table

Each record in a cross-reference table contains only a composite primary key. Normally, primary keys should never be altered. Moreover, they must be unique. This poses a problem for updating the article2cat table. If you make no changes to the selected categories when updating a blog entry, the cross-reference table doesn't need to be updated. However, if the categories are changed, you need to work out which cross-references to delete and which new ones to insert.

Rather than getting tied up in knots working out whether any changes have been made, a simple solution is to delete all existing cross-references and insert the selected categories again. If no changes have been made, you simply insert the same ones again.

PHP Solution 18-5: Adding Categories to the Update Form

This PHP solution amends blog_update_mysqli.php from PHP Solution 17-2 in the previous chapter to allow you to update the categories associated with a blog entry. To keep the structure simple, the only change that can be made to the image associated with the entry is to select a different existing image or no image at all.

1. Continue working with blog_update_mysqli.php from PHP Solution 17-2. Alternatively, copy blog_update_mysqli_04.php from the ch18 folder and save it in the admin folder as blog_update_mysqli.php.

2. When the page first loads, you need to run a second query to get the categories associated with the blog entry. Add the following highlighted code to the conditional statement that gets details of the selected record:

```php
$stmt->free_result();
// get categories associated with the article
$sql = 'SELECT cat_id FROM article2cat
        WHERE article_id = ?';
if ($stmt->prepare($sql)) {
    $stmt->bind_param('i', $_GET['article_id']);
    $OK = $stmt->execute();
    $stmt->bind_result($cat_id);
    // loop through the results to store them in an array
    $selected_categories = [];
    while ($stmt->fetch()) {
        $selected_categories[] = $cat_id;
    }
}
```

The query selects cat_id from all records in the cross-reference table that match the primary key of the selected blog entry. The results are bound to $cat_id, and a while loop extracts the values into an array called $selected_categories.

3. In the body of the HTML page, add a multiple-choice <select> list between the text area and the <select> drop-down menu that displays the list of images. Use another SQL query to populate it, like this:

```php
<p>
    <label for="category">Categories:</label>
    <select name="category[]" size="5" multiple id="category">
        <?php
        // get categories
        $getCats = 'SELECT cat_id, category FROM categories
                        ORDER BY category';
        $categories = $conn->query($getCats);
        while ($row = $categories->fetch_assoc()) {
            ?>
            <option value="<?= $row['cat_id'] ?>" <?php
            if (isset($selected_categories) &&
                in_array($row['cat_id'], $selected_categories)) {
                echo 'selected';
            } ?>><?= safe($row['category']) ?></option>
        <?php } ?>
    </select>
</p>
```

The while loop builds each <option> tag by inserting cat_id in the value attribute and displaying the category between the opening and closing tags. If cat_id is in the $selected_categories array, selected is inserted in the <option> tag. This selects the categories already associated with the blog entry.

4. Save `blog_update_mysqli.php` and select one of the EDIT links in `blog_list_mysqli.php` to make sure the multiple-choice list is populated with the categories. If you inserted a new entry in PHP Solution 18-4, the categories you associated with the item should be selected, as shown in the following screenshot.

Categories:
```
Autumn ▲
Food
Kyoto
People
Temples ▼
```

You can check your code, if necessary, against `blog_update_mysqli_05.php` in the ch18 folder. The PDO version is found in `blog_update_pdo_05.php`.

5. Next, you need to edit the section of code that updates the record when the form is submitted. The new code begins by removing all entries in the cross-reference table that match `article_id` and then inserts the values selected in the update form. Inline comments indicate where existing code has been omitted to save space:

```php
// if form has been submitted, update record
if (isset($_POST ['update'])) {
    // prepare update query
    if (!empty($_POST['image_id'])) {
        // existing code omitted
    } else {
        // existing code omitted
            $done = $stmt->execute();
    }
}
// delete existing values in the cross-reference table
$sql = 'DELETE FROM article2cat WHERE article_id = ?';
if ($stmt->prepare($sql)) {
    $stmt->bind_param('i', $_POST['article_id']);
    $done = $stmt->execute();
}
// insert the new values in articles2cat
if (isset($_POST['category']) && is_numeric($_POST['article_id'])) {
    $article_id = (int) $_POST['article_id'];
    foreach ($_POST['category'] as $cat_id) {
        $values[] = "($article_id, " . (int) $cat_id . ')';
    }
    if ($values) {
        $sql = 'INSERT INTO article2cat (article_id, cat_id)
                VALUES ' . implode(',', $values);
        $done = $conn->query($sql);
    }
}
}
```

The code that inserts the values selected in the update form is identical to the code in step 4 of PHP Solution 18-4. The key point to note is that it uses an INSERT query, not UPDATE. The original values have been deleted, so you're adding them anew.

6. Save blog_update_mysqli.php and test it by updating existing records in the blog table. You can check your code, if necessary, against blog_update_mysqli_06.php in the ch18 folder. The PDO version is found in blog_update_pdo_06.php.

Treating Multiple Queries as a Block in a Transaction

The preceding PHP solution takes a lot on trust. The update sequence involves three separate queries: updating the blog table, deleting references in the article2cat table, and inserting new ones. If any of them fails, $done will be set to false; but if a subsequent one is successful, it will be reset to true. You could easily end up with only a partial update, but be none the wiser unless it was the last part of the series of queries that fails.

One solution might be to run a series of conditional statements preventing any further execution if the preceding query fails. The problem is that you still end up with a partial update. When updating connected records in multiple tables, the whole sequence needs to be treated as a block. If one part fails, the whole sequence fails. The update sequence is processed only if all parts of it succeed. Treating multiple queries as a unified block is known in SQL as a transaction. Implementing a transaction is simple in both MySQLi and PDO.

■ **Note**   To use transactions in MySQL and MariaDB, you must use the InnoDB storage engine.

Using a Transaction in MySQLi

By default, MySQL and MariaDB work in autocommit mode. In other words, SQL queries are executed immediately. To use a transaction, you need to turn off autocommit mode and then invoke the begin_transaction() method on the database connection object like this (assuming $conn is the database connection):

```
$conn->autocommit(false);
$conn->begin_transaction();
```

You then run the sequence of SQL queries as normal, setting a variable to true or false depending on whether the query was executed successfully. If any errors are detected, you can roll back all tables to their original state at the end of the sequence. Otherwise, you commit the transaction processing the sequence as a single block like this:

```
if ($trans_error) {
    $conn->rollback();
} else {
    $conn->commit();
}
```

Using a Transaction in PDO

PDO also works in autocommit mode. Invoking the `beginTransaction()` method on the database connection object turns off autocommit mode. PHP 8 automatically throws an exception as soon as it encounters a problem, so it's not necessary to use a variable to track the success of individual queries. Simply use a `catch` block to roll back the tables to their original state. The basic structure looks like this:

```
try {
    $conn->beginTransaction();
    // run sequence of SQL queries
    // commit the transaction if no problems have been encountered
    $done = $conn->commit();
    // catch the exception if there's a problem
} catch (Exception $e) {
    // roll back to the original state and get the errormessage
    $conn->rollBack();
    $trans_error = $e->getMessage();
}
```

■ **Caution**   Function and method names in PHP are case-insensitive, so `rollBack()` and `rollback()` are equally acceptable for MySQLi and PDO. However, there's a subtle difference between `begin_transaction()` (MySQLi) and `beginTransaction()` (PDO). The PDO method doesn't have an underscore.

Prior to PHP 8, PDO's default error mode was silent. If your server is running an older version of PHP, you need to set the error mode explicitly to throw an exception when it encounters a problem like this:

```
$conn->setAttribute(PDO::ATTR_ERRMODE, PDO::ERRMODE_EXCEPTION);
```

PHP Solution 18-6: Converting Tables to the InnoDB Storage Engine

This PHP solution shows how to convert a table from MyISAM to InnoDB. If you plan to upload the tables to your remote server, it must also support InnoDB (see PHP Solution 18-1).

1.   Select the `phpsols` database in phpMyAdmin, and then select the `article2cat` table.

2.   Click the Operations tab at the top right of the screen.

3.   In the Table options section, the Storage engine field reports which engine the table is currently using. If it says MyISAM, select InnoDB from the drop-down menu, as shown in Figure 18-10.

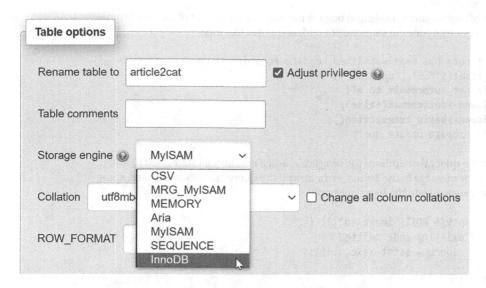

Figure 18-10. *Changing a table's storage engine is very easy in phpMyAdmin*

4. Click Go. Changing the storage engine is as simple as that!

■ **Note**   Each table needs to be converted individually. You cannot change all tables in a database in a single operation.

PHP Solution 18-7: Wrapping the Update Sequence in a Transaction (MySQLi)

This PHP solution improves the script in `blog_update_mysqli.php` by wrapping the sequence of SQL queries that update the `blog` and `article2cat` tables in a transaction, rolling back the database to its original state if any part of the sequence fails.

1. If necessary, convert the storage engine for the `blog` and `article2cat` tables to InnoDB as described in the previous PHP solution.

2. Continue working with `blog_update_mysqli.php` and `blog_list_mysqli. php` from PHP Solution 18-5. Alternatively, copy `blog_update_mysqli_06.php` and `blog_list_mysqli_04.php` from the `ch18` folder to the `admin` folder in the `php8sols` site root, and remove the numbers from the filenames.

3. Initialize an empty array at the top of `blog_update_mysqli.php` to store error messages:

    ```
    $trans_error = [];
    ```

4. Turn off autocommit mode and begin a transaction at the start of the conditional statement that runs the sequence of update queries like this:

```
// if form has been submitted, update record
if (isset($_POST ['update'])) {
    // set autocommit to off
    $conn->autocommit(false);
    $conn->begin_transaction();
    // prepare update query
```

5. After the query that updates the blog table, add a conditional statement to add any error message to the $trans_error array if the query fails. To save space, some of the existing code has been omitted:

```
if (!empty($_POST['image_id'])) {
    // existing code omitted
        $done = $stmt->execute();
    }
} else {
    // existing code omitted
        $done = $stmt->execute();
    }
}
if (!$done) {
    $trans_error[] = $stmt->error;
}
```

6. Add a similar conditional statement to capture any error message from the deletion of existing values in the cross-reference table:

```
// delete existing values in the cross-reference table
$sql = 'DELETE FROM article2cat WHERE article_id = ?';
if ($stmt->prepare($sql)) {
    $stmt->bind_param('i', $_POST['article_id']);
    $done = $stmt->execute();
    if (!$done) {
        $trans_error[] = $stmt->error;
    }
}
```

7. The code to capture any error message from inserting the updated values in the article2cat table needs to be slightly different because it uses the query() method rather than a prepared statement. Instead of the error property of the statement object, you need to access the error property of the database connection object like this:

```
if ($values) {
    $sql = 'INSERT INTO article2cat (article_id, cat_id)
                VALUES ' . implode(',', $values);
    $done = $conn->query($sql);
```

```
    if (!$done) {
        $trans_error[] = $conn->error;
    }
}
```

8. After the sequence of queries, use a conditional statement to roll back or commit the transaction like this (the code goes inside the conditional statement that runs the script when the Update button has been clicked):

```
if ($trans_error) {
    $conn->rollback();
    $done = false;
} else {
    $conn->commit();
}
```

It's necessary to set $done explicitly to false if $trans_error contains any error messages. This is because $done will be set to true by any query that would have succeeded outside of the transaction.

9. The conditional statement that redirects the page needs to be amended to handle the transaction. Add the new code highlighted in bold:

```
// redirect page after updating or if $_GET['article_id']) not defined
if (($done || $trans_error) || (!$_POST && !isset($_GET['article_id']))) {
    $url = 'http://localhost/php8sols/admin/blog_list_mysqli.php';
    if ($done) {
        $url .= '?updated=true';
    } elseif ($trans_error) {
        $url .= '?trans_error=' . serialize($trans_error);
    }
    header("Location: $url");
    exit;
}
```

The conditions are now grouped inside parentheses to make sure they're interpreted correctly. The first pair checks whether $done or $trans_error equates to true. The final condition is made more specific by checking that the $_POST array is empty. This is necessary because !isset($_GET['article_id']) is always true after the Update button has been clicked.

If $trans_error contains any error messages, it equates to true, so a query string is appended to the redirect location. Because $trans_error is an array, it needs to be passed to the serialize() function before it can be concatenated onto the query string. This converts the array to a string that can be converted back to its original format.

10. The final change is in the PHP block above the table in blog_list_mysqli.php. Add the code in bold to display any error messages if the update fails:

```
if (isset($_GET['updated'])) {
    echo '<p>Record updated</p>';
} elseif (isset($_GET['trans_error'])) {
```

```
        $trans_error = unserialize($_GET['trans_error']);
        echo "<p>Can't update record because of the following error(s):</p>";
        echo '<ul>';
        foreach ($trans_error as $item) {
            echo '<li>' . safe($item) . '</li>';
        }
        echo '</ul>';
    }
```

The unserialize() function reverses the effect of serialize(), converting the error messages back into an array, which are then displayed in a foreach loop.

11. Save blog_update_mysqli.php and blog_list_mysqli.php, and update an existing record. The script should work the same as before.

12. Introduce some deliberate errors into the SQL in blog_update_mysqli.php, and test it again. This time, you should see a series of error messages similar to Figure 18-11 when you return to blog_list_mysqli.php.

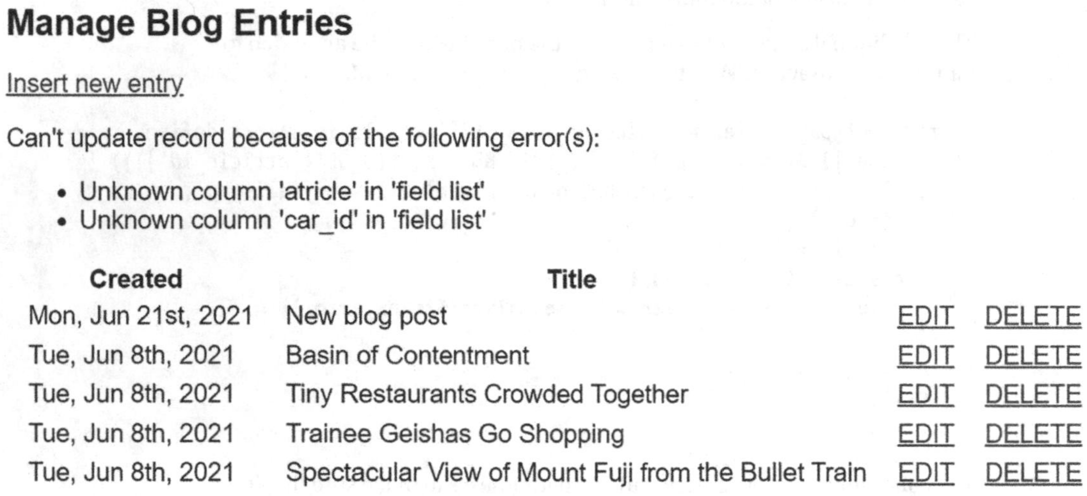

Manage Blog Entries

<u>Insert new entry</u>

Can't update record because of the following error(s):

- Unknown column 'atricle' in 'field list'
- Unknown column 'car_id' in 'field list'

Created	Title		
Mon, Jun 21st, 2021	New blog post	EDIT	DELETE
Tue, Jun 8th, 2021	Basin of Contentment	EDIT	DELETE
Tue, Jun 8th, 2021	Tiny Restaurants Crowded Together	EDIT	DELETE
Tue, Jun 8th, 2021	Trainee Geishas Go Shopping	EDIT	DELETE
Tue, Jun 8th, 2021	Spectacular View of Mount Fuji from the Bullet Train	EDIT	DELETE

Figure 18-11. *The update fails because of errors in the column names*

13. Click the EDIT link for the record you just tried to update and verify that none of the values has changed. You can check your code against blog_update_mysqli_07.php and blog_list_mysqli_05.php in the ch18 folder.

PHP Solution 18-8: Wrapping the Update Sequence in a Transaction (PDO)

This PHP solution improves the script in blog_update_pdo.php by wrapping the sequence of SQL queries that update the blog and article2cat tables in a transaction, rolling back the database to its original state if any part of the sequence fails.

1. If necessary, convert the storage engine for the `blog` and `article2cat` tables to InnoDB as described in PHP Solution 18-6.

2. Continue working with blog_update_pdo.php and blog_list_pdo.php from PHP Solution 18-5. Alternatively, copy blog_update_pdo_06.php and blog_list_pdo_04.php from the ch18 folder to the admin folder in the php8sols site root, and remove the numbers from the filenames.

3. Initialize a variable at the top of the page to keep track of the transaction, and set its value to false:

```
$trans_error = false;
```

■ **Note** PHP 8 automatically throws an exception when it encounters an error in PDO, so the following step is required only if your server is running an older version of PHP. Skip to step 5 if you are running PHP 8 or later.

---

4. Inside the conditional statement that runs the sequence of queries to update the blog and article2cat tables, set PDO to throw an exception when it encounters a problem like this:

```
if (isset($_POST['update'])) {
    $conn->setAttribute(PDO::ATTR_ERRMODE, PDO::ERRMODE_EXCEPTION);
    // prepare update query
    $sql = 'UPDATE blog SET image_id = ?, title = ?, article = ?
            WHERE article_id = ?';
```

5. Wrap all the code that runs the update queries in a try/catch block, and begin a transaction at the beginning of the try block like this:

```
if(isset($_POST['update'])) {
    try {
        $conn->beginTransaction();
        // prepare update query
        // other database queries omitted
    } catch (Exception $e) {
        $conn->rollBack();
        $trans_error = $e->getMessage();
    }
}
```

6. In the existing code, the return value of executing each query is set to $done. This is no longer necessary because we're using a transaction. We'll use $done as the return value of committing the transaction successfully. Locate the following lines (they're around lines 53, 57, and 69):

```
$done = $stmt->execute();
$done = $stmt->execute([$_POST['article_id']]);
$done = $conn->exec($sql);
```

Change them to this:
```
$stmt->execute();
$stmt->execute([$_POST['article_id']]);
$conn->exec($sql);
```

7. Immediately before the catch block, add the code in bold to commit the transaction:

```
    $done = $conn->commit();
} catch (Exception $e) {
    $conn->rollBack();
    $trans_error = $e->getMessage();
}
```

8. The conditional statement that redirects the page needs to be amended to handle the transaction. Add the new code highlighted in bold:

```
// redirect page after updating or if $_GET['article_id'] not defined
if (($done || $trans_error) || (!$_POST && !isset($_GET['article_id']))) {
    $url = 'http://localhost/php8sols/admin/blog_list_pdo.php';
    if ($done) {
        $url .= '?updated=true';
    } elseif ($trans_error) {
        $url .= "?trans_error=$trans_error";
    }
    header("Location: $url");
    exit;
}
```

The conditions are now grouped inside parentheses to make sure they're interpreted correctly. The first pair checks whether $done or $trans_error equates to true. The final condition is made more specific by checking that the $_POST array is empty. This is necessary because !isset($_GET['article_id']) is always true after the Update button has been clicked.

If $trans_error contains any error messages, it equates to true, so a query string is appended to the redirect location.

9. The final change is in the PHP block above the table in blog_list_pdo.php. Add the code in bold to display any error messages if the update fails:

```
if (isset($_GET['updated'])) {
    echo '<p>Record updated</p>';
} elseif (isset($_GET['trans_error'])) {
    echo "Can't update record because of the following error: ";
    echo safe($_GET['trans_error']) . '</p>';
}
```

PDO throws an exception as soon as it encounters an error, so there will be only one error message, even if there are multiple errors.

10. Save blog_update_pdo.php and blog_list_pdo.php, and update an existing record. The script should work the same as before.

11. Introduce a deliberate error in one of the update queries in `blog_update_pdo.php`, and test it again. This time, you'll see the error message when you're returned to `blog_list_pdo.php`.

12. Click the EDIT link for the record you just tried to update and verify that none of the values has changed. You can check your code against `blog_update_pdo_07.php` and `blog_list_pdo_05.php` in the `ch18` folder.

■ **Tip** Transactions are essential in situations where a series of queries should be processed only if certain criteria are met. For example, in a financial database, a transfer of money should go ahead only if sufficient funds are available.

Preserving Referential Integrity on Deletion

In PHP Solution 18-5, there was no need to worry about referential integrity when you deleted records in the cross-reference table because the values stored in each record are foreign keys. Each record simply refers to the primary keys stored in the `blog` and `categories` tables. Referring to Figure 18-1 at the beginning of this chapter, deleting from the cross-reference table the record that combines `article_id` 2 with `cat_id` 1 simply breaks the link between the article titled "Trainee Geishas Go Shopping" and the Kyoto category. Neither the article nor the category is affected. They both remain in their respective tables.

The situation is very different if you decide to delete either the article or the category. If you delete the "Trainee Geishas Go Shopping" article from the `blog` table, all references to `article_id` 2 must also be deleted from the cross-reference table. Similarly, if you delete the Kyoto category, all references to `cat_id` 1 must be removed from the cross-reference table. Alternatively, you must halt the deletion if an item's primary key is stored elsewhere as a foreign key.

The best way to do this is through the establishment of foreign-key constraints. To do so, related tables must use the InnoDB storage engine. If you're using MySQL or MariaDB 5.5 or later, InnoDB is the default. Also, all the `.sql` files that accompany this book select the InnoDB engine. However, if you have existing tables that were created using the MyISAM storage engine, you need to convert them before you can establish foreign-key constraints (see PHP Solution 18-6).

PHP Solution 18-9: Setting Up Foreign-Key Constraints

This PHP solution describes how to set up foreign-key constraints between the `article2cat`, `blog`, and `categories` tables in phpMyAdmin. The foreign-key constraints must always be defined in the child table. In this case, the child table is `article2cat`, because it stores the `article_id` and `cat_id` primary keys from the other tables as foreign keys.

1. Select the `article2cat` table in phpMyAdmin and click the Structure tab.

2. Click Relation view (circled in Figure 18-12) above the structure table (in older versions of phpMyAdmin, it's a link below the structure table).

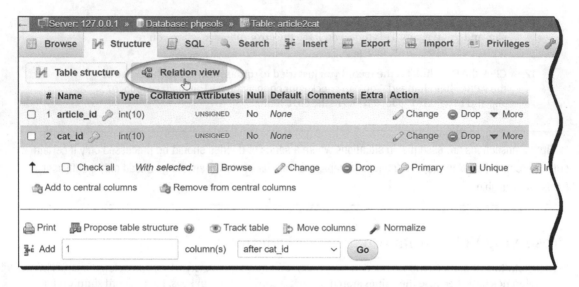

Figure 18-12. *Foreign-key constraints are defined in phpMyAdmin's Relation view*

3. The screen that opens is where you define foreign-key constraints. Leave the Constraint name field blank. phpMyAdmin will automatically generate a name for the constraint.

4. Foreign-key constraints can be set up only on columns that are indexed. The `article_id` and `cat_id` columns in `article2cat` are the table's composite primary key, so they're both listed in the Column drop-down menu. Select article_id. Then select the following settings under Foreign key constraint (INNODB):

   • Database: phpsols

   • Table: blog

   • Column: article_id

   This establishes a constraint between article_id in the parent table (blog) and article_id in the child table (article2cat).

5. Next, you need to decide how the constraint should behave. The ON DELETE drop-down menu has the following options:

   • CASCADE: When you delete a record in the parent table, all dependent records are deleted in the child table. For example, if you delete the record with the primary key `article_id` `2` in the `blog` table, all records with `article_id` `2` in the `article2cat` table are automatically deleted.

   • SET NULL: When you delete a record in the parent table, all dependent records in the child table have the foreign key set to NULL. The foreign-key column must accept NULL values.

- NO ACTION: On some database systems, this allows foreign-key constraint checks to be delayed. MySQL performs checks immediately, so this has the same effect as RESTRICT.

- RESTRICT: This prevents the deletion of a record in the parent table if dependent records still exist in the child table.

■ **Note** The same options are available for ON UPDATE. With the exception of RESTRICT, they are of limited interest because you should change the primary key of a record only in exceptional circumstances. ON UPDATE RESTRICT not only stops changes from being made to the primary key in the parent table; it also rejects any inserts or updates in the child table that would result in foreign-key values that don't have a match in the parent table.

In the case of a cross-reference table, CASCADE is the logical choice. If you decide to delete a record in the parent table, you want all cross-references to that record to be removed at the same time. However, to demonstrate the default behavior of foreign-key constraints, select RESTRICT for both ON DELETE and ON UPDATE.

6. Click the Add constraint link to establish a foreign-key constraint for cat_id using the following settings:

    - Database: phpsols

    - Table: categories

    - Column: cat_id

7. Set ON DELETE and ON UPDATE to RESTRICT. The settings should look like Figure 18-13. Then click the Save button.

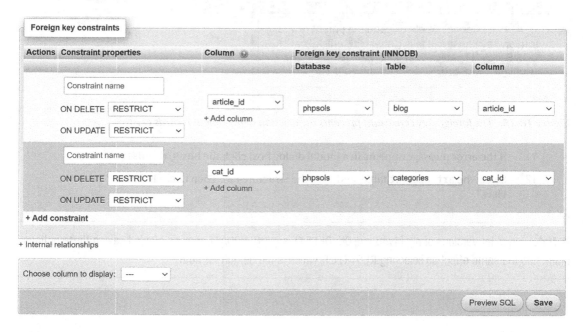

Figure 18-13. Setting foreign-key constraints for the cross-reference table

■ **Note**   The layout of Relation view in older versions of phpMyAdmin is different, combining the Database, Table, and Column drop-down menus in a single drop-down.

8.   If you have not already done so, update at least one blog entry to associate it with a category.

9.   In phpMyAdmin, select the `categories` table and click `Delete` next to a category that you know to be associated with a blog entry, as shown in Figure 18-14.

Figure 18-14. Try to delete a record in the categories table

10.   Click `OK` when phpMyAdmin asks you to confirm the deletion. If you have set up the foreign-key constraints correctly, you'll see an error message similar to that in Figure 18-15.

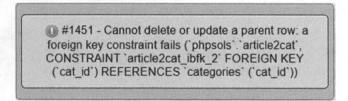

Figure 18-15. The foreign-key constraint prevents the deletion if dependent records exist

11.   If the error message appears in a modal dialog box, click the box to dismiss it.

12.   Select the `article2cat` table, and click the Structure tab. Then click "Relation view."

■ **Note**   In older versions of phpMyAdmin, `ON DELETE` and `ON UPDATE` may be blank. Leaving these options blank has the same effect as selecting `RESTRICT`, which is the default for both.

13. Change both ON DELETE settings to CASCADE, and click Save.

14. Select a record in the blog table that you know is associated with a category. Make a note of its article_id and then delete the record.

15. Check the article2cat table. The records associated with the record you have just deleted have also been deleted.

To continue your exploration of foreign-key constraints, select the blog table, and establish a foreign-key relationship with image_id in the images table. If you delete a record from the images table, the image_id foreign key in the blog table needs to be set to NULL. This is done automatically if you set the value of ON DELETE to SET NULL. Test it by deleting a record from the images table and checking the associated record(s) in the blog table.

■ **Note** If you need to convert an InnoDB table back to MyISAM, you must first remove any foreign-key constraints. Select "Relation view," and click Drop at the top left of each constraint. In older versions of phpMyAdmin, set the "Foreign key (INNODB)" fields to blank, and click Save. After removing the constraints, you can change the storage engine as described in PHP Solution 18-6. Select MyISAM instead of InnoDB.

Creating Delete Scripts with Foreign-Key Constraints

Choosing the values for ON DELETE in InnoDB tables depends on the nature of the relationship between tables. In the case of the phpsols database, it's not only safe but desirable to set the option to CASCADE for both columns in the article2cat cross-reference table. If a record is deleted in either the blog or categories parent table, the related values need to be deleted in the cross-reference table.

The relationship between the images and blog tables is different. If you delete a record from the images table, you probably don't want to delete related articles in the blog table. In that case, SET NULL is an appropriate choice. When a record is deleted from the images table, the foreign key in related articles is set to NULL, but the articles remain intact.

On the other hand, if images are vital to the understanding of articles, select RESTRICT. Any attempt to delete an image that still has related articles is automatically halted.

These considerations affect how you handle deletion scripts. When the foreign-key constraint is set to CASCADE or SET NULL, you don't need to do anything special. You can use a simple DELETE query and leave the rest to the database.

However, if the foreign-key constraint is set to RESTRICT, the DELETE query will fail. To display an appropriate error message, use the errno property of a MySQLi statement object. The MySQL error code for a query that fails as a result of a foreign-key constraint is 1451. After calling the execute() method, you can check for errors in MySQLi as follows (see blog_delete_mysqli_innodb.php):

```php
$stmt->execute();
if ($stmt->affected_rows > 0) {
    $deleted = true;
} else {
    $deleted = false;
    if ($stmt->errno == 1451) {
        $error = 'That record has dependent files in a child table, and cannot be deleted.';
    } else {
        $error = 'There was a problem deleting the record.';
    }
}
```

If you are using PDO, use the errorCode() method. The code for a query that fails as a result of a foreign-key constraint is HY000. After checking the number of affected rows, you can check the error code with a PDO prepared statement, like this (see blog_delete_pdo_innodb.php):

```
$deleted = $stmt->rowCount();
if (!$deleted) {
    if ($stmt->errorCode() == 'HY000') {
        $error = 'That record has dependent files in a child table, and cannot be deleted.';
    } else {
        $error = 'There was a problem deleting the record.';
    }
}
```

The technique is the same if you use the PDO exec() method, which returns the number of affected rows with a non-SELECT query. When using exec(), the errorCode() method is called on the database connection:

```
$deleted = $conn->exec($sql);
if (!$deleted) {
    if ($conn->errorCode() == 'HY000') {
        $error = 'That record has dependent files in a child table, and cannot be deleted.';
    } else {
        $error = 'There was a problem deleting the record.';
    }
}
```

Creating Delete Scripts Without Foreign-Key Constraints

If you can't use InnoDB tables, you need to build the same logic into your own delete scripts. To achieve the same effect as ON DELETE CASCADE, run two consecutive DELETE queries, like this (the code is in blog_delete_mysqli_myisam_cascade.php; the PDO version is in blog_delete_pdo_myisam_cascade.php):

```
$sql = 'DELETE FROM article2cat WHERE article_id = ?';
$stmt->prepare($sql);
$stmt->bind_param('i', $_POST['article_id']);
$stmt->execute();
$sql = 'DELETE FROM blog WHERE article_id = ?';
$stmt->prepare($sql);
$stmt->bind_param('i', $_POST['article_id']);
$stmt->execute();
```

To achieve the same effect as ON DELETE SET NULL, run an UPDATE query combined with a DELETE query, like this:

```
$sql = 'UPDATE blog SET image_id = NULL WHERE image_id = ?';
$stmt->prepare($sql);
$stmt->bind_param('i', $_POST['image_id']);
$stmt->execute();
$sql = 'DELETE FROM images WHERE image_id = ?';
$stmt->prepare($sql);
```

```
$stmt->bind_param('i', $_POST['image_id']);
$stmt->execute();
```

To achieve the same effect as ON DELETE RESTRICT, you need to run a SELECT query to find if there are dependent records before continuing with the DELETE query, like this:

```
$sql = 'SELECT image_id FROM blog WHERE image_id = ?';
$stmt->prepare($sql);
$stmt->bind_param('i', $_POST['image_id']);
$stmt->execute();
// store result to find out how many rows it contains
$stmt->store_result();
// if num_rows is not 0, there are dependent records
if ($stmt->num_rows) {
    $error = 'That record has dependent files in a child table, and cannot be deleted.';
} else {
    $sql = 'DELETE FROM images WHERE image_id = ?';
    $stmt->prepare($sql);
    $stmt->bind_param('i', $_POST['image_id']);
    $stmt->execute();
}
```

Chapter Review

Once you have learned the basic SQL and the PHP commands necessary to communicate with a database, working with single tables is very easy. Linking tables through foreign keys, however, can be quite challenging. The power of a relational database comes from its sheer flexibility. The problem is that this infinite flexibility means there is no single "right" way of doing things.

Don't let this put you off, though. Your instinct may be to stick with single tables, but down that route lies even greater complexity. The key to making it easy to work with databases is to limit your ambitions in the early stages. Build simple structures like the one in this chapter, experiment with them, and get to know how they work. Add tables and foreign-key links gradually. People with a lot of experience working with databases say they frequently spend more than half the development time just thinking about the table structure. After that, the coding is the easy bit!

In the final chapter, we move back to working with a single table, addressing the important subject of user authentication with a database and how to handle hashed and encrypted passwords.

CHAPTER 19

■ ■ ■

Authenticating Users with a Database

Chapter 11 showed you the principles of user authentication and sessions to password-protect parts of your web site, but the login scripts all relied on usernames and passwords stored in a CSV file. Keeping user details in a database is both more secure and more efficient. Instead of just storing a list of usernames and passwords, a database can store other details, such as first name, family name, email address, and so on. Databases also give you the option of using either hashing (one-way and irreversible) or encryption (two-way). In the first section of this chapter, we'll examine the difference between the two. Then you'll create registration and login scripts for both types of storage.

This chapter covers

- Deciding how to store passwords
- Using one-way password hashing for user registration and login
- Using two-way encryption for user registration and login
- Decrypting passwords

Choosing a Password Storage Method

The PHP solutions in Chapter 11 use password hashing—once a password has been hashed, there's no way of reversing the process. This is both an advantage and a disadvantage. It offers the user greater security because passwords stored this way remain secret. However, there's no way of reissuing a lost password, since not even the site administrator can extract the original password from the hashed version. The only solution is to reset the password.

The alternative is to use secret-key encryption. This is a two-way, reversible process that relies on a pair of functions: one to encrypt the password and another to convert it back to plain text, making it easy to reissue passwords to forgetful users. Two-way encryption uses a secret key that is passed to both functions to perform the conversion. The key is simply a string that you make up yourself. Obviously, to keep the data secure, the key needs to be sufficiently difficult to guess and should never be stored in the database. However, you need to embed the key in your registration and login scripts—either directly or through an include file—so if your scripts are ever exposed, your security is blown wide apart.

MySQL and MariaDB offer a number of two-way encryption functions, but `AES_ENCRYPT()` is considered the most secure. It uses the Advanced Encryption Standard with a 128-bit key length (AES-128) approved by the US government for the protection of classified material up to the SECRET level (TOP SECRET material requires AES-192 or AES-256).

© David Powers 2022
D. Powers, *PHP 8 Solutions*, https://doi.org/10.1007/978-1-4842-7141-4_19

Both hashing and secret-key encryption have advantages and disadvantages. Many security experts recommend that passwords should be changed frequently. So forcing a user to change a forgotten password because it can't be decrypted could be regarded as a good security measure. On the other hand, users are likely to be frustrated by the need to deal with a new password each time they forget the existing one. I'll leave it to you to decide which approach is best suited to your circumstances, and I'll concentrate solely on the technical implementation.

Using Password Hashing

In the interests of keeping things simple, I'm going to use the same basic forms as in Chapter 11, so only the username and hashed password are stored in the database.

Creating a Table to Store Users' Details

In phpMyAdmin, create a new table called users in the phpsols database. The table needs three columns with the settings listed in Table 19-1.

Table 19-1. Settings for the users table

Name	Type	Length/Values	Attributes	Null	Index	A_I
user_id	INT		UNSIGNED	Deselected	PRIMARY	Selected
username	VARCHAR	15		Deselected	UNIQUE	
pwd	VARCHAR	255		Deselected		

To ensure no one can register the same username as one that's already in use, the username column is given a UNIQUE index.

The pwd column, which is for the password, allows a string of up to 255 characters to be stored. This is much longer than the 60 characters required by the default hashing algorithm used by password_hash(). But the PASSWORD_DEFAULT constant is designed to change over time as new and stronger algorithms are added to PHP. So the recommended size is 255 characters.

Registering New Users in the Database

To register users in the database, you need to create a registration form that asks for a username and password. The username column has been defined with a UNIQUE index, so the database will return an error if anyone attempts to register the same username as an existing one. In addition to validating the user input, the processing script needs to detect the error and advise the user to choose a different username.

PHP Solution 19-1: Creating a User Registration Form

This PHP solution shows how to adapt the registration script from Chapter 11 to work with MySQL or MariaDB. It uses the CheckPassword class from PHP Solution 11-3 and register_user_csv.php from PHP Solution 11-4.

If necessary, copy CheckPassword.php from the ch19/Php8Solutions/Authenticate folder to the Php8Solutions/Authenticate folder in the php8sols site root, and copy register_user_csv.php from the ch19 folder to the includes folder. You should also read the instructions in PHP Solutions 11-3 and 11-4 to understand how the original scripts work.

1. Copy `register_db.php` from the ch19 folder to a new folder called `authenticate` in the php8sols site root. The page contains the same basic user registration form as in Chapter 11, with a text input field for the username, a password field, another password field for confirmation, and a button to submit the data, as shown in the following screenshot:

2. Add the following code in a PHP block above the DOCTYPE declaration:

```php
if (isset($_POST['register'])) {
    $username = trim($_POST['username']);
    $password = trim($_POST['pwd']);
    $retyped = trim($_POST['conf_pwd']);
    require_once '../includes/register_user_mysqli.php';
}
```

This is very similar to the code in PHP Solution 11-4. If the form has been submitted, the user input is stripped of leading and trailing whitespace and assigned to simple variables. Then an external file called `register_user_mysqli.php` is included. If you plan to use PDO, name the include file `register_user_pdo.php` instead.

3. The file that processes the user input is based on `register_user_csv.php` from Chapter 11. Make a copy of your original file (or use the version in the ch19 folder) and save it in the `includes` folder as `register_user_mysqli.php` or `register_user_pdo.php`.

4. In the file you have just copied and renamed, locate the conditional statement that begins like this (around line 18):

```php
if (!$errors) {
    // hash password using default algorithm
    $password = password_hash($password, PASSWORD_DEFAULT);
```

5. Delete the rest of the code inside the conditional statement. The conditional statement should now look like this:

```
if (!$errors) {
    // hash password using default algorithm
    $password = password_hash($password, PASSWORD_DEFAULT);
}
```

6. The code that inserts the user's details in the database goes inside the conditional statement. Begin by including the database connection file and creating a connection with read and write privileges:

```
if (!$errors) {
    // hash password using default algorithm
    $password = password_hash($password, PASSWORD_DEFAULT);
    // include the connection file
    require_once 'connection.php';
    $conn = dbConnect('write');
}
```

The connection file is also in the includes folder, so you need only the filename. For PDO, add 'pdo' as the second argument to dbConnect().

7. The final section of the code prepares and executes the prepared statement to insert the user's details into the database. Because the username column has a UNIQUE index, the query fails if the username already exists. If that happens, the code needs to generate an error message. The code is different for MySQLi and PDO.

For MySQLi, add the code highlighted in bold:

```
if (!$errors) {
    // hash password using default algorithm
    $password = password_hash($password, PASSWORD_DEFAULT);
    // include the connection file
    require_once 'connection.php';
    $conn = dbConnect('write');
    // prepare SQL statement
    $sql = 'INSERT INTO users (username, pwd) VALUES (?, ?)';
    $stmt = $conn->stmt_init();
    if ($stmt = $conn->prepare($sql)) {
        // bind parameters and insert the details into the database
        $stmt->bind_param('ss', $username, $password);
        $stmt->execute();
    }
    if ($stmt->affected_rows == 1) {
        $success = htmlentities($username) . ' has been registered.
            You may now log in.';
    } elseif ($stmt->errno == 1062) {
        $errors[] = htmlentities($username) . ' is already in use.
            Please choose another username.';
```

```
    } else {
        $errors[] = $stmt->error;
    }
}
```

The new code begins by binding the parameters to the prepared statement.
The username and password are strings, so the first argument to bind_param() is
'ss' (see "Embedding Variables in MySQLi Prepared Statements" in Chapter 13).
After the statement has been executed, the conditional statement checks the
value of the affected_rows property. If it's 1, the details have been inserted
successfully.

■ **Tip**   You need to check the value of affected_rows explicitly because it's −1 if there's an error. Unlike
some programming languages, PHP treats −1 as true.

The alternative condition checks the value of the prepared statement's errno
property, which contains the MySQL error code. The code for a duplicate value
in a column with a UNIQUE index is 1062. If that error code is detected, an error
message is added to the $errors array asking the user to choose a different
username. If a different error code is generated, the message stored in the
statement's error property is added to the $errors array instead.

The PDO version looks like this:

```
if (!$errors) {
    // encrypt password using default encryption
    $password = password_hash($password, PASSWORD_DEFAULT);
    // include the connection file
    require_once 'connection.php';
    $conn = dbConnect('write', 'pdo');
    try {
        // prepare SQL statement
        $sql = 'INSERT INTO users (username, pwd) VALUES (:username, :pwd)';
        $stmt = $conn->prepare($sql);
        // bind parameters and insert the details into the database
        $stmt->bindParam(':username', $username, PDO::PARAM_STR);
        $stmt->bindParam(':pwd', $password, PDO::PARAM_STR);
        $stmt->execute();
        if ($stmt->rowCount() == 1) {
            $success = htmlentities($username) . ' has been registered.
                You may now log in.';
        }
    } catch (PDOException $e) {
        if ($e->getCode() == 23000) {
            $errors[] = htmlentities($username) . 'is already in use.
                Please choose another username.';
        } else {
```

```php
            $errors[] = $e->getMessage();
        }
    }
}
```

The default error mode for PDO in PHP 8 is to throw an exception when something goes wrong, so the code that submits the query to the database needs to be wrapped in a try/catch block.

The prepared statement uses named parameters for the username and pwd columns. The submitted values are bound to it by the bindParam() method, using the PDO::PARAM_STR constant to specify the data type as a string. After the statement has been executed, the conditional statement uses the rowCount() method to check if the record has been created.

If the prepared statement fails, the catch block handles the PDOException. The conditional statement calls the getCode() method on the exception object. If the username already exists in the database, the value returned is 23000. PDO uses error codes defined by the ANSI SQL standard instead of those generated by MySQL. If the error code matches, a message is added to the $errors array asking the user to choose a different username. Otherwise, the error message from the getMessage() method is used.

■ **Note** In both the MySQLi and PDO scripts, replace the code in the else block with a generic error message when deploying the registration script on a live web site. Displaying the value of the statement's error property (MySQLi) or $e->getMessage() (PDO) is intended for testing purposes only.

---

8. All that remains is to add the code that displays the outcome on the registration page. Add the following code just before the opening <form> tag in register_db.php:

```php
<h1>Register user</h1>
<?php
if (isset($success)) {
    echo "<p>$success</p>";
} elseif (isset($errors) && !empty($errors)) {
    echo '<ul>';
    foreach ($errors as $error) {
        echo "<li>$error</li>";
    }
    echo '</ul>';
}
?>
<form action="register_db.php" method="post">
```

9. Save register_db.php, and load it in a browser. Test it by entering input that you know breaks the rules for the strength of the password. If you make multiple mistakes in the same attempt, a bulleted list of error messages should appear at the top of the form, as shown in the next screenshot:

Register User

- Username must be at least 6 characters.
- Only alphanumeric characters, hyphens, and underscores are permitted in username.
- Password must be at least 8 characters.
- Password should include at least 2 number(s).
- Password should include at least 1 nonalphanumeric character(s).

Username: [ ]

Password: [ ]

Retype Password: [ ]

[Register]

10. Now fill in the registration form correctly. You should see a message telling you that an account has been created for the username you chose.

11. Try registering the same username again. This time you should get a message similar to the one shown in the following screenshot:

Register User

- davidp is already in use. Please choose another username.

Username: [ ]

Password: [ ]

Retype Password: [ ]

[Register]

12. Check your code, if necessary, against register_db_mysqli.php and register_user_mysqli.php or against register_db_pdo.php and register_user_pdo.php, all found in the ch19 folder.

Now that you have a username and password registered in the database, you need to create a login script. The ch19 folder contains a set of files that replicates the setup in PHP Solutions 11-5 to 11-7: a login page and two password-protected pages.

PHP Solution 19-2: Authenticating a User's Credentials with a Database

This PHP solution shows how to authenticate a user's stored credentials by querying the database to find the hashed version of the username's password and then passing it as an argument to password_verify() together with the user-submitted password. If password_verify() returns true, the user is redirected to a restricted page.

1. Copy login_db.php, menu_db.php, and secretpage_db.php from the ch19 folder to the authenticate folder. Also copy logout_db.php and session_timeout_db.php from the ch19 folder to the includes folder.

   This sets up the same basic test platform as was used in Chapter 11. The only difference is that the links have been changed to redirect to the authenticate folder.

2. In login_db.php add the following code in a PHP block above the DOCTYPE declaration:

   ```php
   $error = '';
   if (isset($_POST['login'])) {
       session_start();
       $username = trim($_POST['username']);
       $password = trim($_POST['pwd']);
       // location to redirect on success
       $redirect = 'http://localhost/php8sols/authenticate/menu_db.php';
       require_once '../includes/authenticate_mysqli.php';
   }
   ```

   This follows a similar pattern to the code in the login form in Chapter 11. It begins by initializing $error as an empty string. The conditional statement initiates a session if the form has been submitted. Whitespace is trimmed from the user input fields, and the location of the page the user will be redirected to on success is stored in a variable. Finally, the authentication script, which you'll build next, is included.

   If you're using PDO, use authenticate_pdo.php as the processing script.

3. Create a new file called authenticate_mysqli.php or authenticate_pdo.php and save it in the includes folder. The file will contain only PHP script, so strip out any HTML markup.

4. Include the database connection file, create a connection to the database with the read-only account, and use a prepared statement to fetch the user's details.

   For MySQLi use the following code:

   ```php
   <?php
   require_once 'connection.php';
   $conn = dbConnect('read');
   // get the username's hashed password from the database
   $sql = 'SELECT pwd FROM users WHERE username = ?';
   // initialize and prepare statement
   $stmt = $conn->stmt_init();
   $stmt->prepare($sql);
   ```

```
// bind the input parameter
$stmt->bind_param('s', $username);
$stmt->execute();
// bind the result, using a new variable for the password
$stmt->bind_result($storedPwd);
$stmt->fetch();
```

This is such a straightforward SELECT query that I haven't used a conditional statement when passing it to the MySQLi prepare() method. The username is a string, so the first argument to bind_param() is 's'. If a match is found, the result is bound to $storedPwd. You need to use a new variable for the stored password to avoid overwriting the password submitted by the user.

After the statement has been executed, the fetch() method gets the result.

For PDO, use the following code instead:

```
<?php
require_once 'connection.php';
$conn = dbConnect('read', 'pdo');
// get the username's hashed password from the database
$sql = 'SELECT pwd FROM users WHERE username = ?';
// prepare statement
$stmt = $conn->prepare($sql);
// pass the input parameter as a single-element array
$stmt->execute([$username]);
$storedPwd = $stmt->fetchColumn();
```

This code does the same as the MySQLi version does, but uses PDO syntax. The username is passed to the execute() method as a single-element array. Because there's only one column in the result, fetchColumn() returns the value and assigns it to $storedPwd.

5. Once you have retrieved the username's password, all you need to do is to pass the submitted and stored versions to password_verify(). If password_verify() returns true, create the session variables to indicate a successful login and the time the session began, regenerate the session ID, and redirect to the restricted page. Otherwise, store an error message in $error.

Insert the following code after the code you entered in the preceding step. It's the same for both MySQLi and PDO.

```
// check the submitted password against the stored version
if (password_verify($password, $storedPwd)) {
    $_SESSION['authenticated'] = 'Jethro Tull';
    // get the time the session started
    $_SESSION['start'] = time();
    session_regenerate_id();
    header("Location: $redirect");
    exit;
} else {
    // if not verified, prepare error message
    $error = 'Invalid username or password';
}
```

545

As in Chapter 11, the value of $_SESSION['authenticated'] is of no real importance.

6. Save authenticate_mysqli.php or authenticate_pdo.php, and test login_db.php by logging in with the username and password that you registered at the end of PHP Solution 19-1. The login process should work in exactly the same way as in Chapter 11. The difference is that all the details are stored more securely in a database.

You can check your code, if necessary, against login_mysqli.php and authenticate_mysqli.php or login_pdo.php and authenticate_pdo.php, all found in the ch19 folder. If you encounter problems, the most common mistake is creating too narrow a column for the hashed password in the database. It must be at least 60 characters wide, and it's recommended to make it capable of storing up to 255 characters in case future encryption methods generate longer strings.

Although storing a hashed password in a database is more secure than using a text file, the password is sent from the user's browser to the server in plain, unencrypted text. For security, the login and access to subsequent pages should be made through a Transport Layer Security (TLS) or Secure Sockets Layer (SSL) connection.

Using Secret-Key Encryption

The main differences in setting up user registration and authentication for secret-key encryption are that the password needs to be stored in the database as a binary object using the BLOB data type (see "Storing Binary Data" in Chapter 12 for more information) and that the password verification takes place in the SQL query, rather than in the PHP script.

Creating the Table to Store Users' Details

In phpMyAdmin, create a new table called users_2way in the phpsols database. It needs three columns, with the settings listed in Table 19-2.

Table 19-2. *Settings for the users_2way table*

Name	Type	Length/Values	Attributes	Null	Index	A_I
user_id	INT		UNSIGNED	Deselected	PRIMARY	Selected
username	VARCHAR	15		Deselected	UNIQUE	
pwd	BLOB			Deselected		

Registering New Users

The AES_ENCRYPT() function takes two arguments: the value to be encrypted and an encryption key. The encryption key can be any string of characters you choose. For the purposes of this example, I have chosen takeThisWith@PinchOfSalt, but a random series of alphanumeric characters and symbols would be more secure. By default, AES_ENCRYPT() encodes data with a 128-bit key. For the more secure 256-bit key length, you need to set the block_encryption_mode system variable in MySQL to aes-256-cbc (for more details, see https://dev.mysql.com/doc/refman/8.0/en/encryption-functions.html#function_aes-decrypt).

The basic registration scripts for one-way password hashing and secret-key encryption are the same. The only difference lies in the section that inserts the user's data into the database.

■ **Tip** The following scripts embed the encryption key directly in the page. For security, you should define the key in an include file and store it outside the server's document root.

The code for MySQLi looks like this (the full listing is in `register_2way_mysqli.php` in the ch19 folder):

```
if (!$errors) {
    // include the connection file
    require_once 'connection.php';
    $conn = dbConnect('write');
    // create a key
    $key = 'takeThisWith@PinchOfSalt';
    // prepare SQL statement
    $sql = 'INSERT INTO users_2way (username, pwd)
            VALUES (?, AES_ENCRYPT(?, ?))';
    $stmt = $conn->stmt_init();
    if ($stmt = $conn->prepare($sql)) {
        // bind parameters and insert the details into the database
        $stmt->bind_param('sss', $username, $password, $key);
        $stmt->execute();
    }
    if ($stmt->affected_rows == 1) {
        $success = htmlentities($username) . ' has been registered. You may now log in.';
    } elseif ($stmt->errno == 1062) {
        $errors[] = htmlentities($username) . ' is already in use. Please choose another
        username.';
    } else {
        $errors[] = $stmt->error;
    }
}
```

For PDO, it looks like this (see `register_2way_pdo.php` in the ch19 folder for the full listing):

```
if (!$errors) {
    // include the connection file
    require_once 'connection.php';
    $conn = dbConnect('write', 'pdo');
    // create a key
    $key = 'takeThisWith@PinchOfSalt';
    try {
        // prepare SQL statement
        $sql = 'INSERT INTO users_2way (username, pwd)
                VALUES (:username, AES_ENCRYPT(:pwd, :key))';
        $stmt = $conn->prepare($sql);
        // bind parameters and insert the details into the database
        $stmt->bindParam(':username', $username, PDO::PARAM_STR);
        $stmt->bindParam(':pwd', $password, PDO::PARAM_STR);
```

```php
        $stmt->bindParam(':key', $key, PDO::PARAM_STR);
        $stmt->execute();
        if ($stmt->rowCount() == 1) {
            $success = htmlentities($username) . ' has been registered. You may now log
            in.';
        }
    } catch (PDOException $e) {
        if ($e->getCode() == 23000) {
            $errors[] = htmlentities($username) . ' is already in use. Please choose
            another username.';
        } else {
            $errors[] = $e->getMessage();
        }
    }
}
```

Strictly speaking, it's not necessary to use a bound parameter for $key because it doesn't come from user input. If you embed it directly in the query, however, the whole query needs to be wrapped in double quotes, and $key needs to be in single quotes.

To test the preceding scripts, copy them to the includes folder and include them in register_db.php instead of register_db_mysqli.php or register_db_pdo.php.

User Authentication with Two-Way Encryption

Creating a login page with two-way encryption is very simple. After connecting to the database, you incorporate the username, secret key, and unencrypted password in the WHERE clause of a SELECT query. If the query finds a match, the user is allowed into the restricted part of the site. If there's no match, the login is rejected. The code is the same as in PHP Solution 19-2, except for the following section.

For MySQLi, it looks like this (see authenticate_2way_mysqli.php):

```php
<?php
require_once 'connection.php';
$conn = dbConnect('read');
// create key
$key = 'takeThisWith@PinchOfSalt';
$sql = 'SELECT username FROM users_2way
        WHERE username = ? AND pwd = AES_ENCRYPT(?, ?)';
// initialize and prepare statement
$stmt = $conn->stmt_init();
$stmt->prepare($sql);
// bind the input parameters
$stmt->bind_param('sss', $username, $password, $key);
$stmt->execute();
// to get the number of matches, you must store the result
$stmt->store_result();
// if a match is found, num_rows is 1, which is treated as true
if ($stmt->num_rows) {
    $_SESSION['authenticated'] = 'Jethro Tull';
    // get the time the session started
    $_SESSION['start'] = time();
    session_regenerate_id();
```

```
    header("Location: $redirect"); exit;
} else {
    // if not verified, prepare error message
    $error = 'Invalid username or password';
}
```

Note that you need to store the result of the prepared statement before you can access the num_rows property. If you fail to do this, num_rows will always be 0, and the login will fail even if the username and password are correct.

The revised code for PDO looks like this (see authenticate_2way_pdo.php):

```php
<?php
require_once 'connection.php';
$conn = dbConnect('read', 'pdo');
// create key
$key = 'takeThisWith@PinchOfSalt';
$sql = 'SELECT username FROM users_2way
        WHERE username = ? AND pwd = AES_ENCRYPT(?, ?)';
// prepare statement
$stmt = $conn->prepare($sql);
// bind variables by passing them as an array when executing statement
$stmt->execute([$username, $password, $key]);
// if a match is found, rowCount() produces 1, which is treated as true
if ($stmt->rowCount()) {
    $_SESSION['authenticated'] = 'Jethro Tull';
    // get the time the session started
    $_SESSION['start'] = time();
    session_regenerate_id();
    header("Location: $redirect"); exit;
} else {
    // if not verified, prepare error message
    $error = 'Invalid username or password';
}
```

To test these scripts, copy them to the includes folder and use them in place of authenticate_mysqli. php and authenticate_pdo.php.

Decrypting a Password

Decrypting a password that uses two-way encryption simply involves passing the secret key as the second argument to AES_DECRYPT() in a prepared statement, like this:

```
$key = 'takeThisWith@PinchOfSalt';
$sql = "SELECT AES_DECRYPT(pwd, '$key') AS pwd FROM users_2way
        WHERE username = ?";
```

The key must be exactly the same as the one originally used to encrypt the password. If you lose the key, the passwords remain as inaccessible as those stored using one-way hashing.

Normally, the only time you need to decrypt a password is when a user requests a password reminder. Creating the appropriate security policy for sending out such reminders depends a great deal on the type of site that you're operating. However, it goes without saying that you shouldn't display the decrypted password onscreen. You need to set up a series of security checks, such as asking for the user's date of birth or posing a question whose answer only the user is likely to know. Even if the user gets the answer right, you should send the password by email to the user's registered address.

All the necessary knowledge should be at your fingertips if you have succeeded in getting this far in this book.

Updating User Details

I haven't included any update forms for the user registration pages. It's a task that you should be able to accomplish by yourself at this stage. The most important point about updating user registration details is that you should not display the user's existing password in the update form. If you're using password hashing, you can't, anyway.

Where Next?

This book has covered a massive amount of ground. If you've mastered all the techniques covered here, you are well on your way to becoming an intermediate PHP developer, and with a little more effort, you will enter the advanced level. If it's been a struggle, don't worry. Go over the earlier chapters again. The more you practice, the easier it becomes.

You're probably thinking, "How on earth can I remember all this?" You don't need to. Don't be ashamed to look things up. Bookmark the PHP online manual (`www.php.net/manual/en/`) and use it regularly. It's constantly updated, and it has lots of useful examples. Type a function name into the search box at the top right of every page to be taken straight to a full description of that function. Even if you can't remember the correct function name, the manual takes you to a page that suggests the most likely candidates. Most pages have practical examples showing how the function or class is used.

What makes dynamic web design easy is not an encyclopedic knowledge of PHP functions and classes but a solid grasp of how conditional statements, loops, and other structures control the flow of a script. Once you can visualize your projects in terms of "if this happens, what should happen next?" you're the master of your own game. I consult the PHP online manual frequently. To me, it's like a dictionary. Most of the time, I just want to check that I have the arguments in the right order, but I often find that something catches my eye and opens up new horizons. I may not use that knowledge immediately, but I store it at the back of my mind for future use and go back when I need to check the details.

The MySQL online manual (`https://dev.mysql.com/doc/refman/8.0/en/`) is equally useful. The documentation for MariaDB is at `https://mariadb.com/kb/en/library/documentation/`. Make both the PHP and database online manuals your friends, and your knowledge will grow by leaps and bounds.

Index

© David Powers 2022
D. Powers, *PHP 8 Solutions*, https://doi.org/10.1007/978-1-4842-7141-4

■ E

■ F, G

■ H

■ I

Printed in the United States
by Baker & Taylor Publisher Services

Printed in the United States
by Baker & Taylor Publisher Services